FIXED-INCOME PORTFOLIO STRATEGIES

FRANK J. FABOZZI, EDITOR

Visiting Professor
Alfred P. Sloan School of Management
Massachusetts Institute of Technology
and Editor
The Journal of Portfolio Management

PROBUS PUBLISHING COMPANY
Chicago, Illinois

ISBN 1-55738-067-8

Printed in the United States of America

1 2 3 4 5 6 7 8 9 0

Contents and Contributors

Part VI
Strategies with Interest Rate Risk Control Instruments

Part VII
International

PART I

Background

Chapter 1

Introduction

FRANK J. FABOZZI, PH.D., CFA
VISITING PROFESSOR OF FINANCE
SLOAN SCHOOL OF MANAGEMENT
MASSACHUSETTS INSTITUTE OF TECHNOLOGY
AND
EDITOR
THE JOURNAL OF PORTFOLIO MANAGEMENT

The objective of this book is to present recent developments in fixed income portfolio strategies. While reviews of fundamental fixed income principles are sometimes included, the book is *not* an introduction to fixed income securities or fixed income portfolio management. This chapter provides a review of the asset management process and an overview of fixed income portfolio strategies.

REVIEW OF THE ASSET MANAGEMENT PROCESS

Asset management is undertaken in five main steps. First, the objectives and policy guidelines are established by the financial institution. For institutions such as pension funds, the investment objective will be to generate sufficient cash flow from the investment portfolio so as to satisfy its pension obligations. Life insurance companies sell a variety of products, most of which basically guarantee a dollar payment at some time in the future or a stream of dollar payments. The investment objective of a life insurance company is to earn a spread above the rate it has implicitly or explicitly guaranteed policyholders. For institutions such as banks and thrifts, funds are obtained from the issuance of certificates of deposit. The objective is to earn a return on invested funds that is higher than the cost of those funds. For investment companies (mutual funds), the investment objective will be set forth in the prospectus. While there are no liabilities that must be satisfied by the fund, typically a target dividend payout will be established.

The second step in asset management is establishing policy guidelines to satisfy the investment objectives. Setting policy begins with the asset allocation decision; that is, the decision as to how the funds of the institution should be distributed amongst the major classes (cash equivalents, equities, fixed income securities, real estate, and foreign securities). Client and regulatory constraints and tax and financial reporting implications must be considered in establishing an investment policy.

Selecting a portfolio strategy that is consistent with the objectives and policy guidelines of the client or institution is the third step in asset management. The focus of this book is on fixed income portfolio strategies. We'll have more to say about these strategies below.

Once a portfolio strategy is selected, the fourth step is to select the specific assets to be included in the portfolio. This requires an evaluation of individual securities. In an active strategy, this means identifying mispriced securities. In the case of fixed income securities, the characteristics of a bond (that is, coupon, maturity, credit quality, and options granted to either the issuer or bondholder) must be carefully examined to determine how these characteristics will influence the performance of the bond over some investment horizon. For a given portfolio strategy, the manager will seek an efficient portfolio; that is, one designed to provide the greatest expected return for a given level of risk.

The measurement and evaluation of investment performance is the last step in asset management. (Actually, it is improper to say that it is the last step since asset management is an ongoing process.) This step involves measuring the performance of the portfolio, then evaluating that performance relative to a *benchmark* (also called a *normal portfolio*).

OVERVIEW OF FIXED INCOME PORTFOLIO STRATEGIES

Portfolio strategies can be classified as either active strategies or passive strategies. Essential to all active strategies are expectations about the factors that are likely to influence the performance of an asset class. Passive strategies, on the other hand, involve minimal expectational input.

Active fixed income portfolio strategies may involve forecasts of future interest rates, future interest rate volatility or future yield spreads. Active portfolio strategies involving nondollar-denominated bonds will require forecasts of future exchange rates.

A popular type of passive strategy is indexing. The objective of an indexing strategy is to replicate the performance of a predetermined index. While indexing has been employed extensively in the management of equity portfolios, the use of indexing for managing fixed income portfolios is a relatively new practice.

Between these extremes of active and passive strategies have sprung strategies that have elements of both. For example, the core of a portfolio may be indexed with the balance managed actively. Or, a portfolio may be primarily indexed but employ low risk strategies to enhance the indexed portfolio's return. This strategy is commonly referred to as "enhanced indexing" or "indexing plus."

In the fixed income area, several strategies classified as *structured portfolio strategies* have been commonly used. A structured portfolio strategy is one in which a portfolio is designed that will achieve the performance of some predetermined benchmark. These strategies are frequently used when funding liabilities. When the predetermined benchmark is to have sufficient funds to satisfy a single liability, regardless of the course of future interest rates, a strategy known as immunization is often used. When the predetermined benchmark is multiple future liabilities that must be funded regardless of how interest rates change, strategies such as immunization, cash flow matching (or dedication) or horizon matching can be employed. Even within the immunization and cash flow matching strategies, low-risk active management strategies can be employed. Indexing can be considered a structured portfolio strategy where the benchmark is to achieve the performance of some predetermined index. Portfolio insurance—where the objective is to insure that the value of the portfolio does not fall below a predetermined level—is also viewed as a structured portfolio strategy.

To control interest rate risk, portfolio managers can use futures, forwards, options, interest rate swaps and interest rate agreements (caps and floors). Futures, forwards and options can be employed by active portfolio managers to capitalize on expected interest rate movements.

OVERVIEW OF THE BOOK

The focus of this book is on fixed income portfolio strategies. Section II includes three chapters on indexing, covering global indexing and indexing of mortgage-backed securities. The five chapters in Section III discuss immunization and dedicated strategies. Portfolio insurance strategies are covered in the two chapters in Section IV. Bond analysis tools for coping with callable bonds and credit spreads, and for enhancing returns in the government bond market are presented in the four chapters in Section V. Strategies for controlling interest rate risk and international fixed income strategies are covered in Sections VI and VII, respectively. Section VIII has two chapters. The first discusses the impact of new SEC rules governing advertising on mutual fund investment strategies. The second explains how portfolios of guaranteed investment contracts should be managed. Section IX has one chapter dealing with normal portfolios and their applications.

Chapter 2

Global Investing: The Importance of Integrating Asset Selection with Investment Horizon

CHRIS P. DIALYNAS
MANAGING DIRECTOR
PACIFIC INVESTMENT MANAGEMENT COMPANY

The scientific revolution on Wall Street has glamorized the bond business. Today's players are obsessed with the quantification of securities. Duration, convexity, effective duration, delta, gamma and many other descriptive terms are relied upon to relate the risks of securities to the changing of interest rates. The new mathematics of the bond business presumably provides for conscious decisions about the matching of assets with liabilities. While the revolution is important and has been useful, one must always be cautious about scientific analysis and empiricism. Most often, the scientific quantification of portfolio risk as it is done today is a localized analysis of risk. Investing today is, as it always has been, as much an art as a science. Localized risk is trivial. Global risk is of profound importance. Localized risk may be thought of as the quantification of risk at a moment of time, giving an accurate account of risk as long as volatility is constant, the changing of interest rates is slow and smooth and liquidity is abundant. The portfolio insurers believe in localized risk—at least they used to.

Global risk analysis recognizes that the marketplace is not a controlled experiment. Global risk analysis focuses upon the shortcomings of the localized quantities. It recognizes, as has been recognized historically, that while localized analysis may be a best estimate, it will most often be a wrong estimate. We will gain a better understanding of the contrast between local risk and global risk as we progress.

As with most economic analysis involving uncertain cost functions, cost functions which may even change over time, it is difficult to generalize investment strategies. We will assume for simplicity that the plan liability stream is known, is fixed and holds a specified duration[1] and convexity.[2] By fixing the liability stream, we can easily understand that a bond portfolio with known payments containing a higher yield, and greater convexity but matched by maturity and duration, is a no-lose proposition.

Unfortunately, the market place does not readily accommodate portfolio managers with such easy solutions. High yield and high convexity on a global basis are inconsistent. Convexity properties must be purchased and the cost is recognized by the yield sacrificed.

THE POPULAR INDICES

A contrast of the most popular indices will illustrate the point. We will contrast the Shearson Lehman Government Corporate (SLGC) Index with the Shearson Lehman Aggregate Index (SLAG). We can easily substitute the Salomon Broad Index for the SLAG and the inferences are still valid.

Generally speaking, the SLGC has better convexity than the SLAG but a lower yield. The convexity of the SLGC is more global than that of the SLAG because the SLGC contains fewer callable bonds. Loosely speaking, the SLAG sells volatility and the SLGC buys volatility.

The SLAG was designed to include mortgage pass-through securities. The inclusion of mortgage pass-throughs increases the yield of the index but pollutes with non-systematic call risk. Uncertain prepayment rates on the mortgages localizes the duration and convexity to a much greater extent than that of SLGC. Because the expected duration and expected convexity of mortgages is a function of their price, this index can change its colors considerably as rates change. The changes always work to the disfavor of the investor. The higher interest rates are, the greater

---

[1]Duration measures the rate of change in the principal value of a portfolio given small discrete parallel changes in inherent rates.

[2]Convexity measures the extent to which yield changes dramatically, and hence captures changes in principal value not picked up by duration. Convexity also measures the inherent call risk of the portfolio, due to corporate bonds and prepayable mortgages.

the call protection, but the longer the bonds become. Mere changes in expectations for volatility or prepayment rates will change the value of the call protection and also the so called "option-adjusted" duration.

Exhibit 1 shows the variation of the historical relative prices of GNMA's as an indicator of the call protection of the SLAG. Pass-throughs below par offer call protection; those above par offer little protection. We observe an inconsistent, volatile series of GNMA's priced below par. The effect of the changes on the effective duration as calculated by Salomon Brothers is shown.

We find that as interest rates increase, durations increase, and declining rates cause durations to decline. (See Exhibits 2 and 3.) This peculiarity is a portfolio manager's dilemma. Locally, the change in duration is modest. Globally, for example the period from 6/84 to 12/86, the relative duration of the SLAG declined significantly.

The relative difference in durational globality is gleaned from descriptive data about the SLGC and the SLAG. The SLGC non-modified duration changed from

EXHIBIT 1
PERCENT OF OUTSTANDING GNMA PASS-THROUGHS AT OR BELOW PAR VS.
SALOMON BROS. BROAD BOND INDEX EFFECTIVE DURATION

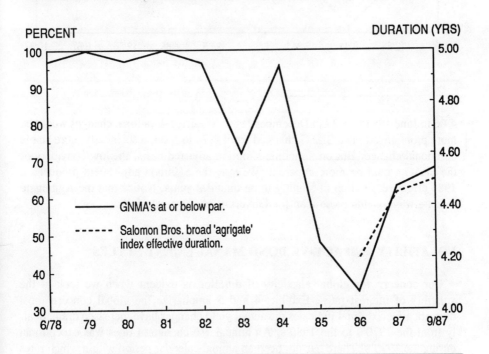

Convexity: relationship between bond
price of bond yield, curvature

change in relationship between

EXHIBIT 2
SLGC DURATION VS. SLAG DURATION

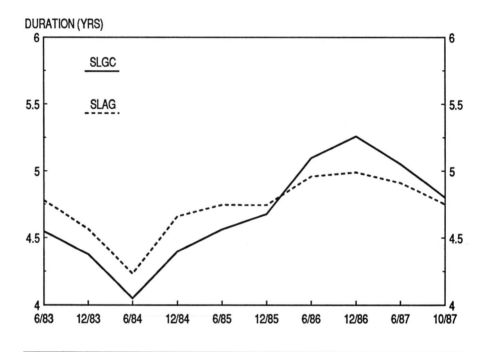

DURATION (YRS)

4.06 in June 1984 to 5.27 in December 1986. Modified durational changes would be more pronounced. The SLAG changed from 4.24 to 5.00, a seemingly more stable durational change. But on a modified, option-adjusted basis, the low convexity of the SLAG would be more apparent. We note the Salomon adjustment produced a 1986 effective duration of slightly more than 4.2 years. Notice that the Aggregate Index always yields more than the Government Corporate Index.

VOLATILITY AND ACTIVE BOND MANAGEMENT STYLES

Our concern for global elasticity of duration is evident when we look at the volatility of interest rates. Exhibits 4 and 5 emphasize the global concern most dramatically. Exhibit 4 indicates the actual yield changes have increased dramatically from the 1970's to the 1980's. An annual 1% change in rates was exceptional during the 1970's. There has not been an annual calendar period within which rates did not change by more than 1% in the 1980's. Exhibit 5 shows the volatility of total

EXHIBIT 3
SLGC YIELD TO MATURITY VS. SLAG YIELD TO MATURITY

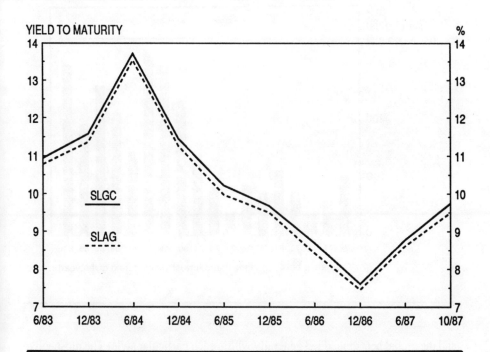

YIELD TO MATURITY

SLGC

SLAG

%

return on 30-year Treasury bonds. We realize that even though the nominal yield volatility increased dramatically during the 80's, the total return variability did not increase as much. This is because a 30-year Treasury bond's duration elasticity is so great. During the 1970's, modified durations were greater because rates were lower and small yield changes exerted profound changes in portfolio values – a subtlety of global consciousness! The 1980's experience can be characterized as more volatility in volatility. How should an investor's preferences between indices vary with volatility? Should they change at all?

We need to digress momentarily to think about why indices exist at all. Selection of a particular index is a statement of risk character. Selection of an index is also a statement of yield/convexity preferences. Indices are a representation of a particular universe available for investment. In other words, they represent the naive capabilities of a passive investor. Finally, in practice, index selection is the yardstick by which the success of artistic prerogative is judged scientifically.

Artistic prerogative means deviating from the indexes. Deviation often results in an active management investment mode. We can look at the popular styles offered

12   Dialynas

EXHIBIT 4
ANNUAL HIGH-LOW YIELD DIFFERENTIAL ON 30-YEAR TREASURY BOND

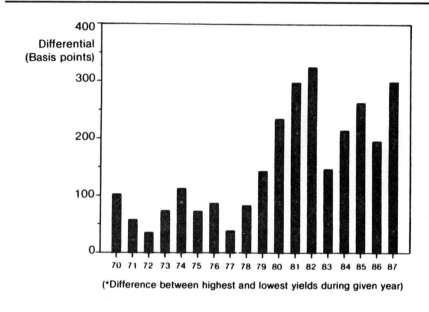

(*Difference between highest and lowest yields during given year)

and the global bets embedded generally within each particular style. The most active style is that of the market timers. These investors rely upon a keen ability to forecast interest rates and vary durations dramatically to reflect the conviction of their forecasts. Second order conditions such as convexity are trivial.

Specialized corporate bond management is another popular active style. With this style the investor is selling convexity, betting on low volatility and taking yield premiums. In return the investor is selling convexity, betting on low volatility and taking yield premiums in return for the bad convexity. This style does well during stable interest rate environments and does relatively poorly in extreme bull and bear markets.

Short maturity bond management explicitly bets against sharply lower rates and against an inversion process in the yield curve. Historically, the yield volatility on short term securities has exceeded that of longer bonds. Therefore, durationally adjusted, portfolios containing a high concentration of short bonds have contained more relative price variability. Moreover, short bonds are not very convex. The importance of a stable environment is most apparent upon recognition that credit risk is bought at narrow premiums relative to credit spreads on longer bonds and improvement in credit worthiness produces trivial gains.

EXHIBIT 5
VOLATILITY OF TOTAL RETURN ON 30-YEAR TREASURY BOND

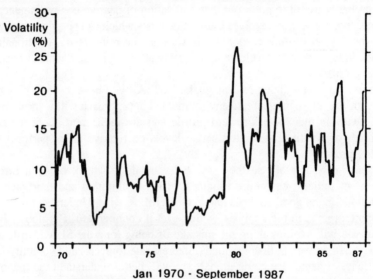

Jan 1970 - September 1987
(6 month moving average of annualized standard deviation)

Specialized mortgage management is yet another popular active style. The mortgage market is a large and very liquid component of the bond market. The market is very complex and is difficult to generalize about. We know, however, that mortgages priced at par offer a downside risk of 20-year bonds and upside potential of 4-year bonds. Given the wide range of potential price character, we can infer that mortgages generally do well during periods of stable interest rates.

The final active style I want to discuss is that of risk-controlled bond management. In this category, artistic perogative is turned over to the manager, but scientific quantification is a necessary quality of the style, since this style decomposes the various sectors of the bond market into a probabilistically weighted set of payments. The style trades off localized influences of volatility with globalized influences. The style focuses on the current state with respect to yield level, volatility and convexity costs. Managers impose their view of localized changes and potential globalized costs when constructing portfolios. The success of artistic perogative is a function of the macroeconomic capabilities of the manager whereas the localized performance is dominated by scientific acumen. These two ingredients are a requirement for good performance since few, if any, investment categories perform well in all markets.

CONCLUDING REMARKS

It is probably useful to point out that replication of passive bogeys is generally not free. Actual replication involves transaction costs which can be substantial when, as with the Aggregate Index, monthly flows must be reinvested. Additionally, most passive indexes contain an element of activity or tilting to them which translates into tracking error.

So, we now have index returns guaranteed. All you have to do is pick the right index for the future interest rate environment. This approach will work if you can be happy with an index's risk/reward profile and are indifferent about the changing dynamics of volatility and interest rate levels on relative index performance and bond returns.

Science conquers all, so they say. It has made its attack on Wall Street. The analysis of indices, customized indices, effective duration and mortgage prepayment modeling is good analysis and very useful. Read it. Understand it. Search for the shortcomings in the analysis — don't let it conquer you. Be global. By being global you will avoid making the mistake of being long the SLAG, instead of the SLGC when you are bullish on bonds. Interest rate forecasts and volatility forecasts are strongly related. By being global, you will better understand the magnitude of the costs of being short volatility in an extremely volatile market. Cleverness carries the day, but wisdom prevails.

PART II
INDEXING

Chapter 3

Indexation and Optimal Strategies in Portfolio Management

MARK L. DUNETZ
VICE PRESIDENT
FIXED INCOME GROUP
KIDDER, PEABODY & CO., INC.

JAMES M. MAHONEY
ASSISTANT VICE PRESIDENT
FIXED INCOME GROUP
KIDDER, PEABODY & CO., INC.

Indexation has become the standard method for tracking market performance and controlling risk. Indices are generally designed to be representative of a broad range of securities and thus be indicative of the return in a particular market. Many investors, however, have specific long-term objectives which are neither consistent nor compatible with overall market structure, such as either maximizing return or funding of a liability. For these investors, a "structured reference portfolio" (SRP)

17

should be designed to reflect specific investment objectives. Whether the investor is attempting to track a generic market portfolio or one which is specifically developed to be representative of his goals, he is engaged in an asset/liability hedging strategy. The liability is the SRP while the asset is the "basket" of securities which the investor is managing. If the basket portfolio is effectively hedged to the SRP, any change in interest rates, in yield curve shape, or in spread relationships will not affect tracking performance. By changing the configuration of the basket portfolio to differ from that of the SRP, the investor takes on controlled risk and has the potential of outperforming the SRP. It is important for the investor to know the tracking parameters of the SRP in order to understand the risks and rewards of altering the structure of the basket portfolio.

This chapter examines how SRPs are designed in the Treasury market and how baskets of securities are constructed to track these portfolios. In addition, several strategies to construct baskets to outperform the SRP are discussed.

APPLICATION OF STRUCTURED REFERENCE PORTFOLIOS IN THE TREASURY MARKET

Three of the major reasons for investing in the Treasury market are speculation, return, and liability funding. Each of these objectives requires the use of a SRP in order to judge investment performance. The speculator, for example, buys securities based on how he perceives the direction of interest rates. If he believes that interest rates will decline, he will invest in long duration bonds; on the other hand, if he believes that interest rates are on the rise, he will invest in bills, thereby deriving a lower yield, but protecting his principal investment. In order to determine if the speculative investor has increased his return, his portfolio's performance should be compared to the general market performance. The SRP would then be the entire Treasury market.

The SRP would also be the entire Treasury market for investors seeking the market return. The basket portfolio would then be designed to track the return performance of the SRP. If the investor alters the composition of the basket portfolio to reflect his view in such areas as the direction of interest rates, the shape of the yield curve, or the level of volatility, his performance will be measured relative to the performance of the SRP. If the investor positions his investments in the marketplace based on such choices, his risk/reward profile relative to the SRP will change. If his views are correct, he will outperform the bogey. If his views are incorrect, he will underperform the bogey. In either case, the distribution of possible returns is under greater control than would be the case if securities were selected in a purely speculative portfolio without understanding of the underlying SRP. By analyzing the configuration of his SRP, the investor has better control of the portfolio he is managing, even when he is investing based on subjective decisions.

An investor with a known liability schedule would be indexed to a portfolio which funds the necessary cash flows. The SRP is then the least cost-dedicated portfolio of Treasuries which funds these liabilities. From this portfolio, decisions can be made about changes in duration, and the maturity and coupon sectors to be weighed more heavily. If the investor makes correct decisions about rich and cheap sectors, his performance will result in additional assets after funding the liabilities. On the other hand, if the investor makes incorrect decisions, his performance will result in a shortfall in the funding of the liabilities and the need for additional cash inflow. Mathematical techniques exist, however, which can be utilized to ensure that a portfolio outperforms the SRP.

ESTABLISHING A STRUCTURED REFERENCE PORTFOLIO IN THE TREASURY MARKET

A structured reference Treasury market portfolio comprises all coupon Treasury issues with maturities of one year or greater weighted by their relative amounts outstanding in the market. Many investors, however, are restricted by the maturity or duration of their investments. For example, an investor may be restricted to no more than 10-year maturities. For these investors, the appropriate structured reference portfolio would be the Treasury market reference portfolio described, with the exclusion of all issues having a maturity in excess of ten years.

The formulation of a structured reference portfolio is more complicated for investors with duration constraints. For example, an investor may be restricted to a duration of 3.5 while the Treasury market reference portfolio has a duration of 4.5. One solution is to formulate a structured reference portfolio starting with issues of one-year to maturity. Successive maturity issues are added until the duration of the reference portfolio is gradually increased to the target duration of 3.5. The reverse strategy can be used to formulate a reference portfolio for investors with duration targets exceeding the market duration. For example, an investor may be restricted to a duration of 5.5 while the market portfolio has a duration of 4.5. A structured reference portfolio for this investor can be created by starting with the Treasury issues of the longest maturities and successively adding issues of decreasing maturity until the duration of the portfolio is gradually decreased to the target duration of 5.5. The strategy of formulating reference portfolios to match duration targets has the advantage of using a laddered structure as the basis of comparison as opposed to a barbell approach which would be biased by changes in the shape of the yield curve.

Exhibit 1 shows the return performance of several structured reference portfolios designed to track sectors of the Treasury market from September to December 1987. During this time, rates increased 100 basis points, and subsequently dropped 150 basis points in mid-October before stabilizing at approximately the same levels as at the beginning of the period. As expected, the duration of the SRPs was the key factor

EXHIBIT 1
STRUCTURED REFERENCE PORTFOLIOS OF THE TREASURY MARKET

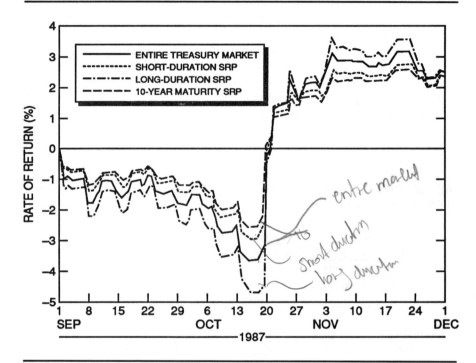

in determining relative performances. For example, the long-duration SRP under-performed the entire Treasury market as rates went up, but outperformed it when rates declined. Since there was little net change in rates by December, however, the long-duration portfolio had approximately the same return as the entire Treasury market for the 3-month period as a whole.

FORMULATING PORTFOLIOS TO TRACK THE REFERENCE PORTFOLIO

Ideally, an investor wishing to track the reference portfolio with low risk would simply buy every issue in the portfolio in the appropriate amounts. Unfortunately, this is not practical. The Treasury market reference portfolio, for example, consists of about 160 issues. A preferable alternative is a "basket" consisting of a manage-able number of issues designed to have the same price and return performance as the reference portfolio. It is then necessary to track the price and return performance of 160 issues with a subset while controlling for two forms of risk: spread risk and market risk.

Spread risk is the risk that the yield difference between two bonds will change. In the Treasury market, spread risk exists between different maturity sectors and different coupon levels. Spread risk between maturity sectors comes from the changing structure of interest rates, For example, when the yield curve steepens, the spread between short-maturity issues and long-maturity issues widens. Therefore, if a Treasury basket portfolio does not have a maturity structure similar to the reference portfolio, there is spread risk and the tracking performance will be affected by changes in the shape of the yield curve.

Spread risk between high and low coupon issues is also a problem in the Treasury market. Many older high coupon issues, because of their lower liquidity and different tax treatment, typically have a positive yield spread to similar maturity current coupon issues. These spreads will widen or narrow under different circumstances. To minimize the effects of coupon level spread risk on tracking performance, the basket portfolio should be designed to have a similar coupon structure as the reference portfolio. On the other hand, the basket portfolio can be structured to take advantage of such differences for increased return at a controllable risk.

Market risk is predominantly duration risk or the chance that the market value of the Treasury basket portfolio and the reference portfolio will not change at the same rate as interest rates change. To minimize market risk it is important that the basket portfolio and the reference portfolio have the same percentage change in price for a given change in rates. Market risk is controlled by structuring the basket portfolio so that it has the same price/yield sensitivity or duration as the reference portfolio. In addition, because duration changes as yields change, the rate of change of duration or the convexity of the two portfolios should be matched as well.

When the Treasury market reference portfolio is formulated, it can be analyzed in terms of maturity structure, coupon levels, and duration. Exhibit 2 indicates these parameters as of September 1987. The maturity structure is analyzed as a series of seven maturity sectors along the yield curve, while the coupon levels are described as low, middle, or high. For each maturity sector, the percentage concentration by market value of the entire Treasury market index is listed. Each maturity sector is also broken down by coupon level. Using optimization techniques, a basket portfolio can be constructed that has a similar maturity structure, coupon levels, and duration as the SRP. The basket is designed to mimic the price performance with little spread risk, while at the same time, attempting to outperform the SRP on a rate of return basis.

Exhibit 3 shows a 21 issue Treasury basket portfolio formulated in September 1987 to track the reference portfolio. To minimize spread risk, the basket portfolio was designed to have a maturity and coupon structure similar to the Treasury market reference portfolio. The two portfolios have a similar percentage concentration in

Look up: Structured Reference Portfolio

EXHIBIT 2
STRUCTURED REFERENCE PORTFOLIO FOR THE TREASURY MARKET RETURN
(SEPTEMBER 1987 PRICES)

Number of issues:	160
Average price:	103.168
Yield:	8.57%
Duration:	4.5
Convexity:	44

	Coupon Rate*			
Maturity range	Low	Mid	High	Totals
1-to-2 Years	15.3%	2.1%	6.2%	23.6%
2-to-3 Years	5.6%	2.2%	4.9%	12.7%
3-to-5 Years	7.8%	1.6%	7.7%	17.1%
5-to-7 Years	4.1%	3.4%	4.1%	11.5%
7-to-10 Years	3.4%	3.4%	3.5%	10.3%
10-to-20 Years	0.7%	0.8%	6.8%	8.3%
20-to-30 Years	3.1%	4.6%	8.8%	16.5%
Totals	40.0%	18.0%	42.0%	100.0%

*Note: The average coupon of the SRP is 9.30%; the mid-coupon rate is 9.30% plus or minus 100 basis points.

Low coupon rate <8.30%
High coupon rate >10.30%

EXHIBIT 3
STRUCTURED REFERENCE PORTFOLIO FOR THE TREASURY MARKET RETURN
(SEPTEMBER 1987 PRICES)

Number of issues:	23
Average price:	104.140
Yield:	8.66%
Duration:	4.5
Convexity:	43

	Coupon Rate*			
Maturity range	Low	Mid	High	Totals
1-to-2 Years	15.0%	3.0%	3.6%	21.6%
2-to-3 Years	5.6%	2.4%	5.0%	13.0%
3-to-5 Years	7.8%	2.0%	8.0%	17.8%
5-to-7 Years	3.9%	4.0%	4.1%	12.0%
7-to-10 Years	2.3%	4.0%	3.5%	9.8%
10-to-20 Years	1.0%	1.0%	7.0%	9.0%
20-to-30 Years	3.0%	5.0%	8.8%	16.8%
Totals	38.6%	21.4%	40.0%	100.0%

method

each of the maturity sectors and coupon categories. In addition, to minimize market risk, the basket portfolio was structured to have the same duration and convexity as the reference portfolio. The basket portfolio also has a higher yield than the market reference portfolio. This is accomplished by optimally selecting issues within the constraints of maturity structure, coupon level, and duration/convexity parameters. Using this approach, a basket portfolio can be designed to track the reference portfolio, while achieving a higher rate of return.

Exhibit 4 shows how the basket portfolio's return (2.58%) exceeded the rate of return of the reference portfolio (2.48%). The higher return is a result of the higher yield of the basket when it was constructed. Over the same period, the price performance of the basket portfolio tracked the price performance of the SRP because the two were duration-matched with a similar maturity and coupon break-down. In fact, regression analysis indicates that there was a correlation between the price performance of the reference portfolio and the basket portfolio of .977, demonstrating the strong tracking performance of the basket portfolio to the SRP.

↳ *use of correlation coeff. to determine tracking performance*

EXHIBIT 4
TREASURY BASKET PORTFOLIO VS. STRUCTURED REFERENCE PORTFOLIO

✻ *frg*

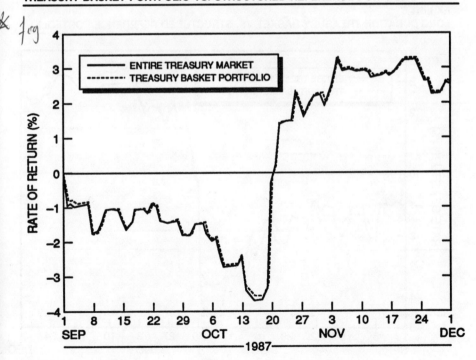

FORMULATING A BASKET PORTFOLIO TO OUTPERFORM THE REFERENCE PORTFOLIO

that

Strategies to outperform the reference portfolio have two basic objectives: maximizing yield by altering coupon or maturity structure, and changing capital gains or losses by altering duration. While both strategies involve altering the risk-neutral basket portfolio based on the investor's subjective inputs about the market, altering duration to affect capital gains or losses is generally the more risky approach of the two.

Remark

To demonstrate this strategy, a basket portfolio was constructed to track the Treasury market SRP in yield and market performance. Based on this basket (duration = 4.5), a long-duration basket (duration = 5.5) was formulated. Exhibit 5 shows the 3-month return performance on the long-duration basket versus the SRP of the entire Treasury market. From September to mid-October 1987, rates rose and the long-duration basket underperformed the SRP. In mid-October, rates dropped dramatically and the long-duration basket outperformed the SRP. By December, however, rates stabilized to their September levels with a slight net decrease. As a result, the long-duration basket slightly outperformed (2.61%) the return of the SRP (2.48%).

EXHIBIT 5
LONG DURATION TREASURY BASKET VS. STRUCTURED REFERENCE PORTFOLIO

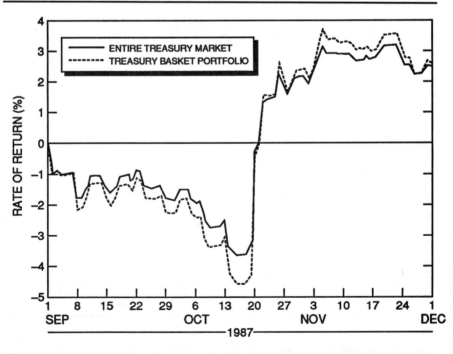

SRP: Structured Reference Portfolio

In addition to altering duration, the investor could have constructed a portfolio having the same duration and maturity structure but with a different coupon break-down than the SRP. Exhibit 6 describes such a portfolio with emphasis on higher coupon, higher yielding securities. The investor is thus taking a risk that the higher coupon yields will tighten or remain stable compared to the current and low coupon yields. In reality, this portfolio outperformed the SRP (2.67% vs. 2.48%) over the period of September to December since spreads did narrow (Exhibit 7). The risks and rewards of this portfolio compared to the duration-altered portfolio are much less dramatic; nonetheless, the approach can be an important technique for inves-tors.

Finally, a portfolio was constructed keeping the duration and coupon similarities to the SRP (Exhibit 8), but with a higher convexity. To construct a highly convex portfolio for a specific duration, the issues must be "barbelled" toward early and late maturities. As shown in Exhibit 9, the high convexity barbell portfolio will have higher price performance than the SRP, the greater the net change in rates. There is little improvement in price performance, however, if rates do not change by much. Although the barbell portfolio has the potential for greater price performance, it is also vulnerable to yield curve risk. For example, if intermediate maturity issues outperform short-and long-maturity issues, then the barbell portfolio will underper-form the SRP.

Exhibit 10 shows the return performance of the barbell portfolio versus the SRP with the long bond rate superimposed. Note that the barbell portfolio began to outperform the SRP in October when rates were very volatile. By late November, however, rates had stabilized close to their September levels. The net change in rates

EXHIBIT 6
TREASURY "HIGH COUPON" BASKET PORTFOLIO TO OUTPERFORM THE TREASURY MARKET RETURN (SEPTEMBER 1987 PRICES)

Number of issues:	14
Average price:	110.902
Yield:	8.70%
Duration:	4.5
Convexity:	43

	Coupon Rate*			
Maturity range	Low	Mid	High	Totals
1-to-2 Years	9.6%	10.4%	0.0%	20.0%
2-to-3 Years	9.8%	0.0%	3.2%	13.0%
3-to-5 Years	0.0%	0.0%	18.0%	18.0%
5-to-7 Years	0.0%	0.0%	12.0%	12.0%
7-to-10 Years	0.0%	0.0%	11.0%	11.0%
10-to-20 Years	0.0%	0.0%	9.0%	9.0%
20-to-30 Years	1.6%	0.0%	15.4%	17.0%
Totals	21.0%	10.4%	68.6%	100.0%

EXHIBIT 7
HIGH COUPON TREASURY BASKET VS. STRUCTURED REFERENCE PORTFOLIO

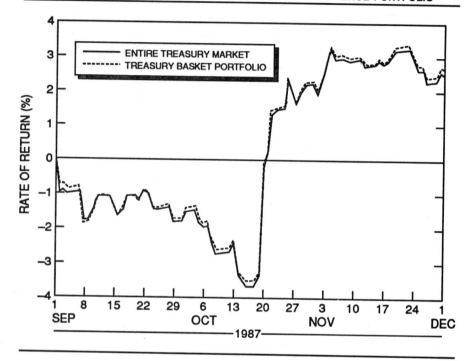

EXHIBIT 8
TREASURY "BARBELL" BASKET PORTFOLIO TO OUTPERFORM THE TREASURY MARKET RETURN (SEPTEMBER 1987 PRICES)

Number of issues:	13
Average price:	100.490
Yield:	8.21%
Duration:	4.5
Convexity:	63

Maturity range	Coupon Rate*			Totals
	Low	Mid	High	
1-to-2 Years	20.2%	18.4%	21.6%	60.2%
2-to-3 Years	0.0%	0.0%	0.0%	0.0%
3-to-5 Years	0.0%	0.0%	0.0%	0.0%
5-to-7 Years	0.0%	0.0%	0.0%	0.0%
7-to-10 Years	0.0%	0.0%	0.0%	0.0%
10-to-20 Years	5.0%	4.8%	0.0%	9.8%
20-to-30 Years	5.0%	10.0%	15.0%	30.0%
Totals	30.2%	33.2%	36.6%	100.0%

EXHIBIT 9
BARBELL TREASURY BASKET VS. STRUCTURED REFERENCE PORTFOLIO

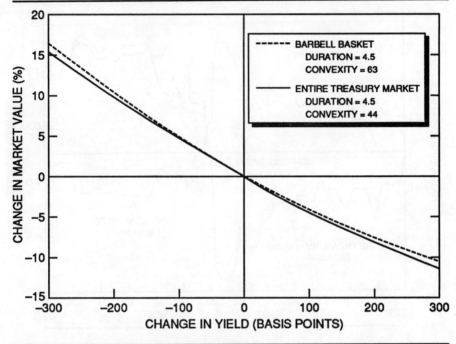

therefore, was not large over the 3-month period as a whole; therefore, the barbell portfolio's return performance was the same as that of the SRP (2.48%).

In summary, if the investor believes he can correctly guess the "rich"/"cheap" sectors or volatility in the market, he should compare his performance continually to that of the SRP to determine whether he is indeed able to outperform the market in the long run.

CONCLUSION

Indexation has generally been used as a technique to track overall market performance and control risk. Investors, however, have begun to require performance bogeys based on their own objectives and constraints. A structured reference portfolio can be designed to be representative of these specific investment goals. The SRP is then the bogey against which the investor can compare his own performance. The SRP should be thought of as a risk-neutral position, free of all subjective opinions the investor might have regarding the direction of interest rates, changes in the shape of the yield curve, market volatility, and spread relationships. The investor can then

EXHIBIT 10
BARBELL TREASURY BASKET VS. STRUCTURED REFERENCE PORTFOLIO

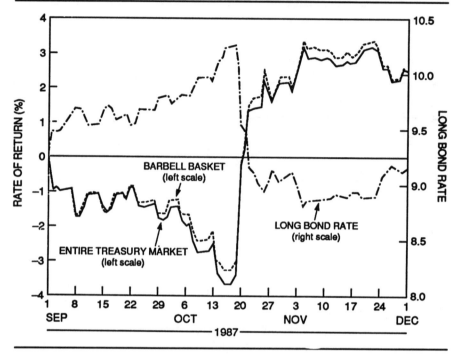

model his portfolio after the SRP in order to achieve the same level of performance. The investor can also attempt to outperform the SRP by altering key parameters based on his own views, while recognizing the potential risks and rewards of doing so.

For instance, an investor wishing to change the convexity of his holdings would not understand the risk he is taking without being familiar with the convexity of the reference portfolio. Therefore, structured reference portfolios should be tailored to the investor's specific objectives and used as a measure of risk control in portfolio management.

Chapter 4

Global Bond Indexation: Concepts, Approaches and Challenges

AGUSTIN R. SEVILLA, PH.D.
VICE PRESIDENT
CHASE INVESTORS MANAGEMENT CORPORATION

FREDERICK NOVOMESTKY, PH.D.
VICE PRESIDENT
CHASE INVESTORS MANAGEMENT CORPORATION

The principal motivation for investing in the global bond markets is that they provide a substantially larger opportunity set than the individual local bond markets. As of the end of 1987, the aggregate value of the major government bond markets was U.S. $3.9 trillion of which the U.S. Treasury market represented 34%. The size of the entire publicly traded debt markets was U.S. $10.6 trillion of which the U.S. bond market comprised 44%.[1] The net effects of a broader universe of bonds are the potential for returns in excess of the domestic alternatives and the ability to diversify risk without significantly reducing total returns.

[1]"How Big is the World Bond Market?—1988 Update" Salomon Brothers Inc, May 20, 1988.

29

Inherent to global investing is the exposure to currency risk. Because of the close links between bond and currency markets, it is possible to efficiently offset exchange rate effects by means of derivative securities. Whether or not to hedge currency exposure and whether to do it symmetrically or asymmetrically is an issue that requires careful consideration. In the short run a large portion of the return on a foreign investment may arise from favorable exchange rate movements. In the long run, risk-adjusted returns across markets may be of the same order of magnitude since currency effects may well average out to zero.

The merits of global bond portfolios apply to both active and passive techniques. The presence of currency exposure makes the implementation of both strategies significantly different from their implementation at the domestic level. The use of passive strategies within countries allows for active country-timing strategies which in turn can be coupled with currency hedging schemes. The outcome will be a very broad range of attainable policies which do not preclude asset-selection abilities.

This chapter is organized as follows: the first section deals with the concept of global bond indices. The second discusses the problem of indexation from a global perspective. The third section examines the effect of currency exposure and considers alternative hedging strategies. The fourth section describes various methodologies for constructing proxy portfolios within each country, then the next section describes the simulation results for a specific technique. The last section highlights operational issues.

GLOBAL BOND INDICES

A global bond index fund is a portfolio of fixed income securities from a number of countries intended to represent the universe of investment opportunities within that group of countries. Each security is assigned a weight proportional to its market value, so that the "ensemble" of bonds within each country represents a "market portfolio." The market portfolios for the various countries are then aggregated with a set of weights that represent the relative values of each market from the investors' perspective.

The use of indexing technology effectively reduces an entire market to a single composite asset thereby enabling the investor to concentrate on the allocation of wealth across these "composite" assets. Different strategies are possible derivations from the standard global bond indexation. Mean-variance analysis provides a convenient method for visualizing the effect of these different strategies on ex-post returns. An efficient portfolio is defined as one with the highest expected return for a given level of risk, or conversely, the portfolio with the lowest risk for a given level of expected return.[2] For an investor who considers a neutrally weighted aggregation of market portfolios of the member countries to be an efficient portfolio, it is logical to use a global bond index that is neutral as to capitalization weights.

---

[2]See H.M. Markowitz, *Portfolio Selection: Efficient Diversification of Investment* (New York: John Wiley, 1970).

Det ☆

N.B.

The investor could also analyze the entire efficient frontier and decide on an allocation where the risk level corresponds to that level which would be undertaken when investing in domestic alternatives (for example, a portfolio of local government securities). The point on the efficient frontier which lies exactly above the domestic alternative illustrates the incremental expected return of an efficient global portfolio in relation to the domestic alternative. The point lying exactly to the left depicts the expected reduction in risk which can be achieved through efficient global diversification.

Exhibit 1 illustrates the efficient frontier paradigm for a U.S. fixed-income investor in relation to the entire range of domestic government bond markets.

The graph shows that at the same level of risk as the local alternative, global diversification would have resulted in a return enhancement of 3.94%. Alternatively, the risk level could have been reduced by 2.81% while still increasing returns by 85 basis points.

EXHIBIT 1
EFFICIENT FRONTIER BASED ON EX-POST RETURNS U.S. PERSPECTIVE
TIME PERIOD: JANUARY 1978 TO DECEMBER 1987

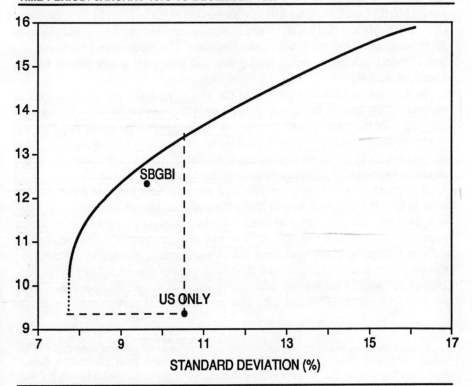

Note: Returns are annualized monthly rates of return.

The process of structuring a global bond fund is involved and complicated, since fixed income securities vary widely across markets in their terms and conditions. Even the calculation of holding period returns, which is a basic function in managing indexed funds, requires detailed knowledge of the intricacies of each market.

Indexation is concerned with the deployment of assets to achieve investment performance relative to the global index. An alternative perspective arises when the focus begins with liabilities. Pension sponsors, or financial institutions, frequently hold liabilities in foreign currencies, for example, the pension payment obligations for the retired employees of a multinational corporation. The liability schedule in each country can be thought of as a portfolio of zero-coupon instruments resembling Treasury bonds which are held *short* by the investor. These obligations can be offset by matching long positions of foreign bonds: a global bond index portfolio can be constructed to match the return pattern of the liability stream.[3]

The main argument is that the liabilities in each country constitute the local index. The country allocation decision is then made as a function of the present value of the liability schedule. The discount factors used in the present value calculations are those derived from the term structure of interest rates in that country.

There are several institutions which publish international bond indices. The most widely recognized is the Salomon Brothers World Bond Index. A refinement of it was created in January of 1985 which concentrates on government securities. Recently, Merrill Lynch has launched its own version of global bond indices. Lombard Odier has published daily total return and price-only indices since 1982. Intersec publishes monthly indices in *Institutional Investor*. The Association of International Bond Dealers publishes weekly total return and price-only return indices for the Eurobond market.

The decision to allocate a portion of the available wealth to a given market as represented by one of the above indices must be substantiated by a long-term perspective of the relative strength between the foreign and the base currencies and to a lesser degree to the stability of interest rate differentials. Long-term views need not necessarily be based on forecasting methods. (A possible alternative is to use Bayesian estimates of correlations between asset classes.)

To illustrate this statement, consider two investors (one based in Japan and the other in the United States) who in mid-1988 evaluate the performance of the Salomon Brothers World Government Bond Index in relation to the performance of their respective domestic fixed-income opportunities, assuming that all securities (locally and internationally) entail equivalent risk. The American investor would conclude that the investment would have been quite attractive over the period of 1985 to mid-1988 or so, while his Japanese counterpart would conclude the opposite. This is illustrated in Exhibits 2A and 2B. The reason for this pattern was the steady

---

[3]An excellent exposition of the concept of "liability returns" and their relevance under FASB 87 can be found in Martin Leibowitz, "Liability Returns: A New Perspective on Asset Allocation" in Frank J. Fabozzi and T. Dessa Garlicki, *Advances in Bond Analysis and Portfolio Strategies*, (Chicago, Il: Probus Publishers, 1987).

EXHIBIT 2A
U.S. GOVERNMENT VERSUS U.S. NON-BASE PORTFOLIO

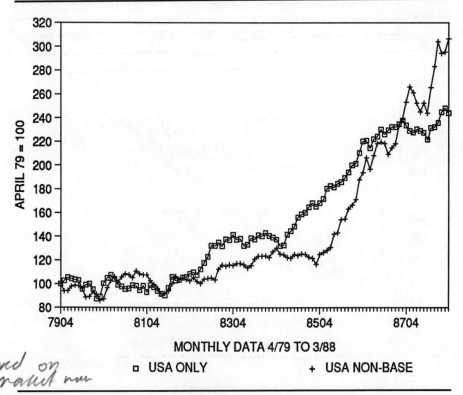

MONTHLY DATA 4/79 TO 3/88

□ USA ONLY   + USA NON-BASE

[handwritten: ...sed on market ???]

[handwritten: must consider currency relationship]

depreciation of the dollar relative to the yen coupled with the fact that the U.S. and Japan comprise the world's two largest debt markets.

THE PROBLEM OF INDEXATION

A portfolio that is "indexed" to a certain market portfolio is one which is constructed so as to replicate the risk and return pattern of the market portfolio as closely as possible. The measure of success most commonly used is "tracking error," which is defined as the standard deviation of the difference between the portfolio return and the markets' return. In what follows, the indexed portfolio will be called the "proxy portfolio" or simply "the proxy." The goal of indexing is to construct and manage a proxy portfolio which will minimize tracking error. A global index will naturally be composed of several country sub-indices, which suggests two approaches to constructing the proxy. One would be to structure the proxy portfolio so as to track the

EXHIBIT 2B
JAPAN GOVERNMENTS VERSUS JAPAN NON-BASE

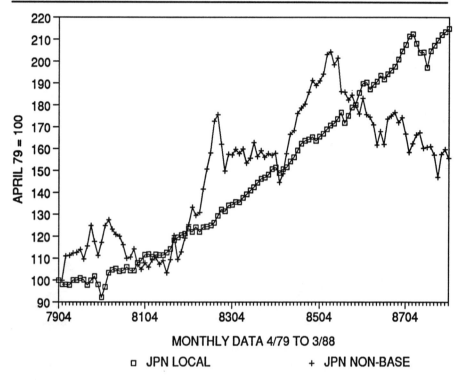

MONTHLY DATA 4/79 TO 3/88

□ JPN LOCAL   + JPN NON-BASE

entire index. An alternative would be to build proxy sub-portfolios for each constituent country and set the values of each component to correspond to the relative weight of the country in the global index.

While the first approach would effectively trade off exact weights in each country with predicted tracking error, it is more complicated to implement. This is primarily for operational considerations, namely the construction procedure would have to deal simultaneously with exchange rates, different settlement and yield conventions across countries and a host of technical details; all of which make comparisons of volatility measures across markets quite difficult.

For example the duration of two bonds from different markets are not directly comparable, as duration is a measure of yield volatility which in turn depends on yield levels.[4] Exhibit 3 depicts representative yields for a cross section of the markets. It is clear from the figure that both levels and volatilities vary widely across markets as do their co-movements.

---

[4]For elaboration see V. Gadkari and C. Thum, "Duration and Volatility in International Fixed Income Markets," in Frank J. Fabozzi (ed.) *Advances and Innovations in Bond and Mortgage Markets* (Chicago, Il: Probus Publishers, 1989).

EXHIBIT 3
TEN-YEAR GOVERNMENT YIELDS AND SPREADS VERSUS TEN-YEAR U.S. TREASURY

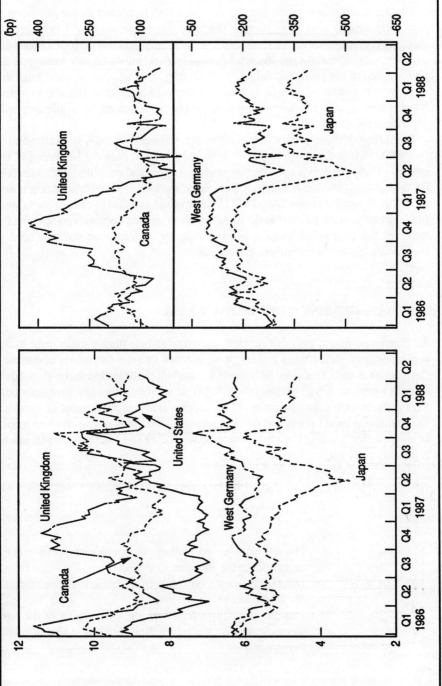

Source: Salomon Brothers, Inc.

The approach where portfolios within countries are treated as pseudo-assets is intuitively simpler and more direct. The portfolio construction and management process becomes specific to each country, so that settlement and custodial issues can be dealt with separately. At the total portfolio level, all that really matters is the performance of the proxy portfolio in each country, and the approach addresses this directly. An additional benefit is that this approach facilitates the use of active country timing schemes whereby returns might be enhanced by a manager with superior forecasting skills.

Regardless of the approach that is taken to construct the proxy, it is important to bear in mind that the construction of proxy portfolios is only the beginning of the process. These portfolios must be monitored carefully and measured with respect to the target index, so as to restructure them as the markets evolve. Rebalancing is also called for as new bonds are issued and because of the exercise of calls or puts. More fundamentally, since the vast majority of the fixed income securities comprising the major global indices are coupon bearing securities, there is an ongoing need to monitor the proper reinvestment of income.

THE MANAGEMENT OF CURRENCY RISK

As mentioned in the previous section, currency effects play a major role in the performance of global bond indices. It was shown that the magnitude of currency fluctuations is such, that over the recent time period, participation in the global debt markets would be very appealing to a U.S. investor; while a Japanese investor would have little incentive to participate. This section analyzes the impact of currency fluctuations on bond indices and describes hedging strategies whose aim is to reduce or eliminate the impact. The interrelation between debt and currency markets can be expressed succinctly as:

$$R_{mkt(i)} = R_{lmkt(i)} + R_{cur(i)} + R_{lmtk(i)} * R_{cur(i)} \tag{1}$$

where

$R_{mkt(i)}$ = The rate of return on market i from a base perspective (i.e., expressed in the investor's currency)

$R_{lmkt(i)}$ = The rate of return on market i expressed in that market's (local) currency[5]

$R_{cur(i)}$ = The rate of return on currency i with respect to the base currency that is, the return from holding one unit of the foreign currency

---

[5]This amount will be perfectly known if the investment is in a money-market instrument as opposed to a bond index.

It follows from this expression that an investment in a given foreign market implicitly consists of three separate parts. This is also the case for a global portfolio, namely:

$$R_{gport} = \sum w(i) * R_{lmkt(i)} + \sum w(i) * R_{curr(i)} +$$
$$\sum w(i) * R_{lmkt(i)} * R_{cur(i)} \tag{2}$$

where

$$w(i) = \text{investment proportion in market } i$$

The above set of equations suggest a simple method of reducing currency exposure. Namely, if it is possible to construct a synthetic security whose return pattern closely resembles the second term in these equations:

$$R_{syn(i)} \approx R_{cur(i)}$$

where

$$R_{syn(i)} = \text{return on synthetic security}$$

Then by holding that synthetic security *short*, the (hedged), return pattern for each market is approximately

$$R_{hmkt(i)} = R_{mkt(i)} - R_{syn(i)} * R_{lmkt(i)}$$
$$\approx (1 + R_{lmkt(i)}) * R_{curr(i)}$$

Alternatively, rewriting:

$$R_{mkt(i)} = R_{lmkt(i)} + (1 + R_{lmkt(i)}) * R_{cur(i)}$$

yields the pattern

$$R_{hmkt(i)} = R_{mkt(i)} - (1 + r_{lmkt(i)}) * R_{syn(i)} \approx R_{lmkt(i)}$$

$$r_{lmkt(i)} = \text{the rate of return in market } i \text{ expressed in local terms}$$

Variants of this last hedging strategy can be derived by seeking that amount (known as the hedge ratio) of the hedging security which either minimizes the variance of the differences between local returns and hedge returns: or that hedge ratio which minimizes the total variance of returns. These two hedging techniques are collectively referred to as "minimum variance" strategies.[6]

---

[6]Bruno Solnik, *International Investments* (Reading, MA: Addison Wesley, 1988).

N.B
N.B
N.B

It is clear that the issue of "how much to hedge" is the principal determinant of the success of a hedging program. In the vast majority of cases rates of return are practically impossible to predict with any degree of accuracy. Bonds however have the interesting property that a portion of their appreciation is fully known in advance. We are referring to coupon income and earnings in the form of accrued interest. If the term structure of interest rates remains unchanged for the duration of the holding period, the "certain appreciation" will equal the realized return. Assuming that coupons are reinvested to the end of the holding period at the prevailing money market rate, it follows that the certain appreciation will be roughly the same for all bonds and that its value will be very close to the beginning-of-period short-term money market rate.

Summarized, let us write,

$$R_{lmkt(i)} = R_{Lshort(i)} + R_{Llong\ (i)} \tag{3}$$

where $R_{Lshort(i)}$ and $R_{Llong(i)}$ are, respectively the "short-end" or "certain return" and the "long-end" or residual return. The residual term will respond principally to movements in the long end of the term structure. Analyzing this decomposition across countries interestingly shows that on average about 90% of the mean return is generated by the "short" component while the residual component generates 90% of total *volatility*. It turns out that the decomposition given in (3) is quite useful in determining hedge ratios. However, in order to comprehend that technique it is necessary to study the behavior of the synthetic securities alluded to earlier. The most widely used instruments are forward-exchange contracts, because of their simplicity and liquidity. It can be shown that the rate of return on these contracts is given by:

Remark

$$R_{for(i)} = R_{cur(i)} - B(i)$$

Formula

where

$$B(i) = \frac{1 + R_{short}}{1 + R_{Lshort(i)}} - 1$$

Notation

R_{short} = the short term rate in the investors *base currency*. *short term rate*

Recalling expression (3), it follows that if the hedge ratio is set equal to the total short-term return, then:

$$R_{hmkt(i)} = R_{mkt(i)} - (1 + R_{Lshort(i)}) * R_{for(i)}$$

$$= R_{short} + (1 + R_{Llong(i)}) * R_{cur(i)}$$

Aggregating this expression at the global portfolio level yields:

$$R_{hgport} = R_{short} + \sum w(i) * (1 + R_{Long(i)}) * R_{curr}(i)$$

This expression shows that hedge ratios defined by the various short-term rates have the effect of converting the global portfolio's return into a part that is basically the base short-term rate plus a portion which depends on movements of the long end of the various bond markets and on currency fluctuations. The net result will be a portfolio whose mean return will be commensurate with the base short-term rate and having a reduced level of risk.

These observations are substantiated by Exhibits 4A and 4B which show the effects of hedging as described above and by using minimum variance techniques. The "perfect hedging" column depicts local returns net of currency effects. It is worthwhile noting that standard-derivations and correlations of "perfectly hedged" bond-indices are very similar to those of the hedged returns. (The sole exception is Australia for which less than 20 observations were available.) The differences in mean returns reflects interest rate differentials, that is, the "cost" of hedging. In general terms, mean returns of currency hedged bond indices will be higher than unhedged returns for those countries having significant negative interest rate differentials with respect to the base. Therefore, to the extent that relative interest rate levels persist through time, hedging with forward-exchange contracts will signify a constant gain or loss depending on investors' numeraire. It is interesting to note that both hedging strategies yield essentially the same distributions of return.

CONSTRUCTING A PROXY PORTFOLIO WITHIN EACH COUNTRY

The problem of constructing an indexed portfolio, in principle, is quite simple: given a set of asset weights $\{w(i)\}$ for the securities comprising the index, the return on the index is:

$$r_{mkt} = \sum_i w(i)r(i)$$

where $\{r(i)\}$ denote asset returns. A proxy portfolio will be defined by a set of weights $\{v(i)\}$, choosing these weights to be equal to the index weights $(v(i) = w(i))$, virtually guarantees exact replication of the indexs' performance. This type of indexed fund is called a "census fund" and it is widely used in the equity area. The technique is not readily amenable to international bond indices primarily for two

EXHIBIT 4A
EFFECTS OF CURRENCY HEDGING ON THE SALOMON BROTHERS WORLD GOVERNMENT BOND INDEX PERSPECTIVE: U.S. MONTHLY DATA
FROM JANUARY 1978 TO DECEMBER 1987

	PERFECT HEDGING		NO HEDGING		SHORT TERM INCOME HEDGING		SINGLE CURRENCY HEDGING	
	Mean	Std. Dev	Mean	Std. Dev	Mean	Std. Dev	Mean	Std. Dev
AUD	13.83%	6.89%	10.56%	19.29%	1.54%	2.78%	5.99%	6.20%
CAN	10.92%	11.68%	9.29%	12.58%	10.18%	11.58%	9.62%	11.87%
FRA	11.28%	5.75%	10.88%	14.28%	9.23%	5.46%	9.14%	5.55%
GER	7.07%	5.81%	10.95%	14.82%	11.42%	5.77%	11.41%	5.89%
JPY	7.86%	5.48%	15.88%	16.06%	12.17%	5.55%	11.90%	5.46%
NET	8.30%	5.39%	11.58%	13.60%	11.45%	5.32%	11.18%	5.48%
SWI	4.00%	3.72%	9.91%	16.33%	10.57%	3.64%	10.66%	3.63%
UKI	12.48%	10.70%	13.23%	17.31%	11.20%	10.60%	11.07%	10.67%
USA	9.41%	10.56%	9.41%	10.56%	9.41%	10.56%	9.41%	10.56%

CORRELATIONS

(NO HEDGING = above diagonal; PERFECT HEDGING = below diagonal)

	AUD	CAN	FRA	GER	JPY	NET	SWI	UKI	USA
AUD		0.041	0.114	0.131	0.089	0.154	0.093	0.208	-0.126
CAN	-0.208		0.233	0.315	0.158	0.320	0.240	0.282	0.665
FRA	-0.011	0.393		0.850	0.655	0.874	0.762	0.442	0.042
GER	0.021	0.577	0.417		0.633	0.949	0.854	0.504	0.204
JPY	-0.030	0.381	0.330	0.598		0.631	0.648	0.407	0.113
NET	-0.011	0.551	0.513	0.753	0.475		0.847	0.536	0.217
SWI	-0.183	0.440	0.260	0.480	0.401	0.467		0.494	0.084
UKI	0.082	0.337	0.233	0.354	0.344	0.363	0.326		0.162
USA	-0.119	0.785	0.232	0.520	0.391	0.570	0.360	0.359	

MINIMUM VARIANCE HEDGING

	AUD	CAN	FRA	GER	JPY	NET	SWI	UKI	USA
AUD		0.090	-0.033	0.086	-0.125	-0.329	-0.010	0.455	-0.242
CAN	-0.154		0.375	0.579	0.375	0.569	0.446	0.339	0.764
FRA	-0.183	0.360		0.378	0.278	0.505	0.200	0.217	0.200
GER	-0.066	0.582	0.387		0.621	0.763	0.461	0.391	0.523
JPY	-0.218	0.387	0.319	0.619		0.505	0.387	0.371	0.421
NET	-0.080	0.556	0.501	0.749	0.499		0.461	0.387	0.582
SWI	-0.122	0.452	0.207	0.473	0.409	0.460		0.351	0.389
UKI	-0.092	0.342	0.209	0.374	0.361	0.376	0.347		0.377
USA	-0.151	0.782	0.198	0.527	0.399	0.580	0.380	0.363	
	AUD	CAN	FRA	GER	JPY	NET	SWI	UKI	USA

SHORT TERM INCOME HEDGING

EXHIBIT 4B
EFFECTS OF CURRENCY HEDGING OF THE SALOMON BROTHERS WORLD GOVERNMENT BOND INDEX PERSPECTIVE: JAPAN MONTHLY DATA FROM JANUARY 1978 TO DECEMBER 1987

	PERFECT HEDGING		NO HEDGING		SHORT TERM INCOME HEDGING		SINGLE CURRENCY HEDGING	
	Mean	Std. Dev	Mean	Std. Dev	Mean	Std. Dev.	Mean	Std. Dev.
AUD	13.83%	6.98%	-9.61%	21.43%	1.15%	2.58%	18.11%	7.18%
CAN	10.92%	11.68%	3.18%	17.74%	6.06%	11.62%	6.30%	11.70%
FRA	11.28%	5.75%	3.64%	11.32%	4.96%	5.57%	4.71%	5.56%
GER	7.07%	5.81%	3.83%	12.93%	7.20%	5.75%	6.80%	5.92%
JPN	7.86%	5.48%	7.86%	5.48%	7.86%	5.48%	7.86%	5.48%
NET	8.30%	5.39%	4.52%	12.11%	7.27%	5.33%	6.94%	5.43%
SWI	4.00%	3.72%	2.55%	12.95%	6.40%	3.68%	6.38%	3.73%
UKI	12.48%	10.70%	6.37%	17.36%	7.05%	10.60%	6.55%	10.68%
USA	9.41%	10.56%	3.45%	17.19%	5.32%	10.56%	5.97%	10.59%

CORRELATIONS

NO HEDGING (upper triangle) / PERFECT HEDGING (lower triangle)

	AUD	CAN	FRA	GER	JPN	NET	SWI	UKI	USA
AUD		0.407	0.154	0.122	-0.171	0.233	0.540	0.240	0.369
CAN	-0.208		0.415	0.486	0.003	0.537	0.337	0.460	0.844
FRA	-0.011	0.393		0.791	0.004	0.822	0.616	0.380	0.314
GER	0.021	0.577	0.417		0.192	0.932	0.782	0.471	0.445
JPN	-0.030	0.381	0.330	0.598		0.114	0.138	0.060	0.018
NET	-0.011	0.551	0.513	0.753	0.475		0.759	0.524	0.508
SWI	-0.183	0.440	0.260	0.480	0.401	0.467		0.410	0.252
UKI	0.082	0.337	0.233	0.354	0.344	0.363	0.326		0.416
USA	-0.119	0.785	0.232	0.520	0.391	0.570	0.360	0.359	
	AUD	CAN	FRA	GER	JPN	NET	SWI	UKI	USA

CORRELATIONS

MINIMUM VARIANCE HEDGING

	AUD	CAN	FRA	GER	JPN	NET	SWI	UKI	USA
AUD		0.276	0.394	0.267	0.354	0.252	0.250	0.690	0.326
CAN	-0.145		0.367	0.582	0.371	0.577	0.452	0.344	0.775
FRA	-0.164	0.364		0.390	0.298	0.501	0.218	0.210	0.186
GER	-0.055	0.584	0.391		0.601	0.751	0.472	0.365	0.513
JPN	-0.213	0.383	0.320	0.614		0.472	0.410	0.365	0.376
NET	-0.067	0.562	0.510	0.748	0.494		0.466	0.373	0.585
SWI	-0.097	0.447	0.230	0.480	0.413	0.469		0.351	0.370
UKI	-0.081	0.338	0.213	0.370	0.355	0.380	0.359		0.352
USA	-0.144	0.788	0.190	0.521	0.391	0.580	0.375	0.359	
	AUD	CAN	FRA	GER	JPN	NET	SWI	UKI	USA

SHORT TERM INCOME HEDGING

*NB gr... is useful way of thinking about bonds & the trends within the market as a whole can be viewed as 2D grid —

Remember

N.B.

N.B - useful way to think about bonds

interrelated reasons: on one hand, liquidity for substantial portions of some country indices can be extremely limited; on the other hand, dealing sizes (round-lots) in bonds are typically much larger than in stocks, thus the amount of capital required to buy a bond census fund would be very large.

A method for circumventing the difficulties of census funds is provided by stratified sampling techniques. In this approach, the universe of bonds is partitioned along broad, well-defined characteristics, e.g., coupon, term to maturity, sector and quality ratings. These partitions define a multidimensional grid where each cell within that grid contains those securities which satisfy all the pertinent criteria. Exhibit 5 illustrates a scheme where bonds are partitioned according to coupon rate and term to maturity. The shaded area (cell A) contains those assets having a coupon rate between 6% amd 8% and a term to maturity between 1 and 3 years.

In a typical formulation, each cell is assigned a "weight" which corresponds to the aggregate market capitalization of the securities within that cell. Stratified sampling algorithms proceed by assigning available funds to the different cells in proportion to

fig

EXHIBIT 5
TWO-DIMENSIONAL GRID ACCORDING TO COUPON RATE AND TERM TO MATURITY

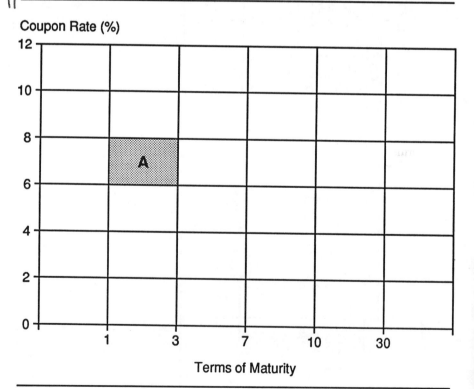

Coupon Rate (%)

Terms of Maturity

their relative weights. Those cells with the largest weights will get the majority of the funds while those with the smallest weights might not get any money at all. These algorithms are usually implemented with linear programming techniques since the allocation of investment proportions to the different cells can be posed as linear constraints, and transactions costs can be modelled as piece-wise linear cost coefficients. The stratified sampling model is as follows:

Stratified Sampling Linear Programming Algorithm

$$\text{Minimize} \left\{ \sum_i tc(i) w(i) \text{ with respect to} \{w(i)\}, \right. \tag{4}$$

such that:

$$\left\{ \underline{a}(i) \le \sum_j a(i,j) w(j) \le \bar{a}(i); i = 1,2,\dots,M \right\}$$

$$\{ \underline{w}(j) \le w(j) \le \bar{w}(j); j = 1,2,\dots N \}$$

where

$tc(i)$	=	represents the cost of transacting in bond i
$w(i)$	=	the proportion of value allocated to bond i
$a(i,j)$	=	1 if bond j is in cell i and 0 otherwise
$a(i),\bar{a}(i)$	=	lower and upper bounds on exposure to cell i
$w(j),\bar{w}(j)$	=	lower and upper bounds on holdings in bond j

In this simple framework, the manager cannot impose constraints on the number of securities held nor on the value of the portfolio in question. Moreover the optimal solution is not constrained to consist of "roundlots" which could potentially lead to un-tradable portfolios. These limitations can be circumvented to some degree by heuristic algorithms applied to the optimal solution. However, these limitations can only be completely resolved by using mixed integer programming techniques which are significantly more complicated and difficult to implement.

The methods outlined above disregard bond price dynamics completely. It is well known that homogeneous groups of bonds move together over time to a very large degree. The underlying force being, of course, the evolution of the term structure of interest rates. A natural extension to the stratified sample model is to incorporate the sensitivity of the proxy portfolio to interest rates. More clearly, the proxy is structured so that its interest rate sensitivity (within each cell) closely matches the sensitivities of the corresponding segments of the benchmark index. The motivation being that the proxy will match the index's characteristics and move in unison with it, thus guaranteeing very tight tracking. This enhancement is accomplished by adding a set of equations of the form:

NB *11*

$$\left\{ \underline{D}(i) \le \sum_j a(i,j) * d(j) * w(j) \le \bar{D}(i); i = 1,2,\ldots,M \right\}$$

to problem (4) for each measure of interest rate sensitivity. Here $d(j)$ denotes the interest rate sensitivity of bond j and $\underline{D}$, $\bar{D}$ denote the lower and upper bounds on the proxy's exposure to that measure (taken relative to the corresponding index exposure).

The best known measures of interest-rate sensitivity are duration and convexity. In spite of the fact that these concepts are based on unrealistic assumptions (a flat yield curve and parallel shifts of that curve); in the vast majority of scenarios these concepts have been used successfully as risk management tools.

More general sensitivity measures can be derived from models that explain the term structure of interest rates as a function of observed market prices.[7] A model of this type provides "fair" valuations for all the constituents of a given bond market. These valuations are expressed as a function of the time value of money, and in addition, yield spreads induced by credit risk and imbedded options. Information about the time value of money is summarized in a set of "discount factors" which effectively give the value of a payment to be received at a specified future date. Individual bonds are modelled as bundles of "pure payments" which are common across all bonds. Within this context a return model is derived by noting that observed changes in bond prices can be expressed as a function of observed changes in model parameters plus a residual (asset-specific) component. From the time series of parameter estimates, a model for investment risk is derived by computing parameter means and covariances.

The base model (4) can be modified to incorporate these concepts by rewriting (5) as a "definition-constraint":

$$\sum_j a(i,j) * d(i,j) * w(j) = D_p(i) \quad ; i = 1,2,\ldots,M \quad (6)$$

and the quadratic term

$$\sum \left[D_p(i) - D_I(i) \right] * V(i,j) * \left[D_p(j) - D_I(j) \right] \quad (7)$$

where $D_I(i)$ is the sensitivity of the index to changes in factor i. $V(i,j)$ denotes the covariance between changes in discount factors i and j.

---

[7]A good summary of the current views on the measurement of the term structure of interest rates can be found in R.J. Shiller and J.H. McCullogh, "The Term Structure of Interest Rates," Cowles Foundation for Research in Economics at Yale University, July 1987.

This last expression transforms the basic model into a quadratic programming model which, although more complicated to implement than linear programming models, they can be solved with existing technology.[8] The incorporation of integer-type constraints is a very new field for which limited results exist as of this writing.

Decision support systems derived from term structure models are inituitively more appealing than simple duration-matching schemes since the core is a model for investment risk. However, the construction of said risk model is quite involved if it is intended to be a predictive model. Typical risk models are essentially sample statistics which by and large will have limited predictive ability.

CASE STUDY: TRACKING THE SBWGBI

This section describes the results that were obtained by applying the concepts which have been outlined in this chapter to the problem of tracking two variants of the Salomon Brothers World Government Bond Index (SBWGBI). One variant is the full index from the perspective of a U.S. investor. The other, which is referred to as the "non-base-U.S. SBWGBI" is formed by removing the U.S. from the full index and valuing the resulting subset in U.S. dollars. The following assumptions were made:

1. The simulation spans January 1985 through December 1987. (The current SBWGBI was created in January of 1985.)
2. Initial amounts of U.S. $25, 50 and 100 million were allocated across countries at the beginning of each simulation with the intention of gauging the effect of portfolio size on tracking error. Amounts assigned to the various countries corresponded to the weight of each country in the index. When this amount fell below U.S. $1 million, those funds were spread out evenly across the other countries and no investment was made in the country in question.
3. Rebalancing took place only at month-end. Transaction costs were taken into account, these differed across countries and across maturities within countries. Bonds were traded only in round-lots as defined for each country. Idle cash as well as coupon receipts are invested at the prevailing Euro CD rate for each country.
4. All issues satisfying the eligibility criteria for the index were considered for inclusion in the proxy. No other securities were considered. The selection algorithm was designed to favor those bonds with large amounts outstanding.

   The simulation program starts out by assigning funds to each country, and in each, an optimal portfolio is constructed (with idle cash invested in Euro CD's).

---

[8]See A.F. Perold, "Solving Large Portfolio Optimization Problems" manuscript, Graduate School of Business Administration, Harvard University, Boston, Massachusetts (1981).

At the end of the month the portfolios are valued and country weights are compared with those of the index. If these weights lie within prescribed tolerances nothing is done, otherwise funds are re-distributed across countries. The next step is to rebalance the country sub-portfolios to account for cash contributions or withdrawals (originated by country weight re-distributions and by coupon and interest income); and also to modify the portfolios' exposure to the index in view of evolving market conditions and switching opportunities. The program proceeds in this fashion until the end of the simulation period at which point a detailed attribution of relative performance takes place. The tables in Exhibit 6 summarize the performance attribution reports.

The algorithm used to buy and sell bonds within the different countries is basically a stratified sampling algorithm (4) with provisions made for definition constraints (5) for interest rate sensitivity. The quadratic objective function (7) has been substituted for a separable, linearized equivalent. A heuristic post-processor is used to ensure that trading takes place only in round-lots (the core algorithm also favors round-lot trades). If limited funds make the problem infeasible, the definition constraints are collapsed across cells to ensure that interest-rate sensitivity of the *entire* index will be matched. This relaxed problem will be feasible by definition.

OPERATIONAL ISSUES

This section contains a brief outline of the government bonds of Canada, France, Germany, Japan, the Netherlands, Switzerland, and the United Kingdom. The purpose is to provide a succinct overview of the subject rather than an in-depth analysis.

We have excluded non-government securities principally because they comprise a relatively small portion of the universe of securities available to international investors. On the other hand, the accurate classification of the many sources of investment risk (volatilities of credit-spread and valuation of imbedded options) makes the subject highly specialized and goes beyond the scope of this chapter.

The bond manager accustomed to U.S. Treasury securities should be aware that the government bond markets of some of the aforementioned countries are not nearly as straight forward. Conversely, a British investor in gilts would consider any of the other markets extremely simple to understand.

As will be seen below, the complicating factors in these markets (as far as analyzing security characteristics is concerned) are imbedded options, mandatory sinking fund provisions, conversion features and non-standard mechanisms for the purchase of securities. Two other major factors are limited liquidity and withholding tax.

EXHIBIT 6
TRACKING ERROR SUMMARY
INDEX: U.S. DOLLAR BASE SALOMON BROTHERS
WORLD GOVERNMENT BOND INDEX
AVERAGE TRACKING ERROR (PROXY - INDEX) IN PERCENT

Quarter	(Portfolio Values in millions)		
	100	50	25
85 - 1	0.01	0.07	0.36
85 - 2	0.01	0.17	0.22
85 - 3	0.02	0.04	0.10
85 - 4	−0.06	−0.01	0.03
86 - 1	−0.02	0.05	0.35
86 - 2	−0.05	0.11	0.06
86 - 3	0.07	0.03	−0.21
86 - 4	−0.04	−0.12	−0.06
87 - 1	0.02	0.04	0.11
87 - 2	−0.04	0.06	0.22
87 - 3	0.04	0.09	0.21
87 - 4	0.15	−0.08	0.07
Average number of positions	60	40	25

INDEX: U.S. DOLLAR NON-BASE SALOMON BROTHERS
WORLD GOVERNMENT BOND INDEX
AVERAGE TRACKING ERROR (PROXY - INDEX) IN PERCENT

Quarter	(Portfolio Values in millions)		
	100	50	25
85 - 1	0.03	0.03	0.23
85 - 2	−0.01	0.01	0.20
85 - 3	−0.08	−0.05	0.04
85 - 4	0.01	−0.07	0.15
86 - 1	−0.05	0.00	0.36
86 - 2	−0.02	−0.04	0.19
86 - 3	−0.02	0.05	0.07
86 - 4	−0.04	−0.03	−0.16
87 - 1	0.01	−0.02	0.17
87 - 2	0.03	0.01	−0.05
87 - 3	0.05	0.19	−0.06
87 - 4	−0.17	0.10	0.35
Average number of positons	50	35	20

The Guilder Market

The Guilder market is characterized by mandatory retirement of debt by fixed payment over the last few years of the bond's life. This is thought to be a complicating factor, but the cash flows of the bond can be determined in advance and can be accounted for accordingly. The redemption schedules are guaranteed as the government cannot repurchase bonds on the open market. Also, it is the amount redeemed that is guaranteed, not which particular issues will be sunk. By registering the bonds with Euro-Clear, Cedel, Giro or Schuldregister the bonds will be sunk proportionately each year. This differs from personally holding the bond when there is uncertainty whether your particular issue will be sunk. The sinking fund bonds have less liquidity than the bullet bonds though reasonable liquidity is assured in a number of issues. The sinking fund bonds have had greater yields than the bullet bonds, because of an international preference for bullet bonds due to lack of familiarity with sinking fund provisions.

U.K. Gilts

U.K. Gilts offer a wide range of maturities with various coupons that are attractive to different investors due to funding requirements and tax status. Further complementing this broad range of securities are the bonds issued partially paid. These bonds are essentially bought on time with a principal payment and then a fixed payment schedule. While initially issued to smooth out cash flows to the Bank of England, their leveraging features have made them attractive for speculative purposes, which in turn has led to increased volatility for partially paid issues. Convertible gilts confer to the bondholder the option for conversion into one of two longer-dated securities. A complicating factor is that not all of the options are necessarily exercised and this might cause the new bonds to be illiquid. Investors need to be careful not only in pricing issues, but also when converting. FOTRA (Free of Tax to Residents Abroad) stocks comprise a significant proportion of the gilt market. The special tax treatment they are accorded is reflected in a premium relative to comparable issues.

The French Treasury

The French Treasury in 1985 settled on a standard form for new bond issues. Prior to 1985 the government bonds took many forms with different options. Pre-1979 Obligation Renouvelables du Tresor, (ORT) bonds were set up with a sinking fund which would work similar to the Dutch bonds. Other bonds had options to convert into variable rate bonds or to extend the life of the bond. The new issues (Obligation Assimilable du Tresor, OAT) are either fixed or floating rate bonds without any of the conversion or sinking fund nuances. These bonds are issued with maturities of 7 to

25 years and already represent a significant portion of the outstanding treasuries. Also of interest to institutional investors are the French Treasury Bills (Bons du Tresor a Fixe et Interest Annual, BTAN), which are issued with maturities of up to 7 years.

German Government Bonds

German government bonds include those issued by the Federal Railroad (Bundesbahn) and the Post Office (Bundespost). All of these bonds are backed by the Federal government and offer investors virtually no credit risk. Strong demand from international investors recently has reduced the yield of the Bundesbank bonds relative to the other government bonds. The Bundesbank bonds have higher liquidity than comparable alternatives. These securities are all "straight bonds" paying annual coupons.

Japanese Government Bonds

There are two main types of Japanese government bonds, coupon bonds and 5-year discount bonds. Maturities range between 2 and 10 years. These bonds are typically issued with call provisions, however to date there is no evidence of the option ever being exercised. A peculiar characteristic of this market is the price behavior of the benchmark bond. This bond is typically (but not always) the most recently issued 10-year bond. A substantial amount of the trading volume in that market is concentrated in this particular issue. This results in a liquidity premium which has exceeded 100 basis points in the recent past.

Switzerland Government Bonds

Switzerland has the smallest amount of outstanding bonds, has limited liquidity and due to the budget surplus this market has been declining. International investors make up only a small portion of the market because of withholding tax considerations.

Canadian Government Bonds

The Canadian government bond market is the largest debt market in that country and is very tightly linked to the U.S. Treasury market. These bonds offer a broad range of coupons (from 3% up to 16¼%) and with maturities between 1 and 42 years. The maturity of the typical recent long bond has been 25 years. These securities are essentially noncallable (with exception of a small older issue). However, there exist several extendable Canadian Government bonds which can be exchanged at the option of the bondholder for bonds maturing at a later date.

Summary

While these many features seem to complicate the portfolio composition, they actually can be used to improve the construction of the portfolio. The sinking fund bonds will increase the cash position of the portfolio without selling any bonds. Likewise the options to convert into long-term securities can allow for a term structure change and avoid transaction costs. These bonds should not be excluded because of their options.

All secondary trading is done through the large securities houses in each country and in some cases foreign houses also. With the exception of Canada, bond prices are quoted on the local stock exchange. The actual trading for the British market is performed on the floor to the London Stock Exchange. Most of the markets settle within two days, with Britain a little faster and Canada and Switzerland a little slower.

International exchanges are also taking advantage of improvements in computer technology by switching to registered bonds from bearer bonds. Switzerland is the only country that has not switched (probably due to banking secrecy).

In addition to the transfer taxes in Japan and Switzerland, interest payments to U.S. investors are subject to withholding taxes of 10% and 5%, respectively. This is the net tax as double taxation treaties allow a refund of most of the tax. In Australia and Britain the net tax is zero for U.S. investors who have filed for the refund.

CONCLUSION

Participation in global bond markets offers a broad spectrum of risk/return alternatives. The decision to hedge some or all of the currency risk depends on the investor's objectives and risk aversion. This decision may be active or passive. Fixed-income indexing strategies, if applied at the individual country level (with global idiosyncrasies accounted for) can yield attractive results and enable the investor to control transaction costs. Active and passive country allocation strategies, coupled with country indexation, offer the investor a framework within which to seek returns in excess of those derived from a market-capitalization country-weighting approach.

Chapter 5

Mortgaged-Backed Securities Indexation

LLEWELLYN MILLER
FIRST VICE PRESIDENT
DREXEL BURNHAM LAMBERT

EDWARD P. KRAWITT*

MICHAEL P. WANDS
ASSOCIATE
DREXEL BURNHAM LAMBERT

Portfolio management strategies can be characterized by the extent to which they depend on the accurate anticipation of uncertain events. For managers of mortgage pass-through securities, the principal uncertainty is the dynamics of interest rates in terms of both volatility and level or more directly, their impact on prices and prepayments. Substantial performance enhancement from favorable prepayments as well as price movement can be obtained through successful timing of the market by

*This chapter was written when Edward P. Krawitt was in the employ of Drexel Burnham Lambert.

reallocating portfolio attributes to benefit extraordinarily from market rallies and defend against market falls over an anticipated interest rate cycle. Secondarily, and more subtly, management tasks concentrate on the ability to identify specific securities that exhibit exceptional value among available bonds suggested by the rate forecasts. Such value may be realized either through favorable correction of mispricing in the short run, or with a combination of positive price moves and advantageous prepayments over a longer investment horizon.

This enhanced performance is accompanied by the risk of inaccurate interest rate forecasts that, if incorporated, lead to results that are worse than average. Extraordinary performance, whether below or above average, is often expressed in terms of total return benchmarks that purport to represent average market performance.

The commonly used sources of market average performance data are regularly published indices or index returns. An index return is the market-value weighted average total return of all securities included by the index. For current purposes the discussion is restricted to the U.S. government agency mortgage pass-throughs. The term *index* interchangeably refers to the universe of securities included in the compilation as well as the time-series of periodic total returns achieved by the securities. If that universe has certain attributes which make it representative of a particular market, then it can be said to reflect the experience of the average investor in that market.

The total returns are typically expressed as the month-to-month percentage change in accumulated value due to price change, accrued interest, coupon payments, principal repayments and reinvestment income from intra-month cash flows. The calculation must also incorporate the change in the market compositon from new issues, scheduled and unscheduled principal repayment. Indices differ by the specifications that determine inclusion of individual securities such as the minimum current outstanding or remaining time to maturity. Typically, the movements in and out of the index are treated as month-end events even if they are mid-month occurrences. Index conventions also vary in reinvestment treatment of intra-month cash flows from ignoring it to assuming a conservative money market rate until month end.

Performance over longer periods can be easily calculated by multiplying the periodic returns for the months under consideration (after making the proper conversion to decimal fractions).

A common comparison between the performance of a portfolio and the performance of an index or among the performances of managed portfolios is based on rates of total return. This is appropriate if the portfolios or indices are of comparable risk. A qualitative comparison based on the types of bonds held in the portfolio or represented by the index may be sufficient to justify a comparison of total returns. Such risk comparisons should include the difference in risk due to credit, calls, prepayment and market value volatility. A serviceable summary measure of risk is the relative variability of returns often expressed as standard deviation of return.

The comparisons should also be based on similar total return calculations. The calculations should weigh contributions of appreciation, coupon income and reinvestment comparably. As mentioned above, reinvestment treatment of mid-month cash flows vary and can affect return comparability.

When return rates alone are used to make comparisons, the time interval chosen may have a bearing on its validity. Small differences in volatility among portfolios can lead to significant differences in rates of return during periods of exceptional volatility. By including a full market cycle, the analysis should minimize most of the aberrations that come from using short intervals.

The validity of comparing portfolios to an index had, until recently, been questioned. The return calculations for indices were considered unrealizable since they excluded transaction costs and more generally because the index itself was not an available investment option. As a response, designers of various indices have attempted to make index results replicable. Investment managers currently offer index funds providing investments that track a target index in performance very closely. Their availability makes index comparisons meaningful because the index is a valid alternative. The providers of such index funds have adopted duplication of the index returns as their performance objective for portfolio management.

Performance fees payable to many investment managers are based on the extent to which they outperform a selected index. For them, the object is to exceed index returns substantially and consistently. Index returns become the lower boundary for acceptable performance rather than the target. This strategy is sometimes called *index-plus* or *enhanced indexing*.

The purpose of the remainder of this chapter is to examine the problems of and alternative solutions to managing an index fund or to implementing an index-plus strategy for mortgage pass-through securities. These index-related strategies are attractive to investors who want to achieve at least market average performance while accommodating their level of confidence in their ability to forecast rates.

To facilitate discussion of the management process, it's helpful to acknowledge that we are really dealing with three distinct portfolios.

The *market portfolio* consists of all the securities that the relevant investor base could purchase or sell, weighted by their actual presence in the market. The distinction between equity and fixed-income, or between taxable and tax-exempt segments may appear contrived. However, for many purposes these market segmentations are observed by institutions and any practical implementation should incorporate that separation.

The *index portfolio* consists of all the securities included in the index. As comprehensive or as representative of the market portfolio as the index is intended to be, practical considerations require observation of some arbitrary rules of exclusion to reflect relative availability in the market of some thinly represented or seldom traded securities. If replicability of the index is a serious consideration in the index construction, then inaccessible securities, and those so thinly traded that reliable pricing is impossible, should be excluded. However, every exclusion obviously increases the gap between the index and market portfolios.

As the index universe is a subset of the market, the investor portfolio, the *index-track fund* or *index-fund* is in turn a subset of the index portfolio. The popular indices include hundreds or thousands of individual issues. For practical reasons the number of securities actually selected must be considerably less than those constituting the index.

INDEX FUND MANAGEMENT THROUGH CONVENTIONAL CELLULAR APPROACH

For a strict indexing objective, the intuitively attractive approach would be to construct a miniature replica of the index portfolio by including every component security in the index in its proper proportion. Since the popular indices track thousands of entries and because generally odd lot holdings are uneconomical, the need for replicating index performance with a relatively small sampling of securities becomes clear. In the mortgage pass-through market, each pool is unique in its prepayment trajectory even if it shares all other features. The number of pools currently totals over 300,000. This collection can be broken down by several features including coupon, program, issue year, or remaining term. When restricted to pool categories that are sufficiently traded, we can reduce the number to 250 generics. If we further restrict selection to regularly traded and liquid generics, the count is about 95.

The mortgage index returns are largely determined by the performance of about 200 representative generics. This still remains too large a sampling of securities except for very large portfolios.

In general, for bond portfolios the most popular alternative is to partition the universe of securities reflected in the index into gross sectors—Treasury, agency, corporate, mortgages—as well as industry, credit rating, coupon and maturity subgroups. For the mortgage sector the results are cells that are homogeneous with respect to bond terms such as coupon, maturity, and agency program. One benefit, if successful, is that the cells may then be effectively managed independently.

The effectiveness of this cell construction is the extent to which the similarity of bond terms translate into homogeneous subsets with respect to total return performance. In the case of mortgage pass-throughs the commonality with respect to prepayment responsiveness to rate dynamics in a market pricing framework is assumed to suggest the similarity in risk-return characteristics.

It's tempting to interpret the goal as the process—mimick the index portfolio performance by a comprehensive sampling of the index portfolio structured to duplicate the weighted average terms as well as distribution of as many bond terms as is practical. The result is a portfolio with a weighted average coupon, maturity and distribution of coupon and maturity among several mortgage-pool programs equal to that of the index portfolio. Cash flows would be reinvested to maintain such averages and distributions. Periodic restructurings would be required to effect adjustments to maintain tracking tolerance when regular reinvestments are insufficient. This approach might be called "index term" tracking.

Accepting the index return as a performance goal, the very effort of tracking bond terms will introduce discrepancies between index and fund performance.

Transaction costs—Typically, the maintenance of the index emulation or tracking tolerance requires a great deal of portfolio turnover—50% a year is not uncommon. Transaction costs are not included in the performance of the popular indices because they are not intrinsic to the market itself even when the typical flow of funds through the market portfolio, due to calls, maturity or change in credit rating induces turnover. However, the "index terms" tracker is committed to incurring the cost of restructuring just to keep up with the pace of the funds flow.

Counterproduction—The very activity of realigning the portfolio can result in degraded performance. The market segment that shows the most growth can many times, not surprisingly, represent the segment with impending oversupply. Oversupply can result in depressed prices, much like any market-traded commodity. This is a more pronounced problem in the corporate sector, but manifests itself to varying degrees in all sectors. The diligent index terms tracker is programmed, under these circumstances, to trade out of favorable sectors and to reallocate into a likely disfavored prospect.

Misrepresentation—The criteria on which matching is based—coupon, credit rating, maturity, industry sector, etc.—may not be complete enough to capture the market valuation process. In most cases, an effective consideration of calls, puts, prepayments and sinking funds is left out of the analysis. These features are important to determining the links between bond descriptions and bond cash flows and price movement.

Inappropriate Measures—The selection of cell representatives is usually based on the "cheapest securities" among those that constitute the cell. Many times the yield calculation used is unrelated to periodic return as reported by indices. Although "what's cheap is cheap" is a viable rule of thumb, a performance criterion that reflected index return calculations would be more helpful. Treatment of reinvestment income is the single largest variable in different return calculations such as total realized return and yield to maturity.

A CASH FLOW MATCHING APPROACH

A more direct approach to matching portfolios is a modification of the cash matching procedure typically used to select dedicated portfolios. Under this technique, securities are selected on the basis of the degree to which asset cash inflow matches the liability outflows. The preferred portfolio is that which meets the liability requirements at the lowest cost. Typically, the cash flow schedules of both the assets and liabilities are fixed and assumed to be known with certainty and neither credit nor market risks need to be considered. The degree of mismatch is the extent to which the asset and liability cash flow schedules differ.

In the case of index matching, the cash flows are associated with a pricing model for the component bonds. The general form of the model is that price is a function of expected cash flows, a schedule of spot discount rates, and factors peculiar to the subject securities such as credit quality, gross maturity, and characteristics of embedded options.

Securities with similar characterizations would be assumed to have pricing models of the same form—that is in their relative weighting of securities' cash flow along the spot rate term structure and in turn their influence on price.

This format could form the basis for partitioning the index portfolio into subsets which exhibit similar price dynamics. For this to utilize a cash-match formulation, it's sufficient that two securities with similar cash flow schedules at a given interest rate environment exhibit similar price sensitivity to interest rates. The exact specification is not necessary.

A first step might be to partition the index portfolio into subsets characterized by: (1) uniform yield-related factors such as cash flow risk due to credit considerations and uncertainty due to option/prepayment features and (2) similarity of cash flow distributions along respective term structures.

Second, securities in an index fund would be separated into their proper subsets. The degree of the match between index portfolio and index fund has two dimensions—the similarity of (1) market value distributions among the subsets and (2) the cash flow schedules within each subset.

A SUBSECTOR EXAMPLE

Consider an index portfolio subset defined by all GNMA single-family coupons between 10% and 12%, with ages between two and six years. These securities share credit and other characteristics that influence cash flow distributions and valuation. Even if the relationship between this cash flow distribution and total return were not well defined or well understood, it is reasonable to assume that the extent to which distributions of cash flows of similar quality match that of the index portfolio is strongly related to the extent of the return match between the two.

At current prepayment levels, the cash flow schedule is represented by the lower schedule in Exhibit 1. This graph displays the difference between the cash flow distribution of the index subset (lower curve) and that of the securities chosen to represent it (upper curve).

For pass-through securities the cash flow schedule is a function of the yield environment to which the bond is subjected—this applies to any bond with an associated contingent claim. For this reason the cash flow distribution comparisons

EXHIBIT 1
MBS CASH FLOW SCHEDULE
GNMA SF 10%-12% VS PORTFOLIO CELL
CURRENT INTEREST RATE ENVIRONMENT

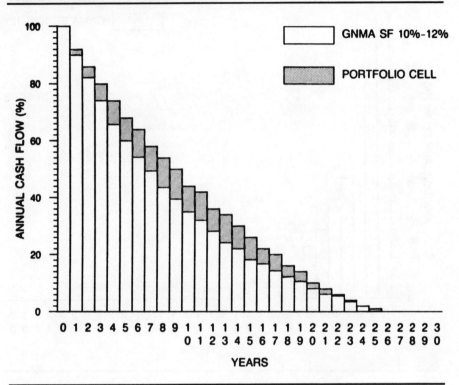

must incorporate the effects of interest rate dynamics. Stated differently, the comparison should include distribution dynamics as well as statics.

Exhibits 2 and 3 show the difference in schedules due to prepayment sensitivity to rates.

For each index-portfolio matching, a measure of similarity indicated by the magnitude of the shaded area between the curves in Exhibit 1 could be minimized under several interest rate conditions, resulting in a portfolio with matching cash flow distribution within small rate ranges and similar cash flow dynamics. Such an optimization is feasible and could conceivably be performed for either the entire portfolio or for the sub-sectors to evaluate purchase opportunities with respect to impact on index tracking. It's feasible, but not very practical under most circumstances.

EXHIBIT 2
MBS CASH FLOW SCHEDULE
GNMA SF 10%-12%
LOW INTEREST RATE ENVIRONMENT

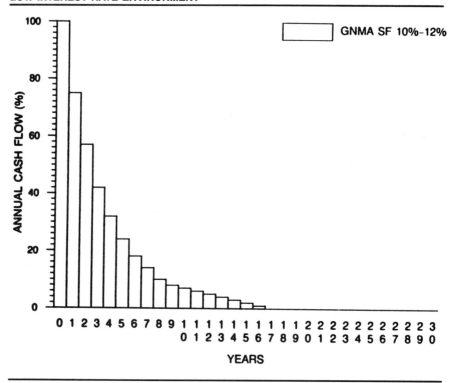

REALIZING THE POTENTIAL OF THE CELLULAR APPROACH

The use of cells in the management process is intended to simplify the identification of candidates for portfolio growth and swaps. Cell definition should alleviate the task of simultaneous consideration of duration, convexity, liquidity and market weights by grouping securities that share the performance-related parameters.

When the approach is implemented correctly the manager may make selections through a multi-step process.

- Determine the market value to be allocated to each meaningfully defined cell.
- Select securities from each cell for either matching the index returns or exceeding index returns.

For cell definition to be useful, the breakdown must carry certain attributes.

EXHIBIT 3
MBS CASH FLOW SCHEDULE
GNMA SF 10%-12%
HIGH INTEREST RATE ENVIRONMENT

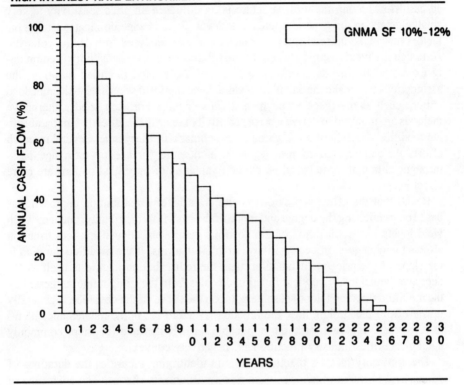

- *Replicatility*—The cell must include pools that are readily available in the market.
- *Scaling to the portfolio size in question*—Smaller portfolios must invest in fewer individual securities to obtain favorable pricing.
- *Homogeneity*—Pools within a given cell should be sufficiently homogenous so that selection can be based on simple calculations using, at most, readily observable parameters such as price, coupon, WAM or WART, and program type plus a relevant return measure.

While both approaches described—cash flow distribution matching and bond terms distribution matching—have serious drawbacks, they have useful features and intuitive appeal. In the following we set forth the mortgage application of a method for assembling and maintaining an index-oriented portfolio that combines and enhances the contributions from the above techniques, while alleviating some of the impracticalities and counterproductivity.

EXPLICITLY OPTION-BASED CRITERIA

The single most relevant feature of the distribution of scheduled or currently expected cash flows along the term structure is its influence on price sensitivity to very small changes in the general interest rate level. Price change dominates among the factors that make up total return for short horizons analyzed in indexing contexts. Although the relationship between this distribuiton and price sensitivity is commonly expressed by the duration calculation and the related modified duration, the assumptions that make the calculation valid do not apply to securities with embedded options such as mortgage prepayments, calls or puts. For such bonds, alternative methods are required to derive a price sensitivity factor that is directly comparable to the modified duration of a conventional benchmark Treasury note. Several research efforts have attempted to produce such a measure for agency mortgage pass-throughs although those based on explicit valuation of imbedded options are more effective.

Recall that the effectiveness of the earlier cash flow distribution approach was based on monitoring the degree and mode of the cash flow distribution changes when yield levels move. In terms of the portfolio return objectives, this redistribution affects the change in price sensitivity. In graphic terms, if the modified duration is the slope of the price/yield function, then the redistribution manifests itself as the degree to which the price/yield function deviates from the straight line suggested by the modified duration (slope) at some point on the curve. If the deviation is generally upward from the straight line, the function is said to be, in the mathematics literature, convex. If downward, the applicable term is concave (or more commonly among securities industry practitioners, negatively convex).

The convexity factor's practical use is in identifying securities the durations of which tend to move in tandem when rate environments change. The advantage of successful duration and convexity matching with index tracking (or any asset-asset match application) is that it results in reduced portfolio rebalancing and thereby lower turnover-induced transaction costs.

Cell definition used in index fund management based on effective modified duration and convexity homogeniety is in general more useful than those based on bond terms. The advantage comes from the more direct approach of emulating index performance rather than the index portfolio's distribution of bond terms. Flow of funds through the index portfolio changes bond terms' distribution, but this dynamic does not necessarily have a one-to-one correspondence to the index portfolio's modified duration, or convexity. There will most likely exist opportunities to realign the price sensitivity match with less turnover than would be suggested by reestablishing the bond term match.

Exhibit 4 displays the distribution of 98 pass-through generics on the convexity, duration plane. Securities in close proximity will share price movement behavior under most interest rate scenarios, including those characterized by changes in

EXHIBIT 4
MORTGAGE MARKET GOOD DURATION VS. GOOD CONVEXITY—FEBRUARY 1987
NOMENCLATURE

Prefix	Sec Type	Coupon	Example
G	GNMA SF	In Percent	G825 = "GNMA SF 8.25%"
FP	GNA GPM	In Percent	GP1225 = "GNMA GPM 12.25%"
G15Y	GNMA 15YR	In Percent	G15Y10 = "GNMA 15YR 10%"
F	FHLMC G/S	In Percent	F9 = "FHLMC G/S 9%"
FP	FHLMC PC	In Percent	FP11 = "FHLMC PC 11%"
FN	FNMA MBS	In Percent	FN95 = "FNMA MBS 9.5%"
F15Y	F G/S 15YR	In Percent	F15Y9 = "F G/S 15YR 9%"
FP15Y	F PC 15YR	In Percent	FP15Y85 = "F PC15YR 8.5%"
FN15Y	FNMA 15YR	In Percent	FN15Y = "FNMA 15 YR 9%"

Note: For securities where two coupon/WAM classes exist, the new class is assumed except when marked with an "*"

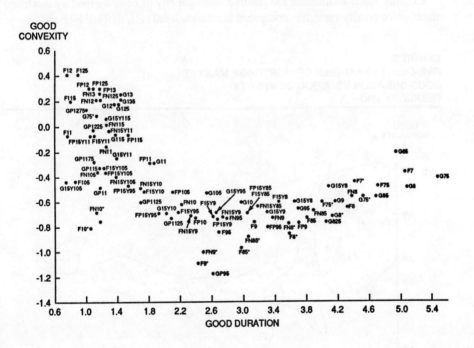

market yield levels, yield curve shapes and yield spreads due to valuation of likely prepayments.

Cells are constructed on the basis of partitioning this universe into clusters of relative homogeneity as measured by distance between points. Because not all generics are equally represented in the market, the partitioning incorporates the relative market value presence of each security so that most clusters have sufficient liquidity to be useful or replicable.

Exhibits 5 and 6 show two possible partitionings of the universe with five and ten cells, respectively. The number of cells chosen should be related to the size of the index fund under consideration since the dollar volume available for purchases determines the number of pools, or other economically obtainable units, that are practical. The maximum number of cells would be such that the smallest cell can be filled with round lot amounts. It should be noted that optimality may be sacrificed if the solution forces a cell to be represented by a single security because either the match may be deliberately missed to achieve round lot volume or the parametric match is accomplished by the incurring of the diseconomies of odd lots.

Exhibits 7 and 8 illustrate the relative homogeneity of cells defined by modified duration/convexity measures compared to conventional cells defined by bond terms.

EXHIBIT 5
FIVE-CELL BREAKDOWN OF MORTGAGE MARKET
GOOD DURATION VS. GOOD CONVEXITY
FEBRUARY 1987

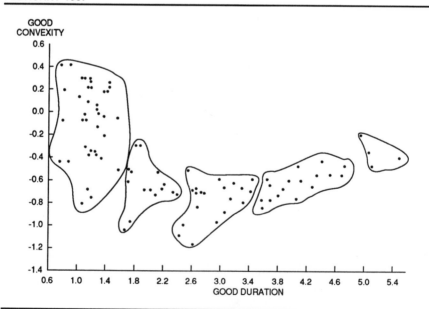

EXHIBIT 6
TEN-CELL BREAKDOWN OF MORTGAGE MARKET
GOOD DURATION VS. GOOD CONVEXITY
FEBRUARY 1987

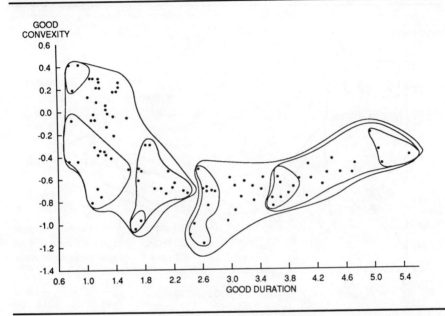

Although the conventional cells have restrictive definitions (see legends), they exhibit significant heterogeneity with respect to prospective price behavior. The new cells combine securities across programs and coupon categories that would not typically be considered alike upon inspection of terms.

The tree is configured so that each cell is a proper subset of another cell further along in the hierarchy. This allows a change in the number of cells without having to split up any cells. Such splitting would necessitate reallocating cell representatives and rebalancing selections to accommodate the new cell definitions.

Movement up or down the hierarchy involves trade-offs. Increased aggregation as one moves down the tree reduces the number of cells to manage and, possibly, the overall number of securities to be selected but corresponding decreases in homogeneity increase the likelihood of misrepresenting the cell through application of naive security selection rules. Moving up the tree increases the homogeneity but increases the number of cells and reduces the possibility of naive security selection. For each portfolio size and style there exists a most appropriate level in the hierarchy. Finally, the actual portfolio is chosen for the desired return.

EXHIBIT 7
CONVENTIONAL MARKET BREAKDOWN VS. GOOD DURATION/GOOD CONVEXITY
CELL DEFINITION
MORTGAGE MARKET—FEBRUARY 1987

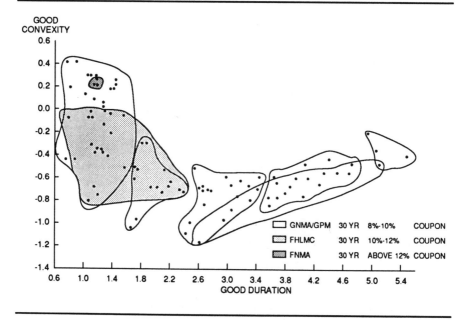

CRITERIA FOR SECURITIES SELECTION

A useful mortgage valuation method should include the following features to be considered useful for indexing as well as other portfolio assembly purposes.

1. The valuations should be rate-anticipation neutral. Validity should not rest on the ability to forecast interest rates or prepayment rates. They should incorporate the effects of the relationship between conditional prepayment rates and interest rate levels for non-generics as well as generics.
2. Return performance should be expressed in terms directly comparable to benchmark Treasury securities, such as yield to maturity, as well as in terms used in the index of interest or some other realizable return measure.

To accommodate the varying cell definition for different portfolio needs, especially with respect to size, a pool classification system in the form of hierarchical trees is used (see Exhibit 9). As one moves through the tree, the level of aggregation increases as the level of homogeneity decreases.

EXHIBIT 8
CONVENTIONAL MARKET BREAKDOWN VS. GOOD DURATION/GOOD CONVEXITY
CELL DEFINITION
MORTGAGE MARKET—FEBRUARY 1987

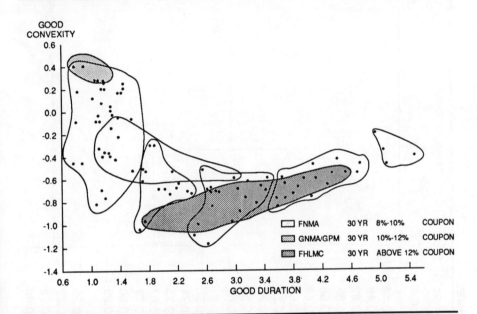

3. Measures of price sensitivity to interest rates should be consistent and reliable across the coupon range. This provides a measure that locates mortgages at appropriate points on the yield curve as well as accommodates the effects of change in the yield curve shape.

To accomplish a useful rate-anticipation neutral, return measure, the mortgage should be subjected to a variety of interest rate scenarios that represent likely environments on some probabilistic basis. Borrowing from option pricing frameworks, a set of arbitrage-free interest rate paths are created for which security cash flows are generated in accordance with a prepayment model. Each cash flow is discounted using the Treasury forward rate plus a spread. The spread that returns the given price on a probability weighted basis is derived. This spread is a constant incremental yield over the Treasury curve that can be used as an indication of relative value regardless of the length of the subject security.

A second index-equivalent measure would use a probalistic scenario-driven scheme but would use return calculation conventions similar to the index and

EXHIBIT 9
HIERARCHICAL TREE OF MORTGAGE PASS-THROUGH MARKET

Sec Type	Coup	Good Dur	Good CVX
FHLMC G S	7.00	4.42	0.44
FHLMC G S	7.50	4.75	0.49
FHLMC G S	7.50	4.03	0.62
FHLMC G S	8.00	4.34	0.63
FHLMC MBS	8.00	4.40	0.56
GNMA 15YR	8.00	4.10	0.49
GNMA SF	7.50	4.57	0.55
GNMA SF	8.00	4.17	0.74
GNMA SF	8.25	4.07	0.77
GNMA SF	8.50	4.70	0.56
GNMA SF	9.00	4.21	0.62
FHLMC G S	8.00	3.59	0.83
FHLMC G S	8.50	3.85	0.74
FHLMC MBS	8.00	3.58	0.75
FHLMC MBS	8.50	3.93	0.67
FHLMC PC	9.00	3.70	0.77
GNMA 15YR	8.50	3.66	0.60
GNMA SF	9.50	3.71	0.65
FHLMC G S	7.00	5.08	0.36
GNMA SF	6.50	4.97	0.22
GNMA SF	7.50	5.52	0.39
GNMA SF	8.00	5.12	0.48

"Number of Cells": 10, 9, 8, 7, 6, 5

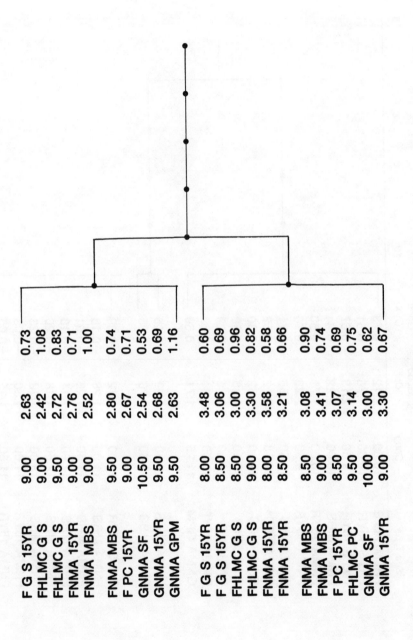

EXHIBIT 9 (Continued)
HIERARCHICAL TREE OF MORTGAGE PASS-THROUGH MARKET

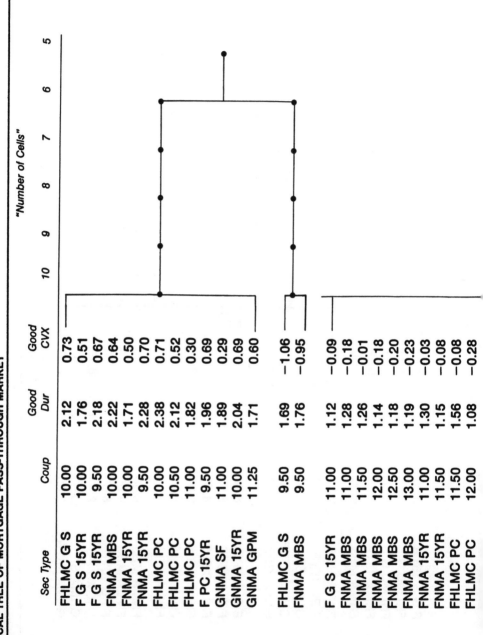

Sec Type	Coup	Good Dur	Good CVX
FHLMC G S	10.00	2.12	0.73
F G S 15YR	10.00	1.76	0.51
F G S 15YR	9.50	2.18	0.67
FNMA MBS	10.00	2.22	0.64
FNMA 15YR	10.00	1.71	0.50
FNMA 15YR	9.50	2.28	0.70
FHLMC PC	10.00	2.38	0.71
FHLMC PC	10.50	2.12	0.52
FHLMC PC	11.00	1.82	0.30
F PC 15YR	9.50	1.96	0.69
GNMA SF	11.00	1.89	0.29
GNMA 15YR	10.00	2.04	0.69
GNMA GPM	11.25	1.71	0.60
FHLMC G S	9.50	1.69	−1.06
FNMA MBS	9.50	1.76	−0.95
F G S 15YR	11.00	1.12	−0.09
FNMA MBS	11.00	1.28	−0.18
FNMA MBS	11.50	1.26	−0.01
FNMA MBS	12.00	1.14	−0.18
FNMA MBS	12.50	1.18	−0.20
FNMA MBS	13.00	1.19	−0.23
FNMA 15YR	11.00	1.30	−0.03
FNMA 15YR	11.50	1.15	−0.08
FHLMC PC	11.50	1.56	−0.08
FHLMC PC	12.00	1.08	−0.28

"Number of Cells"

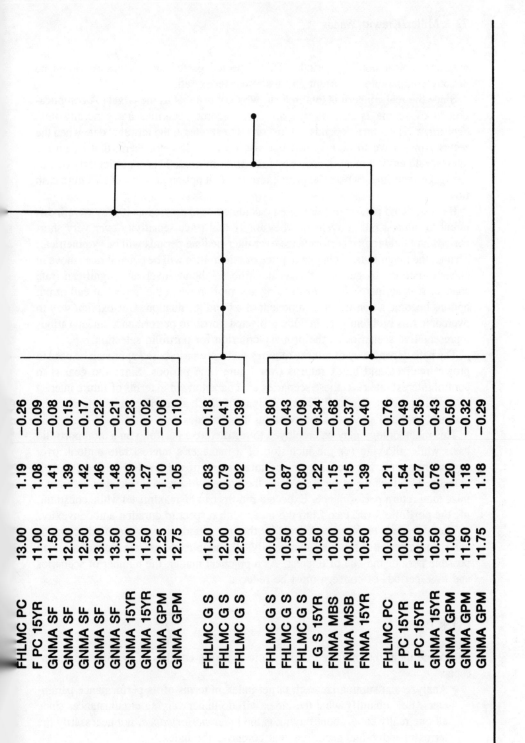

horizons typical holding periods. This expected performance measure would be directly comparable to current and historical index returns.

Since the real concern is total return, why not use that as the target? A complication to overcome is that returns on fixed income securities are generally *path dependent*. The return depends not just on interest rates at the terminal date when the security may have to be revalued but also on how they got there; that is, on the interest rate environment at each previous point in time. This is particularly true of mortgage securities, where the prior exercise of an option may affect all future cash flows.

Because bond parameters are often calculated or expressed as if they were indifferent to interest rate movement, they imply that price sensitivity over very short periods and total return performance over intermediate periods will be symmetrical. That is, the magnitude of change in price or total return will be equal if rates move in either direction. In general, this is not true for bonds over any significant rate change. It is an increasingly misleading assumption when the impact of call or put options become a non-trivial component of a bond's valuation. One explicit way to overcome this problem is to include projected portfolio performance under various representative scenarios as the primary criterion for portfolio selection.

The path dependency of returns requires that a scenario-based approach be used to project realized and index returns over future time periods. Since the goal is to control interest rate risk, these scenarios are characterized in terms of future interest rate environments. Probabilities are assigned to each scenario compatible with the assumed probabilistic process governing interest rates.

This methodology may be employed to restructure a portfolio on a total portfolio basis while allowing for the inclusion of a manager's interest rate outlook over various horizons. By focusing on the total return of the bonds adjusted for their embedded options we at once simplify the process of security selection and maximize total return performance. Expected returns can be maximized while constraining the portfolio's variance from the index with respect to duration and convexity.

The investor's targets are defined by the index returns over specified scenarios and specific periods of time. Theoretically, all possible interest rate scenarios and all possible periods may be of interest. As a practical matter, the number of scenarios and time periods of concern must be reduced.

CONCLUSION

In essence then, the preferred approach to indexing consists of the following concepts:

- Analyze and summarize each target index in terms of its performance parameters, i.e., quantify what the index will do under varying circumstances since all one really cares about buying is the index *performance*, not necessarily the terms of individual securities that comprise the index.

- Construct efficiently the performance equivalent of this target index with an appropriate number of securities.
- Enhance the expected total return prospects by programming the selection of a least-cost portfolio while constraining the prepayment or option exposure to a level equivalent to that of the target index.

The practical implementation is outlined by the following steps as followed in the mortgage pass-through illustration.

- Determine the market-weighted average modified duration and convexity of the index portfolio.
- Assign each pass-through generic to a duration/convexity-defined cell appropriate to the portfolio size.
- Determine the market-weighted average modified duration and convexity of each cell.
- Select candidates to represent each cell based on combinations that achieve the weighted average duration and convexity of each cell while maximizing either (1) OAS option-adjusted spreads, or (2) index-equivalent total return.
- Compare the selected portfolio to the index portfolio with respect to conventional cell characteristics (program, coupon, WAM) to examine degree of mismatch to index.

The last step is important because by matching the index portfolio through projected performance rather than by terms, the investor is betting that certain event risks won't be incurred—in general that the credit, prepayment, and yield characteristics that distinguish GNMA, FHLMC and FNMA programs will not change. The possible excess returns don't always come free of additional risk. One example of a change in the typical spread relationship among agency pass-throughs was the non-recurring tightening of yield spreads to Treasuries among GNMAs that resulted from the demand induced by the advent of the collateralized mortgage obligation. Such bets are part of the risk/return tradeoff that any investor makes. Part of the obligation is to know the magnitude of the tradeoff.

This approach, based on the prepayment-encoding parameters, has even more value in index-related strategies where the objective is to exceed rather than match index returns.

Index strategies can be distinguished in the relative emphasis placed on (1) expected returns (2) duration and convexity parameters, and (3) bond terms.

Conventional strict indexing is exclusively concerned with matching the index's distribution of bond terms and selecting underpriced securities conforming to the index terms constraints—that is, the bond terms tracking mentioned earlier.

A more flexible technique of strict indexing would be similar to conventional indexing with the exception that duration and convexity are the index tracking criteria in place of bond terms. The increased flexibility, especially when coupled with a hierarchical tree categorizing scheme, is the applicability to portfolios of a wide variety of sizes.

However, the greatest benefit to a system that facilitates the explicit and simultaneous control of the three variable categories—expected returns, parameters, and terms—is its applicability to index plus strategies.

Index tracking tolerance can be adjusted with respect to both bond terms and option-adjusted parameters while pursuing above market-average returns. Stated

EXHIBIT 10
SELECTED MBS PORTFOLIO (TOTAL MARKET VALUE = $1.00 BILLION)

Cell	Sec	Type	Coupon	Par Val ($ Bill)	Par Tot (%)	Mkt Val ($ Bil)	Mkt Tot (%)	GOOD Dur	GOOD Cvx
1	FNMA	15YR	8.00	.0403	4.10	.0400	4.00	3.58	−0.58
1	FNMA	MBS	8.50	.0997	10.14	.1000	10.00	3.08	−0.90
1	FNMA	MBS	9.00	.0391	3.98	.0400	4.00	3.41	−0.74
Total	CELL 1			.1791	18.22	.1800	18.00	3.26	−0.79
2	FNMA	15YR	11.00	.0379	3.86	.0400	4.00	1.30	−0.03
2	GNMA	SF	13.50	.0727	7.40	.0800	8.00	1.48	0.21
2	GNMA	GPM	12.25	.0465	4.73	.0500	5.00	1.10	−0.06
Total	CELL 2			.1571	15.98	.1700	17.00	1.33	0.07
3	FNMA	15YR	9.00	.0875	8.90	.0900	9.00	2.76	−0.71
3	FNMA	MBS	9.00	.0489	4.98	.0500	5.00	2.52	−1.00
Total	CELL 3			.1364	13.88	.1400	14.00	2.67	−0.81
4	GNMA	GPM	11.75	.0651	6.62	.0700	7.00	1.12	−0.29
5	FNMA	15YR	9.50	.0478	4.86	.0500	5.00	2.28	−0.70
5	GNMA	SF	11.00	.0371	3.77	.0400	4.00	1.89	−0.29
5	GNMA	GPM	11.25	.0280	2.85	.0300	3.00	1.71	−0.60
Total	CELL 5			.1129	11.49	.1200	12.00	2.01	−0.54
6	FNMA	MBS	8.00	.0608	6.19	.0600	6.00	3.58	−0.75
6	FNMA	MBS	8.50	.0499	5.08	.0500	5.00	3.93	−0.67
Total	CELL 6			.1107	11.26	.1100	11.00	3.74	−0.71
7	FHLMC	G S	8.00	.0713	7.25	.0700	7.00	4.34	−0.63
7	FNMA	MBS	8.00	.0610	6.21	.0600	6.00	4.40	−0.56
7	GNMA	SF	8.25	.0601	6.11	.0600	6.00	4.07	−0.77
Total	CELL 7			.1934	19.57	.1900	19.00	4.27	−0.65
8	GNMA	SF	8.00	.0101	1.03	.0100	1.00	5.12	−0.48
9	FNMA	MBS	9.50	.0096	0.97	.0100	1.00	1.76	−0.95
10	FHLMC	G S	11.50	.0095	0.97	.0100	1.00	0.83	−0.18
Total	PORTFOLIO			.9829	100.00	1.0000	100.00	2.85	−0.55

slightly differently, expected returns can be maximized while constraining the variance of duration, convexity, and coupon maturity from the index portfolio to within required levels.

Although index-orientation has been presented as an essentially passive strategy, the inclusion of the convexity measure in the problem formulation allows for control that incorporates rate anticipation. As mentioned above convexity coefficients are typically expressed as the average of the duration from a straight line made by the price function when yields are raised and lowered. The averaging masks the fact that convexity is not symmetrical. The degree of deviation from a straight line is not equal in both directions. Formulation of the problem in this case would include the convexity coefficient associated with the anticipated interest rate scenario.

Similar treatment can be applied to the expected return value. Since an expected return is a probability weighted average of returns derived from distinct scenarios, it does not necessarily convey the return that would be realized under any particular scenarios, including any particular forecast.

The use of scenario specific convexity and returns helps to reduce tracking variance and select securities that will provide the best returns. However, if a very different interest rate dynamic takes place, it's likely that both tracking and returns will be poorer than if anticipation-neutral measures were used.

As an example, Exhibit 10 shows the index-fund portfolio selected through the duration/convexity based procedure using ten cells. The securities representing each cell are indicated as well as the duration/convexity cell match. The selection was based on a prepayment risk-adjusted return, however it could just as well be made using the expected index-equivalent returns.

Exhibit 11 shows the distribution across subsectors of the selected index-fund portfolio compared to the index portfolio in Exhibit 12. Solutions that incorporate the duration/convexity approach can also be constrained to limit the degree of conventional mismatch to the index portfolio to control the magnitude of the sector bet.

EXHIBIT 11
SUBSECTOR DISTRIBUTION-SELECTED PORTFOLIO

Prog.	GNMA			FHLMC		FNMA		
Coupon	30yr	15yr	GPM	30yr	15yr	30yr	15yr	Totals
8%-Below	0%	0%	0%	0%	0%	0%	0%	0%
8%-10%	7.1%	0%	0%	7.2%	0%	37.5%	17.9%	69.7%
10%-12%	3.8%	0%	9.5%	1.0%	0%	0%	3.9%	18.2%
12%-Above	7.4%	0%	4.7%	0%	0%	0%	0%	12.1%
TOTALS	18.3%	0%	14.2%	8.2%	0%	37.5%	21.8%	100%

EXHIBIT 12
SUBSECTOR DISTRIBUTION-INDEX PORTFOLIO

Prog.	GNMA			FHLMC		FNMA		
Coupon	30yr	15yr	GPM	30yr	15yr	30yr	15yr	Totals
8%-Below	3.2%	0%	0%	2.5%	0%	0.9%	0%	6.6%
8%-10%	20.6%	1.1%	0.3%	15.6%	3.1%	6.3%	1.2%	48.2%
10%-12%	12.4%	0.9%	0.9%	6.4%	0.9%	3.0%	0.7%	25.2%
12%-Above	10.4%	0.1%	1.4%	4.8%	0.2%	3.0%	0.1%	20.0%
TOTALS	46.6%	2.1%	2.6%	29.3%	4.2%	13.2%	2.0%	100%

PART III

Immunization and Dedicated Strategies

Chapter 6

Optimal Funding of Guaranteed Investment Contracts

LLEWELLYN MILLER
FIRST VICE PRESIDENT
DREXEL BURNHAM LAMBERT

NANCY ROTH
VICE PRESIDENT
DREXEL BURNHAM LAMBERT

In this chapter a description of the growing list of features commonly found in guaranteed investment contracts (GICs) is presented and the risks inherent in these features are exmained. With every option built into the contract in an effort to attract investors comes greater uncertainty of the actual amount and timing of funds to be guaranteed. Next, the portfolio strategies currently used to manage the investment of GIC proceeds are discussed. While much attention will be placed on those contract terms that make GICs interest sensitive, it should also be noted that contracts exist that can be effectively managed with the current set of strategies, provided they are applied to the universe of assets for which they were intended. However, for those contract terms that exceed the realm of risk control provided by these strategies, an alternative strategy, Realized Return Optimization (RRO),[1] is presented. RRO is a return-based strategy that explicitly incorporates investor targets and risks in the selection and management of fixed income portfolios.

BACKGROUND

The guaranteed investment contract was first introduced by the insurance industry in the early 1970's. It was a product designed in response to the erratic performance of the stock and bond markets. Its popularity increased with the passage of ERISA (Employee Retirement Income Security Act of 1974) which forced pension plan sponsors to seek more predictable rates of return. Innovations in the basic product have kept pace with changing market needs and the GIC industry, currently at a size of over $100 billion, is a major factor in the insurance industry's successful competition with the traditional bank trust department for private pension dollars.

Another factor that contributes to the substantial growth of the industry is the advent of the investment advisory firms dedicated solely to the management of GIC portfolios. Specialists in this field believe that pension plan sponsors choose GICs on the basis of the guarantee rate alone without paying sufficient attention to the remainder of the contract. By working with the plan sponsor and the insurance company, these specialists help tailor a contract that is more marketable and therefore more popular with depositors. In addition, just as fixed income portfolio management differs from selecting a single bond, GIC portfolio management differs from selecting a single GIC. When purchased in careful combination, portfolios of GICs can provide enhanced long-term return over a single contract. Again, it is these stable yet competitive returns, coupled with controlled risk, that account for the dramatic popularity of this investment vehicle.

CONTRACT TERMS AND LIABILITY-SIDE RISK

The original and most basic form of the product is the *bullet* GIC. This type of contract is characterized by a single deposit, earning interest at the guaranteed rate, until a single maturity. Principal is returned at par, and during the life of the contract, the investor has no access to the money. Bullet GICs are frequently purchased by defined benefit plan sponsors because the total return they provide is known with

---

[1]RRO is introduced in Llewellyn Miller, Uday Rajan and Prakash A. Shimpi, "Realized Return Optimization: A Strategy for Targeted Total Return Investing in the Fixed Income Markets," in Frank J. Fabozzi (ed.), *Institutional Investors Focus on Investment Management* (Cambridge, MA: Ballinger 1988).

certainty and the obligation of these sponsors is the level of benefits rather than contributions.

Another popular category of contracts is the *window* GIC and the more recently developed *dollar window* GIC. Window GICs are characterized by the extended period of time during which they accept contributions at the guaranteed rate. The traditional window GIC accepts contributions for a predetermined period of time, typically a year. The dollar window GIC accepts contributions until a predetermined amount has accumulated. Window GICs are popular with defined contribution plans because the window facilitates the paycheck deduction method of making contributions.

The distinguishing feature of bullets and windows, the length of the deposit period, is not the only contract feature that can vary. Almost every insurance company that underwrites GICs sells a unique product. Some of the more popular variations focus on the following contract terms.

Repayment Schedule

The repayment schedule defines how investors are repaid their principal and interest. Some contracts only allow single sum repayment and some offer the investor the choice between single sum repayment and purchasing an annuity upon maturity. The terms of the annuity may also be guaranteed under some contracts.

Simple Interest versus Compound Interest

Some contracts work like bonds. They pay out the interest earnings periodically and thus shift the reinvestment risk to the investor. Other contracts work more like bank certificates of deposit. The insurance company bears the reinvestment burden by guaranteeing the compounding of the interest income and as a result, these contracts usually have a lower guarantee rate.

Transfers and Withdrawals

Provisions for the withdrawal of funds can vary widely. The most flexible of contracts allow withdrawals at full book value at any time, although they may require some advance notice. Other contracts do not allow for any interim withdrawal without stiff surrender charges. Surrender charges can either be an explicit percentage of book value or an adjustment based on market value. Some contracts represent just one option of a larger 401(K) plan. These contracts allow funds to be switched periodically between the GIC and the competing stock or bond funds and money market accounts; however, recent stipulations have been added to some contracts that prevent switching to a competing fixed income option. Many contracts in the 401(K) setting also allow for loans against the contract value.

Participation

Before GICs were developed, IPG contracts (Immediate Participation Guaranteed) were the dominant investment product of the insurance industry. All investments were deposited into the general account of the insurer and all investors earned whatever the general account earned, i.e., investors participated in the investment experience (gains and losses) of the insurance company. Although GICs replaced IPGs because of their stability, some GICs today allow for a degree of participation. These contracts may stipulate a floor guarantee rate or they may track an index.

Future Commitment

In order to attract investors in a falling rate environment, insurers may guarantee a rate for a future deposit. In a sense this is similar to a window GIC except instead of recurring deposits through a future date, the implication is that no money is deposited until a future date. Thus no money is available to invest at the time the commitment is made. In these situations, insurers can borrow from the general fund to purchase interest rate futures in order to protect themselves from falling rates. In general however, insurance companies are severely limited in the amount and types of investing in which they can participate in the futures and options markets.

Fees and Expenses

Typically, actuarial estimations of administrative fees and expenses are made during the underwriting phase. These estimations are then factored into the guaranteed rate. In some contracts, if the estimations are widely understated, there is a proviso to pass the charges on to the depositor, resulting in a rate lower than the stated guarantee.

The GIC underwriter faces uncertainty from two sources—the assets and the liabilities. The nature of that uncertainty is also twofold—the amount and timing of cash flows. The parameters of the GIC discussed above are the main source of the liability-side uncertainty of how much money will be earning the guarantee rate and when that money will be deposited. Provisions for withdrawals, loans and swapping in and out of competing plans further complicate matters for the insurance company that must make investment commitments for the GIC proceeds. Although in practice options are not always exercised as soon as it makes economic sense to do so, flexible contract terms expose the insurance company to the dual risks of (1) heavy cash inflow when rates are falling and plan participants want to "lock in" at higher rates, and (2) lighter cash inflow or cash withdrawal when rates are rising and plan participants seek better opportunities. In this latter scenario, the insurance company may have to liquidate assets at a loss in order to return money to the contract holder at par. The actuarial term that describes this phenomenon is *cash flow antiselection*.

PORTFOLIO STRATEGIES AND ASSET-SIDE RISK

All the typical risks of the fixed income investor emerge on the asset side. These include asset default risk, asset call risk (or in the case of mortgages, prepayment risk), capital loss (which in the case of GICs can be exacerbated by the potential for short-fall between the market value of the assets and the book value that is guaranteed to the contract holder) and finally, reinvestment risk.

Traditional fixed income portfolio management focuses on three basic matching strategies to address some of these risks. These three strategies—*dedication, immunization* and *active management*—span the spectrum from completely passive to extremely active. In a dedicated portfolio, assets are selected so that the timing and amount of their coupon income and maturing principal exactly offset the liabilities. In an immunized portfolio, the goal is again to assure that the assets selected will cover the liabilities; however, the constraint that all bonds must be held to maturity is relaxed and assumed reinvestment earnings and capital gains contribute significantly toward extinguishing the liabilities. With active management, the riskiest of the three, market moves must be anticipated and the portfolio must be positioned (i.e., deliberately mismatched) to take advantage of yield dynamics.

Dedication is a funding technique that removes all uncertainty due to changes in the interest rate environment. Bonds are held to maturity so no capital loss is realized. If eligible bonds are restricted to Treasury issues or investment grade non-callable corporates, then default and call risks are effectively removed. Finally, if the portfolio is constructed without any reliance on reinvestment income, then changes in short term rates have no effect on the cash inflow schedule. Everything works if the liability cash flow requirements are known with certainty at the time the asset portfolio is being constructed. Since many GICs represent interest rate sensitive liabilities, dedication represents a bet on the future course of interest rates and investors subsequent responses. This type of long term uncertainty defeats the purpose of being dedicated. For those GICs with known liability schedules, like the bullet GIC, dedication may be conceptually attractive but too expensive to be practical.

If dedication is eliminated as a strategy either because of cash flow uncertainty or expense, GIC writers may rely more on immunization. The intent of immunization is to construct a portfolio of assets that will react the same way the liabilities respond to changes in interest rates. Initially an immunized portfolio has a market value equal to the present value of the liabilities. (It is generally assumed that liability cash flows can be analyzed similarly to bonds. The choice of an appropriate discount rate used to calculate a present value, however, is subject to debate.) Then, if rates go down and drive up the present value of the liabilities, the assets will appreciate in value proportionally to cover the excess. Conversely, if rates go up and the value of the assets decline, the liability values will decrease proportionally. Either way, with an immunized portfolio, assets and liabilities begin with equal market value, and regardless of the direction of interest rate changes, liquidation of the assets is always sufficient to fund the economic value of the liabilities.

All of this is accomplished through controlling the weighted average duration of the assets. Duration, in this context modified duration, refers to the percentage change in price resulting from small shifts in yield. Further advances have shown that by constraining the convexity[2] of the assets to be greater than the convexity of the liabilities, the portfolio value will not just move with the liabilities, it will actually dominate the liabilities. Problems arise, however, because duration and convexity only approximate the price behavior of a bond for a given yield. The ability to predict prices based on these two measures diminishes as market yields shift further away from the point at which they were originally calculated. In addition, the price behavior of a bond changes as the bond approaches maturity (or a call date when yields are low enough to make the call likely), thus necessitating periodic rebalancings of the portfolio in order to remain immunized. Finally, when the asset or liability in question is embedded with complicated options, the exercise of which are not as predictable as callable corporate bonds, cash flow simulation itself is an approximation and much is lost in further reducing the description of price behavior to the two parameters duration and convexity. The strong implication, therefore, is that the value of the portfolio cannot be easily controlled by controlling only duration and convexity.

Active management is a strategy that provides no guarantees. If active portfolio managers believe that interest rates will go down, then they will lengthen the modified duration of their portfolios to take advantage of the anticipated price appreciation. Conversely, if they believe that interest rates will rise, the modified duration of the portfolio is shortened in order to soften the impact of any price depreciation. In either case, the duration balance between the assets and liabilities that is so carefully maintained in an immunized portfolio, is removed. Such a strategy is only as good as the rate anticipation itself and the ability to measure bond performance in accordance with these forecasts. While many money managers pursue all strategies with a degree of active management, most rely on some backup set of parameters to guide their portfolio and minimize downside risk.

In summary then, with the exception of dedication of known cash flows, all of the above strategies attempt to assure a goal using approximations rather than including the goal as an explicit parameter. Furthermore, the assumptions generally made about the behavior of liabilities ignore the option characteristics of the liabilities. Clearly, new approaches to asset/liability management which more fully incorporate the interest rate risks on both sides of the balance sheet are required.

---

[2]For a full treatment of duration and convexity, see Kenneth H. Sullivan and Timothy B. Kiggins, "Convexity: The Name is New But You Always Knew What It Was," in *Institutional Investors Focus on Investment Management*.

GICs AND REALIZED RETURN OPTIMIZATION

Flexibility is key in the evolving world of GICs. Extensions to the three basic strategies combining portfolio simulation and optimization tools should be used to derive portfolios with appropriate risk/return profiles. RRO, referred to earlier, is a scenario based strategy that enables the portfolio manager to choose the optimal portfolio that will meet the required repayment schedule of the GIC at a quantifiable level of risk. In the following paragraphs two step-by-step examples of how to apply RRO are presented. The steps for the two examples do not differ conceptually; two are presented only to illustrate differences in the patterns of required returns[3] and the resulting portfolios. The first example is a bullet GIC which is priced at an 85 basis point spread over the current five-year Treasury rate. The second is a window GIC and it is priced at a tighter spread of 55 basis points to reflect the uncertainty of its cash flows. The exact terms of the contracts are described in Exhibit 1.

EXHIBIT 1
TWO SAMPLE CONTRACTS

	BULLET	*WINDOW*
Issue date	*March 1, 1988*	*March 1, 1988*
Maturity date	*March 1, 1993*	*March 1, 1993*
Guaranteed rate	*8.45% effective annual yield*	*8.15% effective annual yield*
Deposits	*$5,000,000 lump sum*	*1 year window*
Withdrawals	*lump sum at maturity*	*allowed every 6 mos. at full book value*
Participation	*none*	*none*

The first step in asset selection is obvious—to understand the plan. Without clear identification of the types of liability options involved, there is no way to purchase assets to hedge these options. To the extent that an insurance company offers a variety of types of contracts, liability options should be reviewed by block of business.

---

[3]Required returns define the targets or the minimum levels of total return that must be earned by the assets in order to ensure sufficient cash flow to support the liabilities. They are calculated in a comparable manner to total rates of return for assets. A detailed example of the components of required return is given in "Realized Return Optimization: A Strategy for Targeted Total Return Investing in the Fixed Income Markets."

The next step is to choose the combination of conditions about which portfolios are to be structured. These conditions should include projected interest rate environments, actuarial estimations and time horizons to the extent that they impact the return targets. The goal of any mathematical model is to reduce an otherwise unmanageable problem to its representative properties. While it is impossible to study all combinations of conditions or changes that could occur during the life of the GIC, it is possible and constructive to derive a representative sampling of scenarios that encompasses the conditions under which a depositor is likely to antiselect.

For the purposes of the example, the five interest rate scenarios depicted in Exhibit 2 were chosen. (Note: The legend at the bottom of the exhibit is defined as follows: SF = steeply falling, MF = moderately falling, MR = moderately rising, SR = steeply rising.) The rates along these paths represent expansions around the current ten-year Treasury rate. The rest of the yield curve, for simplicity, is assumed to shift in parallel. These scenarios were derived from a binomial process that assumes an annual interest rate volatility of 140 basis points. The process is carried out through a five year horizon (since that is the maturity of the two sample contracts) where each step in the process is equivalent to 6 months. Probabilities are assigned to each scenario in accordance with the binomial process and they are used to weight the relative emphasis placed on a scenario at the portfolio selection step. The time horizons chosen are the one, three and five year horizons along these paths.

Cash flow simulation of the liabilities in these rate scenarios is next. The bullet GIC of the example is trivial because it has fixed cash flows that are a function of only the initial deposit and the guaranteed rate, both of which are known at the outset. It is the window GIC that needs further study. Based on the sample contract terms it is known that contributions can be made any time during the first year of the contract but none are allowed after the first year. Withdrawals however, are allowed at any time for the life of the contract at full book value (i.e., no surrender charges). Depositors are assumed to antiselect in the two rising and two falling rate scenarios. The magnitude of the antiselection in each case is modelled by assuming an expected flow of deposits in the flat scenario, and calculating deviations from the expected as an increasing function of interest rate change and a decreasing function of time remaining to maturity.

Estimating the expected deposit schedule in the flat scenario is where actuarial assumptions add value. Window GICs are very much a pension product and standard actuarial measurements regarding the age, mobility, mortality etc. of the population of depositors, as well as any statistics kept on previously issued GICs, can greatly enhance the accuracy of the simulation. In this example, actuarial assumptions were kept very simple. It was asssumed that in the flat scenario, total deposits would equal the five million dollar lump sum required with the bullet GIC but that the contributions would be staggered over the course of the window.

Given the cash flow simulations and the interest rate scenarios, there is enough information to calculate required returns. The results for the two contracts are given

EXHIBIT 2
INTEREST RATE SCENARIOS

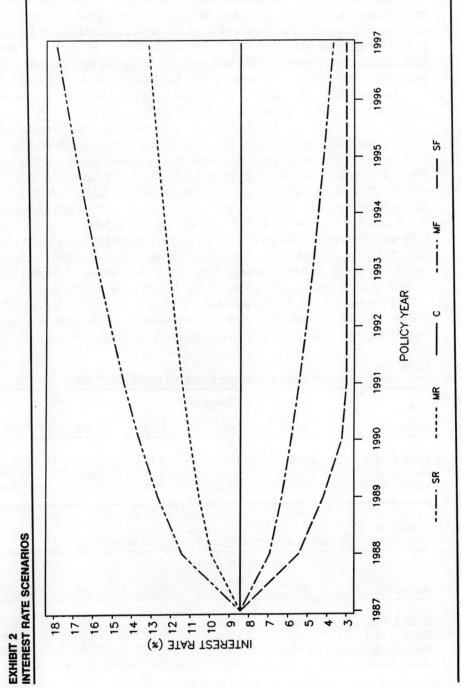

Source: Drexel Burnham Lambert, Fixed Income Research.

in Exhibits 3a and 3b. It is difficult to make too many direct comparisons between the bullet and the window because of the difference in crediting rates. Yet even with the lower crediting rate, the window GIC exhibits higher required returns for each horizon in both rising rate scenarios and higher required returns for the one and three year horizons in the steeply falling rate scenario. In the flat scenario, where no antiselection was assumed, the window GIC has lower required returns because contributions (which, after the window, are equal to the bullet lump sum deposit) are earning the lower crediting rate and are not all credited from day one.

A few observations can be made within each table as well. First, the pattern of returns of the bullet GIC is exactly that of a five year zero coupon bond initially priced at an effective annual yield of 8.45 (8.28 semi-annual equivalent). This is as expected because the cash flows are exactly the same. As for the window GIC, as rates fall, the contract itself gets richer and contributions exceed the expected, both serving to increase the required returns. As rates rise, the contract gets cheaper so that required returns are not as high as under the flat scenario. However, cash outflows in the form of withdrawals from the contract counteract the higher discount rates to keep the required returns from falling very far. Perhaps the most significant observation though, is that at maturity, regardless of the direction or magnitude of the shift in rates, the required returns are higher than under the flat scenario.

Once the required returns are calculated, the scope of the problem is essentially defined. The task that remains is to choose an optimal set of assets that provide at least the required return in each of the representative scenarios. Focusing on realiz-

EXHIBIT 3a
ONE, THREE, AND FIVE YEAR REQUIRED RETURNS FOR BULLET GIC

Horizon	Scenario				
	SF	MF	FLAT	MR	SR
March 1, 1989	20.79	14.46	8.45	2.80	−2.52
March 1, 1991	11.91	10.16	8.45	6.81	5.06
March 1, 1993	8.45	8.45	8.45	8.45	8.45

EXHIBIT 3b
ONE, THREE, AND FIVE YEAR REQUIRED RETURNS FOR WINDOW GIC

Horizon	Scenario				
	SF	MF	FLAT	MR	SR
March 1, 1989	20.82	13.92	7.54	6.00	5.82
March 1, 1991	11.97	10.04	8.17	8.00	7.93
March 1, 1993	8.22	8.10	7.97	8.78	9.63

able return rather than yield allows for more realistic assumptions about reinvestment earnings, pricing spreads and the behavior of assets with interest rate sensitive cash flows. Yields are reasonable measures for assessing relative value of noncallable instruments but they are not good predictors of what will actually be earned over the investment holding period. Calculating asset returns incorporates the quantification of such factors as mortgage prepayments and the value of options in callable bonds.

Optimal asset selection can be approached in several ways. One way is to choose a time horizon and maximize the probability-weighted average return on the assets across scenarios, while maintaining constraints on the individual scenario returns either to the same horizon or across various other time horizons. If a solution can be found, then this formulation assures that the realized returns on the assets are always greater than the required returns defined by the liabilities. If a solution cannot be found, then at least the process has identified those conditions that would result in loss of profitability. Another similar formulation would be to maximize return in the most probable scenario while maintinaing the same floor constraints in the remaining scenarios. Actually, objectives and constraints can be specified with any combination of scenarios and horizons provided both the realized and required returns have been calculated. Distinctions between portfolios selected according to these different objectives depend on the emphasis (i.e., probability) placed on scenarios with high, difficult to beat required returns.

Optimality can also be defined as the minimization of different types of risk. On an individual security basis, the fixed income investor is faced with credit risk, price risk and reinvestment risk. Portfolio credit risk is controlled by imposing diversification constraints on bond rating and on the degree to which any individual bond, issuer or industrial sector is represented in the portfolio. Portfolio price and reinvestment risk are controlled by projecting scenario based asset returns and minimizing the variance of those returns about some target. Formulations of this type usually measure risk in terms of total variance about the mean or expected return. Two unique features of RRO are the ability to minimize only the *downside* variance and to measure that variance about the required returns rather than the mean.[4] Minimizing downside variance will always result in portfolios that either are as good as or dominate those chosen by minimizing total variance. This is because only the variance resulting from underperforming the target is minimized. Furthermore, by measuring variance about the required returns rather than the mean, risk essentially refers to the risk of not being able to fund the GIC in each scenario, rather than the risk of not being able to fund the GIC on average. For situations where there is no downside risk, maximizing the spread over the required returns is an alternative objective.

---

[4]Once again readers are referred to Miller, Rajan and Shimpi, "Realized Return Optimization: A Strategy for Targeted Total Return Investing in the Fixed Income Markets," for a full discussion of downside variance and target returns.

It is important to note that there is no one correct formulation to use in choosing an optimal portfolio to fund GICs. The strength of the analysis is the flexibility to handle many formulations so that different portfolio results can be studied relative to the required returns. For the final step of the example, two optimal portfolios were selected for each sample contract. The portfolios were selected from a universe of assets consisting of mortgage-backed securities, U.S. Treasury notes, bonds and strips, and a mix of callable and noncallable corporate bonds. The resulting portfolio returns for the bullet and window respectively, are listed in Exhibits 4 and 5 (and depicted graphically in Exhibits 6-11). The objective of portfolios 4a and 5a was to maximize the expected return over the five year horizon and the objective of portfolios 4b and 5b was to maximize the spread of the five-year asset returns over the five-year required returns. For all four portfolios, constraints were imposed on each scenario and horizon to insure that the optimal portfolio at least meets the corresponding required returns. Maturity constraints were also imposed on the four portfolios in order to provide a dispersion of cash flow before and after the GIC matures. Finally, constraints were set to limit the percentage of high yield bonds relative to the total portfolio value.

EXHIBIT 4a
ONE, THREE, AND FIVE YEAR PORTFOLIO RETURNS FOR BULLET GIC

MAXIMIZE FIVE-YEAR EXPECTED RETURN

Scenario

Horizon	SF	MF	FLAT	MR	SR
March 1, 1989	25.47	17.53	9.92	3.52	−2.16
March 1, 1991	15.67	11.71	9.49	7.34	5.69
March 1, 1993	10.53	9.46	8.88	8.54	8.45

EXHIBIT 4b
ONE, THREE, AND FIVE YEAR PORTFOLIO RETURNS FOR BULLET GIC

MAXIMIZE FIVE-YEAR SPREAD OVER REQUIRED RETURNS

Scenario

Horizon	SF	MF	FLAT	MR	SR
March 1, 1989	25.93	17.85	10.05	3.45	−2.43
March 1, 1991	15.92	11.93	9.64	7.38	5.59
March 1, 1993	10.73	9.66	9.05	8.63	8.45

EXHIBIT 5a
ONE, THREE, AND FIVE YEAR PORTFOLIO RETURNS FOR WINDOW GIC

MAXIMIZE FIVE-YEAR EXPECTED RETURN
Scenario

Horizon	SF	MF	FLAT	MR	SR
March 1, 1989	20.82	16.31	10.99	6.13	1.47
March 1, 1991	12.74	11.18	10.44	9.13	7.93
March 1, 1993	8.86	9.03	9.69	9.96	10.15

EXHIBIT 5b
ONE, THREE, AND FIVE YEAR PORTFOLIO RETURNS FOR WINDOW GIC

MAXIMIZE FIVE-YEAR SPREAD OVER REQUIRED RETURNS
Scenario

Horizon	SF	MF	FLAT	MR	SR
March 1, 1989	20.82	16.16	10.84	6.07	1.55
March 1, 1991	12.84	11.03	10.28	9.03	7.93
March 1, 1993	8.94	8.93	9.55	9.86	10.13

EXHIBIT 6
ONE-YEAR RETURNS—BULLET GIC

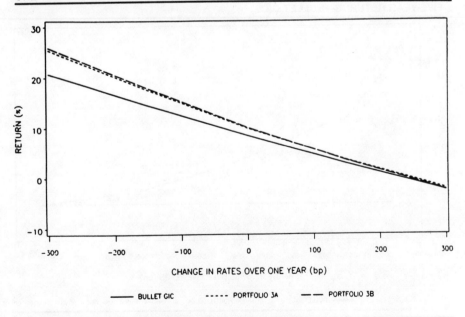

*Source: Drexel Burnham Lambert, Fixed Income Research.

EXHIBIT 7
THREE-YEAR RETURNS—BULLET GIC

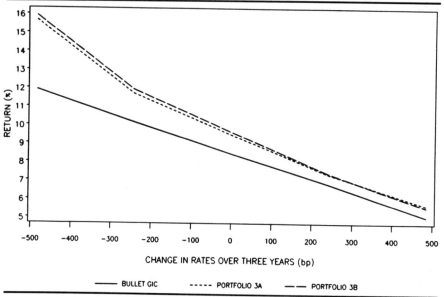

CHANGE IN RATES OVER THREE YEARS (bp)

——— BULLET GIC   - - - - - PORTFOLIO 3A   — — PORTFOLIO 3B

Source: Drexel Burnham Lambert, Fixed Income Research.

EXHIBIT 8
FIVE-YEAR RETURNS—BULLET GIC

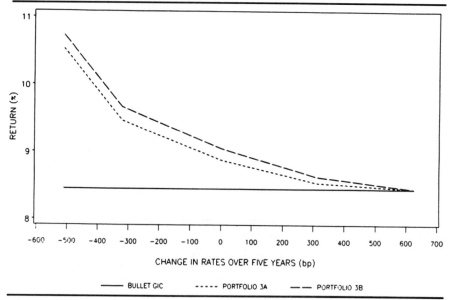

CHANGE IN RATES OVER FIVE YEARS (bp)

——— BULLET GIC   - - - - - PORTFOLIO 3A   — — PORTFOLIO 3B

Source: Drexel Burnham Lambert, Fixed Income Research.

EXHIBIT 9
ONE-YEAR RETURNS—WINDOW GIC

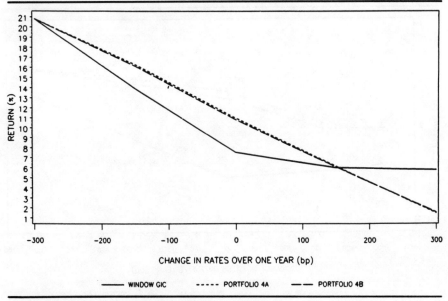

Source: Drexel Burnham Lambert, Fixed Income Research.

EXHIBIT 10
THREE-YEAR RETURNS—WINDOW GIC

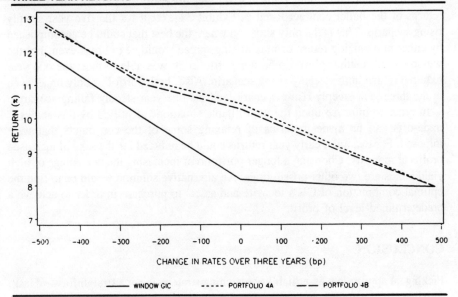

Source: Drexel Burnham Lambert, Fixed Income Research.

EXHIBIT 11
FIVE-YEAR RETURNS—WINDOW GIC

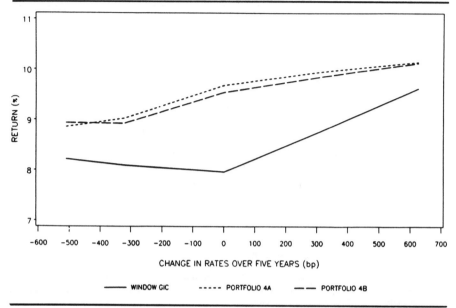

CHANGE IN RATES OVER FIVE YEARS (bp)

——— WINDOW GIC   - - - - - PORTFOLIO 4A   — — PORTFOLIO 4B

Source: Drexel Burnham Lambert, Fixed Income Research.

For the bullet GIC, both portfolios 4a and 4b easily outperform the required returns of the bullet contract listed in Exhibit 3—except for the five year steeply rising scenario. This is the only situation where the best that could be accomplished by either maximizing return or maximizing spread would be to break even. For the window GIC, neither portfolio 5a nor portfolio 5b was able to meet the one year required return in the steeply rising scenario. Also, both portfolios only break even in the three year steeply rising scenario and the one year steeply falling scenario.

In order to improve upon the unprofitable situations identified by this analysis, trade-offs can be made in terms of relaxing some of the constraints that were imposed. For example, early year returns could be reduced for the sake of increased profits at maturity. Choosing a longer portfolio or increasing the percentage of high yield bonds are two other possibilities. An alternative solution would be to find the optimal combination of GICs to write and assets to purchase in order to achieve a predetermined level of profit.

CONCLUSION

Picking an appropriate asset/liability matching strategy is not a straightforward task. Flexible GIC features introduce liability funding issues not conducive to conventional asset/liability management strategies. The investor should study simulation results of the cash flow behavior that occurs under different liability assumptions and different interest rate scenarios. Because solutions reached are not obviously effective, much less optimal, support through simulation where sensitivity to call provision, interest rates and prepayments can be examined becomes an invaluable tool in developing a strategy.

Chapter 7

Finding the Immunizing Investment for Insurance Liabilities: The Case of the SPDA

PETER D. NORIS, CFA
PRINCIPAL
FIXED INCOME RESEARCH
MORGAN STANLEY

SHELDON EPSTEIN, FSA
ASSOCIATE
FIXED INCOME RESEARCH
MORGAN STANLEY

Over the last few years the life insurance world has developed various methods for analyzing and managing interest rate risk. Each method has one primary goal: the determination of an optimal investment strategy that will "immunize" an insurance company's wealth from the ravages of changing interest rates. The most recent and predominant analytical method used for finding this optimal investment strategy is the "actuarial simulation" approach. An actuarial simulation involves creating a

---

Sheldon Epstein is now Vice President, Insurance Strategies Group, Merrill Lynch Capital Markets.

computer model that simulates the performance of an investment strategy versus an insurance company's liabilities. The insurance company's risk manager then tries to find the optimal strategy by testing numerous investment strategies over a wide range of interest rate scenarios. While the simulation approach is powerful, it can rarely discover an "immunizing strategy" for most modern-day insurance company products because no *simple* static or dynamic investment strategy will completely match the variability of the liability cash flows if the liability cash flows are themselves interest-sensitive. Therefore, the simulation approach forces the insurance company manager to settle for an investment strategy that limits the results to an acceptable *range*.

Ironically, the impetus for the development of the simulation technology arose from a perceived shortcoming of another method that had already been shown to achieve *true* immunization. This method, known as "duration matching," sought to protect the insurance company's wealth by matching up the interest rate sensitivities of assets and liabilities. The implementation of duration matching had been well documented and included a simple mathematical formula for determining the "duration" index. However, problems sometimes developed when the duration-matching method was used in an attempt to immunize wealth in situations where the liability cash flows were themselves interest-sensitive. It often appeared to give results that were worse than those achieved through the simulation approach. We will show in this chapter that the failure of duration-matching strategies had everything to do with the *definition* of duration and nothing to do with the concept itself.

This chapter contains a demonstration of proper duration matching for a very interest-sensitive insurance liability, the single premium deferred annuity policy ("SPDA"). We will explain how option-pricing theory can be combined with simulation techniques to derive the duration of an interest-sensitive cash flow stream (irrespective of whether the cash flow arises from an asset or a liability). We will apply this methodology to the SPDA and determine its immunizing investment strategy. Finally, we will validate the strategy by performing a traditional simulation study for the SPDA, where we demonstrate that an investment strategy based upon a proper approach to duration matching will protect the wealth of the insurance company. In the process of validating the immunizing strategy through a simulation model, various key principles with respect to asset/liability management will become apparent.

IMMUNIZATION THROUGH DURATION MATCHING: WHAT IT IS, AND WHAT IT ISN'T

Immunization and Duration Defined

In 1952 F. M. Redington, a British actuary, *defined immunization as "the investment of the assets in such a way that the existing business is immune to a general change in the rate of interest."* [1] The simplest immunization technique involves an asset portfolio that generates cash flows in exactly the right amounts at the due dates of the liabilities, and is otherwise known as "cash flow matching" or "dedication." However, dedication is not feasible in most cases where the asset or liability cash flows are themselves related to the actual level of interest rates.

An alternative immunization method involves an investment strategy that insures that the *market value* of the asset portfolio tracks any movement in market value of the associated liability portfolio as interest rates change. Since the market value of assets or liabilities is also equal to the present value of their cash flows, this method insures that the asset portfolio always has sufficient wealth to either liquidate or mature the liability. Market value immunization is a very powerful and flexible approach to asset/liability management, particularly from the asset portfolio manager's perspective. Because this method is concerned only with the *value* of assets and liabilities, the portfolio manager is not restricted to using only "cash flow matching" investments and may thus consider virtually any fixed income investment for use in the immunizing asset portfolio.

What is needed for market value immunization is a measurement index that defines how the market value of a cash flow stream will change with respect to changes in interest rates. If this single index of price sensitivity is itself susceptible to change (either by the progression of time or by shifts in the level of interest rates), then it may be necessary to also incorporate a rebalancing element in the immunization strategy. This measurement index, which is known as the cash flow stream's "duration," can be derived from the Taylor series expansion of the equation of price as a function of interest rates. The mathematical formulation of duration has been described in other publications, and it is found to be:[2]

$$\text{DURATION} = -\,(d\text{PRICE} / di) / \text{PRICE}$$

In other words, duration is a measure of price sensitivity and is computed by finding out how much the price will change (*d*PRICE) as interest rates change a small amount (*di*). It is turned into a measurement index by taking the ratio of this price change to the beginning price. For the sake of convention, *a negative sign is*

[1]The first reference to immunization was by F. M. Redington in "Review of the Principles of Life-Office Valuations," *Journal of the Institute of Actuaries* (Volume 18, 1952).

[2]The original reference to duration is found in *Some Theoretical Problems suggested by the Movements of Interest Rates, Bond Yields and Stock Prices in the United States Since 1856* by F. R. Macaulay, National Bureau of Economic Research (1938). Other developments are addressed by G. Bierwag, G. Kaufman, and A. Toevs in "Duration: Its Development and Use in Bond Portfolio Management," *Financial Analysts Journal* (July/August 1983). Redington, op. cit., pointed out the use of the Taylor expansion to create a measure of duration for an appropriately small change in interest rates. This formulation ignores the higher order terms of the Taylor expansion and expresses the change in interest rates as a small change in the force of interest δ.

placed in front of the value so that instruments whose prices decrease when interest rates increase (such as bonds) will have positive durations.

How to Immunize a Simplified Insurance Liability

Let us assume that we are an insurance company that is in the business of selling annuities and that we are about to sell the following two simplified insurance products:

(1) A 10-year annuity certain that pays $4,000 every sixth month.
(2) A lump-sum payment of $100,000 at the end of 10 years.

The company's pricing actuary has determined that the products should be sold for premiums of $57,306 and $42,694, respectively, to produce a total profit (ignoring expenses) of $10,827 in present value. (Appendix I contains a more complete development of the pricing and immunization assumptions used in this section.)

The payments described in (1) and (2) above constitute the *liabilities* of our insurance company. Our task is to construct an *investment portfolio* and *reinvestment strategy* that will fund these liabilities and protect the expected profit. To test the prospect of success of an investment strategy, we perform a simulation that considers how much profit is actually earned over a 10-year period. Further, we look at the present value of the profit for each of 100 possible interest rate scenarios. The yields characterizing these interest rate scenarios vary widely, as shown in Exhibit 1 which displays the range of short-term interest rates over all 100 scenarios. Exhibit 1 also highlights three specific interest rate scenarios that we will call high, stable and low.

Testing Simple Investment Portfolios. The first investment portfolios that we will test are composed entirely of constant-maturity bonds. For example, a 20-year bond investment strategy involves using the $89,173 of available premiums (after the expected $10,827 profit has been subtracted from the total $100,000 of premiums) to purchase a 20-year bond. At the end of each quarter (this being a quarterly simulation model) the bond is sold at the prevailing interest rate, any required liability payments are made, and the remaining funds are reinvested in a new 20-year bond.[3] The *success* of this investment strategy will be defined by the ability of the initial $89,173 reserve to fund exactly the entire 10 years of liability payments. Any excess at the end of 10 years means that the reserve was *redundant* and we could have subtracted a larger profit and invested a smaller reserve. Any shortfall means that the reserve was *deficient* and a larger reserve was required, which would have

---

[3]The purpose of the study reported in this chapter is to discover the *characteristics* of an ideal investment strategy. Therefore, while bonds are assumed to be sold at market levels dependent upon the prevailing interest rate, we have assumed no additional transaction costs.

EXHIBIT 1
INTEREST RATE SCENARIOS—6-MONTH YIELDS

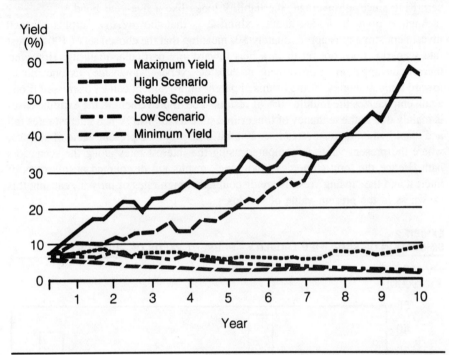

reduced the profit (and maybe even have created a deficit). For the purposes of this chapter, an *immunizing* investment strategy is defined as one that effectively creates neither a redundancy nor a deficiency of reserves in any of the 100 interest rate scenarios.

Exhibit 2 depicts the results of six different constant-maturity investment strategies, from three-month investments to 20-year bonds. The vertical axis is the amount of redundancy (positive numbers) or deficiency (negative numbers) in initial reserve. Each vertical box shows the range of results using that investment strategy for all 100 different interest rate scenarios. There are also markings on each box that show the 20th, 40th, 60th, and 80th percentiles of results, demonstrating their dispersion. Each "diamond" marks the average of all 100 scenarios.

The first thing one notices about Exhibit 2 is that some investment strategies do a better job of "immunizing" than others. In particular, a constant five-year maturity investment strategy seems to contain the least risk of missing the surplus target. Longer or shorter investment strategies have increasing amounts of risk (particularly if one puts less emphasis on the extremes of the 100 scenarios and instead concentrates on the surplus between the 20th and 80th percentiles). This should not be surprising since, on average, the liability looks like a five-year bond.[4]

Another point to notice about Exhibit 2 is that the *average* surplus of each investment strategy is approximately $0, meaning that the chosen set of 100 interest rate scenarios does not result in a bias toward any particular maturity. However, there is an apparent improvement in "upside" versus "downside" as one moves toward long strategies. Some of this apparent improvement can be dismissed if one again emphasizes the middle 60% of results. The improvement in the extreme cases is mainly due to the tendency of longer investments to "win" when interest rates fall and "lose" when interest rates rise. Exhibit 2 displays the present value of surplus, where the present value is computed using the interest rates along the scenario's path. Hence the long strategies' "winning" results are discounted at low rates of interest and the "losing" results are discounted at high rates of interest, causing this skewness in the present value of surplus.

EXHIBIT 2
SIMULATION OF SIMPLIFIED LIABILITY—PRESENT VALUE OF SURPLUS

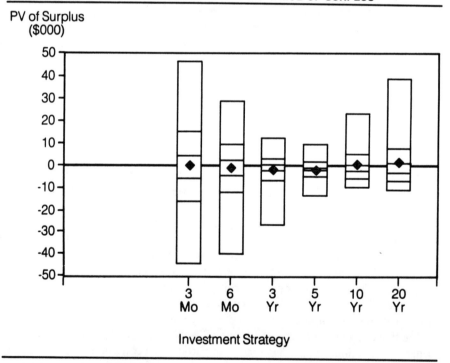

PV of Surplus
($000)

Investment Strategy

---

[4]At issuance, the total liability has the payment characteristics of a 10-year, 8% coupon bond. Over the course of the entire 10 years, the average characteristics are those of a five-year bond.

The final point regarding Exhibit 2 is the *absolute range* of results. Investing in three-month bonds contains some chance that the original reserve is deficient by $44,238—which is more than four times the initially expected profit! Even the best strategy—five-year bonds—contains a substantial probability that the original reserve is either redundant or deficient by thousands of dollars. One can hardly call any of these investment strategies a truly "immunizing strategy."

Duration of a Non-Interest-Sensitive Cash Flow Stream. Earlier we suggested that immunization can be achieved by using an investment strategy which insures that the market value of the asset portfolio tracks any movement in market value of the associated liability as interest rates change. The results of the previous section showed that the investment strategy which came closest to achieving true immunization was also the one which came closest to having the same average cash flow characteristics as the liability. Having the same average cash flow characteristics is one way of assuring that market values will track one another. A more precise way to measure this average is to measure the cash flow's price sensitivity directly by computing its duration.

Exhibit 3 develops the duration of the liabilities and the various investment alternatives. The *duration is simply 100 times the percentage change in price for a one-basis-point drop in interest rates*, assuming all interest rates are expressed on a continuously compounding basis.[5] Another important point of this table is that *liabilities can be managed in aggregate: The duration of a pool of liabilities is equal to its market-value-weighted average duration.*

EXHIBIT 3
MARKET VALUE AND DURATION

	Market Value (at current interest rates)	Market Value (down one basis point)	Percentage Change	Duration*
Liability 1	$51,101.32	$51,124.06	.044%	4.4 years
Liability 2	38,077.54	38,109.63	.100	10.0
Total Liability	$89,172.86	$89,233.69	.068%	6.8 years
3-month bonds	$100,000.00	$100,002.50	.0025%	0.25 years
6-month bonds	100,000.00	100,005.00	.0050	0.50
3-year bonds	100,000.00	100,026.96	.027	2.7
5-year bonds	100,000.00	100,041.08	.041	4.1
10-year bonds	100,000.00	100,065.65	.066	6.6
20-year bonds	100,000.00	100,088.80	.089	8.9

*Note that the duration value is denominated in years because duration is a measure of price change with respect to interest rates, and interest rates are expressed as a percentage *per year.* Alternatively, duration is often a measure of average life (see "Duration Misunderstood"), where the average life is expressed in years.

---

[5]We have chosen to define duration in terms of a one-basis-point drop in the entire term structure of interest rates. The term structure is exhibited in Appendix I.

Duration-Matched Investment Strategy. Because the liability duration of 6.8 years is not precisely equal to the duration of any of the available investments, it is not surprising that none of the available investments performed an adequate job of immunization. We could, however, construct an investment portfolio composed of 10-year and 20-year bonds that would have an average duration of 6.8 years. By investing in this portfolio, the asset duration will equal the liability duration, and theory tells us that the profit should be immunized. Exhibit 4 compares the results of the previously shown constant-maturity investment strategies with the *constant-duration* investment strategy.

What has gone wrong? The new set of results hardly looks better than investing in 10-year bonds and is certainly less "immunizing" than investing in five-year bonds. The problem is not with the initial investment portfolio, which is duration-matched to the initial liability, but with the *reinvestment* strategy. By using a *constant-duration* investment strategy we have ignored the fact that the duration of the liability is continuously changing. Two primary factors contribute to the change in liability duration: (1) as time progresses, the liability ages (known as duration "drift"), and (2) as interest rates change, duration also changes (generally referred to as "convexity"). Exhibit 5 shows the range of liability durations for all 100 interest rate

EXHIBIT 4
SIMULATION OF SIMPLIFIED LIABILITY—PRESENT VALUE OF SURPLUS

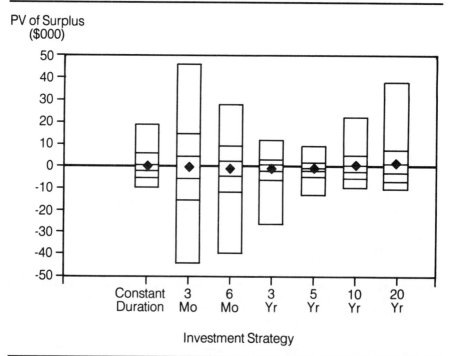

EXHIBIT 5
LIABILITY DURATION

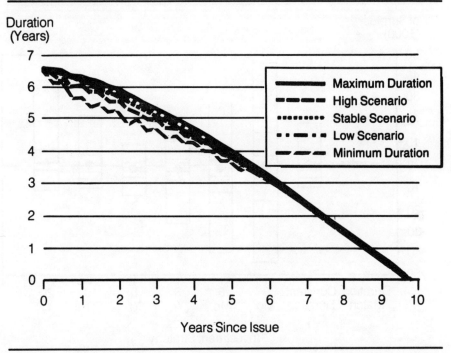

scenarios as well as the actual movement of duration for the three highlighted scenarios. Note that the duration drifts until it reaches zero at maturity. Note also that the level of interest rates influences the duration of the liability (as evidenced by the dispersion of possible durations at any quarter).

Immunization requires rebalancing the asset portfolio. The process of constructing an immunizing asset portfolio requires not only the measurement of an initial duration target, but also the measurement and rebalancing of ensuing liability and asset durations. To test the success of a full *duration-matching* investment strategy, we again perform a simulation. The new investment strategy is to purchase, at the beginning of each quarter, a portfolio of two bonds that has the same duration as the *remaining* liability.[6] By rebalancing every quarter, we can construct an asset portfolio whose duration "replicates" the duration level and drift of the liability. In theory, immunization requires continuous rebalancing in order for the asset portfolio to exactly track the liability's duration. In practice, rebalancing is done only periodically. In this chapter we study the effect of quarterly rebalancing. Also, because we know that any rebalancing and interest rate changes can occur only at the *end* of each

---

[6]The two bonds are selected from the then-current three-month, six-month, one-year, three-year, five-year, 10-year or 20-year maturity current-coupon bonds.

EXHIBIT 6
SIMULATION OF SIMPLIFIED LIABILITY—PRESENT VALUE OF SURPLUS

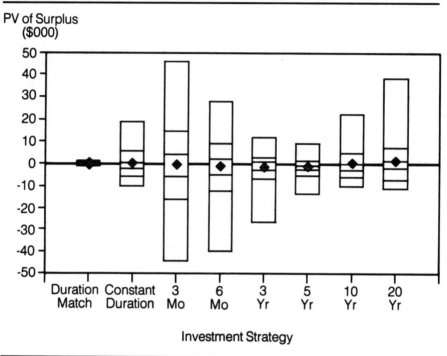

PV of Surplus
($000)

Investment Strategy

quarter, our duration calculation is refined to incorporate only the cash flows remaining after the end of the quarter. This refinement improves the degree of immunization. The degree of immunization could be improved further by also matching the convexity of the asset portfolio to that of the remaining liability. However, Exhibit 6 shows that even with such quarterly rebalancing and lack of convexity match, a substantial degree of immunization is achieved. Appendix I indicates that all 100 scenarios are within $1,247 of the reserve target. We will call these results true immunization.

Duration Misunderstood

The word "duration" is potentially misleading for the measure of price sensitivity that we are trying to quantify. "Duration" was coined by Frederick R. Macaulay in 1938 to describe the average life of a set of cash flows as determined by their average present-value-weighted maturities. "Duration" became synonymous with the price-sensitivity definition when it was shown that the Macaulay duration of a non-interest-sensitive cash flow stream is mathematically equal to its price sensitivity.

However, Macaulay duration fails to equal the price sensitivity whenever the cash flows themselves vary with the level of interest rates. It should have come as no surprise to asset/liability managers that duration, as defined by Macaulay, failed to properly provide an immunizing strategy for interest-sensitive cash flows (such as most insurance liability cash flows). Finding no simple method to adapt Macaulay duration to interest-sensitive cash flows, insurance company risk managers began to implement simulation models in an attempt to discover immunizing investment strategies.

However, if one goes back to the basic market-value definition of duration, it is possible to develop a proper duration measurement for *interest-sensitive* cash flows. As long as we can derive a single market value or price for the cash flows, it is possible to examine the price behavior in various interest rate environments and determine duration numerically. This duration is called *"option-adjusted duration"* because of the way in which the price of the cash flows is determined. The determination of option-adjusted durations involves applying both simulation techniques and option-pricing theory. By using both tools it is possible to express the *immunizing* investment strategy *directly in terms of duration*, in contrast to the actuarial simulation approach in which an initial set of assets and a reinvestment strategy must be specified.

THE THEORY OF PRICING FINANCIAL ASSETS AND ITS RELATION TO INSURANCE SIMULATION MODELS

Option-Pricing Theory

To most people (even to some actuaries and investment managers), "option-pricing theory" is an intimidating phrase. Not only does it involve options, which are often viewed as esoteric instruments and very risky, but it emphasizes theory, which may seem to have little bearing on the real world. But "option-pricing theory" simply refers to the pricing of any instrument whose cash flow is dependent upon the movement of interest rates. These instruments do not have to be the "puts and calls" one normally associates with options; rather they can be the components of any cash flow stream (such as the payments arising from an insurance contract). The theory merely indicates how to derive a fair market value for the cash flow stream.

Why use option-pricing theory? Actuaries already have many "pricing" methods that are used to set an insurance policy's price (i.e., its premium). Unfortunately, these methods were created at a time when interest rate volatility was of little concern. Most traditional actuarial pricing methods use only a *single* interest rate (or interest rate path) assumption. When concerned about the volatility of interest rates, actuaries will choose a "conservative" interest rate assumption to set a policy's price. While this method may perhaps arrive at an acceptable level of profitability, it is hardly a method to use when trying to create an immunizing investment strategy.

In the real world, interest rates vary. A pricing method should account for this fact, and should do so in such a way that a single price is consistent with all reasonably possible scenarios of future interest rate movements. In option-pricing theory, one does not have to make a *subjective* ranking of the likelihood of any given interest rate path occurring, which is a common problem with actuarial simulation techniques. The *price as determined by option-pricing theory is the present value of the cash flow stream, no matter which scenario interest rates follow.*[7] This statement is true because the fair price of an interest-sensitive instrument can also be justified by assuming that *riskless arbitrage* cannot exist. That is, it can be shown that a *hedging portfolio* of fixed-cash-flows bonds can be created that has the same future value as the interest-sensitive instrument.[8] Therefore, in order to prevent riskless arbitrage, the price of the interest-sensitive instrument must also be the present value of the hedging portfolio. Conversely, the value of a cash flow stream determined by applying option-pricing methods is *fully hedgeable*. This is a very important statement to any insurance company manager who is concerned with the ability of a company's assets to satisfy fully the associated insurance liabilities. By using the lessons of option-pricing theory, the investment manager can create a fully immunizing investment strategy.

Option-Pricing Techniques

Most people agree on the characteristics necessary to construct a proper theory of option pricing, but putting the theory into practice has created a cottage industry. One of the input assumptions necessary to option pricing is a properly *unbiased process* that describes the manner in which interest rates behave. This process is used to generate interest rate paths which, when taken as a set, make certain statements about the volatility of interest rates and the probabilistic dynamics of the entire yield curve. Creating such an unbiased set of interest rate paths is the rub. Many types of option-pricing model have been described in the literature, especially models where the interest rate process involves discrete changes in interest rates. A popular form of these models permits interest rates to move according to a discrete binomial process (that is, interest rates can move only to some "up" state or "down" state from one period to the next). Whatever process is used, however, the interest rate paths must conform to proper assumptions concerning the volatility of interest rates and the way in which various parts of the yield curve interact.[9]

---

[7]So long as the yield curve dynamics and volatility on which the price is based continue to apply.

[8]This arbitrage approach is explained by J. Cox, S. Ross, and M. Rubinstein in "Option Pricing: A Simplified Approach," *Journal of Financial Economics* (September 1979).

[9]The characteristics of a proper option-pricing model are explained by R. Bookstaber, D. Jacob, and J. Langsam in "Pitfalls in Debt Option Models," Morgan Stanley Fixed Income Research Publication (April 1986). A conforming model is developed by D. Jacob, G. Lord and J. Tilley in "A Generalized Framework for Pricing Contingent Cash Flows," *Financial Management* (Summer 1987).

All option-pricing models require an initial level of interst rates to be specified. A properly constructed model must use a whole yield curve to seed the interest rate process. The first step in pricing a cash flow stream is to generate a set of interest rate paths from the initial yield curve according to the assumed interest rate process. Next, the relevant cash flows are projected for each time period along each path. If the cash flows are interest-sensitive, their amount and timing will depend upon the path that is followed. The present value of the cash flows for any one path is found by discounting the flows using the period-by-period short-term rates along the path. Finally, these disparate present values from all the paths are averaged appropriately to produce a single market value or price. To verify the accuracy and consistency of the technique, it can be used to value assets whose prices are established through market forces; for example, all U.S. Treasury bonds.

The option-pricing model used in this chapter is based upon a continuous process of interest rate movements that generates paths of entire yield curves. The interest-sensitive cash flows are priced using a large sample of paths.

Similarity to Actuarial Simulation Techniques

The preceding description of option-pricing models sounds very similar to traditional actuarial simulation models. An actuarial simulation involves generating cash flows both for the assumed assets and the liabilities along several interest rate paths. We borrow from simulation techniques in that the cash flow generator for the liability stream is constructed essentially as it would be for a simulation model. However, unlike actuarial simulation models, we do not need to study an assumed *asset* cash flow since the *liability* market value and duration *will dictate the ideal characteristics of the asset portfolio.* The major differences between an option-pricing approach and a simulation approach are that option-pricing models (1) look at one side of the balance sheet at a time, and (2) produce market values (present values) rather than period-by-period results. However, because the generation of period-by-period cash flows is an interim step within an option-pricing model, option-pricing theory as applied to insurance liabilities can be thought of as an *extension* of actuarial simulation models.

In practice, an option-pricing-based model is often used to determine the market value of existing liabilities, which is then compared with the market value of existing assets (where the assets have been valued according to the actual market prices on the date of valuation).[10] The difference between the asset and liability market values is the amount of *market value surplus* (or deficit) in the modeled business. The *match* between asset and liability duration can also be found if the asset duration is determined using a similar option-pricing framework, allowing the analysis of interest-sensitive assets such as callable bonds and mortgage-backed securities.

---

[10]In effect, option-pricing theory is the interest-sensitive analog to a Gross Premium Valuation.

Calculation of Duration and Convexity

The preceding sections have described how option-pricing techniques can be used to derive a market value for an insurance liability cash flow stream. The relative size of the liability market value in relation to the asset market value determines the existence of true economic (as opposed to statutory) surplus or deficit. In order to immunize this surplus or deficit, the next step is to calculate the liability duration so that it can be compared with the asset duration. It also might be helpful to calculate the convexity of the liability so the asset portfolio can be positioned to reduce the need for rebalancing. However, this chapter will emphasize the calculation of duration only.

It is important to remember that duration and convexity are merely indices that describe how much a price will change as interest rates change. The option-pricing model determines a price by generating a set of interest paths, starting from some *initial* yield curve (which is usually the actual yield curve of available investments as of the date of valuation). By shifting the initial yield curve and generating a new set of paths and cash flows starting from the shifted curve, one can reprice the cash flows and so determine how the price varies with movements in interest rates. Studying a number of parallel shifts in the *initial* interest rate *term structure* allows us to determine the duration and convexity of the cash flow stream.[11] Even though we analyze only parallel shifts in the initial term structure, the model allows for nonparallel movements of the yield curves along the various paths. The last section of this chapter will demonstrate that this duration target can be very reliable even when nonparallel shifts occur.

Finally, it should be noted that when *non-interest-sensitive* cash flows are evaluated using an option-pricing model, the duration and convexity values produced are identical to those produced through a simple modification of Macaulay's original formulation. Thus, option-pricing models allow the theory of immunization to be extended to the situation of *interest-sensitive* cash flows.

CASE STUDY: MARKET VALUE AND DURATION OF AN SPDA

This section applies option-pricing techniques to an interest-sensitive insurance liability: the single premium deferred annuity ("SPDA"). We first give a generalized description of the SPDA, highlighting the sources of interest rate risk. We then analyze a specific example, developing assumptions about the interest sensitivity of various product features. These assumptions are incorporated into a model that is

---

[11]The term structure of interest rates refers to time-specific discount rates, sometimes called "spot rates" or "zero-coupon bond yields." The term structure is often derived from information contained in the yield curve of coupon-paying bonds. A discussion of term-structure theory and its uses is contained in A. Toevs and L. Dyer, "The Term Structure of Interest Rates and Its Use in Asset and Liability Management," Morgan Stanley Fixed Income Research Publication (October 1986).

used to calculate the price and duration of the SPDA cash flow. The price will indicate the expected profitability of the SPDA, while the duration will dictate the immunizing investment strategy.

In the next section we utilize a traditional actuarial simulation approach to test the results of the model. We show that by investing in an asset portfolio with the proper duration, the expected profitability of the SPDA can be acceptably immunized against changes in interest rates. The results should be compared with the previous simplified example of immunization to determine the success of the SPDA immunization.

It should also be kept in mind that we are analyzing only one set of assumptions about the interest sensitivity of SPDA product features. However, these techniques can easily be repeated for other sets of assumptions and such sensitivity analysis will indicate to the asset/liability manager the degree of immunization that can ultimately be achieved.

What Is an SPDA?

An SPDA is an insurance product that acts like a savings account for the eventual purchase of an annuity. The purchaser of an SPDA makes a single premium payment, usually at the time the contract is applied for. The premium is credited to the policy account and accrues interest until (1) the account is used to purchase an annuity at the then-current rates, (2) the purchaser dies, or (3) the purchaser decides to withdraw the policy's funds. The interest rate credited is usually a current-market rate, initially guaranteed for a defined period, and then reset periodically by the insurer subject to a minimum guarantee. SPDAs are normally sold as a vehicle to accumulate funds for retirement.

Interest Rate Risks Inherent in an SPDA

There are numerous interest rate risks inherent in an SPDA. Most industry analysts have focused on the risk of disintermediation due to rising interest rates. It is relatively easy for a policyholder to withdraw funds from an SPDA since all products allow access to any or all of the account's accumulated value, usually with some nominal "surrender charge" during the first seven to 10 years after issuance. Most SPDAs also allow a small percentage of the account value, usually 10%, to be withdrawn annually without incurring a charge. In order to avoid taxation on the accumulated interest, the policyholder can surrender the contract and "roll" the proceeds over to a new SPDA. In addition, the policyholder can always convert the SPDA into an immediate annuity that provides a monthly income stream. Thus, from the policyholder's point of view, there usually are no tax considerations involved when deciding whether or not to surrender the policy.

The policyholder's major consideration when deciding whether to surrender is the rate that is being credited by the insurer versus the rates that are currently available in the marketplace as offered by competitive insurers. Since funds are withdrawn at close to book value, a loss to the insurer may occur if the assets supporting the policy account have to be sold at less than their book value. The risk to the insurance company is obviously greatest whenever interest rates suddenly rise. However, just as some homeowners may prepay their mortgage in a high interest rate environment, there will always be a certain percentage of policyholders who surrender for reasons other than interest rates. An additional risk associated with policy surrender is that even though assets may not have to be liquidated below book value, the surrender charge may be inadequate to recover the unamortized acquisition expenses.

A second major risk is associated with the SPDA's credited rate itself. Initially, the insurance company guarantees a fixed credited rate. This fixed rate is then subject to change after the guarantee period expires (most typically, after one year). At the time of issuance, neither the insurance company nor the policyholder knows what the subsequent credited rates will be. The insurance company may have a *credited-rate strategy,* but the actual rate will be subject to market conditions at the time of renewal. Therefore, the insurer has no way of predicting the accreted size of the ultimate SPDA liability.

Another major (and often overlooked) risk inherent in an SPDA is that of falling interest rates. Some SPDAs guarantee the initial interest rate for as long as seven years. This long guarantee period obviously involves the risk that lower reinvestment rates may cause the insurer to have a shortfall in investment income. Even though this risk seems to be mitigated where the insurer has a shorter guarantee reset period, many insurers are loath to reduce their credited rate. This action effectively creates a longer "guarantee" period. Another risk of falling interest rates arises from the minimum interest rate guarantee attached to the SPDA. While this guarantee is usually a "conservative" 4%, it is entirely conceivable that reinvestment rates may fall below the level and stay there for some time.

Case Study: Assumptions

A detailed description of the SPDA used in this case study is contained in Appendix II. While this SPDA does not represent any particular insurer's policy form, its features are typical of many being marketed today. The case study is based upon a single premium of $100,000, which also becomes the initial value of the SPDA account. The amount of the premium available for the insurer to invest is the $100,000 deposit, net of $219 in issuance expenses, $5,000 in commissions, and $2,000 in anticipated profit—namely a "net premium" of $92,781. Recurring expenses consist of a maintenance expense of $25 per annum, which increases at an inflation rate correlated to the interest rate scenario, and a yearly investment expense equal to 25 basis points (.25%) of the outstanding account value.

The SPDA is credited with a guaranteed rate of 7.90% per annum for the first five years. This rate was set in a yield environment where five-year investments yielded 9.22% on a bond-equivalent basis. After the five-year guarantee period, the credited rate is reset annually. It is assumed that the insurer will follow a reset strategy that annually renews the SPDA at 165 basis points below then-current five-year invest-ment yields (with the result rounded to the nearest 10 basis points), subject to a 4% minimum credited rate. Competing insurers are assumed to follow a similar cred-ited-rate strategy, except that their reset margin is 150 basis points below five-year investment yields.

The SPDA policyholder has the right at any time to withdraw any or all of the accumulated cash value. The SPDA in this example applies a surrender charge at the time of surrender. This charge is 6% in the first two policy years and is scaled downward until it is eliminated by the eighth year. There is no free partial surrender provision. Surrenders are assumed to occur at a minimum rate of 4% of in-force account values annually. Additional lapses occur if the SPDA's credited rate be-comes less attractive than an assumed competitor's credited rate. The algorithm for this lapse function is shown in Appendix II.[12] The case study models a 10-year period, at the end of which time all remaining account value is withdrawn.

Market Value and Duration of the SPDA

The first step in deriving the market value of the SPDA is to construct the interest rate scenarios over which the SPDA cash flow will be analyzed. As previously described, these scenarios are generated in such a way that they comport with option-pricing criteria and each path is a sequence of complete yield curves. The actual number of scenarios analyzed is determined more from practical than from theoretical considerations. While "more scenarios" is always better theoretically, we have found that acceptably accurate results (and acceptable computer charges) can be achieved with about 100 scenarios. For the sake of convenience, the scenarios used to value the SPDA happen to be the same scenarios used previously to test the immunization of the simplified insurance liability. Substantially identical results would be achieved with a different set of 100 scenarios generated from the same interest rate process and assumptions. Once again, rather than supply the details of all scenarios, we will highlight only the three scenarios (high, stable, and low) described earlier. Appendix III lists the full 10 years' worth of interest rates from these three scenarios. It is readily apparent that the assumed volatility of interest rates allows for some fairly wild interest rate movements.

Once the interest rate paths have been generated, the next step is to project the SPDA liability cash flows along each path. These cash flows consist of an initial amount (commissions, issuance expenses, and profit) followed by a stream of expenses and surrenders. The details of these cash flows are listed in Appendix III. The total cash flow for the three scenarios is shown in Exhibit 7. Because the

---

[12]A common criticism of using option-pricing models for insurance products is that it is necessary to specify an interest-sensitive withdrawal function. However, the need for this function is also implicit in the actuarial-simulation models that are currently in vogue.

EXHIBIT 7
SPDA CASH FLOWS

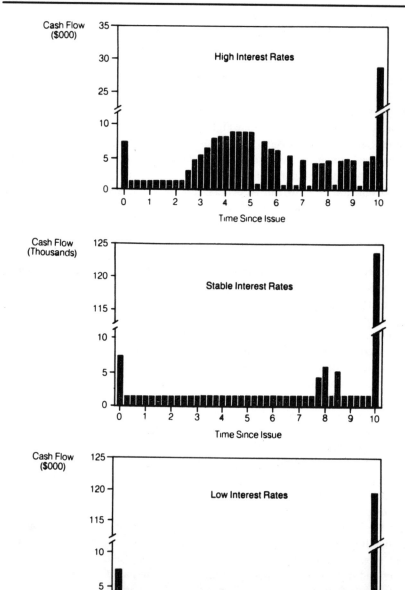

modeled credited-rate strategy is fairly "competitive" (that is, it follows current market rates both up and down), cash surrenders are held to a minimum and the projected cash flows generally extend for a long period of time. Other credited-rate strategies would show different cash flow characteristics. The large amount of cash flow in the tenth year is due to the assumed surrender of all policies still in force at the end of the projection period. Our challenge is to immunize the SPDA's target surplus, notwithstanding the variability of this cash flow.

The cash flows shown are a good example of the various risks inherent in an SPDA. The high interest rate scenario exhibits the risk of early surrender. This is particularly apparent during the period near the end of the five-year guarantee, a time when the surrender charge is decreasing and the fixed credited rate is becoming less attractive as interest rates increase. Even during the final five years, when the credited rate is reset annually, interest-sensitive surrenders are avoided only at the times when the credited rate is competitive. The stable interest rate scenario exhibits only a few interest-sensitive surrenders, when interest rates drift upwards during the eighth and ninth years, but this low surrender rate causes the terminal cash flow to be much higher than in the high interest rate scenario. Finally, the "low" interest rate scenario avoids interest-sensitive surrenders, but the five-year fixed guarantee followed by the 4% minimum guarantee creates a terminal cash flow that is not much smaller than in the stable interest rate scenario.

The market value of the SPDA is found by calculating the average over the 100 interest rate paths of the present values of liability cash flows. The SPDA in our example has a market value of $92,781. One hopes that $92,781 is also the amount of funds available to invest after all up-front expenses and present value of future profits have been subtracted from the SPDA premium. If the amount is greater (less) than $92,781, the expected present value of profits is greater (smaller). The example for this case study has been arranged so that the available SPDA "net premium" is $92,781—exactly equal to the SPDA market value.

This market value is derived from a set of paths based upon the initial current-coupon-bond curve of available investments (listed in Appendix I). In order to calculate the duration of the SPDA, we must also calculate a market value in a shocked interest rate environment. In fact we should calculate market values in *two* more interest rate environments in order to better approximate the duration in the current interest rate environment. These two additional sets of 100 paths have been computed by first shocking the term structure underlying the initial coupon curve both up and down by 100 basis points (on a continuously compounded basis), then generating 100 new interest rate paths and cash flows for each of the new environments.[13] The results of these calculations are:

---

[13]Note that this process is *not* the same as simply adding or subtracting 100 basis points to the rates along each path.

Shock to Initial Term Structure	Market Value	Percentage Change
− 100b.p.	$96,297	
0	92,781	3.8%
100	89,742	−3.3

To calculate the duration of the SPDA we then fit a curve to the above results with the following functional form:

$$MV(S) = e^{a+bS}$$
$$Duration(S=0) = -b$$

where MV denotes market value and S denotes shock to the initial yield curve.

Thus, the option-adjusted duration of the sample SPDA is found to be 3.5 years, which is also roughly the average percentage change in price for a 100-basis-point shift in interest rates from the initial levels.

Comparison with Macaulay Duration

It is interesting to compare the price-sensitivity duration for the SPDA with its Macaulay duration. For any particular interst rate scenario, the Macaulay duration is equal to the average present-value-weighted maturity of the cash flow stream. For the SPDA modeled in this chapter, the range of Macaulay durations over all 100 scenarios is from 2.9 years to 7.9 years. If the average cash flow over all 100 scenarios is used to compute a Macaulay duration, the value is 6.3 years. Practically all of these Macaulay durations are much longer than the price-sensitivity duration of 3.5 years. Why is there a difference?

Macaulay duration merely indicates the average life of the cash flows. For anyone interested in the expected length of time the SPDA liability will remain outstanding, the Macaulay duration is useful. However, for anyone interested in immunizing the profitability of the SPDA, Macaulay duration is meaningless. Before leaving this subject, let us intuitively reconcile the two types of duration. One can think of the SPDA (or for that matter, any cash flow stream) as having two components: (1) an expected amount of cash flow given a "normal" interest rate environment, and (2) an interest-sensitive cash flow that will increase or decrease as interest rates change. The Macaulay-type duration properly accounts for both the length *and price sensitivity* of the *"normal"* component. In our SPDA example, this value is 6.3 years. In order to find the price sensitivity of the *total* SPDA liability, we must *overlay the duration of the interest-sensitive cash flow onto the base duration of 6.3 years.*

Intuitively, we know that the *interest-sensitive* SPDA component has a low or negative duration. Why? First, because the SPDA credited rate is reset to follow somewhat the direction of interest rates, the amount of SPDA cash value increases as interest rates increase. Second, the amount of cash flow required to support the SPDA also increases as interest rates increase, due to the occurrence of additional surrenders. Any instrument that has increased cash flow or value as interest rates increase has a low or negative duration.

In the case of the SPDA, because we must overlay a negative duration for the "interest-sensitive" component onto the more positive duration of 6.3 years for the "normal" component, we know that the price-sensitivity (option-adjusted duration) of the SPDA must be less than its average maturity (Macaulay duration). This relationship can also be expressed mathematically, as described in Appendix IV.

IMMUNIZING THE PROFITABILITY OF THE SPDA

We now wish to test the effectiveness of using the option-adjusted duration measure of price sensitivity to immunize the profitability of our representative SPDA. We will first test the success of constant-maturity investment strategies in order to give the reader an appreciation of the amount of risk inherent in mismatched investment strategies. As in an earlier section, where we examined a non-interest-sensitive insurance liability, we will use an actuarial simulation to gauge the extent of the immunization. Once again, the test is conducted using the 100 different interest rate scenarios that were shown in Exhibit 1 and highlighted in Appendix III.[14]

Constant-Maturity Investment Strategies

Exhibit 8 shows the results for various constant-maturity investment strategies. As before, the vertical axis is the amount of redundancy (positive numbers) or deficiency (negative numbers) in the initial SPDA reserve and the vertical boxes indicate the range of results using that investment strategy for all 100 different interest rate scenarios. The additional markings show the 20th, 40th, 60th and 80th percentiles and each "diamond" marks the average of all 100 scenarios.

Exhibit 8 is a good illustration of how an actuarial simulation approach is normally used to decide upon an optimal investment strategy. On the basis of the six constant-maturity investment strategies, an insurance company risk manager might decide that three-year bonds offer the least risk in backing the SPDA. Alternatively, the risk manager might choose to test other investment strategies, using three-year bonds as a baseline. In any event, such testing would continue until the risk manager was satisfied with the results.

As was the case in testing constant-maturity investment strategies against the simplified insurance liability, the average result is close to $0, indicating a lack of bias in the scenarios. The SPDA results in Exhibit 8 also exhibit some of the

---

[14]We use the same 100 scenarios merely for convenience. Similar results are obtained for any set of 100 scenarios generated by the same method.

EXHIBIT 8
SIMULATION OF SPDA LIABILITY—PRESENT VALUE OF SURPLUS

PV of Surplus
(% of Premium)

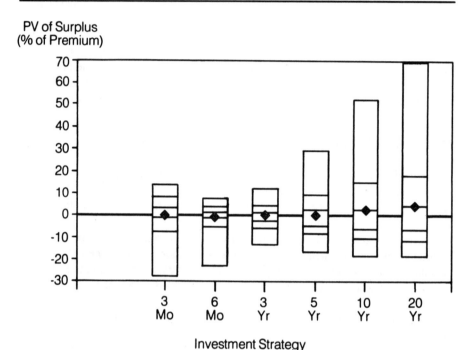

Investment Strategy

skewness shown in the study of the simplified insurance liability. Most of this skewness is due to the same effects noted earlier (i.e., the effect of high interest/discount rates being associated with generally "losing" scenarios using long investments, and generally "winning" scenarios using short investments), but the interest-sensitivity of the liability introduces another effect. Because high interest rate scenarios generally result in increased surrenders, any gain or loss achieved by investing in short or long investments does not have a chance to accrue. Conversely, the minimal surrenders in low interest rate scenarios permit any gain or loss to build to a large amount.

Still, the "optimal" investment strategy of three-year bonds is hardly an immunizing strategy. Exhibit 9 contains the values that were used to generate Exhibit 7. One can see that in at least 40% of the scenarios (those above the 80th and below the 20th percentiles) the size of the redundancy or deficiency is large, especially when compared with the profit target of $2,000. This variability is probably unacceptable, even using the three-year bond strategy.

Some risk managers might be willing to live with variability, as long as there is not much probability that an unacceptable *deficiency* will occur. Exhibit 9 also shows

EXHIBIT 9
SPDA—SIMULATION RESULTS FOR VARIOUS INVESTMENT STRATEGIES: PRESENT VALUE OF ENDING SURPLUS

	3-Month Bonds	6-Month Bonds	3-Year Bonds	5-Year Bonds	10-Year Bonds	20-Year Bonds
Maximum Redundancy	$13,771	$7,335	$11,773	$29,030	$52,147	$69,616
80th Percentile	$8,132	$3,940	$4,113	$9,260	$14,652	$17,616
60th Percentile	$3,211	$1,653	$1,140	$2,354	$2,742	$4,502
Average	($58)	($702)	($421)	$584	$2,537	$3,793
40th Percentile	($888)	($1,065)	($2,382)	($4,526)	($6,182)	($6,504)
20th Percentile	($7,815)	$5,271)	($5,719)	($8,216)	($10,570)	($11,514)
Maximum Deficiency	($28,137)	($23,376)	($13,569)	($16,676)	($18,477)	($18,437)
Number of Scenarios Deficient by $2,000	36	35	41	44	49	50

the number of scenarios in which a reserve deficiency exceeded the target profit of $2,000. Using a three-year bond investment strategy, this amount of deficiency occurred in an unacceptable 41 out of 100 scenarios.

Duration-Matched Investment Strategy

Testing a duration-matched investment strategy for an SPDA is a very computer-intensive exercise. For each interest rate scenario to be tested, the duration of the remaining SPDA liability must be recalculated every quarter as one proceeds along a path. Since the calculation of an accurate duration requires the generation and evaluation of 300 interest rate paths (100 valuation paths for each of the current and shocked interest rate environments), and we conducted a 40-quarter study for each of 100 different interest rate scenarios, the test of the duration-matched investment strategy required the generation and evaluation of 1,200,000 separate interest rate scenarios![15] Insurance company risk managers can be thankful that the real world follows only one interest rate path at a time and that it is necessary to evaluate just the three sets of 100 scenarios each time a valuation is performed.

Exhibit 10 shows several duration paths taken by the SPDA over the 10-year evaluation period. The SPDA exhibits the duration drift that is characteristic of any aging cash flow stream. However, unlike the simplified insurance liability exhibited in Exhibit 5, the duration of the SPDA generally drifts from 3.5 at inception to zero at the five-year point, and then exhibits an annual saw-toothed pattern. The reasoning behind the pattern has to do with the nature of the credited rate guarantee. This SPDA has a credited rate that is fixed for the first five years and then reset annually. Still, there is significant variability around this baseline drift pattern.[16] As a general

---

[15]If one wanted to test a *convexity*-matched investment strategy, a total of five separate market values should be evaluated in order to arrive at an accurate convexity calculation. The test would thus require 2,000,000 separate scenarios.

[16]The amount and direction of this variability is indicative of high positive convexity.

EXHIBIT 10
SPDA DURATION

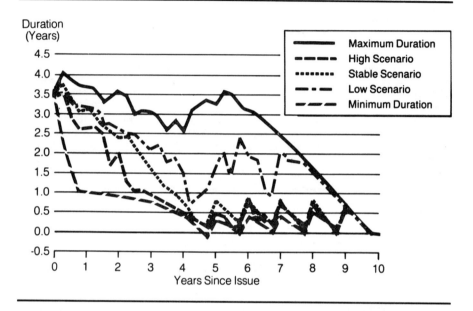

rule, lower interest rates lead to a higher duration (mostly because there is a greater chance that the credited rate will be subject to the guaranteed 4% minimum) and higher interest rates lead to a lower duration (interest-sensitive surrenders occur).

Once the paths of SPDA duration have been calculated, they can be used to test a duration-matched investment strategy. As with the test of the simple insurance liability, the modeled investment strategy is to purchase, at the beginning of each quarter, a portfolio of two bonds that has the same duration as the remaining liability. Exhibit 11 appends the results of this duration-matching strategy to the previous figure of the constant-maturity investment strategies. Exhibit 12 appends the numeric results to the values in Exhibit 9.

The duration-matching investment strategy provides a dramatic improvement in risk control. The profit target of $2,000 is now achieved in 94 out of 100 scenarios. Table 3 also indicates that 89% of the scenarios are *within* $2,000 of the target surplus and 44% are within $1,000. It should also be noted that these results were obtained even though the portfolio was rebalanced only quarterly and that the two-bond asset portfolio matched only the *duration* of the SPDA liability. Better immunization could be obtained with more frequent rebalancing and/or a greater degree of convexity match. Still, this test proves the possibility of immunizing one of the most highly interest-sensitive insurance liabilities—the SPDA.

EXHIBIT 11
SIMULATION OF SPDA LIABILITY—PRESENT VALUE OF SURPLUS

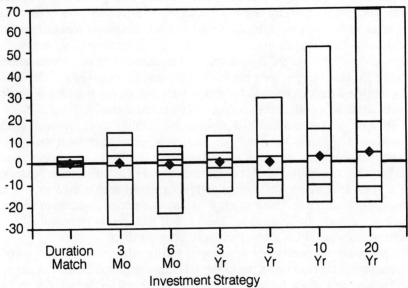

PV of Surplus
(% of Premium)

Investment Strategy

EXHIBIT 12
PRESENT VALUE OF SURPLUS

	Duration Match	3-Month Bonds	6-Month Bonds	3-Year Bonds	5-Year Bonds	10-Year Bonds	20-Year Bonds
Maximum Redundancy	$2,929	$13,771	$7,335	$11,773	$29,030	$52,147	$69,616
80th Percentile	$1,403	$8,132	$3,940	$4,113	$9,260	$14,652	$17,616
60th Percentile	$685	$3,211	$1,653	$1,140	$2,354	$2,742	$4,502
Average	$140	($58)	(702)	($421)	$584	$2,537	$3,793
40th Percentile	($387)	($888)	($1,065)	($2,382)	(4,526)	($6,182)	($6,504)
20th Percentile	($1,141)	($7,815)	($5,271)	($5,719)	($8,216)	($10,570)	($11,514)
Maximum Deficiency	($4,818)	($28,137)	($23,376)	($13,569)	($16,676)	($18,477)	($18,437)
Number of Scenarios							
Deficient by $2,000	6	36	35	41	44	49	50
Between:							
($2,000) to $2,000	89	20	29	28	14	8	5
($1,000) to $1,000	44	12	15	13	9	4	2

CONCLUSION

This chapter explains the principles involved in achieving the immunization of profit arising from a very interest-sensitive insurance liability, the SPDA. The practical application of these principles has been validated through the use of an actuarial simulation model. Only by properly measuring the price sensitivity of the SPDA can an immunizing investment strategy be formulated. The proper measurement of price sensitivity, known as duration, requires the use of option-pricing theory. Option-pricing theory permits the establishment of an immunizing investment strategy for the SPDA, even though future interest rate movements are unknown. The immunization achieved through these techniques is quite successful, resulting in the original profit target being attained in 94 out of 100 tested scenarios.

We have also shown that two popular asset/liability tools, actuarial-simulation models and Macaulay duration, can create suboptimal investment strategies when used in an attempt to immunize interest-sensitive liabilities. An actuarial simulation is, however, an important tool in examining the risk of any investment strategy and it is also an integral part of the option-pricing model that is used to develop the duration-matched investment strategy. Macaulay duration is shown to be a component of price-sensitivity duration, and by itself will usually be biased significantly upward from the SPDA's true price-sensitivity duration.

The techniques outlined in this chapter can be adapted to the analysis of other interest-sensitive cash flows, including other insurance liabilities. The use of these techniques will allow insurance company risk managers to quantify the market values of assets and liabilities and adopt a sounder approach to the reduction of asset/liability risk.

APPENDIX I (SEE PAGES 124-131)

APPENDIX II

SPDA Case Study Assumptions

Policy Size: An assumed single new-issue block totaling $100,000 of premium.

Time Frame Modeled: Quarterly cash flows for 10 years. At the end of the 10-year period, all remaining in-force policies are assumed to surrender their full account value.

Interest Rate Guarantee: The initial guarantee is 7.90%, annual effective, for five years. After the expiration of the five-year period, the guarantee is reset annually according to the credited-rate strategy described below.

Credited-Rate Strategy: The initial five years have a fixed credited rate of 7.90%. On each policy anniversary after the fifth year, the insurer sets its credited rate by deducting a margin of 165 basis points from the five-year current-coupon bond rate.

Surrender Charges: The surrender charges are applied to the total policy account value that has accrued to the time of surrender. The amount paid to the policyholder at any time period is the account value less the surrender charge. All surrenders are subject to the surrender charge (that is, no free surrender).[17] The SPDA does not contain a provision in which the surrender charge is adjusted downward if it would cause the return of less than the original premium to the policyholder (commonly referred to as a "money-back guarantee"). The surrender charge scale is as follows:

Policy Year	Surrender Charge
1	6%
2	6
3	5
4	4
5	3
6	2
7	1
8+	0

Surrenders: There is an assumed number of baseline (non-interest-sensitive) surrenders that equals 4% of the account value annually. Interest-sensitive surrenders are in addition to the baseline surrenders. The function for determining interest-sensitive surrenders is explained in "Modeling the Surrenders."

Expenses: The following expenses are assumed:

Commissions: 5% as an up-front expense. There is also a "chargeback" that results in commission being recaptured if the policy lapses within the first policy year. The chargebacks for the first four quarters are 95%, 95%, 45%, and 45%, respectively.

Issuance Expense: $150 as an up-front expense.

Maintenance Expense: $25 per policy, per year, expensed quarterly. This amount inflates at an annual rate equal to 2% less than the yield on three-month investments.

Investment Expense: An annual expense equal to 25 basis points of the account value. The annualized expense is paid on a quarterly basis.

---

[17]If a free withdrawal corridor exists, it is often modeled as an adjustment to the gross surrender-charge scale. For example, the existence of a 10% corridor would result in a first-year 6% surrender charge being modeled as a 5.4% surrender charge.

APPENDIX I
SIMPLIFIED INSURANCE LIABILITY PRICING ASSUMPTIONS

Maturity	Coupon-Bond Yields	Spot Rates	Delta	Discount Factor	Liab. #1 Cash Flow	Present Value	Liab. #2 Cash Flow	Present Value
0.5	7.14%	7.14%	7.02%	0.9655	$4,000	$3,862	$ 0	$ 0
1.0	7.86	7.88	7.72	0.9257	4,000	3,703	0	0
1.5	8.27	8.30	8.13	0.8852	4,000	3,541	0	0
2.0	8.62	8.67	8.48	0.8439	4,000	3,376	0	0
2.5	8.80	8.85	8.66	0.8053	4,000	3,221	0	0
3.0	8.90	8.96	8.76	0.7688	4,000	3,075	0	0
3.5	9.00	9.06	8.86	0.7333	4,000	2,933	0	0
4.0	9.08	9.15	8.95	0.6991	4,000	2,796	0	0
4.5	9.16	9.24	9.03	0.6661	4,000	2,665	0	0
5.0	9.22	9.31	9.10	0.6344	4,000	2,538	0	0
5.5	9.29	9.39	9.18	0.6036	4,000	2,414	0	0
6.0	9.36	9.47	9.26	0.5739	4,000	2,296	0	0
6.5	9.42	9.55	9.33	0.5453	4,000	2,181	0	0
7.0	9.48	9.62	9.40	0.5180	4,000	2,072	0	0
7.5	9.53	9.68	9.45	0.4921	4,000	1,968	0	0
8.0	9.57	9.73	9.50	0.4675	4,000	1,870	0	0
8.5	9.61	9.78	9.55	0.4441	4,000	1,776	0	0
9.0	9.64	9.82	9.59	0.4219	4,000	1,688	0	0
9.5	9.67	9.86	9.62	0.4008	4,000	1,603	0	0
10.0	9.70	9.89	9.66	0.3807	4,000	1,523	100,000	38,072
				Market Value		$51,101		$38,072
				Profit		6,205		4,623
				Premium		$57,306		$42,694

SIMULATION RESULTS FOR VARIOUS INVESTMENT STRATEGIES: PRESENT VALUE OF ENDING SURPLUS

	Duration Match	Constant Duration	3-Month Bonds	6-Month Bonds	3-Year Bonds	5-Year Bonds	10-Year Bonds	20-Year Bonds
Maximum Redundancy	$1,247	$19,067	$46,018	$28,162	$11,894	$9,240	$22,745	$38,490
80th Percentile	348	5,998	14,925	9,200	3,159	1,876	5,307	7,578
60th Percentile	70	575	4,567	2,514	224	(89)	125	1,016
Average	1	386	(100)	(1,299)	(1,788)	(1,170)	351	1,394
40th Percentile	(136)	(2,005)	(5,555)	(4,481)	(2,248)	(1,990)	(2,268)	(2,879)
20th Percentile	(421)	(5,405)	(15,839)	(12,005)	(6,383)	(4,674)	(5,433)	(6,440)
Maximum Deficiency	(810)	(9,895)	(44,238)	(39,853)	(26,596)	(13,211)	(9,534)	(10,516)

APPENDIX I (CONT'D)
SIMPLIFIED LIABILITY CASH FLOWS

HIGH INTEREST RATE SCENARIO

Time (Quarter)	Yield Curve							Total Outflow	Market Value	Duration
	0.25	1	3	5	10	20				
0	7.14%	7.86%	8.90%	9.22%	9.70%	9.91%		$ 0	$89,173	6.57
1	7.65	8.09	8.85	9.15	9.63	9.86		0	91,810	6.33
2	9.49	9.78	10.27	10.44	10.69	10.71		4,000	84,168	6.28
3	10.28	10.58	10.83	10.94	11.10	11.05		0	84,284	6.00
4	10.37	10.63	10.57	10.64	10.76	10.72		4,000	84,316	6.08
5	10.04	10.11	10.00	10.10	10.26	10.29		0	89,163	5.87
6	10.06	10.01	10.09	10.29	10.51	10.55		4,000	86,201	5.87
7	11.90	11.76	11.74	11.83	11.80	11.60		0	82,128	5.53
8	10.91	10.74	10.70	10.79	10.81	10.72		4,000	85,140	5.62
9	12.61	12.56	12.48	12.46	12.22	11.89		0	80,804	5.28
10	13.22	13.55	13.91	14.02	13.80	13.37		4,000	72,924	5.19
11	13.03	13.15	13.35	13.42	13.22	12.83		0	77,613	4.97
12	14.13	14.05	13.96	13.87	13.47	12.98		4,000	74,950	4.98
13	15.69	15.54	15.22	14.94	14.29	13.63		0	74,169	4.69
14	13.53	13.76	14.17	14.22	13.96	13.50		4,000	74,370	4.69
15	13.88	14.00	14.31	14.31	14.00	13.52		0	76,709	4.44
16	16.15	15.94	15.60	15.23	14.52	13.82		4,000	72,958	4.42
17	15.74	15.52	15.04	14.60	13.89	13.20		0	77,496	4.19
18	16.50	16.41	15.94	15.45	14.63	13.85		4,000	73,591	4.13
19	18.02	17.65	16.64	15.90	14.81	13.89		0	75,092	3.88
20	19.34	19.23	18.43	17.68	16.49	15.42		4,000	69,068	3.79

21	22.15	21.85	20.59	19.58	18.05	16.75	0	67,404	3.50
22	20.93	20.45	19.02	18.03	16.61	15.42	4,000	69,852	3.48
23	24.29	23.68	21.71	20.38	18.53	17.04	0	67,474	3.20
24	25.39	24.74	22.60	21.18	19.21	17.62	0	64,896	3.12
25	27.44	26.56	23.96	22.31	20.09	18.34	0	65,703	2.85
26	25.54	25.00	23.05	21.69	19.75	18.13	4,000	66,249	2.78
27	27.27	26.42	23.99	22.42	20.26	18.51	0	68,048	2.52
28	32.12	30.76	27.19	25.07	22.30	20.17	4,000	62,898	2.40
29	32.93	31.86	28.53	26.41	23.60	21.41	0	64,600	2.14
30	35.51	34.73	31.61	29.46	26.52	24.23	4,000	60,790	2.01
31	38.64	37.22	33.17	30.66	27.38	24.88	0	63,150	1.75
32	39.51	37.92	33.53	30.88	27.47	24.89	4,000	63,316	1.61
33	42.66	41.04	36.31	33.44	29.76	27.01	0	65,393	1.35
34	45.31	43.60	38.56	35.51	31.64	28.77	4,000	64,946	1.18
35	42.90	41.29	36.63	33.79	30.13	27.37	0	72,357	0.93
36	47.37	44.99	39.02	35.66	31.49	28.41	4,000	72,693	0.73
37	51.24	48.99	42.73	39.14	34.70	31.47	0	77,997	0.48
38	56.02	52.97	45.43	41.34	36.43	32.89	4,000	81,242	0.25
39	54.33	50.72	42.57	38.36	33.32	29.67	0	91,784	0
40	51.34	48.45	41.20	37.28	32.49	28.97	104,000	0	0

STABLE INTEREST RATE SCENARIO

Time (Quarter)	Yield Curve						Total Outflow	Market Value	Duration
	0.25	1	3	5	10	20			
0	7.14%	7.86%	8.90%	9.22%	9.70%	9.91%	$ 0	$ 89,173	6.57
1	6.71	7.17	8.03	8.43	9.09	9.46	0	95,057	6.38
2	7.00	7.43	8.35	8.85	9.60	9.96	4,000	90,266	6.35
3	7.51	8.00	8.89	9.45	10.21	10.52	0	89,070	6.04
4	6.99	7.42	8.08	8.64	9.47	9.89	4,000	91,682	6.15
5	6.22	6.47	7.05	7.64	8.56	9.13	0	99,509	5.99
6	6.57	6.61	7.08	7.60	8.43	8.97	4,000	98,491	6.01
7	7.75	7.85	8.45	8.99	9.69	10.03	0	93,274	5.66
8	7.42	7.50	8.06	8.58	9.26	9.64	4,000	93,941	5.70
9	6.53	6.50	6.80	7.19	7.82	8.34	0	104,426	5.56
10	7.03	7.02	7.18	7.45	7.92	8.33	4,000	101,611	5.53
11	7.53	7.60	7.87	8.16	8.57	8.88	0	99,964	5.24
12	7.67	7.81	8.27	8.63	9.09	9.36	4,000	95,547	5.18
13	7.74	7.87	8.34	8.69	9.15	9.41	0	97,468	4.93
14	7.72	7.82	8.24	8.56	8.98	9.25	4,000	96,462	4.90
15	7.22	7.24	7.54	7.80	8.23	8.57	0	102,338	4.69
16	7.08	7.11	7.42	7.65	8.07	8.42	4,000	101,177	4.63
17	6.61	6.81	7.38	7.75	8.32	8.70	0	102,636	4.37
18	6.35	6.55	7.14	7.53	8.15	8.58	4,000	101,746	4.31
19	5.60	5.82	6.50	6.98	7.76	8.31	0	106,216	4.07
20	6.43	6.55	7.02	7.37	7.97	8.40	4,000	102,627	3.97

21	6.24	6.38	6.86	7.22	7.85	8.30	0	105,267	3.73
22	6.03	6.14	6.56	6.91	7.55	8.02	4,000	104,505	3.63
23	5.99	6.17	6.71	7.12	7.82	8.28	0	105,717	3.38
24	6.21	6.46	7.13	7.60	8.36	8.77	4,000	102,127	3.25
25	5.75	5.94	6.55	7.03	7.84	8.33	0	106,127	3.01
26	6.10	6.31	6.96	7.46	8.25	8.68	4,000	102,767	2.87
27	5.56	5.79	6.52	7.09	8.00	8.51	0	106,041	2.63
28	5.56	5.72	6.33	6.84	7.71	8.22	4,000	104,541	2.48
29	6.07	6.17	6.64	7.06	7.79	8.21	0	105,497	2.23
30	8.01	8.21	8.75	9.11	9.63	9.72	4,000	98,599	2.06
31	8.17	8.50	9.30	9.79	10.39	10.45	0	99,880	1.81
32	7.42	7.83	8.89	9.56	10.41	10.56	4,000	99,224	1.64
33	8.04	8.39	9.39	10.02	10.79	10.87	0	100,672	1.39
34	7.33	7.61	8.52	9.16	10.00	10.18	4,000	100,180	1.19
35	7.66	8.05	9.17	9.89	10.78	10.89	0	101,718	0.94
36	7.84	8.21	9.30	10.02	10.90	10.99	4,000	99,804	0.73
37	7.80	8.17	9.26	10.01	10.90	10.99	0	101,988	0.48
38	8.40	8.56	9.25	9.78	10.75	10.47	4,000	99,810	0.25
39	8.84	9.05	9.74	10.23	10.81	10.74	0	101,800	0
40	10.06	10.03	10.25	10.48	10.75	10.53	104,000	0	0

LOW INTEREST RATE SCENARIO

Time (Quarter)	Yield Curve						Total Outflow	Market Value	Duration
	0.25	1	3	5	10	20			
0	7.14%	7.86%	8.90%	9.22%	9.70%	9.91%	$ 0	$ 89,173	6.57
1	7.33	7.82	8.69	9.07	9.64	9.91	0	91,741	6.32
2	7.83	8.28	9.19	9.64	10.26	10.50	4,000	86,447	6.29
3	7.58	7.95	8.60	9.05	9.71	10.03	0	91,884	6.10
4	7.67	7.99	8.38	8.77	9.37	9.70	4,000	92,118	6.17
5	8.28	8.37	8.50	8.78	9.24	9.52	0	95,008	5.95
6	8.95	8.94	9.14	9.44	9.86	10.04	4,000	89,805	5.91
7	7.42	7.34	7.58	7.93	8.49	8.89	0	99,946	5.77
8	7.65	7.53	7.63	7.89	8.30	8.64	4,000	99,046	5.78
9	6.50	6.52	6.79	7.13	7.68	8.15	0	105,105	5.57
10	6.23	6.23	6.40	6.67	7.17	7.68	4,000	106,114	5.57
11	6.26	6.24	6.36	6.59	7.03	7.52	0	108,772	5.33
12	5.98	5.99	6.20	6.46	6.94	7.46	4,000	107,386	5.29
13	5.42	5.42	5.63	5.89	6.41	7.01	0	112,538	5.07
14	6.47	6.38	6.36	6.47	6.76	7.19	4,000	107,596	4.99
15	6.29	6.15	6.07	6.11	6.37	6.81	0	111,394	4.76
16	5.51	5.57	5.81	6.01	6.45	6.97	4,000	109,450	4.68
17	5.76	5.92	6.35	6.63	7.12	7.58	0	108,075	4.41
18	5.52	5.60	5.90	6.13	6.63	7.14	4,000	108,381	4.34
19	5.05	5.15	5.49	5.77	6.34	6.93	0	111,882	4.10
20	4.88	4.96	5.28	5.55	6.15	6.75	4,000	110,611	4.01

21	4.29	4.39	4.77	5.09	5.79	6.49	0	114,359	3.77
22	4.65	4.76	5.14	5.46	6.12	6.75	4,000	110,404	3.65
23	4.04	4.09	4.37	4.67	5.35	6.09	0	115,225	3.41
24	4.00	4.14	4.58	4.96	5.73	6.46	4,000	111,692	3.28
25	3.73	3.89	4.39	4.83	5.69	6.47	0	113,790	3.03
26	4.19	4.39	5.00	5.49	6.38	7.06	4,000	109,139	2.89
27	3.90	4.13	4.86	5.44	6.47	7.20	0	111,133	2.64
28	3.12	3.24	3.75	4.24	5.25	6.14	4,000	112,002	2.49
29	3.13	3.28	3.84	4.35	5.39	6.26	0	112,981	2.24
30	2.95	3.09	3.65	4.17	5.22	6.13	4,000	110,689	2.07
31	2.67	2.80	3.34	3.85	4.93	5.88	0	112,504	1.83
32	2.63	2.77	3.32	3.84	4.94	5.89	4,000	109,558	1.64
33	2.43	2.55	3.05	3.55	4.63	5.61	0	110,946	1.39
34	2.32	2.47	3.05	3.60	4.75	5.75	4,000	107,870	1.20
35	2.45	2.58	3.13	3.66	4.78	5.73	0	108,534	0.95
36	2.19	2.32	2.85	3.39	4.53	5.54	4,000	105,587	0.73
37	2.05	2.19	2.76	3.31	4.49	5.53	0	106,345	0.48
38	1.83	1.92	2.34	2.81	3.89	4.95	4,000	103,057	0.25
39	1.91	2.01	2.44	2.90	3.95	4.97	0	103,517	0
40	2.10	2.21	2.65	3.12	4.15	5.11	104,000	0	0

Profit: The profit goal is 2% of the gross single premium, and is treated as an up front expense.

Insurer's Investment Strategy: The option-pricing techniques used in this analysis do not require any "investment strategy" per se to be specified, since the ultimate output of the analysis defines the immunizing investment strategy. However, we must make an assumption about the initial investment *environment* in order to value the liability. This investment assumption can take two forms: (1) We assume a particular *initial yield curve* of available investments and analyze what profit (or loss) will be supported, or (2) we assume a particular *profit target* and solve for the yield spread above Treasuries needed to support the target. These two methods are usually referred to as "valuation mode" and "pricing mode," respectively. For the purposes of the study reported in this chapter we have assumed that the insurer can invest in current-coupon bonds having the yields shown in Appendix I. The valuation of the SPDA liability will show that these yields are sufficient to support the 2% profit target.

Interest Rate Volatility: Because we are using the initial yield curve to generate interest rate scenarios, we must also make an assumption about the future volatility of interest rates. The volatility used in this study is equivalent to an annual volatility of 20% on the movement of three-month interest rates and 12% on the movement of 20-year interest rates. We also assume that there would be an 85% correlation between three-month and 20-year interest rates. A volatility of 20% can be approximately interpreted to mean that if interest rates begin the year at 10%, there is a 68.3% probability that the end-of-year rate will be between 8.19% and 12.21%.

Modeling the Surrenders

In order to model the interest-sensitive surrenders (i.e., above the 4% baseline), it is first necessary to model the following:

(a) The interest rate *credited* to the policy account, including rates that apply after the initial rate guarantee period expires.

(b) The rate a *competitor* offers on new policies.

As an example, the SPDA policy may have an initial interest rate that is guaranteed for three years. After this rate expires, the policy may allow for the credited rate to be reset annually. To model the initial and renewal credited interest rates, it is necessary to choose an interest rate crediting *strategy*. The modeled strategy can be as simple as deducting "X" basis points from off the then current "Y"-year U.S. Treasury bond rate, or it can be more complicated. The competitor's strategy can be defined in a similar fashion. Often, in order to be conservative, the competitor's rate is modeled according to a "higher of" formula. That is, we assume that the competitor will credit the higher of two rates: a current "new money" rate, and a rolling average "portfolio" rate. The competitor's rate changes quarterly in our quarterly model, while the policy rate changes only when guarantee periods expire. Since the model uses interest rate paths for which complete current yield curves are specified at each point in time, it is always possible to construct both the competitor's and the insurer's credited rates.

The actual volume of interest-sensitive policy surrenders can be expected to exhibit some policyholder "inertia." For purposes of the study reported in this chapter, we have reflected such inertia in two ways. First, the competitor's rate must exceed the insurer's rate by at least a specified "threshold" amount before the average policyholder will consider surrendering. This threshold generally varies by the age of the policy. Second, since the policyholder may be more likely to surrender only after it has been economically feasible to do so for an extended period of time, the model causes interest-sensitive surrenders to increase as the situation of a competitor's rate exceeding the credited rate persists for several time periods.

SPDAs carry surrender charges to inhibit interest-sensitive surrenders before the insurer has a chance to recover acquisition expenses. The surrender charge can be considered to provide an added *hurdle* spread that a *competitor's* rate must cover in order to induce the policyholder to surrender. The size of this hurdle is a function of how the policyholder decides to "amortize" the surrender charge. The longer the time period over which the policyholder is willing to recover the surrender charge, the lower the hurdle will be. Also, as the surrender charge lessens, the hurdle will lessen.

All of the characteristics described above can be incorporated into a surrender function that depends on an interest-sensitive index.

Define:

D_t	=	Interest-sensitive index at time t.
I_t	=	Insurer's crediting rate at time t.
C_t	=	Competitor's crediting rate at time t.
SC_t	=	Surrender charge at time t.
H	=	Policyholder's "horizon" for recovering SC.
L_t	=	Policyholder inertia threshold at time t.

Then, the interest-sensitive index is defined as follows:

$$D_t = C_t - I_t - L_t - [1 - (1 - SC_t)^{-1/H}]$$

It can be seen that the interest-sensitive index is positive only if the competitor's rate exceeds the sum of the insurer's rate, the inertia threshold, and the amount needed to amortize the surrender charge over the policyholder's horizon.

Define:

S	=	Strength parameter.
M	=	Memory parameter between 0 and 1.
p	=	Power parameter.
wq_t	=	Annual effective surrender rate at time t.
bq_t	=	Base annual effective surrender rate at time t.
J_t	=	1 if D_t is positive, and 0 othersise.

Then:

$$wq_t \quad = \quad bq_t + J_t S \left(\sum_{k=0}^{t} M^{t-k} D_k \right)^p$$

The total surrender rate at any time is equal to the base surrender rate plus an interest-sensitive surrender rate. The interest-sensitive surrenders apply only if the current-period interest-sensitive index is positive. They also depend on all of the interest-sensitive indices that have occurred up to the current period, each weighted by the appropriate policyholder memory factor.

The various index values used in this report are:

S	=	Strength parameter	=	100%
M	=	Memory parameter	=	90%
p	=	Power parameter	=	64%

These index values produce the following representative surrender rates:

Spread of Competitor's Rate Over Insurer's Credited Rate Plus Threshold	Annualized Interest-Sensitive Lapses					
	Consecutive Quarters					
	1	2	3	4	. . .	8
100 basis points	5.2%	7.9%	9.9%	11.6%		16.0%
300	10.6	16.0	20.1	23.4		32.3
500	14.7	22.2	27.8	32.4		44.8

APPENDIX III (SEE PAGES 135-140)

APPENDIX III
SPDA CASH FLOWS

HIGH INTEREST RATE SCENARIO

Time (Quarter)	Yield Curve						Credited Rate	Competitors' Rate	Lapse Rate	$_t P_x$	Account Balance	Cash Surrender Benefit	Expense	Total Outflow	Market Value	Duration
	0.25	1	3	5	10	20										
0	7.14%	7.86%	8.90%	9.22%	9.70%	9.91%	7.90%	7.70%	0.0000	1.0000	$100,000	$ 0	$7,219	$7,219	$92,781	3.52
1	7.65	8.09	8.85	9.15	9.63	9.86	7.90	7.60	0.0102	0.9898	100,884	973	11	984	94,071	3.53
2	9.49	9.78	10.27	10.44	10.69	10.71	7.90	8.90	0.0102	0.9798	101,776	981	13	994	90,807	2.93
3	10.28	10.58	10.83	10.94	11.10	11.05	7.90	9.40	0.0102	0.9698	102,676	990	44	1,034	90,538	2.60
4	10.37	10.63	10.57	10.64	10.76	10.72	7.90	9.10	0.0102	0.9600	103,584	999	44	1,043	92,512	2.62
5	10.04	10.11	10.00	10.10	10.26	10.29	7.90	8.60	0.0102	0.9503	104,500	1,008	72	1,079	95,212	2.65
6	10.06	10.01	10.09	10.29	10.51	10.55	7.90	8.80	0.0102	0.9406	105,424	1,017	72	1,089	95,977	2.47
7	11.90	11.76	11.74	11.83	11.80	11.60	7.90	10.50	0.0102	0.9311	106,356	1,026	73	1,099	93,351	1.71
8	10.91	10.74	10.70	10.79	10.81	10.72	7.90	9.60	0.0102	0.9216	107,296	1,035	74	1,108	96,696	1.98
9	12.61	12.56	12.48	12.46	12.22	11.89	7.90	11.20	0.0102	0.9122	108,245	1,055	74	1,129	94,932	1.27
10	13.22	13.55	13.91	14.02	13.80	13.37	7.90	12.50	0.0242	0.8902	107,653	2,536	74	2,610	93,827	1.03
11	13.03	13.15	13.35	13.42	13.22	12.83	7.90	11.90	0.0404	0.8542	105,285	4,212	72	4,284	93,232	1.05
12	14.13	14.05	13.96	13.87	13.47	12.98	7.90	12.70	0.0489	0.8124	102,058	4,985	70	5,055	90,337	0.94
13	15.69	15.54	15.22	14.94	14.29	13.63	7.90	14.30	0.0618	0.7622	97,586	6,174	67	6,241	85,859	0.80
14	13.53	13.76	14.17	14.22	13.96	13.50	7.90	12.70	0.0799	0.7013	91,509	7,631	63	7,694	82,597	0.73
15	13.88	14.00	14.31	14.31	14.00	13.52	7.90	12.80	0.0881	0.6395	85,046	7,891	59	7,949	77,187	0.63
16	16.15	15.94	15.60	15.23	14.52	13.82	7.90	14.80	0.0958	0.5782	78,376	7,969	54	8,023	70,665	0.50
17	15.74	15.52	15.04	14.60	13.89	13.20	7.90	14.40	0.1125	0.5132	70,896	8,715	49	8,764	64,766	0.37
18	16.50	16.41	-15.94	15.45	14.63	13.85	7.90	15.00	0.1255	0.4488	63,185	8,799	44	8,843	58,110	0.24
19	18.02	17.65	16.64	15.90	14.81	13.89	7.90	16.70	0.1397	0.3861	55,402	8,726	38	8,765	51,560	0.08
20	19.34	19.23	18.43	17.68	16.49	15.42	17.70	17.80	0.1595	0.3245	47,459	8,736	33	8,769	44,758	0.47

HIGH INTEREST RATE SCENARIO

Time (Quarter)	Yield Curve						Credited Rate	Competitors' Rate	Lapse Rate	$_tP_x$	Account Balance	Cash Surrender Benefit	Expense	Total Outflow	Market Value	Duration
	0.25	1	3	5	10	20										
21	22.15	21.85	20.59	19.58	18.05	16.75	17.70	20.80	0.0102	0.3212	48,930	492	34	526	45,892	0.39
22	20.93	20.45	19.02	18.03	16.61	15.42	17.70	19.70	0.1440	0.2750	43,627	7,191	30	7,221	41,364	0.18
23	24.29	23.68	21.71	20.38	18.53	17.04	17.70	23.10	0.1366	0.2374	39,234	6,083	27	6,111	37,072	0.16
24	25.39	24.74	22.60	21.18	19.21	17.62	24.10	24.20	0.1440	0.2032	34,980	5,768	24	5,792	33,392	0.79
25	27.44	26.56	23.96	22.31	20.09	18.34	24.10	26.40	0.0102	0.2011	36,545	371	26	397	34,733	0.34
26	25.54	25.00	23.05	21.69	19.75	18.13	24.10	24.30	0.1296	0.1751	33,574	4,948	23	4,971	32,037	0.41
27	27.27	26.42	23.99	22.42	20.26	18.51	24.10	26.30	0.0102	0.1733	35,076	356	25	381	33,618	0.15
28	32.12	30.76	27.19	25.07	22.30	20.17	31.30	31.50	0.1174	0.1530	32,676	4,303	23	4,326	31,621	0.84
29	32.93	31.86	28.53	26.41	23.60	21.41	31.30	32.00	0.0102	0.1514	34,623	355	24	379	33,259	0.43
30	35.51	34.73	31.61	29.46	26.52	24.23	31.30	34.30	0.1025	0.1359	33,264	3,798	23	3,821	31,641	0.36
31	38.64	37.22	33.17	30.66	27.38	24.88	31.30	38.00	0.1062	0.1215	31,824	3,783	22	3,805	30,368	0.20
32	39.51	37.92	33.53	30.88	27.47	24.89	38.80	39.00	0.1251	0.1063	29,805	4,261	21	4,282	28,929	0.81
33	42.66	41.04	36.31	33.44	29.76	27.01	38.80	42.10	0.0102	0.1052	32,022	328	23	351	30,595	0.39
34	45.31	43.60	38.56	35.51	31.64	28.77	38.80	44.80	0.1197	0.0926	30,596	4,162	22	4,183	29,095	0.30
35	42.90	41.29	36.63	33.79	30.13	27.37	38.80	42.30	0.1342	0.0802	28,753	4,456	20	4,476	27,845	0.12
36	47.37	44.99	39.02	35.66	31.49	28.41	47.20	47.40	0.1368	0.0692	26,941	4,269	19	4,288	26,542	0.73
37	51.24	48.99	42.73	39.14	34.70	31.47	47.20	51.10	0.0102	0.0685	29,373	301	21	322	28,250	0.37
38	56.02	52.97	45.43	41.34	36.43	32.89	47.20	56.50	0.1317	0.0595	28,093	4,261	20	4,281	26,622	0.25
39	54.33	50.72	42.57	38.36	33.32	29.67	47.20	55.30	0.1586	0.0500	26,036	4,908	19	4,926	25,310	0.00
40	51.34	48.45	41.20	37.28	32.49	28.97	0.00	0.00	1.0000	0.0000	0	28,678	0	28,678	0	0.00

STABLE INTEREST RATE SCENARIO

Time (Quarter)	Yield Curve 0.25	1	3	5	10	20	Credited Rate	Competitors' Rate	Lapse Rate	$_tP_x$	Account Balance	Cash Surrender Benefit	Expense	Total Outflow	Market Value	Duration
0	7.14%	7.86%	8.90%	9.22%	9.70%	9.91%	7.90%	7.70%	0.0000	1.0000	$100,000	$ 0	$7,219	$7,219	$ 92,781	3.52
1	6.71	7.17	8.03	8.43	9.09	9.46	7.90	6.90	0.0102	0.9898	100,884	973	11	984	96,825	3.73
2	7.00	7.43	8.35	8.85	9.60	9.96	7.90	7.40	0.0102	0.9798	101,776	981	13	994	96,482	3.42
3	7.51	8.00	8.89	9.45	10.21	10.52	7.90	7.90	0.0102	0.9698	102,676	990	44	1,034	95,785	3.07
4	6.99	7.42	8.08	8.64	9.47	9.89	7.90	7.10	0.0102	0.9600	103,584	999	44	1,043	99,801	3.13
5	6.22	6.47	7.05	7.64	8.56	9.13	7.90	6.10	0.0102	0.9503	104,500	1,008	72	1,079	104,565	3.15
6	6.57	6.61	7.08	7.60	8.43	8.97	7.90	6.10	0.0102	0.9406	105,424	1,017	72	1,089	105,412	2.96
7	7.75	7.85	8.45	8.99	9.69	10.03	7.90	7.50	0.0102	0.9311	106,356	1,026	73	1,098	101,962	2.56
8	7.42	7.50	8.06	8.58	9.26	9.64	7.90	7.10	0.0102	0.9216	107,296	1,035	73	1,108	104,033	2.42
9	6.53	6.50	6.80	7.19	7.82	8.34	7.90	5.70	0.0102	0.9122	108,245	1,055	74	1,129	108,646	2.45
10	7.03	7.02	7.18	7.45	7.92	8.33	7.90	6.00	0.0102	0.9030	109,202	1,064	75	1,139	108,196	2.23
11	7.53	7.60	7.87	8.16	8.57	8.88	7.90	6.70	0.0102	0.8938	110,168	1,074	75	1,149	107,350	1.88
12	7.67	7.81	8.27	8.63	9.09	9.36	7.90	7.10	0.0102	0.8847	111,142	1,083	76	1,159	107,641	1.57
13	7.74	7.87	8.34	8.69	9.15	9.41	7.90	7.20	0.0102	0.8758	112,125	1,104	76	1,181	108,493	1.32
14	7.72	7.82	8.24	8.56	8.98	9.25	7.90	7.10	0.0102	0.8669	113,116	1,114	77	1,191	109,429	1.13
15	7.22	7.24	7.54	7.80	8.23	8.57	7.90	6.30	0.0102	0.8581	114,116	1,124	78	1,201	111,095	0.98
16	7.08	7.11	7.42	7.65	8.07	8.42	7.90	6.20	0.0102	0.8493	115,125	1,134	78	1,212	111,896	0.78
17	6.61	6.81	7.38	7.75	8.32	8.70	7.90	6.20	0.0102	0.8407	116,143	1,156	79	1,235	113,312	0.51
18	6.35	6.55	7.14	7.53	8.15	8.58	7.90	6.00	0.0102	0.8322	117,170	1,166	80	1,246	114,322	0.28
19	5.60	5.82	6.50	6.98	7.76	8.31	7.90	5.50	0.0102	0.8237	118,206	1,176	80	1,256	115,951	0.15
20	6.43	6.55	7.02	7.37	7.97	8.40	5.70	5.90	0.0102	0.8154	119,251	1,187	81	1,268	115,442	0.77

STABLE INTEREST RATE SCENARIO

Time (Quarter)	Yield Curve						Credited Rate	Competitors' Rate	Lapse Rate	P_x	Account Balance	Cash Surrender Benefit	Expense	Total Outflow	Market Value	Duration
	0.25	1	3	5	10	20										
21	6.24	6.38	6.86	7.22	7.85	8.30	5.70	5.70	0.0102	0.8071	119.688	1.203	81	1.284	116.323	0.56
22	6.03	6.14	6.56	6.91	7.55	8.02	5.70	5.40	0.0102	0.7989	120.126	1.208	82	1.289	117.054	0.40
23	5.99	6.17	6.71	7.12	7.82	8.28	5.70	5.60	0.0102	0.7908	120.566	1.212	82	1.294	117.839	0.13
24	6.21	6.46	7.13	7.60	8.36	8.77	6.00	6.10	0.0102	0.7828	121.007	1.216	82	1.299	118.786	0.75
25	5.75	5.94	6.55	7.03	7.84	8.33	6.00	5.50	0.0102	0.7748	121.536	1.234	82	1.317	120.087	0.60
26	6.10	6.31	6.96	7.46	8.25	8.68	6.00	6.00	0.0102	0.7669	122.067	1.240	83	1.322	120.429	0.31
27	5.56	5.79	6.52	7.09	8.00	8.51	6.00	5.60	0.0102	0.7592	122.601	1.245	83	1.328	121.616	0.11
28	5.56	5.72	6.33	6.84	7.71	8.22	5.20	5.30	0.0102	0.7514	123.136	1.250	83	1.334	121.710	0.79
29	6.07	6.17	6.64	7.06	7.79	8.21	5.20	5.60	0.0102	0.7438	123.441	1.266	84	1.350	121.459	0.54
30	8.01	8.21	8.75	9.11	9.63	9.72	5.20	7.60	0.0102	0.7363	123.746	1.269	84	1.353	120.680	0.26
31	8.17	8.50	9.30	9.79	10.39	10.45	5.20	8.30	0.0312	0.7133	121.412	3.912	82	3.994	119.590	0.08
32	7.42	7.83	8.89	9.56	10.41	10.56	7.90	8.10	0.0466	0.6801	117.234	5.727	79	5.806	117.137	0.73
33	8.04	8.39	9.39	10.02	10.79	10.87	7.90	8.50	0.0102	0.6732	118.270	1.213	80	1.293	117.803	0.49
34	7.33	7.61	8.52	9.16	10.00	10.18	7.90	7.70	0.0424	0.6446	115.435	5.105	78	5.183	115.610	0.28
35	7.66	8.05	9.17	9.89	10.78	10.89	7.90	8.40	0.0102	0.6381	116.455	1.195	79	1.273	116.742	0.03
36	7.84	8.21	9.30	10.02	10.90	10.99	8.40	8.50	0.0102	0.6316	117.485	1.205	79	1.285	117.744	0.72
37	7.80	8.17	9.26	10.01	10.90	10.99	8.40	8.50	0.0102	0.6252	118.661	1.217	80	1.297	119.021	0.49
38	8.40	8.56	9.25	9.78	10.45	10.47	8.40	8.30	0.0102	0.6189	119.849	1.229	81	1.310	119.756	0.25
39	8.84	9.05	9.74	10.23	10.81	10.74	8.40	8.70	0.0102	0.6126	121.048	1.242	82	1.323	120.901	0.00
40	10.06	10.03	10.25	10.48	10.75	10.53	0.00	0.00	1.0000	0.0000	0	123.514	0	123.514	0	0.00

LOW INTEREST RATE SCENARIO

Time (Quarter)	Yield Curve						Credited Rate	Competitors' Rate	Lapse Rate	$_1P_x$	Account Balance	Cash Surrender Benefit	Expense	Total Outflow	Market Value	Duration
	0.25	1	3	5	10	20										
0	7.14%	7.86%	8.90%	9.22%	9.70%	9.91%	7.90%	7.70%	0.0000	1.0000	$100,000	$ 0	$7,219	$ 7,219	$ 92,781	3.52
1	7.33	7.82	8.69	9.07	9.64	9.91	7.90	7.60	0.0102	0.9898	100,884	973	11	984	94,416	3.52
2	7.83	8.28	9.19	9.64	10.26	10.50	7.90	8.10	0.0102	0.9798	101,776	981	13	994	93,691	3.16
3	7.58	7.95	8.60	9.05	9.71	10.03	7.90	7.50	0.0102	0.9698	102,676	990	44	1,034	96,922	3.23
4	7.67	7.99	8.38	8.77	9.37	9.70	7.90	7.30	0.0102	0.9600	103,584	999	44	1,043	98,967	3.15
5	8.28	8.37	8.50	8.78	9.24	9.52	7.90	7.30	0.0102	0.9503	104,500	1,008	72	1,079	99,709	3.00
6	8.95	8.94	9.14	9.44	9.86	10.04	7.90	7.90	0.0102	0.9406	105,424	1,017	72	1,089	98,678	2.67
7	7.42	7.34	7.58	7.93	8.49	8.89	7.90	6.40	0.0102	0.9311	106,356	1,026	73	1,098	104,591	2.76
8	7.65	7.53	7.63	7.89	8.30	8.64	7.90	6.40	0.0102	0.9216	107,296	1,035	73	1,108	105,057	2.62
9	6.50	6.52	6.79	7.13	7.68	8.15	7.90	5.60	0.0102	0.9122	108,245	1,055	74	1,129	108,500	2.49
10	6.23	6.23	6.40	6.67	7.17	7.68	7.90	5.20	0.0102	0.9030	109,202	1,064	75	1,139	110,400	2.44
11	6.26	6.24	6.36	6.59	7.03	7.52	7.90	5.10	0.0102	0.8938	110,168	1,074	75	1,149	111,126	2.30
12	5.98	5.99	6.20	6.46	6.94	7.46	7.90	5.00	0.0102	0.8847	111,142	1,083	76	1,159	112,154	2.12
13	5.42	5.42	5.63	5.89	6.41	7.01	7.90	4.40	0.0102	0.8758	112,125	1,104	76	1,181	114,006	2.22
14	6.47	6.38	6.36	6.47	6.76	7.19	7.90	5.00	0.0102	0.8669	113,116	1,114	77	1,191	112,049	1.80
15	6.29	6.15	6.07	6.11	6.37	6.81	7.90	4.90	0.0102	0.8581	114,116	1,124	78	1,201	112,809	1.87
16	5.51	5.57	5.81	6.01	6.45	6.97	7.90	4.50	0.0102	0.8493	115,125	1,134	78	1,212	113,987	1.53
17	5.76	5.92	6.35	6.63	7.12	7.58	7.90	5.10	0.0102	0.8407	116,143	1,156	79	1,235	113,750	0.78
18	5.52	5.60	5.90	6.13	6.63	7.14	7.90	4.60	0.0102	0.8322	117,170	1,166	80	1,245	114,311	0.92
19	5.05	5.15	5.49	5.77	6.34	6.93	7.90	4.30	0.0102	0.8237	118,206	1,176	80	1,256	115,317	1.13
20	4.88	4.96	5.28	5.55	6.15	6.75	4.00	4.10	0.0102	0.8154	119,251	1,187	81	1,267	115,832	1.72

LOW INTEREST RATE SCENARIO

Time (Quarter)	Yield Curve						Credited Rate	Competitors' Rate	Lapse Rate	$_tP_x$	Account Balance	Cash Surrender Benefit	Expense	Total Outflow	Market Value	Duration
	0.25	1	3	5	10	20										
21	4.29	4.39	4.77	5.09	5.79	6.49	4.00	3.60	0.0102	0.8071	119,204	1,198	81	1,279	117,330	2.01
22	4.65	4.76	5.14	5.46	6.12	6.75	4.00	4.00	0.0102	0.7989	119,156	1,198	81	1,279	116,500	1.44
23	4.04	4.09	4.37	4.67	5.35	6.09	4.00	3.20	0.0102	0.7908	119,108	1,197	81	1,278	118,575	2.40
24	4.00	4.14	4.58	4.96	5.73	6.46	4.00	3.50	0.0102	0.7828	119,061	1,197	81	1,278	118,254	1.95
25	3.73	3.89	4.39	4.83	5.69	6.47	4.00	3.30	0.0102	0.7748	119,013	1,209	81	1,289	118,907	1.89
26	4.19	4.39	5.00	5.49	6.38	7.06	4.00	4.00	0.0102	0.7669	18,965	1,208	81	1,289	117,906	1.12
27	3.90	4.13	4.86	5.44	6.47	7.20	4.00	3.90	0.0102	0.7592	18,918	1,208	81	1,288	118,374	0.96
28	3.12	3.24	3.75	4.24	5.25	6.14	4.00	2.70	0.0102	0.7514	18,870	1,207	81	1,288	120,674	2.07
29	3.13	3.28	3.84	4.35	5.39	6.26	4.00	2.90	0.0102	0.7438	18,822	1,219	80	1,299	120,444	1.83
30	2.95	3.09	3.65	4.17	5.22	6.13	4.00	2.70	0.0102	0.7363	18,775	1,218	80	1,299	120,859	1.81
31	2.67	2.80	3.34	3.85	4.93	5.88	4.00	2.40	0.0102	0.7288	18,727	1,218	80	1,298	121,488	1.76
32	2.63	2.77	3.32	3.84	4.94	5.89	4.00	2.30	0.0102	0.7214	18,680	1,217	80	1,298	121,322	1.57
33	2.43	2.55	3.05	3.55	4.63	5.61	4.00	2.00	0.0102	0.7141	18,632	1,217	80	1,297	121,565	1.43
34	2.32	2.47	3.05	3.60	4.75	5.75	4.00	2.10	0.0102	0.7068	18,585	1,216	80	1,297	121,291	1.21
35	2.45	2.58	3.13	3.66	4.78	5.73	4.00	2.20	0.0102	0.6996	18,537	1,216	80	1,296	120,742	0.97
36	2.19	2.32	2.85	3.39	4.53	5.54	4.00	1.90	0.0102	0.6925	18,490	1,215	80	1,296	120,632	0.73
37	2.05	2.19	2.76	3.31	4.49	5.53	4.00	1.80	0.0102	0.6855	18,443	1,215	80	1,295	120,204	0.49
38	1.83	1.92	2.34	2.81	3.89	4.95	4.00	1.30	0.0102	0.6785	18,395	1,214	80	1,295	119,717	0.25
39	1.91	2.01	2.44	2.90	3.95	4.97	4.00	1.40	0.0102	0.6717	18,348	1,214	80	1,294	118,959	0.00
40	2.10	2.21	2.65	3.12	4.15	5.11	0.00	0.00	1.0000	0.0000	0	119,514	0	119,514	0	0.00

APPENDIX IV

This appendix discusses the relationship between the price-sensitivity and Macaulay measures of duration. Although the supporting mathematics are too onerous for presentation in this chapter, we believe that a qualitative description adds insight to the important differences between the two measures.

The relationship can be expressed symbolically as:

$$D_{PS} = D_M - \Delta D_{CFS},$$

where D_{PS} is *price sensitivity* duration, D_M is *Macaulay* duration, and ΔD_{CFS} is the *cash-flow-sensitivity* correction term.

For the purpose of this chapter, and in most of the asset/liability analysis done by the authors, it has been found that a "parallel shock" to the *initial* term structure is sufficient to calculate a duration measure D_{PS} that produces acceptable results even though nonparallel shocks generally occur in the real world. The degree of immunization that was demonstrated earlier in this chapter for the SPDA is evidence of this conclusion.[18]

For an interest-sensitive cash flow stream, D_M is a generalization of the classical Macaulay definition. The generalized formula involves summations of expressions over all interest rate paths in the arbitrage-free sample. Unless the cash flows depend only on their time of occurrence, t, and not on the particular path of interest rates followed, these summations over paths do not reduce to the simple factors of t found in the classical formula for Macaulay duration. Nevertheless, D_M can still be interpreted as an average time of payment of cash flow stream.

The cash-flow-sensitivity correction term expresses the contribution to the price-sensitivity duration measure that arises *explicitly* from the interest-rate sensitivity of the various cash flows.[19] This correction term will likely be positive if cash flows increase as interest rates increase. Insurance products usually behave so that if interest rates increase, earlier cash flows increase, while later cash flows may decrease. The calculation of ΔD_{CFS} involves present values, and thus applies relatively greater weight to *changes in* the earlier part of the cash flow stream than to *changes in* the later part. This implies that most insurance liabilities have positive cash-flow-sensitivity correction terms, and thus price-sensitivity durations that are less than Macaulay durations.

---

[18]It is (theoretically) possible to calculate a stochastic derivative of the price function that would give an even more accurate measure of price sensitivity.

[19]The Macaulay duration term itself will be influenced somewhat by any dependence of the cash flows on interest rates. The interest-rate sensitivity of the cash flows leads to the inability to recover the simple factors of t found in the classical formula.

Chapter 8

Funding SPDA Liabilities: An Application of Realized Return Optimization

LLEWELLYN MILLER
FIRST VICE PRESIDENT
DREXEL BURNHAM LAMBERT

PRAKASH A. SHIMPI, A.S.A.
ASSOCIATE VICE PRESIDENT
DREXEL BURNHAM LAMBERT

UDAY RAJAN
VICE PRESIDENT
DREXEL BURNHAM LAMBERT

The single premium deferred annuity (SPDA) is a life insurance product designed to provide the purchaser or policyholder with retirement income. The premium paid by the policyholder earns interest which is accumulated on a tax-deferred basis. The premium and interest are retained by the insurance company until the policy matures or is terminated before maturity at which time it is distributed as either an annuity or a cash lump sum.

Competition in the SPDA market has led to aggressive crediting rate strategies with high interest rates offered to policyholders. This has shifted the attractiveness of the product from retirement vehicle to investment vehicle. SPDA issuers are in competition not only with each other but also with alternative investments that have comparable tax advantages. The policyholders have become more aware of the investment implications of the product and are no longer content to hold on to their policies through all investment environments. As a result, SPDA issuers are concerned with situations where policyholders are likely to withdraw funds. To attract new policyholders and encourage them to maintain their policies, the competitive crediting rates are accompanied by various interest rate guarantees.

A high crediting rate strategy is good for gaining market share. It poses serious problems, however, for the investment manager charged with investing the premiums such that the SPDA cash outflows are met as they fall due. The ability to credit at high rates depends on the returns earned by the issuer on the invested premiums. Although this point is well understood by the actuaries who supply major inputs in the setting of crediting rates and by the investment managers who invest the funds, there is an inconsistency in the way the investment targets are specified.

Conventional actuarial measures of profit are based on book values. The assets, for example, are evaluated according to book yields. The crediting rate strategy incorporated in the design of an SPDA is also based on book values. The rate credited is usually specified as a spread below the book yield on assets, e.g., 150 basis points. It is normal practice for the investment manager to be given the current crediting rate and instructed to earn that plus some required spread. The inconsistency arises because the investment manager is used to evaluating assets in terms of realized returns, not book yields.

Book yields and realized returns do not generally track each other. Book profits tend to be high when interest rates rise and low when they fall. Realized returns on assets, in contrast, fall due to depressed market values when rates rise and rise due to increased market values when rates fall.

Investment managers who recognize this discrepancy in targets are forced to search for high returns in the investment market so as to sustain the aggressive crediting strategy. This exposes the issuer to the risk of underfunding the SPDA liability because the assets are not managed in accordance with the liability requirements.

Investment managers would benefit from the ability to evaluate the liabilities in a framework compatible with their asset evaluations, i.e., in terms of total returns. They need investment targets which specify the funding requirements of the SPDA liabilities. This chapter presents an analysis of the SPDA liabilities and introduces an application of realized return optimization, an investment strategy which identifies not only the return targets but also a useful measure of risk.

THE SPDA LIABILITIES

Elements of the SPDA contract

An SPDA is an annuity contract issued by an insurance company. The SPDA policyholder makes a single payment at the date of issue to purchase a stream of annuity payments commencing at the maturity date. The contract also provides the policyholder with an option to receive a lump sum at maturity in lieu of the annuity. Some of the more important features are summarized in the following paragraphs.

Each policy account is credited with interest at a rate guaranteed at purchase or reset periodically as stipulated in the contract. At any point in time, a policyholder's account value comprises the single premium paid plus the accumulated interest credited to that date. The contract may be surrendered at any time prior to maturity in exchange for a cash sum equal to the account value less any applicable surrender charges. Partial withdrawals of cash are also allowed, subject to appropriate withdrawal penalties. Upon death of a policyholder, the full value of the account is paid without penalty or probate delay.

In addition to the surrender and withdrawal options, SPDA issuers offer the policyholders a number of guarantees.

1. The policyholder will always receive the full value of the account, less applicable charges, despite adverse investment performance of the insurance company.
2. An initial crediting rate is normally guaranteed for up to five years.
3. A minimum guaranteed rate provides a floor for the crediting rate throughout the life of the policy, irrespective of the investment performance of the insurance company.
4. A "bailout option" allows a policyholder to withdraw funds without penalty whenever the crediting rate is reset below some critical level, e.g., 150 basis points below the previous crediting rate.

The features of a typical SPDA policy including expenses, mortality and simplified lapse rate assumptions are summarized in Exhibit 1. The numerical illustrations used in this chapter are based on this policy.

The product features contribute to uncertainty both in the cash flows required to meet the SPDA liabilities and in the valuation of outstanding obligations. These uncertainties are discussed next.

Sources of Liability Cash Flow Uncertainty

SPDAs are interest sensitive insurance products since the cash flows needed to pay off the policyholders depend on movements in interest rates. There are two main sources of interest sensitivity.

EXHIBIT 1
SPDA PRODUCT DESCRIPTION

Issue date	1 August 1987
Issue age	40 years
Deferred period	25 years
Premium per policy	$100,000
Number of policies	1000
Initial rate guarantee period	3 years
Interest guarantee	3 years: current rate, 7% lifetime: 4%
Death benefit	annuity value
Surrender charge	Year 1: 7% 2: 6% 3: 5% 4: 4% 5: 3% 6: 2% thereafter: 0%
Premium tax	0.05% at issue
Issue expenses	$100 per policy
Maintenance expenses	$20 per year, after first year increasing by 4% per year.
Commissions	2.5%
Commission trailers	0.25% from year 3
Mortality rate	male, non-smoker 60% 1965-70 Basic
Lapse rate	Year 1: 6% 2: 7% 3: 8% 4: 6% thereafter: 5% Add 3% per 100 bp rise and deduct 1% per 100 bp fall in interest rates
Interest rate spread	1.5%
Reserves	equal to account value

The first is the range of options offered to each policyholder. These influence policyholder behavior in varying degrees as interest rates change. For instance, the withdrawal option permits the policyholder to withdraw any amount up to the total account value, less applicable penalties, at any time. When interest rates rise, this option becomes valuable to a policyholder who has investment alternatives offering higher returns. The issuer's problems are compounded by the fact that rising rates lead to depressed asset values, which may have to be realized to meet withdrawals.

The second source of interest rate sensitivity is the issuer's option to determine the rate credited to the policyholder accounts. By crediting at a rate which is competitive, the issuer can encourage policyholders to maintain their policies. The value of this option to the issuer is reduced by the interest rate guarantees offered; in falling interest rate environments, the issuer may end up crediting policyholders at a rate in excess of that earned on the investments.

The reaction of the policyholders and the insurance company to changes in interest rates determines how these options are exercised and, therefore, the liability cash flows.

The Value of Outstanding Obligations

Apart from the uncertainty due to the interest sensitivity of the cash flows, there is another type of uncertainty associated with the value of outstanding obligations. It arises because there is no universally accepted method for determining this value.

The account value represents the total amount attributable to the policy holders and can therefore be used as the value of outstanding obligations. In the early years of a policy, this overstates the liability because surrender and withdrawal penalties are ignored. One solution is to use the cash surrender value, since this is the amount which can be withdrawn immediately by a policyholder. The implication of this on the investment strategy is that the market value of the assets must always equal or exceed the cash surrender value. In rising interest rate environments, this may prove too onerous a requirement due to falling asset values.

An alternative method is to use the actuarial reserves calculated under the National Association of Insurance Commissioners (NAIC) guidelines. Essentially, the NAIC recommends projecting the cash surrender value at various intervals up to the maturity date, discounting each of these to the current valuation date and selecting the largest discounted cash surrender value to be the actuarial reserve. In most cases, this turns out to be close to the current cash surrender value and therefore has the same effect on the investment strategy.

The cash surrender value methods are acceptable when the adequacy of funding is framed in terms of book values and the assets need not be marked to market. The cash surrender value is simply the book value of future obligations. It can be considered the market value of future obligations only if all policyholders are expected to surrender their policies immediately.

For investment purposes, market values of assets are more relevant than book values. In order to test the adequacy of the funding, the asset-liability comparison should be made in terms of market values. The market value of the liabilities is calculated as the present value of the projected liability cash flows. Depending on the interest rate assumptions and the SPDA policy features, this may be greater or less than the current cash surrender value.

Each insurance company will have its own view about how its liabilities should be valued. There are other valuation techniques besides the three mentioned here. The liability funding strategy used must be capable of targeting the value of future obligations, however it may be computed, as the long term market value requirement.

The Investment Problem

The insurance company should invest the premiums so that the cash flows required by the SPDAs are met as they fall due. Funding SPDAs is complicated by the uncertainty associated with the liability cash flows. Liability uncertainty impacts an investment strategy in two ways.

1. *Short-term liquidity requirements:* The investments should generate sufficient cash to meet the immediate liability cash payments. When liability cash flows are uncertain, the liquidity requirement proves to be a moving target. In situations where additional cash is available from new business premiums, this constraint on the investments is less severe.
2. *Long-term market value requirements:* The investments should have sufficient market value to ensure that all outstanding SPDA obligations can be met. Since the outstanding obligations are the future liability cash payments, the market value requirement is also a moving target.

Any investment strategy selected to fund SPDA liabilities should accommodate both short and long term requirements under uncertainty. Realized return optimization, discussed below, is a strategy which does this.

Applicability of Option Pricing Methods to Valuing the Liabilities

Since the SPDA contracts incorporate options, it may seem appropriate to use option pricing methods to find the value of outstanding obligations. The assumptions under which the option pricing methods operate and the realities of the SPDA contracts often are incompatible, however.

The basic assumption of option pricing is that an option is exercised only when it is economically preferable to do so. SPDA options are often exercised when it seems financially sub-optimal. Therefore, it can be hard to predict when these options will be exercised. This situation is similar to that of mortgage-backed securities. Option pricing methods can be used with mortgage-backed securities, however, because extensive prepayment data are available to aid in the projection of future prepayment patterns, even those which appear uneconomic. Also, an active secondary market in these securities exists to aid in testing the accuracy of the pricing assumptions. There are insufficient data on SPDA withdrawal and surrender experience and no secondary market exists for these policies.

Another reason against using option pricing methods to value the liabilities is the interaction between the options of the policyholders and the issuer. The rate at which policyholders withdraw funds is influenced by the crediting rate, while the crediting rate set by the issuer is influenced by the withdrawal experience of the policyholders. Separation of the option components for valuation purposes is not straightforward.

Using a Scenario-based Approach to Value the Liabilities

SPDA liabilities are path dependent, that is, the cash flow at any time in the future depends not only on the interest rate environment at that time but also on the interest rates at all preceding points. As stated previously, both the policyholders and the insurance company exercise their options in response to changes in interest rates. As cash is withdrawn at each point in time, the amount available for withdrawal in the future reduces. Concurrently, however, the interest credited to the policyholder accounts increases the amount available for future withdrawals. These features make the liability cash flows path dependent. A scenario-based valuation approach which captures this path dependency is therefore the recommended approach.

Estimates of liability cash flow and market value requirements at each point in time can be derived using explicit assumptions about policyholder and issuer behavior along an interest rate path. These estimates enable the quantification of short and long term investment targets across a range of interest rate scenarios. The adequacy of any portfolio of assets selected to fund the SPDA liabilities can be measured by its success in meeting these targets.

Sensitivity analyses can be performed to determine the effect of changes in the assumptions on the investment targets. This feature of a scenario-based approach is particularly useful because of the uncertainties associated with policyholder behavior. The investment manager of the insurance company can use the results of the sensitivity analyses to identify risky situations, such as where a large number of withdrawals force the liquidation of assets at low market values, and tailor the investment strategy accordingly.

A scenario-based approach encourages the investment manager to make estimates about the range of likely interest rate paths over the investment horizon. Interest rate paths can be generated to reflect the expected rate volatility in the fixed income markets. Because the paths are specified explicitly, the manager can include those scenarios which are of greatest concern.

EXHIBIT 2
INTEREST RATE SCENARIOS

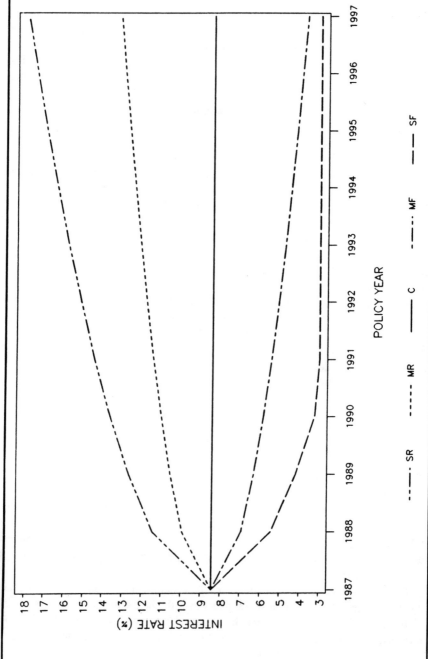

Scenario definitions need not be limited to interest rates alone. Other variables, such as the surrender rate, can be used to specify scenarios. The interest rate environment is, however, the dominant factor which influences the behavior of policyholders and the issuer, so the scenarios are generally a function of interest rates.

An example of interest rate scenarios is graphed in Exhibit 2. The scenarios are labeled:

SR   — steeply rising
MR   — moderately rising
C   — constant
MF   — moderately falling
SF   — steeply falling

The scenarios reflect projections of the yield on 10-year Treasury notes, starting at a rate of 8.43%. For simplicity, the scenarios shown here have interest rates which change in one direction only, i.e., rise, fall or remain constant. In practice, scenarios which have interest rates rising over some periods and falling over others would be included in the analysis.

Both the policyholders and the insurance company exercise their options according to the changes in rates. For illustration, the insurance company is assumed to credit policyholders at a spread of 150 basis points below the scenario rate, although the book yield on assets is usually used as the benchmark. The project lapse rate experience in each scenario (Exhibit 3) is graphed in Exhibit 4. The lapse rate refers to the rate at which the existing policyholders withdraw their funds. This influences the liquidity and market value requirements of the insurance company.

EXHIBIT 3
PROJECTED LAPSE/WITHDRAWAL RATE (%)

Policy			Scenario		
Year	SR	MR	C	MF	SF
1987	15.00	10.50	6.00	4.50	3.00
1988	10.72	8.86	7.00	6.38	5.75
1989	10.85	9.41	8.00	7.52	7.05
1990	8.43	7.23	6.00	5.60	5.77
1991	7.10	6.05	5.00	4.64	5.00
1992	6.92	5.96	5.00	4.68	5.00
1993	6.77	5.90	5.00	4.71	5.00
1994	6.65	5.81	5.00	4.72	5.00
1995	6.56	5.78	5.00	4.75	5.00
1996	6.44	5.72	5.00	4.75	5.00
1997	5.27	5.69	5.00	4.77	5.00

EXHIBIT 4
PROJECTED SPDA LAPSE/WITHDRAWAL RATES

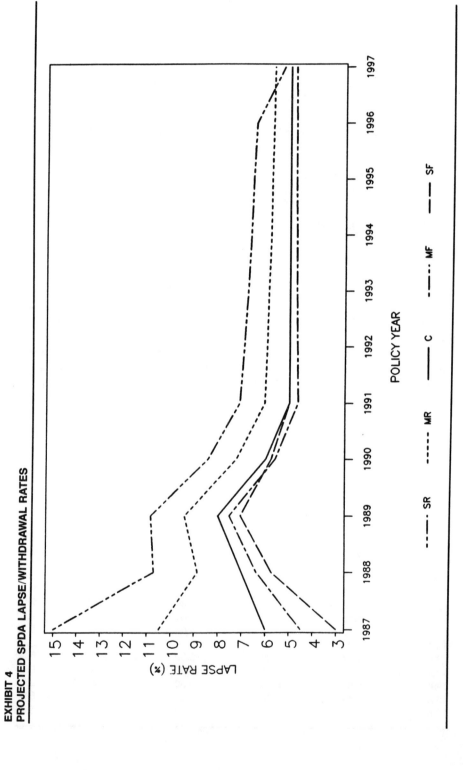

The confluence of the interest rate environments, the crediting rates and the lapse rates produces estimates of the cash flows (Exhibit 5) and account values (Exhibit 6). A comparison of Exhibits 4 and 7 shows that the fluctuations in cash flows in the early years correspond to the fluctuations in the lapse rates. In the later years, the high crediting rates in the rising rate scenarios produce large policyholder account values so that even stable lapse rates produce high cash flow requirements. The account value build-up in the early years is essentially flat across scenarios, with the rising rate scenarios having the lower values (Exhibit 8). This is explained by the larger withdrawals experienced in these scenarios. In the later years, the effect of the higher crediting rates is dominant and the account values in the rising rate scenarios are much higher than those in the other scenarios.

EXHIBIT 5
PROJECTED SPDA CASH FLOW ($ MILLION)

Policy Year	SR	MR	Scenario C	MF	SF
1987	18.47	13.95	9.46	7.96	6.46
1988	10.24	8.81	7.24	6.67	6.08
1989	10.41	9.41	8.32	7.93	7.54
1990	8.46	7.55	6.52	6.13	6.39
1991	7.51	6.59	5.60	5.12	5.55
1992	7.82	6.80	5.76	5.17	5.55
1993	8.32	7.15	5.97	5.26	5.60
1994	8.77	7.37	6.08	5.23	5.54
1995	9.34	7.70	6.19	5.22	5.49
1996	9.96	8.02	6.31	5.18	5.44
1997	9.06	8.42	6.43	5.17	5.39

EHIXIBIT 6
PROJECTED SPDA ACCOUNT VALUE ($ MILLION)

Policy Year	SR	MR	Scenario C	MF	SF
1987	90.88	95.69	100.51	102.11	103.72
1988	89.10	94.47	99.91	102.19	104.49
1989	88.19	93.21	98.23	100.99	103.80
1990	90.41	94.56	98.59	99.32	101.57
1991	94.69	97.49	99.99	98.34	100.18
1992	99.95	100.91	101.38	97.30	98.79
1993	106.25	104.80	102.76	96.22	97.40
1994	113.64	109.20	104.13	95.11	96.00
1995	122.21	114.07	105.19	93.96	94.58
1996	132.14	119.47	106.84	92.79	93.16
1997	145.22	125.39	108.16	91.59	91.73

EXHIBIT 7
PROJECTED SPDA CASH FLOWS

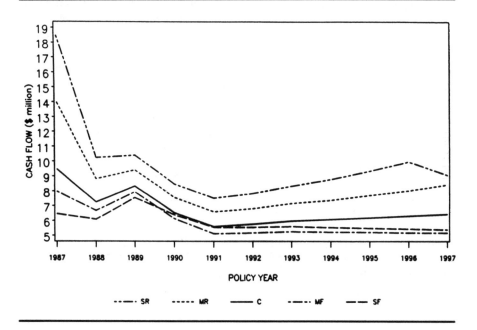

Limitations of Liability Duration and Convexity as Investment Targets

Conventionally, duration[1] and convexity are used to measure the market value sensitivity of the liabilities to changes in interest rates. They are, however, summary measures and, as discussed below, cannot capture the full effect of the path dependency of the SPDA liabilities. As indicated before, pricing SPDA liabilities is difficult. Determining the price response to interest rate changes is much more complex, unless several unrealistic and restrictive assumptions are made.

Investment strategies which use duration and convexity as targets require a single duration number to represent the sensitivity of the market value of liabilities to changes in interest rates and a single convexity value to represent the sensivitity of duration to changes in interest rates. These parameters have useful interpretations for a restricted class of bonds under a limited set of conditions. The option-loaded SPDA

---

[1]Two measures of duration are commonly used—modified duration and Macaulay duration. Modified duration measures the price sensitivity of a stream of payments to interest rate changes. The Macaulay duration of a stream of payments is the weighted average time to receipt of the payments, where the weights are the present value of each payment. In this chapter, the term duration refers to modified duration.

EXHIBIT 8
PROJECTED SPDA ACCOUNT VALUE

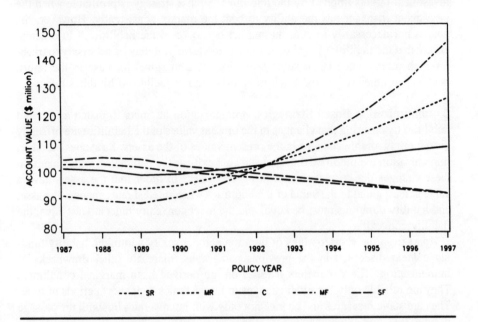

liabilities under volatile and extended interest rate fluctuations do not fit the circumstances conducive to conventional duration and convexity analysis.

Any funding strategy used to meet SPDA liabilities must be able to recognize the inherent uncertainty in the cash flows. Currently used liability funding strategies are not able to accommodate both the short and long term requirements under uncertainty. A new strategy, realized return optimization, has been developed to do so. It is discussed in the following sections.[2]

THE INVESTMENT STRATEGY

Current Investment Strategy Alternatives

Generally, there are three standard investment strategies used to fund the liabilities arising from SPDA contracts.

[2]The strategy is introduced in Llewellyn Miller, Uday Rajan and Prakash A. Shimpi, "Realized Return Optimization: A Strategy for Targeted Total Return Investing in the Fixed Income Markets," in Frank J. Fabozzi (ed.), *The Institutional Investor Focus on Investment Management* (Cambridge, MA: Ballinger Publishing, 1989).

1. "Active" Investment Strategies. The investment manager invests to maximize the total or realized return on the asset portfolio with only peripheral regard for investment targets implied by the liabilities. Such a strategy is profitable when the investment manager has the ability to beat the market consistently. However, the goal is not necessarily to beat the market but to "beat the liabilities." In order to ensure that the liabilities are always funded adequately, it may be necessary to trade-off high return potential in some scenarios for a marginal increase in the return potential in other scenarios. Such trade-offs are not facilitated by this strategy.

2. Immunization Based Strategies. Immunization attempts to match assets and liabilities by ensuring that changes in the present values of the liabilities are offset by even more favorable changes in the present values of the assets. Strategies based on immunization use modified duration and convexity as the parameters which measure these changes due to movements in interest rates. In order that the assets have a value at least equal to the value of the liabilities when interest rates change, the asset and liability durations must be equal and the asset convexity must at least equal the liability convexity.

Apart from the shortcomings of duration and convexity within the liability funding context discussed in the previous paragraphs, there are other drawbacks of immunization. The parameters it relies on are derived from marginal conditions. They are reliable only for small changes in interest rates over short periods of time. They are static measures and change not only with interest rates but with the passage of time. It is more likely than not that the asset and liability durations and convexities respond differently to the passage of time, resulting in a mismatch. To maintain the relationships between the asset and liability parameters, the asset portfolio may require excessive rebalancing (with the associated transaction costs) that could be mitigated through more appropriate analysis.

Conventional immunization works effectively only under parallel shifts of the yield curve. Historically, however, the yield curve has often experienced changes in shape, with short-term rates being more volatile than long-term ones. Duration analysis may yield misleading solutions under such conditions.

3. Portfolio Insurance Portfolio insurance attempts to protect the return on an asset portfolio over a given period. It concentrates on controlling the ending value of the asset portfolio over some relatively short period. It involves dynamic allocation of the portfolio between a riskless asset and a risky asset. This requires constant monitoring of the price changes of the risky asset. It is a market following strategy. For instance, when the risky asset starts to underperform, the portfolio switches out of the risky and into the riskless asset. If the positions are not switched in time, the strategy can fail. In order to raise the floor return of the asset portfolio, an immunized portfolio is used in place of the riskless asset. Doing so exposes portfolio insurance to the problems inherent in immunization.

For the reasons outlined above, these three strategies often are inadequate when applied to funding SPDA liabilities. A strategy which does work well is realized return optimization (RRO).

Realized Return Optimization

Realized return optimization is a liability funding strategy which relies on the measure of greatest concern to investment managers, total return. The strategy ensures that the return earned on the assets is at least equal to the return required to fund the liabilities.

RRO uses a scenario-based approach which focuses on the ability of the selected asset portfolio to meet the liabilities under a range of interest rate scenarios. Asset and liability cash flows are projected along each scenario. Then, using projections of asset prices and the value of future SPDA obligations, the returns that need to be earned to meet the liabilities and the returns that can be earned by the asset portfolio over various periods of time are computed.

The first set of returns, those that need to be earned, are termed required returns (RQ). The second set, those that can be earned, are called realized returns (RR). These return measures focus on the interaction between the cash flows and the market values of the assets and liabilities. Since they are computed over a number of investment horizons and across a range of interest rate scenarios, the strategy considers explicitly the short term liquidity and the long term market value requirements which are at the root of the SPDA liability funding problem.

Computing Required and Realized Returns

The required return over a particular time horizon and interest rate scenario depends on:

a.   funds available for investment at the beginning of the period;
b.   liability cash flow requirements accumulated to the end of the period;
c.   interest paid on short term borrowings; and
d.   the value of the future SPDA obligations measured at the end of the period.

For example, in the moderately rising rate scenario, the liability cash flow requirement at the end of the first year is $13.97 million and the account value is $95.69 million (there are no short term borrowings). The total amount needed at the end of the first year is $109.66 million. The single premium available for investment at the beginning of the first year is $100 million. Therefore, the required return in the first year in this scenario is (109.66 − 100)/100, which is 9.66%. (See Exhibits 5, 6 and 11.)

The required return depends on the method used to compute the value of outstanding obligations. For instance, when the cash surrender value is used instead of the

EXHIBIT 9
PROJECTED SPDA CASH SURRENDER VALUE ($ MILLION)

Policy			Scenario		
Year	SR	MR	C	MF	SF
1987	84.52	88.99	93.47	94.96	96.46
1988	83.75	88.80	93.92	96.06	98.22
1989	83.78	88.55	93.32	95.94	98.61
1990	86.79	90.78	94.65	95.35	97.51
1991	91.85	94.57	96.99	95.39	97.17
1992	97.95	98.89	99.35	95.35	96.81
1993	106.25	104.80	102.76	96.22	97.40
1994	113.64	109.20	104.13	95.11	96.00
1995	122.21	114.07	105.19	93.96	94.58
1996	132.14	119.47	106.84	92.79	93.16
1997	145.22	125.39	108.16	91.59	91.73

account value, the RQ is lower. This is because the cash surrender values (Exhibit 9) are lower than the account values during the first six years as a result of the penalties imposed on withdrawal. The difference between the two values narrows over the years as the surrender penalty gets smaller, as shown in Exhibit 10. The effect of the surrender penalty is significant. In the MR scenario, the cash surrender value at the end of the first year is $88.99 million. Adding the first year cash flow gives the total amount needed, $102.96 million. The corresponding required return of 2.96% is much lower than the 9.66% required when the account value is used.

To illustrate the funding strategy, the account value is used as the value of outstanding obligations. The required returns for 1, 3 and 10 years in each of the 5 scenarios are listed in Exhibit 11.

The realized return of an asset, given a time horizon and interest rate scenario, depends on the:

a.   asset value at the beginning of the period;
b.   asset cash flows received during the period;
c.   reinvestment income earned on asset cash flows during the period; and
d.   asset value at the end of the period.

The coupon income in one year from each $100 invested in a 10% 10-year bond priced at par is $10. If, in a given scenario, the first coupon can be invested at 8% until the end of the year, the reinvestment income is ($5 × 4%), which is $0.20. The value of the bond at the end of the period under this scenario is projected to be $95.[3]

---

[3]Pricing models are required to project both cash flows and asset values. For examples of such models, see Andrew D. Langerman and William J. Gartland, "Callable Corporate Bonds: Pricing and Portfolio Considerations," in *Institutional Investor Focus on Investment Management*, and David J. Askin, Woodward C. Hoffman and Steven D. Meyer, "Evaluation of the Option Component of Mortgage Securities," Chapter 28 in Frank J. Fabozzi (ed.), *The Handbook of Mortgage-Backed Securities*, (Chicago, IL: Probus Publishing, 1988).

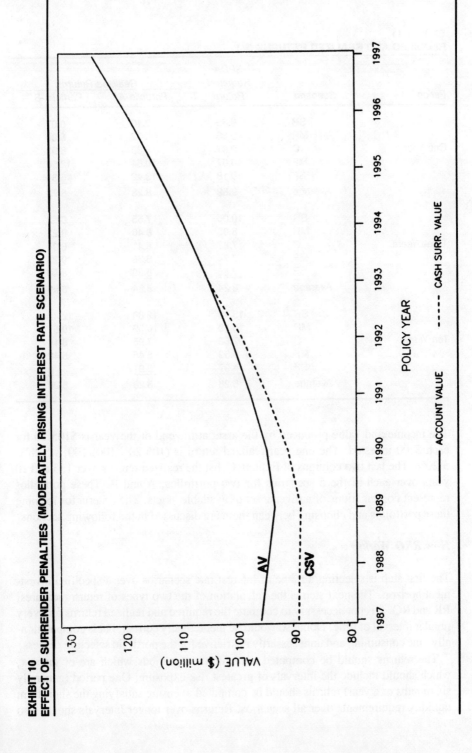

EXHIBIT 10
EFFECT OF SURRENDER PENALTIES (MODERATELY RISING INTEREST RATE SCENARIO)

EXHIBIT 11
REQUIRED AND REALIZED RETURNS (%)

Period	Scenario	SPDA Required Return	Realized Returns	
			Portfolio A	Portfolio B
One Year	SR	9.35	2.10	0.07
	MR	9.66	5.72	5.00
	C	9.97	8.33	8.93
	MF	10.07	10.84	12.66
	SF	10.18	13.42	15.39
	Average	9.89	8.23	8.73
Three Years	SR	10.06	7.55	6.62
	MR	8.95	8.40	8.23
	C	7.87	8.41	8.94
	MF	7.74	8.38	9.23
	SF	7.66	8.20	8.26
	Average	8.24	8.34	8.65
Ten Years	SR	13.49	12.86	12.47
	MR	10.59	10.59	10.51
	C	7.68	7.95	8.14
	MF	5.39	5.45	5.42
	SF	4.97	3.91	3.70
	Average	8.28	8.28	8.28

The income and value produced by the asset at the end of the year is $105.20 for each $100 invested. The one-year realized return is $(105.20 - 100)/100$, which is 5.20%. The last two columns of Exhibit 11 list the realized returns over 1, 3 and 10 years over each of the 5 scenarios for two portfolios, A and B. These portfolios represent combinations of a diverse set of available assets. The criteria for forming these portfolios and choosing between them are discussed in the following sections.

How RRO Works

The first step is selecting a range of interest rate scenarios over a specified investment horizon. The next step is the calculation of the two types of return measures, RR and RQ. It is not necessary to compute the required and realized returns for every regular interval of time. Doing so would be theoretically correct, but is computationally time consuming and unnecessarily restrictive for the portfolio selection process.

The returns should be computed only for those periods which are of interest, which should include the intervals of greatest risk exposure. One period (generally six months or a year) returns should be computed to ensure satisfying the short term liquidity requirements over all scenarios. Returns over longer intervals should also

.be calculated to provide a view to the medium and long term market value requirements of the SPDA business. In the illustration, returns over three years are computed to monitor the adequacy of the asset portfolio over the initial interest rate
guarantee period. Ten-year returns are used to test the longer term adequacy.

Once these returns are obtained, the investment strategy is fairly straightforward.
The realized return on the asset portfolio selected should exceed the required return
in all scenarios and over all time periods specified. By doing so, both the cash flow
and market value constraints of funding are dealt with over multiple time horizons
and divese shifts in interest rates. These are not accommodated by immunization or
any other popular investment strategy.

It may not always be possible for the asset portfolio to achieve the required return
in every scenario and over every time interval. RRO identifies these risky situations
and provides the investment manager with the opportunity to develop appropriate
hedging strategies. Comparing the RQ and RR values in Exhibit 11, the risky
situations for portfolios A and B can be identified. The comparisons for the 1-, 3-,
and 10-year returns are graphed in Exhibits 12, 13 and 14, respectively. The risky
situations correspond to the areas of the graphs where the RR line of a portfolio falls
below the RQ line.

EXHIBIT 12
ONE-YEAR RETURNS

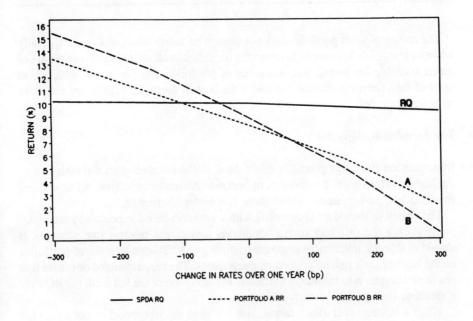

CHANGE IN RATES OVER ONE YEAR (bp)

—— SPDA RQ   ----- PORTFOLIO A RR   — — PORTFOLIO B RR

EXHIBIT 13
THREE-YEAR RETURNS

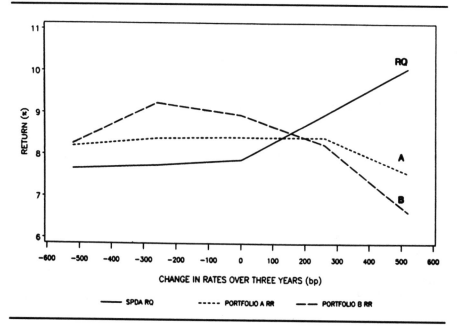

The choice of asset portfolio may not always be immediately obvious, especially when all portfolios are unable to cover the liabilities in all situations. From the set of assets available for investment, a number of portfolios may be formed which meet most of the return constraints. To select the best of these, an investment objective must be quantified.

The Investment Objective

Immunization strategies generally select the duration matched portfolio which earns the highest return over the investment horizon. A similar objective can be utilized for RRO but, as explained below, there is a better alternative.

The objective should be compatible with a scenario-based approach by recognizing explicitly the different return conditions under each interest rate scenario. It should enable the investment manager to distinguish between alternative portfolios on the basis of their risk and return characteristics. The recommended objective that has these features is to minimize the downside deviation of the RR from the RQ over a specified time period in each scenario.

When a strategy specifies a target, risk refers to the likelihood of not achieving that target. Liability funding seeks to ensure that the asset portfolio value does not

EXHIBIT 14
TEN-YEAR RETURNS

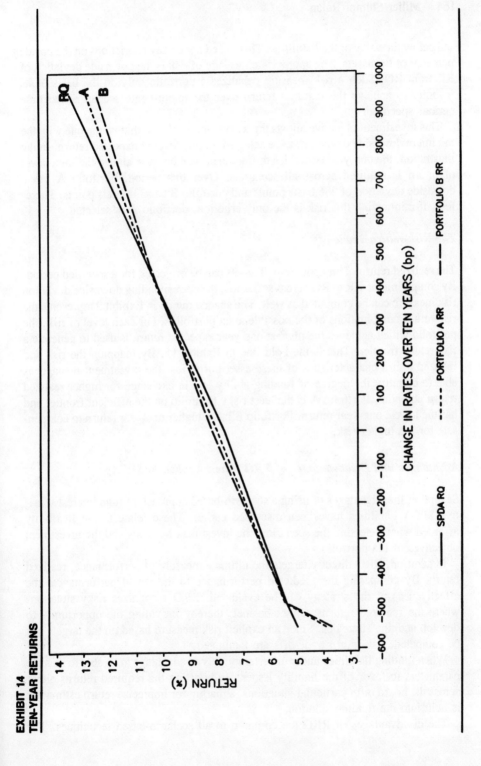

RETURN (%)

CHANGE IN RATES OVER TEN YEARS (bp)

RQ   A   B

——— SPDA RQ   ----- PORTFOLIO A RR   ——— PORTFOLIO B RR

fall below the value of the liabilities. There need not be any restrictions on the upside potential of the assets. The appropriate measure of risk is the downside deviation of RR from RQ. Such a risk measure penalizes a portfolio only on the basis of its inability to achieve the required return over the interest rate scenarios and time periods specified.

This investment objective allows the least risky portfolio, that is, the one with the minimum downside deviation, to be selected for any level of expected return. In the illustration, the one-year period is considered critical because almost the same level of return is required across all scenarios. Over this period, portfolio A has a downside deviation of 286 basis points and portfolio B has 335 basis points. Therefore, if minimizing this risk is the only criterion, portfolio A is selected.

The Risk-return Trade-off

The realized return of any portfolio of assets can be projected for a specified period. By comparing the RR to RQ across scenarios, the corresponding downside deviation risk measure can be computed as well. The shaded region in Exhibit 9 represents the risk-return combinations of the possible asset portfolios. For each level of risk, the portfolio which achieves the highest one-year expected return is used to generate a risk-return frontier. This is the bold line in Exhibit 15. By mapping the risk and realized return characteristics of these asset portfolios, the investment manager is able to quantify the degree of funding ability lost in exchange for higher realized return potential. Portfolio A is the least risky portfolio on the efficient frontier and has the lowest one-year return. Portfolio B has a higher one-year return to compensate for the higher risk.

Advantages and Disadvantages of RRO When Applied to SPDAs

Several of the advantages of using a scenario-based approach to fund interest sensitive SPDA liabilities have been discussed earlier. These relate to the flexibility afforded when selecting the scenarios, the investment horizons and the investment objectives of the portfolio.

In addition, RRO directly targets the ultimate measure of performance, realized return. By comparing the predicted performance to the actual performance, the effectiveness of the strategy can be evaluated. RRO recognizes risky situations where the required returns cannot be met, thereby providing the opportunity to develop hedging strategies. Since an explicit risk measure based on the targets can be computed, risk-return trade-offs are facilitated.

When funding liabilities under uncertainty, it is an advantage to be able to bias the parameters in favor of the liability issuer. By boosting the required returns either across the board or in particular situations, a margin for imprecise return estimation is built into the funding solution.

The disadvantages of RRO are common to all scenario-based techniques. The

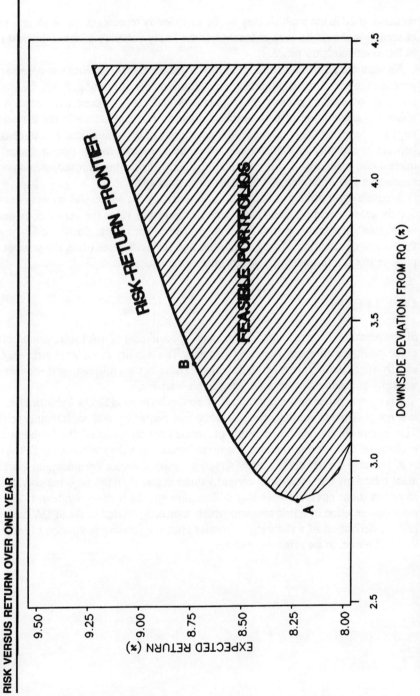

EXHIBIT 15
RISK VERSUS RETURN OVER ONE YEAR

scenarios used in the analysis may not be sufficiently representative. A diverse range of scenarios should be used to incorporte the likely volatility of future interest rates in the asset selection process.

An accurate cash flow simulation model for the SPDA liabilities is necessary to generate the cash flow and market value requirements of funding. Actuarial simulation may be used to project these quantities under any interest rate scenario and under any assumption of new business growth. The confidence in the investment targets depends on the confidence in the accuracy of the simulation. The trade-off is between the quality of the estimates of required returns for all time horizons and interest rate scenarios of concern and the quality of one duration and one convexity number as specifications of the investment strategy.

Accurate asset pricing models also are necessary for successful implementation. Sophisticated pricing models have been developed to value the option components of callable corporate bonds and mortgage-backed securities. These models permit the accurate evaluation of these securities and facilitate forecasting the price at any point in the future under any given interest rate scenario.

CONCLUSION

Single premium deferred annuities present a peculiar set of asset selection problems to the insurance company portfolio manager. The liability funding requirements are usually specified in terms of book yields. These can be misleading if interest rate volatility is assumed to be a non-negligible variable.

It is inappropriate to use immunization strategies to fund SPDA liabilities because it is not possible to estimate their duration and convexity with sufficient precision. This is due to the combined result of various option features, the "sub-optimal" exercise of options and the absence of an active secondary market for SPDAs.

A scenario driven optimization strategy, realized return optimization, provides asset selections that meet both current valuation and liquidity requirements. It also identifies those circumstances that will require special hedging strategies. The explicit computation of a risk measure which is directly related to the SPDA liabilities and the derivation of a risk-return frontier enable a funding institution to trade off risk and return in an effective manner.

Chapter 9

Duration, Immunization and Volatility for Taxable Debt Securities

GRANT MCQUEEN
PH.D. CANDIDATE
UNIVERSITY OF WASHINGTON

ROGER CLARKE, PH.D.
MANAGING DIRECTOR
TSA CAPITAL MANAGEMENT

IVAN CALL, PH.D.
PROFESSOR OF FINANCE
BRIGHAM YOUNG UNIVERSITY

Although originally conceived simply as a measure of the timing of a bond's cash flow, duration has proven to have other benefits. Fisher and Weil show how immunization is achievable when the investment horizon equals a bond's duration.[1] Fisher[2]

[1]L. Fisher, and R. Weil, "Coping with the Risk of Interest Rate Fluctuations: Return to Bondholders for Naive and Optimal Strategies," *Journal of Business* (October 1971).

[2]L. Fisher, "An Algorithm for Finding Exact Rates of Return," *Journal of Business* (January 1966).

and Hopewell and Kaufman[3] further extend the usefulness of duration by establishing a direct relation between a bond's duration and the sensitivity of the price of a bond to interest rate fluctuations.

These papers, along with most of the subsequent duration literature, address the specific case of duration without regard to taxes, that is, pre-tax duration. However, for a taxable investor or for the manager of a taxable bond portfolio, pre-tax duration is misleading. For example, a common immunization technique is to purchase a zero coupon bond with duration (and maturity) equal to the investment horizon, eliminating both the price and reinvestment risk. This immunization strategy will fail for the taxable investor since a zero coupon bond does have cash flows (outflows to pay taxes) prior to maturity.

Hessel and Huffman[4] and Kalotay[5] discuss after-tax duration; however, each of these papers looks at specific categories of bonds. Hessel and Huffman analyze the after-tax duration of bonds purchased in the secondary market at a discount and conclude that all the before-tax duration results still hold. However, their conclusion is the result of focusing only on the specific case of market discounts where after-tax cash flows are positive, thus ignoring the case of original issue discounts (OID).

On the other hand, Kalotay excludes market discounts and premiums and looks at the specific case of after-tax duration on OIDs. Kalotay observes that the negative after-tax cash flows of OIDs can result in their duration being greater than their maturity, and explains the effect of taxes on immunization strategies.

The purpose of this chapter is first, to develop a general closed-form expression for the duration of a bond with the possibility of an original issue discount, a market discount, an acquisition premium, and a premium, and second, to use this expression to extend immunization strategies and the determinants of bond volatility to an after-tax environment.[6] In the next section the tax treatment for OID, discount and premium bonds, are discussed. In the third section three different expressions of after-tax duration will be developed depending upon whether the bond is purchased at a market discount, acquisition premium, or premium. Our formulas extend previous work in that they are: 1) closed-form, 2) general, encompassing OID, discount, and premium bonds, and 3) current, reflecting the tax law changes of 1982, 1984, 1985, and 1986. After establishing the general duration expressions, we show

---

[3]M. Hopewell, and G. Kaufman, "Bond Price Volatility and Term to Maturity: A Generalized Respecification," *American Economic Review* (September 1973).

[4]C. Hessel, and L. Huffman, "The Effect of Taxation on Immunization Rules and Duration Estimates," *Journal of Finance* (December 1981).

[5]A. Kalotay, "An Analysis of Original Issue Discount Bonds," *Financial Management* (Autumn 1984) and A. Kalotay, "The After-tax Duration of Original Issue Discount Bonds," *Journal of Portfolio Management* (Winter 1985).

[6]In this chapter we concentrate on after-tax duration of bonds under the most recent tax laws. The law makes a distinction in how income shall be determined depending upon when a bond was originally issued and when it was purchased, as is explained in the next section. For after-tax duration on debt securities under previous tax laws see R. Clarke, I. Call, and G. McQueen, "Closed-form Duration Formulas for Taxable Debt Securities, A Note," Working Paper.

how the cases explored by Hessel and Huffman and Kalotay along with the case of zero coupon bonds all are special cases encompassed by our general formulas. In the fourth section we use the duration formulas to: a) examine the determinants of a bond's after-tax duration and volatility, b) discuss the effects of recent and pending tax laws, and c) examine immunization strategies.

TAX LAWS

A bond is said to have an OID if when issued to the public the discount from its stated redemption price is larger than a prescribed *de minimus* amount defined in the tax code.[7] The investor is required to report the amortized discount as interest income each year even though there may be no cash payment of interest to the investor. For bonds issued before July 1, 1982 the OID must be amortized over the life of the issue using a straight line method, whereas OID bonds issued on or after July 1, 1982 are amortized using a compound interest method. The required compound rate is the yield to maturity at the time of the original sale. The tax basis of a bond with OID, the adjusted issue price (AIP), increases for each year by the amount of the OID that is amortized for that year. Thus a schedule of the accrued interest and the AIP for each year is fixed at the time the bond is first sold and remains the same no matter who subsequently purchases the bond.

Market discount is measured at the time the purchaser buys the bond in the secondary market and equals the excess of the stated redemption price over the basis of the bond immediately after acquisition.[8] If the bond also has an OID, the stated redemption price is treated as being equal to the AIP. The market discount accrues as ordinary income using either the straight line or compound interest accrual method; however, unlike the OID, the accrued income is usually reported and taxed in the year of disposition.[9,10]

For premium bonds the investor may opt between postponing the loss until disposition or amortizing the premium and receiving a tax shield for the negative amortization. Unlike the market discount, amortization of premiums is preferred because by early recognition the present value of the tax shield is increased. For

---

[7]The *de minimus* amount is defined as being less than ¼ of one percent of the stated redemption price at maturity multiplied by the number of years to maturity. As an example, on a 20 year bond the allowed discount could be .25% × 20 years or 5.0%. Thus, if the original issue discount were 5.0% or less, there would be no original discount in the eyes of the tax code. If the original issue price were less than 95 (OID>5%) then there would be an OID. The issuer is required to print on each bond its OID.

[8]Like OID, market discount is zero if less than the *de minimus* amount.

[9]The investor may elect to recognize income on market discount bonds as income in the year to which it is attributable rather than postponing its recognition until the year of disposition of the bond. For most investors this election would not be advantageous.

[10]Market discount on bonds issued before July 18, 1984 is classified as capital gain at the time the bond is sold whereas the market discount on bonds issued after this date is classified as ordinary income. However, the importance of distinguishing between capital gain and ordinary income was diminished by the Tax Reform Act of 1986.

bonds issued before September 27, 1985, "any reasonable" method of premium amortization is allowed, but for bonds issued after this date the compound interest amortization is required.

An acquisition premium occurs when an OID bond is purchased in the secondary market at a price above the adjusted issue price but below the stated redemption price. Amortization of the acquisition premium serves to reduce the amount of OID reportable as income in each period. For bonds purchased on or before July 18, 1984, the amount of OID income in each period is reduced (but not below zero) by straight line amortization of the acquisition premium. For bonds purchased after July 18, 1984, acquisition premium is amortized by reducing the OID that would other-wise accrue by a constant fraction determined at the time of purchase. The numera-tor of the fraction is the total amount of premium to be amortized and the denomina-tor is the aggregate amount of unaccrued OID at the time of purchase.

GENERAL DURATION EXPRESSIONS

Throughout our analysis we will use the following notation:

P_o = the purchase price of the bond
P^i = the original issue price of the bond
P = the par value of the bond
Y^i = the original before-tax yield to maturity of the bond
Y = the before-tax yield to maturity of the bond when purchased
Y^a = the after-tax yield to maturity of the bond when purchased
M^i = the maturity of the bond when issued
M = the maturity of the bond when purchased
CF^a_t = the after-tax cash flow of the bond in period t. The flows depend on the investor's marginal tax rate and the tax laws applying at the time the bond was issued.[11]
τ = the investor's marginal income tax rate
D^a = the after-tax duration of the bond

The traditional after-tax duration of the bond is:[12]

---

[11]CF^a_t, τ, and D^a can be different for investors in different marginal tax brackets; however, to simplify notation these three terms are not indexed by i.

[12]Equation (1) is the duration measure derived by Macaulay which discounts all cash flows by the prevailing average yield to maturity for the bond [See: F. Macaulay, *Some Theoretical Problems Suggest-ed by the Movements of Interest Rates, Bond Yields, and Stock Prices in the United States Since 1856* (New York: National Bureau of Economic Research, 1938)]. Bierwag and Kaufman develop two other duration measures using forward rates to discount the cash flows depending on whether all the interest rates in the term structure change by the same amount (additive shock) or by the same percentage (multiplicative shock) [See: G. Bierwag, and G. Kaufman, "Coping With Risk of Interest Rate Fluctu-ations: A Note," *Journal of Business* (July 1977)]. The Macaulay measure will be used throughout this article.

$$D^a = \frac{\sum_{t=1}^{M} \frac{tCF_t^a}{(1+Y^a)^t}}{P_o} \tag{1}$$

In general, the periodic after-tax cash flow in period t for any bond can be written as:

$$CF_t^a = (1-\tau)C - T_t \tag{2}$$

where:

C = the coupon payment

T_t = the tax liability, in period t, that results from amortization of the OID less amortization of any premium.

At maturity, in addition to the periodic cash flow, the principal is returned less any terminal tax liability which must be paid, giving:

$$CF_M^a = (1-\tau)C - T_M + P - \bar{T}_M \tag{3}$$

where:

$\bar{T}_M$ = the terminal tax liability in period M that results from purchasing the bond at a market discount.

Substituting (2) and (3) into (1), the after-tax duration can be written as:

$$D^a = \frac{\sum_{t=1}^{M} t\left[(1-\tau)C - T_t\right](1+Y^a)^{-t}}{P_o} + \frac{M\left(P - \bar{T}_M\right)(1+Y^a)^{-M}}{P_o}$$

Following the framework developed by Chau[13] and Babcock[14], shown in Appendix A, the after-tax duration can be written as:

---

[13]J. Chua, "A Closed Form Formula for Calculating Bond Duration," *Financial Analysts Journal* (May/June 1984).

[14]G. Babcock, "Duration as a Weighted Average of Two Factors," *Financial Analysts Journal* (March/ April 1985).

$$D^a = \frac{(1-\tau)C}{P_o Y^a}\left[(1+Y^a)\text{PVIFA}^a - \frac{M}{(1+Y^a)^M}\right] + \frac{MP}{P_o(1+Y^a)^M}$$

$$-\sum_{t=1}^{M}\frac{tT_t(1+Y^a)^{-t}}{P_o} - \frac{M\bar{T}_M}{P_o(1+Y^a)^M} \tag{4}$$

where PVIFA^a is the present value annuity factor at rate Y^a for M periods. Equation (4) will be simplified in the next four subsections. In its present form it is helpful to examine the four terms that comprise after-tax duration.

The first term in Equation (4) captures the influence of the after-tax coupon payments on duration. The second term captures the effect of the return of principal on duration. These first two terms are not impacted by recent changes in the tax laws. However, the last two terms are sensitive to the tax law features. The third term is generated by the periodic tax liability, T_t, which arises if the bond has an original issue discount or was purchased with a premium. This cash flow (tax payment or tax credit) influences duration in an opposite direction to the coupon payment, hence the term is subtracted from the other terms. The fourth term captures any terminal tax liability at maturity, $\bar{T}_M$, which arises if the bond was purchased at a market discount and the investor deferred the taxes from the market discount until the bond's maturity. This terminal tax component is also subtracted since it acts to reduce the after-tax proceeds from the redemption of the bond.

Compound Interest Amortization of OID

For bonds issued on or after July 1, 1982, the investor must use the compound interest amortization method for the OID and is taxed on the imputed income. The tax liability each period depends on the change in adjusted issue price (AIP):

$$T_t = \tau\left(\text{AIP}_t - \text{AIP}_{t-1}\right)$$

$$= \tau\left(Y^i P^i - C\right)\left(1 + Y^i\right)^{t+(M^i-M)-1} \tag{5}$$

The change in adjusted issue price used in Equation (5) is derived in Appendix B.

The periodic tax liability component of the duration calculation, the third term in (4), is:

$$\frac{\sum_{t=1}^{M} t T_t \left(1 + Y^a\right)^{-t}}{P_o} = \frac{\tau \left(Y^i P^i - C\right)\left(1 + Y^i\right)^{\left(M^i - M\right)}}{P_o \left(1 + Y^a\right)} \left[\sum_{t=1}^{M} \frac{t \left(1 + Y^i\right)^{t-1}}{\left(1 + Y^a\right)^{t-1}} \right]$$

$$= \frac{\tau \left(Y^i P^i - C\right)\left(1 + Y^i\right)^{\left(M^i - M\right)}}{P_o \left(1 + Y^a\right)} \left[\frac{\left(1 + r\right)^M \left(rM - 1\right) + 1}{r^2} \right]$$

(6)

where:

$$(1 + r) = \left(1 + Y^i\right) / \left(1 + Y^a\right)$$
$$r = \left(Y^i - Y^a\right) / \left(1 + Y^a\right)$$

and the last equality follows from the relationship (A4) derived in Appendix A.

Terminal Tax Liability With Compound Interest Amortization of OID

In Appendix B the adjusted issued price at time $t = 0$, which may be different than the initial issue date, is:

$$\text{AIP}_o = P^i \left(1 + Y^i\right)^{\left(M^i - M\right)} - C \left[\frac{\left(1 + Y^i\right)^{\left(M^i - M\right)} - 1}{Y^i} \right]$$

(7)

The tax liability at the maturity of a market discount bond will be:

$$\overline{T}_M = \tau \left(\text{AIP}_o - P_o\right)$$

$$= \tau \left[P^i \left(1 + Y^i\right)^{\left(M^i - M\right)} - C \left(\frac{\left(1 + Y^i\right)^{\left(M^i - M\right)} - 1}{Y^i} \right) - P_o \right]$$

(8)

Amortization of Acquisition Premium

For OID bonds purchased after July 18, 1984 the acquisition premium is amortized by reducing the amount of OID reported as income each period. The OID income is reduced by multiplying by the following constant fraction:

$$\frac{P - P_o}{P - AIP_o} = \frac{P - P_o}{P - \left[P^i (1 + Y^i)^{M^i - M} - C \left(\text{FVIFA}^i \right) \right]} \tag{9}$$

where FVIFA^i is the future value annuity factor at rate Y^i for $M^i - M$ periods. Since acquisition premium is amortized over the life of the bond, no terminal tax liability occurs, thus the forth term in (4) is zero.

Amortization of Premium

When a bond sells at a premium any OID is fully offset by the acquisition premium, leaving only the amortization of the premium. For bonds issued after September 27, 1985, compound interest amortization is required; hence, the tax liability each period depends on the change in the adjusted issue price.

$$T_t = \tau \left(AIP_t - AIP_{t-1} \right)$$

This tax term has the same equation as the tax liability for OID bonds; however, two differences are important to note. First, with OID bonds T_t is positive, signifying a tax liability, whereas for market premiums the term is negative, signifying a tax credit. Second, the adjusted issue price for OID bonds is measured from the time of original issue, whereas for market premiums it is measured from the time of purchase. Since the tax equation for premium has the same form as in the OID case, we can use steps similar to those in the subsection on OID amortization and in Appendix B to show that for market premium the third term in (4) is:

$$\frac{\sum_{t=1}^{M} t T_t (1 + Y^a)^{-t}}{P_o} = \frac{\tau (YP - C)}{P_o (1 + Y^a)} \left[\frac{(1 + q)^M (qM - 1) + 1}{q^2} \right] \tag{10}$$

where:

$$(1+q) = (1+Y)/(1+Y^a)$$
$$q = (Y - Y^a)/(1+Y^a)$$

Finally, unlike market discount, premium has no terminal tax liability so the last term in Equation (4) is zero.

Complete Duration Formulas

Substituting these components (Equations 6, 8, 9, and 10) into (4) results in three closed-form expressions for the after-tax duration of a bond. For a bond issued on or after July 1, 1982 and purchased at *market discount*, $P_o < AIP_o$, the after-tax duration is:

$$D^a = \frac{(1-\tau)C}{P_o Y^a}\left[(1+Y^a)PVIFA^a - \frac{M}{(1+Y^a)^M}\right]$$

$$- \frac{\tau(Y^i P^i - C)(1+Y^i)^{(M^i-M)}}{P_o(1+Y^a)}\left[\frac{(1+r)^M(rM-1)+1}{r^2}\right]$$

$$+ \frac{MP}{P_o(1+Y^a)^M}$$

$$- \frac{M\tau}{P_o(1+Y^a)^M Y^i}\left[(Y^i P^i - C)(1+Y^i)^{(M^i-M)} - (Y^i P_o - C)\right] \quad (11)$$

For OID bonds issued on or after July 1, 1982, and purchased at an *acquisition premium*, $AIP_o < P_o < P$, after July 18, 1984, the after-tax duration is:

$$D^a = \frac{(1-\tau)C}{P_o Y^a}\left[(1+Y^a)\text{PVIFA}^a - \frac{M}{(1+Y^a)^M}\right]$$

$$- \frac{\tau(Y^i P^i - C)(1+Y^i)^{(M^i - M)}}{P_o(1+Y^a)}\left[\frac{(1+r)^M (rM - 1) + 1}{r^2}\right]$$

$$\left[\frac{P - P_o}{\left[P - \left[P^i(1+Y^i)^{M^i - M} - C(\text{FVIFA}^i)\right]\right]}\right] + \frac{MP}{P_o(1+Y^a)^M} \quad (12)$$

For *premium* bonds, $P_o > P$, issued after September 27, 1985, the after-tax duration is:

$$D^a = \frac{(1-\tau)C}{P_o Y^a}\left[(1+Y^a)\text{PVIFA}^a - \frac{M}{(1+Y^a)^M}\right]$$

$$- \frac{\tau(YP - C)}{P_o(1+Y^a)}\left[\frac{(1+q)^M (qM - 1) + 1}{q^2}\right] + \frac{MP}{P_o(1+Y^a)^M} \quad (13)$$

Equations (11), (12), and (13) have several advantages over the after-tax duration formulas existing in the literature. First, these formulas encompass OID, market discount, acquisition premium, and premium bonds. Second, the equations are closed-form, simplifying the calculation. Third, the formulas are current, reflecting the tax law changes of 1982, 1984, 1985, and 1986.

It is interesting to note how some special cases can be derived from our general equations. Duration for the Hessell and Huffman case of a market discount bond originally issued at par so that $P^i = P$ and $Y^i = C/P^i$ is:

$$D^a = \frac{(1-\tau)C}{P_o Y^a}\left[(1+Y^a)\text{PVIFA}^a - \frac{M}{(1+Y^a)^M}\right] \quad (14)$$

$$+ \frac{M}{P_o(1+Y^a)^M}[P - \tau(P - P_o)]$$

If a bond issued after July 1, 1982 is limited to exclude market discounts and premiums (i.e. purchased on the original issue date so that $P_O = P^i$, $M = M^i$, and $Y = Y^i$), then we have a closed duration formula for the specific case analyzed by Kalotay:

$$D^a = \frac{(1-\tau)C}{P_o Y^a}\left[(1+Y^a)\text{PVIFA}^a - \frac{M}{(1+Y^a)^M}\right]$$

$$-\frac{\tau(YP_o - C)}{P_o(1+Y^a)}\left[\frac{(1+r)^M(rM-1)+1}{r^2}\right] + \frac{MP}{P_o(1+Y^a)^M} \tag{15}$$

A zero coupon bond issued on or after July 1, 1982 and purchased at a market discount will have a duration of:

$$D^a = -\frac{\tau Y^i P^i(1+Y^i)^{(M^i-M)}}{P_o(1+Y^a)}\left[\frac{(1+r)^M(rM-1)+1}{r^2}\right] \tag{16}$$

$$+\frac{MP}{P_o(1+Y^a)^M} - \frac{M\tau}{P_o(1+Y^a)^M}\left[P^i(1+Y^i)^{(M^i-M)} - P_o\right]$$

Finally, if the investor is in a zero tax bracket, the duration of a zero coupon bond is equal to the current maturity:

$$D^a = \frac{MP}{P_o(1+Y^a)^M} = M \tag{17}$$

This result follows since by definition $P_o = P(1+Y^a)^{-M}$ for a zero coupon bond in a zero tax bracket environment.

TAXES, DURATION, IMMUNIZATION AND VOLATILITY

Volatility

Besides playing a role in immunization, duration relates the change in the price of the bond to a change in the yield to maturity. Writing the price of the bond as:

$$P_o = \sum_{t=1}^{M} CF_t^a \left(1 + Y^a\right)^{-t} \tag{18}$$

allows us to differentiate with respect to $(1 + Y^a)$, which, with some rearranging, gives:

$$\frac{dP_o}{P_o} = -D^a \frac{d\left(1 + Y^a\right)}{\left(1 + Y^a\right)} \tag{19}$$

which has the same form as the familiar before-tax measure of interest rate sensitivity:

$$\frac{dP_o}{P_o} = -D \frac{d\left(1 + Y\right)}{\left(1 + Y\right)} \tag{20}$$

Here we see that after-tax duration not only measures the life of a bond but also is a measure of a bond's volatility, where volatility is defined as the percentage change in price for a given change in after-tax interest rates.[15,16]

---

[15]Although duration as a measure of volatility has been criticized, Bierwag, et. al. show that some of the criticism is the result of major errors in deriving testable implications. They conclude that, although not perfect, duration measures are "likely to outperform maturity as a measure of interest rate risk for portfolios of default-free bonds." [See G. Bierwag, G. Kaufman, C. Latta, and G. Roberts, "Duration: Response to Critics," *Journal of Portfolio Management* (Winter 1987)].

[16]Equating (19) and (20) gives an expression for the change in gross after-tax yield to maturity for a change in the gross before-tax yield to maturity.

$$d(1 + Y^a) = \frac{D(1 + Y^a)}{D^a(1 + Y)} \; d(1 + Y)$$

The change in the gross after-tax yield to maturity is proportional to the gross before-tax yield to maturity and the proportion depends on the relative duration and gross yields to maturity before and after taxes. The change in after-tax yield to maturity is tax-bracket specific and also depends on the tax law prevailing at the time the bond was issued.

Duration[17]

Having established a direct relationship between a bond's duration and price volatility, we can now explore the determinants of bond volatility in a taxable environment. These determinants are coupon, term to maturity, yield to maturity, and the marginal tax rate. The coupon and the marginal tax rate have negative and positive effects on duration respectively. However, the effect of term to maturity and yield to maturity are ambiguous, depending on whether the bond sells at a market discount, an acquisition premium, or premium.

The inverse relationship between duration and the size of the coupon, as seen in Exhibits 1 and 2 for bonds issued before and after July 1, 1982 respectively, has an intuitive explanation. Bonds with higher coupons pay relatively more of the cash flows during the early years of the bond's life. Therefore, holding everything else constant, the higher the coupon, the lower the duration and volatility.

EXHIBIT 1
AFTER-TAX DURATION AT VARIOUS COUPON RATES OF A POST-1982 10 YEAR BOND YIELDING 12% BEFORE TAX (ISSUED BEFORE JULY 1, 1982)

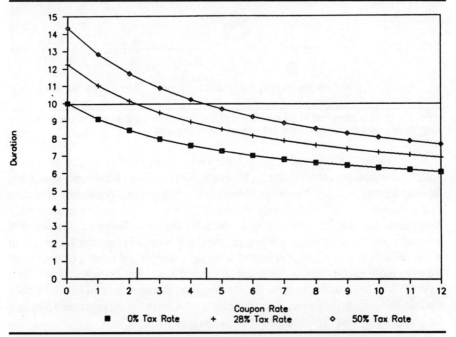

Note: The bond is assumed to be purchased at the original issue date so there is no market discount or premium involved, only the original issue discount.

[17]Fuller and Settle analyze the determinants of duration and bond volatility in a non-tax environment; this subsection parallels their paper but in an after-tax environment. [See R. Fuller, and J. Settle, "Determinants of Duration and Bond Volatility," *The Journal of Portfolio Management* (Summer 1984)].

EXHIBIT 2
AFTER-TAX DURATION AT VARIOUS COUPON RATES OF A 10 YEAR BOND YIELDING
12% BEFORE TAX
(ISSUED ON OR AFTER JULY 1, 1982)

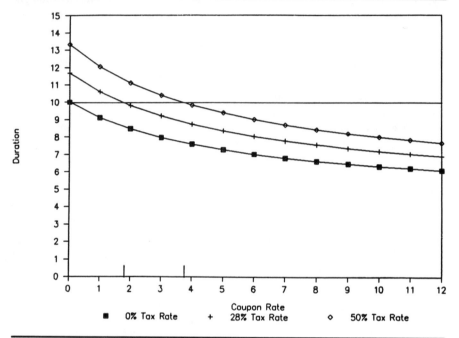

Note: The bond is assumed to be purchased at the original issue date so there is no market discount or premium involved, only the original issue discount.

Traditionally, duration and bond volatility were thought of as strictly increasing functions of maturity (see Exhibit 3). However, Hopewell and Kaufman showed that for deep market discount bonds, as M increases duration initially increases but then peaks, decreases, and finally levels off (see Exhibit 4).[18] This pattern of increasing then decreasing duration also exists in the after-tax case. However, the negative effect of maturity on duration is of less practical importance in the after-tax case than in the before-tax case since it occurs at levels of maturity and market discount that are even more uncommon in our financial environment. For example, even with a 1,000 (6% to 16%) basis point increase, the market discount bond in Exhibit 4 does not start to decrease until remaining maturity is over 20 years, 30 years, and 50 years for a 0%, 28%, and 50% marginal tax rate respectively.

---

[18]For a thorough discussion of the relationship between duration and maturity, see C. Hsia, and J. Weston, "Price Behavior of Deep Discount Bonds," *Journal of Banking and Finance* Vol. 5 (1981).

EXHIBIT 3
AFTER-TAX DURATION AT VARIOUS MATURITIES FOR A 6% COUPON BOND
CURRENTLY SELLING IN THE SECONDARY MARKET TO YIELD 6% BEFORE TAX

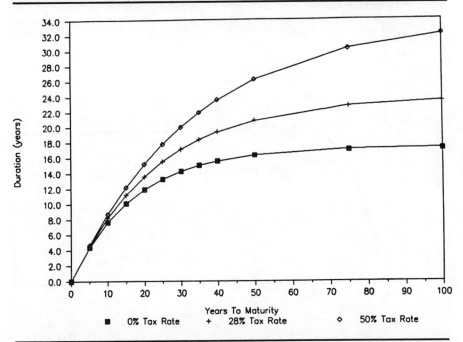

Note: For each maturity the bond was originally issued 5 years earlier at par. For example, the 20 year maturity bond was originally issued with a 6% yield to maturity and a 25 year maturity but currently has 20 years of remaining maturity.

Exhibit 5 illustrates the relation between duration and the level of yield to maturity for a bond issued after July 1, 1982 with a 4% coupon and a 12 year maturity that is purchased at various yields when the bond has 10 years left to maturity. Fuller and Settle show that in a non-tax environment, yield to maturity has an unambiguously negative effect on duration. This happens because yield to maturity acts as a discount rate in the duration formula (see Equation (1)). As the discount rate increases, the present value of distant cash flows diminishes; thus, more weight is given to early cash flows relative to later cash flows and duration decreases. When taxes are introduced, the negative "discount rate" effect of yield to maturity on duration is counteracted in two ways. First, for original deep discount bonds the interim cash flows can be negative; consequently, the "discount rate" effect works in the opposite direction to increase duration. Second, for a given coupon rate, as the yield to maturity increases the bond may sell at a smaller premium. When the smaller premium is amortized, a smaller tax shield results, reducing the value of the interim cash flows relative to the final cash flow and increasing duration. These three effects

EXHIBIT 4
AFTER-TAX DURATION AT VARIOUS MATURITIES FOR A 6% COUPON BOND
CURRENTLY SELLING IN THE SECONDARY MARKET TO YIELD 16% BEFORE TAX

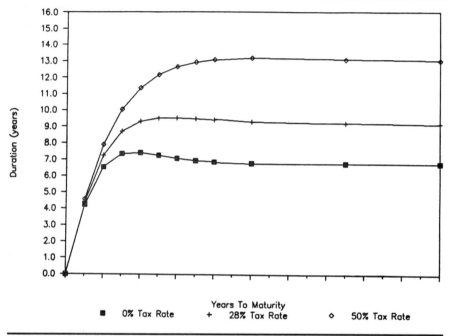

Note: For each maturity the bond was originally issued 5 years earlier at par. For example, the 20 year maturity bond was originally issued with a 6% yield to maturity and a 25 year maturity but currently has 20 years of remaining maturity.

are illustrated in Exhibit 5. At low interest rates the influence of the premium and the OID dominate, thus increasing the yield to maturity increases duration. At higher interest rates, when the bond sells at a market discount, the discount rate influence dominates and duration is a decreasing function of the yield to maturity.

Understanding the effect of coupon and yield to maturity illuminates the positive influence that taxes have on duration. An increase in the marginal tax rate effectively lowers both the after-tax coupon and the after-tax discount rate, both of which cause an increase in duration. The influence of taxes on duration is illustrated in Exhibits 1 through 5 which show duration at 50%, 28%, and 0% marginal tax rates.

Tax Laws

We now turn to the effects of recent and pending tax laws. Comparing Exhibits 1 and 2 shows that the tax law of 1982 requiring compound interest amortization of OIDs decreases the duration of all OID bonds issued after July 1, 1982 (the amount of the

EXHIBIT 5
AFTER-TAX DURATION OF A 10 YEAR BOND WITH A 4% COUPON, CURRENTLY
SELLING IN THE SECONDARY MARKET AT VARIOUS YIELDS TO MATURITY
(ISSUED ON OR AFTER JULY 1, 1982 AND PURCHASED ON OR AFTER
SEPTEMBER 27, 1985)

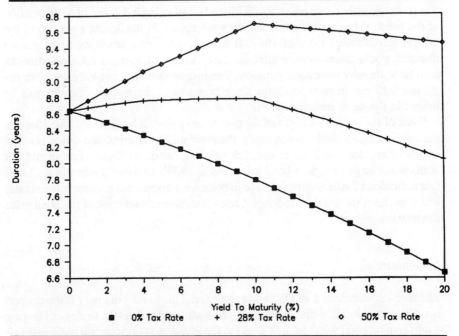

Note: The bond was originally issued two years earlier (12 year maturity) with an OID to yield 10% before tax. The OID bond sales in the secondary market at a premium when YTM < 4%, at an acquisition premium when 4% < YTM < 10%, and at a market discount when YTM > 10%.

decrease in duration affected by the 1982 law is greatest for zero coupon bonds). By requiring compound interest amortization of OID, the 1982 tax law increases early after-tax cash flows and decreases distant after-tax cash flows relative to straight line amortization.

The 1984 tax law requires that the market discount be taxed at ordinary rates for all bonds issued after July 18, 1984 (no longer allowing favorable capital gains treatment). Our duration formula could be modified to show this change by allowing for a second tax rate, τ_c, in the final term of (11). The obvious effect of the 1984 tax law is to decrease the final after-tax cash flows of market discount bonds, thus decreasing duration in cases of market discount.

The Tax Reform Act (TRA) of 1986 began a process of gradually lowering marginal tax rates over several years until the top marginal rates for individuals are 33%, and 34% for corporations. As shown above, the lower marginal tax rates result in higher levels of after-tax duration. The TRA of 1986 also mandated the compound interest method of amortizing market premiums which results in a slight shift of part of the early cash flows to later periods, consequently increasing duration. Finally, in 1986, straight line amortization of acquisition premium was changed for bonds purchased after July 19, 1984, resulting in higher levels of duration.

On October 29, 1987, the House passed a proposal to begin requiring investors to pay taxes annually on discount bonds instead of allowing a deferral until disposition of the bonds. The proposed tax rule does not appear in the Senate's version of the Budget Reconciliation Act of 1987. If passed, the annual amortization of market discount would lower interim after-tax cash flows and increase the final after-tax cash flow, thereby increasing duration. The proposed change could be easily incorporated into our general formulas since presumably the market discount will be treated in the same manner as OID.

Some of the tax law changes of the past several years have increased the after-tax duration of bonds and consequently their volatility, whereas the other tax law changes have decreased the after-tax duration of bonds. However, one should not attribute the large swings in bond prices in the 1980's to these changes in tax laws. Our definition of volatility is a change in price for a given change in the interest rate, and it has been the changes in interest rates that have caused most of the bond price fluctuations.

Immunization

The after-tax duration of an OID bond can exceed the bond's maturity if the coupon is sufficiently low (Exhibits 1 and 2).[19] The traditional before-tax strategy of buying a zero coupon bond with maturity equal to the investment horizon will obviously fail for a taxable investor. Instead, the investor should buy a sufficiently low coupon bond with duration, maturity, and investment horizon being equal. For a bond issued before July 1, 1982, this would be a bond whose coupon payments would exactly offset the tax liability, resulting in zero net interim cash flows. In the pre-1982 case, the tax liability each period comes from straight line amortization of the difference between the bond's par value and the initial purchase price:

$$T_t = \frac{\tau\left(P - P^i\right)}{M^i} \tag{21}$$

With the coupon offsetting the tax liability, the full value of the bond comes at maturity, making the duration equal to the maturity of the bond. Using Equations (2) and (21), we can solve for the coupon which will offset the tax liability and permit duration to equal maturity.

---

[19]See Kalotay, "An Analysis of Original Issue Discount Bonds."

$$C = \frac{\tau(P - P^{i})}{M^{i}(1 - \tau)} \qquad (22)$$

$$= \frac{\tau \cdot P \cdot Y \cdot \text{PVIFA}}{M^{i}(1 - \tau) + \tau \cdot \text{PVIFA}}.$$

where PVIFA is the present value annuity factor at rate Y for M periods.

For a bond issued post-1982, the tax liability is not constant each period. The coupon payments would only offset the changing tax liability on average over the life of the bond but it would be possible to have a low coupon bond with a duration equal to maturity.

For example, using Exhibit 1, an investor in a 28% marginal tax bracket who bought a pre-1982 issued bond yielding 12% with a 2.19% coupon would have a 10 year bond with zero net cash flows in the interim years. The coupon payment would just equal the tax liability and the duration would equal maturity. For an investor with a 50% marginal tax rate, a bond with a 4.37% coupon would accomplish the same thing. Under the new tax law, although taxes vary each period, the level of the coupon at which duration would equal maturity is 1.74% and 3.68% for investors with 28% and 50% marginal tax rates respectively.

SUMMARY

In the preceding analysis, the closed-form expressions for the after-tax duration of a bond have been derived. The expressions encompass all bonds (OID, market discount, acquisition premium, and premium), are closed form, and reflect the most recent tax laws. After deriving general duration formulas, specific cases were looked at including the Hessel and Hoffman case of market discount and the Kalotay case of OID, along with the specific case of zero coupon bonds.

These duration formulas were used first to examine the determinants of bond volatility in an after-tax environment. They are coupon, term to maturity, yield to maturity, and the marginal tax rate. A bond's after-tax duration increases with the marginal tax rate, and decreases with the level of coupon. Practically, after-tax duration increases with maturity; however, for bonds with deep market discounts, duration increases, decreases, then finally levels off as maturity increases. After-tax duration generally decreases with yield to maturity, yet for bonds with deep OID and bonds that sell at a premium, duration can increase with yield to maturity. We analyzed the specific effects of recent and pending tax laws on duration. Lastly, we used the duration formulas to develop after-tax immunization which is accomplished by buying a particular low coupon bond with duration, maturity, and the investment horizon all being equal.

APPENDIX A
MATHEMATICAL RELATIONSHIPS USED IN THE DURATION CALCULATIONS

Two relationships are frequently used in the analysis in the chapter. The first is the relationship:

$$\sum_{t=1}^{M} t\,(1+r)^{-t} = \frac{1}{r}\left[(1+r)\,\text{PVIFA} - \frac{M}{(1+r)^{M}}\right] \tag{A1}$$

where PVIFA is the present value annuity factor at rate r for M periods given as:

$$\text{PVIFA} = \frac{(1+r)^{M} - 1}{r\,(1+r)^{M}} = \sum_{t=1}^{M} (1+r)^{-t}$$

Equation (A1) is derived by Chua in the following way. Let S be equal to:

$$S = \sum_{t=1}^{M} t(1+r)^{-t} \tag{A2}$$

If the expression $\text{PVIFA} + S/(1+r) - S$ is formed, all but one of the terms in the summations cancel out, leaving:

$$\text{PVIFA} + \frac{S}{(1+r)} - S = \frac{M}{(1+r)^{M+1}} \tag{A3}$$

Solving for S gives (A1).

The second relationship used in deriving the closed form expression is:

$$G = \sum_{t=1}^{M} t(1+r)^{t-1} \tag{A4}$$

$$= \frac{(1+r)^{M}(rM - 1) + 1}{r^{2}}$$

This is derived as follows. Let F be the compound value annuity factor:

$$F = \sum_{t=1}^{M} (1+r)^{t-1} \qquad \text{(A5)}$$

$$= \frac{(1+r)^M - 1}{r}$$

If we form the expression $F + G - G/(1+r)$, most of the terms in the summations will cancel, leaving:

$$F + G - \frac{G}{(1+r)} = (M+1)(1+r)^{M-1} - (1+r)^{-1} \qquad \text{(A6)}$$

Solving for G and substituting in the value for F gives (A4).

APPENDIX B
ADJUSTED ISSUE PRICE USING CONSTANT RATE AMORTIZATION

The adjusted issue price of a bond with an OID which is amortized using the constant rate amortization can be written as:

$$AIP_0 = P^i$$

$$AIP_1 = AIP_0(1+Y^i) - C$$

$$AIP_2 = AIP_1(1+Y^i) - C$$

$$\vdots$$

In general, the relationship will be:

$$\text{AIP}_j = \text{AIP}_{j-1}\left(1 + Y^i\right) - C \tag{B1}$$

$$= P^i\left(1 + Y^i\right)^j - C \sum_{k=1}^{j}\left(1 + Y^i\right)^{k-1}$$

$$= P^i\left(1 + Y^i\right)^j - C\left[\frac{\left(1 + Y^i\right)^j - 1}{Y^i}\right]$$

where:
- AIP_j = the adjusted issue price in period j
- P^i = the initial issue price of the bond
- Y^i = the initial before-tax yield to maturity on the issue date
- C = the coupon interest payment

The gain in adjusted issue price from one period to the next is considered taxable income to the investor and is equal to:

$$\text{AIP}_j - \text{AIP}_{j-1} = P^i\left(1 + Y^i\right)^j - C\sum_{k=1}^{j}\left(1 + Y^i\right)^{k-1} \tag{B2}$$

$$- P^i\left(1 + Y^i\right)^{j-1} + C\sum_{k=1}^{j-1}\left(1 + Y^i\right)^{k-1}$$

$$= \left(Y^i P^i - C\right)\left(1 + Y^i\right)^{j-1}$$

If the bond was issued some time previous to the time of purchase by the investor, we can write the change in adjusted issue price with respect to the investor's time of purchase as:

$$\text{AIP}_t - \text{AIP}_{t-1} = \left(Y^i P^i - C\right)\left(1 + Y^i\right)^{t + \left(M^i - M\right) - 1} \tag{B3}$$

where the date j from the original time line is shifted by the difference between initial maturity when issued and maturity when purchased to conform to the new time line.

Chapter 10

Beyond Cash Matching

T. DESSA FABOZZI, PH.D.
VICE PRESIDENT
FINANCIAL STRATEGIES GROUP
MERRILL LYNCH CAPITAL MARKETS

TOM TONG
VICE PRESIDENT
STRUCTURED INVESTMENTS GROUP
MERRILL LYNCH CAPITAL MARKETS

YU ZHU, PH.D.
VICE PRESIDENT
STRUCTURED INVESTMENTS GROUP
MERRILL LYNCH CAPITAL MARKETS

Since Hodges and Schaefer proposed the cash matching model more than a decade ago,[1] cash matching has become an important portfolio strategy and has been widely applied in asset/liability management.[2] The purpose of this chapter is to propose

---

[1]See S. D. Hodges and S. M. Schaefer, "A Model for Bond Portfolio Improvement," *Journal of Financial and Quantitative Analysis*, June 1977.

[2]Direct applications of this strategy include debt defeasance, pension fund (or insurance company) liability funding, and others.

three new strategies which use cash matching as their core. These strategies demonstrate that cash matching can easily be adapted and extended to a broad range of applications with different investment objectives. After a brief review of the cash matching strategy,[3] we introduce consecutively the symmetric cash matching, multifund optimization and reversed cash matching strategies. Examples are given for each strategy.

REVIEW OF CASH MATCHING

The cash matching strategy uses an optimization procedure to select a least expensive bond portfolio to fund a liability stream. Strict application of the cash matching strategy would structure a portfolio such that the cash inflows exactly match liability outflows. If there exists a complete capital market, this asset creation becomes trivial because a zero coupon bond would be available whose maturity matches each future liability date. In reality, the capital market is not complete and, since the number of securities available are limited, a perfect match is hardly possible. Because the matching of cash inflows to liabilities is not perfect, a portfolio is set up such that cash flows occurring on or before a liability date are used to meet the liability. A surplus usually exists on the liability date, which is then used to satisfy future liability requirements. In this way, the risk of shortfall is eliminated.

Because the cash matching strategy is based on matching cash inflows and outflows, the resulting portfolio's performance (assuming zero reinvestment) will not be affected by future interest rate fluctuations. Thus, its interest rate risk is minimal.[4] The up-front cost of a cash matching strategy may be higher than other popular bond portfolio strategies, such as immunization.[5] This is partially due to the fact that it requires stricter constraints. Also, securities applicable for the cash matching strategy are limited.[6] However, the cash matched portfolio does not need rebalancing after it is structured, and, unless a bond issue defaults, the risk that the liability will not be met is minimal. As discussed in a recent paper by Maloney and

---

[3]We will use cash matching and dedication strategies interchangeably in this chapter. Some researchers distinguish the two strategies. For an example, see Logue and Maloney, "Neglected Complexities in Structured Bond Portfolios," *The Journal of Portfolio Management*, Winter 1989, pp. 59-68. According to their definitions, the base strategy we are using for comparison and extension is dedication, although we will refer to it as cash matching.

[4]In practice, a conservative reinvestment rate is usually assumed. As will be demonstrated in symmetric cash matching, changes in this assumed reinvestment rate will affect the portfolio's performance. In addition, there exists default risk which may be related to the level of interest rates.

[5]The immunization strategy matches durations of assets and liabilities. If future interest rate movements follow the theoretical assumptions implied in the strategy, the present value of the assets will always be greater than or equal to the present value of the liabilities. However, this strategy needs frequent rebalancing and does not guarantee that the liability stream will be covered.

[6]Securities whose cash flows are uncertain, such as mortgage-backed securities and callable bonds, are not suitable for cash matching.

Logue,[7] if transaction costs are considered, the total cost of an immunized portfolio may not be lower than the corresponding portfolio constructed using a cash matching strategy.

SYMMETRIC CASH MATCHING

Cash matching uses only cash flows occurring on or before a liability date to meet the liability. An extended cash matching strategy which we will call "symmetric cash matching" uses cash flows occurring both before and after the liability date to meet a particular liability. We have chosen the name symmetric cash matching because the cash flows used to meet the liability stream can lie symmetrically around the liability date although, in actuality, both the resulting cash flow timing and amount which result from the employment of this technique are rarely symmetric.

Symmetric cash matching requires that the firm incur short-term borrowing when using the cash flows beyond the liability date to satisfy the liability. The short-term borrowed funds are repaid immediately upon the receipt of cash flows from the investment portfolio. Thus, the borrowing may occur for a period of one day to the number of days until the next liability date. Liability needs are still met with the portfolio cash flow, but the cash flow structure is less rigid than under a straight cash matching strategy. Security selection with symmetric cash matching becomes easier and the cost may be lower.[8] Also, since the short-term debt is backed by the portfolio's cash inflow, risk is minimized.

To understand the benefits of symmetric cash matching we will compare it to a cash matching portfolio strategy. In both cases, linear programming will be employed to find the optimal portfolio required to fund the liability stream.

An Illustration of Symmetric Cash Matching

Suppose XYZ company must meet a liability stream totaling $105,262,000 over the period from February 1988 to February 1994. The company wishes to construct a bond portfolio to fund this liability stream. In the analysis, the firm specifies a borrowing rate of 8% for short-term loans (less than six months, the time period between liability dates) and a reinvestment rate for mismatched funds of 6%. The firm also limits the universe of bonds for the constructed portfolio to noncallable Treasury securities, thus avoiding default, call, and event risks.

The liability stream the portfolio manager wishes to fund is as follows:

---

[7] See Maloney and Logue, "Neglected Complexities in Structured Bond Portfolios."

[8] A symmetric cash matching strategy may not represent the lower cost solution over a straight cash matching approach in all cases. It will be most beneficial when the liability dates are between cash flow dates for the bonds in the portfolio.

Date	Liability	Date	Liability
2/10/88	$3,912,500	2/10/91	$ 8,112,000
8/10/88	5,913,500	8/10/91	13,112,500
2/10/89	3,650,000	2/10/92	12,368,750
8/10/89	3,650,000	8/10/92	11,637,500
2/10/90	3,650,000	2/10/93	11,275,000
8/10/90	6,650,000	8/10/93	10,881,250
		2/15/94	10,450,000

A straight cash matched solution will result in the purchase of 13 Treasury securities at a total dollar cost of $78,640,000. The cash flows from this portfolio and the liability stream are illustrated in Exhibit 1. As can be seen from the exhibit, the cash flows from the bond portfolio are more than sufficient to cover the current liabilities, resulting in a positive ending cash balance in each period. These funds will be reinvested at an annual reinvestment rate of 6%. At the end of the investment horizon, the firm is left with a surplus of $665.

We reoptimized the problem using a symmetric cash matching technique for two cases. In the first case, we allowed the firm to borrow 100% of the liability due each period. In the second case, we allowed the firm to borrow only 50% of the liability due each period. In both cases, the amount borrowed was repaid immediately from subsequent bond portfolio cash flows.

In the case where borrowing 100% of the liability was allowed, the solution resulted in the purchase of 13 Treasury securities (although a different basket of securities than suggested under the dedication strategy) at a total dollar cost of $78,030,000. The cash flows from this portfolio and liability stream are illustrated in Exhibit 2. As can be seen from the "borrowing inflows," the firm borrows funds in each period tó meet the current liability. The resulting cash surplus at the end of the investment horizon is $150. When the firm is allowed to borrow only 50% of the liability in each period, the cost of the portfolio will be $78,320,000 and the solution requires the purchase of 21 bonds. The cash balance at the end of the horizon is $1,060. The cash flows from this solution are shown in Exhibit 3. From this exhibit, it is easy to understand why we have chosen the name of symmetric cash matching for this strategy.

We see that the firm can save close to $600,000 on the initial cost of constructing the bond portfolio by using symmetric cash matching when the the firm is permitted to borrow 100% of the liability. When the firm is only allowed to borrow 50% of its liability in each period, it still can save over $300,000 on the portfolio construction cost. Both cases represent a substantial savings to the firm compared to a straight cash matching strategy. The firm is afforded greater savings when allowed to borrow more of the liability flow. This is due to the greater flexibility allowed in constructing the portfolio.

Although the borrowing rate is 200 basis points above the reinvestment rate, using symmetric cash matching allows a better match of the timing of liability payments to

EXHIBIT 1
CASH MATCHING STRATEGY
RATES: REINVESTMENT 6%   BORROWING 8%

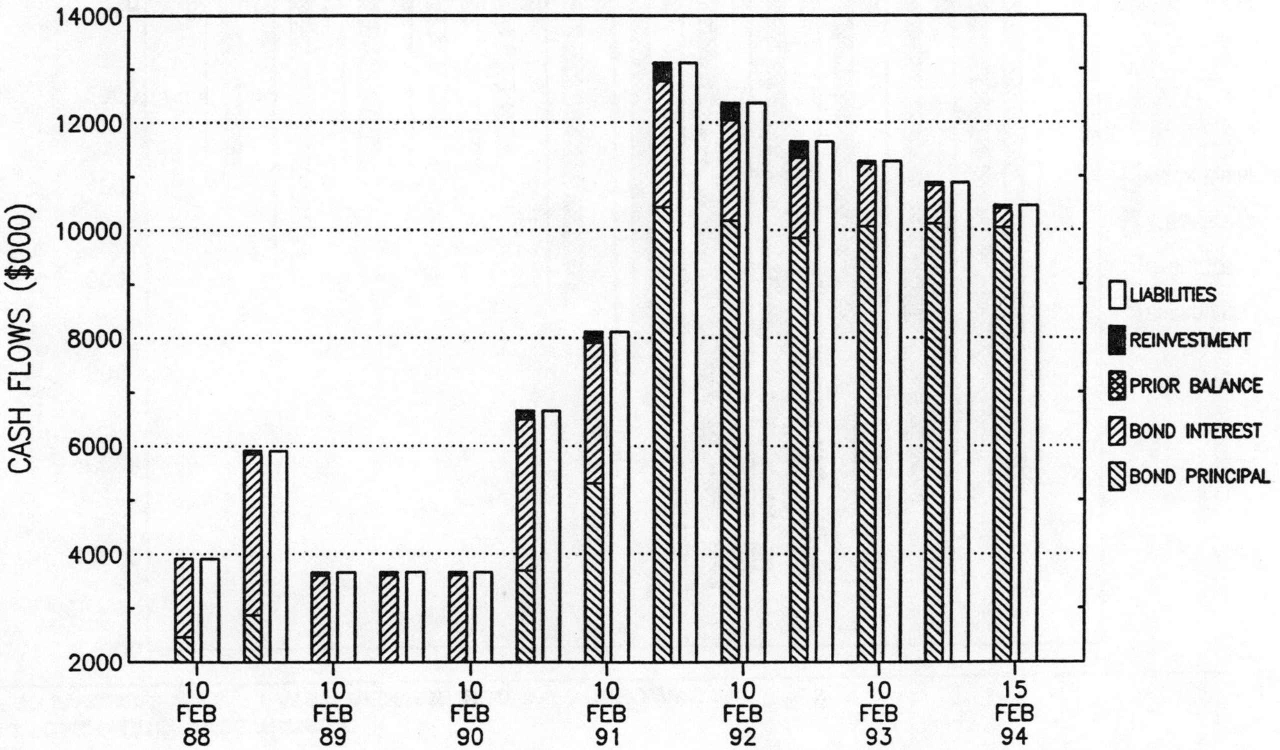

Legend:
☐ LIABILITIES
■ REINVESTMENT
▨ PRIOR BALANCE
▨ BOND INTEREST
▨ BOND PRINCIPAL

CASH FLOWS ($000)

14000 12000 10000 8000 6000 4000 2000

10 FEB 88   10 FEB 89   10 FEB 90   10 FEB 91   10 FEB 92   10 FEB 93   15 FEB 94

EXHIBIT 2
SYMMETRIC CASH MATCHING STRATEGY
BORROWING MAXIMUM: 100%   RATES: REINVESTMENT 6%, BORROWING 8%

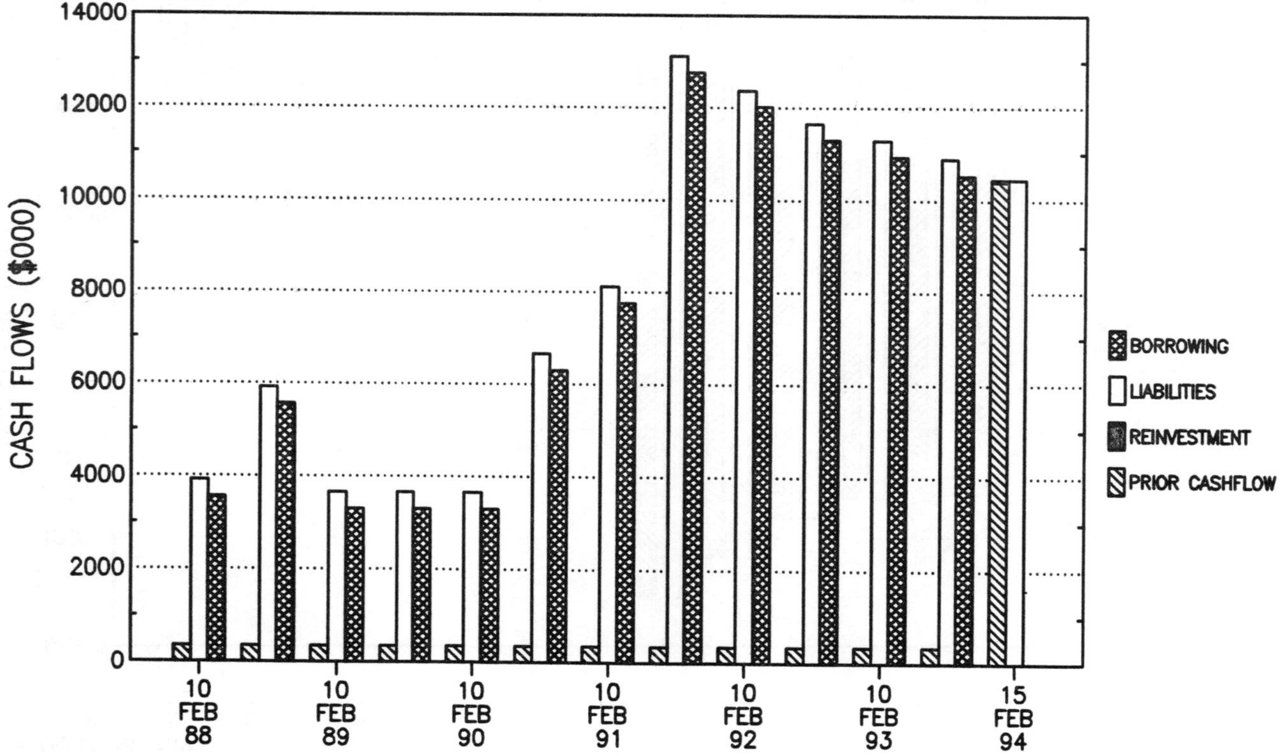

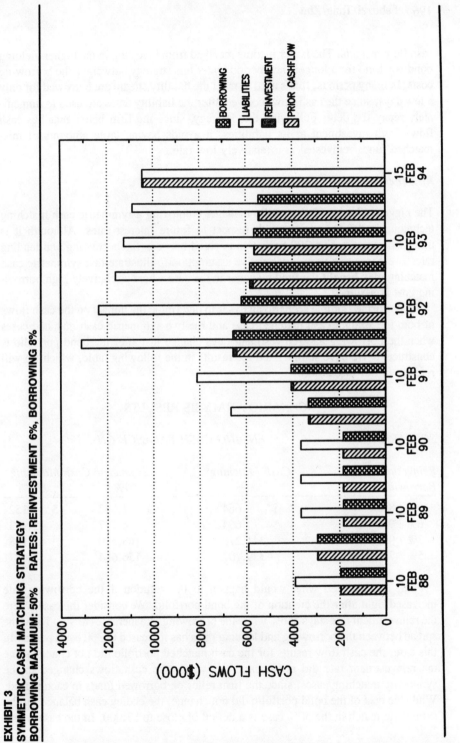

EXHIBIT 3
SYMMETRIC CASH MATCHING STRATEGY
BORROWING MAXIMUM: 50%   RATES: REINVESTMENT 6%, BORROWING 8%

cash flow receipts. The larger income received from investing in the higher yielding bond portfolio for a longer time period under this strategy outweighs the borrowing costs. In many periods, funds used to meet the liability stream are borrowed for only a few days, since the cash flow received after the liability dates are used to immediately repay the debt. Following this strategy, since the firm better matches cash flows from investment to its liabilities, it avoids having large amounts of mismatched funds reinvested at a relatively low rate.

Risk Incurred With Symmetric Cash Matching

The biggest concern of a portfolio manager employing a symmetric cash matching technique is the uncertainty with respect to future interest rates. Although it is unrealistic to assume a 200 basis point spread between the borrowing and lending rates, we chose this very conservative assumption to illustrate that symmetric cash matching may benefit the fund manager in the case where a relatively high borrowing cost is assumed.

We performed simple scenario analyses to determine the impact on the cash flows of both the straight cash matched case and the two symmetric cash matched cases when the borrowing and reinvestment rates change just after the bond portfolio is constructed. We have summarized the results in the following table, which we will refer to in our discussion.

SCENARIO ANALYSIS RESULTS

SCENARIO:	ENDING CASH BALANCE ON 2/15/94:		
Reinvestment/	Cash Matching	Symmetric Cash Matching	
Borrowing		50%	100%
6% / 8%	$ 664	$ 1,062	$ 152
6% / 9%	664	−6,717	−15,903
7% / 9%	341,278	163,510	−3,168
5% / 7%	−339,707	−156,684	2,487

First, we analyzed what would happen to the solution if the borrowing rate increased right after the creation of the bond portfolio. We consider the case where the reinvestment rate stays at 6% while the borrowing rate increases to 9%. Thus, the spread between the borrowing and lending rates has increased to 300 basis points. In this case, the cash flow results for the cash matched portfolio did not change since the reinvestment rate did not change. However, the cash flows changed in the symmetric matching cases, since the firm relies on borrowed funds in each period. While the cost of the bond portfolio did not change, the ending cash balance for the symmetric match in the 50% case is a deficit of close to $7,000. In the case where

100% borrowing of the liability was allowed, the deficit amounted to approximately $16,000. Thus, a symmetric cash matching portfolio will be adversely affected if borrowing costs rise while reinvestment rates remain constant. However, the magnitude of these deficits are low relative to the size of the liability stream and the initial savings from using symmetric cash matching to construct the bond portfolio. Since the deficit is in future value terms, its present value is lower.

Next, we took the initial case and shifted both interest rates up by 100 basis points (parallel shift) so that the spread between these two rates remains the same as in the initial case. Thus the new borrowing rate is 9% and the new reinvestment rate is 7%. Again we assume that the change occurs immediately after the portfolio construction. For this scenario, the ending balance in the 50% symmetric cash matched portfolio was a gain of approximately $163,500. A negative balance of close to $3,000 occurred in the 100% case. The cash matched portfolio reported a gain of over $340,000. This example demonstrates the impact of reinvestment income on the portfolios. In the 50% case, the gain in reinvestment income outweighs the higher borrowing cost since, in most cases, the borrowing occurs only for a short time after the liability date.[9] The 100% case reported a small negative ending balance. Since this case relies more heavily on short-term borrowing, the borrowing costs outweigh the benefits of additional reinvestment income. As can be seen in this example, the variance in cash flows resulting from symmetric cash matching are lower than the straight cash matching strategy. This is because the impact of a change in the borrowing rate partly offsets the effect of a change in the reinvestment rate on portfolio cash flows.

When we shifted both interest rates down by 100 basis points (with a borrowing rate equal to 7% and a reinvestment rate of 5%), the cash matched portfolio resulted in a negative ending cash balance of over $300,000, again demonstrating its strong reliance on reinvestment income. The symmetric cash matched portfolio for the 50% case resulted in a loss of over $150,000 and the 100% case reported a small gain of approximately $2,500. The shortfall in the 50% borrowing case resulted from the lost reinvestment income outweighing the fall in short-term borrowing costs. In the 100% case, the gain from a reduction in borrowing cost outweighed the loss in reinvestment income from interim cash flows.

In the scenario analysis results presented above, we can see that there is a tradeoff between a lower initial cost of constructing the portfolio with the possible risk of a rise in borrowing costs and the benefit to be derived from a cash matched portfolio if reinvestment rates rise above those assumed in the portfolio construction. However, if reinvestment rates fell during the period, the portfolio manager could lose a substantial amount of income that he was relying on in the cash matched portfolio. Since future interest rates are uncertain and the portfolio manager of a structured investment fund is not in the business of predicting interest rates, this interest rate

---

[9]Because we chose a large spread between the borrowing rate and the reinvestment rate, the optimal solution will only utilize borrowed funds for short time periods.

play should not be considered when constructing a portfolio to fund a liability stream.

Summary of Symmetric Cash Matching

Symmetric cash matching allows a firm to better match cash flows from a portfolio to liability needs. By allowing the firm to meet liability cash flows from both cash inflows occurring before the liability date and from borrowing cash inflows expected just beyond the liability date, the firm may be able to realize substantial savings on the cost of constructing the portfolio. The more flexibility the manager is afforded in terms of borrowing interim cash flows, the better the firm is able to match cash outflows to actual and expected cash inflows from the bond portfolio. Even if a restriction is placed on the amount of the liability which can be borrowed each period, the cost savings may be substantial over a straight cash matched strategy.

The difference in bond default risk of a cash matched versus a symmetric matched fund is insignificant if both strategies choose bonds from the same quality rating universe to construct the funding portfolio. All borrowing is backed by the expected cash inflows and is of very short duration, since loans are repaid as cash flows are received. Thus, the higher cost of borrowing is more than outweighed by the better matching of cash flows, allowing a higher yielding portfolio to be purchased.

In addition, in a symmetric cash matched portfolio, since the impact of a change in the reinvestment rate to some extent offsets the impact of the change in the borrowing rate (assuming that both rates move in the same direction), the risk of an adverse change in reinvestment rates is lower than in a cash matched fund. This is because a straight cash matched portfolio relies heavily on the assumed reinvestment rate when the portfolio is constructed.

MULTIFUND OPTIMIZATION

In this section, we will describe a strategy to optimally create several distinct but linked portfolios to satisfy various aspects of one particular objective. Each portfolio would have a specific universe of bonds from which to choose as well as its own liability and other specialized constraints. We demonstrate that these portfolios in a multifund problem should be constructed simultaneously, minimizing the total cost of the portfolios while meeting the individual fund constraints. We will refer to this strategy as "multifund cash matching." This strategy represents a more efficient and less costly solution than a naive approach, which optimizes each fund separately.

A Multifund Problem

Consider for example a municipality which issues bonds to finance a construction project—say, a bridge. It expects that the first stage of the construction project will take three years. After completion of the first phase, the municipality will start to collect income in the form of tolls which will be used to repay the issued debt and finance future expenditures. The proceeds of the bond issue will be used for two purposes: (1) to meet the expenses of the project and (2) to service the issued debt.

Two separate portfolios are to be formed. A "construction fund" will be set up to finance the expected costs for the first phase of the project. This fund will consist of a portfolio of bonds structured so that the investment income from the portfolio will be sufficient to fund the project. Next, a "capitalized interest fund" will be set up to service the debt during the initial phase of the project (in this case, three years), while project income is not yet forthcoming.

Considering possible delays in the completion of the project and uncertainty in future income from the project, sometimes one or more "debt service reserve funds" are constructed to service the debt beyond the period serviced by the capitalized interest fund. For simplicity, in this example, we consider only one construction fund and one capitalized interest fund, although our analysis could be easily extended to cases involving more than two funds.

In practice, a very conservative investment strategy is employed for the capitalized interest fund to insure full servicing of the debt. Investments in this fund may be restricted to only Treasury securities and it is usually " grossly funded." This means that at all times during the life of the fund, the fund will have sufficient income to service interest payments on the municipal debt, even with zero return on the investment.

The pool of securities available for investment in the construction fund is less restrictive. In addition to Treasury securities, government agency bonds and high-quality corporate bonds are considered. Surpluses in earnings from the capitalized interest fund are transferred to the construction fund during the period, although there are restrictions on the cash flow considered to be transferable.[10]

Multifund Solution versus Naive Cash Matching

The portfolios for the separate funds can be structured individually by applying a cash matching strategy to each fund. However, this would be an inefficient approach since it ignores the fact that all funds are serving a common objective and are linked through intra-fund cash flows. The multiple fund strategy takes into consideration the linkage among funds. This strategy constructs all funds simultaneously, such that

---

[10]In addition to interest income from investment, bond accretion and amortization may have an important impact on the amount of permissible cash flow from the capitalized interest fund to the construction fund. For a premium bond, the amount of amortization is often deducted from its interest income and not allowed to be transferred to the construction fund. Sometimes the amount of accretion on other discount bonds in the portfolio can be used to offset the amortization. The most conservative strategy and the one used in our example is with amortization, but without accretion. Of course, the amortization (accretion) method is also important. Also, in most cases, accrued interest is not permitted to flow out of this fund.

each portfolio meets its own liability requirements and other constraints. At the same time, the strategy channels permissible surpluses from the capitalized interest fund and debt servicing reserve funds to the construction fund to minimize the overall cost of financing.

The procedure for structuring the construction fund and the capitalized interest fund is as follows:[11]

(1) Minimize the total cost of the portfolios;
(2) For the capitalized interest fund:
    a. It must be grossly funded;
    b. The cash flow from this portfolio on each debt service date must be sufficient to service the debt; and
    c. Permissible surpluses can be transferred to the construction fund;
(3) For the construction fund, all the cash flows from its bond portfolio plus the permissible surpluses from other funds must meet construction draw requirements on or before the draw dates specified.

An Illustration of Multifund Optimization

Suppose ABC Port Authority has just issued fixed rate revenue bonds to finance its construction project. It plans to set up one construction fund and one capitalized interest rate fund to finance this project. The construction fund has the following payment schedule:

Date	Liability	Date	Liability
6/1/88	$1,000,000	6/1/89	$2,200,000
7/1/88	1,000,000	7/1/89	650,000
8/1/88	1,350,000	8/1/89	575,000
9/1/88	1,300,000	9/1/89	1,165,000
10/1/88	1,181,000	10/1/89	1,490,000
11/1/88	1,150,000	11/1/89	2,458,000
12/1/88	1,665,000	12/1/89	3,891,000
1/1/89	1,850,000	1/1/90	3,296,000
2/1/89	2,005,000	2/1/90	1,635,000
3/1/89	2,115,000	3/1/90	1,148,000
4/1/89	2,800,000	4/1/90	1,831,000
5/1/89	2,245,000		

Total Liabilities: $40,000,000

---

[11]A debt service fund can be struetured which is similar to the capitalized interest fund.

The capitalized interest fund has debt service requirements as follows:

Date	Liability
8/1/88	$2,317,504
2/1/89	2,317,504
8/1/89	2,317,504
2/1/90	2,317,504
4/2/90	772,501

Total Liabilities: $10,042,517

Both funds are restricted to purchase only U.S. Treasury bonds and government agency bonds. In addition, the assumed reinvestment rate is zero and the amortized amount of premium bonds in the capitalized interest fund cannot be transferred to the construction fund.

Multifund Solution: The optimal portfolios for the construction fund and the capitalized interest fund using the multifund optimization strategy are presented in Exhibits 4 and 5. The total cost for the two funds is $45,477,877 ($35,472,044 for the construction fund and $10,005,833 for the capitalized interest fund). All requirements for each fund are satisfied.

Naive Solution: For comparison purposes, a naive method is also used to construct these portfolios. The naive method for structuring the two portfolios involves two steps. First, the capitalized interest fund is constructed. Since this must be grossly funded and the interest income after amortization may be eligible for transferral to the construction fund, the fund's objective is to maximize a weighted average of cash flow surplus. The weights are defined by the timing of their receipt. The closer in time is the cash flow surplus, the higher is the corresponding weight.[12] The next step is to structure the construction fund. The objective here is to minimize the portfolio cost, taking into consideration permissible cash flow transfers from the capitalized interest fund.

The solutions, although not presented here, meet all the requirements set by ABC Port Authority. The same dollar amount is invested in the capitalized interest fund and the total cost of the construction fund is $35,531,076. This is $59,032 (or 17 basis points) higher than the multifund solution. The outcome of this *ad hoc* approach is considered satisfactory.

Comparison: The reason for the closeness in the multifund and the naive solutions is that, in the case of only two funds (construction and capitalized interest fund), it is

---

[12]For instance, these weights can be proportional to the prices of discount bonds maturing at corresponding surplus dates, but this is not necessarily the best selection.

EXHIBIT 4
CONSTRUCTION FUND—BOND SELECTION
SETTLEMENT DATE: 2/01/1988

Bond	Coupon	Maturity	Par Amount	Price	Flat Price	Accrued	Full Price	Yield
FD HOME L	8.800	06/27/1988	570	100.68750	573,918.75	4,737.33	578,656.08	6.99851
FD HOME L	9.150	07/25/1988	810	101.09375	818,859.38	1,235.25	820,094.63	6.80230
FD HOME L	6.350	08/25/1988	910	99.65625	906,871.88	25,040.17	931,912.05	6.96763
FD HOME L	8.000	09/26/1988	930	100.70777	936,582.30	26,040.00	962,622.30	6.84970
FD HOME L	6.350	10/25/1988	940	99.46875	935,006.25	15,917.33	950,923.58	7.08659
T-NOTE	6.250	11/30/1988	1,335	99.56250	1,329,159.38	14,362.19	1,343,521.57	6.78753
FD HOME L	10.700	12/27/1988	1,610	103.15625	1,660,815.63	16,269.95	1,677,085.58	7.02534
FD HOME L	11.375	01/25/1989	1,560	103.96875	1,621,912.50	2,957.50	1,624,870.00	7.12120
FD HOME L	15.100	02/27/1989	4,320	107.06250	4,625,100.00	279,048.00	4,904,148.00	8.07361
FD HOME L	6.900	04/25/1989	2,070	99.56250	2,060,943.75	38,088.00	2,099,031.75	7.26404
T-NOTE	8.000	05/31/1989	1,915	101.12500	1,936,543.75	26,370.49	1,962,914.24	7.08481
FD HOME L	7.700	06/26/1989	510	100.62500	513,187.50	3,817.92	517,005.42	7.21543
FD HOME L	14.125	07/25/1989	290	109.12500	316,462.50	682.71	317,145.21	7.50682
T-NOTE	7.750	08/31/1989	1,125	100.73360	1,133,253.05	36,887.02	1,170,140.07	7.24320
FD HOME L	14.550	09/25/1989	1,260	110.56250	1,393,087.50	64,165.50	1,457,253.00	7.59931
FD HOME L	9.350	10/25/1989	2,350	103.06250	2,421,968.75	57,982.99	2,479,951.74	7.42160
FD HOME L	11.550	11/27/1989	3,670	106.43750	3,906,256.25	75,357.33	3,981,613.58	7.68198
FD HOME L	8.250	12/26/1989	3,170	101.19057	3,207,741.07	23,973.13	3,231,714.20	7.56040
FD HOME L	6.550	01/25/1990	2,610	97.93750	2,556,168.75	2,849.25	2,559,018.00	7.68997
FD HOME L	11.900	03/26/1990	1,690	108.43750	1,832,593.75	69,829.86	1,902,423.61	7.56718
			33,645		34,686,432.69	785,611.92	35,472,044.61	

EXHIBIT 5
CAPITALIZED INTEREST FUND—BOND SELECTION
SETTLEMENT DATE: 2/01/1988

Bond	Coupon	Maturity	Par Amount	Price	Flat Price	Accrued	Full Price	Yield
FD HOME L	9.150	07/25/1988	2,090	101.09375	2,112,859.38	3,187.25	2,116,046.63	6.80230
FD HOME L	11.375	01/25/1989	2,150	103.96875	2,235,328.13	4,076.04	2,239,404.17	7.12120
FD HOME L	14.125	07/25/1989	2,190	109.12500	2,389,837.50	5,155.63	2,394,993.13	7.50682
FD HOME L	11.200	01/25/1990	2,260	106.50000	2,406,900.00	4,218.67	2,411,118.67	7.60563
FD HOME L	11.900	03/26/1990	750	108.43750	813,281.25	30,989.58	844,270.83	7.56718
			9,440		9,958,206.26	47,627.17	10,005,833.43	

possible to find a set of weights by trial and error that would produce a reasonably good solution. This is a time consuming process. If more than two funds are involved, the process of choosing weights for the naive solution becomes more complicated and the difference between the multifund solution and the naive approach may be substantial. Multifund cash matching is clearly the better choice.[13]

Summary of Multifund Optimization

We demonstrated the benefits from using multifund optimization for the case where a firm or municipality must construct several funds to service one objective. Since the multifund optimization technique optimizes all funds simultaneously and considers all intra-fund cash flows, it represents the most efficient solution to this problem. Although a naive approach may come close to the optimal solution in the case of a limited number of funds, the complexity of the problem increases as the number of funds increases. The naive approach will lead to a suboptimal solution to the multifund problem.

REVERSED CASH MATCHING

In many cases, a firm faces the situation where it expects to receive a set of cash inflows with a large degree of predictability.[14] A relevant question to ask is: How can the firm benefit from these cash flows in the current period? One possible answer is that the firm can issue debt supported by the cash inflows, freeing current funds while immediately defeasing the issued debt. This represents a low-risk financing strategy for the firm. We call this strategy "reversed cash matching."[15]

In a cash matching strategy, a portfolio manager is faced with a liability stream which he expects to fund with an optimal combination of assets, such that the cash flows from the assets in each period are sufficient to cover the liability requirements. With optimal debt issuance, the situation is reversed. The firm expects to receive measurable future cash flows and desires to issue debt in the current time period to be backed by these expected cash flows. Optimization techniques are employed to find an optimal combination of debt issues (i.e., liabilities) which are fully supported by the expected inflows.

In the following sections, we use simple examples to demonstrate how reversed cash matching may be employed by the firm to find the optimal basket of debt to issue, thus maximizing the current dollar takeout to the firm. Since the debt will be

---

[13]There is a potential computational difficulty in the multi-fund strategy. As the number of funds increases, the size of the problem grows rapidly and the ordinary simplex method fails to remain efficient, even if a large computer is used. This difficulty can be mitigated by taking advantage of a block diagonal structure of the problem.

[14]Leasing and other account receivables are examples of these cash flows.

[15]This strategy can also be called optimal debt issuance. However, the strategy only optimizes a local set of bond issues as opposed to the global structure of the firm's debt.

fully supported by the expected cash inflows, risk is minimized. We will apply reversed cash matching to a leasing company which desires to issue the optimal amount of debt, maximizing the current dollar takeout while fully funding the liability stream with expected leasing receivables. An extension of this strategy is discussed next. Here a firm desires to issue debt, invest the proceeds in the securities markets, and earn the maximum spread between the cost of the debt and the investment income from the securities. The optimal amount of both debt and assets for the firm are determined jointly, maximizing the current dollar takeout to the firm.

An Application of Reversed Cash Matching

The Problem: In January 1988, XYZ Leasing Company projects that it will receive $1,577,118 in leasing revenues each quarter for the next nine years. The firm has decided that it wants to issue commercial paper and/or medium-term notes to be fully backed by the expected lease receivables. The borrowing rates expected for the debt issues are determined by the current rates on Treasury bills and notes with similar maturities and adding the appropriate spreads for the credit risk associated with the debt of XYZ Leasing Company. At the time of the analysis the following rates were suggested:

Maturity	Treasury Rate (percent)	Spread (basis pts.)	Rate for XYZ Debt (percent)
6-month	6.60%	60 bp	7.20%
9-month	6.96	60	7.56
12-month	7.08	65	7.73
2-year	7.77	75	8.52
3-year	8.05	85	8.90
4-year	8.22	95	9.17
5-year	8.37	105	9.42
7-year	8.61	120	9.81
10-year	8.83	130	10.13

Based on this information, a universe is set up consisting of 18 possible debt issues whose maturities span from 6 months to 9 years, the desired maturity range specified by XYZ Company. The borrowing rates on debt issues for maturities between those specified above, such as 8-year securities, were interpolated from the information given. It is assumed that the debt is issued at par. Initially, for simplicity, we shall omit reinvestment income.

A mixed integer programming model[16] will be employed to determine the optimal

---

[16]The model represents a mixture of both linear and integer programming, where integer variables are included in the analysis.

debt issuance for this firm. The objective is to maximize the total dollar value of bonds to be issued, subject to the following constraints:

(1) The receivables are sufficient to cover all interest and principal payments due each period on the issued debt.
(2) A minimum and maximum dollar size are specified for each issue.
(3) A limit is specified on the allowable number of separate bond issues.

Additional constraints could be included in the optimization program based on the requirements of the firm.

We included constraint (3) because a firm will usually place a limit on the number of separate new issues it will float at any one time for practical and administrative reasons. In our example, the number of separate bond issues is limited to eight.

The Solution: The optimal solution to the problem concludes that XYZ Leasing Company should issue eight bonds with total proceeds of $37,310,000 and maturities ranging from 1988 to 1996. The debt portfolio, shown in Exhibit 6, has an average maturity of 5.77 years and an average duration of 4.36 years. The cash flow results considering both the leasing income and debt payments are shown graphically in Exhibit 7. The leasing cash flow is sufficient to fully service the debt requirements, with a surplus balance resulting in each period.

This solution demonstrates that with optimal debt issuance, the firm can take advantage of expected future cash inflows in the current time period by issuing debt which is fully backed by the expected cash inflows. This strategy benefits the firm by minimizing risk associated with the debt issued (since the firm is, in effect, pre-defeasing debt) while freeing up capital in the current time period. In this case, XYZ Leasing Company was able to use expected receivables to back current optimal debt issuance for an initial dollar takeout of over $37 million.

Comparison Solutions—Relaxing the Constraints: The constraints employed in the optimization can be tailored to meet the particular needs of the firm requesting the issuance. In the example above, we employed some assumptions which may be unrealistic for a firm using this strategy. Several of the constraints used for the initial solution will be relaxed here to determine their impact on the dollar takeout for the firm.

1. Allowing for the Reinvestment of Mismatched Funds.
Assuming a reinvestment rate of zero for mismatched funds is very conservative and often unrealistic. In most cases the firm will not keep funds idle, but will reinvest them in income-producing vehicles. We reoptimized the problem, assuming various reinvestment rates, and will present only summary results here. The following table shows the results for the initial problem as well as the results obtained from allowing for the reinvestment of mismatched funds at rates of 2%, 4%, 6% and 8%, respectively.

EXHIBIT 6
REVERSED CASH MATCHING I—BOND ISSUANCE
SETTLEMENT DATE: 1/04/1988

Bond	Coupon	Maturity	Par Amount	Price	Flat Price	Accrued	Full Price
1	7.200	06/15/1988	2,990	100.00	2,990,000.00	0.00	2,990,000.00
2	7.730	12/15/1988	1,680	100.00	1,680,000.00	0.00	1,680,000.00
3	8.130	06/15/1989	1,590	100.00	1,590,000.00	0.00	1,590,000.00
4	8.520	12/15/1989	1,660	100.00	1,660,000.00	0.00	1,660,000.00
5	8.900	12/15/1990	3,460	100.00	3,460,000.00	0.00	3,460,000.00
6	9.170	12/15/1991	3,780	100.00	3,780,000.00	0.00	3,780,000.00
7	9.420	12/15/1992	4,120	100.00	4,120,000.00	0.00	4,120,000.00
8	10.000	12/15/1996	18,030	100.00	18,030,000.00	0.00	18,030,000.00
					37,310,000.00		37,310,000.00

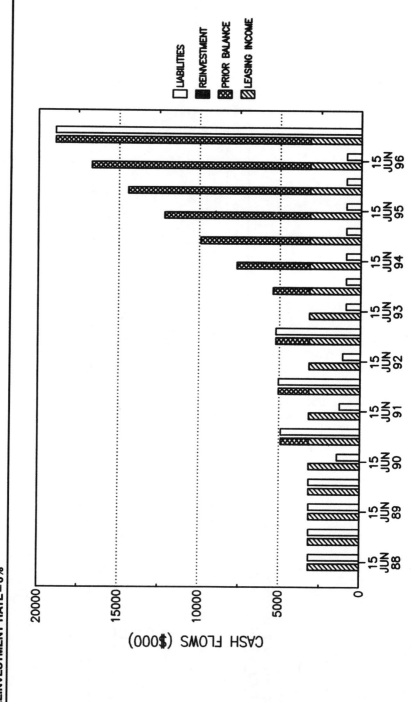

EXHIBIT 7
REVERSED CASH MATCHING I
REINVESTMENT RATE=0%

Comparison Solutions

Reinvestment Rate	Dollar Takeout
0%	$37,310,000
2	38,730,000
4	39,010,000
6	39,290,000
8	39,570,000

As can be seen from the table, the higher the reinvestment rate, the larger is the dollar takeout to the firm.[17] These rates were chosen for comparison purposes only. The actual reinvestment rate for the firm will probably be a rate between the classifications given. Thus it seems reasonable to estimate that the firm's initial takeout can exceed $39 million.

2. Relaxing the Constraint on the Allowable Number of Debt Issues.

In most cases, the firm may wish to set a limit on the number of separate debt issues to be brought to the market at any one time. If this constraint is removed from the analysis, the optimal solution suggests the issuance of 11 securities. As a result, the dollar takeout to the firm is increased by $1,410,000. If a more restrictive limit on the number of bonds to be issued was imposed, restricting the debt to a maximum of six issues, the optimal solution would consist of six issues for a total dollar takeout of $35,420,000 which is $1,890.000 less than the solution involving a maximum of eight issues, and $3,300,000 less than when no limit was placed on the number of issues. Thus, this constraint has an important impact on the profitability of the strategy.

Determining The Optimal Debt/Assets Portfolio

The reversed cash matching strategy can be applied to the case where the firm wishes to issue debt and immediately defease the debt with the proceeds of a corporate bond portfolio set up for this purpose. The debt will be backed by the bond portfolio, as opposed to leasing receivables. Therefore, the need is to construct the optimal combination of these two portfolios simultaneously, the debt portfolio and the asset portfolio. If the total amount of debt to be issued is given, the firm's objective becomes to service the entire debt portfolio with the minimum dollar

---

[17]The relatively large discrepancy between the dollar takeout in the 0% and the 2% reinvestment cases is due mainly to the different debt structures suggested in the solution to these cases. The case with 0% reinvestment of mismatched funds suggests the issuance of very short-term bonds along with one large issue due in December 1996. The 2% reinvestment case allows a more level debt structure, resulting in a lower cost of funds. In addition, allowing higher reinvestment rates suggests structures similar to the 2% case. Although higher reinvestment rates improve the dollar takeout, their incremental effects on the final solution become gradual.

investment in the asset portfolio, thus maximizing the current dollar value. Again, an example facilitates our explanation.

The Problem: In this case, the firm wishes to issue approximately $25 million of debt and invest the proceeds in non-callable corporate bonds. The following rates are specified for the debt:

Maturity	Interest Cost (%)
6-month	7.08
12-month	7.38
2-year	7.55
3-year	7.78
4-year	7.95
5-year	8.20
6-year	8.30
7-year	8.36
8-year	8.45

These data are used to construct a universe of 16 new issues with a maturity span of six months to eight years from the present date. Again, mixed integer programming is used. The objective function minimizes the cost of the asset portfolio to be purchased to defease the issued debt, subject to the following constraints:

(1) The cash flow from assets is sufficient to cover all interest and principal payments due each period on the issued debt.
(2) A minimum and maximum dollar size are specified for each issue.
(3) A limit is specified on the allowable number of separate bond issues.

We assume no reinvestment of mismatched funds. In addition to the constraints employed in the previous case, other constraints may be used. For example, a limit on the number of corporate bonds to be purchased for the asset portfolio can be imposed as well as a limit on the average credit quality of the asset portfolio or the quality of each issue purchased. Below, we report results only for the mixed integer case, where the maximum number of issues to be sold is constrained to equal eight.

Solution: The optimal debt solution for this debt issuance/investment problem where the asset portfolio is constrained to include only non-callable corporate bonds of the highest credit rating (rated Aaa by Moody's Investor Service), suggests that the firm issue six medium-term notes with a total market value of $25,030,000. The optimal asset portfolio consists of 12 corporate bonds to be purchased at a total cost of approximately $23,799,000. This solution demonstrates that the firm can immediately take out approximately $1,231,000 ($25,030,000 - 23,799,000) from this

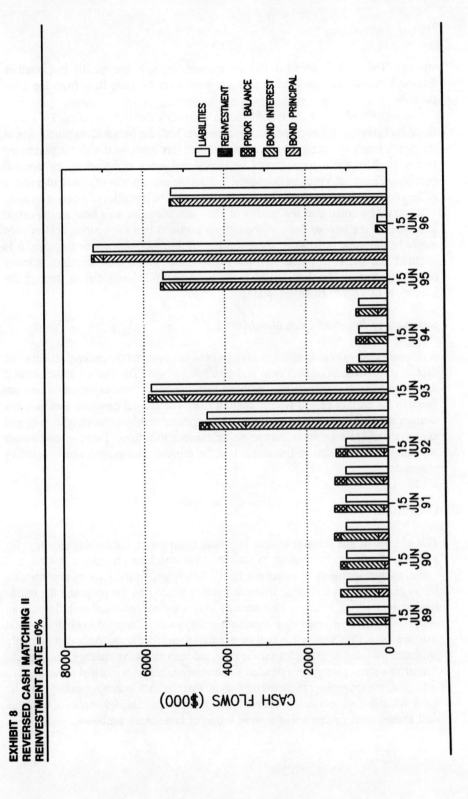

EXHIBIT 8
REVERSED CASH MATCHING II
REINVESTMENT RATE = 0%

LIABILITIES
REINVESTMENT
PRIOR BALANCE
BOND INTEREST
BOND PRINCIPAL

CASH FLOWS ($000)

8000
6000
4000
2000
0

15
JUN
89

15
JUN
90

15
JUN
91

15
JUN
92

15
JUN
93

15
JUN
94

15
JUN
95

15
JUN
96

strategy. The cash flows from this investment strategy, graphically presented in Exhibit 8, show that the debt is well serviced with the cash flow from the asset portfolio.

The success of this optimal debt issuance strategy depends upon market conditions. By investing in the corporate bond market, both the firm and the purchasers of the firm's issues are subject to event and default risk associated with the purchased issues. Each of these risks should be considered when constructing the optimal portfolio. Constraints may be employed to limit the exposure to any particular sector of the corporate bond market to ensure that a diversified portfolio of assets is chosen.

It should be noted that the quality of the asset portfolio may bear an important influence on the cost of debt. Although we assumed that the coupon cost of debt would be the same regardless of the asset portfolio, this may not be the case. It is possible that the firm could obtain a higher credit rating and therefore a lower borrowing cost on the debt issued if the asset portfolio dedicated to funding the liability is of very high credit quality.

Summary of Reversed Cash Matching

A reversed cash matching strategy may be used to construct the optimal structure of debt or combinations of both debt and assets for a firm. The first example showed that reversed cash matching may enable a firm to benefit from expected future cash flows in the current period with minimum risk. The second demonstrated that this strategy may also be applied to construct an optimal combination of both debt and assets to provide maximum current dollar takeout to a firm. Thus, reversed cash matching allows a firm to free capital in the current time period while incurring minimal risk.

CONCLUSION

This chapter details three new strategies built upon the cash matching strategy. By allowing short term borrowing, symmetric cash matching provides a flexible and cost-effective approach to finance a firm's liabilities. In the case of constructing loosely linked portfolios with different liability schedules, we proposed the multi-fund cash matching strategy. This strategy makes use of intra-fund cash flows in an optimal way. The reversed cash matching strategy can be applied to obtain optimal issuance of a firm's debt backed by predicted cash inflows. Although we only presented two simple examples for the reversed cash matching strategy, the application of this strategy can be extended to structure other asset-backed securities.

In sum, the strategies presented here show that the cash matching strategy can be more versatile and less costly than originally expected. Skillful application of this well known strategy can solve a wide scope of investment problems.

PART IV

Portfolio Insurance

Chapter 11

Portfolio Insurance in the Fixed Income Market

 EROL HAKANOGLU, PH.D.
VICE PRESIDENT
FINANCIAL STRATEGIES GROUP
GOLDMAN, SACHS & CO.

ROBERT KOPPRASH, PH.D., C.F.A.
MANAGING DIRECTOR
HYPERION CAPITAL MANAGEMENT
AND
VICE PRESIDENT
RANIERI & WILSON CO.

EMMANUEL ROMAN
ASSOCIATE
FINANCIAL STRATEGIES GROUP
GOLDMAN, SACHS & CO.

We are grateful to Fischer Black for the intellectual guidance, perceptive comments, and invaluable suggestions he contributed to this project. We would also like to thank Jeff Horing and Jeff Zajkowski for their vital assistance with the empirical research and Ron Krieger for his exceptional efforts in developing the manuscript. Robert Kopprasch was a vice president at Goldman, Sachs when this chapter was written.

215

PROTECTING PORTFOLIOS

Portfolio insurance is designed to give the investor the ability to limit downside risk while allowing some participation in upside markets. This return pattern has seemed attractive to many investors, who have poured up to $70 billion into various portfolio insurance products. Most of this money has been in equity portfolios, although an accelerating amount seems to be in fixed income accounts.

There is little doubt that the market crash of October 19, 1987, has cast a shadow on portfolio insurance and may even threaten its continued viability in the equity market. Criticism has come from all sides. On the one hand, some regulators and non-users of portfolio insurance have blamed the crash partly on program selling from insured portfolios. On the other hand, many portfolio insurance investors were unhappy with the performance of their investments. Some of those who were in protected portfolios, but whose managers elected not to trade (as required by the strategy) as the market was tumbling, found that their portfolios fell below the supposed protection level.

Nevertheless, the promised pattern of a protected portfolio remains attractive, and we anticipate that many investors will continue to allocate funds toward this type of protection, albeit with a new awareness of the risks. In addition, the trend toward increased debt allocation by pension funds in light of FASB 87 will increase interest in fixed income based portfolio insurance. In light of this potential interest, this chapter extends to fixed income instruments the methodology of constant proportion portfolio insurance (CPPI), originally developed for equity investments by Fischer Black[1] and André Perold.[2] We show that a CPPI strategy using only fixed income instruments is a viable alternative to traditional forms of portfolio insurance.

Why Portfolio Insurance?

Portfolio insurance promises a return pattern that captures some portion of the upward moves in the market while providing a floor value for the portfolio.[3] As Exhibit 1 indicates, the stylized return pattern (solid line) resembles that of a portfolio combined with a put option on the entire portfolio. In fact, if puts on an investor's portfolio (or a substantially similar portfolio) were available with the sizes and expiration dates desired by the investor, there would be little reason (other than regulatory and accounting constraints or credit considerations) not to consider them. The decision on whether to use actual puts or portfolio insurance would then be made on the basis of price and convenience. However, long-term puts are generally

---

[1]Fischer Black and Robert Jones, "Simplifying Portfolio Insurance," *Journal of Portfolio Management,* Fall 1987.

[2]André F. Perold, "Constant Proportion Portfolio Insurance," Harvard Business School Working Paper, 1986.

[3]The method assumes that prices move without *jumps.* Such price gaps can cause the floor to be violated.

EXHIBIT 1
COMPARISON BETWEEN SYNTHETIC PUT AND CPPI

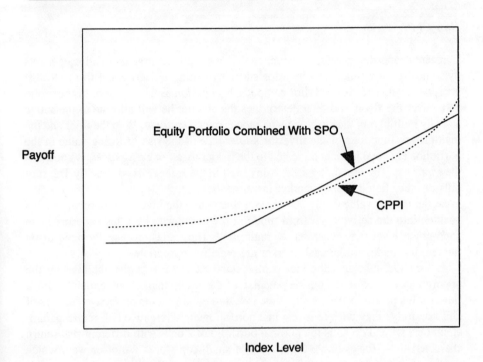

not available, especially on a portfolio that is likely to change in composition during the option period. For this reason, investors desiring put-like protection have had to create it through portfolio insurance.

Usually, such puts are created synthetically by using a variant of the option pricing model developed by Black and Scholes,[4] which involves modeling the behavior of the underlying asset (in this case the portfolio). But this type of model cannot handle many of the peculiarities of a portfolio that changes over time. The constant proportion model provides an alternative approach and produces a return pattern that differs from the synthetic put option (SPO) approach but retains such attractive

---

[4]Fischer Black and Myron Scholes, "The Pricing of Options and Corporate Liabilities," *Journal of Political Economy*, 81, 1973.

features as upside potential and limited downside risk. Exhibit 1 compares the stylized patterns of an SPO and a CPPI portfolio.[5]

How CPPI Works

Constant proportion portfolio insurance uses a simplified strategy to allocate assets dynamically over time. The investor starts by setting a *floor* equal to the lowest acceptable value of his portfolio, computes his *cushion* as the excess of his portfolio value over the floor, and then determines the amount he will allocate to the active asset by multiplying the cushion by a predetermined *multiple*. Both the floor and the multiple are functions of the investor's *tolerance* of the risk of losing value in the portfolio. The total amount allocated to the riskier asset, or *active asset*, is known as the *exposure*. The remaining asset is invested in the *reserve asset*, usually Treasury bills or other liquid money market instruments.

As the market value of the active asset fluctuates, the investor will rebalance his position into the active asset from time to time in order to keep his exposure at an appropriate level (i.e., cushion × multiple).[6] The trades are usually done using futures, but trades in the cash market are equally appropriate.[7]

As we have indicated, the idea behind standard CPPI is to give the investor the opportunity to capture the upside potential of the equity market while maintaining a floor for his portfolio. However, some investors who find the protective features of CPPI desirable may wish to invest in a portfolio with alternative risk-return parameters. One way to do so is to choose a portfolio of stocks with different risk-return characteristics—for example a portfolio of small-cap stocks. Another way, which we emphasize in this chapter, is to invest in a basket of fixed-income instruments.

CPPI FOR FIXED INCOME PORTFOLIOS

In many ways, constant proportion portfolio insurance in the fixed income market is similar to the CPPI practiced in the equity market. It operates with a floor, a tolerance, a cushion, a multiple, etc. But there are subtle differences. For example,

---

[5]For a detailed comparison of SPO and CPPI, see Fischer Black and Ramine Rouhani, "Constant Proportion Portfolio Insurance and the Synthetic Put Option: A Comparison," in Frank J. Fabozzi (ed.), *Institutional Investor Focus on Investment Management* (Cambridge, MA: Ballinger Publishing, 1989).

[6]The investor who wishes to be on the opposite side of the transaction should see Fischer Black and Erol Hakanoglu, "Simplifying Portfolio Insurance for the Seller," in *Institutional Investor Focus on Investment Management*.

[7]Short-term options can also be used. They provide the advantage of changing in price sensitivity in the proper direction as the market moves.

in the equity market, instruments are usually available that allow the investor to exactly capture a particular risk-return pattern. This is less likely to be the case in the fixed income market. The investor's target return pattern may be captured only imperfectly by his intended investment. Further, no actual bond portfolio may be available that corresponds exactly to the intended investment. These problems may necessitate refinements in the definition of the active asset, as well as corrections to the calculation of exposure in fixed income CPPI. We explore these issues and some related complications in Appendix A.

In the discussion that follows, we will assume that the investor—a fund manager who wishes to set a floor for the value of his portfolio—can invest in only one active asset and one reserve asset. The floor may correspond to the present value of the liabilities of, say, a corporate pension fund. The difference between the current portfolio value and the actual floor is the cushion. The manager invests part of the portfolio in a reserve asset that has an acceptable minimum rate of return; he invests the rest of the portfolio in the active asset, which has an expected return exceeding that of the reserve asset. The amount in the active asset is the exposure. The manager will try to maintain the proportion of his exposure to his cushion as a constant, his multiple.

To demonstrate the method, we will use a hypothetical portfolio with the following characteristics:

Initial value of portfolio:	$100 million
Initial value of floor:	$90 million
Initial value of cushion:	$10 million
Multiple:	5
Active asset:	Bond portfolio with duration of 6.2 years
Reserve asset:	Bond portfolio with duration of 5 years
Tolerance:	8% move in cushion

Exhibit 2 (a) illustrates the initial portfolio allocation. The CPPI investor would put $50 million (= cushion of $10 million × multiple of 5) into a bond portfolio with a duration of 6.2 years because of its desired risk-return characteristics. He would put the remaining $50 million into a bond portfolio with a duration of 5 years in order to track the liabilities, which also have a duration of 5 years. Exhibit 2(b) and (c) illustrate how the strategy works when a market movement occurs, in this case a rise in the value of the active asset to $52 million, bringing the portfolio value to $102 million. The cushion has expanded by 20%—well beyond the tolerance—to $12 million. The multiple of 5 implies a new active holding of $60 million. The investor enters into transactions that substitute $8 million of the active asset for $8 million of the reserve asset.

EXHIBIT 2(a)
INITIAL PORTFOLIO ALLOCATION (millions of $)

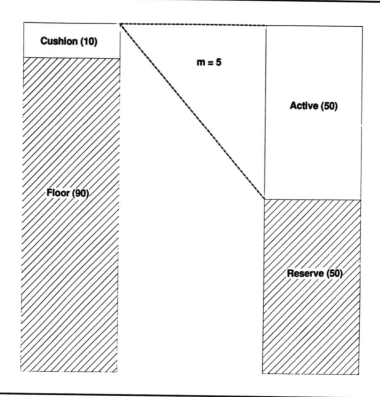

The Volatility Spectrum and Maturity Choices

Fixed income investors have a wide array of volatilities to choose from, just within the Treasury market. From bills to long bonds, with a wide range in between, investors can choose from nearly overnight securities to 30-year bonds, i.e., from durations of almost zero to approximately 10. Because duration is a measure of the price sensitivity of the portfolio to interest rate changes, investors use it as a proxy for overall portfolio volatility.[8]

Because of the high correlation of yield movements of securities with similar durations, investors can substitute "nearby" securities for the active asset, as long as

---

[8]*Duration* approximates the percentage change in the value of a bond for a change in interest rates of 1 percentage point (100 basis points). *Dollar duration* is the dollar change in the value of $1 million par amount of the bond for a change in interest rates of 1 percentage point.

EXHIBIT 2b
PORTFOLIO ALLOCATION AFTER A MARKET MOVE (millions of $)

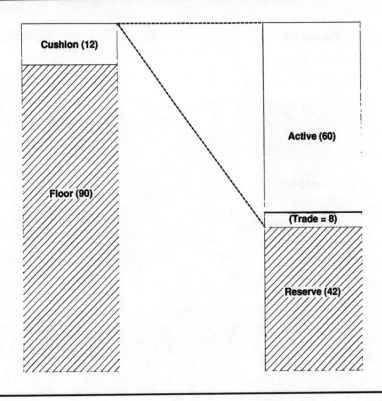

the overall dollar volatility is preserved.[9] But more significantly, the investor can use the overall volatility determined by the CPPI methodology in structuring his portfolio, without distinguishing between active and reserve assets. If the investor has the freedom of choosing securities all along the yield curve, many combinations of securities can preserve the desired volatility level. In the example above, the investor may think that bonds with a duration of 10 are relatively cheap and select accordingly for his portfolio, keeping control of the overall volatility exposure of the portfolio. However, he should be careful about including subjective views in the strategy.[10] Keeping these considerations in mind, the investor has a high degree of freedom in choosing the particular maturities and the resulting yield curve risk of the portfolio.

[9]Simple weighting techniques can be used to preserve the overall volatility.
[10]For a brief discussion of this point, see Appendix B.

EXHIBIT 2c
PORTFOLIO ALLOCATION AFTER REBALANCING (millions of $)

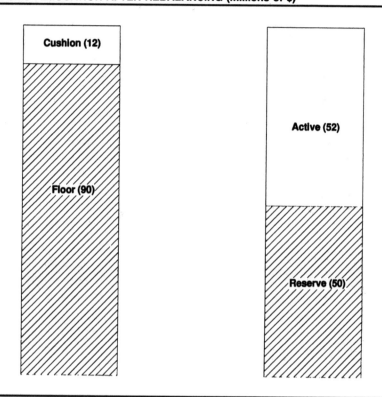

Duration as a Measure of Portfolio Volatility

While the equity investor using CPPI has an exposure that is determined solely by the active asset, the fixed income CPPI investor may have substantial exposure to volatility in the reserve asset as well. As a result, several differences between equity CPPI and fixed income CPPI immediately become apparent:[11]

- the investor must carefully monitor the value of the reserve asset as well as that of the active asset;
- the overall portfolio—not just the active component—has a target volatility level, as measured by the portfolio duration; and
- because of the high correlation between variations in the active and reserve

---

[11]Actually, these differences do not arise exclusively because of the active asset; they result partly from the choice of the reserve asset.

assets, the investor is not concerned as much with the source of volatility as with the overall level.

In equity-based CPPI, exposure is measured as the dollar value of the active asset. The reserve asset is usually Treasury bills, assumed to have no volatility. In the fixed income version of CPPI, however, the reserve asset can exhibit volatility, which may be highly correlated with the volatility of the active asset, as in the example above. In fixed income CPPI, the active and reserve asset portfolios can be combined into a single duration measure. The investor can then manage his exposure by adjusting the overall portfolio volatility, without regard to "arbitrary" distinctions between active and reserve assets.

In this section, we will take duration as a measure of portfolio volatility and try to extend the CPPI strategy to take into account the volatility exposure. We call this extended strategy "duration-adjusted CPPI."

The duration (d_p) of the total portfolio (P) is a simple linear combination of the durations of the two underlying assets:

$$d_p = d_a f_a + d_r f_r \tag{1}$$

where f_a is the fraction of active assets in the portfolio and f_r the fraction of reserve assets.

Note that since he has set the multiple (m) to 5 and the initial cushion (C) to 10, the investor starts with $f_a = f_r = 0.5$.

Thus,

$$d_p = (6.2)(0.5) + (5.0)(0.5) = 5.6 \tag{2}$$

The amount in the active asset, A, is given by:

$$A = mC \tag{3}$$

Combining equations (1) and (3) leads to the following equation:[12]

$$d_p - d_r = (d_a - d_r)m\frac{C}{P} \tag{4}$$

which can be written as:

$$e_d = m_d c \tag{5}$$

---

[12]For the derivation of equations (4) and (5), see Appendix C.

where:

$$m_d = m(d_a - d_r) = \text{duration-adjusted multiple.}$$

$$c = \frac{C}{P} = \text{proportional cushion.}$$

$$e_d = (d_p - d_r) = \text{duration exposure.}$$

Thus, the investor can manage his CPPI portfolio in a duration context, in which the exposure is measured in terms of the extension of duration from the reserve asset to (a maximum of) that of the active asset.

Exhibit 3 depicts the relationships of equations (4) and (5).

As the value of the active asset rises relative to that of the reserve asset, the proportional cushion expands, causing the target duration of the portfolio, d_p, to increase toward the duration of the active asset, d_a. On the other hand, when the reverse happens, the cushion shrinks, causing d_p to decrease more closely to d_r, the duration of the liabilities (and of the reserve asset). At the limit, as d_p approaches d_r, the value of the reserve asset approaches that of the floor (i.e., liabilities) and the portfolio becomes immunized. Therefore, a strategy of immunization or dedication can be thought of as a simple, static case of fixed income CPPI. The duration-adjusted CPPI strategy protects the value of the assets from falling below the value of the liabilities (assuming no downward price jumps).

Trading Using CPPI

Simple CPPI requires the investor to trade when the market moves sufficiently. The investor determines how large a move is necessary by specifying a *tolerance*, that is, the amount by which his actual exposure can vary from the target exposure (cushion × multiple) before a trade is necessary.

In contrast, with duration-adjusted CPPI we target the duration of the portfolio. Therefore, *we must redefine the tolerance as the maximum acceptable percentage change in the duration exposure $(d_p - d_r)$*. Thus, a tolerance of 8% means that the proportional cushion (and the portfolio duration in excess of the duration of the liabilities) must change by 8% before a rebalancing trade is required.

A larger tolerance reduces whipsawing, but at the expense of tracking accuracy if the market exhibits a trend. A low tolerance improves theoretical accuracy, but at the expense of higher (more frequent) transaction costs.[13]

A *capped portfolio* occurs when the investor becomes fully invested in the active asset. The portfolio manager could short a Treasury security matching his liabilities in order to be invested at a level above 100% in the active asset; his portfolio then will be *uncapped*.

---

[13]We give historical evidence of this effect later in this chapter.

EXHIBIT 3
DURATION-ADJUSTED CPPI

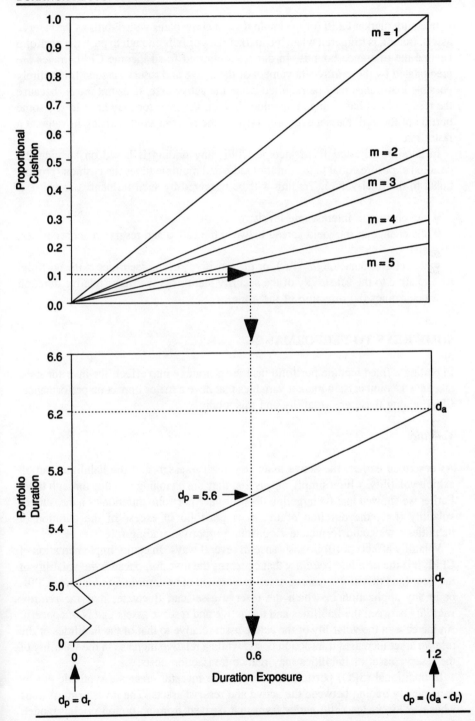

In equity market CPPI (or in simple fixed income plans with T-bills as the reserve asset), trading is triggered when the market rises or falls enough to push the portfolio beyond the tolerance bounds. In duration-adjusted fixed income CPPI, trades are precipitated by the *relative* movement of the active and reserve assets. It is entirely possible that trades may be required when the active asset does not move, because the reserve asset has changed in value. In fact, the investor may have to *sell* some portion of the active asset even in a rally, if the reserve asset is rising in value at a faster rate.

In duration-adjusted fixed income CPPI, any trading is based on keeping the duration exposure equal to the duration-adjusted multiple times the cushion (proportional to the total value). Trading will be triggered by such influences as:

- the change in interest rate levels;
- the change in the yield spread between the active and reserve asset securities; and
- the relative duration $(d_a - d_r)$, or the sensitivity of the securities in the portfolio relative to the sensitivity of the security that tracks the floor (relative duration determines the direction of the trade).

SOME KEYS TO PERFORMANCE

In putting a fixed income portfolio insurance strategy into effect, the investor must take into account certain market variables that have a major impact on performance. Chief among these are volatility and mispricing.

Volatility

As described earlier, the active asset, the reserve asset, and the liabilities can all exhibit volatility, which simply means that they are changing in value through time. Earlier we showed that by targeting the "surplus" portfolio duration as a measure of volatility (i.e., the duration of the asset portfolio in excess of the duration of liabilities), we could formulate a constant proportion trading rule.

Volatility affects portfolio insurance in several ways. In equity implementation of CPPI, it is the *absolute volatility* that concerns the investor, because the volatility of the floor (and that of the reserve asset) is assumed to be zero. In fixed income CPPI, or in any application in which the reserve asset can fluctuate, it is the *relative volatility* between the liabilities and the active and reserve assets that is of concern. An increase in the volatility of the active asset relative to that of the liabilities or the reserve asset increases transaction costs, while a relative increase in the volatility of the reserve asset or liabilities may reduce transaction costs.

In traditional (SPO) portfolio insurance, the investor creates a synthetic put by dynamically trading between the active and reserve assets. The investor must trade whenever his *hedge ratio* varies from that derived from an option pricing model.

One required input to the option formula is the expected volatility over the life of the synthetic put. The investor must estimate volatility, and his forecast may be erroneous. This would cause the investor to use an incorrect hedge ratio, and the resulting positions in the active and reserve assets would be inappropriate. Thus, changes in volatility or an incorrect estimate can affect the floor as well as the upside performance of the portfolio.

CPPI requires no volatility estimate for its implementation (although investors still may wish to estimate volatility to get an idea of the cost). With fixed income CPPI, volatility itself affects trading insofar as it causes the cushion to change (see Exhibit 4), but it is not a parameter that determines the actual duration exposure. When volatility is high, the investor will probably trade more often, and the high volatility will cost more in terms of performance lag (although the investor could diminish this effect by gearing the multiple to the volatility). For SPO portfolio insurance, the experienced volatility has an impact on performance, but the level alone is not sufficient to predict the effect, because the cost is "path dependent." This means simply that the changing level of volatility interacts with the level of

EXHIBIT 4
IMPACT OF VOLATILITY ON PERFORMANCE

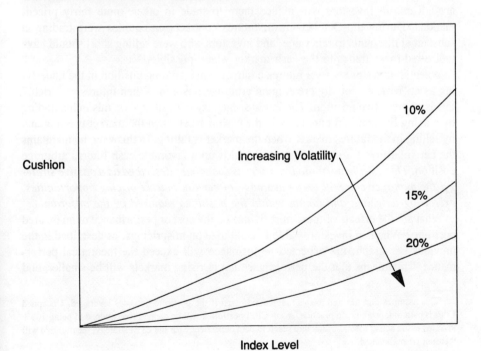

Index Level

market prices in such a way that knowing the average volatility is not enough to predict performance. For a CPPI program, on the other hand, the ultimate cost is a function of the experienced volatility.[14]

Mispricing

Financial theory commonly assumes that assets are priced "properly" in the economy and are traded continuously through time. The extent to which the pricing assumption is violated can affect the performance of an insured portfolio. Two critical questions that arise are the impact of mispricing on the trading pattern and the effect this has on the cost of insurance.

Trading in a CPPI portfolio program, as in any program, will best be served by using an active asset that is traded in a liquid market. For some assets, the cash market provides the necessary liquidity; in others, futures are more liquid. CPPI does not specify which markets should be used, but the relative liquidity and the relative pricing will serve as a guide. For the investor who needs to lower his sensitivity to the active asset, "cheap" futures contracts will not be attractive to short. But the investor who needs to increase his exposure will find cheap futures highly attractive to purchase. The direction of mispricing and the direction of the trade will determine the relative attractiveness of specific vehicles. Mispricings that are adverse to investors will induce them to trade in other, more fairly priced, markets. During the October crash, futures contracts on equities were trading at substantial discounts to fair value, and investors who were selling short should have redirected these trades to the cash market where possible.[15]

When an investor shorts a futures contract against a long position in the underlying asset, he is essentially creating an arbitrage position. When futures are "rich," this is an attractive position. The investor may try to capitalize on this in his trading by making his required purchases in the cash market when the market is rising and by selling in the futures market when the market is falling. In this way, he maintains the net volatility at a proper level and builds up a favorable cash-futures arbitrage position. *Thus, while portfolio insurance is sometimes described as a passive strategy, the manager can still take advantage of certain market pricing opportunities, exercising judgment and timing within the positions required by the program.*

What are the effects of these mispricings on the cost or performance of an insured portfolio? When an investor is able to capitalize on mispricings, as described in the previous paragraph, the expected performance will exceed the theoretical performance. This means that the performance lag in rising markets will be smaller, and

---

[14]This assumes that the multiple is maintained, even if the portfolio becomes leveraged. Uncapped CPPI is path independent. In practice, many CPPI portfolios will be capped (constrained to being 100% invested in the active asset), which will result in path dependency for the CPPI strategy; the multiple will then not be maintained.

[15]See Appendix B for a brief discussion of the theoretical implications of mispricing. As we previously warned, investors should be cautious about incorporating their subjective views into a CPPI strategy.

the achieved floor in declining markets will be higher. On the other hand, when an investor is forced to trade in an adversely mispriced market, the cost will be higher, resulting in a greater lag in rising markets or a lower floor in falling markets.

Because of the uncertainty of the timing and direction of mispricings, it is impossible to predict the exact impact on performance. In general, if the investor can trade in the most favorable market, mispricings will not do major damage and may in fact improve expected performance. One adverse scenario could occur when an investor is fully invested in the reserve asset. If the reserve asset declines (simply because it was overvalued) but the investor's liabilities do not fall in value, the portfolio will fall below its floor level (relative to the liabilities). Another adverse scenario involves futures mispricing. In the case of equities, if the investor is transacting in the futures market rather than the cash market, futures mispricing generally hurts him. This may also be true for fixed income portfolios.

IMPLEMENTING THE CPPI STRATEGY

We are now ready to demonstrate the implementation of CPPI. We will first discuss the issues in choosing the reserve and the active assets. We will then examine the implications of using corporate bonds as the active asset, concentrating on the impact of changes in Treasury-corporate spreads. In the next section, we will present historical simulations results, using a portfolio based on the example introduced earlier in this chapter.

Choosing the Reserve Asset

For the fixed income CPPI investor—who may be acting for, say, a pension fund or an insurance company—the structure of the liabilities the institution faces is a major influence on the choice of the reserve asset. One major objective of the investor is to maintain a floor on his portfolio relative to his liabilities. If the portfolio value falls below this floor, he may not be able to meet the obligations. In order to manage this risk, the investor has to understand how his liabilities behave through time and what forces affect them.

Once a fund manager has estimated a projected liability stream, perhaps by actuarial means, his problem is to construct a portfolio of securities that funds these liabilities. He must ensure that two necessary conditions are met. First, the present value of the portfolio of securities must at least be equal to the present value of the liabilities. Second, the sensitivities of the present values of the asset and liability portfolios to changes in the interest rate should be the same. For many liability streams, these two conditions are sufficient for full funding. For others, however, portfolios composed of fixed income instruments alone are not sufficient. In such cases, it may be necessary to add equity-based securities to a fixed income portfolio to capture the effects of, say, inflation and productivity.

Pension obligations provide a good example of liabilities that may require more than just fixed income instruments to fund (and therefore a reserve asset portfolio that is not simply fixed income). Pension fund liabilities can be measured by the accumulated benefit obligation (ABO) and the projected benefit obligation (PBO). Both measure a pension plan's obligations at a given time. The ABO is a measure of the value of accrued benefits of the pension plan, based on pay history and past service. The PBO differs from the ABO in that it includes an adjustment for the effect of future wage and pay increases. Fixed income securities are sufficient to model the ABO. However, since the PBO reflects future compensation levels, which are generally affected by inflation and productivity changes, a portfolio constructed to model the PBO should include instruments correlated with inflation and productivity (e.g., equities, real estate, or fixed income instruments that behave somewhat like equities, such as high yield bonds). Under certain conditions, the inflation component of the PBO can be funded by fixed income instruments alone—for example, if wage inflation is fully incorporated in prices.[16]

These issues are fundamental to the selection of the reserve asset. Fortunately, the CPPI strategy provides the flexibility to choose both fixed income and equity instruments to meet liabilities.

Choosing the Active Asset

The choice of an active asset may prove to be more difficult than the selection of a reserve asset. The investor would like to expose himself to a higher return-higher risk asset. But which one should he choose? And how high is *higher*, in terms of both risk and return? Recent experiences in the equity market have taught many managers what "high risk" really means.

The expected return of corporate bonds probably exceeds the expected return of Treasury bonds of similar coupons and maturities. Thus, one obvious choice for the active asset is a portfolio of corporate bonds, either actively managed or passively mimicking a corporate bond index. If the investor wishes to choose a basket of securities with a lower or higher duration than that of such an index (that is, if he would like less or more risk in his portfolio), there is nothing in the CPPI strategy that stops him from doing so.

When the prices of Treasury bonds change because of interest rate movements, the prices of corporate bonds usually change also. The change in corporate prices is due both to changes in interest rates and to changes in the spread off Treasuries. Depending on the relative direction of the changes between rates and spreads, investors holding corporate bonds do better, worse, or as well as investors holding the corresponding Treasury bonds. The prices of the two types of bonds are positively correlated. But the correlation is not perfect because of the spread—which reflects

---

[16]For a full discussion of this question, see Laurie S. Goodman and William J. Marshall, "*Inflation, Interest Rates, and Pension Liabilities,*" in Robert Arnott and Frank J. Fabozzi (eds.), *Asset Allocation* (Chicago, IL: Probus Publishing, 1988).

default risk, call risk, differences in tax treatment, and liquidity. Over the past two years, for example, the correlation between monthly changes in the 7-year Treasury coupon bond and the Moody's Corporate Bond Index has been 0.75.

The fund manager's views on interest rates and spreads will help to determine the choice of assets and parameters to implement the CPPI strategy. There are nine possible scenarios—generated by combinations of Treasury rates rising, falling, or staying the same while corporate spreads over these rates widen, narrow, or remain flat. We will describe in some detail three of these scenarios for the joint movement of the rates and spreads, indicating how a hypothetical investor's strategy would work under each of them.

To do so, we will continue to use the example introduced in the second section of this chapter. The floor is set to the present value of the liabilities and is tracked closely by the behavior of a bond with a duration of 5 years. We will assume that the active asset is a corporate bond with a duration of 6.2 years. The initial corporate spread is 100 basis points. Based on a multiple of 5, a floor of $90 million and an initial portfolio of $100 million, we start with $50 million in the active asset and $50 million in the reserve asset. The total portfolio duration is 5.6 years, and the duration-adjusted multiple is 6. We assume a tolerance of 8%.

Rate and Spread Scenarios

Let us assume the yield of the Treasury bond falls by 100 basis points. Since the duration of both the reserve asset and the liabilities is 5, the price of the reserve asset and the value of the liabilities both rise by 5%. Exhibit 5 summarizes the three possible scenarios for corporate yields, which we discuss below.

EXHIBIT 5
SCENARIOS WHEN TREASURY RATE FALLS 100 BASIS POINTS (millions of $)

Percentage change in Treasury bond's price:			5%
Reserve asset holdings before rebalancing:			$52.5
Floor:			$94.5

		Spreads	
	Widen	Same	Narrow
Change in corporate yield (bp)	−50	−100	−150
Change in price (%)	+3.1	+6.2	+9.3
Active (before trading)	$51.55	$53.1	$54.65
Portfolio value	$104.05	$105.6	$107.15
Nominal cushion	$9.55	$11.1	$12.65
Proportional cushion (%)	9.18	10.51	11.81
After Trading			
Active	$47.75	$53.1*	$63.25
Reserve	$56.4	$52.5*	$43.9
Portfolio duration (years)	5.55	5.61*	5.71

*Move below tolerance: no trade or no change.

Treasury Rate Falls and Spread Widens: Assume the corporate yield falls only by 50 basis points. The value of the active asset rises to $51.55 million (a 3.1% increase, corresponding to a 50 basis points fall for a duration of 6.2) while the reserve asset holdings rise 5%, to $52.5 million. The portfolio is worth $104.05 million, and the floor is $94.5 million. The cushion in nominal terms declines to $9.55 million, and the proportional cushion (as a percentage of the portfolio value) is down by 8.2% to 9.18%. The percentage drop exceeds the tolerance of 8%, triggering a trade. By selling $3.8 million worth of the active asset and buying the same amount of the reserve asset, the investor ends up having $47.75 million in corporate bonds and $56.4 million in Treasuries. The portfolio duration target is now 5.55 years.

Treasury Rate Falls and Spread Remains the Same: Assume that Treasury and corporate yields both fall by 100 basis points, so that the spread is still 100 basis points. The value of the active asset holdings is $53.1 million. The reserve asset holdings amount to $52.5 million and the floor is $94.5 million. The portfolio value becomes $105.6 million and the nominal cushion is up by 11% to $11.1 million. The porportional cushion is up only 5.1%, which is not enough to trigger a trade. That is, portfolio duration is above its target level, but not by enough to signal a readjustment.

Treasury Rate Falls and Spread Narrows: Assume the corporate bond yields falls by 150 basis points, narrowing the spread to 50 basis points. The active asset holdings are now worth $54.65 million, the reserve $52.5 million. The floor is at $94.5 million and the portfolio is now worth $107.15 million. The value of the nominal cushion is $12.65 million, and the proportional cushion is up by 18.1%. This percentage change is well above the tolerance level. A trade of $8.6 million is triggered from the reserve into the active asset. After rebalancing, the portfolio duration is 5.71 years, its exact target level.

Other Scenarios: In Exhibits 6 and 7, we summarize six other scenarios resulting from Treasury yields rising or staying the same while spreads widen, narrow, or remain the same.

HISTORICAL PERFORMANCE

To examine how the CPPI strategy would have performed over the six year period 1982-1987, we assume that the liabilities behave as a 7-year Treasury bond (with a duration of approximately 5 years).

EXHIBIT 6
SCENARIOS WHEN TREASURY RATE RISES 100 BASIS POINTS (millions of $)

Percentage change in Treasury bond's price:		-5%
Reserve asset holdings before rebalancing:		$47.5
Floor:		$85.5

	Spreads		
	Widen	*Same*	*Narrow*
Change in corporate yield (bp)	+150	+100	+50
Change in price (%)	-9.3	-6.2	-3.1
Active (before trading)	$45.35	$46.9	$48.45
Portfolio value	$92.85	$94.4	$95.95
Nominal cushion	$7.92	$8.9	$10.45
Proportional cushion (%)	8.53	9.43	10.89
After Trading			
Active	$36.75	$46.9*	$52.25
Reserve	$56.1	$47.5*	$43.7
Portfolio duration (years)	5.48	5.60*	5.65

*Move below tolerance: no trade or no change.

EXHIBIT 7
SCENARIOS WHEN TREASURY RATE STAYS THE SAME (millions of $)

Percentage change in Treasury bond's price:		0%
Reserve asset holdings before rebalancing:		$50.0
Floor:		$90.0

	Spreads		
	Widen	*Same*	*Narrow*
Change in corporate yield (bp)	+50	0	-50
Change in price (%)	-3.1	0.0	+3.1
Active (before trading)	$48.45	$50.0	$51.55
Portfolio value	$98.45	$100.0	$101.55
Nominal cushion	$8.45	$10.0	$11.55
Proportional cushion (%)	8.58	10.0	11.37
After Trading			
Active	$42.25	$50.0*	$57.75
Reserve	$56.2	$50.0*	$43.85
Portfolio duration (years)	5.52	5.66*	5.68

*Move below tolerance: no trade or no change.

Choosing the Assets

The investor matches his liability stream with the reserve asset, a 7-year Treasury bond. If the price of the active asset falls dramatically, he will move totally into the reserve asset and still be able to fund his liabilities.

For the active asset, the investor chooses a basket of corporate bonds. To conduct our simulations, we have constructed an index of corporate bonds based on data obtained from Moody's Investors Service. The index is composed of equal proportions of investment grade bonds.[17] From a practical point of view, our approach is flexible enough to allow the investor to choose for himself a basket of bonds with different risk-return characteristics. A less risk-averse investor, for example, might want to include a few high yield securities in his basket.

Simulation Results

Let us look at how a hypothetical pension fund would have performed using the CPPI strategy over the last six years, starting at the beginning of 1982 and targeting a specific volatility and duration for the overall portfolio. Assume that the fund manager selects the basket of corporate bonds described earlier as the active asset. He faces a liability stream that seems to have a duration of 5 years, and chooses the reserve asset to be the 7-year Treasury bond, which has a duration of approximately 5 years.

Say the current portfolio is worth $100 million, and the manager wants to set a floor of $90 million. With his views on interest rates and spreads as well as his attitude toward risk, he decides on a multiple of 5. He therefore starts with a nominal cushion of $10 million (a proportional cushion of 0.1, or 10%), $50 million in corporate bonds, and $50 million in the 7-year Treasury bond; his portfolio duration is 5.6 years. His duration-adjusted multiple is 6 and his duration exposure is 0.6. His tolerance is 5%, i.e., he is willing to rebalance between the active and the reserve part of the portfolio for moves in asset prices that change his portfolio duration (or proportional cushion) by 5% or more. Let us assume the trading costs amount to 0.75% of the dollar amount traded, and trades occur at closing prices. Using daily data, we find that over the 6-year period, he trades only 63 times, an average of less than one trade a month.

At the beginning of 1982, the yield spread between the corporate bond basket and the 7-year Treasury bond was 110 basis points. By the end of 1982, interest rates had

---

[17]For the most recent part of our sample, we checked the consistency of our results by using the actual Moody's Corporate Bond Index traded on the COMEX. The correlation between the two indexes is approximately 0.75. The Moody's index comprises 80 bonds selected by pre-specified classification rules, including duration, quality, and rating. At least 40 issuers are represented. The Moody's index reflects total return, in that coupon accruals are added each day to the level of the index. The average duration of bonds in the Moody's index is approximately 6.2 years.

fallen 400 basis points and the spread had widened to 265 basis points. The value of the portfolio had risen to $135.2 million. The floor was $120.7 million, leaving him with a proportional cushion of 0.107, or 10.7% (the nominal cushion was up 45% to $14.5 million). The asset portfolio consisted of $72.5 million in corporate bonds and $62.7 million in the 7-year Treasury bond. His portfolio duration at that point was 5.64 years. If he had instead followed a simple buy-and-hold strategy—by investing $90 million in the Treasury bond that moved with the $90 million liabilities and $10 million in the corporate bond index—he would have ended with a value of only $134.5 million. So over the first year, CPPI outperformed an uninsured portfolio by $0.7 million.

During 1983, rates moved up 150 basis points from the end of 1982 and spreads narrowed to 130 basis points. At the end of 1983 the value of the CPPI portfolio was $146.9 million. The floor was $125.2 million, leaving the investor with a nominal cushion of $21.7 million and a proportional cushion of 0.148, or 14.8%. The portfolio contained $108.5 million in corporate bonds and $38.4 million in the 7-year Treasury bond, implying a portfolio duration of 5.89 years and a duration exposure of 0.89. If he had instead followed the buy-and-hold strategy described above, he would have ended 1983 with a portfolio worth only $140.6 million. So over the two-year period, the manager fared better by $6.3 million using our strategy. Over the entire six years of the simulation, he did better by $36.28 million.

Exhibit 8 lists the cumulative year-end portfolio values and cushions from the beginning of 1982 to the end of 1987.

In Exhibit 9, we present the cumulative year-end portfolio values for two buy-and-hold strategies: investing the entire portfolio in corporate bonds (a risky strategy, which does not guarantee a floor) and investing 10% in the corporate bonds and 90% in the Treasury bond. Exhibit 10 summarizes non-cumulative simulation results for each year from 1982 through 1987, comparing the outcomes with those of the two buy-and-hold strategies.

Transaction Costs

For a fund manager contemplating the use of portfolio insurance, one of the major concerns is how volatility will affect the returns on the insured portfolio. This concern is well justified in light of recent events in the market.

The higher the volatility, of course, the larger the number of trades and hence the higher the transaction costs. Furthermore, the cost of volatility increases as the tolerance level decreases: more trading is needed to maintain equality between (1) the ratio of the portfolio duration exposure to the proportional cushion and (2) the duration-adjusted multiple. The higher the volatility, the more often the investor must rebalance his holdings.

In Exhibit 11, we illustrate the effect of different tolerance levels during 1982-87,

EXHIBIT 8
INSURED PORTFOLIO PERFORMANCE (millions of $)

Active asset:	Basket of corporate bonds with a duration of 6.2
Reserve asset:	Seven-year Treasury bond with a duration of 5
Initial portfolio:	100
Initial floor:	90
Initial cushion	10
Initial portfolio duration:	5.6 years
Initial duration exposure:	0.6 years
Initial active asset exposure:	50
Multiple:	5
Duration-adjusted multiple:	.6

Tolerance: Rebalance after a 5% move in portfolio duration or proportional cushion
Trading Cost: 0.75% of amount traded

Final Portfolio Values

To the end of:	From the Beginning of:					
	1982	1983	1984	1985	1986	1987
1982	135.21					
1983	146.94	108.62				
1984	170.89	126.14	115.37			
1985	224.44	165.28	149.59	128.94		
1986	281.54	207.11	184.46	158.13	121.29	
1987	272.25	200.28	177.98	152.89	117.67	97.71

Final Cushion Values

To the end of:	From the Beginning of:					
	1982	1983	1984	1985	1986	1987
1982	14.50					
1983	21.73	15.11				
1984	28.17	19.55	12.93			
1985	44.51	30.90	20.43	15.47		
1986	56.31	41.42	33.65	25.65	16.42	
1987	54.45	40.05	29.41	22.38	14.36	8.66

EXHIBIT 9
BUY-AND-HOLD PORTFOLIO PERFORMANCE (millions of $)

100% in Corporate Bonds
Initial Portfolio Value: 100

Final Portfolio Values

To the end of:	From the Beginning, of: 1982	1983	1984	1985	1986	1987
1982	137.81					
1983	154.29	112.28				
1984	180.76	131.55	117.01			
1985	239.08	173.99	154.76	131.71		
1986	299.92	218.27	194.15	165.23	125.23	
1987	290.25	211.06	187.74	159.77	121.10	96.96

10% in Corporate Bonds
90% in 7-year Treasury Bonds
Initial Portfolio Value: 100

Final Portfolio Values

To the end of:	From the Beginning of: 1982	1983	1984	1985	1986	1987
1982	134.49					
1983	140.64	104.74				
1984	160.80	119.74	114.15			
1985	203.84	151.78	144.64	126.63		
1986	240.08	178.72	170.22	149.00	117.39	
1987	235.97	175.68	167.34	146.49	115.42	98.75

using the same initial conditions as those in Exhibit 10. We can make the following observations:

- The choice of the tolerance level does not significantly affect the final value of the portfolio. For a tolerance level of 1%, the final value of the portfolio is $270.21 million. The final value is $270.95 million for a tolerance level of 7% and $271.8 million for a tolerance level of 10%.[18]

---

[18]Looking at the historical volatility, *ex post*, we can identify an optimal tolerance level for a given set of parameters and time period. For our sample, a tolerance level of 6% would have been optimal. Our results are also affected by the use of historical closing price data. Because tolerance levels could be penetrated during the day but might return to within tolerance by the close, a real investor would trade at least as often as the frequency shown in our results. If the market whipsawed, our results would reflect too low a level of transaction costs; for trending markets, our results would underperform those of a real investor.

EXHIBIT 10
SIMULATION RESULTS WITH THE STRATEGY RESTARTED EACH YEAR (NON-CUMULATIVE) (millions of $)

Active asset:	Basket of corporate bonds with a duration of 6.2
Reserve asset:	Seven-year Treasury bond with a duration of 5
Initial portfolio:	100
Initial floor:	90
Initial cushion	10
Initial portfolio duration:	5.6 years
Initial duration exposure:	0.6 years
Initial active asset exposure:	50
Multiple:	5
Duration-adjusted multiple:	6

Tolerance: Rebalance after a 5% move in portfolio duration or proportional cushion

Trading Cost: 0.75% of amount traded

	CPPI Strategy						Buy-and-Hold Strategies	
Year	Portfolio Value	Cushion	Floor	Total Amount Traded	Largest Sell	Largest Buy	100% in Corporate Bonds	10% in Corporate Bonds
1982	135.21	14.50	120.71	79.17	-7.09	5.68	137.81	134.49
1983	108.62	15.11	93.51	32.67	-3.68	3.42	112.28	104.74
1984	115.37	12.93	102.44	21.46	-2.93	2.65	117.01	114.15
1985	128.94	15.47	113.47	26.33	-3.28	3.51	131.71	126.63
1986	121.29	16.42	104.87	35.18	-5.23	3.89	125.23	117.33
1987	97.71	8.66	89.05	42.64	-3.91	3.87	96.96	98.75

EXHIBIT 11
EFFECTS OF TOLERANCE ON PORTFOLIO PERFORMANCE, 1982-87 (millions of $)

Tolerance	Portfolio Value	Floor	Cushion	No. of Trades Buy	Sell	Trading Cost (million $)
1%	270.21	206.97	54.04	263	181	5.321
3%	271.47	206.97	54.29	91	50	2.707
5%	272.25	206.97	54.45	44	19	1.796
7%	270.95	206.97	54.19	29	13	1.663
10%	271.83	206.97	54.36	18	6	1.283
20%	275.05	206.97	55.01	7	1	0.604

- The higher the tolerance level, the lower the number of trades. But as the tolerance level increases, the size of the average trade increases, as does the size of the largest trade.[19] An important concern for the investor is that the amount traded be reasonable; he does not want to have to sell 50% of the portfolio in a single trade. Over our 6-year simulation, the largest trade was $10.5 million on October 19, 1987. We checked the result for several multiples and obtained similar outcomes: higher tolerance levels meant fewer but larger trades. Keep in mind that for a given set of parameters, the size of the trade hinges in part on the starting date of the program, since the amount traded depends on the cushion. For a given multiple, the value of the cushion will vary with the date the program was started. As a consequence, the amount traded will also vary.

CONCLUSIONS

Three main conclusions emerge from this chapter.

First, CPPI is a promising method of managing a portfolio of fixed income securities dynamically over time. It gives the investor a coherent way to allocate his assets while staying out of the stock market. Compared with a simple buy-and-hold strategy, CPPI with fixed income instruments does well on the downside and with low volatility, although it may give poor results with high volatility.

Second, CPPI using fixed income instruments presents a viable alternative to traditional forms of portfolio insurance. CPPI avoids some of the drawbacks of the SPO strategy and gives the investor enough flexibility to decide not only on the choice of securities for the active and the reserve assets but also on whether to trade in cash or future contracts.

Finally, by targeting the total portfolio duration, the investor has control over his

---

[19]More precisely, the distribution of trades for low tolerance levels has very thin tails, and most of the trades are centered around the mean. For high tolerance levels, most of the trades are large in absolute terms and their distribution becomes bimodal—trades are either large buys or large sells.

volatility exposure. The strategy works in such a way that, unless jumps occur in the fixed income market, in his *worst*-case scenario he ends up with a duration-matched portfolio. The simulations for the past six years show that the value of the sample portfolio went from $100 million at the beginning of the 1982 to $275.25 million by the end of 1987, always remaining above the floor—even during October 1987. To achieve this result, the strategy required less than one trade per month; the total trading cost of following the strategy during the past six years was less than 2% of the initial portfolio value.

APPENDIX A.
CONCEPTUAL ISSUES IN FIXED INCOME CPPI

In adapting CPPI to fixed income instruments, we can refine our approach by making a few conceptual adjustments in certain CPPI concepts, generalizing some of the ideas and terminology of equity-based CPPI.

The Active Asset

In simple equity CPPI, the investor attempts to capture the upside return pattern of the equity market. Let us call the equity portfolio that captures this pattern his *target asset*. We will then call his intended investment the *active asset*. (This is probably the target asset when it is available, but the target asset may not even be a real asset.) We will use the term *hedge asset* to refer to the actual investment. If the investor is forced (or prefers) to trade in a different vehicle, however, his hedge asset will not be identical to the active asset. For example, if the investor was trying to capture the upside of the S&P 500, that index would be his target asset; his normal active asset might be a portfolio of 50 stocks currently selected for convenience, liquidity, or other reasons. His hedge asset is what he actually buys. This example may be strained in the case of equities, but it accurately conveys an idea of the situation the investor will encounter in the debt market.

In the fixed income case, a pension fund manager may, for example, have a liability that has a duration of 7 years. Since he presumably wants his assets to outperform the liability in a rally, a bond with a duration of, say, 10 years could be the target asset. If the closest investment is a Treasury bond with a duration of 9.8 years, that would be the active asset. But if the manager felt that the Treasury instrument was currently "rich" relative to its neighbors on the yield curve, he might use a different bond or combination of bonds—or perhaps futures contracts or options—as the actual trading vehicle (the hedge asset).

In the case of equity CPPI, we may easily adopt the simplification that the actual portfolio matches the target asset perfectly. But if we look at the problem more generally, as we must do when we address the fixed income market, we will see that this simplification does not always hold.

Let us consider the exposure value (that is, the cushion × the multiple) to be a more general measure of the volatility necessary in the portfolio rather than the dollar amount to be invested in the risky asset. Returning to the equity example, we see that if the required exposure is $1 million, then $1 million invested in a market portfolio would be the correct amount. But if the investor happened to hold a high beta portfolio, a lower amount would be the appropriate *volatility equivalent*. The simple equity CPPI formula for exposure implicitly assumes that the ratio of the volatilities of the active and the hedge asset is 1.0, but this isn't necessarily the case. Thus, we should substitute for the original formula the following expression:

$$\text{exposure} = \text{multiple} \times \text{cushion} \tag{6}$$

$$\text{volatility-adjusted exposure} = \text{multiple} \times \text{cushion} \times \beta_a/\beta_h \tag{7}$$

where β_a is the beta of the active asset and β_h is that of the hedge asset.[20]

The active and the hedge asset have different volatilities; they may also be less than perfectly correlated. This could affect the accuracy of the hedging process and the predictability of the return pattern.

Take the case of mispricing, described in the third section of the chapter. An investor may have different target, active, and hedge assets. For a given CPPI strategy and parameters, the investor can construct two "equivalent" portfolios that appear markedly different. For example, if he needs to be 50% invested in the active asset, he may hold 50% in the active asset and the rest in the reserve, or he may hold 100% in the active asset and be short 50% in the hedge asset. The equivalence of these positions will not be maintained if the active asset and the hedge asset are mispriced relative to each other.

The Reserve Asset

The reserve asset in SPO portfolio insurance is usually Treasury bills. This is a convenient choice because it is rather easy to accept that the return on the T-bills is uncorrelated with the return on the active asset. This approach provides a fixed floor for the portfolio. A more general formulation uses a floating floor, based on some liability pricing rate, perhaps a 7-year Treasury. This is most appropriate for pension funds, because it protects the fund's surplus. Thus, it is often called *surplus insurance*. The CPPI approach to surplus insurance allows both a volatility to the reserve asset and a non-zero correlation between it and the active (or the target, or the hedge) asset. In the extreme, if the reserve asset had the same volatility as the hedge asset, and if they were perfectly correlated, the actual allocation between them would be irrelevant. For many fixed income cases, the reserve asset will exhibit *some* volatility and is likely to be correlated with the hedge asset and target asset. It may be

---

[20]Since we are using duration as a measure of volatility, in this context the volatility-adjusted exposure is the same as the duration exposure introduced in the second section of the chapter.

necessary to trade even when the active asset does not change in value, because the reserve asset is fluctuating.

APPENDIX B.
MISPRICING AND EQUILIBRIUM MODELS

Managers of fixed income portfolios often have views on the yield curve and look at particular sections of the curve to be relatively "cheap" or "rich" at any given time. The question is whether this is consistent with the theory behind the CPPI approach. Here we consider the case where the portfolio is uncapped. Perold[21] derives conditions under which CPPI is an optimal investment strategy. He tells us that, for a certain class of utility functions (the so-called HARA), CPPI is the only path-independent strategy that maximizes investors' expected utility.

Some of Perold's results are based on earlier work by Merton.[22] Like most equilibrium models, Merton's intertemporal capital asset pricing model assumes that assets are properly priced in the economy and that prices fully reflect all information available to investors at any time. Considering one sector of the yield curve as being cheap or rich implies that investors use an embedded model of equilibrium for the term structure to arbitrage mispricings in the yield curve. CPPI theory does not tell us anything about relative prices in the economy. Selecting a different sector of the yield curve to trade based on its cheapness may invalidate the optimality of the strategy. An investor may incorporate his views into the implementation of the strategy by increasing the multiple when he is bullish on the active asset. While it is possible to use the CPPI strategy in conjunction with subjective views on possible arbitrage opportunities, the formal conditions for doing so remain an open research question.

APPENDIX C.
DERIVATION OF THE DURATION EXPOSURE

Starting with equations (1) and (3) from pages 8-9:

$$d_p = d_a f_a + d_r f_r \qquad (1)$$

and

$$A = mC \qquad (3)$$

---

[21]André F. Perold, *op. cit.* (See footnote 2)

[22]Robert C. Merton, "An Intertemporal Capital Asset Pricing Model," *Econometrica*, 41, September 1973.

where:

$$f_a = \frac{A}{A+R} = \frac{A}{P} \tag{8}$$

$$f_r = \frac{R}{A+R} = \frac{R}{P} \tag{9}$$

we get:

$$d_p = d_a m \frac{C}{P} + d_r (1 - m \frac{C}{P}) \tag{10}$$

$$d_p - d_r = (d_a - d_r) m \frac{C}{P} \tag{4}$$

$$e_d = d_p - d_r \tag{11}$$

$$m_d = m(d_a - d_r) \tag{12}$$

$$c = \frac{C}{P} \tag{13}$$

which gives:

$$e_d = m_d c \tag{5}$$

Note that a given percentage change in c implies the same percentage change in e_d.

Chapter 12

Portfolio Protection for Fixed Income Portfolios, Balanced Portfolios, Surplus Protection

ETHAN S. ETZIONI
VICE PRESIDENT
OPTION MANAGEMENT DIVISION
OPPENHEIMER CAPITAL

The purpose of this chapter is to examine the application of portfolio protection for fund sponsors that want to protect a fixed income or balanced portfolio or a specific surplus level. This will entail an introduction to U.S. Treasury bond futures and their proper use in such a strategy. The chapter is intended to be a methodical guide that also touches upon some of the obstacles and controversies. Fixed income and balanced programs are analyzed in their own right, and are used as stepping stones towards *surplus protection*. It is assumed that the reader is familiar with the basic application of portfolio protection to an equity portfolio.

The chapter draws on a variety of disciplines which are not usually all familiar to one person: futures hedging, option pricing, fixed income investments, tax law, actuarial analysis, financial accounting, pension management and a minor dose of

The author wishes to thank Rob Bluestone, Eugene Brody and William Dreher for their thoughtful comments.

math. A reader interested primarily in the conceptual aspect of surplus protection may skip directly to that section.

U.S. TREASURY BOND FUTURES

A probable tool in any of these programs is the U.S. Treasury bond futures contract that trades on the Chicago Board of Trade. The liquidity in this contract is phenomenal. For example, on August 5, 1987, 304,417 contracts traded, representing an underlying face value of $30.4 billion. By comparison, on the same day, 87,996 S&P 500 contracts traded representing an underlying value of $14.2 billion, while the volume on the New York Stock Exchange was 192,700 shares with a value of $7.7 billion.

The contract calls for the delivery of $100,000 face value of U.S. Treasury bonds with at least fifteen years to maturity or the earliest call date. At any point in time, there are about thirty bonds eligible for delivery. A typical duration of the cheapest bond to deliver is about ten years at current levels of interest rates.

Nominally, the contract is based on an 8% bond with twenty years to maturity. For other deliverable bonds, the invoice price is adjusted by a conversion factor. The factor is calculated by pricing the bond to yield 8% to the earlier of maturity or call date. At any point in time, there is one bond that is expected to be cheapest to deliver on a certain futures expiration month. Generally, futures are priced off that bond.

In a positive yield curve environment, the bond futures are expected to sell at a discount to the cash, because the yield on the bonds is higher than their financing cost. By contrast, equity futures generally trade at a premium to the spot index. However, there are several peculiarities to the bond futures contract of which one should be aware. The seller (the short) has the option of selecting which bond to deliver. At times, several bonds are close to being the cheapest to deliver. Therefore, the futures trade at an additional discount to reflect the value of this option. The value of this option increases with the number of bonds that are close to being cheapest and the amount of time remaining to the futures delivery month.

A second feature is the "wild card option." The short may deliver any day on the expiration month and may tender the delivery notice each day until 8 P.M.. If, after the bond futures market closes at 3 P.M. there is some major negative news, the short may still tender a delivery notice. He will be invoiced based on that day's futures price yet he can buy the bond either that day until about 5:30 P.M. or the next day at a substantially lower price. Also, in a negative yield curve environment, it may be advantageous to make early deliver. All these factors affect the pricing of the contract and suggest that the "long" should roll out to a further expiration before the beginning of the delivery month.

It should be noted that there are price move limits on the bond futures of two points the first day a limit is reached and three points thereafter. These limits may hinder the performance of the portfolio protection. Finally, the trading hours for this contract are 9:00 A.M.–3:00 P.M. (E.S.T.) versus 9:30 A.M.–4:15 P.M. for the S&P 500 futures. Obviously, there are times when one cannot trade simultaneously in both markets (a potential obstacle for surplus protection).

APPLICATION OF FIXED INCOME FUTURES

Let us assume that a manager wants to fully hedge (not portfolio protection) a $100 million (market value) fixed income portfolio with an average duration of eight years and a 9% yield to maturity. Also assume (for simplicity) that all yield changes are parallel along the yield curve (admittedly, a very tentative assumption).

The first step is to calculate the dollar impact on the portfolio due to changes in interest rates. This is usually measured in dollars per yield change of one basis point (known as the "dollar value of an O one" or $VO1). The $VO1 is essentially the derivative of the value of the portfolio or fixed income instrument with respect to yield, and can be shown to equal the modified duration multiplied by the full price (including accrued interest) divided by 10,000. Modified duration is equal to Macaulay duration divided by one, plus half the yield to maturity (assuming semi-annual coupons).

To continue the example, given that the yield to maturity on this portfolio is 9%, the modified duration would be 7.66 (8/(1 + .09/ 2)). The $VO1 for this portfolio would be $76,600 (.01 × 7.66% × $100,000,000). This is a rough estimate. A more precise approach would be to calculate the aggregate of the $VO1 for all the securities in the portfolio.

As of the close on July 13, 1987, the cheapest bond to deliver on the September futures contract was the one with a coupon of 13 1/4%, a maturity date of May 15, 2014, a call date of May 15, 2009 and a current market value of $1,440,000. This bond trades on a yield to call basis, currently 8.82. The $VO1, based on the forward price of the bond on September 30, 1987, is $1,258 per million dollar par value (the last delivery day on the contract). To get the $VO1 for the futures contract it is necessary to divide $1,258 by 10 and then by the conversion factor of 1.5347, equal to 82 per futures contract. Therefore, to hedge the portfolio, it is necessary to sell 934 contracts ($76,600/82). A more accurate approach for calculating the $VO1 might be to take a weighted average of several bonds that are close to being cheapest to deliver.

The percentage change in price as a result of a basis point change in yield (%VO1) is essentially identical to the modified duration. To get back from $VO1 to %VO1, one should divide the $VO1 by the full price. Here the %VO1 using the full price of the 13¼'s is equal to .0871% (1,258/1,444,000). The %VO1 (or modified duration) is important for comparing the volatility of different securities.

One final adjustment must be made to take interest on variation margin into consideration. To demonstrate the logic for this adjustment, let us assume that a fixed income portfolio hedged by futures will be liquidated on the futures expiration date and the futures closed out. If the portfolio is fully hedged, any gain in the portfolio will be fully offset by losses in the futures and vice-versa. However, the losses on the futures will be paid for right away in the form of variation margin, while the gain will not be realized until the portfolio is sold. Therefore, the futures position should be reduced by dividing by one plus the interest rate between now and expiration. Using two months to expiration and an interest rate of 6.5%, the adjustment factor is 1.011 and the corrected quantity of futures contracts is 924 (934/1.011).

FIXED INCOME PORTFOLIO PROTECTION

We believe that portfolio protection on fixed income assets is a timely strategy to consider. On one hand, bonds have provided very attractive returns in recent years and it is reasonable to expect that bonds will provide higher returns than cash equivalents over any given long horizon. On the other hand, the volatility of bonds has increased dramatically. Hence, it is clear that a portfolio protection program that would limit the downside risk on a bond portfolio and yet capture most of the upside, would give a manager staying power to maintain or increase his fixed income portfolio. This would increase long term returns, the principal benefit of a portfolio protection program.

Given the methodology of utilizing bond futures, we are ready to move along with fixed income portfolio protection. The first most important input is the volatility or standard deviation of the portfolio. For the 13¼'s, the annualized standard deviation using the logarithm of daily returns for the year prior to this analysis is 14.3%. Let us also assume a short-term risk free rate of 6.5%.

Assuming that we are dealing only with equal changes in yield for all securities, it is possible to infer the volatility of a fixed income portfolio from the ratio of its %VO1 to the %VO1 of the above bond. Using the previously mentioned portfolio, the %VO1 is equal to the modified duration divided by 10,000 or .0766%. The ratio of the %VO1 of the portfolio and of the 13¼'s is .88 (= .0766/.0871). Therefore, the expected volatility of this portfolio would be 12.6% (14.3 × .88). Alternatively, if daily data of returns for the actual portfolio is available, the annualized standard deviation of the logarithm of the returns should be used.

Based on the work of Hayne Leland, it is possible to factor in transaction costs by increasing the volatility.[1] Our experience in equity portfolio protection indicates that a 5% increase is appropriate. Therefore, we propose using a volatility of 13.2%. Exhibit 1 presents the estimated cost, required hedge ratio, and number of futures contracts for a one year protection horizon. Obviously, the protection cost is less

---

[1]Hayne E. Leland, "Option Pricing and Replication with Transactions Costs," *The Journal of Finance*, Vol. XL, No. 5, December 1985.

than that for a comparable equity portfolio. This is due to the somewhat lower volatility.

Some of the risks in a fixed income portfolio protection program are similar to an equity program: 1) unexpected increase in volatility and 2) unfavorable mispricing of the futures. Another obstacle is the lack of a good index to use as the reference point, such as the S&P 500. Perhaps, the yield on the current long bond should be used. Then the assumed value of the fixed income portfolio can be monitored on a current basis using its $VO1. The Salomon or Lehman indexes are difficult to use because they are shorter term and their composition is more inclusive than the few government bonds the futures contract is based on.

If the portfolio consists of securities other than government bonds, such as corporate bonds or mortgages, there might be an adverse widening of the yield spread. In the case of junk bonds or convertible bonds, it might make sense to combine a large position in fixed income futures with a small position in equity futures. In any case, it is not possible to hedge away specific credit risk.

Another risk might be different changes in yield along the yield curve, or different changes in yield for different securities. If it is anticipated that a certain security or portfolio will have uneven yield changes, its "yield beta" should be used to adjust its $VO1.[2] In the case of fixed income portfolios with shorter durations, the futures on the Treasury notes might be a more suitable vehicle. In any case, it is necessary to monitor the underlying portfolio and adjust to any changes in its characteristics.

With regard to the use of futures, there is the risk that changes in the "cheapest to deliver" will prevent the futures from declining at the expected rate in the case of an interest rate rise. Also, the underlying bonds might start trading on a yield to maturity basis instead of yield to call as they trade at the time of this writing.

Some theoreticians might point out that the return distribution of a bond is not lognormal. This would invalidate the applicability of the option pricing model and therefore hinder its use in fixed income portfolio protection. However, the return distribution of a bond is close enough to lognormal to make this point of no practical relevance.

In the case of fixed income portfolio protection, dealing in the cash market, i.e., shorting government bonds, is a much more plausible alternative than in equity portfolio protection, especially for smaller portfolios. For one, no uptick is required. Secondly, it is easier to get a fair return on the proceeds from the short sale by doing a reverse repurchase agreement. Thirdly, one could short only one government bond; there is no need to short a basket as in the equity market, thus transaction costs are lower. Also, margin requirements for government bonds are much more liberal than for equities. Finally, it is possible to select the actual bond to short, thereby specifying the duration of the hedge to equal the duration of the portfolio.

---

[2]Robert W. Kopprasch, "Understanding Duration and Volatility," Chapter 5 in Frank J. Fabozzi and Irving M. Pollack (eds.) *The Handbook of Fixed Income Securities* (Homewood, IL: Dow Jones - Irwin, 1987).

EXHIBIT 1
FIXED INCOME PORTFOLIO PROTECTION

Deductible (%)	Cost (%)	Initial Hedge Ratio (%)*	Yield Sensitivity Ratio**	Number of Contracts	Underlying Value of Futures to Be Sold ($MM)
0	2.56	28.2	934 (= 76,600/82.0)	263	26.3
5	1.31	16.7	934	156	15.6
10	.58	8.5	934	79	7.9

Assumptions: Portfolio value $100MM, duration 8 years, yield to maturity 9%.
One year protection horizon, portfolio volatility 13.2%, risk free rate 6.5%.
Protection cost is externally financed.
*Adjusted for interest on variation margin.
**Yield sensitivity ratio = $V01 portfolio/$V01 futures contract

Problems with this approach include: restrictions on shorting securities by pension plans, the possibility of a squeeze in the particular issue short, and strong relative performance of this issue.

PORTFOLIO PROTECTION FOR BALANCED PORTFOLIOS

The combination of equity portfolio protection and fixed income portfolio protection does not pose any difficult conceptual problems. The basic procedure is to sell equity futures according to the prescribed hedge ratio against the equity portion of the portfolio and fixed income futures in the same proportion. This method achieves a gradual and even shift of the portfolio into cash as is normally the case in portfolio protection.

Portfolio protection on two or more asset classes is quite different than getting the highest return of the various assets.[3] Clearly, getting the higher return entails creating a more complex and expensive option. This multi-asset option is less costly than the aggregate value of the calls on each asset separately, but substantially more costly than a put on the aggregate portfolio value.

Why not first sell equity futures until that portion of the portfolio is completely covered and then sell fixed income futures? This approach is inferior, because it interjects path dependence and therefore results in higher cost uncertainty. For example, if the market fluctuates in a trading range around the initial level, the program would be buying and selling equity futures. If these fluctuations occur after a large decline, the trading would be in fixed income futures, clearly leading to different results. Also, when only equity futures are outstanding, the correlation between the futures and the portfolio would be lower, leading to an increased risk of tracking error.

A major advantage of balanced portfolio protection is that the protection cost is less than the aggregate cost of protecting the equity component and the fixed income component separately. This is due to the low correlation between equity returns and bond returns which results in a lower combined volatility. The formula for calculating the combined standard deviation is as follows:

$$
\begin{array}{ccccccc}
 & & & & \text{Variance} & & \\
\text{Variance} & & \text{Variance} & & \text{Fixed} & & \text{Covariance} \\
\text{Balanced} & = & \text{Equity} & + & \text{Income} & +2\times & \text{of Two} \qquad (1) \\
\text{Portfolio} & & \text{Component} & & \text{Component} & & \text{Components}
\end{array}
$$

$$
P^2 \times SDP^2 = E^2 \times SDE^2 + FI^2 \times SDFI^2 + 2 \times RHO \times E \times FI \times SDE \times SDFI
$$

---

[3]Oldrich A. Vasicek, "Getting the Best of N Asset Returns," presented at the Institute for International Research Conference, June 1986.

where:

P	= Portfolio value
SDP	= Portfolio standard deviation
E	= Equity value
SDE	= Equity standard deviation
FI	= Fixed income value
SDFI	= Fixed income standard deviation
RHO	= Correlation between equity returns and fixed income returns

For example, consider a portfolio that consists of $60 million equity (beta = 1) and $40 million fixed income (with the same characteristics as in the previous example). Using daily data for the past year, the standard deviations are 17.0% and 12.6%, respectively. The correlation of stock returns with bond returns using daily data for the 3 years prior to this analysis is .37 (a larger historical data base is preferable when estimating correlation). The combined standard deviation from equation (1) is 12.9%. The 5% allowance for transaction costs brings the volatility to 13.5%. Figures for one year policies are presented in Exhibit 2.

If the portfolio has a cash equivalent component, the equity and fixed income futures can be reduced accordingly. This will result in the protection cost being incurred in the form of opportunity cost on the cash rather than losses on the futures.

SURPLUS PROTECTION

Surplus protection, also known as *dynamic asset liability management*, has great intuitive appeal.[4] For one, the focus of pension plans, mandated by FASB 87, is shifting to surplus rather than just assets. A deficit would show up as a liability on the balance sheet and may affect pension expense and pension contribution. Secondly, in surplus protection, the risk-free or reserve asset is the equivalent of a dedicated bond portfolio, rather than cash equivalents as in conventional portfolio protection. The higher expected returns from bonds relative to cash will contribute to the lower protection cost. Cash in this environment appears to be inferior, having both substantial risk relative to liabilities and lower expected returns. Finally, the positive correlation between equity returns and the liability returns diminishes the relative standard deviation substantially and therefore lowers the protection cost even further. Zurack and Somes cite as an example September 11, 1986.[5] On this day, the

---

[4]Mark Kritzman, "What's Wrong with Portfolio Insurance," *The Journal of Portfolio Management*, Fall 1986, 13-16.

[5]Mark A. Zurack and Steven P. Somes, "Pension Plans, Portfolio Insurance and FASB Statement No. 87: An Old Risk in a New Light," *Financial Analysts Journal*, January-February 1987.

EXHIBIT 2
PORTFOLIO PROTECTION FOR A BALANCED PORTFOLIO

Deductible (%)	Cost (%)	Initial Hedge Ratio (%)*	Value of Equity Futures ($MM)	Number of Equity Futures Contracts Short**	Yield Sensitivity Ratio	Number of Bond Futures Contracts Short	Underlying Face Value of Bond Futures Contracts ($MM)
0	2.67	28.5	17.1	110	374 (=934×40/100)	107	10.7
5	1.39	17.2	10.3	66	374	64	6.4
10	.63	8.9	5.3	34	374	33	3.3

Assumptions: Portfolio components: $60MM equity, $40MM fixed income (same as in previous example), one year protection horizon, portfolio volatility 13.5%, risk free rate 6.5%. Protection cost is externally financed.

*Adjusted for interest on variation margin.

**Using S&P 500 contracts, with the index currently at 310.

market had a big decline, but because interest rates rose, liabilities also fell. Hence, the surplus was left nearly unchanged and there was no need to rebalance. However, when the stock market crashed in October 1987, interest rates fell so pension fund surplus fell even faster and bigger adjustments became necessary.

The analytical solution to surplus protection can take two forms. One, based on Margrabe's model,[6] would have us look at the surplus as a ratio. All returns would be measured relative to liabilities and we would have to specify a minimum return or deductible as a ratio. With this approach, like regular portfolio protection, one can determine the cost and the hedge ratio using the standard option pricing model. The volatility and risk-free rate would be based on relative returns.[7]

The ratio of assets to liabilities is of particular importance under several legislative regulations and proposals. Under the Omnibus Budget Reconciliation Act of 1987 the minimum and maximum funding requirement are expressed as ratios.

On one hand, the act established a maximum funded limit of 150% of "current liability" (similar to the Accumulated Benefit Obligation). Any contributions beyond this limit would not be deductible and would be subject to an excise tax. On the other hand, if the ratio drops below 100%, new stringent minimum funding requirements will be imposed. The investment implications for a fund that is in the middle of this range for the moment and wants to maintain a stable funding policy, is to engage in a strategy that is equivalent to buying an out-of-the-money put and selling an out-of-the-money call on the surplus. The put would protect against a drop below 100% while by writing a call, the fund would transfer the potential appreciation beyond 150% in return for a premium. This strategy, in addition to containing the surplus ratio within the 150%-100% band, will also be more economical. The proceeds from the call sale will help defray or may even exceed the cost of the put. Of course, we are not talking about actually trading calls or puts on the pension surplus, but about dynamically replicating them via a surplus protection program. Interestingly, the hedge ratio of such a program in relation to the surplus level would take on the shape of a bowl, as shown in Exhibit 3.

In addition, under a still pending proposal, recapture of pension assets would be permitted only to the extent that assets exceed 125% of liabilities. If assets dropped below this ratio, the corporation would be required to fund the difference before any recapture would be possible.

Nevertheless, specifying the surplus as a ratio is not always desirable. A plan sponsor would probably be more interested in preserving a specific dollar surplus

---

[6]William Margrabe, "The Value of an Option to Exchange One Asset for Another," *The Journal of Finance*, Vol. XXXIII No. 1, March 1987.

[7]The interest rate plays two roles in the Black-Scholes model. First, it acts as a proxy for the risk adjusted expected appreciation of the underlying asset. For this purpose the risk-free rate should be set to zero. The second role is to discount the value of the option to the present where the actual (not the relative) risk-free rate should be used.

EXHIBIT 3
SURPLUS PROTECTION REQUIRED HEDGE RATIO

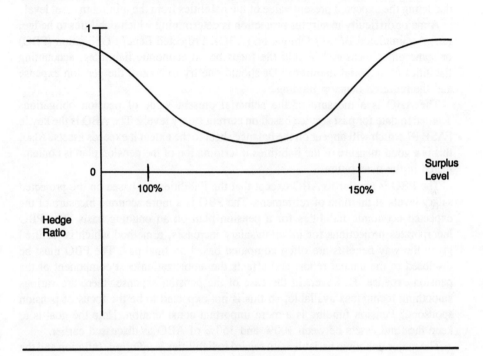

rather than a specific ratio to the liabilities. Also, the Omnibus Budget Reconciliation Act mandates variable premiums payable to the Pension Benefit Guaranty Corporation based on the absolute level of underfunding. While prior to this law there was a flat premium of $8.50 per plan participant effective in 1988, the rate will be $16 per participant plus $6 per participant for every $1,000 of underfunding of the plan per participant up to a maximum total rate of $50 per participant. This feature of the law would suggest focusing on the absolute deficit level in the case of a deficit near this range.

Protecting a certain dollar surplus/deficit can be considered as a special case of balanced portfolio protection, where the fixed income component of the portfolio is negative. The standard deviation should be calculated using equation (1), but substituting a minus instead of a plus in front of the covariance term. The expected assets and present value of liabilities at the end of the protection horizon should be calculated. The assets should be increased by the risk-free rate plus any expected contributions, less anticipated plan disbursements. Then the estimated cost and hedge ratio can be calculated using Black's formula for options on futures/forwards.[8] Here the deductible and the cost would be specified as a percent of the assets. Once this step is complete, we can calculate the minimum surplus level by deducting the expected present value of the liabilities from the minimum asset level.

A major difficulty in surplus protection is determining which liabilities to hedge, i.e., Accumulated Benefit Obligation (ABO), Projected Benefit Obligation (PBO) or some other measure? Should the focus be on economic liabilities, accounting liabilities or actuarial liabilities? Or should one try to control the pension expense and the required pension funding?

The ABO is a measure of the actuarial present value of pension obligations accrued to date for past service based on current salary levels. The ABO is the key in FASB 87 which will appear on the balance sheet to the extent it exceeds assets. Also, this is a good measure of the liabilities if termination of the pension plan is contemplated in the near future.

The PBO is similar to ABO except that the liabilities are based on the projected salary levels at the time of retirement. The PBO is a more accurate measure of the expected economic liabilities for a pension plan on an ongoing basis. The PBO incorporates projections for inflation/salary increases, a method which is justified given the way benefits are often computed based on final pay. The PBO must be disclosed in the annual report and affects the amortization cost component of the pension expense. However, in the case of the pension expense, there are various smoothing techniques available, so this is not expected to be the focus of pension sponsors.[9] Pension funding is a more important consideration. Here the goal is to keep the fund assets between 100% and 150% of ABO as discussed earlier.

The major unknown variable with regard to liabilities is *inflation*. Inflation and the resulting salary increases cause the liabilities to change, making liability estimates more difficult to formulate. Even if we could completely hedge the PBO with a dedicated bond portfolio (this would entail a very long duration portfolio), inflation would cause the liabilities to rise with no commensurate increase in assets. Bonds are clearly not an effective hedge against inflation. It is surprising that no liquid vehicle exists that would enable the trading and transfer of inflation risk. In some countries, Israel for example, there are inflation-indexed bonds that serve this purpose. There is a futures contract on the Consumer Price Index that is listed on the Coffee, Sugar and Cocoa Exchange. Unfortunately, its volume is nearly zero.

High inflation is a serious risk that plan sponsors should address. With the mounting government debt and the continued huge budget deficits it appears likely that within the next few years the government will face the terrible choice of an outright default on U.S. obligations or the printing of money to pay down the debt. The choice is likely to be the latter.

---

[8]Fischer Black, "The Pricing of Commodity Contracts," *Journal of Financial Economics* 3, 1976, 167-179.

[9]Zurack and Somes, "Pension Plans, Portfolio Insurance and FASB Statement No. 87: An Old Risk in a New Light."

Leibowitz makes a strong assertion that bonds are the best available vehicle to hedge liability returns.[10] He argues that typical plan liabilities have very long durations, while most pension assets have very short durations. However, Leibowitz ignores inflation and its effect on liabilities.

If not bonds, then what is the appropriate reserve asset to hedge away inflation risk? Ibbotson and Sinquefield show that cash equivalents are the best available inflation hedges while stocks are fair inflation hedges.[11] Cash equivalents benefit from the increase in short term interest rates that occurs during inflationary periods.

In the absence of effective inflation hedges, it does not make sense to focus on such a long term liability measure as the PBO. In a "final pay" plan, the only component of the liabilities that is not affected by inflation is the benefits for retired employees that are not subject to COLA (Cost of Living Adjustments). However, there are pension plans that calculate the benefits using other formulas such as "career average plans" and "flat dollar plans." In these plans, the "inflation free" component is substantially greater.

From an economic point of view, only the inflation free component should be hedged. From an accounting and funding point of view, the more inclusive ABO should be hedged. The decision would be based on corporate priorities as defined by senior management.

The mechanics for surplus protection are demonstrated with the following example. Consider a pension sponsor that desires a one year surplus protection program. The expected ABO a year from now (including benefits accrued through the coming year) at current interest rates is $70 million. The $VO1 is .1% of $70 million or $70,000. No contribution by the corporation into the pension plan is expected. Total assets of $100 million consist of $60 million in equity, $30 million in fixed income with the same characteristics as in previous examples, and $10 million in cash equivalents. The expected surplus if assets (including income) and interest rates remain unchanged is $30 million. For the purpose of this example, we need to assume that the only uncertainty regarding the ABO is the discount rate a year from now (the ABO will of course be affected by other factors such as mortality and turn over).

The first step of the solution is to net out the fixed income component against the ABO. The net $VO1 is $47,0 00 ($70 million × .1% − $30 million × .0766%) and the net %VO1 is .067% ($47,000/$70 million). The implied volatility of the ABO, again arrived at by multiplying the volatility of the 13 1/4's by the ratio of the %VO1, is 11.0% (14.3 × .067/.087). Obviously, the fixed income component has reduced the volatility of the ABO substantially.

The combined volatility can now be calculated using equation (1), as mentioned earlier, a minus is substituted for the plus in front of the covariance term. The cash

[10]Martin L. Leibowitz, "Pension Asset Allocation Through Surplus Management," *Financial Analysts Journal*, March-April 1987.

[11]Roger G. Ibbotson and Rex A. Sinquefield, "Stocks, Bonds, Bills and Inflation: Year by Year Historical Returns (1926-1974)," *The Journal of Business*, January 1976, 11-47.

component is assumed to have zero volatility. Also, once the dollar volatility is arrived at, it is converted into a percent volatility be dividing by the total assets of $100 million (not by the expected surplus of $30 million). The result is 10.3% and with the adjustment for transaction costs 10.8%.

The cash component of the portfolio constitutes part of the reserve asset and therefore reduces the need to sell equity futures and buy bond futures. Exhibit 4 summarizes the results.

In surplus protection, using the cash instrument instead of the futures is even more realistic than in fixed income portfolio protection. In this case, we are long the bond so there is no risk of difficulty in the collateral market. However, there still remains the problem of pension fund restrictions on margin and relative performance of the specific issue.

PORTFOLIO PROTECTION AND THE OCTOBER, 1987 CRASH

In the wake of the failure of many portfolio protectors to meet the expected floor of their programs, the investment community has largely written off portfolio protection as a viable strategy. We do not support this view.

When the crash occurred and equity futures went to huge discounts, institutions pursuing a portfolio protection program should have cashed in their protection policy. The disaster against which the protection was meant to protect occurred. So why wait until some predefined termination date if the protection proceeds could be collected with a premium immediately? Of course, inherent in that decision is the judgment that from that point on the risk of an immediate further collapse is reduced. But investment management requires that such judgments be made. Just the existence of equity futures contracts trading at 10-15% discounts from the spot value is an enormous market inefficiency begging to be exploited. Unfortunately, when everybody is panicking there is no natural buyer of these contracts. We believe that a portfolio protector short futures is in a unique position to buy futures under such conditions. At some point, the futures must be bought back anyhow. Here there is an enormous incentive to do so right away.

In any case, an investment strategy should not be based on one day that is not likely to repeat itself any time soon. Even the bear market that followed the 1929 crash was much more gradual than the crash itself.

Finally, if we accept that the markets are somewhat efficient, a higher volatility will be associated with higher expected returns on equities. Yet equity ownership will be and feel more risky. Hence, the benefit of portfolio protection is augmented, albeit one must pay the higher price.

If one desires an absolute foolproof portfolio protection program they may buy index puts. However, once they realized the substantial premium they must pay for this certainty they will quickly be dissuaded.

This entire discussion relates to equity portfolio protection which, of course,

EXHIBIT 4
SURPLUS PROTECTION COSTS

Deductible (%)	Cost (%)	Initial Hedge Ratio (%)*	Required Hedge Net of Cash	Value of Equity Futures Short ($MM)	Number of Equity Futures Contracts Short **	Yield Sensitivity Ratio	Number of Bond Futures Long	Underlying Face Value of Bonds Futures ($MM)
0	1.77	25.0	15.0	9.0	58	573 (=47,000/82.0)	86	8.6
5	.75	12.5	2.5	1.5	10	573	14	1.4
10	.26	4.9	0	—	—	—	—	—

Assumptions: $60 MM equity, $30MM fixed income, $10MM cash, $70MM expected ABO, one year protection horizon, combined volatility 10.8%, risk free rate 6.5%.

All percentage figures are based on $100MM.
Protection cost is externally financed.
*Adjusted for interest on variation margin.
**Using S&P 500 contracts, with the index currently at 310.

impacts balanced portfolio protection and surplus protection. However, fixed income markets and futures have not exhibited similar jumps and they are equally important in the implementation of these programs.

CONCLUSION

Surplus protection can be achieved at a surprisingly low cost relative to the portfolio protection cost of protecting an equity portfolio alone. The low cost is due primarily to the significantly positive correlation between the stock returns and the changes in the present value of liabilities due to fluctuations in the discount rate. This positive correlation reduces the relative volatility substantially.

Secondly, a fixed income portfolio is a more desirable reserve asset than cash because of its higher long term returns. Finally, the ABO can be reduced to the extent of any fixed income component in the portfolio weighted by the relative sensitivity to changes in yield. Also, the required hedge can be reduced by the amount of the cash equivalents resulting in even further cost savings.

From an economic point of view, surplus protection should only cover "inflation free liabilities" such as benefits for retired employees not subject to COLA. Other measures of liability are very sensitive to inflation which cannot be effectively hedged. The accountants, however, focus on the ABO. If avoiding a liability on the balance sheet or controlling the required funding of the plan are important concerns, then ABO should be used.

The major benefit of both portfolio protection and surplus protection, to just briefly reiterate, is the ability to have a more aggressive asset allocation on average, thereby increasing expected returns. We believe portfolio/surplus protection continues to be a wise strategy despite recent bad press.

The perils, however, are numerous. To mention a few of them in order of importance: gap moves in stocks, unexpected low correlation between equity returns and liability returns, unexpected high volatility of stocks or interest rates, mispricing in futures contracts, non-parallel yield shifts and peculiarities of the bond futures.

Nevertheless, the purpose of a pension plan is to be able to meet benefit requirements, not just accumulate assets in a vacuum. Maximizing assets without regard to liabilities makes no more sense than maximizing revenues without regard to expenses and profits. This fact, combined with the lower cost of protecting assets-less-liabilities make a compelling argument for the use of surplus protection.

PART V
Bond Analysis Tools

Chapter 13

Spread-Duration: A New Tool for Bond Portfolio Management

MARTIN L. LEIBOWITZ, PH.D.
MANAGING DIRECTOR
SALOMON BROTHERS INC

WILLIAM S. KRASKER, PH.D.
VICE PRESIDENT
SALOMON BROTHERS INC

ARDAVAN NOZARI, PH.D.
VICE PRESIDENT
SALOMON BROTHERS INC

The sensitivity of bond portfolio values to changing interest rates has been the subject of extensive research in recent years. For bonds with well-defined cash flows, such as most Treasury issues, the interest rate sensitivity is closely represented by the "modified duration," which describes how the price of the bond changes

The authors wish to express their appreciation to Thomas Klaffky, Y.Y. Ma, Steve Mandel, and Leo Schlinkert for their role in the formulation of the spread-duration concept and for their many helpful suggestions.

with small variations in its yield. For typical corporate bonds and mortgage-backed securities, which have embedded option features and, hence, cash flows that depend on the path of interest rates, we can still examine the price response to changes in the general level of rates. This sensitivity, usually called the "effective duration," provides portfolio managers with a method of controlling their interest rate exposure.

This duration measure is a valuable tool for estimating and controlling the volatility of fixed-income portfolios, as long as overall changes in interest rates represent the sole source of risk. However, a portfolio that includes corporate bonds generates returns that depend not only on changes in interest rates, but also on the changes in the spreads of the bonds that comprise the portfolio. A portfolio selection procedure that ignores this spread variability will be driven, for example, toward high-yield bonds, because it will understate their true risk. In this chapter we discuss the concept of "spread-duration," which represents the sensitivity of a portfolio to spread changes in the corporate bond market. (Although our discussion concentrates on the corporate market, the same ideas can be usefully applied to a variety of asset classes.)

For clarity, we begin by examining the effect of a spread change on a portfolio consisting of a single corporate bond. Subsequently, we will consider portfolios that combine a corporate bond with a Treasury bond. The spread-duration—the sensitivity of the portfolio value to the bond's spread change—depends on the product of the duration of the corporate bond and its weight in the portfolio.

Finally, we will consider spread-duration for general portfolios. For these, the key quantities are the empirically derived "sector spread betas," which describe how the spreads in subsectors of the corporate market tend to change, given a change in spread for the *corporate market as a whole*. The spread-duration of a general portfolio is defined as a weighted average of the durations of the various corporate sectors comprising the portfolio, in which the weight of each sector is the product of its sector spread beta and its market value percentage in the portfolio.

PRICE/YIELD RELATIONSHIPS WITHOUT SPREAD VARIABILITY

For simplicity, we focus on zero-coupon bonds. Exhibit 1 shows a hypothetical Treasury STRIPs curve. In this graph the vertical axis is the yield, and the horizontal axis is the bond's maturity. The 5-year Treasury zero-coupon bond with an 8.2% yield is highlighted on the curve. In addition, we include a corporate zero-coupon bond that has the same 5-year maturity, but trades at a higher yield.[1] The 150-basis-

---

[1]For clarity of exposition, our example uses a hypothetical corporate zero-coupon bond. In more general cases, we would have to include consideration of coupon effects, optional calls and sinking fund features. This would require an extensive discussion of the role of interest rate volatility and its relationship to more sophisticated versions of the spread and duration concepts (such as the option-adjusted spread and the effective duration). However, this additional complexity is not required for our main purpose.

EXHIBIT 1
YIELDS AND MATURITIES—THE CASE OF EQUAL DURATIONS

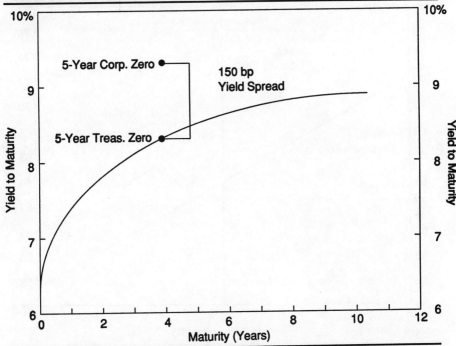

point spread is simply the vertical "yield distance" between the corporate bond and the Treasury bond.

First, consider the price response of these securities to changes in Treasury yields, assuming that the corporate bond maintains a constant spread. Exhibit 2 illustrates the prices of the two bonds as functions of the change in the Treasury yield. The Treasury bond has a slightly steeper curve, which implies a greater absolute price sensitivity to any particular yield change. However, the percentage price changes for the two securities—their returns—are nearly equal because of their essentially equal durations. Thus, apart from credit risk, the securities have virtually identical risk characteristics.

THE EFFECT OF SPREAD CHANGES

Exhibit 3 contains a representation of the effect of a change in spreads. The upper two curves are the same as those in Exhibit 2, while the bottom curve shows the price of the corporate bond for different shifts in the yield curve, given a 50-basis-point increase in its spread relative to the Treasury curve. The magnitude of the drop

EXHIBIT 2
BOND PRICES VERSUS YIELD CURVE SHIFT

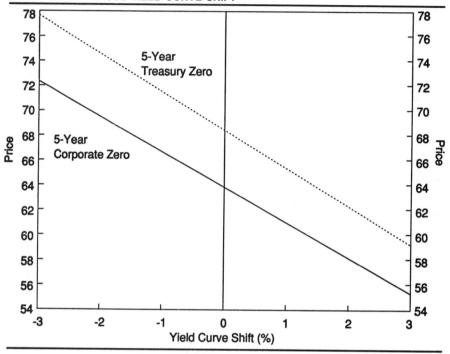

in price—the vertical distance between the two solid curves—represents the sensitivity of the corporate bond to spread changes. The actual price change of the corporate bond, in a general setting in which both interest rates and spreads change, is represented in Exhibit 3 as a combination of two changes: (1) a spread change that determines the location of the bond's price curve in the figure; and (2) a change in interest rates that determines a particular point on the curve.

We can isolate the effect of a spread change on the bond's return by assuming that interest rates remain unchanged. This leads to Exhibit 4, in which the bond return is depicted as a function of its spread change. The return per unit change in spread—the slope of the curve in the figure—can be regarded as the spread-duration relative to a benchmark portfolio consisting of just this bond. In this case, the spread-duration of 4.77 years coincides with the corporate bond's modified duration, because a spread change has the same effect as a general change in yields.[2]

---

[2]While the "Macaulay duration" for a zero-coupon bond of maturity N years is N, the proper measure of its instantaneous price sensitivity is called the "modified duration" which has the value N/(1 + Y/200) for a bond with yield Y. Thus, the 5-year corporate zero at a yield of 9.7% has a modified duration of 5/(1 + 9.7/200) = 4.77 years.

EXHIBIT 3
EFFECT OF SPREAD CHANGE

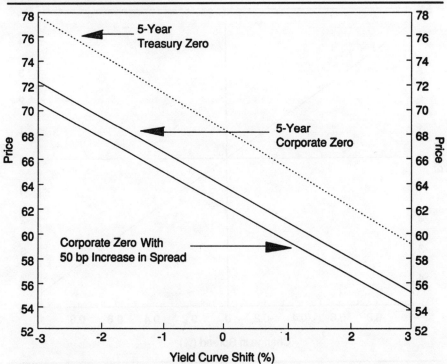

THE CASE OF UNEQUAL DURATIONS

Thus far, we have focused on the case of equal durations. Assume instead that the corporate bond has a 7-year maturity, as depicted in Exhibit 5. Exhibit 6 shows how the returns on the two securities vary as a function of the shift in the yield curve. The curve for the corporate bond is steeper, reflecting its greater sensitivity to yield changes. The slopes of the curves are simply the modified durations: 6.7 years for the corporate bond and 4.8 years for the Treasury bond.

Exhibit 7 combines the effects of changes in interest rates and spreads on the returns of these two bonds. The middle curve in the exhibit shows the difference in the returns (corporate over Treasury) as a function of the shift in the yield curve, assuming that there is no change in the corporate bond's spread. Because of the corporate bond's longer duration, it will outperform or underperform the Treasury bond, depending on whether the yield curve shift is down or up. The top and bottom curves represent spread changes of −50 basis points and +50 basis points, respectively. Analogous to Exhibit 3, the difference in the returns has two components—the difference generated by the interest rate change, which reflects the duration gap, and the additional return to the corporate bond because of the spread change. In our

EXHIBIT 4
CORPORATE BOND RETURN VERSUS SPREAD CHANGE

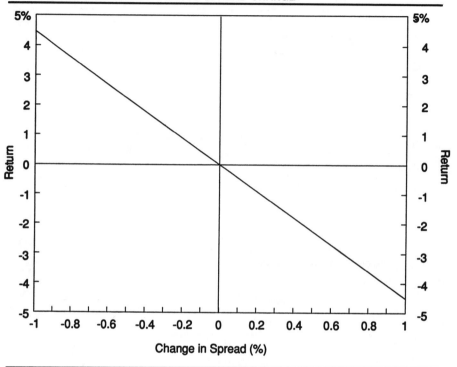

Change in Spread (%)

representation, the second component determines the appropriate curve, while the first determines the location on that curve. The spread-duration is 6.7 years, which, once again, coincides with the modified duration of the 7-year corporate zero.

SPREAD-DURATION OF A SIMPLE PORTFOLIO

We now turn our attention to portfolios. Consider a simple portfolio that consists of a 60%/40% mix of the 5-year Treasury bond and the 7-year corporate bond. As shown in Exhibit 8, the duration of this portfolio is the market-value-weighted average of the durations of the bonds that it comprises, and the portfolio yield (the internal rate of return) is approximately the weighted average of the individual yields, weighted by the product of market value and duration. (Notice that, in general, the portfolio will not lie on the straight line between the two bonds in a yield curve diagram such as Exhibit 8.)

EXHIBIT 5
YIELDS AND MATURITIES—THE CASE OF UNEQUAL DURATIONS

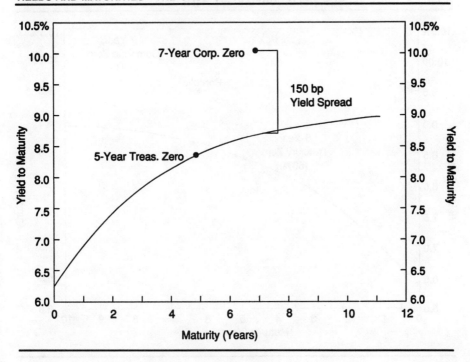

Exhibit 9 graphs the portfolio return as a function of the change in the corporate spread. The slope of the curve, 2.68, is the spread-duration, which, in this case, is the product of the duration of the corporate bond, 6.7, and its weight, 0.4, in the portfolio.

SPREAD-DURATION FOR GENERAL PORTFOLIOS

We can extend the concept of spread-duration to general portfolios by first defining a general benchmark "spread change" in the corporate market. We consider the market-weighted average change in spread of all the securities in the corporate component of the Salomon Brothers Broad Investment-Grade Bond Index[SM] (the Broad Index) as such a benchmark. We then empirically estimate the sector "spread betas" for various subsectors of the corporate component of the Broad Index. These betas represent the amount by which the market-weighted average spread in each sector tends to change, given a change in the overall corporate spread. Finally, we

EXHIBIT 6
BOND RETURNS VERSUS YIELD CURVE SHIFT WITH UNEQUAL DURATIONS

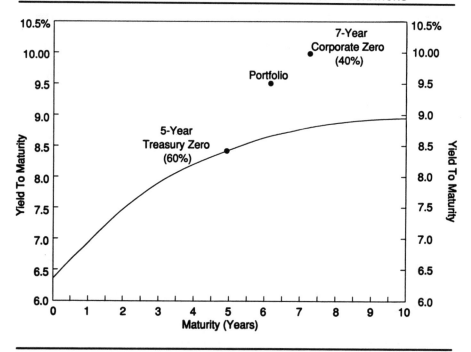

define the portfolio spread-duration as a weighted average of the durations of the sectors comprising the portfolio, in which the weight of each sector is the product of its sector spread beta and its market value percentage in the portfolio.

For example, consider a portfolio consisting 65% of Treasury bonds with a 6-year duration, and 35% of BBB-rated corporates with a 4-year duration. The sector spread beta is zero for Treasuries, and is approximately 1.3 for BBB securities. Thus, the portfolio spread-duration is 1.82 years, which is computed as follows:

65% Treasury	$0.65 \times 6 \times 0.0 =$ ⎯⎯ 0
35% BBB Corporate	$0.35 \times 4 \times 1.3 = \underline{1.82}$
Portfolio Spread-Duration	1.82

We can illustrate the effectiveness of this approach by applying it to the corporate sector of the Broad Index itself. Exhibit 10 contains the scatterplot of the sequence of incremental monthly returns from the corporate sector of the Broad Index, net of the part of the return due to the shift in a Treasury benchmark, versus the overall

EXHIBIT 7
DIFFERENCE IN RETURNS VERSUS YIELD CURVE SHIFT

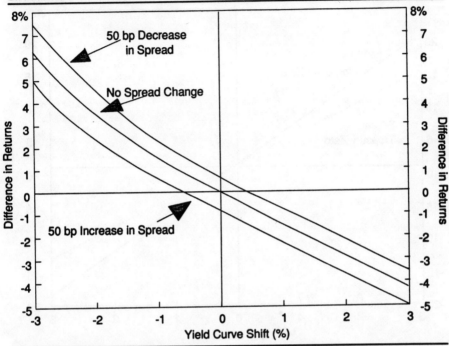

corporate spread change over the corresponding month. The slope of the line drawn through the scatterplot is the average (1984-88) spread-duration for the Broad Index corporates. The tightness of the scatter around this theoretical line suggests that the spread-duration can be a useful measure of the sensitivity of a portfolio to spread changes.

CONCLUSION

The power of the spread-duration is derived from its simplicity and corresponding ease of application. It provides a compact, one-dimensional measure of spread risk over short-term horizons. However, it should be pointed out that this simplicity entails certain costs. As with all duration measures, the spread-duration should be expected only to approximate incremental returns associated with modest changes in market spreads. To capture the effects of large market movements, we must turn to a broader set of more complex tools that can address other factors such as convexity,

EXHIBIT 8
PORTFOLIO YIELD AND DURATION

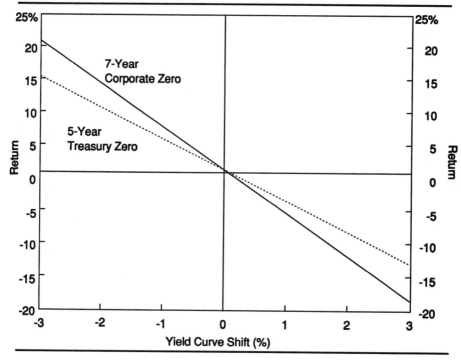

optional characteristics, various yield curve effects, etc. As with the basic modified Macaulay duration, the spread-duration concept has the virtue of being so simple and so intuitive that it can be readily incorporated into the day-to-day management of fixed-income portfolios.

Traditionally, a portfolio manager focuses on the percentage of corporate bonds in his or her portfolio, or perhaps the percentages within each credit sector, as a measure of the portfolio's credit risk. This approach may be appropriate for long-term horizons, where the risk consists of the possibility of actual defaults. However, with the increasing focus on short-term return as a measure of performance, portfolio managers need a correspondingly short-term gauge of credit risk. The spread-duration, by measuring the sensitivity of the portfolio return to spread changes over the short term, provides such a yardstick.

Spread-duration greatly facilitates the comparison of portfolios. For example, two portfolios, comprising very different securities, will nevertheless have similar risk characteristics if they have the same duration and spread-duration. This improved

EXHIBIT 9
PORTFOLIO RETURN VERSUS SPREAD CHANGE

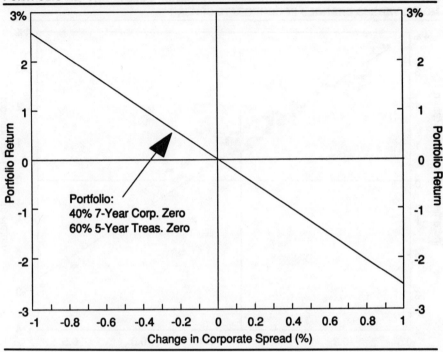

assessment of short-term spread risk can facilitate the comparison and control of overall portfolio risks, as well as help to construct portfolios that are actively oriented to exploit perceived market opportunities in specific sectors. Indeed, the very heart of duration-constrained active management is sector spread management. For these reasons, we believe that the spread-duration concept represents a fundamental new tool that should prove valuable for active management as well as for various structured strategies.

EXHIBIT 10
INCREMENTAL BROAD INDEX CORPORATE RETURNS ADJUSTED BY YIELD CURVE
MOVES VERSUS CHANGES IN CORPORATE SPREAD

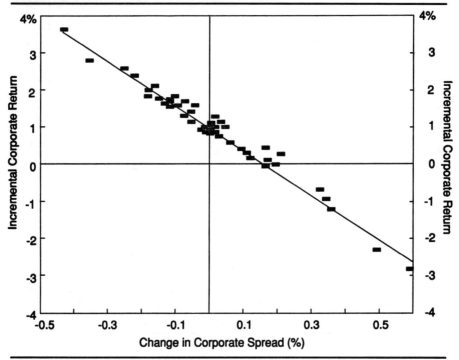

Change in Corporate Spread (%)

Chapter 14

The Analysis of Credit Barbells: An Application of the Spread-Duration Technique

MARTIN L. LEIBOWITZ, PH.D.
MANAGING DIRECTOR
SALOMON BROTHERS INC

WILLIAM S. KRASKER, PH.D.
VICE PRESIDENT
SALOMON BROTHERS INC

ARDAVAN NOZARI, PH.D.
VICE PRESIDENT
SALOMON BROTHERS INC

In the previous chapter, we introduced the concept of credit spread-duration as a measure of the sensitivity of a portfolio's value to changes in corporate spreads. Spread-duration is defined as a weighted average of the durations of the various

The authors wish to express their appreciation to Thomas Klaffky, Y.Y. Ma, Steve Mandel, and Leo Schlinkert for their role in the formulation of the spread-duration concept and for their many helpful suggestions.

sectors comprising the portfolio. The weight of each sector is the product of its market value weight in the portfolio and a parameter, "beta," that describes how spreads in that sector respond to changes in overall corporate spreads. By setting the spread-duration at appropriate values, a portfolio manager can gain significant control over his portfolio's exposure to changing spreads.

In this chapter we focus on "credit barbells." A credit barbell is a portfolio that maintains a specified duration and spread-duration through a combination of two (or more) sectors having differing credit ratings and/or durations. Credit barbells often have advantages over single-sector portfolios with the same risk characteristics, such as higher yields, more desirable cash flow patterns, better liquidity, etc. Using the spread-duration technique, a portfolio can be tailored to achieve these or other goals, while maintaining the same exposure to yield curve shifts and corporate spread changes.

SPREAD-DURATIONS FOR DIFFERENT CREDIT SECTORS

Exhibit 1 graphs the portfolio return as a function of an instantaneous change in the corporate spread, for several different spread-durations. (The overall level of interest rates is assumed to remain constant.) The larger the spread-duration, the steeper is the slope, reflecting the greater responsiveness of the portfolio value to changes in yields in the corporate sector as a whole. We refer to the corporate sector of the Salomon Brothers Broad Investment-Grade Bond Index℠ (Broad Index) as a proxy for this corporate sector as a whole.

For a portfolio consisting entirely of bonds from a single homogeneous credit sector, the spread-duration will be proportional to the ordinary modified duration. The constant of proportionality, or "spread beta," will reflect the relative sensitivity of each subsector's yield spread to changes in the Broad Index corporate spread. In general, the spread betas for individual subsectors will tend to vary inversely with the quality level: Lower-grade credits will have a larger beta value. This relationship is depicted in Exhibit 2, in which we have taken beta values of 0.8, 0.9, 1.0, and 1.3, for AAA, AA, A, and BBB sectors, respectively. This implies, for example, that a portfolio consisting solely of AA-rated bonds with a modified duration of 5 years would have a spread-duration of 5.0 years $\times 0.9 = 4.5$ years.

It is possible in principle (and desirable in application) to partition the corporate sector into smaller subsectors and then to determine the spread-duration of each subsector. However, for illustrative purposes, we will deal only with the above four aggregated rating classes.

From the duration and spread-duration, we can approximate the expected response of the portfolio to any combination of yield curve shifts and changes in the

EXHIBIT 1
THE SPREAD-DURATION CONCEPT

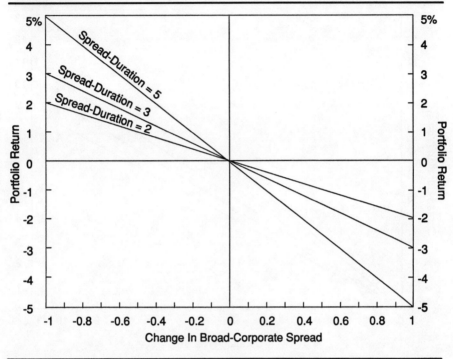

corporate spread. Assume, for example, that the yield curve shifts down by 100 basis points, while the corporate spread narrows by 20 basis points. For a portfolio with a duration of 5 years and a spread-duration of 5 years, the approximate return would be 6.00% as follows:

$$5 \times 1.0 = 5.00\%$$
$$5 \times 0.2 = \underline{1.00\%}$$

Approximate Return 6.00%.

CREDIT BARBELLS ACROSS DURATION

A portfolio manager will often have specific targets for the sensitivity of the portfolio to changes in the level of interest rates and to changes in the corporate spread.

EXHIBIT 2
SPREAD-DURATION FOR VARIOUS CREDIT SECTORS

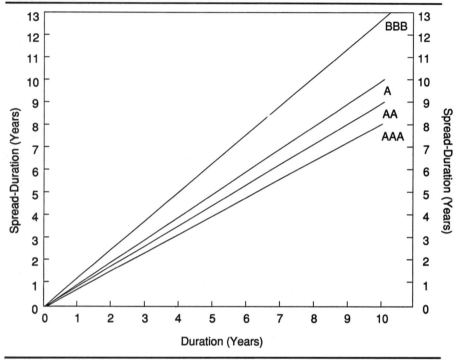

These targets translate into values for the duration and spread-duration. However, there is usually a wide spectrum of vastly different portfolios that can satisfy any given duration and spread-duration target. For example, suppose a manager wants to maintain a 5-year duration and a 5-year spread-duration. Since the sector "beta" for A-rated corporates is taken to be 1.0, the portfolio manager could invest entirely in 5-year A-rated bonds. This would correspond to the homogeneous Portfolio I shown in Exhibit 3.

There are many other nonhomogeneous portfolios—credit barbells—that have the same risk characteristics (identical values for the duration and the spread-duration). The simplest example is a portfolio that combines low-duration and high-duration bonds within a single rating sector. In Exhibit 4, Portfolio II is equally weighted between 3-year duration and 7-year duration A-rated bonds. This barbell has the same 5-year duration and 5-year spread-duration as the initial homogeneous Portfolio I, and thus the same exposure to interest rate and spread changes (though not necessarily to other forms of credit risk, particularly default risk).

EXHIBIT 3
SIMPLE PORTFOLIO OF 100% A-RATED 5-YEAR DURATION BONDS

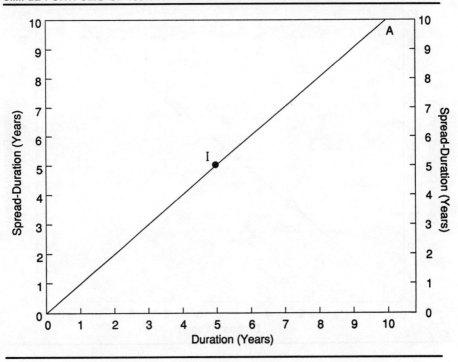

CREDIT BARBELLS ACROSS RATING CLASSES

Another example of a credit barbell is one in which bonds of different rating levels, but identical durations, are combined in proportions that achieve the intended spread-duration. In Exhibit 5, Portfolio III has a mix of 25% BBB-rated bonds and 75% AA-rated bonds, all having a 5-year duration. The portfolio maintains the 5-year duration and also retains the spread-duration of 5 years:

25% BBB	$0.25 \times 5 \times 1.3 = 1.625$
75% AA	$0.75 \times 5 \times 0.9 = 3.375$
Portfolio Spread-Duration	5.000

It is not necessary to restrict a credit barbell to securities of a single duration or rating sector. In Portfolio IV, longer-duration AA-rated bonds are combined with

EXHIBIT 4
CREDIT BARBELLS ACROSS DURATION

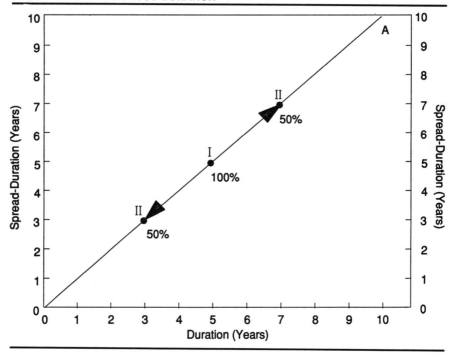

shorter-duration BBB-rated bonds to obtain a portfolio with the same duration and spread-duration as in Portfolio I.

VARYING THE PROPORTION OF CORPORATE BONDS

Thus far we have examined portfolios that contain only corporate bonds. However, the same analysis applies to portfolios that combine corporate bonds with Treasury bonds. It should be evident that Treasuries have a spread-duration of zero. In Exhibit 7, Portfolio V has a duration of 5 years and a spread-duration of one year. The Treasury curve is depicted as a horizontal line corresponding to the Treasury's spread-duration of zero. The same duration/spread-duration levels as those of Portfolio V can be reached with Portfolio VI, comprised 80% of 5-year duration Treasury bonds and 20% 5-year duration A-rated corporate bonds.

Exhibit 8 shows another alternative, Portfolio VII, which also achieves the same

EXHIBIT 5
CREDIT BARBELLS ACROSS RATING CLASSES

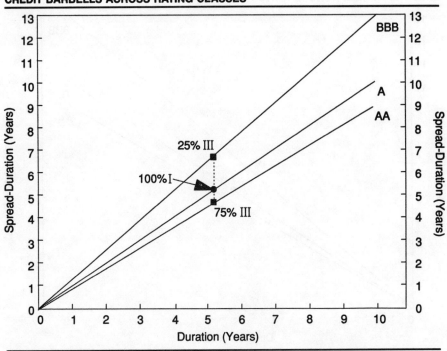

duration/spread-duration targets. This portfolio has 75% of its holdings in Treasury bonds with a duration of 5.33 years and 25% in A-rated bonds with a 4-year duration. This portfolio has a duration of 5 years,

75% Treasuries	$0.75 \times 5.33 = 4.00$
25% A-Rated Corporates	$0.25 \times 4.00 = \underline{1.00}$
Portfolio Duration	5.00

and a spread-duration of 1 year,

75% Treasuries	$0.75 \times 5.33 \times \ 0 = \ \ \ 0$
25% A-Rated Corporates	$0.25 \times 4.00 \times 1.0 = \underline{1.00}$
Portfolio Spread-Duration	1.00

EXHIBIT 6
CREDIT BARBELLS ACROSS RATING AND DURATION

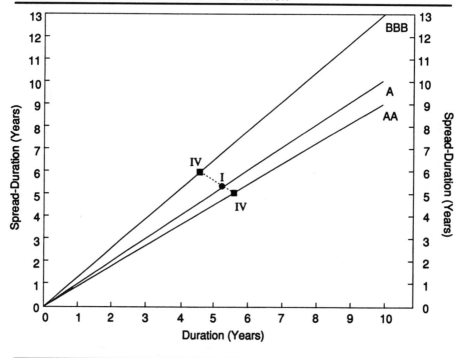

Exhibit 9 provides an alternative graphical representation of the effect of varying the proportion of corporate bonds. Portfolio VIII holds 20% in A-rated corporate bonds with a duration of 4 years and 80% in Treasury bonds with a 5-year duration, so that the portfolio duration is 4.8 years and the spread-duration is $(0.2 \times 4 \times 1.0) = 0.8$ years. By increasing the weighting of the corporate bonds to 30%, while decreasing their duration to 2.67 years, the spread-duration remains constant. If, at the same time, we increase the duration of the remaining Treasury bonds to 5.71 years, we obtain Portfolio IX, which maintains the overall duration at 4.8 years.

The portfolio manager can achieve further flexibility by altering the sector distribution within the overall corporate component. In Exhibit 10, the holdings of corporate bonds are changed from 20% A-rated with a duration of 4 years (Portfolio X) to 10% BBB-rated with a duration of 6.15 years (Portfolio XI). Under this change, the spread-duration remains constant at $0.1 \times 6.15 \times 1.3 = 0.8$ years. (To maintain the overall duration at 4.8 years, the duration of the Treasury component must then be decreased to 4.65 years.)

EXHIBIT 7
COMBINING CORPORATES AND TREASURIES WITH THE SAME DURATION

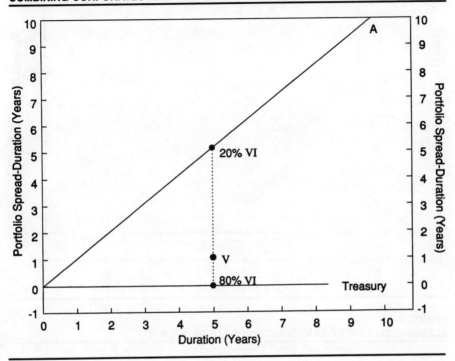

DURATION TRADE-OFFS

Exhibit 11 illustrates the trade-off between the durations of the corporate and Treasury components of the portfolio as the percentage of corporates increases, in order to hold both the duration and spread-duration constant at 5 years and 1 year, respectively. (For simplicity, the corporate sector is assumed, in this example, to have a spread beta of 1.0.) When the percentage of corporates is very small, the duration of the corporate component must be correspondingly large to achieve any desired spread-duration. At this point, the duration of the Treasury component will be nearly equal to the difference between the desired portfolio duration and the desired spread-duration. On the other hand, when the percentage of corporates is very large, the duration of the corporates itself approximates the spread-duration, and the duration of the Treasury component must swing widely in the appropriate direction to bring the overall duration into line.

EXHIBIT 8
COMBINING CORPORATES AND TREASURIES WITH DIFFERENT DURATIONS

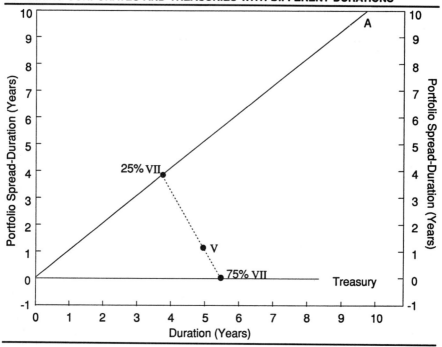

EXHIBIT 9
ALTERNATIVE VIEW OF VARYING CORPORATE PROPORTION

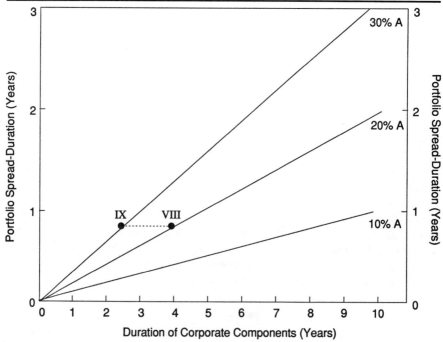

EXHIBIT 10
VARYING CORPORATE PROPORTION AND CREDIT CLASSES

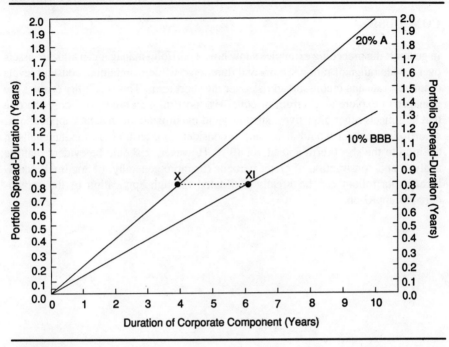

EXHIBIT 11
CORPORATE/TREASURY DURATION TRADE-OFF TO ACHIEVE SPECIFIC RISK TARGETS

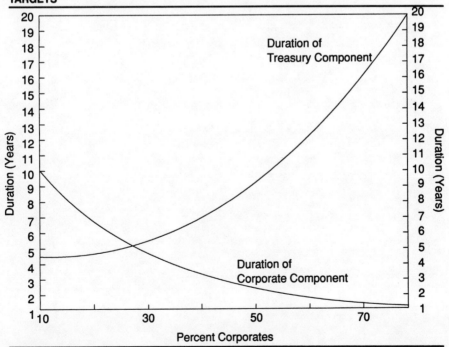

CONCLUSION

In general, the preceding examples show how a portfolio manager can allocate assets over a wide range of rating sectors and durations, while maintaining constant levels of interest rate and credit-spread risk over the short term. This flexibility enables the manager to explore a spectrum of equal-risk portfolios in order to choose the one that best meets other objectives, such as yield maximization. In actual applications, a portfolio manager would also want to consider long-term credit fundamentals in addition to the short-term spread volatility. However, it should be evident that the analysis and construction of credit barbells (or more generally, of "optimal" fixed-income portfolios) can be greatly facilitated through application of the spread-duration approach.

Chapter 15

Structuring Portfolios in an Uncertain Volatility Environment: Enhancement Opportunities With Callable Securities

STEVE MANDEL
DIRECTOR
SALOMON BROTHERS INC

Y. Y. MA
VICE PRESIDENT
SALOMON BROTHERS INC

ARDAVAN NOZARI
VICE PRESIDENT
SALOMON BROTHERS INC

GARY SHKEDY
ANALYST
SALOMON BROTHERS INC

Interest rate volatility plays a central role when evaluating a portfolio of securities with embedded options such as callable corporate bonds and mortgage securities. In the past few years, though, the volatility of interest rates has varied dramatically. For instance, since January 1987, the annualized 20-day yield volatility for the 30-year U.S. Treasury bond has fluctuated from below 6% to above 27% (see Exhibit 1). In this chapter, we present a methodology for constructing portfolios with the potential for enhanced returns while reducing the investor's reliance on a volatility assumption.

Investors seeking value in the fixed-income market are often challenged by its size and diversity. For instance, as of May 1988, there were more than 4,700 issues in the Salomon Brothers Broad Investment-Grade Bond Index with a total outstanding market value of more than $2.2 trillion. The securities in the corporate market are particularly varied and many have embedded option features that render traditional measures of value such as yield to maturity inappropriate. Indeed, more than 75% of the securities in the corporate sector have some sort of a call feature. Mortgage securities also have prepayment features that require special consideration.

To address this challenge, two interrelated concepts of *option-adjusted spread* (*OAS*) and *effective duration* have been developed.[1] OAS is the yield spread of the bond over the Treasury yield curve, adjusted for its option features, while effective duration is a measure of a bond's interest rate sensitivity. These measures take the embedded options of the security into account and are, thus, more precise than the traditional yield spread measures, such as the yield-to-maturity spread or the yield-to-call spread, and modified duration. Of course, for instruments with no option characteristics, OAS and effective duration are essentially equivalent to the yield-to-maturity spread and modified duration.

A drawback to the OAS and effective duration measures is that an estimate of interest rate volatility is required to calculate them. Indeed, these two measures can be quite sensitive to this estimate. In this chapter, we present a methodology to structure portfolios of fixed-income securities that would result in enhanced returns over a *baseline* portfolio without incremental exposure to interest rate volatility risks. The baseline could be an existing portfolio, the corporate and/or mortgage sectors of the Salomon Brothers Broad Investment-Grade Bond Index or any other customized index. Our methodology uses OAS to determine value and effective duration to control interest rate sensitivity, but it *does not rely* on a single volatility assumption. Hence, it is appropriate for investors who seek enhanced returns over a baseline but are uncertain about the level of volatility.

The authors would like to express their gratitude to their colleagues in the Bond Portfolio Analysis Group for their thoughtful comments.

[1]For detailed descriptions see William M. Boyce, Mark Koenigsberg and Armand H. Tatevossian, *The Effective Duration of Callable Bonds: The Salomon Brothers Term Structure-Based Option Pricing Model*, Salomon Brothers Inc, April 1987 and Michael Waldman and Mark Gordon, *Evaluating the Option Features of Mortgage Securities: The Salomon Brothers Mortgage Pricing Model*, Salomon Brothers Inc, September 1986.

EXHIBIT 1
ANNUALIZED 20-DAY VOLATILITY OF U.S. TREASURY 30-YEAR YIELD

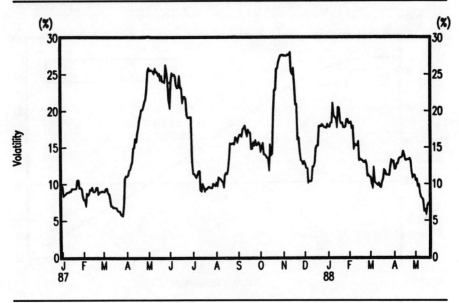

THE IMPORTANCE OF VOLATILITY ASSUMPTION

OAS and effective duration are calculated using an option-pricing model and depend on an estimate of interst rate volatility. For bonds with no embedded options, OAS and effective duration are independent of the volatility assumption. However, for securities with embedded options, OAS and effective duration depend on the volatility assumption. Exhibit 2 depicts the relationship of the OAS as a function of volatility for one noncallable and one callable bond: for a callable bond, OAS decreases as assumed volatility increases. As the volatility assumption increases, the value of the call option will increase. Because the investor has sold this call option, then, for a given price for the callable bond, increasing the assumed volatility increases the price of the underlying (noncallable) bond and thus decreases the OAS.

Exhibit 3 illustrates the pattern of effective duration versus the volatility assumption for three different bonds: one trading to call, one trading to maturity and one noncallable. We note that, for bonds that effectively trade to call, effective duration increases as volatility assumption increases. Conversely, for bonds trading to maturity, effective duration decreases as the volatility assumption increases. Intuitively, for a bond that effectively trades to call, higher volatility increases the probability

EXHIBIT 2
OPTION-ADJUSTED SPREAD VERSUS VOLATILITY ASSUMPTION

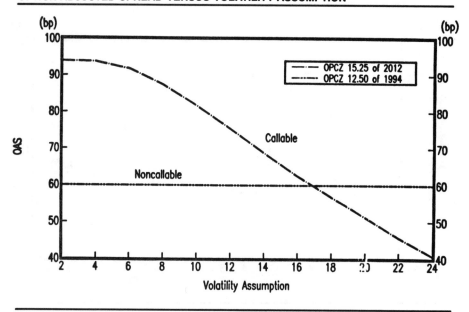

EXHIBIT 3
EFFECTIVE DURATION VERSUS VOLATILITY ASSUMPTION

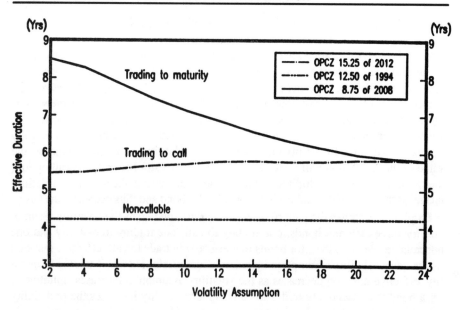

that the bond would not be called at its next call date, and thus the effective duration increases. On the other hand, for a bond trading to maturity, as the volatility assumption increases the probability that it would be called earlier increases and therefore the effective duration decreases.

Exhibits 2 and 3 demonstrate that any single volatility assumption may inaccurately portray the OAS and effective duration.

A PORTFOLIO EXAMPLE

The portfolio selection process can be described in a simplified manner as defining an *objective* and a set of *constraints*. In this context, investors seek portfolios that optimize their objective without violating any of their constraints. To the extent that the objective and constraints involve OAS and effective duration, the volatility assumption is crucial to the portfolio selection process.

To see the effect of the volatility assumption on portfolio structuring, consider a universe of 15 corporate bonds and a baseline portfolio that consists of an equally market-weighted combination of all the bonds in this sample universe. Exhibit 4 tabulates the OAS and effective duration of these securities at three volatility assumptions: 8%, 16% and 24%.

As a first example, we assume a volatility of 16% and construct a portfolio by maximizing OAS subject to matching the effective duration of the baseline. Exhibit 5 depicts this optimal portfolio and displays its OAS and effective duration under other volatilities. We observe that the OAS advantage changes dramatically at volatilities other than 16%. For example, an OAS advantage of approximately 35 basis points at 16% volatility would diminish to 8 basis points at 8% volatility.

Focusing on effective duration reveals that there could be a potentially significant interest rate sensitivity mismatch at volatilities other than 16%. For example, if the correct volatility were 8%, there would be an effective duration mismatch of almost one full year.

For a second example, we assume volatility to be 24% and construct a portfolio in a manner similar to the previous one: maximizing OAS subject to an effective duration constraint (see Exhibit 6). Comparing this portfolio with the one constructed assuming 16% volatility, we observe that both comprise the same two securities: one noncallable and one callable. However, the portfolio with the higher volatility assumption has 63.59% of its total market value in the noncallable bond, while the one with the lower volatility assumption has only 23.71% in the noncallable bond. This behavior should not be surprising as it is evident from Exhibit 2 that larger volatility assumptions make the OAS of noncallable bonds more attractive. Furthermore, in this example, the dependency of effective duration on the volatility assumption has contributed to the weighting of the bonds.

These simple examples illustrate the importance of the volatility assumption: different volatility assumptions can result in portfolios with dramatically different

EXHIBIT 4
BASELINE PORTFOLIO

Bond	Status	Yield To Worst	Duration To Worst	Option-Adjusted Spread			Effective Duration			Market Weight
				8%	16%	24%	8%	16%	24%	
A	NC	9.00%	4.72%	79bp	79bp	79bp	4.72yrs	4.72yrs	4.72yrs	6.67%
B	NC	8.95	5.97	60	60	60	5.97	5.97	5.97	6.67
C	M	9.65	8.13	98	58	C	7.28	5.72	4.78	6.67
D	M	9.30	8.35	73	63	40	8.36	7.54	6.47	6.67
E	M	9.45	7.98	86	60	19	7.60	6.30	5.45	6.67
F	M	9.43	8.32	87	66	30	8.07	6.90	5.81	6.67
G	M	9.75	8.69	99	62	23	7.65	6.79	6.08	6.67
H	M	9.95	9.47	118	72	27	7.91	6.56	5.99	6.67
I	M	9.65	9.57	95	60	18	8.70	7.19	6.06	6.67
J	M	9.70	9.28	87	51	24	7.64	7.13	6.84	6.67
K	M	9.67	10.08	88	42	0	8.36	7.00	6.20	6.67
L	M	10.10	9.26	96	24	-37	6.02	4.84	4.52	6.67
M	C	9.51	5.84	108	88	70	5.95	6.12	6.14	6.67
N	C	10.05	0.44	147	10	-122	1.65	1.37	1.20	6.67
O	C	9.29	0.86	95	-24	-132	2.92	2.65	2.37	6.67
Total		9.56%	7.13%	94bp	51bp	7bp	6.59yrs	5.79yrs	5.24yrs	100.00%

NC Noncall Life. M Yield to Maturity<Yield to Call. C Yield to Call<Yield to Maturity. bp Basis points.

EXHIBIT 5
OPTIMAL PORTFOLIO ASSUMING 16% VOLATILITY

Bond	Status	Market Weight
A	NC	23.71%
M	C	76.29

	Option-Adjusted Spread			Effective Duration		
	8%	16%	24%	8%	16%	24%
Optimal Portfolio	102bp	86bp	73bp	5.66yrs	5.79yrs	5.81yrs
Baseline	94	51	7	6.59	5.79	5.24
Difference	8bp	35bp	66bp	-0.93yrs	0.00yrs	0.57yrs

NC Noncall Life.   M Yield to Maturity<Yield to Call.   C Yield to Call<Yield to Maturity.   bp Basis points.

EXHIBIT 6
OPTIMAL PORTFOLIO ASSUMING 24% VOLATILITY

Bond	Status	Market Weight
A	NC	63.59%
M	C	36.41

	Option-Adjusted Spread			Effective Duration		
	8%	16%	24%	8%	16%	24%
Optimal Portfolio	90bp	83bp	76bp	5.17yrs	5.23yrs	5.24yrs
Baseline	94	51	7	6.59	5.79	5.79
Difference	-4bp	32bp	69bp	-1.42yrs	-0.56yrs	0.00yrs

NC Noncall Life.   M Yield to Maturity<Yield to Call.   C Yield to Call<Yield to Maturity.   bp Basis points.

characteristics. And, hence, to the degree that these portfolios would perform differently, the assumed volatility will have a major impact on their relative performance.

A VOLATILITY-ROBUST APPROACH

The wide fluctuations in interest rate volatility, combined with the fact that the assumed volatility will have a significant impact on relative performance, requires investors to take a deliberate position on volatility. Those who are confident about the level of interest rate volatility can structure their portfolios accordingly. For those who are uncertain about the level of volatility, we present a volatility-robust strategy.

To accomplish this, we construct a portfolio whose dependence on volatility is identical to that of the baseline's. Hence, we require that all the volatility-dependent constraints be satisfied not only under a single volatility assumption, but under a range of volatilities. For example, because effective duration changes with the

EXHIBIT 7
OAS OF THE BASELINE AND THE OPTIMAL PORTFOLIOS, CONSTRUCTED SUBJECT TO IDENTICAL CONSTRAINTS, AT DIFFERENT VOLATILITIES

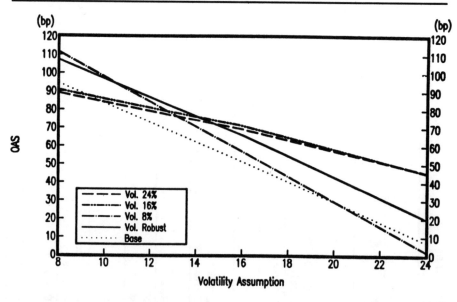

volatility assumption, the effective duration of the portfolio should be constrained to match that of the baseline across a range of volatilities.

Ensuring that the OAS advantage of the portfolio over the baseline is not affected by changes in the volatility assumption is more complex. To accomplish this, we maximize the minimum OAS advantage over the baseline across a range of volatility assumptions. To illustrate, refer back to the previous example and consider four portfolios constructed with *identical* constraints but different objectives. The constraints are to match the effective duration of the baseline at volatilities of 8%, 16% and 24%. The first three portfolios have as their objective maximizing OAS computed at 8%, 16% and 24%, respectively, while the last portfolio uses the volatility-robust objective. Exhibit 7 displays the OAS values of these portfolios as well as those of the baseline under a range of volatility assumptions. Exhibit 8 focuses on the relative OAS advantage of these portfolios over the baseline as a function of volatility. These figures demonstrate that the volatility-robust objective offers an OAS advantage of approximately 13 to 15 basis points across the range of volatilities.

Exhibit 9 displays the portfolio using the volatility-robust approach. Comparing this portfolio with the ones assuming a single volatility, as in Exhibits 5 and 6, we realize that it is a more diversified portfolio whose OAS and effective duration have the same volatility dependence as those of the baseline.

EXHIBIT 8
OAS ADVANTAGE OVER THE BASELINE OF OPTIMAL PORTFOLIOS, CONSTRUCTED SUBJECT TO IDENTICAL CONSTRAINTS, AT DIFFERENT VOLATILITIES

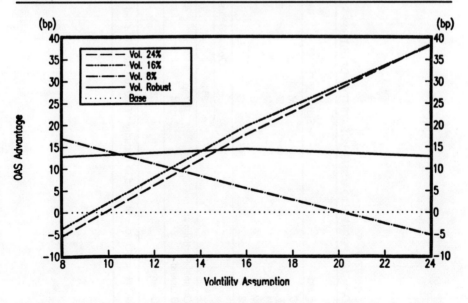

EXHIBIT 9
OPTIMAL PORTFOLIO USING VOLATILITY-ROBUST APPROACH

Bond	Status	Market Weight
C	M	18.84%
F	M	23.63
H	M	18.06
M	C	28.54
N	C	10.93

	Option-Adjusted Spread				Effective Duration		
	8%	16%	24%		8%	16%	24%
Optimal Portfolio	107bp	66bp	20bp		6.59yrs	5.79yrs	5.24yrs
Baseline	94	51	7		6.59	5.79	5.24
Difference	**13bp**	**15bp**	**13bp**		**0.00yrs**	**0.00yrs**	**0.00yrs**

NC Noncall Life.   M Yield to Maturity<Yield to Call.   C Yield to Call<Yield to Maturity.   bp Basis points.

CONCLUSION

Creating fixed-income portfolios with enhanced returns is a complicated task. A wide range of factors such as changes in supply and credit ratings as well as movement of interest rates affect performance. For securities with embedded options, such as callable corporate bonds and mortgage securities, the complexity is further compounded by changes in the volatility of interest rates. Interest rate sensitivity of a portfolio is controlled by its effective duration, which in turn depends on the volatility assumption. The measure of the relative value of securities with embedded options also depends on the volatility assumption.

The methodology presented in this chapter can readily incorporate traditional means of addressing supply and credit ratings as well as many other important factors involved in portfolio structuring. The methodology can be used in creating portfolios whose interest rate sensitivity (effective duration) and measure of their relative value (OAS) have the same volatility dependence as those of the baseline. The methodology creates portfolios that tend to be more diversified and that do not embody the duration mismatch problem associated with assuming a single volatility. Furthermore, these portfolios offer an OAS advantage over the baseline across a range of volatility assumptions. Hence, in today's environment of uncertain interest rate volatility, our methodology is a new approach for constructing portfolios with a potential for enhanced return to investors who are reluctant to take a positon on the level of volatility.

Chapter 16

Duration-Equivalent Butterfly Swaps

N.R. VIJAYARAGHAVAN, PH.D
VICE PRESIDENT
DREXEL BURNHAM LAMBERT

MONTE H. SHAPIRO
ASSOCIATE
DREXEL BURNHAM LAMBERT

As volatilities in the Treasury market have reached unprecedented levels, strategies to take advantage of yield curve movements can play an important role in fixed income portfolio management. The focus of this chapter is to reintroduce investors to a spread strategy, the butterfly swap, which can be used to take advantage of the shape and volatility of the yield curve. The strategy involves a swap between the following:

- A security (A) of a given maturity.
- A portfolio of two securities (B) and (C). The maturity of (B) is shorter than that of (A) and the maturity of (C) is longer than that of (A).

The *butterfly swap* involves no net increase or decrease in the market value of the overall portfolio. Typically, the swap is constructed by assigning equal market value weights to the two securities B and C. In other words, $1 market value of security A is swapped for a portfolio of $0.5 market value of security B and $0.5 market value of security C. However, such a swap generally increases or decreases the duration of the portfolio. The purpose of the swap is to provide a pick-up in yield to maturity.

A *duration-equivalent butterfly swap* maintains the risk level of the portfolio (as defined by its duration), in addition to maintaining its market value. This is achieved by allowing the market value weights assigned to securities B and C to vary from 0.5, while they still sum to 1. This chapter discusses the details of constructing such duration-equivalent swaps. Further, the pick-up in yields will, in general, be different for short holding periods than for holding periods until maturity. The specific assumptions about yield curve movements also define the expected performances of such swaps. These additional aspects often are ignored in analysis of this type.

Before discussing the swap itself, a brief review of the concepts of duration and convexity is provided. These concepts help explain the expected performance of the swap and illustrate how it can be employed to enhance portfolio performance.

DURATION

Duration is now commonly used by investors to help measure the interest rate risk of their fixed income portfolios. Duration provides a measure of the percentage price sensitivity of the portfolio (or a security) relative to a small change in its yield. The solid curve in Exhibit 1 illustrates the actual relationship between the percentage change in price and the change in yield for a bond. As shown in the exhibit, the initial yield of the bond is 10%. The dotted line represents the estimated percentage change in price for small changes in the yield of this security. This approximation, which appears as a straight line that is tangential to the curve at that current yield, is the duration of the security at that current yield. Duration is simply a measure of the steepness (mathematically known as the slope) of this straight line. The steeper this line, the greater the duration. When duration is greater, the price changes are larger for a given yield change. This supports the use of duration as a measure of risk. Duration is also useful as a hedging tool as it can be employed to offset the potential price changes of one security with those of another.

Consider the following example.

Price (including accrued interest) of bond = $100
Initial yield = 10%
Present yield = 9%
Change in Yield = 9% − 10% = −0.01

When the yield of the bond falls from 10% to 9%, Exhibit 1 illustrates how the straight line approximates the expected percentage price increase.

EXHIBIT 1
PRICE-YIELD CURVE

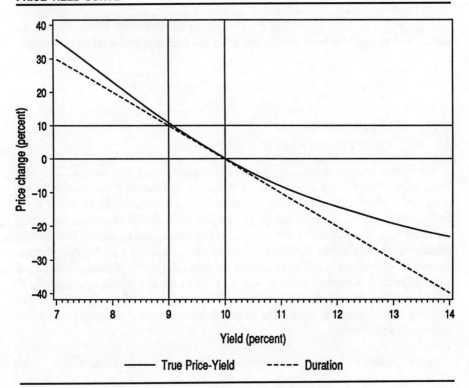

Approximate new price of bond, as estimated by the line
$$= (100) + (0.1) \times (100) = \$110.$$

Duration is defined as:

$$\text{Duration} = -\frac{\% \text{ price change}}{\text{yield change}}$$

$$= -\frac{0.1}{(-.01)} = 10$$

The Use of Duration as a Hedging Tool

Duration is a useful tool for quantifying and hedging risk. This is illustrated with a simple example. Consider the following two bonds.

Bond 1 Price (including accrued interest): 100
    Duration: 10

Bond 2 Price (including accrued interest): 110
    Duration: 5

If the yields on both bonds fall by 1% (notice the important assumption of the same yield change for both bonds) the price changes are predicted as follows:

Price change on Bond 1
   $= -$ (Duration) $\times$ (Yield change) $\times$ (Price)
   $= -$ (10) $\times$ ($-.01$) $\times$ (100) $= \$10$

Price change on Bond 2
   $= -$ (5) $\times$ ($-.01$) $\times$ (110) $= \$5.50$

These price changes implicitly include any changes in accrued interest. To hedge Bond 1 with Bond 2, the price change for one must offset the price change for the other for a given change in yield. Suppose $100 par value of Bond 1 has to be hedged. Its expected price change is $10 for the yield change shown above. Using the two bonds, the quantity of Bond 2 which produces a price change of $10 must be calculated. As seen above, $100 par value of Bond 2 produces a $5.50 price change. Therefore, to produce a $10 price change for Bond 2, (10 / 5.50)(100) = $182 par value of Bond 2 is needed. In other words, $182 of Bond 2 is sold to hedge a $100 long position in Bond 1, which produces a hedge ratio of 1.82 : 1. A direct way of deriving this number is to use the ratio of price-weighted durations or "dollar durations" as follows:

Dollar Duration = Modified Duration $\times$ (Price + Accrued Interest)

$$\text{Hedge Ratio} = \frac{[\text{Dollar Duration}] \text{ for Bond 1}}{[\text{Dollar Duration}] \text{ for Bond 2}}$$

and by substituting,

$$\frac{10 \times 100}{5 \times 110} = 1.82 \text{ of Bond 2 for each Bond 1}$$

Duration measures the percentage price sensitivity to yield changes. In hedging applications, the absolute price sensitivity to yield changes is a more relevant measure. Dollar duration captures this absolute price sensitivity and therefore appears in the hedge ratio as shown above.

CONVEXITY

Looking at Exhibit 1, the duration line (the straight line) is a fairly good approximation for percentage price changes of the bond as long as the yield changes are small.

It is evident, however, that the duration line does not track the true price-yield relationship for large yield changes. The difference between the duration-predicted and observed values distorts both the measurement of risk and the hedge ratios. Therefore, it is useful to understand and quantify this difference which is explained by the "convexity" of the price-yield curve.[1]

Two bonds are shown in Exhibit 2 which have the same duration at current prices. However, the price-yield relationship for Bond 2 (solid line) has a more pronounced curvature than that of Bond 1 (dashed line). For reference, the duration line is also shown in the exhibit. As mentioned earlier, duration helps to measure approximately the percentage change in price for a given change in yield. Notice that the approximation is closer for Bond 1 than for Bond 2.

Since the curvature of the price-yield relationship for Bond 2 is greater than that of Bond 1, the deviations from the approximation provided by duration are larger for Bond 2 than for Bond 1. The important point is that when yields change, not only do

EXHIBIT 2
CONVEXITY EXPLANATION

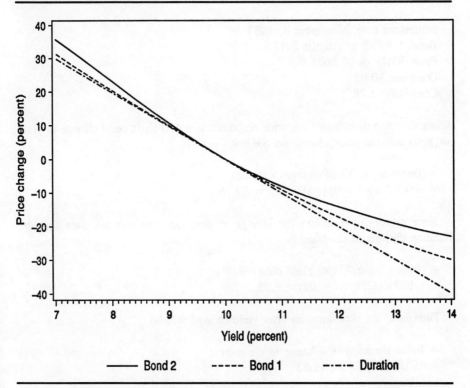

---

[1]This is discussed in detail in Kenneth Sullivan and Timothy Kiggins, "Convexity: The Name Is New But You Always Knew What It Was."

prices change, but durations change as well. Convexity (loosely defined) is a measure of the change of a bond's duration for a given yield change. The greater the change in duration, the greater the convexity. Convexity is defined as:

$$\text{Convexity} = -\frac{\text{Change in Duration}}{100 \times \text{Change in Yield}}$$

The factor 100 in the denominator is used merely to express convexity in conveniently smaller units. As higher yields reduce duration, the negative sign above enables convexity to be expressed as a positive number.

It is seen from this explanation that when yields change, using duration (at the initial yield) to predict price changes produces errors. As duration itself changes when the yield changes, there is no single duration number associated with the yield change. The duration increases continuously during a fall in yield and decreases continuously during a rise in yield. Indirectly, convexity captures the average duration during a yield change (of any level) for calculating price changes, as is shown in the following example:

Settlement date: November 4, 1987
Bond: 8.875% of August 2017
Price: 97:18 or 97.5625
Duration: 10.05
Convexity: 1.78

Using duration to estimate the price response, a -100 basis point change in yield suggests that the price change on the bond is

$-(\text{Duration}) \times (\text{Yield change}) \times (\text{Price})$
$= -(10.05) \times (-.01) \times (97.56) = \$9.76$

Since convexity measures the change in duration, one can calculate that the duration change on the bond is

$-100 \times (\text{Convexity}) \times (\text{Yield change})$
$= -100 \times (1.78) \times (-.01) = 1.78$

Therefore, the new duration after yield change will be

$=$ Initial duration $+$ Change in duration
$= 10.05 + 1.78 = 11.83$

The average duration during the yield change is

(Initial duration + Final duration) / 2
= 10.94

Using the average duration, one can recompute the expected price change as

$-$(Average duration) $\times$ (Yield change) $\times$ (Price)
$= -(10.94) \times (-.01) \times (97.56) = \$10.67$

Therefore, the error in predicting price change using initial duration is

$10.67 $-$ $9.76 = $0.91

This is almost a 10% error at this yield change level.

This error could have been directly calculated from the convexity number as[2]

$\frac{1}{2} \times (100 \times C) \times$ (yield change)$^2 \times$ Price
$= \frac{1}{2} \times (100 \times 1.78) \times (.01)^2 \times 97.56 = \$0.90$

Note that the calculation is similar for *any* level of yield changes.

From the above example, it is seen that when yield changes are large, the errors in predicted price changes are larger. Additionally, the larger the convexity of the bond, the worse the errors are.

As a practical matter, investors should prefer larger convexities, other things being equal. A bond with a larger convexity gains value at a faster rate when yields fall and loses value at a slower rate when yields rise. The crucial assumption is that yield changes are the same for different bonds. In other words, when investors expect only parallel yield curve movements they should always prefer to hold securities with large convexities. However, when yield curve shifts are not parallel, shape change risk has to be considered explicitly when making investment decisions. This risk is discussed in a later section.

Duration and Convexity Along the Yield Curve

It is useful to examine a representative set of bonds with varying durations and study their yields and convexities. As shown in Exhibit 3, the current on-the-run securities (as of November 20, 1987) are chosen for this purpose. Note that their durations are dependent on both their terms to maturity and their coupons.

---

[2]Mathematically, duration relates to the first term of the Taylor series expansion of prices with respect to yields. Convexity relates to the second term of the expansion.

EXHIBIT 3

	Duration	Convexity	Yield
2-year	1.78	0.041	7.71
4-year	3.20	0.127	8.21
5-year	3.96	0.195	8.35
7-year	5.00	0.321	8.66
10-year	6.54	0.568	8.84
30-year	10.15	1.809	8.93

Bonds with the same duration may have different convexities. This is a result of the difference in the cash flow structures; a bond with cash flows that are distributed over a longer period of time tends to have a larger convexity. Looking at Exhibit 3, it is obvious that as the maturity of the bond increases, both duration and convexity increase, but convexity increases more rapidly. Exhibits 4 and 5 show the yield curve and the convexity curve, both defined with respect to duration. The yield curve tapers off with higher duration but the convexity curve increases rapidly with duration. The swaps presented subsequently in this chapter demonstrate one of the

EXHIBIT 4
YIELD CURVE

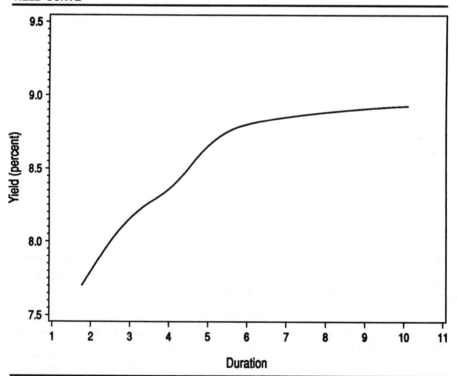

EXHIBIT 5
CONVEXITY CURVE

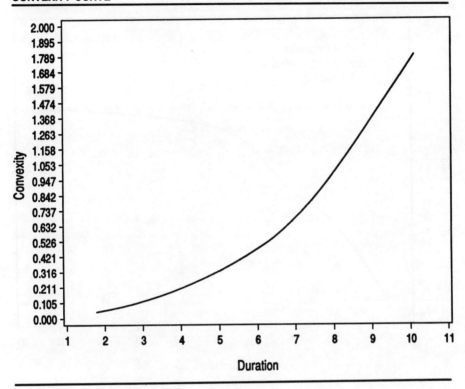

ways in which investors can systematically take advantage of the observed yield-convexity tradeoffs available in the market.

DURATION-EQUIVALENT BUTTERFLY SWAPS

As shown in the previous section, convexities of securities increase much more rapidly than yields with their duration. This can be used advantageously by combining two securities (a barbell) with different durations (or maturities) to mimic another security (a bullet) whose duration (maturity) lies between the two. Exhibits 6 and 7 depict the yield and convexity profiles of two securities with nominal maturities of 7 and 30 years. The securities are combined in such a way that the combination has the same duration as that of a 10-year security. The convexity of the barbell is higher than that of the bullet as seen in Exhibit 7. The yield of the barbell, however, turns out to be marginally lower than that of the bullet, as seen in Exhibit 6. Therefore, it appears that convexity has a price. The market usually prices

EXHIBIT 6
YIELDS—BARBELL VS. BULLET

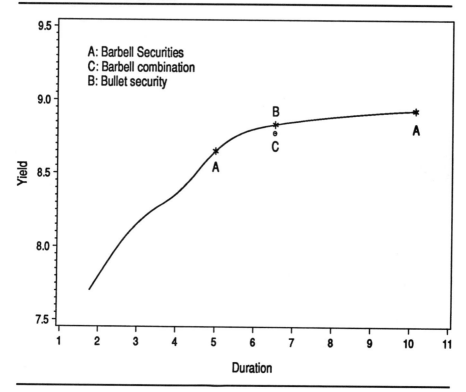

A: Barbell Securities
C: Barbell combination
B: Bullet security

convexity (which is a desired feature) with lower yields to maturity. On occasions, the market is priced such that it is possible to pick up both yield and convexity. This provides attractive investment opportunities for those who can recognize them.

A representative selection of swaps illustrating the respective gains in yield and convexity for November 20, 1987 settlement are provided in Exhibit 8. Obviously, many other combinations of securities are possible. Exibit 8 indicates the relative weights of each security to be used for this selection of swaps. The yields of the barbells are calculated on a combined cashflow basis and should be interpreted as their internal rates of return, if held until maturity.

The gain in convexity implies that if rates move either up or down, these barbells should outperform the bullets. This can be tested by assuming a one-month holding period (although holding periods of other lengths could be used as well) and parallel yield curve shifts of varying amounts. Exhibit 8 shows the relative performance of the barbells versus the bullets under these scenarios, which confirms the hypothesis.

EXHIBIT 7
CONVEXITY—BARBELL VS. BULLET

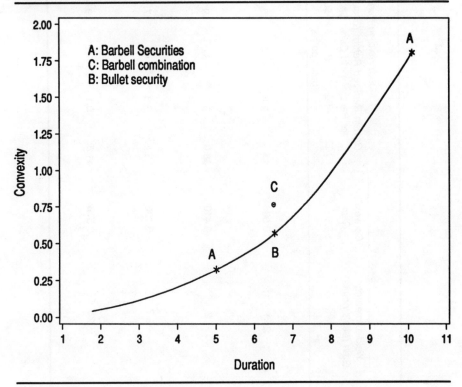

For example, the 2-year and 10-year combination, held in amounts of $5.4 million and $4.6 million respectively, outperforms the duration-equivalent $10 million investment in the 5-year bullet by 13.0 and 26.6 basis points for +/− 100 basis point yield curve shifts, respectively. Smaller gains in holding period returns are obtained with the barbell for +/− 50 basis point moves. This performance comes at a cost of only 1.1 basis points loss in return if the yield curve does not change between now and the end of the holding period. Notice that when the 30-year bond is used on the long end of the barbell, the gains in holding period returns and convexities when rates change increase as well.

Exhibit 8 also shows that if the swapped securities are held until maturity, the internal rate of return is 21.1 basis points higher for the barbell than for the bullet. This number represents the yield gain for a holding period until maturity. For two of the four cases shown, there are yield (until maturity) as well as convexity gains.

The gains in net returns for all the cases are shown in Exhibit 9. Note that there is a

EXHIBIT 8
DURATION-EQUIVALENT SWAPS

Data for settlement on November 20, 1987

| | Barbell | Bullet | | Modified Duration | Barbell | | 1 Month Holding Period Gain in Realized Return (basis points) for Parallel Yield Curve Shifts of | | | | |
Term	Amount $	Term	Amount $		Yield-to-maturity Gain (basis points)	Convexity Gain	+100	+50	0	-50	-100
									(basis points)		
Swap 1											
2-year	5.4MM	5-year	10MM	3.96	21.1	0.088	13.0	2.6	-1.1	5.3	26.6
10-year	4.6MM										
Swap 2											
2-year	6.1MM	7-year	10MM	5.00	1.2	0.410	38.0	8.2	-3.6	19.3	104.1
30-year	3.9MM										
Swap 3											
7-year	7.0MM	10-year	10MM	6.54	-5.7	0.199	13.4	3.3	-1.5	7.1	43.2
30-year	3.0MM										
Swap 4											
2-year	4.3MM	10-year	10MM	6.54	-.25	0.578	41.8	10.1	-4.1	19.0	112.0
30-year	5.7MM										

EXHIBIT 9
SWAPS PROFIT POSITIONS FOR PARALLEL SHIFT*

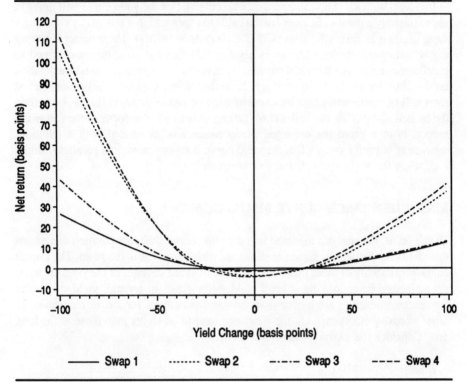

*See Exhibit 8 for description of the four swaps.

small loss in yields in all cases if rate changes are less than (approximately) $+/-25$ basis points. The actual absolute yield volatilities observed for Treasuries are in the 60-130 basis point range. These numbers represent monthly volatilities in the range of 17-40 basis points. Therefore, yield level variations of $+/-25$ basis points, required to gain from these trades, seem to be extremely plausible under current market conditions.

However, for larger yield changes, there are gains for all the swaps. For example, an investor who believes strongly that there will be a parallel yield curve shift of -50 basis points during the holding period, should swap the 10-year for a 2-year and 30-year combination. The yield gain in a month is about 19 basis points, or \$19,000 on a \$10 million position. Even if the actual yield curve shift turned out to be exactly the opposite, say, $+50$ basis points instead of -50 basis points, the investor still gains 10.1 basis points, or \$10,100 on a \$10 million position! It should, therefore, be clear that with parallel yield curve movements, the direction of the yield changes is relatively unimportant to produce gains from convexity. Note, however, that the gains are, in general, not symmetric for yield changes in different directions.

Investors with short holding periods who believe that the yield curve will move in approximately a parallel fashion are thus able to capture higher returns by choosing a swap which maximizes the convexity (i.e., buying volatility). The investor is betting that 1) the yield curve volatility is high and 2) that the volatility is confined to parallel movements of the yield curve. The investor is not required to take a position on the direction of the yield changes. Note that investors who believe that interest rates will be stable can profit by executing the converse strategy; that is, by selling the barbell and buying the bullet (i.e., selling volatility). The focus of the following section is to explore the expected performance risk associated with a duration-equivalent butterfly swap when the yield curve does not move in a parallel fashion; i.e., when the yield curve flattens or steepens.

RISK WHEN YIELD CURVE SHAPE CHANGES

To this point, the analysis assumed that the yield curve shifts are parallel; this means that yield changes are the same for all the securities involved in the swap. The impact on the profitability of these positions, because of shape changes of the yield curve, is not addressed when looking at level yield shifts alone. In general, yield volatilities for shorter maturities are higher than the yield volatilities for longer maturities. In other words, yield changes at the short end tend to be larger than those at the long end. Consider the example discussed earlier.

Bond 1 Price: $100
        Duration: 10 years

Bond 2 Price: $110
        Duration: 5.5 years

Assuming that yields shift 1% for both bonds, the hedge ratio is 1.82.
    Assume now that the yield change for Bond 2 is twice that for Bond 1.

Yield change of Bond 1 $= -1\%$

Yield change of Bond 2 $= -2\%$

Price change for $100 par value of Bond 1 $=$
    $-(\text{Duration}) \times (\text{Yield change}) \times (\text{Price}) =$
    $-(10) \times (-.01) \times (100) = \$10$

Price change for $100 par value of Bond 2 $=$
    $-(5)(-.02) \times (110) = \$11$

·Note that originally the hedge ratio was calculated to be 1.82, i.e., $182 par value of Bond 2 hedges $100 par value of Bond 1.

Had the investor hedged with $182 par value of Bond 2, the price change now would be

$$\frac{182 \times (11)}{100} = \$20$$

For a hedge ratio of 1.82, the price change ratio would be $20 to $10 or 2.0. This results in an overhedged position.

As $10 of price change per $100 par value of Bond 1 happens simultaneously with a $11 price change per $100 par value of Bond 2, the correct hedge ratio in this situation is 10/11 = 0.90. In other words, if every $100 par value of Bond 1 had been hedged with $90 par value of Bond 2, the respective price changes would both be equal to $10. The result, theoretically, is a perfect hedge. Note, however, that in such a situation where different maturities have different yield changes, construction of a perfect hedge utilizing only a single security imposes additional demands; i.e., an accurate prediction of the association of the yields changes for the security and the hedge is required. (For example, the perfect hedge mentioned above works only because of the knowledge that a 1% change in yield of Bond 1 simultaneously happens with a 2% yield change in Bond 2.) Therefore, it is apparent that simple duration hedging does not eliminate all risk.

Similarly, with yield curve shape changes, convexity may not be the correct measure of potential gains due to yield volatility. Assume that there are two bonds that have the same duration but have different convexities due to different maturities. If yields change instantaneously, the higher convexity bond will outperform the other bond, assuming the same investment (market value) in both bonds. In Exhibit 10, the net differential performance of the higher convexity bond over the lower convexity bond is shown by the solid curve for various yield changes. This assumes that the yield changes are the same for both bonds. However, in the same exhibit, with the assumption that the higher convexity bond (assumed to be of longer maturity) has only half the yield change of the other, the net differential performance of the higher convexity bond will change as shown by the dashed line. Clearly, the net differential performance increases more dramatically when yields rise but falls when yields drop. In general, the nature of this net performance differential will depend upon

1. the absolute convexity levels of the securities and
2. the association of the yield changes across securities

These principles imply that the complex interaction among these factors leads to different profiles of net returns under different scenarios.

Similarly, the higher observed convexity of a barbell over a bullet does not always

EXHIBIT 10
PROFITS WITH YIELD CURVE SHAPE CHANGE

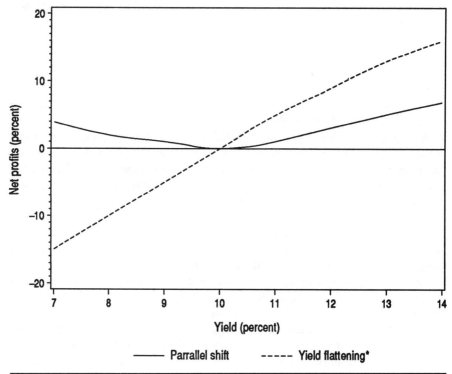

*Yield flattening: Long yield change = Half of short yield change.

ensure better performance. The differential performance of the barbell over the bullet, instead of being positive for both directions of yield changes, could be negative in one direction if the curve changes shape. These illustrations show the pitfalls in mechanically relying on duration and convexity measures as guides for hedging and arbitrage when yield curve shape changes are likely.

THE EFFECT ON SWAP PERFORMANCE

In an earlier section the performance of a selection of swaps was analyzed under parallel yield curve shifts. Duration and convexity were found to be relevant measures in predicting the performances of the swaps in those cases. However, in the last section, with the possibility of yield curve shape changes, these measures were shown to be inadequate in predicting the performances of the swaps. The effect of yield curve shape changes on the performance of the swaps is now incorporated into the analysis.

In Exhibit 11, each swap is analyzed for two cases of flattening and two cases of steepening of the yield curve. For simplicity, yield curve shape changes are represented by different amounts of yield changes for each security in the swap. For example, in the first case, the shorter maturity barbell security has a yield change of +100 basis points, the longer maturity barbell security has a yield change of +50 basis points and the bullet (with intermediate maturity) has a yield change of +75 basis points. This case, therefore, corresponds to the yield curve moving up over the entire maturity spectrum, but by larger amounts at the lower end; i.e., the yield curve flattens in shape. Notice, however, that for a given case, the yield curve shape changes are different for the various swaps because of differences in the maturities of the securities in the different swaps.

EXHIBIT 11
BARBELL OVER BULLET
PROFILE OF GAIN IN HOLDING PERIOD REALIZED RETURN WITH YIELD CURVE SHAPE CHANGES

	Case 1	Case 2	Case 3	Case 4
Swap 1	46.1	51.4	−57.3	−61.9
Swap 2	65.3	68.7	−83.2	−80.3
Swap 3	−8.8	−7.6	15.6	16.1
Swap 4	107.0	121.0	−144.0	−161.5

Description of Cases
Yield change

Security	Case 1	Case 2	Case 3	Case 4
Short Maturity Barbell	+100	+50	−50	−100
Bullet	+ 75	+25	−25	− 75
Long Maturity Barbell	+ 50	0	0	− 50

The differences in realized rates of return for a one-month holding period are shown in Exhibit 11 and also are plotted in Exhibit 12. Note, for the latter, that the variable on the X-axis is the yield change for the shorter maturity security of the barbell.

These numbers show that for each swap the returns are positive for one direction of yield changes but are negative for the other. The reason for this behavior was discussed in the last section. Given the possibility of yield curve shape changes, the riskiness of the barbell and the bullet are not the same, even though their durations are equal. Exhibit 11 helps identify the performance risk under the various shape

EXHIBIT 12
SWAPS PROFIT POSITIONS FOR SHAPE CHANGE OF YIELD CURVE

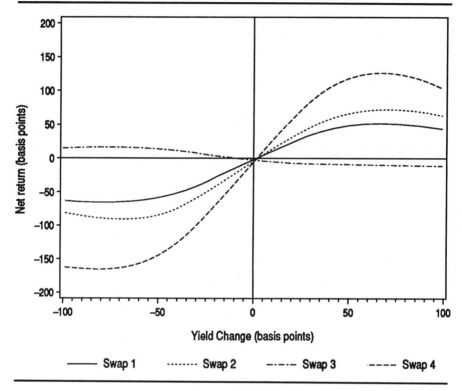

change cases. For example, for the 2-year/10-year combination versus the 5-year bullet (swap 1), if the yields rise 100 basis points for the 2-year security, 75 basis points for the 5-year and 50 basis points for the 10-year, the one-month holding period return gain is 46.1 basis points. For investors who expect an increase in yield levels accompanied by a flattening of the yield curve, this strategy produces a significant pick-up in return. They should execute this swap. On the other hand, if yield levels fall and the yield curve steepens to the same degree, this strategy produces a loss of 61.9 basis points. An investor who strongly believes that yields are likely to go up with an accompanying flattening of the curve, should execute the 2-year/30-year for 10-year swap (swap 4) to profit from the situation. For a moderate increase in yields (+ 50 basis points at the short end) this strategy will produce a gain of 121.0 basis points ($121,000 on a $10 million position) in one month. For larger yield increases (+ 100 basis points at the short end), the gains are 107 basis points ($107,000 on a $10 million position). Although the numbers used above were for illustrative purposes, such calculations could be tailored to suit the individual investor's specific outlook on yield changes in different maturity sectors.

As in the parallel yield curve shift cases, investors who believe that interest rate and yield curve shape changes will be in the opposite direction can profit by executing the swaps in the opposite direction. For example, swap 4 could be used by those who expected rates to fall and the curve to steepen. In this case, the 10-year should be bought and the 2- and 30-year sold. This produces a one month holding period gain of 161.5 basis points if rates fell by 100, 75 and 50 basis points on the 2-year, 10-year and 30-year securities respectively.

The three swaps shown that involve the 2-year security (swaps 1, 2 and 4) have similar return difference profiles; that is, they produce large return gains if yields rise and the yield curve flattens and large return losses if the yields fall and the curve steepens. The swap of 7-year and 30-year for the 10-year (swap 3) produces a different return profile. In this case, the investor gains if yields fall and the curve steepens. In general, the net returns from the swap will depend not only on the net convexity gains, but also on the *absolute* convexity levels of the bullet and the barbell and the *exact shape change* of the yield curve. For the case of the swap of the 7-year and 30-year combination for the 10-year, a moderate convexity gain is achieved from a high-convexity bullet. In the other cases, either the net gain in convexity is high or the gain is achieved from low-convexity bullets. Further, as mentioned earlier, the shape changes are strictly not the same across the swaps, because of differences in the maturities of the swap securities. These factors contribute to the differences in performance profiles.

Given the behavior of the swaps for various yield scenarios, the performance of being long the duration-equivalent butterfly can be summarized as follows.

1. For level shifts of the yield curve (either up or down), buying the barbell and selling the bullet produces profits if volatility exists.
2. If the yield curve does not move at all, there might be a small sacrifice in yield during the holding period.
3. With yield curve shape changes, the positive returns are usually magnified in one direction, but turn negative in the other. A swap, under these conditions, implies a position in the direction of the changes of yields. Note that this was not implied with parallel yield curve shifts.

If an investor is required to take a position on the direction of yield changes, it might be tempting to conclude that swaps with single securities would achieve the same or better results than swaps with barbells. Note, however, that barbells *also* give the additional advantage of producing gains from the *parallel shift component* of the yield curve movements, when there are shape as well as level changes to the yield curve. Therefore, it has an *embedded option* to gain from the parallel shift component of yield curve movements. Depending on one's belief about the relative contribution of this component to overall yield curve movement volatility, one may gain from this strategy.

Another practical detail to consider explicitly in evaluating shape changes (relevant to the swap securities) is the choice of securities. Bonds which are likely to move off-the-run within the holding period will lose value (increase in yield) due to the change in the liquidity premium. In other words, yield spreads for such securities considered for the swap will behave differently than those of the spreads of the equivalent on-the-run securities because of security-specific factors. For example, if the shorter maturity barbell security is going off-the-run during the holding period its yield is likely to increase. This causes a flattening of the yield curve for such a swap relative to another swap which utilizes an on-the-run short maturity barbell security, that remains on-the-run during the holding period.

CONCLUSION

This chapter develops the concept of duration-equivalent butterfly swaps as a return-enhancement tool for fixed income portfolio managers. The use of such a tool maintains the risk level of the portfolio (as measured by its duration), while simultaneously allowing the investor to capture the benefits from yield curve volatility. Such a strategy works independently of the direction of yield changes as long as the volatility of yields is confined to approximately parallel movements. Note, however, that the gains may not be symmetric in different directions of yield changes. When volatility is high and the yield curve also changes shape, the strategy can still be used. The investor now, however, must tailor the strategy to specific beliefs about the direction and the nature of the yield curve shifts. In any case, if the realized changes in the yield curve have a large parallel shift component and a small shape change component, investors stand to gain from these swaps (regardless of their positions on the direction of change of the yield curve) because of the embedded option.

PART VI

Strategies with Interest Rate Risk Control Instruments

Chapter 17

Hedging with Futures and Options

LAURIE S. GOODMAN, PH.D.
VICE PRESIDENT
GOLDMAN, SACHS & CO.

Futures and options are valuable tools for portfolio managers. Used appropriately, they can transform the risk-return profile of the portfolio into a more desirable configuration. In this chapter, we investigate the hedging uses of futures and options with fixed income portfolios. The first section describes how to define your risk, how to examine your desired risk-return profile, and how to choose between futures and options. The second section focuses on hedging with futures, the third on hedging with options, and the last on hedging fixed income instruments with embedded options.

RISK IDENTIFICATION AND CONTROL

You would take several preliminary steps before setting up a futures or options hedge. The first step is to define your risk. The second is to identify your desired risk-return profile. The third is to determine which instrument, or combination of instruments, can be used to generate the desired profile.

The author would like to thank Jane Brauer for her insightful comments on an earlier draft, and Ron Krieger for editing the chapter. Michelle Deligiannis provided valuable research assistance.

Define Your Risk

Risk identification generally consists of analyzing your portfolio to see what types of risks are present. There are two basic risk positions—symmetric risk and asymmetric risk. With symmetric risk, the gain when interest rates rise by 10 basis points is roughly the same magnitude as the loss when rates fall by 10 basis points. Thus if you hold a long position in 30-year Treasury bonds, you face symmetric risk. If rates go down you gain by roughly the same amount as if rates go up. The amount of symmetric risk you face can be quantified—it is the price sensitivity of your portfolio to a small change in rates. It is often called the *duration* of your portfolio.

By contrast, if you hold a bond with an embedded option, such as a mortgage security or a corporate bond with a call option, you would face an element of asymmetric risk. Your loss if interest rates rise is greater than your gain if interest rates fall. Most corporate bonds have call features. We can think about the holder of a mortgage-backed security as long a bond and short a call option. That is, as interest rates go down, the homeowner has the right to call the mortgage and refinance his house at the new low rates. The amount of asymmetric risk in a portfolio is often called *convexity.*

Identifying Your Desired Risk-Return Profile

After identifying the risks, the next step is to identify the desired risk-return profile. You must decide which risks reward you sufficiently for keeping them and which you wish to lay off. If you are a money manager with a long position in a 30-year Treasury security, and you expect interest rates to rise more than is reflected in the term structure of interest rates, you may want to neutralize this position by hedging. That is, you may want to turn the long bond position, in effect, into a position in a money market instrument. Conversely, if you have a long position in a 30-year Treasury security and you expect interest rates to fall, you will not want to hedge your position.

You may also want to convert a symmetric risk position into an asymmetric risk position. That is, if you hold a portfolio of 30-year Treasury bonds, the purchase of a put option will place a maximum loss on your position, while preserving your upside. The portfolio will gain if rates decline. The option can be put if rates rise. If interest rates remain steady you will lose the option premium.

In sum, if you are a portfolio manager with a long symmetric position, you have three alternatives: keep the long symmetric position, neutralize the long symmetric position or convert the long symmetric position into an asymmetric position by purchasing puts.[1] Combinations of these alternatives are, of course, possible. Thus, if you hold a long symmetric bond position and choose to shorten but not eliminate

---

[1] In this chapter, we do not consider call writing strategies. Call writing does reduce the maximum loss, if interest rates rise, by the amount of the premium. Call writing is not, however, done to hedge. It is done to gain additional income, and we do not consider it a hedging strategy in the true sense of the word.

your position, the return will be a combination of the long symmetric position and the neutralized position.

If you begin with asymmetric risk you again have three alternatives: keeping the asymmetric position, neutralizing the option by converting to a symmetric risk position, or neutralizing the position entirely. For example, assume that you hold a current coupon mortgage security, say a GNMA 10. As rates go up, the security will drop in price. As rates fall, the mortgage security will go up in price, but not by as much as it would in the absence of the call option. If rates are expected to remain steady you may be satisfied with your position. If you expect rates to fall over the near term but are reluctant to sell the security, you may want to neutralize the option position that is embedded in the mortgage-backed security. You can do this by purchasing an option. This will leave you with a long position in a bond. You can also convert your asymmetric risk to a money market position by hedging both the option position and the underlying position.

Which Instrument or Instruments Should Be Used to Hedge?

Futures positions are generally used to neutralize symmetric risk. Futures are very actively traded, and it is possible to execute a very large order at one time rather than "working the order." Futures contracts exist on a number of different interest rate instruments—including Treasury bonds, 10-year Treasury notes, 5-year Treasury notes, Treasury bills, Eurodollars, municipal bonds, and corporate bonds.[2] Treasury bond futures are by far the most actively traded of the futures instruments, with a daily trading volume of 304,500 and an open interest of approximately 445,000 in mid-1988. Exhibit 1 shows the open interest (the number of contracts outstanding) and trading volume for futures on different contracts.

In contrast to futures, options are usually used to convert symmetric risk to asymmetric risk. Options can be either exchange-traded or over-the-counter and can be written on either physical bonds or bond futures. Exchange-traded options on futures have very low transactions costs. Exhibit 1 shows the volume and open interest on each of these contracts. Looking at the options on bond futures, you can see that the open interest on the options is actually larger than on the underlying futures. The trading volume is, however, somewhat smaller. There are exchange-traded options on physical bonds on the Chicago Board Options Exchange, but their volume is considerably lower than that of the options on bond futures.

Over-the-counter options allow the portfolio manager to minimize his basis risk. The portfolio manager can choose the instrument on which he wants to buy an option. Thus, if the portfolio manager holds a specific bond, the 8⅞ of 2017, for example, he can buy options on that particular bond.

The choice of OTC options versus exchange-traded options, or options on futures versus options on bonds, depends on your need to tailor the hedge to a specific date,

---

[2]While there are the two corporate bond contracts, neither one currently trades.

EXHIBIT 1
VOLUME AND OPEN INTEREST ON U.S. FUTURES EXCHANGES*

Contract and Exchange	Volume	Open Interest
Chicago Board of Trade		
U.S. Treasury 30-Year Bond	304,500	445,000
Bond Future Option	88,900	574,200
U.S. Treasury 10-Year Note	19,700	87,800
Note Future Option	4,000	58,300
Municipal Bond Buyer Index	6,500	11,700
U.S. Treasury 5-Year Note	1,600	11,300
Chicago Mercantile Exchange		
90-day Eurodollar Time Deposits	92,400	452,700
Eurodollar Options	8,000	103,100
91-Day U.S. Treasury Bills	5,200	19,600
Financial Exchange New York		
U.S. Treasury 5-Year Note	2,800	9,400
5-Year Note Future Option	2,000	2,200

*Average daily figures for June-July 1988 (rounded to nearest 100).

security, or strike price, as well as on the liquidity of the market. Exchange-traded options, if appropriate, can be less costly than OTC options, since they eliminate the dealer's bid-asked spread. Sometimes, however, exchange-traded options will not meet your needs. Expiration dates on exchange-traded options are spaced three months apart, strike prices are spaced two points apart, and the longest expiration date is only nine months out. Moreover, they are based on only a small universe of bonds. The advantage, however, is that exchange-traded options are more liquid—if you no longer need the option, you can resell it at any time. By contrast, OTC options often can only be resold to the original seller, entailing fairly large transactions costs.

HEDGING WITH FUTURES

Having decided to hedge a cash instrument with futures, you, as a portfolio manager, must then decide which futures to short. You will normally choose the futures contract that most closely matches the cash position. For example, if you were trying to hedge municipal bonds, you would normally use municipal bond futures rather than Treasury bond futures. This judgment may be tempered by liquidity considerations. Let us take three examples of this:

- While corporate bond futures exist, they basically do not trade. Thus, you will probably use Treasury bond futures to hedge a corporate bond position.

- There is no mortgage futures contract. Most portfolio managers would like to use 5-year note futures for premium mortgages. However, these contracts are not yet liquid enough to hedge large positions, so the 10-year note futures is often used.
- In the municipal area, if you have a large municipal position to protect and are afraid of moving the market, you initially may want to short both municipal futures and the more liquid bond futures. Over time, you can buy back the bond futures and sell more municipal futures.

After deciding which contract(s) to short, you must decide how many. If you are using a single instrument to hedge, there are four procedures for determining hedge ratios:

- Duration hedging
- Factor hedging
- Regression hedging
- Regression/Duration hedging

The choice of procedure depends largely on the circumstances. We will discuss each in turn.

Duration Hedging

The objective of any hedge is to match the change in price of your portfolio with the change in price of the hedge. That is, we want a hedge in which equation (1) holds:

$$\Delta P_B = HR \times \Delta P_{FUT} \tag{1}$$

where ΔP_B = the change in the price of the bonds in your portfolio
                HR = the hedge amount
                ΔP_{FUT} = the change in the price of a futures contract

Duration is a linear approximation to the change in price of a bond or a bond portfolio for a given change in interest rates. That is, the change in price of a bond or portfolio can be approximated by equation (2):

$$\Delta P_B = D_B \times P_B \times \Delta r \tag{2}$$

where P_B = the price of the bonds in your portfolio
                D_B = the duration of the bonds in your portfolio
                Δr = the change in interest rates

The change in the price of the futures contract, can be similarly approximated, as given by equation (3):

$$\Delta P_{FUT} = D_{FUT} \times P_{FUT} \times \Delta r = D_{CTD} \times P_{FUT} \times \Delta r \tag{3}$$

where D_{FUT} = the duration of the futures contract, which is close to the duration of the cheapest-to-deliver bond (D_{CTD}).[3]

More precisely, the duration of the futures is the duration of the cheapest-to-deliver bond from delivery to maturity.

Substituting (2) and (3) into (1) and assuming that the change in interest rates is the same for the cash and futures, we obtain equation (4):

$$D_B \times P_B = HR \times D_{CTD} \times P_{FUT} \tag{4}$$

The left hand side of (4) is the dollar duration (duration times price) of your portfolio. $D_{CTD} \times P_{FUT}$ is the dollar duration of a futures contract.

As an example, assume we want to hedge $10,000,000 par of the 8⅞ of 2017. The modified duration of the bond is 9.92 years and the price plus accrued interest is 100.67. The duration of the futures is 10.34 years and the price is 88¹⁵⁄₃₂. The hedge amount required is $10,900,000 (109 contracts) or a hedge ratio of 1.09.

Factor Hedging

Factor hedging is the simplest way to hedge. No calculations are necessary. It can be used when the bonds to be hedged are Treasury securities that are deliverable against the Chicago Board of Trade note or bond futures contract. We shall, however, see that duration hedging is preferable when the Treasury bond to be hedged is not the cheapest to deliver.

The note and bond futures contracts specify that a range of securities is deliverable. In the case of the bond contract, any bond with at least 15 years to first call (if applicable) or maturity (on a non-callable bond) is deliverable. Each bond is equated to a hypothetical 8% instrument by means of the delivery factors. For example, the 7¼ of 2016 has a factor of .9175 for March 1989 delivery. This means that at delivery, the bond would have an invoice price equal to the closing futures price times its factor plus accrued interest. This is given by:

Invoice Price of Bond = (Futures Price × Factor) + Accrued Interest

Thus, the fair futures price is one that makes the futures price times the factor equal to the price of the bond at delivery.

---

[3]"Cheapest to deliver" is discussed later.

Prior to maturity, you should hold F futures to hedge \$100,000 par amount of a cash bond, where F is the factor. That is, the theoretical price of the bond prior to maturity will be the futures price times the factor less the net carry. (The net carry is the current yield on the bond less the cost of the borrowed funds necessary to own the bond between now and delivery.) Thus, as interest rates change, the change in the bond price would be roughly the change in the futures price times the (constant) factor.

In actuality, this relationship holds better for certain bonds than for others. Some bonds are substantially more expensive than this relationship would dictate. The bond for which this relationship comes the closest to holding is known as the cheapest to deliver.[4]

Factor hedging works well when the bond to be hedged is the cheapest-to-deliver bond. In this case, factor hedging is very close to duration hedging. Recall that in duration hedging, the dollar duration of the futures position is equated to the dollar duration of the cash position as given by:

$$P_{CTD} \times D_{CTD} = HR \times P_{FUT} \times D_{CTD}$$

We know the price of the cheapest-to-deliver bond is roughly equivalent to the price of the futures times the factor. Substituting on the left hand side of the above equation, we find that the hedge ratio must be roughly the factor, as given by equation (5):

$$P_{FUT} \times \text{factor}_{CTD} \times D_{CTD} = HR \times P_{FUT} \times D_{CTD} \qquad (5)$$

For bonds other than the cheapest to deliver, this does not work so well. If the duration of the futures is roughly the duration of the cheapest-to-deliver bond, the factor of the bond to be hedged would be an incorrect hedge ratio. We could, of course, do a "duration correction" to the hedge ratio, as follows:

$$P_B \times D_B = P_{FUT} \times D_{CTD} \times HR \qquad (6)$$

where $HR = D_B / D_{CTD} \times \text{factor}_B$

This correction assumes that the price of the futures times the bond's factor is reasonably close to the price of the bond. This is often not the case. Furthermore, if you are going to do a duration correction, you would find it just as easy to use a duration hedge.

---

[4]We have oversimplified this discussion to establish the point in a concise manner. Because of the presence of delivery options, the cheapest-to-deliver bond will be slightly less expensive than the futures times the factor less the net carry. Moreover, if there are several bonds that are relatively close to being the cheapest to deliver, the duration of the futures may actually be a combination of these rather than having exactly the duration of the cheapest bond.

In short, factor hedging is a simpler way to construct a futures hedge than duration hedging. However, it is less generally applicable than duration hedging. Factor hedging can be used only on Treasury securities, and it is inapplicable if the bond to be hedged is not deliverable on the futures contract. It works well if the Treasury bond or note to be hedged is the cheapest to deliver or is a Treasury bond or note with a duration close to the cheapest-to-deliver bond or note. It works less well if the bond to be hedged has very different characteristics from the cheapest-to-deliver bond.

We have seen that duration hedging has an advantage over factor hedging in that it can be used for all instruments, not just Treasury securities. Duration hedging does have an important drawback in that it assumes that yields change by the same amount for all instruments. This is obviously not the case. For example, 10-year Treasury yields may increase by 10 basis points, while 10-year corporate yields increase by 20 basis points. Even within the Treasury sector, if 10-year Treasury yields increase by 10 basis points, 5-year Treasury yields could increase by 5 basis points or 20 basis points. This is where regression hedging is useful.

Price Regression Hedging

Regression hedging takes into account the fact that the yield on the instrument to be hedged will not move exactly in line with that of the hedging vehicle. Regressions allow the user to pick the hedge ratio that minimizes the squared errors from the hedge. In price terms, you generally run a regression of the form:

$$P_B = a + b\, P_{FUT} + e \tag{7}$$

where e represents a residual, or error term.

Note that all prices are per $100 par amount. The regression can also be run in terms of price changes as given by equation (8).

$$\Delta P_B = b\Delta P_{FUT} + e \tag{8}$$

The beta (b) of the regression is the hedge ratio for $100 par amount. When the regression is run in terms of levels, as in equation (7), there is usually a great deal of autocorrelation in the error terms. This causes some doubt as to the validity of the results, so most market participants tend to run the regression in terms of price changes as in equation (8). The only problem with running in terms of price changes is that if the prices are non-synchronous (3:00 futures prices and 3:30 cash prices, for instance), the bias will be much greater than if the regression were run in terms of levels.

The regression approach has a serious drawback in that the results are very sensitive to the frequency of the data (daily, weekly, monthly) and the period used.

The conventional wisdom in this area is that the data frequency should correspond to the length of the hedge period. Thus, if you plan to hedge for two weeks, you should use biweekly data.

The length of the sample period for which you run the regression should depend primarily on how long a period you believe the past experience is relevant. For example, if you were estimating the beta of a regression with GNMA 10s on the left-hand side and Treasury bonds on the right-hand side, the results in a market rally would not be relevant to a period of stable rates. Moreover, this judgment occasionally must be modified to make sure you have enough observations to run a regression. For example, with daily data, a nine-month observation period is more than sufficient. With monthly data it is not.

It should be noted that if the correlation between the instrument to be hedged and the futures is 1.0, regression hedging and duration hedging are equivalent. That is, the beta of the regression is simply the correlation between the instruments times the relative variability. In symbols:

$$b = \rho(P_B, P_{FUT}) \times \text{Stan Dev}_{FUT}/\text{Stan Dev}_B \qquad (9)$$

where $\rho(P_B, P_{FUT})$ = Correlation between the price change of the bond and futures
Stan Dev_B = standard deviation of the bond price
Stan Dev_{FUT} = standard deviation of the futures price

The relative variability (ratio of standard deviations of the futures and the bond) is equal to the ratio of the dollar durations (per $100 par).

Regression/Duration Hedging

Most market participants use a combination of regression and duration hedging. That is, they first find the duration hedge ratio. This is then modified by the beta from a yield regression. The regression is generally performed using yield levels, as follows:

$$Y_B = a + b \ Y_{FUT} + e \qquad (10)$$

The yield on the cheapest-to-deliver bond is taken as a proxy for the yield on the futures. The regression is sometimes run in terms of first differences, as follows:

$$\Delta Y_B = b \Delta Y_{FUT} + e \qquad (11)$$

The regression run on yield levels generally has much less of an autocorrelation problem. Moreover, the betas of equations (10) and (11) are very close.

The regression correction is then made to modify the duration hedge ratio. This is done by multiplying the duration hedge ratio by the beta, as given by equation (12).

$$RHR = DHR \times beta \qquad (12)$$

where $RHR =$ the regression hedge ratio
              $DHR =$ the duration hedge ratio

In the previous example, we calculated the duration hedge ratio to be 1.09. If the beta on the yield regression was .80, the regression/duration hedge ratio would be .8 times 1.09, or .872. That is, 87 bond futures of $100,000 each are necessary to hedge the $10,000,000.

Note that each of the approaches discussed above has limitations. Factor hedging can be used only for Treasury securities, and is not accurate for bonds other than the cheapest-to-deliver. Regression hedging relies on past experience providing a guide to the future. It is dependent on the time period chosen and the availability and frequency of the data. Duration hedging works well for small parallel changes in yield levels. It doesn't work well for larger changes in yield or for changes in the shape of the yield curve. Apart from these limitations, all the techniques discussed so far involve hedging a bond position with a single futures contract.

Hedging with Multiple Instruments

Single instruments are generally used to hedge a portfolio. However, there are two circumstances in which you should use more than one instrument. The first is if you want to hedge a very large amount, and liquidity is a concern. In the examples mentioned earlier, if you wanted to hedge GNMA 11's, a premium instrument, 5-year note futures would be the instrument selected. However, there is not enough liquidity in this to hedge a large position. Thus, you would initially hedge a part of your portfolio with 5-year note futures and the remainder with 10-year note futures or bond futures. Similarly, if you wanted to hedge a very large municipal position, you would initially sell some municipal bonds and some Treasury bond futures. As circumstances permitted, you would buy back the bond futures and sell more municipal futures.

In these circumstances, the hedge is sequential, and the dynamics of determining hedge ratios are similar to those of a single instrument.

Step 1: Determine how large a futures position in your desired instrument you want to undertake.

Step 2: Determine how much of your cash position this will hedge.

Step 3: Determine how much of your second-choice instrument is necessary to hedge the remaining cash position, using the techniques discussed in the previous section.

The second circumstance calling for multiple instruments occurs when the characteristics of your cash position would be most closely matched by a combination of two instruments. For example, if you hold a large cash position in the 2-year note, you may want to use a combination of Eurodollar futures and the 5- or 10-year note, as this provides greater protection against changes in the shape of the yield curve than would any single position. This hedge is different from the multiple instrument hedge discussed above, as the amount of each of the two futures to use is jointly determined. One way to do this is to use generalized duration hedging — that is, to match the first two moments of the price-yield relationship, rather than only the first moment as is done with a duration hedge.[5]

Generalized Duration Hedging[6]

Duration approximates the price-yield relationship of a bond with a straight line. The slope of the line is the duration of the instrument. However, the actual price-yield relationship is curvilinear, as shown in Exhibit 2. Duration provides a good approximation of the percent change in price for small changes in interest rates, at which point the straight line is tangent to the curve. For large changes in rates, duration can be substantially off.

Assume the yield curve will change shape such that the yield change on any two bonds will have the relationship given by equation (13):

$$\Delta Y_2 = \Delta Y_1 \, m_2/m_1 \tag{13}$$

where m_1 is the maturity of bond 1 and m_2 is the maturity of bond 2.

It can be shown that, in this instance, the correct hedge ratio will be P_1C_1/P_2C_2, where C is the convexity. If changes in the shape of the yield curve cannot be

---

[5]The first two moments of the price-yield relationship refer to the first two terms in a Taylor series expansion for the percent change in bond price around the initial interest rate.

[6]A more in-depth discussion of this can be found in Laurie S. Goodman and N.R. Vigayaraghavan, "Combining Various Futures Contracts to Get Better Hedges," in Frank J. Fabozzi (ed), *Advances in Futures and Options Research*, Volume 3, JAI Press, 1989, or Laurie S. Goodman and N.R. Vigayaragahavan, "Generalized Duration Hedging with Futures Contracts," *Review of Research in Futures Markets*, Volume, 6, Number 1, 1987.

EXHIBIT 2
THE PRICE-YIELD RELATIONSHIP

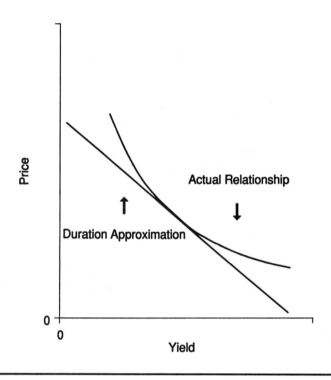

characterized in exactly this manner, convexity will help, but will not completely hedge against changes in slope.[7]

Nonetheless, it appears that hedging duration and convexity will provide protection against large changes in interest rates and small slope changes. We can hedge duration and convexity by using two futures instruments, F_1 and F_2. We essentially find H_1 and H_2, the amount of each futures instrument to be purchased such that equations (14) and (15) hold simultaneously.

$$P_B \times D_B = H_1 \times P_{F1} \times D_{F1} + H_2 \times P_{F2} \times D_{F2} \qquad (14)$$

$$P_B \times C_B = H_1 \times P_{F1} \times C_{F1} + H_2 \times P_{F2} \times C_{F2} \qquad (15)$$

---

[7]A fuller discussion on this point can be found in G.O. Bierwag, George G. Kaufman and Cynthia M. Latta, "Duration Models: A Taxonomy," *The Journal of Portfolio Management*, Fall 1988.

That is, we are solving two equations for two unknowns. The duration and convexity of each of the futures contracts is the duration and convexity of the cheapest-to-deliver bond. The hedge position selected for a bond that has a duration and convexity less than one of the futures and greater than the other will utilize positive quantities of each of the futures.

Generalized duration hedging does not allow for differential changes in yields across sectors. For example, if corporate yields changed by more or by less than Treasury yields, this method would not take such changes into account. Moreover, there are higher order moments, such as changes in curvature, which will make the hedge less effective.

Thus, there are a number of different methods to choose a futures hedge ratio. Each has its advantages and drawbacks. To choose the appropriate method, the user must consider the instruments involved and how accurate the hedge should be.

PURCHASING PUT OPTIONS TO HEDGE ASYMMETRIC RISK

As we discussed earlier, options offer a risk profile that differs substantially from that of futures. They are, therefore, an alternative structuring tool in the control of risk. In contrast to the symmetric return profile for futures, options have an asymmetric risk/reward profile that can be used to protect against price declines while allowing the investor to profit if the market rallies.

The decision to use a short hedge or a long put to hedge a bond portfolio depends on your views on the direction and magnitude of interest rate changes in the future, your comfort level regarding unfavorable outcomes, and your investment goals. If you strongly believe that rates will rise substantially, you should choose a short hedge to lock in its return. However, if you want to protect yourself from a possible rise in rates — but you also believe that rates may fall — a put option, which limits the loss while allowing for upside potential, may be more appropriate. A long put added to a portfolio has the risk characteristics of a call option — upside potential with limited downside risk. If rates rise, this option strategy will cost more than a short hedge. It will perform far better than an unhedged bond, as it will provide a floor on the return. In the event that rates fall, this strategy will have a greater return than a short hedge.

A Simple Example

Let us consider an example in which you, the investor, are hedging a call-free bond portfolio with Treasury bond puts. For this example, assume that your portfolio consists of one bond — the 8⅞ Treasury bond of 8/15/17, now at 98-12. As rates rise, the market value of the portfolio declines, and as rates fall, the market value of the portfolio rises. This asset has symmetric risk — the same type of gain/loss occurs in the opposite direction when rates fall/rise.

Next, suppose that you expect rates to rise in the near future and want to protect against this risk. You strongly believe that rates will not fall, and you are willing to forego gains if rates do fall in exchange for protection if rates rise. In other words, you are looking for a symmetric "risk-free," or neutral, return on your portfolio. In this case, you would choose a symmetric hedge — a short cash or futures position — to offset your long cash position. Options would not suit your risk needs. The returns to an unhedged portfolio, a portfolio hedged with futures, and a portfolio hedged with options are shown in Exhibit 3. Note that the position hedged with futures provides a return comparable to that of a "risk-free" money market instrument under all interest rate scenarios.

Suppose instead that you now expect rates to fall over the next month but want protection if rates rise. For the protection, or insurance, against an adverse change in interest rates, you are prepared to pay a premium. If you are right, your gain is the market move less the premium. If you are wrong, you lose only your premium.

EXHIBIT 3
COMPARISON OF AN UNHEDGED PORTFOLIO, A PORTFOLIO HEDGED WITH PUTS AND A PORTFOLIO HEDGED WITH FUTURES

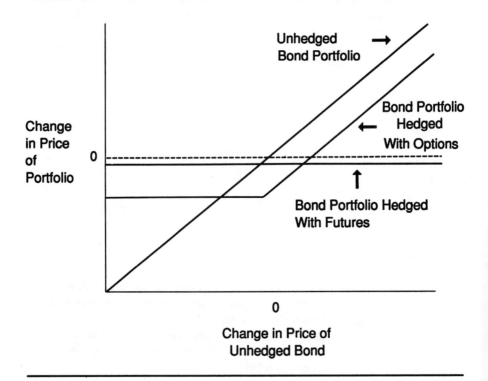

The purchase of a four-week, at-the-money Treasury put on the 8⅞ of 2017 at a price of 1.56 points, when combined with the bond you own, would give you your desired profile by allowing you to benefit from a decline in interest rates. In this transaction, you would purchase a put option entitling you to sell the 8⅞ of 2017 at 98-12 (the strike price) at any time before the expiration date of the option. The strike could be defined in terms of yield instead of price. For example, the option could have been specified to sell the 8⅞ at a 9% yield.

If the price falls below the put's strike price, then you would realize a loss on the portfolio, but you would also realize an offsetting profit on the puts in the following way. Suppose the 8⅞ falls to a price of 95-12. The portfolio then falls by three points. But the option has value in either of two ways. By purchasing the Treasury securities in the open market at 95-12 and "putting" them, or selling them to the writer of the option at the price represented by the strike price, i.e., 98-12 — you have a put that, as exercised, is worth three points. Alternatively, you could sell the put itself back to the writer; the value of the put is the same three points of the so-called "intrinsic value" — the difference between the open market price and the strike price. Thus, if the market price falls below the strike price, the gain of three points from the put will offset your three-point loss on the portfolio, less the cost of the option, for a capital loss of 1.56 points instead of three points on the unhedged bond. If the price falls by an amount equal to the cost of the option, the hedged position will have a capital loss of 1.56 as will the unhedged bond. On the other hand, if prices do not fall below the strike price, the option will expire worthless, reducing the minimum return at all prices above the strike price, as seen in Exhibit 3. If prices have risen three points, for example, the hedged position will have a capital gain of 1.44 points, versus three points for the unhedged position. If prices rise substantially, of course, the hedged position will consistently produce a return somewhat smaller than the unhedged position. This is the cost of the unused insurance. Note that to compute the holding period return, you must include the coupon income.

Options at Different Strike Prices

Put options are similar to insurance. You, the investor, pay a premium for protection against rising interest rates. The size of this premium depends on the strike price, which is determined by the desired "deductible." Of course, the less the protection, the lower the price.

The strength of your market opinion helps to determine which strike price to choose — whether to protect a cash position against any and all adverse movements, or to protect only against a larger movement (at a lower premium cost).

For example, suppose that you are the manager of a fixed income portfolio. You want to earn a certain minimum rate of return over the next month, but you expect rates to rise. You could buy an "at-the-money" put option, in which the market price is the strike price; an out-of-the-money option, in which the market price is higher than the strike price; or an in-the-money option in which the market price is lower than the strike price. Exhibit 4 shows the return profile of the long 8⅞ bond hedged with puts in and out of the money by two points, as well as by an at-the-money put.

An in-the-money option, if exercised today, has intrinsic value. In our example, this intrinsic value is two points. The price of the option, which incorporates both intrinsic value and time value, must be greater than that. In this case the price is 2.85. If rates fall (prices rise), the bond hedged with the in-the-money put option will underperform the unhedged bond by $2.85. It will underperform the bond hedged with the at-the-money option (cost $1.56) by $1.29 ($2.85 minus $1.56). If prices fall by more than $.85, the bond with the in-the-money option will outperform the unhedged bond by an amount dependent on the price. Under the same circumstances, the bond with the in-the-money option will outperform the bond with the at-the-money option by $.75 ($1.56 minus $.85), as shown in Exhibit 4.

An out-of-the-money option is the least likely to be exercised and is, therefore, the least expensive option hedging alternative. A one-month option two points out of the

EXHIBIT 4
COMPARISON OF AT-THE-MONEY, OUT-OF-THE-MONEY, AND IN-THE-MONEY OPTION HEDGES

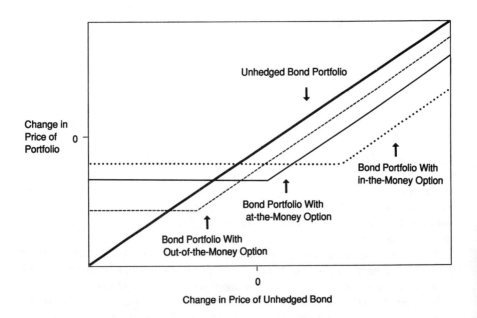

-money sells for $.72. Thus, if rates fall (prices rise), the bond hedged with an out-of-the-money option will underperform the unhedged bond by $.72. On the other hand, if prices do fall, the first few points will be a direct loss to your return, as will be the premium. Prices must fall more than $2.72 (the out-of-the-money amount plus the premium) for the hedged bond to outperform the unhedged bond. An at-the-money put, with strike at today's price, fits somewhere between the in- and out-of-the-money options.

Costs

In contrast to futures, options protection is expensive because it is one-sided — if rates go up, you gain; if rates go down, you do not lose. The explicit cost for being able to obtain this payoff structure is the option premium.[8]

Because the costs are not small, you must decide what risk you are willing to bear. You can reduce the cost of the option if you choose an out-of-the-money option and/ or if you shorten the expiration date. For example, if you are protecting against an adverse change in Federal Reserve policy within the next three weeks, a two-month option represents an unnecessary cost.

Option prices are also a function of volatility. The more volatile the market, the higher the hedging cost for a market maker, and therefore the higher the price to the buyer. Of course, in volatile markets you will have a higher level of concern about asset protection than in stable markets. Consequently, you will be more willing to pay for this protection. Exhibit 5 shows some options price estimates of a put option on the 8⅞ U.S. Treasury of 2017, as well as the 8⅛ of 1998. As you can see, with 15% volatility, the price of a one-month at-the-money option on the 8⅞ is $1.23. The price is $2.12 at 21% volatility.

Calculating Hedge Ratios

If you want to change symmetric risk into asymmetric risk using options, the hedging principles are exactly the same as for futures: you want the price changes on the instrument underlying the option to be the same as those on the instrument to be hedged. This is given by equation (16):

$$HR = \Delta P_B / \Delta P_H \tag{16}$$

where: ΔP_B = the change in the price of your portfolio
ΔP_H = the change in the price of the instrument underlying the option

---

[8]The buyer of an option is not required to post margin. Therefore, the cost is precisely the premium.

EXHIBIT 5:
REPRESENTATIVE PUT PRICES (IN 32NDS)

Coupon: 8.875%
Maturity: 30 years

	1 Month to Expiration Volatility					3 Months to Expiration Volatility				
Strike Price	*9.0%*	*12.0%*	*15.0%*	*18.0%*	*21.0%*	*9.0%*	*12.0%*	*15.0%*	*18.0%*	*21.0%*
2 Pt OTM*	0-10	0-19	0-27	1-05	1-15	1-03	1-20	2-05	2-22	3-07
1 Pt OTM	0-20	0-30	1-08	1-18	1-28	1-17	2-02	2-20	3-05	3-21
ATM**	1-03	1-13	1-23	2-01	2-12	2-02	2-19	3-04	3-22	4-07
1 Pt ITM***	1-23	2-00	2-10	2-20	2-29	2-22	3-06	3-23	4-07	4-24
2 Pt ITM	2-15	2-23	2-31	3-08	3-17	3-12	3-27	4-11	4-27	5-12

Coupon: 8.125%
Maturity: 10 years

	1 Month to Expiration Volatility					3 Months to Expiration Volatility				
Strike Price	*9.0%*	*12.0%*	*15.0%*	*18.0%*	*21.0%*	*9.0%*	*12.0%*	*15.0%*	*18.0%*	*21.0%*
2 Pt OTM	0-03	0-06	0-11	0-15	0-21	0-15	0-24	1-02	1-12	1-23
1 Pt OTM	0-09	0-14	0-20	0-26	1-00	0-26	1-05	1-15	1-26	2-04
ATM	0-22	0-28	1-03	1-09	1-15	1-11	1-21	2-00	2-10	2-20
1 Pt ITM	1-12	1-17	1-22	1-28	2-01	2-00	2-09	2-19	2-28	3-06
2 Pt ITM	2-08	2-11	2-14	2-18	2-23	2-25	3-00	3-08	3-17	3-26

*OTM = Out-of-the-money
**ATM = At-the-money
***ITM = In-the-money

Thus, if you were buying an over-the-counter option on a Treasury bond that you held, you would purchase the same par amount of options as bonds (a 1:1 hedge ratio).

If you were using an option on one bond to hedge a similar bond you would want to use a duration hedge. That is, you would use the ratio of the dollar durations. This can be written as in equation (17):

$$P_B \times D_B = HR \times P_H \times D_H \tag{17}$$

For options on bond futures, the underlying hedging instrument is the bond futures. In this case we would have equation (18):

$$P_B \times D_B = HR \times P_{FUT} \times D_{CTD} \tag{18}$$

Recall that a duration hedge assumes that the yield on the hedging instrument will move by the same amount as the yield on the portfolio to be hedged. If you believe that rates will not move equally, you can run a regression either with prices or with yields. If you regress yield, you then adjust the duration hedge by the relative volatility of yields based on the "beta," or the slope of the regression equation. The optimal regression hedge ratio is then given by multiplying the duration hedge ratio by the beta obtained from the yield regression, as discussed in the futures section (equation (12)).

Simulating Options With Futures

There are situations in which you as an investor cannot find an exchange-traded put option to meet your needs. In order to create the desired payoff structure for the hedging instrument, in such a case, you have three alternatives: (1) you can purchase a tailor-made put option over-the-counter; (2) you can simulate such a put option by adjusting the size of the short cash or futures hedge frequently according to a specific portfolio strategy; or (3) you can continually replace some of your long bonds with money market instruments and vice versa using a dynamic asset allocation model so that your portfolio return looks like that of an option.

Futures, because of their greater liquidity and low transactions costs, are often chosen as a way to simulate an option. Moreover, the creation of a synthetic option enables you to create an option-like return at the exercise (strike) price and expiration date of your choosing. If tailoring the exercise price and expiration date on exchange-traded options is important to you, this strategy may be viewed as a less expensive alternative to OTC option purchases. A synthetic strategy does, however, require that you adjust positions frequently as the market changes.

To understand synthetic options, you have to understand the concept of the "delta" of an option. The delta of an option is the hedge ratio of the option to the underlying instrument — that is, the change in the price of the option relative to the change in the price of the underlying instrument.

We discussed the return profile of the option at expiration earlier in the chapter. To review a bit, when the market price is at the option strike price, the option is "at-the-money." If the price rises, the put becomes worthless. If the price falls, the put becomes valuable. The lower line in Exhibit 6 shows the return of the put at expiration. The curved line shows the price of the option one month before expiration. The slope of the curved line is the delta or hedge ratio. The higher the price of the underlying security, the less likely the put is to be exercised and, therefore, the fewer futures are needed as a hedge. The lower the price, the more likely the put is to be exercised, and the more futures contracts are needed as a hedge. When the bond is priced at-the-money, the hedge ratio is .5. This means that the price of one at-the-money put will move half as much as the futures contract. If the market rallies, the

EXHIBIT 6
PUT OPTION PROFILE

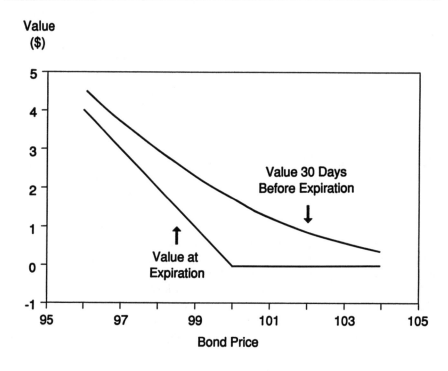

position is overhedged; if it drops, the position is underhedged. Because the hedge ratio changes as the price changes, you frequently have to readjust. In- and out-of-the-money deltas do not need to be adjusted as frequently as at-the-money deltas, because they do not change as much as at-the-money options when the price of the underlying bond changes. You can calculate the delta by using conventional option pricing formulas, such as the Black-Scholes model.

The creation of a synthetic option using futures contracts requires that you multiply the number of futures contracts required to hedge the bond by the delta of the option.

Earlier in this chapter, we explained how you would compute the number of options on bond futures to hedge a portfolio. Equation (19) shows you how to compute the number of futures to be sold (purchased) to create a long position in a synthetic put (call) option.

$$\Delta P_B \times \text{delta} = DHR \times \Delta P_{FUT} \tag{19}$$

where delta is the delta on the synthetic option.

Rewriting, we obtain equation (20):

$$DHR = \frac{P_B \times D_B \times \text{delta}}{P_{FUT} \times D_{CTD}} \tag{20}$$

The cost of creating a synthetic option is the loss that results from selling futures contracts as the price falls and buying them back as the price rises. For example, assume you want to create an at-the-money put option. This will pay off if prices fall. If prices rise, the option will expire worthless. With a synthetic option, if prices rise continuously, you will be buying back more and more of your initial short position at higher and higher prices, realizing losses. These losses will add up to the option premium. As prices fall, you will be selling a larger and larger short position. You will experience gains approximately equal to the payoff on the synthetic option less its theoretical premium.

You may choose to create a synthetic option in order to achieve the desired expiration date for a particular strike price. You may also choose to create a synthetic option if you believe the market will be less volatile than an OTC or exchange-traded option implies. In this case, the cost of the synthetic option will be less than the cost of purchasing an option from an option writer. That is, if volatility is lower than expected, the ex-post cost of the synthetic option will be lower than the ex-ante price quote on an OTC option. If volatility is higher, the reverse will be true.

Thus, options can be used to hedge by creating an asymmetric risk profile from a symmetric risk profile. This is done by the purchase of put options. A user must decide (1) the strike price desired on the option, which is determined by the user's desired return profile, (2) the type of options (over-the-counter or exchange-traded), and (3) the quantity of options to buy (the hedge ratio). We have reviewed all of these decisions.

HEDGING ASSETS WITH EMBEDDED OPTIONS

Situations in which you would like to hedge bonds with embedded options are extremely common; most corporate bonds and virtually all mortgage-backed securities have embedded option provisions. These securities are usually purchased because they look "cheap" relative to the alternatives. After purchasing the securities, you as a portfolio manager must decide if you want to keep the current profits on the securities, achieve a symmetric risk profile — that is simply offset the embedded call option — or achieve a neutral or zero risk position. The asymmetric position would be desirable if rates were expected to remain steady. If rates were expected to fall, you might want to offset the call options. You could also take advantage of falling rates by lengthening your portfolio. If rates were expected to rise, you would want to neutralize the position.

We first look at offsetting the option. It is important to realize that in order to offset the option you have written, you must purchase an option. This is often difficult, since exchange-traded options go out a maximum of nine months and long-term over-the-counter options are very expensive. To offset an embedded call on a bond when the first exercise date is five years off, or to offset the implicit call on a mortgage-backed security, the most accurate hedge would be to customize the option. In principle, this can be done by means of synthetic options. But it is rarely done in practice because of the hassle involved in readjusting the futures hedge. Moreover, it is hard to tell exactly what the hedge ratio should be on a mortgage security. As a practical matter, some portfolio managers simply buy exchange-traded call options. They figure out how many call options would be needed if rates dropped a specific amount, say 100 basis points.

Relatively few portfolio managers who hold bonds with embedded options are interested solely in hedging out the option position. If you expect rates to fall, you would lengthen your portfolio. If you expect rates to rise, you would shorten it. Thus, a more relevant concern to portfolio managers is neutralizing a portfolio that contains embedded options. There are two ways this could be done. The first is to use a duration hedge and alter the hedge ratio on a frequent basis.

Duration hedging must be used extremely cautiously when hedging a callable bond. Callable bonds have a duration that can be calculated as follows:

$$D_{CB} = \frac{(D_{NCB} \times P_{NCB} - D_O \times P_O)}{P_{CB}} \qquad (21)$$

where: $D_{NCB} \times P_{NCB}$ is the dollar duration of a non-callable bond
$D_O \times P_O$ is the dollar duration of the option
D_{CB} is the duration of the callable bond

The problem with using duration hedging to hedge a callable bond is shown in Exhibit 7 for a 10% 10-year bond, callable at par after 5 years. At low interest rates, the bond has a duration equal to that of a bond maturity at the call date. At high interest rates, the bond has a duration based on its time to maturity. When the bond sells for a price close to par, its duration can change rapidly. A 10% 10-year non-callable bond has a duration of 6.23 when it is priced at par. If interest rates went up to 12%, the bond would have a duration of 5.95. By contrast, a 10% 10-year callable bond has a duration of 5.48 at 10% interest rates and a duration of 5.91 at a 12% rate. Note that while the duration is lower at higher interest rates for non-callable bonds, the reverse is true for callable bonds. That is, callable bonds have negative convexity, whereas non-callable bonds have positive convexity. Note also the absolute change in duration is considerably higher for the callable bond: .43 years rather than .28 years. Current coupon and premium mortgages also have large negative convexity — that is their duration increases rapidly as interest rates rise.

Duration hedging a callable bond with futures is equivalent to establishing a short futures hedge and constructing a synthetic option position to offset the embedded call. The synthetic call involves a long position in bond futures. This is more than

EXHIBIT 7
THE DURATION OF A CALLABLE BOND

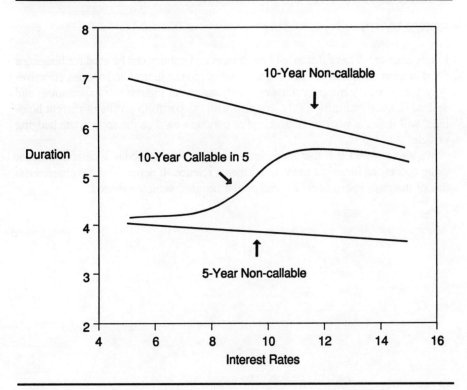

offset by the short futures position on the non-callable host bond. The synthetic option must be adjusted fairly frequently. Thus, if you were to use a duration hedge for an instrument with an embedded option, you must be sure to adjust the hedge ratio frequently. This is less important for an instrument with symmetric risk.

An alternative approach is a variation of the generalized futures hedging. We can find a combination of an option and a futures contract that has the same duration and convexity as the callable bond. This can be done by solving for HR_F and HR_O, the hedge ratio for the futures and option, respectively, in equations (22) and (23):

$$P_{CP} \times D_{CB} = HR_F \times P_F \times D_F + HR_O \times P_O \times D_O \qquad (22)$$

$$P_{CP} \times D_{CB} = HR_F \times P_F \times C_F + HR_O \times P_O \times C_O \qquad (23)$$

Again, we solve for two unknowns in two equations. This approach is rarely used, as it is complicated to calculate, it must be adjusted frequently and many portfolio managers are reluctant to buy expensive, short-term options as part of a hedge for a longer-term instrument.

CONCLUSION

In this chapter we have discussed how futures and options can be used for hedging a fixed income portfolio. We showed that in order to use futures and options effectively, you as a money manager must explicitly state your interest rate expectations and desired risk/return profile. This, coupled with the portfolio profile of current holdings, will indicate whether futures and/or options would be the appropriate hedging vehicle.

We also showed that the derivation of hedge ratios to hedge a cash instrument using options or futures is more an art than a science. It depends on the characteristics of the cash instruments as well as the hedging vehicle selected.

Chapter 18

Hedging with Eurodollar Futures

DANIEL NADLER
QUANTITATIVE STRATEGIES GROUP
SHEARSON LEHMAN HUTTON

Emerging as the futures contract of choice for managing the risks associated with the volatility of short-term interest rates, Eurodollar futures have become an integral part of the fixed-income marketplace. Many financial institutions are using Eurodollar futures to hedge short-term liabilities and other asset/liability mismatches. While some institutions look to forward rate agreements, interest rate swaps, and other over-the-counter products to manage these risks, the Eurodollar futures market provides an effective alternative. The purpose of this chapter is to demonstrate how Eurodollar futures can be used to manage short-term interest rate risk.[1]

I would like to thank the following for their respective contributions: Mark Pitts, Stan Jonas, Georges Courtadon, Doreen Davidow, Rebecca Horowitz, and Hasan Latif.

[1]An excellent overview of hedging interest rate volatility in general is provided in "Hedging with Interest Rate Futures," in Mark Pitts and Frank J. Fabozzi, *Interest Rate Futures and Options* (Chicago: Probus Publishing, 1989).

345

THE FUNDAMENTALS

The Eurodollar Futures Contract

Eurodollars are deposits of U.S. dollars in institutions outside the United States. Because short-term Eurodollar lending and borrowing is so common, the International Monetary Market introduced the Eurodollar Time Deposit futures contract in 1981. Created to provide a means for managing the risks inherent in lending and borrowing Eurodollars, the futures contract is tied to the London Interbank Offered Rate (LIBOR), the rate at which Eurodollars are offered among top-tier international banks. Basically, the contract is designed to protect interest expense (income) on $1 million for 90 days from fluctuations in 3-month LIBOR. Highlights of contract specifications are presented in Exhibit 1.

EXHIBIT 1
CONTRACT HIGHLIGHTS

Exchange:	International Monetary Market (IMM) of the Chicago Mercantile Exchange
Months traded:	March, June, September, December
Contract size:	$1,000,000
Price quotation:	100 minus annualized futures yield (simple, or add-on, interest)
Minimum fluctuation in price:	.01% (1 basis point) @ $25/basis point
Daily trading limit:	None
Settlement:	Cash, based upon the rate at which three-month Eurodollar Time Deposits are being offered by the London market (LIBOR)
Last day of trading:	2nd London business day prior to 3rd Wednesday of contract month
Settlement date:	Last day of trading
Hours of trading:	7:20 a.m. – 2:00 p.m. (Chicago) 7:20 a.m. – 9:30 a.m. (last day of trading)

The Eurodollar futures contract is quoted and traded in terms of a price which is equal to 100 minus the annualized futures interest rate. For example, a Eurodollar price of 92.00 is simply another way of saying that the futures LIBOR rate is 8.00%. The $25 price value of a one basis point change in the futures price follows from the fact that simple interest on $1 million for 90 days is equal to

$$\$1,000,000 \times [\text{rate} \times 90/360],$$

and that a one basis point (.01%) change in rate means a $25 change in interest expense (income).

Eurodollar futures trade in 12 contract months on a March, June, September, December cycle out for 3 years. This makes it possible for a financial institution to hedge changes in short-term interest rates for up to three years. The final settlement price for the contract is set equal to 100 minus 3-month LIBOR, on the last trading day. Three-month LIBOR, in turn, will be determined by the rate at which 3-month Eurodollar Time Deposit funds are being offered to major banks by the London market. Since Eurodollar futures do not have an underlying cash security and consequently do not call for actual delivery, settlement is made in cash. In other words, unlike other open futures contracts which call for delivery of the underlying commodity after the last day of trading, open Eurodollar contracts are automatically offset at the final settlement price. This cash settlement feature is probably a major factor contributing to the contract's liquidity.

Eurodollar Futures Pricing

In order to fully understand hedging with Eurodollar futures, a basic knowledge of futures pricing is warranted. Not unlike more traditional commodities, a "carry" argument (presented below) is used to establish a fair price for a Eurodollar futures contract. When market prices deviate significantly from theoretical prices, arbitrage (riskless profit) opportunities arise. Arbitrageurs, in turn, force market prices back in line with theoretical prices, thereby ensuring market efficiency. In order to illustrate this point, consider the following spot yield curve:

Maturity (in months)	LIBOR
1	7.000%
2	7.125%
3	7.250%
5	7.500%
6	7.500%

Suppose we are trying to price the Eurodollar futures contract which stops trading exactly 60 days from today. Furthermore, consider a LIBOR borrower whose financing horizon is 5 months (150 days). The borrower is simply concerned with his interest expense (in dollars) over the 5-month period. He should be indifferent as to whether the money is borrowed for 5-months term, at the rate r_5, or if it is borrowed for 2 months at the rate r_2 and then refinanced for the remaining 3 months at today's futures interest rate 2 months forward $f_{3,2}$. Consequently,

$$[1 + r_5 \times 150/360] = [1 + r_2 \times 60/360] \times [1 + f_{3,2} \times 90/360]$$

Using the rates in our spot yield curve and solving for $f_{3,2}$, we find that $f_{3,2} = 7.66\%$. In other words, the fair price for the Eurodollar futures contract which stops trading in 60 days (2 months forward) is equal to $100 - 7.66 = 92.34$.[2]

If the Eurodollar futures price differed from 92.34, market forces should quickly return it to equilibrium. Suppose for example that the price was 92.20, which corresponds to a forward rate of 7.80%. Our 5-month borrower would prefer borrowing at 7.50% for 5 months to borrowing at 7.125% for 2 months and refinancing at 7.80%. On the other hand, lenders (investors) would prefer the "synthetic" strategy. At this point, the arbitrageur steps in and borrows for 5 months at 7.50%. Simultaneously, he invests the borrowed money for 2 months at 7.125% and buys futures, consequently driving its price higher, in order to lock in the 7.80% reinvestment for the 3-month period, 2 months forward. At the end of the 5 months, the arbitrageur repays the borrowed money (with interest) and finds that the interest income from the synthetic 5-month investment exceeds his interest expense. Arbitrageurs should continue to exploit the inefficiency until the futures price reaches 92.34.[3] The opposite argument can be made for futures which are overpriced. Finally, futures prices for longer maturities can be derived analogously.

Eurodollar Strip Rate

Having completed our discussion on the pricing of Eurodollar futures contracts, an introduction of the Eurodollar strip rate seems appropriate. In the first place, one should not confuse a Eurodollar strip with the strip rate. Whereas the strip generally refers to the execution of a series of Eurodollar futures contracts, in sequence, in more than one contract month, the strip rate is the rate of return (expressed in money-market terms) which can be realized by earning spot LIBOR of appropriate maturity until settlement of the nearby Eurodollar contract and then compounding the earnings, each quarter, at the rates implied by futures prices. For example, using the data presented above, we calculate the 5-month strip rate s_5 as follows:

$$[1 + s_5 \times 150/360] = [1 + r_2 \times 60/360] \times [1 + f_{3,2} \times 90/360]$$

where r_2 is 2-month LIBOR spot (7.125%) and $f_{3,2} = 7.66\%$, the rate implied by today's Eurodollar futures price, 2 months forward. Solving for s_5 we find that $s_5 = 7.50\%$, which should not surprise anyone. In fact, if s_5 were not equal to 7.50%, arbitrage would be possible. The argument is identical to that just described in that the 5-month Eurodollar strip rate is the rate implied by the "synthetic" strategy.

Because the 2-year Eurodollar strip is popular, another example (using the data below) is presented. In addition, it gives us a chance to clear up any uneasiness about strip rate calculations.

---

[2]Transaction costs, fees, taxes, and bid-asked spreads are ignored.

[3]The return to equilibrium may occur due to changes in spot yields rather than futures prices. In either case, a sophisticated marketplace should insure fair pricing.

Futures Contract Month	Price	Implied Rate
Sep 87	92.34	7.66%
Dec 87	92.00	8.00%
Mar 88	91.80	8.20%
Jun 88	91.61	8.39%
Sep 88	91.41	8.59%
Dec 88	91.20	8.80%
Mar 89	90.99	9.01%
Jun 89	90.80	9.20%

Suppose that the Sep 87 contract stops trading exactly 60 days from now and that 2-month LIBOR spot equals 7.125%. Furthermore, suppose that 91 days separate each contract month. The 2-year strip rate s_{2y} is calculated as follows:

$$[1 + s_{2y} \times 365/360]^2 = [1 + .07125 \times 60/360] \times [1 + .0766 \times 91/360] \times$$
$$[1 + .08 \times 91/360] \times [1 + .082 \times 91/360] \times \ldots \times [1 + .0901 \times 91/360] \times$$
$$[1 + .092 \times 33/360]$$

Solving for s_{2y} we find that the 2-year strip rate is equal to 8.58%.[4]

Eurodollar futures mathematics used to perform strip rate calculations and contract pricing will be needed in order to implement a successful hedging program. The mathematical concepts used in this section will be applied repeatedly in upcoming sections where we concentrate on hedge ratio and target rate calculations.

HEDGING WITH EURODOLLAR FUTURES

Hedge Ratios and Target Rates

Hedge ratios and target rates are perhaps the two most important elements of a hedging program. The hedge ratio determines how many futures contracts are needed to minimize risk. The target rate provides a way to measure whether or not the hedge was successful. The purpose of this section is to explain the mechanics of hedge ratio and target rate calculations. By presenting a sequence of examples, starting out with a straightforward case and relaxing simplifying assumptions one at a time, many of the more subtle issues surrounding hedging with Eurodollar futures will be isolated and revealed.

Consider a financial institution that will be borrowing $100 million for the 90-day period beginning on the last trading day (hereafter, IMM date) of the Sep 87

---

[4]Note the 33-day interest period associated with the Jun 89 futures contract. This is so that the period of time covered by the strip corresponds to the 730-day "2-year" period.

Eurodollar contract, 60 days from "today." Furthermore, suppose that the borrowing rate will be set equal to 3-month LIBOR on that date and that today's Sep 87 futures price is 92.34. Before detailing any of the calculations, three issues merit consideration. First, because Eurodollar futures contracts are tied to 3-month LIBOR, the futures rate will converge to 3-month LIBOR spot on the last trading day (see Exhibit 2). In other words, 3-month LIBOR zero days forward is equal to spot. Second, the issue of whether to buy or sell Eurodollar contracts must be addressed. Basically, short-term borrowers fearing rising interest rates should sell Eurodollar futures whereas investors fearing a decline in rates should buy futures. Finally, the hedge lift date will be the date on which the borrowing rate is determined. When the rate is established, the uncertainty disappears and the hedge should be unwound.

Returning to our example, since the financial institution will be borrowing dollars and consequently fears an increase in 3-month LIBOR over the next 60 days, it should sell contracts. As far as the hedge ratio is concerned, the basic idea is to equate the interest rate sensitivity of the futures position to that of the "cash security" being hedged. In other words,

$$\text{Hedge Ratio} \quad = \quad \frac{\text{Dollar Volatility of Hedged "Security"}}{\text{Dollar Volatility of Futures Contract}}$$

Since actual interest expense will equal $100,000,000 × [3-month LIBOR × 90/360], the incremental expense caused by each basis point increase in 3-month LIBOR is $2,500. Recall that the price value of a one basis point (PVBP) change in the Eurodollar contract is $25. Consequently, the hedge is to sell 2,500/25 = 100 Sep 87 Eurodollar contracts.

Concerning the target rate, it is the interest rate implied by futures prices that we attempt to lock in through hedging and *not* current spot rates. In our example, since the borrower's rate is set on an IMM date, convergence to the futures rate is assumed. Therefore, the target for the hedge is set equal to the rate at which the borrower can sell 100 Sep 87 futures contracts. If the sale is transacted at 92.34, the target rate for the hedge would be equal to 7.66%. In other words, the targeted interest expense is $1,915,000 = $100,000,000 × [.0766 × 90/360].

In order to illustrate how the hedge performs, consider the following scenario. Suppose that by the time the $100 million is borrowed 60 days later, 3-month LIBOR has risen to 10.00% (futures settle at 90.00). The actual interest expense would be $2,500,000. However, having sold 100 contracts at 92.34, the futures (hedging) gain would be 234 basis points × $25/basis point × 100 contracts = $585,000. Consequently, the interest expense net of futures gains, or effective interest expense, equals $1,915,000, the target for the hedge. A moment's reflection reveals that the actual borrowing rate (which equals the settlement futures rate) minus (plus) futures gains (losses) equals the contracted futures rate, i.e., the target rate for the hedge.

With the most straightforward example behind us, we move on to construct hedges where a variety of factors are considered. By working through this section carefully, the reader will learn how to:

EXHIBIT 2
CONVERGENCE—SPOT LIBOR VS. EURO FUTURES

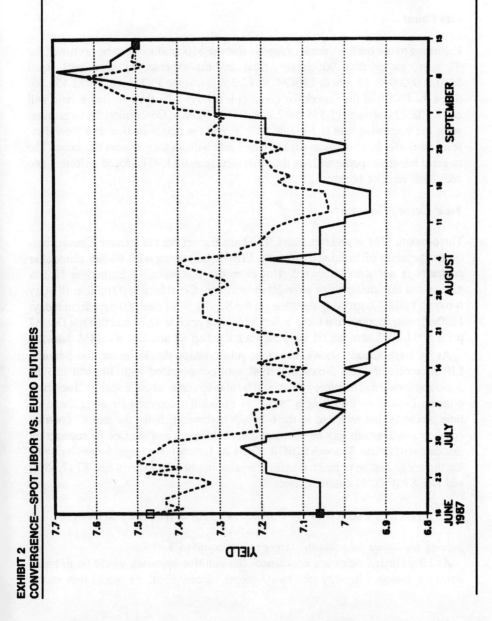

- incorporate actual day counts
- hedge 6-month LIBOR and other yield curve or maturity mismatches
- hedge the financing of variation margin
- hedge for rate resets which do not coincide with IMM dates, and
- hedge short-term rates other than LIBOR such as CD and commercial paper rates.

Day Count

Returning to our basic example, suppose that the $100 million is to be borrowed for 92 days, rather than 90 days. Actual interest expense, in turn, will equal $100,000,000 × [3-month LIBOR × 92/360], and the PVBP will be $2,555.56. Since the PVBP of the Eurodollar contract is always $25, the new hedge ratio will equal 102.22 contracts (2,555.56/25, or 100 × 92/90). Concerning the target rate, since the borrowing rate is 3-month LIBOR and the determination date (hereafter, reset date) also has not changed, the target rate will, in fact, remain the same. The targeted interest expense will, on the other hand, equal $1,957,555.56 reflecting two additional days of borrowing.

Yield Curve Mismatch

Three-month LIBOR and 6-month LIBOR are distinct rates of interest. Consequently, the problem of hedging a 6-month LIBOR borrowing with 90-day Eurodollar contracts is not straightforward. However, our discussion of Eurodollar futures pricing and Eurodollar strips provides the solution. Consider a $100 million 182-day 6-month LIBOR borrowing resetting on the Sep 87 IMM date, 60 days from today. Furthermore, suppose that today's Sep 87 futures price is 92.34 and that the Dec 87 price is 92.00. There are 91 days between the Sep 87 and Dec 87 IMM dates.

As we have already shown, arbitrage relationships should insure that 6-month LIBOR spot will equal 3-month LIBOR spot compounded with 3-month LIBOR 3 months forward. Therefore, we should be able to create a hedge against changes in 6-month LIBOR by executing a "strip" of Eurodollar contracts covering the same time period as that reflected in the 6-month borrowing. Since the Sep 87 contract converges to 3-month spot on the reset date and the price of the Dec 87 contract on that date will reflect 3-month LIBOR 3 months forward, the target 6-month rate L_6 for the hedge can be computed using the rates implied by today's Sep 87 (7.66%) and Dec 87 (8.00%) contract prices:

$$[1 + L_6 \times 182/360] = [1 + .0766 \times 91/360] \times [1 + .08 \times 91/360]$$

Solving for L_6 we find that the target rate is equal to 7.91%.

As far as hedge ratios are concerned, the intuitive approach would be to break down the 6-month liability into two 3-month pieces. First, we would lock in the

Sep 87 rate of 7.66% (representing 3-month LIBOR spot) for 91 days by selling 101.11 Sep 87 contracts ($100 \times 91/90$). Then, we would lock in the Dec 87 rate of 8.00% (representing 3-month LIBOR 3 months forward) for the next 91 days by selling 101.11 Dec 87 contracts. Actually, this is only part of the story. It turns out that the correct number of Sep 87 contracts is $103.16 = 100 \times 91/90 \times [1 + .08 \times 91/360]$. And, the correct number of Dec 87 contracts is $103.07 = 100 \times 91/90 \times [1 + .0766 \times 91/360]$. In other words, selling the strip of 103.16 Sep 87 contracts and 103.07 Dec 87 contracts should provide an effective hedge against changes in 6-month LIBOR.[5] Finally, since the 6-month rate will be determined on the Sep 87 IMM date, and any uncertainty will consequently be eliminated, the hedger must be careful to unwind the entire strip on that date. The same analysis can be extended to hedging 9-month LIBOR or any other maturity.

Before examining the issue of variation margin financing, it is important to make the following remark about yield curve mismatches. If the hedger in our 6-month LIBOR example used the definition of hedge ratio presented earlier in this section in the strictest sense, he would have calculated the hedge ratio to be equal to 202.22. We see that this is approximately equal to $103.16 + 103.07$. To the degree that changes in 3-month LIBOR are equal to changes in 6-month LIBOR, the hedge created by "stacking" 202.22 contracts in the Sep 87 contract month would be equally effective. In fact, if spreads between contract months remained constant, so too would be the hedge accomplished by shorting 202.22 contracts in any contract month. (If spreads between futures contract months remained constant, 3-month LIBOR and 6-month LIBOR would not experience equal changes in yield.) Since we know that spreads do not necessarily remain constant, and since we know that changes in 3-month LIBOR are not necessarily equal to changes in 6-month LIBOR, the strip will provide a more effective hedge to the degree that it captures changes in the shape of the yield curve. In other words, changes in 6-month LIBOR which are caused by changes in 3-month LIBOR 3 months forward (rather than changes in 3-month LIBOR) will be hedged effectively by a strip, though not through stacking. The use of Sep 87 and Dec 87 contracts is ideal because they span a period of time identical to that spanned by 6-month LIBOR spot on the Sep 87 IMM date.

Variation Margin Financing

Recall that the hedge ratio is designed to equate the interest rate sensitivity of a futures position to that of the "security" being hedged. Hedging the financing of variation margin, or "tailing" the hedge, may be regarded as fine-tuning the basic hedge and is designed to equate these interest rate sensitivities on a present value basis.

To illustrate, let's return to our base example of a hedge created to lock in an upcoming 3-month LIBOR reset on $100 million for a 90 day interest period. Furthermore, recall that on the day the hedge is initiated, Sep 87 Eurodollars are

---

[5]The correct hedge ratios are justified by an elementary calculus computation.

trading for 92.34 and that the borrower's expected (targeted) interest expense is $1,915,000, to be paid at the end of the interest period exactly 90 days after the rate reset.

EXHIBIT 3

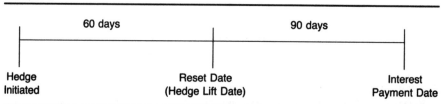

Our base example demonstrated how shorting 100 Sep 87 contracts would lock in the target rate. However, the story does not end here. To insure that participants in the futures markets fulfill their contractual obligations, and in turn insure the integrity of the futures contracts themselves, the futures exchanges have devised a system whereby all gains and losses are marked to market on a daily basis. That is, all gains and losses are recognized as they occur and are not deferred until futures delivery. Returning to our example, suppose that the change in the Eurodollar futures price from 92.34 to 90.00 occurred on the first day (just after the hedge was initiated) and that futures prices remained constant from then until the reset date. According to exchange rules and regulations, the gain on 100 futures contracts of $585,000 will be credited to the hedger's (borrower's) account by the following day. The realized gain will then be available to the hedger for short-term interest bearing investment. Consequently, the hedger's gain on the futures position with interest to the payment date will exceed the difference between targeted and actual interest expense. Conversely, had futures prices moved in the other direction, the difference (gain) between actual and targeted interest expense would not be enough to compensate the borrower for hedging losses including financing costs. In order to equate the two, the hedger must tail his futures position so that gains or losses on the hedge will be equal, but opposite to, losses or gains on the cash side on a present value basis.

To illustrate this technique, recall that the hedge was initiated exactly 60 days prior to the reset date and suppose that the borrower's rate for lending and borrowing variation margin cash flow is 7.00%. Note that there are 150 days between the day on which the hedge is initiated and the day on which the actual interest payment will be made (60 days to the reset date plus 90 days from then until the payment date, as shown in Exhibit 3). Had the borrower sold 97.2 futures contracts ($100/[1 + .07 \times 150/360]$), gains or losses on the futures position on that day, with interest to the payment date 150 days later, would equal (with only rounding errors) the loss or gain on the cash side: 97.2×234 basis points $\times$ $25/basis point $\times [1 + .07 \times 150/360] = $585,205$. This is known as tailing the hedge and is designed to compensate for the effects of financing futures gains or losses to the hedging horizon.[6]

Clearly, the futures position will need to be adjusted through time as the number of days to the reset date declines toward zero. This is because the tail does not depend upon the date on which the hedge was established, but rather upon the number of days remaining until the offsetting transaction occurs (in this case, the payment date). It should also be noted that even on the reset date, the number of contracts will still be somewhat less than 100 due to the fact that interest is being paid on an add-on basis. In other words, futures gains (or losses) as of the reset date will be invested (or financed) for the remaining 90 days to the interest payment date. Since the adjustments for both marking to market (in this case 60 days) and add-on interest (90 days) are similar in nature, we have lumped the two together.

Finally, the borrowing/lending rate, which also affects the tail, will not be constant but should move in the same direction as rates implied by futures prices. In other words, the funds rate should increase when futures prices decline and vice-versa. This too will necessitate adjustments to the futures position. Closer inspection reveals a slight advantage for the short hedger: The hedger who is shorting futures contracts will be able to invest futures gains at a higher than expected (tailed) rate and will finance futures losses at lower than expected rates.

Target Date, Delivery Mismatch

The examples presented up to this point have been constructed assuming that the target date for the hedge coincided with a Eurodollar futures delivery date (IMM date). Consequently, convergence to spot LIBOR has been a realistic assumption, and in turn, the hedges performed as anticipated. Hedging for dates other than IMM dates presents a problem of a very different nature. In order to minimize the risks caused by the date mismatch, a "composite" contract strategy is applied.[7]

As with other commodity contracts, we define the basis as the cash price minus the futures price. As Exhibit 4 illustrates, with Eurodollars, the only thing absolutely predictable about the basis is that it converges to zero at futures delivery. Since the relationship between spot LIBOR and a futures contract (the basis) is not always predictable, LIBOR hedges will not necessarily, or even likely, be near perfect except on the four futures settlement dates during any given year. (Variation margin financing adjustments to the hedge ratio cause even the most straightforward hedges to be imperfect.) However, since in broader terms, spot LIBOR and the nearby Eurodollar contract move together, the contract month next following the target date is frequently used to hedge LIBOR resets which do not coincide with a contract

---

[6]For the sake of clarity, simple interest was chosen. The actual tail should depend upon the hedger's margin financing arrangements and will most likely need to reflect interest compounding.

[7]See Mark Pitts and Robert W. Kopprasch, "Reducing Inter-Temporal Risk in Financial Futures Hedging," *Journal of Futures Markets*, 1984.

EXHIBIT 4
BASIS—SPOT LIBOR VS. EURO FUTURES

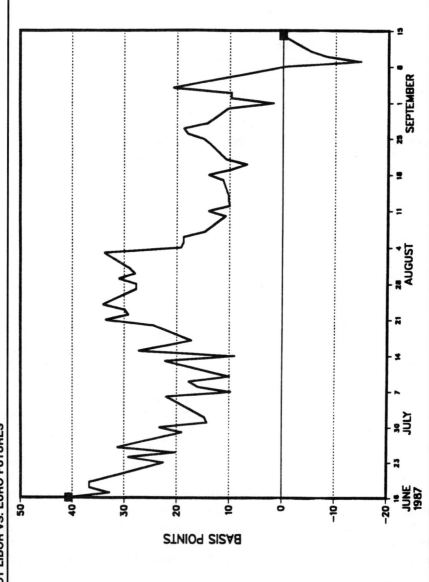

settlement date. An alternative strategy for hedging the date mismatch is the "composite" contract strategy which suggests transactions in both the contract months preceding and next following the target date. Since the strategy surrounds the target, the approach is intuitively appealing. It may, in fact, be viewed as an attempt to create a futures contract whose delivery date coincides with the target date.

In order to determine whether the composite strategy is also analytically appealing, we have simulated 3-month LIBOR hedges for both strategies over the period June 1985 to August 1987. Exhibit 5 summarizes our results for the hedging error.[8] Clearly, the composite strategy provides a more effective hedge than the alternative. This is perhaps best illustrated by looking at confidence intervals. Assuming normal distribution of errors and making the leap of faith that the mean error reverts to zero over longer periods of time, we can be 95% confident that we realize our target ± 26 basis points (2 standard deviations) if the composite strategy is applied whereas the 95% confidence interval for the next contract strategy widens to the target ± 40 basis points. If 26 basis points itself seems excessive, consider how much short-term rates can move over extended periods of time. Finally, as one would expect, in general, the nearer to an IMM date the target is, the more effective the hedge.

EXHIBIT 5
SUMMARY OF HEDGING ERROR FOR COMPOSITE AND NEXT CONTRACT STRATEGIES

Error Term	Composite Strategy	Next Contract
Standard deviation	13.2 bp	19.9 bp
Mean	−5.4	−15.4
Maximum	54.2	80.9

Having established the risk parameters for the composite strategy, we return to the base example to illustrate exactly how the strategy is applied. Suppose the financial institution will be borrowing $100 million for the 90-day period beginning October 10, 1987, rather than on the Sep 87 IMM date, September 14. Furthermore, suppose that the borrowing rate will be set equal to 3-month LIBOR on October 10 and that today's Sep 87 and Dec 87 futures prices are 92.34 and 92.00, respectively. (Remember, "today" is 60 days prior to September 14.) The Dec 87 IMM date is December 14 (see Exhibit 6).

---

[8]The hedging error is the difference between the effective rate and the target rate. Unlike Pitts and Kopprasch, we define the target rate for the next contract strategy to be the same as for the composite strategy. We feel this is a more reasonable approach but do not believe it significantly alters the results. It should also be noted that, as Pitts and Kopprasch pointed out, there is nothing special about the hedge initiation date. In fact, regardless of how long the period for which the composite hedge is in place, the error will be the same.

EXHIBIT 6

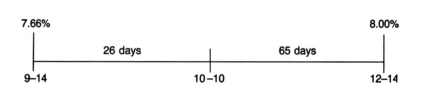

To begin with, calculate the hedge ratio exactly as before. Since this example is identical to the base case except for the target date, the hedge ratio is equal to 100.[9] Then based upon where the target date is with respect to the relevant IMM dates, linearly weight the futures transaction among the two contract months. In our example, since there are 65 days from the target to the IMM date next following, and a total of 91 days between IMM dates, sell 100 × 65/91 = 71.43 Sep 87 contracts and 100 × (1 − 65/91) = 28.57 Dec 87 contracts. As one would hope, since October 10 is closer to the Sep 87 IMM date, more Sep 87 contracts are shorted than Dec 87 contracts.

As far as the target rate is concerned, use the same weighting and calculate a weighted average futures rate. In our example, 7.76% (65/91 × 7.66 + 26/91 × 8.00) would be the target. This is equivalent to assuming that LIBOR will move linearly from 7.66% to 8.00% over the 91-day period.

Finally, since the Sep 87 contract settles on September 14 and the risk needs to be hedged with a full 100 contracts through October 10, roll the 71.43 Sep 87 contracts into Dec 87 on the last trading day of the Sep contract. On October 10, the hedger should unwind the entire position.

Cross-Hedging

Because futures contracts tied to commercial paper rates do not exist and since those tied to domestic CD rates are fairly illiquid, managing the risk associated with these and other domestic short-term rates of interest is not as straightforward as hedging LIBOR risk. However, as Exhibits 7 and 8 illustrate, most short-term rates are very highly correlated with one another. Exhibit 7 presents correlation coefficients for 3-month T-bill and 3-month commercial paper rates with respect to 3-month LIBOR, for the period January 1984 to August 1987. Although each rate does not respond to market forces identically in every situation (as reflected in the relatively poor correlation for one week changes), the long-term impression is that, at least histori-

---

[9]For the sake of clarity, variation margin financing is ignored as in the base example. The tail, if included, would be measured to the interest payment date in exactly the same manner as detailed in the previous section.

cally, cross-hedging with a LIBOR-based contract should provide effective risk management.

EXHIBIT 7
CORRELATION WITH LIBOR

	1-Week Changes	1-Month Changes	3-Month Changes
T-bill	.498	.783	.901
CP	.726	.858	.958

The issue of cross-hedging itself is the subject of extensive academic study and is beyond the scope of this chapter. We present a simple, idealized cross-hedging technique for illustrative purposes but do not suggest that this method is better, or worse, than any other.

Recall that the hedge ratio equals

$$\frac{\text{Dollar Volatility of Hedged ``Security''}}{\text{Dollar Volatility of Futures Contract}} = \frac{\text{PVBP Hedged ``Security''}}{\text{PVBP Futures Contract}}$$

The PVBP of the Eurodollar futures contract is known to be \$25. Furthermore, the PVBP, or incremental interest expense (income), of the "security" to be hedged can be determined with respect to the non-LIBOR rate given a one basis point change in said rate. Therefore, the uncertainty surrounding hedging non-LIBOR based short-term rates with Eurodollar futures contracts centers around the relationship between the rate in question and the LIBOR rate with similar maturity. In other words, by how many basis points will the rate in question change for every one basis point change in LIBOR?

Regression analysis is a statistical technique which can be used to measure this relationship. Based upon historical data, simple linear regression solves the equation

$$[\text{Change in Yield}_i \text{ in question}] = \text{Beta} \times [\text{Change in LIBOR}_i] + e_i$$

for Beta by minimizing the variance of the residual terms e_i over the sample period. The hedge ratio for a cross-hedge follows immediately and is equal to the hedge ratio calculated to capture LIBOR multiplied by Beta.

Before applying regression results to cross-hedging problems, it is important to consider the following. Statistics generated by the regression includes a coefficient of determination, R^2, which is a measure of the degree to which the variability of the yield in question is explained by the linear relationship. In other words, it is an indicator of the percentage of risk which can be eliminated by hedging. R^2 ranges from zero to one; an R^2 near one indicates an almost perfect fit. As for the target rate, because cross-hedging employs the use of statistical inference, the hedger is really

EXHIBIT 8
DOMESTIC SHORT-TERM RATES

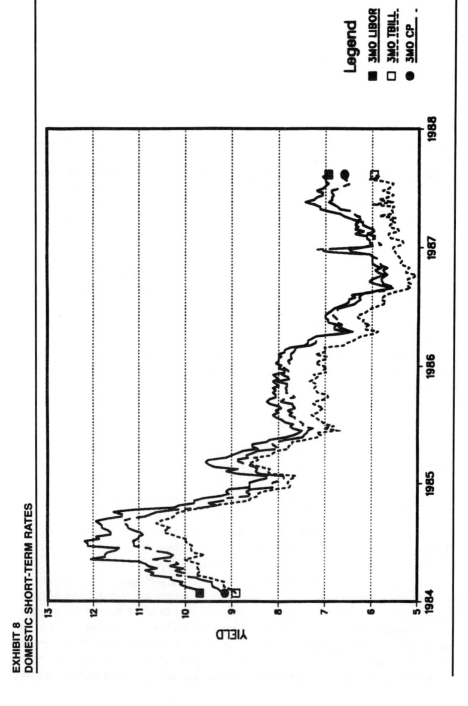

Legend
■ 3MO LIBOR
□ 3MO TBILL
● 3MO CP

targeting a range of rates rather than a specific rate. In general, the closer R^2 is to one the smaller the targeted range.[10]

Consider a commercial paper (CP) issuer which expects to sell $100 million worth of 90-day paper 60 days from now. Because a hedge against rising rates will be in place for 60 days, we performed a regression on the historical relationship between changes in 90-day commercial paper rates over 60-day periods and changes in 3-month LIBOR over 60-day periods and found that[11]

$$\text{Change in 90-day CP} = .93 \times [\text{Change in 3-month LIBOR}]$$

Furthermore, suppose that the Eurodollar futures contract which stops trading 60 days from now is trading for 93.00. Disregarding the hedge for variation margin financing, the issuer would sell 100 contracts in order to lock in a 7.00% LIBOR rate for 90 days. Because 90-day CP has historically been 93% as volatile as 3-month LIBOR, the issuer alters the basic hedge by the Beta and sells only 93 contracts. Finally, the target CP rate is 6.76% = .25 + .93 (7.00%). The .25 intercept is obtained by assuming that the average CP and LIBOR rates satisfy the same equation.

Exhibit 9 illustrates how the hedge will perform as a function of where 3-month LIBOR will be in 60 days when the hedge is lifted and the paper is sold. (We use 93.00 as the transacted futures price rather than 92.34 as in the base example in order to simplify the exposition in the exhibit.) As illustrated by the example, cross-hedging will be very effective if the actual sale rate for commercial paper is exactly equal to that indicated by the historical relationship. To the degree that this is not true, hedging effectiveness will vary.

The cross-hedging example raises other issues of importance which revolve around the fact that different rates of interest are often quoted in dissimilar terms. For example, in the case of 90-day CP rates, the PVBP for each $1 million worth of 90-day CP is equal to $25 just like the Eurodollar contract. On the other hand, the CP rate is a discount rate of interest whereas 3-month LIBOR is an add-on rate. Consequently, the CP hedge is "tailed" only to the sale date, i.e., the beginning of the interest period, whereas the LIBOR borrowing is tailed to the end of the interest period. Even more striking are the adjustments which need to be made for certain domestic CDs which pay interest compounded daily. Clearly, the PVBP of an interest bearing security that pays $[(1 + \text{rate} \times 1/360)^{\text{days}} - 1]$ is greater than the PVBP of a security that pays $[(1 + \text{rate} \times \text{days}/360) - 1]$. In this case, adjustments should be made to the hedge ratio in order to construct the most effective hedge. Other differences do exist among short-term debt securities. The more esoteric problems should be addressed on a case by case basis.

---

[10]A more lengthy explanation can be found in Chapter 9 of Pitts and Fabozzi, *Interest Rate Futures and Options*.

[11]It should be noted that these results are a function of the sample period over which the regression was performed. Nowhere are we implying that this is *the* yield relationship.

EXHIBIT 9
PERFORMANCE OF HEDGE

(A) 3-Month LIBOR	(B) Actual Sale Rate for CP	(C) Actual Sale Price for CP	(D) ED Futures Price	(E) Hedge Gain/Loss (−93.0 contracts)	(F) Effective Sale Price	(G) Effective Sale Rate
6.00%	5.830%	$98,542,500	94.00	($232,500)	$98,310,000	6.76%
6.50	6.295	98,426,250	93.50	(116,250)	98,310,000	6.76
7.00	6.760	98,310,000	93.00	0	98,310,000	6.76
7.50	7.225	98,193,750	92.50	116,250	98,310,000	6.76
8.00	7.690	98,077,500	92.00	232,500	98,310,000	6.76
8.50	8.155	97,961,250	91.50	348,750	98,310,000	6.76
9.00	8.620	97,845,000	91.00	465,000	98,310,000	6.76
9.50	9.085	97,728,750	90.50	581,250	98,310,000	6.76
10.00	9.550	97,612,500	90.00	697,500	98,310,000	6.76

Column A   is a range of possible values for 3-month LIBOR as of the sale date.

B   is equal to .25 + .93 × Column A.

C   is based on the fact that commercial paper trades on a discount basis and consequently is priced equal to $100,000,000 × [1 − CP rate × 90/360].

D   is the final settlement price for the Eurodollar contract. Convergence insures that Column D = 100 − Column A.

E   is the gain/loss achieved by selling 93 futures contracts at 93.00. Column E = 93 contracts × (93.00 − Column D) × $25/basis point.

F   is the effective sale price for commercial paper which equals the actual sale price plus (minus) futures gains (losses).

G   is backed into using the formula for Column C and the value in Column F.

Residual Hedging Risks

The methods outlined in the preceding pages can be used to manage short-term interest rate risk effectively. However, a hedger should be aware of the residual risks of hedging with Eurodollar futures. Although some of these have already been mentioned, a brief summary is warranted.

The risks can be broken down into three categories. The first is yield curve risk. This is the risk associated with hedging a LIBOR-based rate other than 3-month LIBOR with 90-day Eurodollar contracts. By synthetically creating hedges for 6-month LIBOR and other maturity mismatches using Eurodollar strips, we are relying on market efficiency to produce the most effective hedge. Whereas IMM hedges for 6-month LIBOR in particular are generally very successful, those for 1-month LIBOR, for instance, can be riskier.

The second category of risk is basis risk, which is caused by the uncertainty surrounding the relationship between spot LIBOR and a Eurodollar futures contract on any day other than its last trading day. Whereas strategies such as the composite can be used to minimize this risk, Exhibit 5 shows that even this strategy can falter. Note for instance the 54 basis point maximum error. Furthermore, there are no guarantees that future experience will conform to expectations based upon historical observations.

The third category of risk is cross-hedge risk. Successful cross-hedges will depend on the ability to accurately measure the relationship between the volatility of LIBOR and that of any other short-term rate. Although an in-depth analysis of cross-hedging is beyond the scope of this chapter, we presented a straightforward technique for measuring this relationship in order to illustrate how the results can be applied to determine hedge ratios and target rates. Hedge effectiveness will depend upon how accurate the formulated relationship is. In addition, even the most sophisticated methods for quantifying the yield relationship will be subject to the degree to which the future behaves like the past.

Before we present applications of the hedging methods described in this section, the reader should consider the following remarks: First of all, most hedges will necessitate some combination of techniques. For example, a commercial paper issuer hedging 180-day paper will incorporate the synthetic 6-month strip, regression analysis, and perhaps the composite strategy. In addition, all futures hedges will need to be tailed. Second, it should be noted that the date on which a hedge is initiated is, in large part, irrelevant as it relates to the hedge ratio. In fact, it only affects the calculation of the tail. Finally, the risk caused by an inability to transact fractions of contracts, though relatively small for hedges of tens and hundreds of millions of dollars, should not be overlooked for hedge programs of smaller size.

HEDGING EXAMPLES

Understanding the mechanics of hedging with Eurodollar futures is only part of effective short-term interest rate risk management. The ability to apply the basics to

EXHIBIT 10
DATA FOR HEDGING EXAMPLES

Today's date:	8-12-1987		
Financing rate:	6.50%		

Futures:	*Contract Month*	*Price*	*Days to Next Contract*
	Sep 87	92.34	91
	Dec 87	92.00	91
	Mar 88	91.80	91
	Jun 88	91.61	98
	Sep 88	91.41	91
	Dec 88	91.20	84
	Mar 89	90.99	98
	Jun 89	90.80	91
	Sep 89	90.62	91

CD/LIBOR relationship: 6-month CD = 1.11% + .86 × [6-month LIBOR]*

*See footnote 10.

solve real problems is also required. The purpose of this section is to demonstrate how the techniques presented earlier can be used to solve problems. Since it would be impossible to present all the different applications of hedging with Eurodollar futures in this section, we have confined our discussion to two examples. The first is a bank which rolls certificates of deposit and the second is an issuer of floating-rate notes. Both institutions, fearing a rise in short-term rates, decide to use Eurodollar futures to protect borrowing costs. Both the bank and the issuer create hedges which conform to the methods detailed in this chapter. For each problem, a brief discussion of the hedging procedure is presented along with the recommended futures position. A sketch of the calculations is also included. The data in Exhibit 10 will be used for both examples.

Rolling CD Issuances

Many commercial banks, as well as thrifts, fund themselves short term through 3- or 6-month certificates of deposit (CDs). Every week or so, a portion of the entire holding is refunded by "rolling" maturing deposits into new ones at then current rate levels. Clearly, a rising rate environment will result in higher interest expense for CD issuers.

Consider a bank that has $130 million worth of 6-month (26-week) deposits at all times and that each week 1/26 or $5 million is rolled into a new 26-week deposit. Furthermore, suppose that the bank expects a rise in short-term rates in the upcoming months and consequently decides to hedge its rollover risk for 9 months. Anticipating rate stability for the next 4 weeks however, the first rollover to be hedged is

EXHIBIT 11
EURODOLLAR FUTURES POSITION FOR ROLLING CD ISSUANCE EXAMPLE

Contract:	Total Number
Jun 87	0.0000
Sep 87	− 29.7806
Dec 87	− 84.4873
Mar 88	− 108.5610
Jun 88	− 78.5120
Sep 88	− 24.6635
Dec 88	0.0000

the deposit maturing on September 14 (Sep 87 IMM date). The bank, in its effort to hedge the September 14 rollover and the 38 rollovers (9 months worth) which follow, establishes the Eurodollar futures shown in Exhibit 11.

At first glance, the recommended position may seem somewhat surprising. However, consider the following. Each of the 39 distinct hedges against rises in 6-month CD rates will require approximately 8.6 contracts in total ($5 million for 6 months, adjusted for Beta = .86). Furthermore, $8.6 \times 39 = 335.40$, which is not very different from the total number of contracts recommended.

We detail the calculations for the first two rollovers and present the results for the remaining 37 in Appendix A. The recommended position is simply the sum of 39 distinct hedges.

The first hedge is a hedge for $5 million worth of 182-day CDs resetting on the Sep 87 IMM date, September 14. Since the Sep 87 futures price is 92.34, and the Dec 87 price is 92.00, 6-month LIBOR L_6 targeted for the hedge is found by solving the following equation for L_6:

$$[1 + L_6 \times 182/360] = [1 + .0766 \times 91/360] \times [1 + .08 \times 91/360]$$

Having calculated $L_6 = 7.91\%$, we can solve for the targeted 6-month CD rate which is equal to $1.11\% + .86 \times [7.91]$, or also 7.91% by pure coincidence.

As far as the hedge ratios are concerned, one should sell $(5 \times 91/90) \times [1 + .08 \times 91/360]) = 5.16$ Sep 87 contracts and $(5 \times [1 + .0766 \times 91/360] \times 91/90) = 5.15$ Dec 87 contracts in order to lock in 6-month LIBOR for 182 says. Since there are 33 days until the reset date plus an additional 182 days from then until interest is actually paid, adjust these numbers for variation margin financing by dividing $[1 + .065]^{215/365.25}$. (Unlike the section which introduced tailing and assumed simple interest financing, this calculation and the ones that follow reflect interest compounding.) Finally, since 6-month CDs have been only 86% as volatile as 6-month LIBOR, multiply by .86 and find that selling 4.27 Sep 87 contracts and 4.27 Dec contracts is the hedge consistent with the arguments presented earlier in this chapter.

EXHIBIT 12

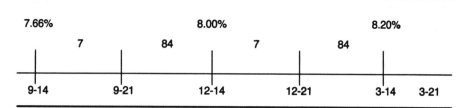

The second rollover illustrates a new "twist." To begin with, recognize that we are hedging the exact same risk as in the first rollover, except that the second rollover date is September 21 (non IMM) (see Exhibit 12). In order to determine the target rate for the hedge, apply the composite contract strategy along with compounding and regression. We find that the targeted 3-month LIBOR spot rate equals 7.69% (7.66 × 84/91 + 8.00 × 7/91) and that 3-month LIBOR 3 months forward is equal to 8.02% (8.00 × 84/91 + 8.20 × 7/91). L_6 in turn equals 7.93% and the targeted 6-month CD rate also happens to be 7.93%.

Concerning hedge ratios, start with the 4.27 and 4.27 calculated for the first rollover. Since the target for 3-month LIBOR spot is 7.69% rather than 7.66%, and since the target for 3-month LIBOR 3 months forward is 8.02% rather than 8.00%, compounding which affects the number of contracts is slightly different. In addition, because interest is paid 7 days later, the tail is adjusted to reflect 222 days of variation margin financing rather than only 215 days. (Note: 4.27 and 4.27 are unchanged to two decimal places.) Finally, since this represents the number of contracts we wish to sell whose last trading days are September 21 and December 21 respectively, and since these contracts do not exist, apply the composite contract strategy and sell 3.94 (4.27 × 84/91) Sep 87 contracts, 4.27 (4.27 × 7/91 + 4.27 × 84/91) Dec 87 contracts, and 0.33 (4.27 × 7/91) Mar 88 contracts. Note the use of three contract months to hedge a 6-month rate when the reset date does not coincide with an IMM date.

The target rates and hedge ratios for the remaining 37 rollovers are calculated similarly (see Appendix A). Basically, hedges range from 4.27 Sep 87 contracts, 4.27 Dec 87 contracts, and 0.00 Mar 88 contracts (4,4,0) to (0,4,4) as the target moves from the Sep 87 IMM date to the Dec 87 IMM date. Hedges of the form (3,4,1), (2,4,2), and (1,4,3) will also be needed. As the target date moves beyond the Dec 87 IMM date, similar analysis reveals that transactions in the Jun 88 and Sep 88 contract months are also required.

Adjustments to the futures position should be made as time passes. In addition to the normal adjustments to maintain an effective hedge for variation margin financing, the bank must unwind (buy back) contracts each week as an old deposit matures and a new one is issued. Finally, although the bank hedged only 39 CD rolls, additional hedges can be added to extend the period of interest rate protection. It should be recognized, however, that if futures interest rates rise in the interim, the bank will simply be "locking in" higher CD rates.

Floating Rate Notes

Consider an issuer that can generate floating-rate funds quite easily in relation to its access to fixed funds. However, given its current rate outlook, the issuer is reluctant to incur floating-rate debt. By issuing a LIBOR based floating-rate note and simultaneously shorting Eurodollar futures, the issuer can effectively fix his cost of funds.

Suppose that on September 14, 1987, the issuer plans to sell $100 million worth of floating-rate notes maturing in two years. Furthermore, suppose that the rate will float off 3-month LIBOR and that the interest accrual periods will coincide with Eurodollar futures delivery dates. In other words, resets occur on IMM dates and interest accruals will go from one IMM date to the next. The Eurodollar strip shown in Exhibit 13 can be used to lock in the issuer's LIBOR resets for each of the upcoming eight quarters.

Since the hedge for the floating-rate note is essentially eight distinct hedges, each protecting against increases in 3-month LIBOR on $100 million for 84, 91 or 98 days, the calculations are fairly straightforward. Again, we detail calculations for the first two resets.

For the Sep 87 reset, the target rate will be $100 - 92.34 = 7.66\%$. The hedge ratio is simply $(100 \times 91/90)$ divided by $[1.065]^{124/365.25}$ which equals 98.97. There are 124 days from August 12 thru December 14, the date on which interest accruals for the September 14 reset will be paid. As for the Dec 87 reset, the target is

EXHIBIT 13
EURODOLLAR FUTURES POSITION FOR FLOATING-RATE NOTE EXAMPLE

Date: 8-12-1987
Financing rate: 6.50%

Contract	Total Number
Jun 87	0.0000
Sep 87	−98.9723
Dec 87	−97.4316
Mar 88	−95.9148
Jun 88	−101.5623
Sep 88	−92.8397
Dec 88	−84.4660
Mar 89	−96.8925
Jun 89	−88.5710
Sep 89	0.0000

8.00% and the hedge ratio is 97.43, reflecting 215 days of variation margin financing.

Note how the recommended futures position becomes gradually smaller as you move into the more distant contract months. Just as the number of Dec 87 contracts is less than the number of Sep 87 contracts, this is caused by the hedge for variation margin financing. The relatively large positions in the Jun 88 and Mar 89 contract months, as well as the relatively small position in Dec 88, are a direct result of the number of days in the relevant interest accrual periods.

The Eurodollar strip which appears in Exhibit 14 hedges exactly the same floating-rate note except, in this case, the issuer is concerned with his total cost of funds. In other words, in an attempt to replicate a zero coupon security, the issuer must hedge not only interest on principal but also the cost of financing each of the payments through the maturity date. The example assumes that the issuer can finance his payments at 3-month LIBOR.

EXHIBIT 14
EURODOLLAR FUTURES, POSITION FOR FLOATING-RATE NOTE EXAMPLE HEDGING TOTAL COST

| Date: | 8-12-1987 |
| Financing rate: | 6.50% |

Contract	Total Number
Jun 87	0.0000
Sep 87	− 98.9723
Dec 87	− 99.3182
Mar 88	− 99.7492
Jun 88	− 107.8117
Sep 88	− 100.8033
Dec 88	− 93.7026
Mar 89	− 109.6952
Jun 89	− 102.7336
Sep 89	0.0000

On December 14, the issuer will make an interest payment, net of futures gains (losses), of $1,936,277.78 = $100,000,000 × [.0766 × 91/360]. Consequently, the issuer wants to hedge increases in 3-month LIBOR for the upcoming 91 days, not on $100,000,000, but rather on $101,936,277.78. The hedge ratio, in turn, will equal (100 × [1 + .0766 × 91/360] × 91/90) divided by [1.065]$^{215/365.25}$ = 99.32. For March 14, 1988, the issuer wants to hedge principal ($100,000,000) plus the March 14 interest payment ($2,022,222.22 = $100,000,000 × [.08 × 91/360]) plus the December 14 interest payment with interest to March 14 ($1,975,433.62 = $1,936,277.78 × [1 + .08 × 91/360]). In other words, the issuer sells $(100 \times [1 + .0766 \times 91/360] \times [1 + .08 \times 91/360] \times 91/90)$ divided by $[1.065]^{306/365.25} = 99.75$ Mar 88 contracts. The process is carried out to the maturity date. Note that the recommended futures position is somewhat larger than in the previous example. In fact, since each interest payment is approximately $2 million, it is approximately $[(2 \times i) - 2]$ contracts greater (in each contract month) where i corresponds to the ith reset date.

This example illustrates how the goals of a hedger can have an effect on the appropriate futures position. The hedger must consider his own needs and, in turn, establish a futures position which best addresses those needs. In other words, there is no single best Eurodollar strip but rather tremendous flexibility in hedging with strips.

SUMMARY

The primary purpose of this chapter was to acquaint the reader with Eurodollar futures and to detail exactly how they can be used to manage short-term interest rate risk. By working through the sections carefully, an understanding of the mechanics of hedging with Eurodollar futures can be achieved. Finally, we included a few examples to show how the hedging techniques can be used to solve concrete problems.

APPENDIX A

Number of Eurodollar contracts needed to hedge the 39 6-month CD rollovers.

Rollover Date		Sep 87	Dec 87	Mar 88	Jun 88	Sep 88
September	14	4.27	4.27			
	21	3.94	4.27	.33		
	28	3.61	4.26	.66		
October	5	3.28	4.26	.98		
	12	2.95	4.25	1.31		
	19	2.62	4.25	1.63		
	26	2.29	4.24	1.96		
November	2	1.96	4.24	2.28		
	9	1.63	4.23	2.60		
	16	1.30	4.23	2.93		
	23	.97	4.22	3.25		
	30	.65	4.22	3.57		
December	7	.32	4.21	3.89		
	14		4.21	4.21		
	21		3.88	4.20	.32	
	28		3.55	4.20	.65	
January	4		3.23	4.19	.97	
	11		2.90	4.19	1.29	
	18		2.58	4.18	1.61	
	25		2.25	4.18	1.93	
February	1		1.93	4.17	2.25	
	8		1.60	4.17	2.57	
	15		1.28	4.17	2.88	
	22		.96	4.16	3.20	
	29		.64	4.16	3.51	
March	7		.32	4.15	3.83	
	14			4.15	4.14	
	21			3.82	4.15	.32
	28			3.49	4.14	.64
April	4			3.17	4.13	.95
	11			2.85	4.13	1.27
	18			2.53	4.12	1.59
	25			2.21	4.12	1.90
May	2			1.89	4.11	2.22
	9			1.58	4.11	2.53
	16			1.26	4.10	2.84
	23			.94	4.09	3.16
	30			.63	4.09	3.47
June	6			.31	4.08	3.78
		29.79	84.48	108.55	78.52	24.67

(with rounding error)

APPENDIX B: THE BUTTERFLY

Hedging assets and/or liabilities which float off short-term interest rates is made possible, in part, by the existence of Eurodollar futures. Because Eurodollars trade in 12 contract months, hedging as far out as 3 years is easily accomplished by applying the techniques presented earlier in this chapter. In order to hedge against fluctuations in short-term rates for more than 3 years, the 12th contract is often used as a proxy for more distant contracts. This is known as "stacking" and is essentially a bet that the spread between the 12th contract and the more distant contract will remain constant. The "butterfly" strategy is an alternative to stacking which assumes only that the difference between two consecutive spreads remains constant. Historical observation shows that the butterfly tends to be significantly more stable than outright spreads and is consequently the preferred hedging technique.

Consider a hedger that wants to buy the 13th Eurodollar contract F_{13} which does not begin trading until 3 months from now. Buying F_{12} in lieu of F_{13} supposes that

$$D F_{12} = D F_{13}$$

where $D F_{12}$ is the change in F_{12} and $D F_{13}$ is the change in F_{13}. This implies that

$$D [F_{12} - F_{13}] = 0$$

and therefore

$$F_{12} - F_{13} = K, \text{ a constant}$$

In other words, stacking will provide an effective hedge if the spread remains constant.

On the other hand, suppose we assume only that the difference between two consecutive spreads (the butterfly) remains constant:

$$[F_{11} - F_{12}] - [F_{12} - F_{13}] = K$$

This implies

$$F_{11} - 2F_{12} + F_{13} = K$$

and

$$D F_{11} - 2D F_{12} + D F_{13} = 0$$

and therefore

$$D F_{13} = 2D F_{12} - D F_{11}$$

where D means "change in." In this case, buying the 12th contract two times and selling the eleventh contract once will be equivalent to a long position in F_{13}.

Exhibits 15 and 16 demonstrate the relative stability of the butterfly to the spread since October 1984 and support our preference for the butterfly strategy.

EXHIBIT 15
STACKING VS. BUTTERFLY STRATEGY

	Butterfly	Spread
Standard deviation (three-month changes)	1.91 bp	8.32 bp
Butterfly	$= F_{10} - 2F_{11} + F_{12}$ since mid June 1987	
	$F_6 - 2F_7 + F_8$ prior to June 1987	
Spread	$= F_{11} - F_{12}$ since mid June 1987	
	$F_7 - F_8$ prior to June 1987	

In order to hedge the next distant contract, F_{14}, the butterfly strategy can be extended in the following manner:

$$[F_{12} - F_{13}] - [F_{13} - F_{14}] = K$$

which implies

$$F_{12} - 2F_{13} + F_{14} = K$$

and

$$D F_{12} - 2D F_{13} + D F_{14} = 0$$

and

$$D F_{14} = 2D F_{13} - D F_{12}.$$

F_{13} does not exist but we have already observed that $D F_{13} = 2D F_{12} - D F_{11}$. Consequently

$$D F_{14} = 2 [2D F_{12} - D F_{11}] - D F_{12}$$

EXHIBIT 16
STACKING VS. BUTTERFLY STRATEGY

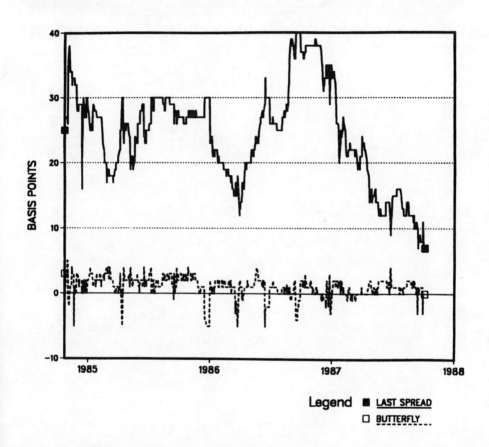

Legend ■ LAST SPREAD
□ BUTTERFLY

and therefore

$$D F_{14} = 3D F_{12} - 2D F_{11}$$

In other words, in lieu of buying F_{14}, buy F_{12} three times and sell F_{11} twice. The butterfly strategy can be extended similarly for even more distant contracts out to about 4 years. To the extent that butterflies are stable, hedges will be effective.

Chapter 19

Applying Futures and Options to Restructure Bond Portfolio Returns

YU ZHU, PH.D.
VICE PRESIDENT
STRUCTURED INVESTMENTS GROUP
MERRILL LYNCH CAPITAL MARKETS

In recent years the financial futures and interest rate options markets have undergone a period of very rapid growth. The most remarkable example is the Treasury bond futures market: the daily volume of T-bond futures has far exceeded that of the underlying bonds. Since futures and options are levered instruments (i.e., they are comprised of both positions in the underlying securities and borrowing), the funds needed to carry out transactions are much lower than that of cash transactions. The tremendous volume and liquidity in futures and options markets make transactions in these markets operationally efficient in the sense of low cost and fast execution. The development of new products in financial futures and options markets provides a wide range of strategies for bond portfolio management in controlling interest rate risk. Their important role as hedging instruments is well known. Many hedging strategies would be very difficult if not impossible to implement without these derivative products.

In this chapter we discuss three strategies that apply futures and options to reshape a bond portfolio's return structure according to specific needs. These models are the extended duration hedge model, the duration hedge model with convexity adjustment, and the bond portfolio option replication model.

FLAT RETURN STRUCTURE AND DURATION HEDGE

A typical return structure of a bond portfolio is illustrated as the solid line in Exhibit 1. When interest rates move up, the portfolio return drops and even becomes negative. As interest rates fall, the portfolio, on the other hand, generates higher returns. The simplest and most common objective of hedging a bond portfolio is to protect the value of the portfolio by locking in today's price. A perfect hedge changes the portfolio's downward sloping curve into a flat line, which guarantees that the portfolio will earn a riskless rate regardless of interest rate changes.

EXHIBIT 1
DIFFERENT BOND PORTFOLIO RETURN STRUCTURES—
COMPARISON OF HEDGED AND UNHEDGED PORTFOLIOS

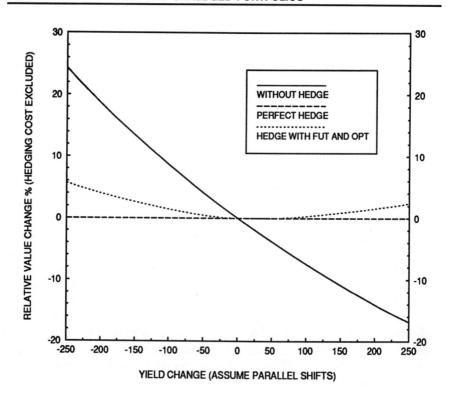

One convenient way to reach this objective without changing the portfolio composition is to buy or sell Treasury bond futures contracts. Though many techniques are available, the most widely used method is the so called "duration hedge." By taking a long or short position in futures market, we can construct a hedged portfolio such that the duration of the hedged portfolio is equal to the target duration.[1] For an instantaneous hedge, the target duration is zero. In general, the target duration is the investment horizon or the duration of the liabilities. The number of futures contracts to hedge a given portfolio can be calculated by the following equation:[2]

$$D_B + X_F D_F = D_T, \tag{1}$$

where

D_B = the duration of the portfolio;

D_F = the duration of the futures contract;[3]

D_T = the target duration;

X_F = N F / B; F is the contract price, B is the portfolio value, and N is the number of contracts.

It is well known that the duration hedge will only be effective if the yield curve is subject to an instantaneous change or an infinistesimal parallel shift. For a large parallel shift or a non-parallel shift in the yield curve, the above simple duration hedge may not produce the desired flat return structure.

---

[1] In bond portfolio management this hedged portfolio is usually called an immunized portfolio.

[2] Here we assume that the bond portfolio and the hedging instruments have the same yield volatility and are perfectly correlated. This is, of course, a strong assumption. To handle more general cases, Equation (1) can be extended as follows:

$$D_B + X_F D_F \, YVF = D_T,$$

where YVF stands for the yield volatility factor. YVF reflects the ratio of implied interest rate movement of futures contract with respect to corresponding portfolio yield change. It can be easily shown that

$$YVF = \sigma_F / r_{BF}\sigma_B,$$

where σ_F and σ_B are the (absolute) yield volatilities of corresponding securities and r_{BF} is their correlation coefficient. In this chapter we always assume that YVF is one for simplicity.

[3] There are many different methods in calculating the duration of T-bond futures contract. The simplest one is to assume that the duration of the futures is equal to the duration of the cheapest to deliver bond from the delivery date and calculated based on the futures price and the conversion factor. Jones and Krumholz suggest using the cash and carry relationship of the futures contract, F. J. Jones and B. A. Krumholz, "Duration Adjustment and Asset Allocation with Treasury Bond and Note Futures Contracts," in F. J. Fabozzi and T. D. Garlicki (eds.) *Advances in Bond Analysis & Portfolio Strategies*, (Chicago, IL: Probus Publishing Company, 1987). These two methods give slightly different results. Chen, Park and Wei apply a term structure model and produce a quite different duration measure for a futures contract (A. H. Chen, H. Y. Park and K. J. Wei, "Stochastic Duration and Dynamic Measure of Risk in Financial Futures," in *Advances in Futures and Options Research*, F. J. Fabozzi (ed.), Vol. 1, 93–111, JAI Press, 1986).

Empirical evidence suggests that yield curve movements can be described by a combination of parallel shifts, tilts, bends, etc. In technical terms, we say that the shocks to the yield curve can be modeled as a polynomial function of time t:

$$y = a_0 + a_1 t + a_2 t^2 + \cdots + a_{k-1} t^{k-1} \qquad (2)$$

In order to hedge a portfolio against these different components of yield curve changes, the ordinary concept of duration should be generalized. Recall that the duration of a bond is calculated as a weighted average of time to cash payments, $\{t_1, \cdots, t_T\}$:

$$D = \Sigma \, t_i \, w_i \qquad (3)$$

where the weights w_i are determined by the present values of the cash payments C_i:

$$w_i = \frac{C_i}{(1+y)^i} \Big/ \sum_j \frac{C_j}{(1+y)^j}$$

In the above expression y is the bond yield. Since (3) only contains t_i, this duration measure will be called "the first order duration," or $D^{(1)}$. By matching the first order durations, we are able to hedge the risk of parallel shift in interest rates, which corresponds to the first component (a_0) in Equation (2). To hedge the risk of non-parallel shifts in interest rates, we extend the ordinary concept of duration by introducing higher order durations. The second order duration is defined as the weighted average of the square of time to cash payments, i.e.,

$$D^{(2)} = \Sigma \, t_i^2 \, w_i.$$

Similarly, the k-th order duration is

$$D^{(k)} = \Sigma \, t_i^k \, w_i.$$

Thus, different from the ordinary duration, which is only one number, the extended duration becomes a vector. In the extended duration hedge model,[4] we use

---

[4]See M. Granito, *Bond Portfolio Immunization* (Lexington, MA: Lexington Books, 1984). The extended duration hedge model is simply a matrix form of Equation (1):

$$D_B + D_F X_F = D_T,$$

where

$$D_B = \{D_B^{(1)}, \cdots, D_B^{(k)}\}'$$
$$D_T = \{D_T^{(1)}, \cdots, D_T^{(k)}\}'$$

more than one futures contracts so that the duration vector of the hedged portfolio will match that of the target. We shall illustrate the extended model in the following example.

Example 1

Suppose XYZ Insurance Company owns a portfolio with seven bonds (Exhibit 2). The flat cost of the portfolio is \$94.89 million, and its duration is 6.07 years. The portfolio manager wants to use futures to hedge his portfolio for an investment horizon of three years.

To do this, the first step is to choose appropriate hedging instruments. Assuming $k = 2$ (i.e., we only consider the first and second order durations), we pick up the near term T-bond futures and T-note futures as the hedging instruments. We then calculate the duration vector of the portfolio and the duration matrix of the futures contracts; the solution is readily obtained by solving the extended duration hedge model. The solution presented in Exhibit 3 shows that we need to sell 215 T-bond futures contracts and 167 T-note futures contracts in order to reduce the portfolio duration to the target level. The convexity of the portfolio after the hedge is placed, becomes much smaller, suggesting that after the hedge the return structure becomes flatter.

The intuition of using more than one futures contract to hedge a portfolio is quite clear. A portfolio may contain long, intermediate and short term bonds. A combination of bond futures, note futures and bill futures can match the characteristics of the portfolio better than a single futures contract. These characteristics are reflected not only in the first order moment (ordinary duration), but also in higher order moments. Hence, by taking into consideration higher order durations, the hedged portfolio will perform better in absorbing interest rate shocks.

$$X_F = \{X_1, \cdots, X_k\}',$$

and D_F is the $k \times k$ duration matrix of k futures contracts,

$$DF = \begin{bmatrix} D_{F1}^{(1)} & \cdots\cdots & D_{F1}^{(k)} \\ \cdot & & \cdot \\ \cdot & \cdot & \cdot \\ \cdot & & \cdot \\ D_{Fk}^{(1)} & \cdots\cdots & D_{Fk}^{(k)} \end{bmatrix}$$

We note that the definition of the duration vector in this chapter is based on the assumed interest rate process as given by Equation (2). Assuming that the discount function follows a k-factor stochastic process, Nelson and Schaefer derive a duration vector in a more general form (J. Nelson and S. Schaefer, "The Dynamics of the Term Structure and Alternative Portfolio Immunization Strategies," in *Innovations in Bond Portfolio Management: Duration Analysis and Immunization*, George G. Kaufman, G. O. Bierwag and Alden Toevs (eds.), JAI Press, 1983).

EXHIBIT 2
NET BOND PORTFOLIO REPORT—DEDICATED PORTFOLIO ANALYSIS SYSTEM

XYZ INSURANCE COMPANY—Settlement Date 5/03/1988

Bond Descriptor	Coupon	Maturity	Round	Par Amount	Price	Flat Price	Accrued	Full Price	Accrued Yield	Accrued
T-bond	10.500	02/15/1995	1.000	7,913	109.28125	8,647,425.31	178,042.50	8,825,467.81	8.65740	2.25000
T-bond	10.375	05/15/1995	1.000	14,000	108.78125	15,229,375.00	678,365.38	15,907,740.38	8.67940	4.84547
T-bond	12.625	05/15/1995	1.000	12,000	121.21875	14,546,250.00	707,554.94	15,253,804.94	8.54710	5.89629
T-bond	11.500	11/15/1995	1.000	13,000	115.28125	14,986,562.50	698,214.28	15,684,776.78	8.69170	5.37088
T-bond	15.750	11/15/2001	1.000	10,000	151.84375	15,184,375.00	735,576.92	15,919,951.92	9.03410	7.35577
T-bond	11.625	11/15/2002	1.000	8,758	119.50000	10,465,810.00	475,494.43	10,941,304.43	9.16890	5.42926
T-bond	11.875	11/15/2003	1.000	13,000	121.75000	15,827,500.00	720,982.15	16,548,482.15	9.21340	5.54602
				78,671.000		94,887,294.81	4,194,230.60	99,081,528.41		

Market Weighted by Flat Price:
Average Maturity of the Portfolio (from Settlement) is: 10.375 Years
Average Yield of the Portfolio is: 8.86
Average Duration of the Portfolio is: 6.066 Years

EXHIBIT 3
PORTFOLIO HEDGE REPORT—
DEDICATED PORTFOLIO ANALYSIS SYSTEM

XYZ INSURANCE COMPANY—Settlement Date 5/03/1988

Futures /Options Hedge:

Futures and Options	Expiration	Contracts	Price	Cost ($1000)
Futures T-bond Sep 88 CBT	9/30/1988	−215.00	86.88	−18,678.13
Futures T-note Sep 88 CBT	9/30/1988	−167.00	93.09	−15,546.66

	Unhedged Portfolio	Hedged Portfolio
Flat Cost	94,887,297.81	94,887,297.81
Full Cost	99,081,528.42	99,081,528.42
Duration	6.07	3.01
Convexity	0.52	0.10
Net Hedge Cost ($1000)		0.00

DURATION HEDGE WITH CONVEXITY ADJUSTMENT BY FUTURES AND OPTIONS

A successful duration hedge produces an asset with a flat (or near flat) return structure. In the case of an instantaneous hedge, for example, the portfolio will earn an instantaneous riskless return. For a horizon hedge, the rate of return on the hedged portfolio should equal the return on a zero coupon bond. Therefore, while the hedge protects the portfolio in a rising interest rates environment, it eliminates gains if interest rates fall. This is not always a desirable outcome. However, by applying options as well as futures, we are able to meet the target duration and, at the same time, increase the portfolio's convexity. As a result, we create an asset not only with a floor return but also with a convex return structure. With interest rates moving in either direction, the hedged portfolio will always have a return higher than the floor (Exhibit 1). This desirable result, of course, can only be realized at a cost and only if the assumptions of the model are reasonable.[5]

Let us first define the often encountered concept of convexity. In Exhibit 1, at the current yield level, the duration describes the slope of the curve, while the convexity reflects its curvature. The definition of convexity is:[6]

---

[5]It is important to note that a higher convexity does not guarantee a higher return if interest rates move in a non-parallel fashion.

[6]When reported, the convexity number is usually divided by 100. It can be shown that for a bond, the convexity is related to its first order and second order durations in the following simple way:

$$V = [D^{(1)} + D^{(2)}] / (1 + y)^2.$$

$$V = \frac{1}{B} \frac{d^2B}{dy^2}$$

Suppose bond B_1 and bond B_2 have the same duration, but bond B_1 has a larger convexity. Under the assumption of a parallel shift of the yield curve, bond B_1 is preferred to bond B_2 due to the following reasons. The values of both bonds will decrease if interest rates rise, but the value of B_1 decreases at a lower rate. On the other hand, should interest rates fall, bond B_1 would appreciate faster.

In the duration hedge model, if we want to reduce the duration of the hedged portfolio, we usually sell futures contracts. However, selling futures contracts reduces the convexity as well as duration. For example, if we set both $D^{(1)}$ and $D^{(2)}$ of the hedged portfolio equal to zero, the convexity will also become zero. If a portfolio manager wishes to decrease the duration of the portfolio and, at the same time, increase its convexity, then both option and futures should be employed. Because a put option has the property of negative duration and positive convexity, the combination of the put and a futures contract can serve this purpose well. On the other hand, if one wants to extend the portfolio duration and increase its convexity, call options may be selected. To determine the hedge ratio, we solve the following equations:

$$D_B + X_F D_F + X_o D_o = D_T \tag{4}$$
$$V_B + X_F V_F + X_o V_o = V_T$$

where the subscript "o" denotes variables of the option, and D_T and V_T are the target duration and convexity, respectively. In a duration hedge, only positions in bond futures markets are taken, so up-front costs need not be paid, although the margin requirements must be met. By using options to adjust duration and convexity, certain explicit hedging costs will be incurred.

Example 2

Exhibit 4 shows that in order to reduce the duration of portfolio XYZ Insurance Company (Exhibit 2) from 6.07 to about 3 years and increase the convexity from 0.52 to 2.0, we should sell 120 September T-bond futures contracts, and buy 372 September 88 puts on T-bond futures. Comparing this result with Example 1, we find that here we need to sell only about a third the total number of futures contracts required using the straight duration hedge. Therefore, when interest rates move up, the gain from selling futures contracts will be less than in the first example, but the put options will generate additional profits. On the other hand, if interest rates fall, the value of the puts will decrease, but will always be greater than or equal to zero. Again, because we sell less futures contracts, the gains from the cash position will not be totally offset by the loss in the futures markets. This is why the return

EXHIBIT 4
DEDICATED PORTFOLIO ANALYSIS SYSTEM—
PORTFOLIO HEDGE REPORT

XYZ INSURANCE COMPANY—Settlement Date 5/03/1988

Futures /Options Hedge:

Futures and Options	Expiration	Contracts	Price	Cost ($1000)
Futures T-bond Sep 88 CBT	9/30/1988	– 120.00	86.88	– 10,425.00
Futures T-bond CBT Aug/88	8/20/1988	372.00	3.06	1,139.25

	Unhedged Portfolio	Hedged Portfolio
Flat Cost	94,887,297.81	96,026,547.81
Full Cost	99,081,528.42	100,220,778.42
Duration	6.07	3.01
Convexity	0.52	2.00
Net Hedge Cost ($1000)		1,139,250.00

structure of a hedged portfolio with both option and futures will exhibit a nice convex shape similar to the dotted line in Exhibit 1.

We note that the convexity of the hedged portfolio is quite sensitive to yield changes. To reduce this sensitivity, we can apply optimization techniques to select a portfolio of options instead of using only one option as the hedging instrument. By optimizing, the convexity of the hedged portfolio will remain at the desired level for a wide range of yield changes, and the return structure will be more preferable.

ONE-SIDED HEDGE AND OPTION REPLICATION TECHNIQUE

The third strategy is the so called one-sided hedge. The objective of this strategy is to protect the portfolio value against any losses due to rising interest rates, and to preserve portfolio gains when interest rates fall. Since the payoff of this strategy is the same as the payoff of a portfolio with an insurance policy, it is commonly referred to as a portfolio insurance strategy. The simplest way to implement this strategy is to buy a put option on the portfolio. Since put options for a given bond portfolio are usually not available, synthetic put options can be created by dynamically allocating assets to risky and riskless investments. However, the dynamic hedging method suffers from high transaction costs due to frequent trading in volatile markets, and it performs poorly when markets do not move as "smoothly" as the theoretical model predicts.

It is interesting to note that the dynamic hedging method and the previous duration hedge method (with or without convexity adjustment) adopt a similar technique in asset replication: they adjust the composition of the portfolio to match the derivatives of the payoff function of the synthetic asset. For the duration hedge, we match dB/dY of that portfolio (the derivative of portfolio value with respect to yield) to that of the target asset, e.g., a zero coupon bond. In the case of dynamic hedging, an option is replicated by matching the deltas—the derivatives of options with respect to the underlying security's price. Since these derivatives are constantly changing over time, frequent rebalancing is required.

We employ a different method to replicate an option on a bond portfolio. Instead of matching derivatives, we use exchange listed options to match the payoff functions directly. Because the market for bond options generally does not have sufficient liquidity, we choose options on the Treasury bond futures as the replication instruments. Obviously we still need to roll these options over if the hedge horizon is longer than their time to expiration. Nonetheless, this method manages to avoid many of the difficulties of the dynamic hedging method.

Theoretical justification of option replication techniques has been documented in several academic papers.[7] Although the theory is profound, the idea can be explained in a simple way.

For simplicity, we only consider two dates: today, t_0, and a future date, t_1. At time t_1, there are N states of the world (for example, N different future interest rate scenarios). Imagine that we have the same number (N) of securities, security 1, . . . , security N. Security i pays \$1 if state i occurs and nothing otherwise. Since these securities have such simple payoff functions, they are called "primitive securities." It is obvious that if we know the prices of these primitive securities then, given the payoff function of any complex security, we can calculate the price of that complex security immediately. For example, if a security (option) pays \$100 in states 1 and 2, \$50 in state 3 and \$0 in all other states (4 to N), then its price should be

$$P = 100 \, (p_1 + p_2) + 50 \, p_3$$

We can say that this security is equivalent to a portfolio of primitive securities with 100 security 1, 100 security 2 and 50 security 3. In the real marketplace, we do not have these primitive securities. Otherwise security pricing would become a trivial matter. However, owing to their nonlinear payoff patterns, call and put options expiring at time t_1 with different strike prices can be used to "construct" these primitive securities. They then can be used to synthesize complex assets. If we have a sufficient number of calls and puts, we would be able to synthetically create a security with any customized payoff at time t_1.

---

[7]See, for example, S. A. Ross, "Options and Efficiency," *Quarterly Journal of Economics* (February 1976), 75-89. In order to replicate a long term option with listed short term options, a common misconception is to buy a short term option with the same exercise price. For example, suppose we are to create a one-year put option with strike price at 100 on a security currently priced at 100. One would naturally suggest to buy a 3-month put option with the same strike price (100) and roll it over after 3, 6 and 9 months. Unfortunately, as we shall show in the following discussion, this is not the correct way of replicating a long term option.

For replicating a long term option with expiration $T > t_1$, we need a model to calculate its payoff function at t_1. Then a portfolio of primitive securities can be used to replicate that payoff. Theoretically, the number of the future states of the world is infinity, so we should have an infinite number of securities with linearly independent payoff functions in order to create enough primitive securities for each state of the future world. But the number of exchange traded options are limited. Furthermore, practical considerations such as liquidity and transaction costs discourage us from using all these listed short term options. Therefore, the replication cannot be perfect. The objective of our model is only to make the replication as good as possible.

Based on the above analysis, if there are M replication instruments and N future states of the world, the option replication model in its simple form can be written as

Minimize:
$$\sum_i |TARGET\ PAYOFF_i - \sum_j X_i\ PAYOFF_{ij}|^2 \tag{5}$$

Subject to:
$$\sum (X_j{}^+ - X_j{}^-)\ P_j < C$$

$$\sum (X_j{}^- P_j \mid X_j < 0) < SC$$

$$X_j = X_j{}^+ - X_j{}^-$$

$$X_j{}^+ > 0 \quad X_j{}^- > 0$$

$$j = 0, 1, \ldots, M; \quad i = 1, 2, \ldots, N.$$

The objective function is to minimize the discrepancy between the target payoff and the synthetic payoff, where X_j is the number of instrument j with price P_j. In the constraints, superscript " $+$ " means a buy solution and " $-$ " means a sell solution, C is the upper limit of hedging cost and SC is the maximum dollar amount of short sale allowed. One can easily impose other constraints.[8]

We note that in model (5) the target payoff is the theoretical payoff of an option on a bond portfolio. It can be shown that an option on a portfolio of securities will not behave in the same way as a portfolio of options on each of the individual securities with proportional exercise prices. For example, suppose we want to buy a one-year call option on a portfolio of ten bonds with strike price equal to the portfolio cost. One naive way to calculate the option value is to compute the sum of the values of options on each bond with strike prices equal to the corresponding bond prices. It is a feasible solution, but the total cost of the call would most likely be higher than its

---

[8]For example, one may want to introduce transaction costs and different probabilities for each scenario. Or one can restrict his net exposure in terms of the total number of put or call contracts.

true value. Thus, even if we have options on each bond in a portfolio, the combination of these options is not equivalent to the option on the portfolio.

Interestingly, the correct way to calculate an option on a bond portfolio is still based on a portfolio of options. Let us explain this in some detail. First, the bond portfolio is viewed as a stream of cash flows, i.e., a portfolio of zero coupon bonds. It can be shown that in a one-factor term structure option model framework, an European option on a bond portfolio is equivalent to a portfolio of options on each zero coupon bond. In contrast with the "naive" method, the strike prices of these options are not so simple. They have to be calculated by the bond portfolio option model.[9]

Example 3

To illustrate the performance of the option replication model, we replicate a one-year put option on the portfolio of XYZ Insurance Company (Exhibit 2) based on histori-

EXHIBIT 5
10-YEAR TREASURY BOND YIELD (JANUARY 1986–APRIL 1987)

---

[9]Readers interested in technical details are referred to F. Jamshidian, "Pricing of Contingent Claims in the One-Factor Term Structure Model," Merrill Lynch Capital Markets, 1987.

cal daily closing prices. Options on T-bond futures are selected as the replication instruments.

In the first quarter of 1986, interest rates fell sharply. The yield on the 10-year Treasury note went down from 9.04% on January 2, 1986 to 7.198% on April 15 of the same year (Exhibit 5). Anticipating that interest rates will rise again, the portfolio manager would like to purchase a put option on the portfolio to lock in its gain. The put option will expire on April 15, 1987 with a strike price equal to the portfolio's initial value on April 16, 1986. Applying the bond portfolio option replication model, the first basket of options together with a cash equivalent instrument was selected on April 16, 1986 (Exhibit 6).[10] As expected, the basket had a net long position in puts and a net short position in calls. The total cost was about 5.8% of the portfolio flat cost. A comparison between the target payoff and the synthetic payoff is shown in Exhibit 7. It can be seen that the replication was not perfect, but the tracking error seems to be acceptable. The discrepancy between the two curves is attributed to the limited number of replication instruments used and the other constraints imposed on the model.

This option replication portfolio was rebalanced on August 18, 1986. On this first rebalancing date, we liquidated the first option portfolio and obtained a value of $735,000. As predicted by the model, this amount of money was enough to purchase

EXHIBIT 6
PORTFOLIO HEDGE REPORT—
DEDICATED PORTFOLIO ANALYSIS SYSTEM

Settlement Date 4/16/1986—XYZ Insurance Company				
Option Replication:				
PUT	*Expiration = 4/15/1987*	*Strike = 100%*		*Rebalance = 8/18/1986*
Futures and Options	*Expiration*	*Contracts*	*Price*	*Cost ($1000)*
Call T-bond CBT Sept/104	8/23/1986	−51.50	3.97	−204.46
Call T-bond CBT Sept/108	8/23/1986	−8.31	2.27	−18.86
Call T-bond CBT Sept/110	8/23/1986	44.56	1.67	74.42
Put T-bond CBT Sept/100	8/23/1986	20.78	2.03	42.18
Put T-bond CBT Sept/102	8/23/1986	8.86	2.75	24.37
Put T-bond CBT Sept/106	8/23/1986	51.60	4.69	242.00
Put T-bond CBT Sept/108	8/23/1986	−15.23	5.94	−90.47
Treasury 3-month	7/16/1988	0.58	98.55	566.27
	Net Hedge Cost			635.45
	Unhedged Portfolio Cost			10,839.21
	Hedged Portfolio Cost			11,474.66

---

[10] In practice, the number of contracts should be rounded to the nearest integer.

EXHIBIT 7
USING OPTIONS TO REPLICATE A GIVEN PAYOFF FUNCTION
(PERIOD 1: 04/16/1986–08/18/1986)

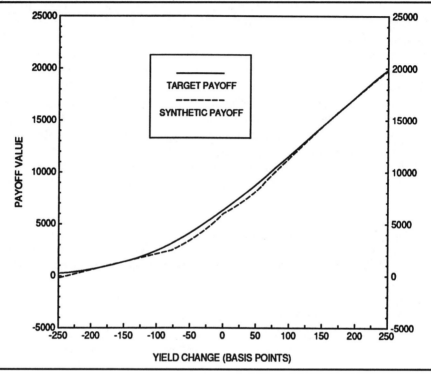

the second basket of options as specified by the model. On the subsequent two rebalancing dates, November 14, 1986 and February 20, 1987, we found that the liquidation values were also sufficient to cover the rebalancing costs. Exhibits 8, 9 and 10 illustrate the replication results for these three periods. Note that the accuracy of the replication was quite satisfactory, especially for the high interest rate scenarios. This is important because the main purpose of the hedge is to protect the portfolio against rising interest rates. The replication of the last period was almost perfect (Exhibit 10). This is not surprising because in the last period the original long term option became a short term option, which was easier to replicate with a set of short term options.

At the end of the one year hedge program, the bond portfolio lost $816,361, or about 7.53% of the original portfolio value. This loss was partially offset by the 61% gain in the option portfolio. Exhibit 11 compares the performance of the hedged portfolio and the unhedged portfolio. It can be seen that the creation of a synthetic

EXHIBIT 8
USING OPTIONS TO REPLICATE A GIVEN PAYOFF FUNCTION
(PERIOD 2: 08/18/1986—11/14/1986)

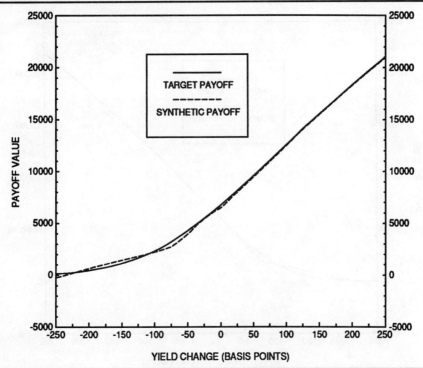

put option makes the hedged portfolio value much less volatile. Exhibit 12 illustrates that the value of the synthetic option was moving in the opposite direction of the bond (unhedged) portfolio.

It should be emphasized that the bond portfolio option replication model is not restricted to replicating a put option. In fact, it can also be applied to replicate any European option, whether simple or complex, so long as the payoff function is given.

Example 4

Assume an insurance company has the intention to construct a bond portfolio to meet a certain liability stream. A dedicated cash matched portfolio would be an appropriate solution. Unlike our previous and more commonplace examples, the company

EXHIBIT 9
USING OPTIONS TO REPLICATE A GIVEN PAYOFF FUNCTION
(PERIOD 3: 11/14/1986—02/20/1987)

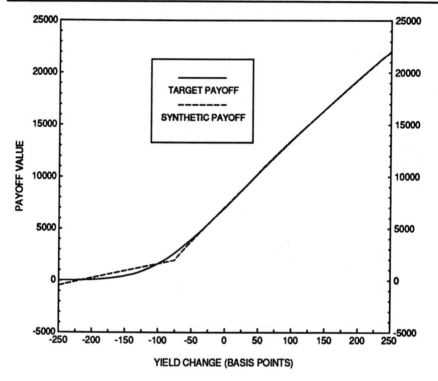

EXHIBIT 10
USING OPTIONS TO REPLICATE A GIVEN PAYOFF FUNCTION
(PERIOD 4: 02/20/1987–04/15/1987)

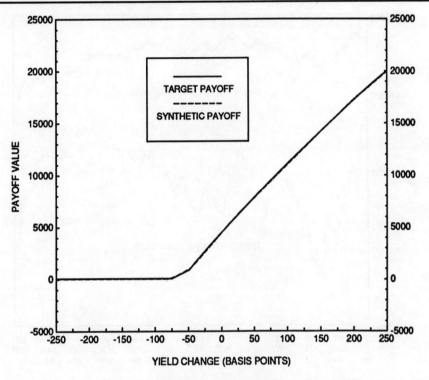

EXHIBIT 11
XYZ INSURANCE COMPANY: A CASE STUDY
HEDGE A BOND PORTFOLIO BY A SYNTHETIC PUT (1)

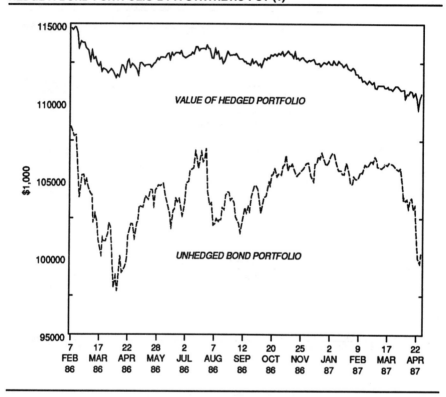

EXHIBIT 12
XYZ INSURANCE COMPANY: A CASE STUDY
HEDGE A BOND PORTFOLIO BY A SYNTHETIC PUT (2)

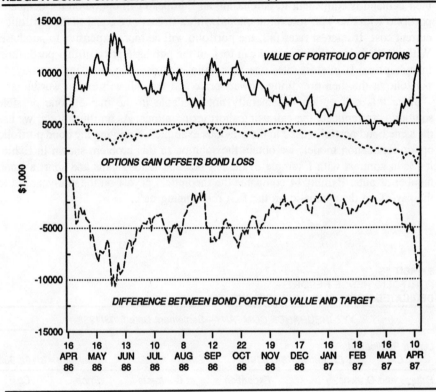

only wants to set up the portfolio now, and actually buy the portfolio one year from now at today's price. Carefully analyzing the company's request, it can be found that their demand is equivalent to purchasing an European call option on the dedicated portfolio with one year to expiration and with a strike price equal to the portfolio's current cost. If interest rates fall, the portfolio will be more expensive to purchase. With a call option, the company can lock in the purchase price of that portfolio at today's price. If interest rates one year from now rise, the company can buy the portfolio at the then prevailing (lower) price and the call will expire worthless.

Since this call option is generally not available in the market, one possible solution is to replicate the call using short term options. As an illustration, we use the same bond portfolio used in the previous examples. Applying the bond portfolio option replication model, we obtain the solution to this problem shown in Exhibit 13. In contrast with Example 3, the net position is long calls and short a small number of puts. Exhibit 14 compares the theoretical payoff on the one-year put to the payoff on the synthetic on the first rebalancing date.

EXHIBIT 13
PORTFOLIO HEDGE REPORT—
DEDICATED PORTFOLIO ANALYSIS SYSTEM

XYZ INSURANCE COMPANY—Settlement Date 5/03/1988				

Option Replication:
CALL	Expiration = 5/03/1989	Strike = 100%	Rebalance = 8/18/1988	

Futures and Options	Expiration	Contracts	Price	Cost ($1000)
Call T-bond CBT Aug/82	8/20/1988	73.00	5.67	414.05
Call T-bond CBT Aug/86	8/20/1988	126.00	2.94	370.13
Call T-bond CBT Aug/88	8/20/1988	137.00	1.92	263.30
Call T-bond CBT Aug/90	8/20/1988	−825.00	1.19	−979.69
Call T-bond CBT Aug/92	8/20/1988	981.00	0.69	674.44
Put T-bond CBT Aug/80	8/20/1988	39.00	0.55	21.33
Put T-bond CBT Aug/82	8/20/1988	−53.00	0.89	−47.20
Treasury 3-month	8/02/1988	0.24	98.47	236.86

	Unhedged Portfolio	Hedged Portfolio
Flat Cost	94,887,297.81	95,840,496.56
Full Cost	99,081,528.42	100,034,727.17
Duration	6.07	7.30
Convexity	0.52	2.22
Net Hedge Cost ($1000)		953,198.75

EXHIBIT 14
OPTION REPLICATION—XYZ INSURANCE COMPANY
(CALL, EXP=5/03/1989, STRIKE=100% REBALANCE=8/15/1988)

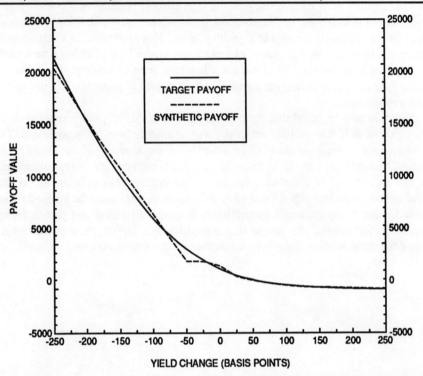

CONCLUSION

Broadly speaking, the objective of bond portfolio management is to create a new asset or replicate an asset that satisfies investors' needs. A dedicated cash matched portfolio creates an asset whose cash flow matches the liability stream. Actually, the purpose of immunizing a portfolio is to replicate a zero coupon bond or a money market instrument. These assets can be characterized by their return structures; therefore, bond portfolio management essentially involves constructing a portfolio to meet a predefined return structure.

From this point of view, the importance of applying futures and options in bond portfolio management cannot be overstated. The applications are of course not restricted to the three strategies discussed in this chapter. Without exaggeration, we can say that the applications of futures and options have opened a new dimension in bond portfolio management because, at least theoretically, futures and options can be viewed as building blocks from which we can mold any specific bond portfolio return structure.

However, in reshaping portfolio return structure, non-trivial costs will be incurred. Explicit costs include transactions fees, costs of purchasing options, interest costs due to mark-to-market requirement with futures, etc. In addition, there is an implicit cost—mainly the expected yield-give-up. This reminds us of a fundamental law in modern finance: one cannot expect to earn higher than a riskless return while hedging away all the risk. Thus, as in any financial decision making, it is important to evaluate a hedging strategy in terms of both its degree of protection and its explicit and implicit costs.

It should also be noted that there exists, in this world, no perfect replication. A synthetic asset is always different in one way or another from the genuine one. The performance of replication critically depends on the accuracy of the assumptions behind the replication model in describing the actual marketplace. A typical example is the assumption of constant volatility in the option replication model. If this assumption (together with several other assumptions) were true, the synthetic asset would enjoy many attractive properties such as self-financing and path independence. Unfortunately, this assumption is questionable. Hence, these properties are not guaranteed when rolling over the basket of short term options.

Chapter 20

Synthetic Asset Strategies

ROBERT P. LECKY, JR.
VICE PRESIDENT
THE FIRST BOSTON CORPORATION

Investors often need a *cash flow* that is unavailable in the capital markets. To create a desired cash flow, an investor can combine an existing cash market instrument with a risk management tool, such as *interest rate swaps, currency swaps* and *forwards, caps and floors, futures,* and *options.* The resulting instrument is called a *synthetic asset.*

Synthetic assets are commonly created because investors want to change a fixed cash flow into a floating cash flow, or vice versa. Similarly, investors can change the characteristics of a fixed cash flow (e.g., change a zero coupon bond into a full coupon bond) or those of a floating cash flow (e.g., change the index, from 3-month Treasury bill to 3-month LIBOR). In creating synthetic assets, investors can specify characteristics such as yield, maturity, duration, and credit. The term of the risk management tool employed should represent the investors' views on changes in interest rates and/or intermarket spreads.

The objective of this chapter is two-fold. First, risk management tools are described and compared, and, second, various trading strategies are described. These

The author would like to thank the following colleagues at First Boston for their contribution to this report: Stephen Chapin, Gregg Cohen, Robert Cohen, Peter Karpen, Harry Kavros, Phillip Moineau, Edward Ocampo, Dharshni Peries, Mark Polhill, Steven Schwimmer, and Dexter Senft.

fall into two categories. The first strategy is to create synthetic floating rate assets. This strategy should appeal to traditional floating rate buyers, including *commercial banks (domestic and foreign), insurance companies, thrifts,* and *money managers.* The second strategy is to create synthetic fixed rate assets. This strategy should appeal to traditional fixed rate investors, including *insurance companies* and *money managers.*

Examples in this chapter are typically of transactions in which the asset and the risk management tool have the same maturity. Transactions can be structured, however, to provide any mismatch an investor desires. Market timing or outlook, product structure, or any combination of both can determine the structure of a synthetic transaction.

BENEFITS AND RISKS

The benefits associated with synthetic assets include:

- Investors usually receive a higher yield than is otherwise available on capital market instruments.
- Investors create assets that are otherwise unavailable.
- New or different credits and structures can be obtained.
- Investors can transform the characteristics of an asset without realizing gains or losses.
- Investors can take advantage of inefficiencies inherent in new and developing markets.

The risks associated with synthetic assets include;

- Decoupling synthetic assets prior to maturity may be more costly than generic trading because one is dealing with at least two markets/products: one for the cash market instrument and one for the risk management tool. The bid-to-offer spread for risk management tools with maturity longer than three years is generally 5-15 basis points.
- As with other products, yield curves, prepayment speeds, exchange rates, and intermarket spreads must be monitored.

CASH MARKET INSTRUMENTS AND RISK MANAGEMENT TOOLS

Securities that can be used to create synthetic fixed rate assets include:

Floating rate certificates of deposit (U.S. and Euro)
Floating rate notes (FRNs) (U.S. and Euro)

Floating rate mortgage-backed securities
Foreign currency notes
Preferred stock (floating rate)

Securities that can be used to create synthetic floating rate assets include:

Term CDs (U.S. and Euro) and medium term deposit notes
Intermediate corporates (U.S. and Euro)
Medium-term notes
Fixed rate mortgage-backed securities
Whole loans
Taxable municipals
Private placements
High yield notes
Foreign currency notes
Preferred stock (fixed rate)

Risk management tools commonly used with cash market securities to create synthetic assets are:

Interest rate swaps
Interest rate options
Interest rate futures/forwards
Interest rate caps, floors, collars, and corridors
Currency futures/forwards
Currency swaps

Each risk management tool is unique. Exhibit 1 indicates the most important characteristics of each.

As shown in Exhibit 2, the various risk management tools can be grouped into two categories, which meet the needs of the two basic investor segments: *cash flow accounts* and *performance accounts*.

The cash flow account usually has a buy and hold strategy. It looks to purchase a synthetic asset where there is yield enhancement and where the maturity of the underlying cash market instrument usually matches the maturity of the risk management tool.

Conversely, the performance account more likely makes short-term market decisions. It uses risk management tools that are highly liquid and have short maturities. In most cases the creation of a synthetic asset by combining a cash market instrument and a risk management tool(s) with similar maturities will not appeal to this investor segment.

One can look at risk management tools, such as interest rate and currency rate

EXHIBIT 1
CHARACTERISTICS OF RISK MANAGEMENT TOOLS

Risk Management Tool	Available Maturities/ Currencies	Longest Term	Minimum Trade Size	Bid-Ask Spread	Credit Exposure	Documentation	Other Characteristics
Exchange Traded Interest Rate Futures: Short Term	3-mo T-Bill 3-mo LIBOR	T-Bill: 2 years (8 contracts) LIBOR: 3 years (12 contracts)	1MM	1-5 bp	Low. Daily Margin Required.	Standardized	M, J, S, D Cycle
Long Term	5 yr, 10 yr, 30 yr	2 years (8 contracts)	100M	5 yr: 4/32 10 yr: 1/32 30 yr: 1/32			
Exchange Traded Interest Rate Options: Short Term	3-mo T-Bill 3-mo LIBOR	1 year (4 contracts) 2 years (8 contracts)	1MM	T-Bill: 5-10 bp LIBOR: 1-3 bp	Low. Daily Margin Required.	Standardized	M, J, S, D Cycle T-Bill options are extremely illiquid.
Long Term	5 yr, 10 yr, 30 yr	9 months	100M	2/32-4/32	Low. Daily Margin Required.	Standardized	F, M, A, N Cycle
OTC Interest Rate Options	2-30 years	5 years	1MM	2/32-4/32	Medium. Buyer exposed to writer. No clearing house.	Not Standardized	Custom tailored. Less liquid than ET options. Not very liquid past 1 year.
Interest Rate Swaps	1-10 years	10 years	5MM	Up to 10 bp	Medium. Exposure normally limited to net difference checks. No exchange of principal. No clearing house.	ISDA Standard Document with modifications made by each dealer.	3/6-mo LIBOR index is most liquid. 3-mo T-Bill 1-mo CP Prime and Fed Funds available.

Interest Rate Forwards	3 mo-30 years	1 year +	25MM	1/4-3/4 pt	Medium. No clearing house.	Not Standardized	Available on most Treasuries and MBS.
Interest Rate Caps/Floors	3/6-mo T-Bill 3/6-mo LIBOR	10 years	10MM	1/4-3/4 pt	High. No credit enhancement protection.		3-mo LIBOR is the only liquid index.
Currency Futures	£, DM, Yen, C$, SF	2 years (8 contracts)	Depends on currency	1-3 bp	Low. Daily Margin Required.	Standardized	M, J, S, D Cycle
Currency Forwards	1-2 years: A$, NZ$ 1-5 years: £, DM, YEN, C$, SF	5 years	1MM	A$, NZ$: 10-20 bp, £, DM: 10-20 bp, Yen, C$: 20-30 bp, SF: 30-40 bp	Medium. No clearing house.	Not Standardized	More flexible than currency swaps.
Currency Swaps	2-7 years: £, DM, Yen, C$, SF, A$, NZ$	7 years	5MM	10-15 bp	High. Principal and/or interest risk. No clearing house.		Commercial Banks are usually counterparties.

EXHIBIT 2
PRODUCTS FOR DIFFERENT TYPES OF ACCOUNTS

	Risk Management Tool	Most Liquid Terms	Longest Term
	Interest Rate Swaps	2-7 years	10 years
	Interest Rate Caps/ Floors	2-7 years	10 years
Cash Flow Accounts	Currency Forwards	A$, NZ$: out to 2 years £, C$: out to 3 years SF, DM, Yen: out to 5 years	10 years
	Currency Swaps	A$: out to 5 years NZ$: out to 3 years C, £, SF, DM, Yen: 2-7 years	10 years

	Risk Management Tool	Most Liquid Terms	Longest Term
	Exchange Traded Futures	6-12 months	2 years
Performance Accounts	Exchange Traded Options	out to 6 months	Short Term: 1 yr Long Term: 9 mo
	OTC Options	out to 6 months	10 years
	Currency Futures	out to 6 months	10 years

swaps and caps and floors, simply as extensions of futures and options. There are, however, risk management tools that have similar characteristics and have *overlapping* lives (see Exhibit 3).

Where this overlapping occurs, most inefficiences have been arbitraged out; however, there are situations where it is more economical to use one tool versus another. Other non-quantifiable factors, such as credit approval and documentation, should be taken into account as well.

EXHIBIT 3
COMPARISON OF RISK MANAGEMENT TOOLS

Risk Management Tools	Period of Overlapping Lives	Similar Characteristics
Exhange Traded Futures, Forwards and Interest Rate Swaps	1-3 years	Can change type of cash flow (e.g., floating to fixed). Can change frequency of payment (i.e., annual to semiannual).
Exchange Traded Futures and Interest Rate Caps/Floors	1-3 years	Set/remove minimum/maximum rate. Set/remove option characteristics.
Exchange Traded Options and Interest Rate Caps/Floors	9 mo - 1 year	Set/remove minimum/maximum rate. Set/remove option characteristics.
Currency Futures and Currency Forwards	3 mo - 2 years	Change currency of principal and/or interest.
Currency Futures and Currency Swaps	1½ - 2 years	Change currency of principal and/or interest.
Currency Forwards and Currency Swaps	2 - 5 years	Change currency of principal and/or interest.

RISK MANAGEMENT TOOLS

Interest Rate Swaps

The generic interest rate swap is a transaction in which one party pays or receives a fixed rate at a specified spread to a stated maturity of a U.S. Treasury issue versus receiving or paying 3/6-month LIBOR, 3-month Treasury bills, 1-month commercial paper, or prime rate.[1]

The key elements in interest rate swaps include:

1. Swaps spreads

   - In the 1-3 year area, fixed rate swaps levels (the swap curve) versus 3/6-month LIBOR are driven by the TED spread (the spread between U.S.

[1]For more information on interest rate swaps, see *Interest Rate Swaps* (First Boston, October 1987).

Treasury bill futures and Eurodollar futures). The swap curves versus Treasury bills, commercial paper, and prime are all driven by spot market levels, intermarket spreads, historical spreads, currency values, and market expectations.

- In the 4-10 year area, the swap curve is influenced by primary and secondary corporate note spreads, the shape of the Treasury yield curve, money market yields, intermarket spreads, currency values, and market expectations.

2.   Credit

- Credit approval is a must. A swap is a long-term credit relationship. The credit exposure in a swap is tied to the potential default of the counterparty and is quantified by the current market value of the fixed rate flows. *Both* counterparties must realize the credit risks and therefore might require credit enhancement.
- Where credit enhancement is deemed necessary, a mark-to-market document that allows *either* counterparty to ask for collateral whose value is equal to the present value of the swap exposure is used.
- In another form of credit enhancement, up front collateral that is tied to a specified percentage of the notional amount of the swap multiplied by the number of years to maturity is required. The collateral that is acceptable typically includes cash, U.S. Treasuries and agencies, GNMAs, FNMAs, FHLMCs, and Letters of Credit of certain AAA institutions.

3.   Documentation

- The International Swap Dealers Association (ISDA) has recently produced the 1987 standard document for interest rate swaps. The vast majority of ISDA members will also use this document.

Exchange Traded and OTC Interest Rate Options

The OTC options market exists because it offers the investor the ability to trade options on a broad number of issues with terms that are not available in exchange traded option contracts. There are many strategies that investors can use in the options market. Before discussing these it might be useful to define basic option terms.

A *call* option is the right but not the obligation to buy a specific underlying security at a predetermined price (the strike or exercise price). Conversely, a *put* option is the right but not the obligation to sell a specific underlying security at a predetermined strike price.

The option *premium*, or price, has two components: *intrinsic value* and *time value*. Intrinsic value is the amount by which a put or call option is *in the money*. A call option is in the money if the underlying security has a value greater than the exercise price of the option. A put option is in the money if the underlying security is worth less than the exercise price. Out of the money describes an option with no intrinsic value. A call option is *out of the money* when the underlying security is worth less than the exercise price, and a put option is out of the money when the underlying security is worth more than the exercise price. *At the money* describes an option for which the underlying security is selling at (or very near) the exercise price. Time value is the portion of the option premium that is not intrinsic value. It is the total option premium less the amount the option is in the money. Out-of-the-money options have premiums consisting entirely of time value. The *term* of an option, or time to expiration, is the amount of time the holder (owner) of an option has the right to exercise the option.

There are numerous methods of valuing interest rate options, which are beyond the scope of this chapter. This chapter will focus on the use of OTC options to hedge interest rate swaps (corporates) with embedded options. Holders of callable corporate notes have implicitly sold calls on a proxy non-callable security to the issuer of the callable corporate note. They are compensated with higher yield.

Call options embedded in a corporate note can cause its price/yield spread relationship to vary with its non-callable proxy. When rates rise the callable corporate trades more closely to its final maturity (duration extension); when rates drop the callable corporate's price might not appreciate as fast because the issue could be called (duration contraction). This situation is called *negative convexity*.

Being long a corporate and short a call is equivalent to being short a put. In other words, both positions have similar returns. To turn a callable bond into a non-callable bond, the call must be repurchased. This will allow comparison with the swap market, which is non-callable. Thus, to hedge a callable corporate an investor would buy a weighted amount of puts. This combination of embedded short calls and long puts is equivalent to a forward sale of the underlying non-callable proxy security. Once a fixed rate corporate that has a call has been hedged, its fixed cash flows can be swapped to a floating basis on a matched maturity basis. Other applications appear in Exhibit 4. The *pricing condition* that options must satisfy is:

return (long cash + long put + short call) = risk-free rate to date of option expiration

Credit and Margin: The volatility and term of the option and the creditworthiness of the option seller will determine a counterparty's credit policy. The following margin alternatives are available:

1. The counterparty usually reserves the right to ask for margin collateral from the option seller if the option goes in the money.

2. The counterparty may require an escrow receipt where the underlying security is held in escrow.
3. The counterparty may require collateral in the form of cash or cash equivalent (i.e., Treasuries) equal to a certain percentage of the par amount of the underlying security.

Exchange Traded Interest Rate Futures

A financial futures contract is a transferable agreement to buy or sell a particular financial instrument, known as the *underlying security*, at a particular point in time, known as the *delivery date*, at a predetermined price. Since a futures contract is an agreement to buy or sell at a fixed price, profits or losses will be generated as the price of the underlying security changes.

The pricing of a futures contract is determined by today's expectations of the future price of the underlying security. The price of a futures contract will be the price of the underlying security adjusted by *carry*. Carry is the spread between the interest earned from holding a security and its financing costs. Carry will generally be positive for interest rate futures in an upwardly sloping yield curve environment. As a result, futures prices will generally be lower than prices in the cash market. Since carry will decline as the delivery date approaches, the prices of the underlying security and the futures contract will *converge*.

The difference between the price of the underlying security and the price of the futures contract is known as the *basis*. The basis will contract over time as the cash and futures price converge. *Basis risk*, which is the fluctuation in the basis, arises from temporary supply and demand disparities between the cash and futures markets, or uncertainty as to which security will be delivered for any given contract.

This chapter will focus on the IMM contracts featuring 3-month Treasury bills and 3-month Eurodollar Time Deposits by combining a strip of contracts that will match the life of the underlying asset. The 3-month Treasury bills trade in 8 consecutive 3-month periods (2 years) while the 3-month Eurodollar Time Deposits trade in 12 consecutive 3-month periods (3 years). Thus the maximum term of a maturity-matched synthetic asset using 3-month Treasury bill futures or 3-month Eurodollar Time Deposits is 2 and 3 years, respectively.

Credit and Margin: Futures contracts have very limited credit risk due to the clearing house. The clearing house is a corporation connected with the exchange through which all futures contracts are reconciled, guaranteed, and settled. The clearing house effectively becomes the counterparty to each trade by positioning itself between the buyer and seller. Investors therefore do not have to look to the credit of the party taking the opposite side of the trade. The clearing house also oversees the margin requirements and the daily mark-to-market process. Margin requirements protect the integrity of the exchange and ensure market participants that contractual obligations will be fulfilled. The daily mark-to-market process limits the dollar exposure to a default to a one-day move in interest rates.

Caps/Floors/Collars/Corridors

An interest rate *cap* (ceiling) is a series of put options on a floating interest rate (such as LIBOR, commercial paper, or Treasury bills) that is sold by one party to another. A cap agreement specifies the floating rate to be used (e.g., 3-month LIBOR), the length of time of the agreement (maturity), and a predetermined *strike level* or rate. If rates go above this predetermined strike level, the seller of the cap must pay the buyer the difference between the actual rate and the strike rate.

A cap may be said to be in the money, at the money, or out of money, depending on the relationship between the strike rate and actual rates. Most caps are out-of-the-money options whose strike rates are higher than current market rates. The value of these put options increases as the actual rates rise, volatility increases, and/or the yield curve steepens.

The opposite of a cap is an interest rate *floor*. A floor represents a series of call options on a floating interest rate. A floor agreement stipulates that if actual rates go below the predetermined strike rate, then the seller of the floor must pay the buyer the difference between the actual rate and the strike rate. Like a cap, floors may be written in, at, or out of the money, with the majority being out of the money. The value of these call options increases as rates go down.

An interest rate swap is simply a combination of a cap and a floor, known as an interest rate *collar*. A swap can be created by constructing a collar whose cap and floor strikes are equivalent. A collar typically has different strike rates for the cap and floor (e.g., an 8% cap and a 6% floor). The major difference between a swap and a typical collar is that the collar restricts the counterparty's rate exposure to a range of interest rates (e.g., 6% to 8%). A swap, on the other hand, limits the exposure to a single fixed interest rate (e.g., 7%).

Collars can be used by either bullish or bearish investors to reduce their all-in cost of purchasing puts or calls. A bullish investor would sell a collar (sell a cap and buy a floor) to hedge against falling rates; a bearish investor would buy a collar (buy a cap and sell a floor). In both cases, the net premium is reduced by the offsetting price received for the option sold.

An interest rate corridor is also a combination of a cap and a floor. However, a corridor is created by selling *both* an interest rate cap *and* an interest rate floor. This strategy fits an investor who believes that interest rates will trade in a specific range over the life of the corridor. For example, suppose an investor sold an 11% 3-month LIBOR cap and an 8% 3-month LIBOR floor for 2 years. The bet is that 3-month LIBOR will not deviate between the two strikes (8 and 11%). The investor is paid up front for this transaction and can use the proceeds to enhance their income/yield.

Interest rates swaps, caps, floors, collars, currency swaps and forwards are all

EXHIBIT 4
APPLICATIONS AND RAMIFICATIONS OF USING RISK MANAGEMENT TOOLS IN

	Interest Rate Swaps		Interest Rate Caps/Floors			
	Floating rate security combined with receiving fixed and paying floating.	Fixed rate security combined with receiving floating and paying fixed.	Floating rate security combined with the sale/purchase of an out-of-the-money cap/floor:		Fixed rate security combined with the sale/purchase of an out-of-the-money cap/floor:	
	Synthetic Fixed	Synthetic Floating	Sell Cap	Buy Floor	Buy Cap	Sell Floor
Interest Rates Increase	Value decreases. Losses limited to how high interest rates rise.	Value increases. Profit limited by how high short-term interest rates rise.	Value decreases as market rates approach, hit, or exceed the exercise rate of the cap.	Value decreases slightly as market rates move away from the exercise rate of the floor.	Value of a fixed rate security decreases. Value of the cap increases as it gets closer to being in the money.	Value of fixed rate security decreases. Profit from the sale of floor enhances return. Value of the floor declines as rates move away from exercise price.
Interest Rates Unchanged	Value unchanged.	Value unchanged.	Value unchanged. Over time, the value of the cap will decay as the cap approaches expiration.	Value unchanged. Over time, the value of the floor will decay as the floor approaches expiration.	Value unchanged. Cost of purchasing the cap decreases total return.	Value unchanged. Sale of floor increases total return.
Interest Rates Decrease	Value increases. Profits limited by amount of drop in interest rates.	Value decreases. Losses limited to drop in interest rates.	Value increases as market rates move away from the exercise rate of the cap.	Value increases as market rates move toward the exercise rate of the floor.	Value of underlying security cap increases.	Value of fixed rate security increases. Profit from sale of floor might not be sufficient to offset liability of the floor as the market rate approaches the exercise price of the floor.

extensions of basic futures and options. As noted above, listed futures and options have relatively short lives and may have inflexible structures and/or dates. Swaps, forwards, caps, floors, and collars can have maturities of up to 10 years and generally can be constructed to fit the investor's specifications.

Each risk management tool affects the value of the underlying cash instrument. These instruments can be complicated and difficult to value. Exhibit 4 gives a general look at the market exposure dynamics of using interest rate swaps, caps, floors, collars, and listed options.

CREATING SYNTHETIC ASSETS

	Collars/Corridors		*Interest Rate Options*			
	Floating rate security combined with the purchase of an out-of-the-money:	Floating rate security combined with the sale of an out-of-the-money:	Floating rate security combined with the purchase of an out-of-the-money, over-the-counter:	Fixed rate security combined with the sale/purchase of an out-of-the-money, over-the-counter call/put:		
					Sale of a Call	*Purchase of a Put*
	Collar	*Corridor*	*Call*	*Put*		
	Value of security stays the same or decreases if market rates approach the exercise rate of the cap.	Value of the floater is unchanged or decreases as market rates approach the strike of the cap.	Value of floater is unchanged but value of the call decreases.	Value of the floater is unchanged but value of the put increases.	Value of fixed rate security declines but the profits from selling the call offset the risk of call being exercised.	Value of fixed rate security declines. Value of put increases.
	Value unchanged. The value of the collar will decay as it approaches expiration.	Value unchanged. The value of the corridor will decline over time as it approaches expiration.	Value unchanged. Over time, the value of the call will decay.	Value unchanged. Over time, the value of the put will decay.	Value unchanged. Proceeds from sale of the call tend to outweigh exposure to this call being exercised.	Value unchanged. Over time the value of the put will decay.
	Value of security will stay the same or increase if market rate approaches the exercise rate of the floor.	Value of the floater is unchanged or decreases as market rates approach the strike of the floor.	Value of floater stays the same and the value of call will increase.	Value of floater stays the same but the value of the put decreases.	Value of fixed rate security increases. The sale of the call limits price appreciation as market rates approach exercise rate of the call. Sale of proceeds add to income.	Value of fixed rate security increases. Value of the put declines.

Credit and Margin: Floors, caps and corridors are agreements between two parties that commit one side to making possible payments in the future. A long-term credit relationship is therefore created. Collars commit both sides of the agreement to making possible future payments; the credit relationship is therefore even more complicated. Unfortunately, there is no single, universally accepted method of valuing caps, floors, collars and corridors. This makes a mark-to-market process difficult to manage over the life of the agreement. Up front collateral requirements, mark-to-market provisions, and other credit enhancements are therefore difficult to apply. As a result, the credit approval process may be more selective since the seller of the agreement is an unsecured creditor to the buyer (in the case of caps, floors and corridors), and each party to the agreement is an unsecured creditor to the other in the case of collars.

Currency Forwards

Investors can enhance yield versus alternative investments by investing in foreign currency issues fully hedged into U.S. dollars. This strategy can be implemented by agreeing to sell forward the future foreign currency coupon and principal payments at a predetermined exchange rate. These prices, or forward foreign exchange rates, reflect the interest rate differentials between the currency and the dollar markets. This results in gradually changing forward foreign exchange rates over the life of the contracts to produce an uneven stream of U.S. dollar inflows. If an investor purchases a foreign currency note that has higher interest rates than the U.S. market and sells a corresponding amount of forward foreign exchange contracts, then the initial U.S. dollar flows are favorable to the investor but there is an offsetting principal loss at maturity. If the currency depreciates, the investment value of the foreign currency bond is adversely affected, but a compensating profit is made on the forward foreign exchange contracts (since the currency may be bought at a lower price than that for which it was originally sold). If the currency appreciates, then the gain on the foreign currency bond position is offset by a loss on the short sale of the forward contracts. Conversely, if an investor purchases a note denominated in a currency with lower interest rates than the U.S. market, then the U.S. dollar flows, after the execution of forward foreign exchange contracts, would initially appear unattractive with a principal gain at maturity. Most transactions using currency forwards convert non-dollar fixed into dollar fixed or floating. However, non-dollar floating swapped to dollar fixed or floating can be executed as well.

(1) Features

- Very flexible; can be customized with respect to maturity, payment frequency, and principal amount.
- Can be executed in small blocks (e.g., $500,000).
- In short maturities (1-3 years), are often more liquid than currency swaps.
- Can be easily reversed with offsetting forward contracts.
- Range of maturities is generally 1 week to 5 years, up to 3 years being the most liquid.
- From time to time can provide investors with more attractive hedged dollar yield than can be achieved via the currency swap market.
- In order to generate a floating rate return, forward contracts must be combined with an interest rate swap.

(2) Credit

- Subject to mutual approval by investor and counterparty. Usually a major money center bank.

(3) Documentation

- Forward foreign exchange confirmation telexes.

(4) Timing

- It is generally necessary to obtain an order, subject to credit, at an agreed yield target to the investor good for at least 1 to 2 days.

Currency Swaps

Investors can use currency swaps to create a return on a foreign currency denominated security into U.S. dollars (or vice versa). This return can be a fixed *or* floating rate. The investor contracts to exchange a predetermined set of foreign currency cash flows for U.S. dollars. The principal exchange at maturity is generally executed at the spot exchange rate prevailing at the time the swap is executed. In addition, the currency and dollar interest flows are even, giving both sets of cash flows a bond-like structure. Thus, unlike forward foreign exchange contracts, a currency swap reflects the interest rate differential between the currency and dollar markets in differing currency and dollar coupon rates rather than through varying exchange rates. As in foreign exchange contracts, any appreciation or depreciation of the foreign currency against the dollar will affect the dollar return of the currency investment. This, however, will be offset by an equal and opposite economic effect on the currency swap transaction. The investor is thereby left with a fully hedged asset package.

(1) Features

- Can most easily accommodate bullet, non-call structures. Amortizing structures are less common but can be negotiated.
- Can be executed in maturities of 2 to 10 years. Usually 2- to 7-year maturities are most liquid.
- From time to time can provide investors a more attractive hedged dollar yield than can be achieved with currency forwards.
- Currency swaps are generally indexed to U.S. dollar LIBOR. A fixed rate return in a foreign currency is usually swapped to a floating rate basis in U.S. dollars at a spread above LIBOR. However, can be combined with an interest rate swap to create a fixed rate return.

- Usually less liquid than foreign exchange forwards in maturities up to 3 years.
- Principal blocks of less than $5,000,000 are generally not economical.

(2) Credit

- Subject to mutual approval by customer and counterparty. Usually large bank names.

(3) Documentation

- Subject to mutually acceptable documentation to be provided by swap counterparty. Virtually all major swap market principals now provide documentation conforming to ISDA's 1987 Standard Interest Rate and Currency Exchange Agreement.

(4) Timing

- It is generally necessary to obtain an order, subject to credit, at an agreed yield target to the customer, good for at least 1 to 2 days.

CREATING SYNTHETIC FLOATING RATE ASSETS

In this section and the one to follow, various synthetic asset trading strategies are described. In this section, the focus is on creating synthetic floating rate assets. Each strategy will be explained by using an example.

Fixed to Floating Using Interest Rate Swaps

An investor wants to buy a single-A or better U.S. regional bank CD that floats off of LIBOR with a maturity of 2 years. The investor has a preference for Pittsburgh National Bank and wants a yield to maturity (YTM) spread of LIBOR flat. Suppose that there is no Pittsburgh National paper available, and if there were it would be at a YTM spread of 3-month LIBOR -6.25. Suppose, also that by combining a 2-year Pittsburgh National Bank fixed rate medium term note (MTN) with an interest rate swap the investor can receive 3-month LIBOR flat. This is depicted at the top of page 413.

The asset and swap flows from the investor's perspective are shown in Exhibit 5.

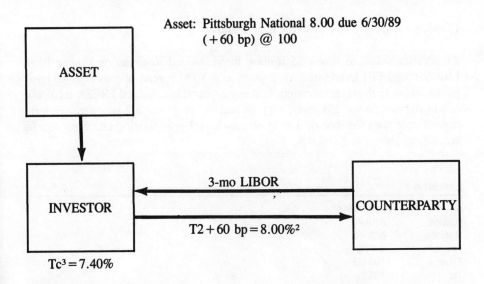

Asset: Pittsburgh National 8.00 due 6/30/89
(+60 bp) @ 100

EXHIBIT 5
ASSET AND SWAP FLOWS FROM INVESTOR'S PERSPECTIVE

| | | Swap Flows | | |
| | Pittsburgh National Asset Flows | Swap Fixed Outflows | Swap Floating Inflows | |
Period				Net
6/30/87	−100.00	—	—	−100.00
9/30/87	—	—	3-mo LIBOR/4	3-mo LIBOR/4
12/31/87	4.00	−4.00	3-mo LIBOR/4	3-mo LIBOR/4
3/31/88	—	—	3-mo LIBOR/4	3-mo LIBOR/4
6/30/88	4.00	−4.00	3-mo LIBOR/4	3-mo LIBOR/4
9/30/88	—	—	3-mo LIBOR/4	3-mo LIBOR/4
12/31/88	4.00	−4.00	3-mo LIBOR/4	3-mo LIBOR/4
3/31/89	—	—	3-mo LIBOR/4	3-mo LIBOR/4
6/30/89	104.00	−4.00	3-mo LIBOR/4	3-mo LIBOR/4 + 100

IRR on Synthetic Asset: LIBOR flat

---

[2]Note that the 8.00% fixed coupon pays semiannually (8.00%/2).
[3]Tc = Interpolated Treasury Curve.

Fixed to Floating Using Interest Rate Futures

An investor wants to invest $5 million in an A-rated Regional or Yankee Bank LIBOR-based FRCD maturing in 3 years at a YTM spread of plus 5 to 10 basis points. Suppose the investor cannot find any 3-year single A-rated FRCDs at LIBOR +5 to 10 basis points. However, suppose that by combining a 3-year medium-term deposit note with the sale of a strip of futures a 3-year floating rate asset can be created, as shown in Exhibit 6.

EXHIBIT 6

Asset:	BNP Paris
Ratings:	AAA/AA+
Maturity:	6/20/90
Coupon:	8.60%
Price:	100.00
Tc:	7.90%

EURODOLLAR FUTURES CONTRACTS

		Price	Yield
Sep 87	Contract	92.58	7.42
Dec	Contract	92.31	7.69
Mar 88	Contract	92.09	7.91
Jun	Contract	91.89	8.11
Sep	Contract	91.70	8.30
Dec	Contract	91.51	8.49
Mar 89	Contract	91.33	8.67
Jun	Contract	91.17	8.83
Sep	Contract	91.02	8.98
Dec	Contract	90.88	9.12
Mar 90	Contract	90.74	9.26
Jun	Contract	90.61	9.39

Bond equivalent yield (BEY) of Medium-Term Deposit Note: 8.600%
Bond equivalent yield (BEY) of Eurodollar Futures Strip: 8.526%*

IRR on Synthetic Asset: LIBOR + 7.4 bp

* Assumes that the cost of money for variation margin calls washes between excess and debit.

The investor would sell the 12 Eurodollar futures and combine this with the purchase of a 3-year BNP New York Branch medium-term deposit note at 8.60%. As in the previous example, the payment dates and settlement date on the deposit note coincide with the maturities of the futures contracts.

Floating to Floating Using Interest Rate Swaps

An investor wants to buy a 2-year floating rate asset of a bank tied to one-month commercial paper at a spread of 1-month CP + 25 basis points. Suppose there is no bank paper available at one-month commercial paper + 25 basis points; however, an investor discovers that via a floating-to-floating rate swap, a swap dealer can create a 2-year bank FRCD at LIBOR + 6.25 basis points and swap this to one-month commercial paper + 25.25 basis points. This situation is depicted below.

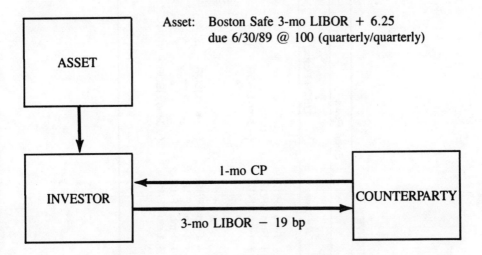

Exhibit 7 summarizes the asset and swap flows from the investor's perspective. The commercial paper flows are the one-month commercial paper rate paid out monthly (thus each month the rate is divided by 12); the LIBOR flows are 3-month LIBOR paid quarterly (thus the 3-month rate is divided by 4).

Floating to Floating Using Interest Rate Futures

An investor wants a LIBOR-based A-rated regional bank FRCD maturing in 2 years that has a 0 to +5 basis points YTM spread. Suppose a dealer does not have what the investor needs. However, a dealer is able to show the investor a 2-year A-rated FRCD at LIBOR +2 basis points by buying a Treasury bill-based FRCD and 8 consecutive contracts (a strip) of TEDs. The investor would buy Treasury bill futures and sell the Euro futures. If the TED widens, the investor would benefit from this hedge while the value of the FRCD would decline. If the TED spread narrows the investor would lose on the hedge but the FRCD should appreciate as the YTM spread narrows, as summarized in Exhibit 8.

EXHIBIT 7
ASSET AND SWAP FLOWS FROM INVESTOR'S PERSPECTIVE

Period	Boston Safe Asset Flows	Swap Flows		Net
		CP Flows	LIBOR Flows	
6/30/87	– 100	-	-	– 100
7/30/87	•	+ 1-mo CP/12	-	+ 1-mo CP/12
8/30/87	• •	+ 1-mo CP/12	-	+ 1-mo CP/12
9/30/87	(3-mo LIBOR + 6.25)/4	+ 1-mo CP/12	(–3-mo LIBOR – 19)/4	+ 1-mo CP/12 + 25.25/4
	• • • •	• • •	• • •	• • •
3/30/89	(3-mo LIBOR + 6.25)/4	+ 1-mo CP/12	(–3-mo LIBOR – 19)/4	+ 1-mo CP/12 + 25.25/4
4/30/89	•	+ 1-mo CP/12	-	+ 1-mo CP/12
5/30/89	•	+ 1-mo CP/12	•	+ 1-mo CP/12
6/30/89	(3-mo LIBOR + 6.25)/4 + 100	+ 1-mo CP/12	(–3-mo LIBOR – 19)/4	+ 1-mo CP/12 + 25.25/4 + 100

IRR on Synthetic Asset: 1-mo CP + 25.25 bp

EXHIBIT 8

Asset:	XYZ FRCD
Ratings:	A₂/A-
Maturity:	6/21/89
Index:	3-month T-Bill
Reset/Repay:	Q/Q
Margin:	120 bp
Price:	Par
Settlement Date:	6/15/87

		Eurodollar Futures Contract		T-Bill Futures Contract	
		Price	Yield	Price	Yield
Sep 87	Contract	92.58	7.42	93.94	6.06
Dec	Contract	92.31	7.69	93.69	6.31
Mar 88	Contract	92.09	7.91	93.48	6.52
Jun	Contract	91.89	8.11	93.29	6.71
Sep	Contract	91.70	8.30	93.08	6.92
Dec	Contract	91.51	8.49	92.91	7.09
Mar 89	Contract	91.33	8.67	92.70	7.30
Jun	Contract	91.17	8.83	92.49	7.51

BEY of Eurodollar futures strip	8.175*
BEY of T-Bill futures strip	6.994
YTM Spread of FRCD (BEY)	120 bp
TED Spread (BEY)	118 bp

IRR on Synthetic Asset: LIBOR + 2 bp

* Assumes that the cost of money for variation margin calls washes between excess and debt.

Investors can thus protect the purchase of the Treasury bill FRCD against any credit concerns the banking sector in general might have. They have not, however, completely protected themselves against the individual credit of the FRCD. In effect they have locked in a return of Treasury bill + 120 basis points (BEY) with an additional 2 basis points for protection. These computations do *not* include any reinvestment.

Adjustment Swaps

Before we discuss various types of adjustment swaps, it might be helpful to discuss the concept of an adjustment swap. There are certain types of investors who for certain reasons (e.g., tax treatment, accounting treatment, etc.) prefer to purchase generic or synthetic assets under the following scenarios:

- An investor buys fixed or floating rate notes at a discount and enters into an interest rate swap with the counterparty in which he or she pays fixed or floating at a rate equal to the coupon on the note. That rate is less than the market rate on a swap of that maturity. In part to compensate the counterparty for receiving less than the market rate on this swap, the investor makes a one-time payment to the counterparty. This payment is normally equal to the difference between the par value and the purchase price of the notes, and is either paid for up front or at maturity. Any difference between what the investor pays the counterparty and what the counterparty requires as compensation for receiving a sub-market coupon is repaid to the investor over the life of the swap in the form of a premium on the swap payment it receives.

- The opposite situation is one in which the investor buys bonds at a premium, pays an above market rate on the swap equal to the bond coupon, and receives an up front or back end payment from the counterparty. That payment is normally equal to the premium on the bond. The payment, less whatever the counterparty requires to pay the investor the margin he or she desires over the normal swap payment, compensates the investor for paying an above market coupon on the swap.

Adjustment swaps allow investors to smooth out and adjust the dollar flows connected with specific investments. Swap coupons can be set equal to bond coupons. Swap margins or above market coupons can be exchanged for up front or back end payments. The adjustment trade allows the investor to rearrange asset flows into a structure that, for various reasons, he or she finds more attractive.

There are complex tax and accounting issues that relate to these transactions. Therefore, there will be times when swap dealers are more active or less active in pursuing these types of trades. In all the adjustment swaps discussed in this chapter a discount instrument (fixed or floating) is converted into a par instrument (fixed or floating). The investor also pays the swap dealer an up front payment, *not* a backend payment.

Adjustment Swap Using Interest Rate Swaps: Par for Par/Flat Swap

An investor wants to invest $5 million in a non-bank A-rated or better floating rate asset at par for 9-10 years at LIBOR + 35-40 basis points. The investor wants the floater to be at par with no accrued interest (flat).

Suppose there are no 9- to 10-year non-bank A-rated or better floaters available that trade at LIBOR + 40 basis points. However, suppose the swap shown at the top of page 418 can be arranged.

The investor will pay the swap dealer 5.09% of principal up front that will be invested to pay the investor an above market floating rate, and the swap dealer will pay the investor 3.31875% up front for the accrued interest, to settle the issue flat.

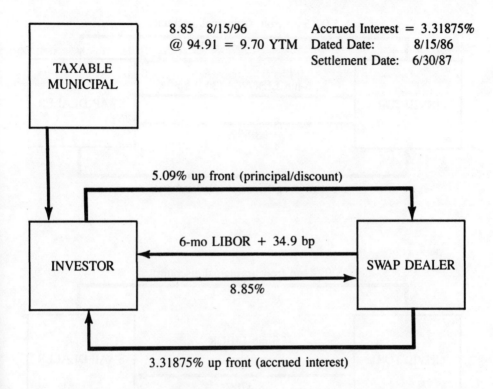

8.85   8/15/96   Accrued Interest = 3.31875%
@ 94.91 = 9.70 YTM   Dated Date: 8/15/86
                        Settlement Date: 6/30/87

TAXABLE
MUNICIPAL

5.09% up front (principal/discount)

INVESTOR

6-mo LIBOR + 34.9 bp

8.85%

SWAP DEALER

3.31875% up front (accrued interest)

Tc = 8.30%

Therefore, the gross flows paid to the swap dealer by the investor will be 1.77125%. The accrued interest of 3.31875% will be paid at the first coupon payment date. The principal of 5.09% will be amortized over the life of the swap.

Exhibit 9 shows the asset and swap flows from the perspective of the investor.

A swap with an up front payment of cash to the swap dealer is really two transactions:
1. A self-amortizing payment (here 5.09% made to the swap dealer until 8/15/96).
2. A swap whereby the swap dealer receives Tc + 100 basis points or 9.30% versus paying 6-month LIBOR flat.

This is shown below:

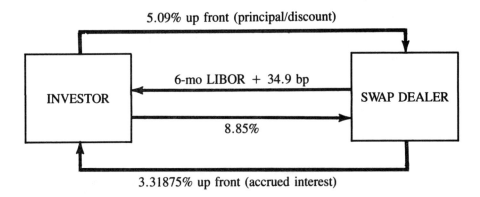

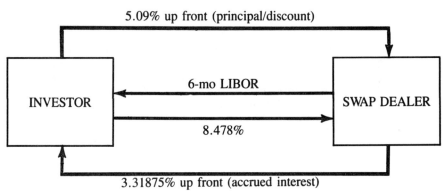

Tc = 8.30%

EXHIBIT 9
ASSET AND SWAP FLOWS FROM THE INVESTOR'S PERSPECTIVE

Period	Asset	Swap Fixed Flows	Swap Floating Flows	Net
6/30/87	−94.91	−1.77125	—	−96.681
8/15/87	4.425	−4.425	(6-mo LIBOR + 34.9)/2	(6-mo LIBOR + 34.9)/2
2/15/88	4.425	−4.425	(6-mo LIBOR + 34.9)/2	(6-mo LIBOR + 34.9)/2
•	•	•	•	•
•	•	•	•	•
•	•	•	•	•
2/15/96	4.425	−4.425	(6-mo LIBOR + 34.9)/2	(6-mo LIBOR + 34.9)/2
8/15/96	104.425	−4.425	(6-mo LIBOR + 34.9)/2	(6-mo LIBOR + 34.9)/2

IRR on Synthetic Asset: LIBOR + 34.9 bp

EXHIBIT 10
CASH FLOWS ON FULL FIXED RATE COUPON FROM INVESTOR'S PERSPECTIVE

Amount =	5.09%
Maturity =	8/15/96 (18.25 periods)
Reinvestment Rate =	8.30%
6/30/87	−5.09%
8/15/87	+.4112%
2/15/88	+.4112%
•	•
•	•
•	•
2/15/96	+.4112%
8/15/96	+.4112%

The up front receipt of principal is a self-amortizing payment to the investor as shown in Exhibit 10. The two semiannual payments for the loan would be subtracted (.4112 + .4112 = .8223) from the level at which the investor would pay fixed (9.30%) versus receiving LIBOR flat to arrive at the rate (8.478%) at which the investor would pay fixed versus receiving LIBOR flat.

Adjustment Swap Using Interest Rate Swaps: Zero Coupon Swapped to Floating Coupon

An investor is shown an attractively priced zero coupon issue and wants to invest in this issue, but only if it can float to 3/6-month LIBOR. A swap dealer shows the trade on page 422.

The swap dealer will reinvest the 60.05%, or $3,025,000, on the $5,000,000 notional amount at 9.30% and pay the customer LIBOR + 42.69 basis points. The swap flows would be as shown in Exhibit 11.

The up front receipt of principal is a self-amortizing payment to the investor as shown in Exhibit 12. Note that the investor could receive a fixed coupon of 9.78% (4.864 x 2), which is equivalent to receiving 6-month LIBOR +42.69 basis points.

Adjustment Swap Using Interest Rate Swaps: Discount Floating Coupon Swapped to Full Floating Coupon

An investor is shown an attractive floating rate note that is trading at a discount. The investor, however, wants current income and thus wants to buy the bonds at par and receive the current market YTM spread. Suppose a swap dealer is willing to receive

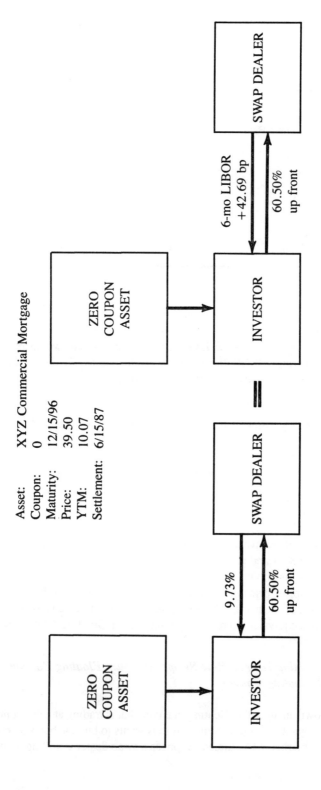

EXHIBIT 11
ASSET AND SWAP FLOWS FROM INVESTOR'S PERSPECTIVE

Period	Asset	Swap Fixed Flows	Swap Floating Flows	Net
6/15/87	(−39.50) + (−60.50)			−100.00
12/15/87	0	●	(6-mo LIBOR + 42.69 bp)/2	(6-mo LIBOR + 42.69 bp)/2
⋮	●	●	●	●
	●	●	●	●
12/15/95	0	●	(6-mo LIBOR + 42.69 bp)/2	(6-mo LIBOR + 42.69 bp)/2
6/15/96	100.00	●	(6-mo LIBOR + 42.69 bp)/2	100 + (6-mo LIBOR + 42.69 bp)/2

IRR on Synthetic Asset: LIBOR + 42.69 bp

EXHIBIT 12
CASH FLOWS ON FULL FLOATING RATE COUPON
SPREAD FROM INVESTOR'S PERSPECTIVE

Reinvestment Rate:	9.30%
Number of Payments:	19
6/15/87	−60.50%
12/15/87	+4.864%
•	•
•	•
•	•
12/15/95	+4.864%
6/15/96	+4.864%

the difference between par and the discount price and will in turn pay the investor the yield equivalent of this dollar price differential. The swap is summarized below:

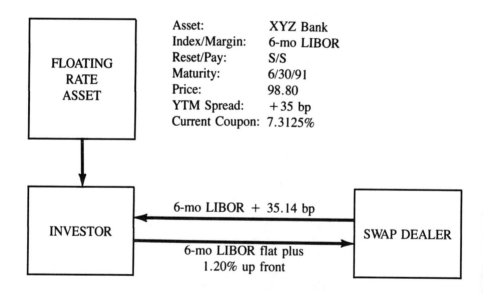

Asset:	XYZ Bank
Index/Margin:	6-mo LIBOR
Reset/Pay:	S/S
Maturity:	6/30/91
Price:	98.80
YTM Spread:	+35 bp
Current Coupon:	7.3125%

The swap dealer will receive 100% − 98.80% or $60,000 on a $5 million transaction. Again, assuming a reinvestment rate of 8.80%, the flows would be as shown in Exhibit 13. The investor would annually receive 6-month LIBOR +35.14 basis points (.1757 x 2) over the life of the asset.

EXHIBIT 13
CASH FLOWS OF FLOATING RATE COUPON FROM INVESTOR'S PERSPECTIVE

Reinvestment Rate:	8.80%
Number of Payments:	8
6/30/87	−1.20%
12/31/87	+.1757%
6/30/88	+.1757%
•	•
•	•
•	•
12/31/91	+.1757%
6/30/92	+.1757%

IRR on Synthetic Asset: LIBOR + 35.14 bp

Amortizing Swap Using Interest Rate Swaps

An investor wants floating rate LIBOR-based assets at various spreads and maturities. A swap dealer has lead managed a substantial number of asset backed securities and actively makes a secondary market in the product. The dealer's asset swap desk constantly monitors trading levels of numerous securities and has noticed an opportunity with an asset backed security in the secondary market. Suppose the asset swap desk proposes the following transaction:

Asset:
- Security: Credit Card Receivables
- Size: $400 MM
- Coupon: 6.90% (semi 30/360)
- Ratings: AAA/AAA
- Payment: Monthly with a 2-week delay
- Lockout period: Interest only for 18 months
- Principal: Commences in period 19 until the principal is fully amortized.
- Payment Rate: 21.72% monthly (assumed)
- Average Life: 21.5 months
- Final Maturity: 23.5 months

Using an 18%, 21.72%, and 25% payment rate, the notes would amortize principal at the following levels:

Swap Period	Coupon Period	18%	Benchmark Payment Rate 21.72%	25%
#1	#19	$ 66.65mm	$ 81.53mm	$ 94.65mm
#2	#20	66.65mm	81.53mm	94.65mm
#3	#21	66.65mm	81.53mm	94.65mm
#4	#22	66.65mm	81.53mm	94.65mm
#5	#23	66.65mm	73.88mm	21.40mm
#6	#24	66.65mm	---	---
#7	#25	.10mm	---	---
		$400.00mm	$400.00mm	$400.00mm

Under the assumed 21.72% pay rate, the swap dealer would create an amortizing swap to cover periods 19-23, as shown below.

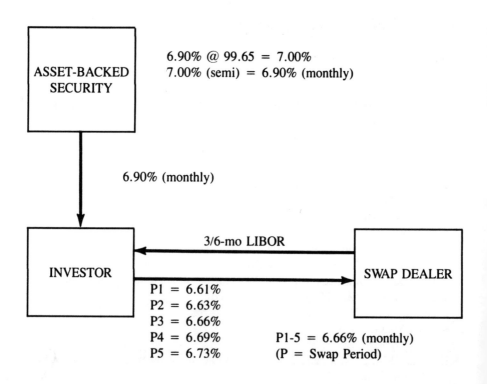

ASSET-BACKED SECURITY

6.90% @ 99.65 = 7.00%
7.00% (semi) = 6.90% (monthly)

6.90% (monthly)

INVESTOR

3/6-mo LIBOR

SWAP DEALER

P1 = 6.61%
P2 = 6.63%
P3 = 6.66%
P4 = 6.69%   P1-5 = 6.66% (monthly)
P5 = 6.73%   (P = Swap Period)

The fixed rate amortizing asset pays interest only for periods 1-18. After period 18 principal and interest are paid on an uncertain schedule. However, payment assumptions can be made as noted in the 18%, 21.72%, and 25% scenarios.

An investor wants to convert the fixed rate coupon to a floating rate LIBOR based coupon. From a cash flow perspective, the investor has to make an assumption about the payment flows (the payment rate scenario of 21.72% was used in this example). The next step is for the investor to look at his fixed rate flows using the market and issue levels mentioned above.

The fixed rate cash flows on a $5 million investment based on 6.90% monthly would be as shown in Exhibit 14. As the $5 million investment is assumed to follow this amortization schedule, the investor would commit to floating the fixed flows by paying the swap dealer a fixed rate and receiving 3/6-month LIBOR. The swap dealer will receive fixed at five different time intervals.

The swap dealer will receive five fixed rate flows for periods 1-19 (6.61%), 1-20 (6.66%), 1-22 (6.69%), 1-23 (6.73%) at a weighted level of 6.66% (monthly). Thus the investor will receive 6.90% and pay 6.66%, netting .24%.

The risk is that the amortization of the asset does *not* follow the 21.72% payment rate. Thus, the asset life could either be longer or shorter than the terms of the swap. A sensitivity analysis using 18% and 25% payment rates (both are outside the historical payment rates), however, would show the following:

SURPLUS/SHORTFALL vs 21.72%

	Payment Rate Scenario	
	18%	25%
Period 19 (Shortfall)/Surplus	$14.88mm	$(13.12mm)
20	14.88mm	(13.12mm)
21	14.88mm	(13.12mm)
22	14.88mm	(13.12mm)
23	7.23mm	52.48mm
24	(66.65mm)	
25	(.10mm)	

Since the swap expired before the asset paid down under the 18% payment rate scenario, the investor, who is no longer receiving a floating rate (LIBOR flat) on the swap, would need to borrow to carry the asset. The sensitivity analysis assumes that the investor finances the remaining asset at LIBOR + 200 basis points. The mirror of this would be the 25% payment rate scenario in which the asset will pay down more quickly than the swap leaving the investor with the need to invest the swap flows into an asset. The assumption is that the investor invests at LIBOR − 200 basis points. In both cases the investor's return over LIBOR was reduced by only 5 basis points to LIBOR + 19 basis points as shown below:

EXHIBIT 14

Period	1-19	1-20	1-21	1-22	1-23	TOTAL
0	-$1,019,125.00	-$1,019,125.00	-$1,019,125.00	-$1,019,125.00	-$923,500.00	-$5,000,000.00
1	+5,859.97	+5,859.97	+5,859.97	+5,859.97	+5,310.13	28,750.00
2	+5,859.97	+5,859.97	+5,859.97	+5,859.97	+5,310.13	28,750.00
3	+5,859.97	+5,859.97	+5,859.97	+5,859.97	+5,310.13	28,750.00
•	•	•	•	•	•	•
19	+1,024,984.97					
20		+1,024,984.97				
21			+1,024,984.97			
22				+1,024,984.97		
23					+928,810.13	+5,028,750.00

SENSITIVITY ANALYSIS
(spread to LIBOR)

	Payment Rate Scenario:		
	18%	21.72%	25%
LIBOR + 200 bp	+ 19bp	—	—
LIBOR + 0 bp	—	+ 24bp	—
LIBOR − 200 bp	—	—	+ 19bp

Swaption Using Interest Rate Swaps and OTC Options

An investor wants to invest in a 7- to 10-year synthetic floating rate commercial mortgage. The synthetic floating rate spreads to LIBOR are generous; however, the investor does *not* want to take *any* prepayment risk. The asset swap desk of a dealer says that there are no non-callable commercial mortgages available, but proposes the following transaction:

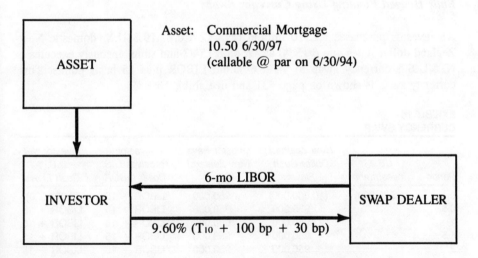

Asset: Commercial Mortgage
10.50 6/30/97
(callable @ par on 6/30/94)

T_{10} = 8.30%

This transaction allows the investor to neutralize the issuer's call option on the commercial mortgage by paying the swap dealer 30 basis points to buy a call option on the swap. Therefore, if interest rates dropped dramatically and the issuer calls the commercial mortgage on 4/15/94, the investor can call the swap back from the swap dealer. Exhibit 15 shows the investor's swap flows.

EXHIBIT 15
ASSET AND SWAP FLOWS FROM INVESTOR'S PERSPECTIVE

Period	Commercial Mortgage Asset Flows	Swap Fixed Flows	Swap Floating Flows	Net
6/30/87	−100	—	—	−100
12/31/87	+5.25	−4.80	6-mo LIBOR/2	6-mo LIBOR/2 + .45
•	•	•	•	•
•	•	•	•	•
•	•	•	•	•
6/30/94*	+5.25	−4.80	6-mo LIBOR/2	6-mo LIBOR/2 + .45
•	•	•	•	•
•	•	•	•	•
•	•	•	•	•
12/31/96	+5.25	−4.80	6-mo LIBOR/2	6-mo LIBOR/2 + .45
6/30/97	+105.75	−4.80	6-mo LIBOR/2	6-mo LIBOR/2 + 100.45

IRR on Synthetic Asset: LIBOR + 90 bp

* If call is exercised by issuer, investor calls swap from swap dealer @ 100.

Fully Hedged Floating Using Currency Swaps

An investor purchases NZ$10 million of XYZ Corp. 19% U.S. domestic New Zealand dollar notes due 6/15/90 at par on 6/15/87 and simultaneously executes a NZ$/U.S.$ currency swap to yield 6-month LIBOR plus 15 basis points. This currency swap is shown on page 431 and in Exhibit 16.[4]

EXHIBIT 16
CURRENCY SWAP

Period	US $ Investment	New Zealand Dollar Cash Flows	Investor Pays New Zealand Dollars	Investor Receives U.S. Dollar LIBOR	Investor Net U.S. $ Cash Flows
0	(5,800,000)	(10,000,000)	950,000	LIBOR + 15	(5,800,000)
0.5		950,000	950,000	LIBOR + 15	LIBOR + 15
1		950,000	950,000	LIBOR + 15	LIBOR + 15
1.5		950,000	950,000	LIBOR + 15	LIBOR + 15
2		950,000	950,000	LIBOR + 15	LIBOR + 15
2.5		950,000	10,950,000	LIBOR + 15	LIBOR + 15
3		10,950,000			5,800,000

IRR (S/A)	9.762%
IRR (ANN)	10.000%

IRR on Synthetic Asset: LIBOR + 15 bp

---

[4]Investors who want to fix these floating U.S.$ LIBOR flows can use interest rate swaps as explained later in this chapter.

1. Interest Payments

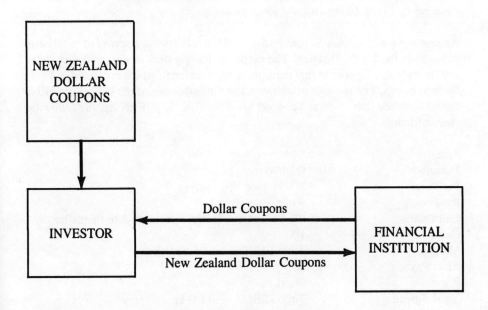

2. Principal Repayment

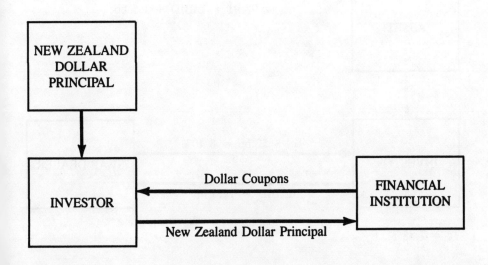

CREATING SYNTHETIC FIXED RATE ASSETS

Floating to Fixed Using Interest Rate Swaps

An investor wants a AAA Sovereign 5-year fixed rate asset at a spread of + 60 basis points over the 5-year Treasury. The corporate trading desk of a swap dealer states that the only AAA-paper in that maturity is supranational, which is offered at Tc + 50 basis points. The dealer's asset swap desk finds that one of the U.K. Euro FRNs can be swapped into fixed at Tc + 66 bp. This U.K. Euro FRN has the following characteristics:

Size:	$4 billion
Maturity:	9/24/96
Put Date:	9/1/91 (one time only)
Put Price:	99.25
Call Date:	9/1/91 and any interest payment date thereafter
Call Price:	100
Margin:	3-mo LIBID − 12.5 bp
Reset/Pay:	Q/Q
Price:	98.91
YTM Spread:	3-mo LIBOR − 11.0 bp

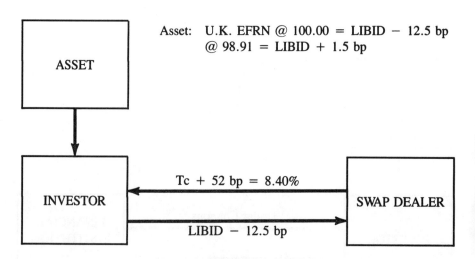

Asset: U.K. EFRN @ 100.00 = LIBID − 12.5 bp
@ 98.91 = LIBID + 1.5 bp

Tc = 7.88%

EXHIBIT 17
ASSET AND SWAP FLOWS FROM INVESTOR'S PERSPECTIVE

| | | Swap Flows | | |
Period	U.K. Asset Flows*	Swap Fixed Inflows	Swap Floating Outflows	Net
6/30/87	−98.91	—	—	−98.91
9/21/87	(3-mo LIBID-12.5/4)	8.40/2	−(3-mo LIBID-12.5/4)	4.20
•	•	•	•	•
•	•	•	•	•
•	•	•	•	•
9/01/91	(3-mo LIBID-12.5/4) + 99.25	8.40/2	−(3-mo LIBID-12.5/4)	103.45

IRR on Synthetic Asset: 8.40% (Tc + 52 bp)

* Assumes issue trades on 9/1/91 at 99.25.

The asset and swap flows from the investor's perspective are summarized in Exhibit 17. The investor will essentially pass on the U.K. coupon to the swap dealer, receive 8.40%, plus accrete 14 basis points or the difference between LIBOR − 11 basis points and LIBID − 12.5 basis points. Thus a return spread of +52 basis points plus + 14 basis points, or +66 basis points will be generated. Note that the U.K. floater pays quarterly and that the fixed rate flows are semiannual.

Floating to Fixed Using Interest Rate Futures

An investor wants to invest $5 million in an A-rated regional bank fixed rate asset maturing in 2 years at a spread of plus 70 basis points to the 2-year Treasury. Neither the corporate trading nor the medium-term note desks of a swap dealer can find any paper at those spread levels. The asset swap desk, however, discovers that by combining a 2-year FRCD with the purchase of a strip of futures a 2-year fixed rate asset can synthetically be created, as described in Exhibit 18.

The investor would buy the 8 Eurodollar futures contracts and combine this with the purchase of a 2-year Signet/Virginia FRCD at 3-month LIBOR flat. In order to minimize any mismatches, the swap dealer would try to have the payment dates on the FRCD coincide with the maturities of each of the Eurodollar futures contracts. Additionally, in this example the settlement date of the FRCD is the same day as the expiration of the front (June) contract; thus, there is no stub period to account for.

Gap Swap Using Interest Rate Swaps

An investor has a liability maturing in June 1991 that costs 9.00% (T4 = 8.00%). With this fixed cost at 4-year Treasuries + 100 basis points this investor is looking for an A-rated fixed rate investment at 4-year Treasuries plus 140 to 150 basis points (9.40% to 9.60%). Since no A-rated paper due in 6/91 trades at Tc + 70 basis

EXHIBIT 18

Asset:	Signet/Virginia FRCD
Ratings:	A₂/A
Maturity:	6/21/89
Margin:	Flat
Reset/Pay:	Q/Q
Price:	Par
Settlement Date:	6/15/87
Tc:	7.50%

EURODOLLAR FUTURES CONTRACTS

		Price	Yield
Sep 87	Contract	92.88	7.12
Dec	Contract	92.54	7.46
Mar 88	Contract	92.22	7.78
Jun	Contract	91.97	8.03
Sep	Contract	91.75	8.25
Dec	Contract	91.57	8.43
Mar 89	Contract	91.40	8.60
Jun	Contract	91.29	8.71

IRR on Synthetic Asset: 8.215% (Tc + 71.5 bp)*

* Assumes that the cost of money for variation margin calls washes between excess and debit.

points, a swap dealer proposes that the investor consider buying a floating rate note maturing in June 2000 that is trading at a steep discount to par but is callable at any coupon refix at par. The details are shown on page 435.

There are, however, the following risks to this transaction:

(1) The FRNs could be called at any coupon refix at par. Since the issue trades at 95.00, a call at par would seem extremely unlikely. However, one could run a scenario analysis for return levels at various points in time and assume asset replacement or liability (swap) replacement levels. Making 5.00 points on this trade, however, would certainly be welcome.

(2) If the FRN is not called prior to the maturity of the swap, then the investor is left outright with a FRN that has 9 years left to maturity. The uncertainty is what to do with this asset. If the note is not called the investor can either sell the asset or enter into another interest rate swap for any part of the remaining life of the FRN asset.

What follows is an analysis of three possible rates of return cash flows resulting from three different scenarios of this gap swap.

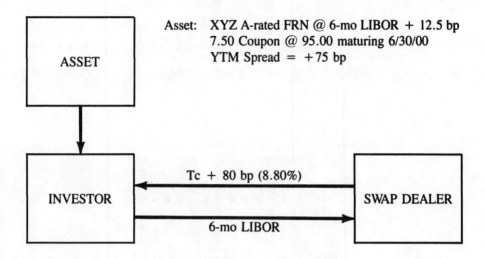

Asset: XYZ A-rated FRN @ 6-mo LIBOR + 12.5 bp
7.50 Coupon @ 95.00 maturing 6/30/00
YTM Spread = +75 bp

Tc = 8.00%

Scenario #1: "XYZ" FRN is called at par on 6/30/89. The investor decides to reinvest proceeds in a 2-year non call A-rated FRCD with a LIBOR flat coupon, and continue to receive 8.80% on the existing swap. This is shown in Exhibit 19.

The return characteristics for this scenario are an 8.80% fixed return for 2 years, the asset FRN margin of 12.5 basis points, plus the profit of 5.00 points on the called FRNs (100-95.00). This is equivalent to buying a fixed rate instrument with a coupon of 8.925% (8.80 + .125) at a discount of 95.00. After 2 years this 8.925 @ 95.00 would be called at par, and the proceeds reinvested in a LIBOR flat FRN @ par receiving 8.80. The combined cash flows of these two transactions would provide an IRR of 10.43%, or Tc (8.00%) + 243 basis points.

Scenario #2: "XYZ" FRN is not called and the swap matures. The FRN is bid for at 92.00. The investor decides to sell the FRN and close out the gap swap. The asset and swap flows from the investor's perspective are shown in Exhibit 20.

The return characteristics from this scenario are an 8.925% (8.80 + .125) fixed return plus a loss of 3 points on the sale of the FRN at the maturity of the swap. The total IRR to the investor is 8.72%. Thus the investor would net a spread of only +72 basis points to the Treasury curve (Tc = 8.00%).

Scenario #3: "XYZ" FRN is not called and the swap matures. The FRN is bid for at 98.00. The investor decides to "roll over" this transaction for another 4 years at

EXHIBIT 19
ASSET AND SWAP FLOWS FROM INVESTOR'S PERSPECTIVE

Period	XYZ FRN Asset Flows	Swap Flows		Net
		Swap Fixed Flows	Swap Floating Flows	
6/30/87	−95.00			−95.00
12/31/87	(6-mo LIBID + 12.5bp)/2	—	(−6-mo LIBOR)/2	+.125/2 + 4.40
• • •	• • •	• • •	• • •	• • •
6/30/89	(6-mo LIBOR + 12.5 bp)/2 + 100	8.80/2	(−6-mo LIBOR)/2	104.40 + .125/2
6/30/89	−100.00	8.80/2		−100.00
12/31/89	(6-mo LIBOR)/2	8.80/2	(−6-mo LIBOR)/2	4.40
• • •	• • •	• • •	• • •	• • •
6/30/91	(6-mo LIBOR)/2 + 100	8.80/2	(−6-mo LIBOR)/2	104.40

IRR on Synthetic Asset: 10.43% (Tc + 243 bp)

EXHIBIT 20
ASSET AND SWAP FLOWS FROM INVESTOR'S PERSPECTIVE

| | XYZ FRN | Swap Flows | | |
| | | Swap Fixed | Swap Floating | |
Period	Asset Flows	Flows	Flows	Net
6/30/87	−95.00	—	—	−95.00
12/31/87	(6-mo LIBOR + 12.5 bp)/2	8.80/2	(−6-mo LIBOR)/2	+.125/2 + 4.40
•••	•••	•••	•••	•••
12/31/90	(6-mo LIBOR + 12.5 bp)/2	8.80/2	(−6-mo LIBOR)/2	+.125/2 + 4.40
6/30/91	(6-mo LIBOR + 12.5 bp)/2 + 92	8.80/2	(−6-mo LIBOR)/2	+.125/2 + 4.40 + 92.00

IRR on Synthetic Asset: 8.72% (Tc + 72 bp)

EXHIBIT 21
ASSET AND SWAP FLOWS FROM INVESTOR'S PERSPECTIVE

Period	XYZ FRN Asset Flows	Swap Flows		Net
		Swap Fixed Flows	Swap Floating Flows	
6/30/87	−95.00	—	—	−95.00
12/30/87	(6-mo LIBOR + 12.5 bp)/2	8.80/2	(−6-mo LIBOR)/2	+4.40 + .125/2
•	•	•	•	•
•	•	•	•	•
•	•	•	•	•
12/31/90	(6-mo LIBOR + 12.5 bp)/2	8.80/2	(−6-mo LIBOR)/2	+ 4.40 + .125/2
6/30/91	(6-mo LIBOR + 12.5 bp)/2 + 98.00	8.80/2	(−6-mo LIBOR)/2	102.40 + .125/2

IRR on synthetic asset: 10.06% (Tc + 206 bp)

the then market swap levels (these future swap levels are neither given nor calculated). From the investor's perspective, the asset and swap flows would be as shown in Exhibit 21.

A *sensitivity analysis* of the three scenarios indicates the following:

	IRR	SPREAD TO Tc (8.00%)
Scenario #1	10.43%	+243 bp
Scenario #2	8.72	+72
Scenario #3	10.06	+206

A price/return sensitivity analysis (at 6/30/91) would reveal the following:

Price Variation		Return Variation	Spread to Tc (8.00%)
+ 5.00	(100.00)	10.49%	+249 bp
+ 4.00	(99.00)	10.27	+227
+ 3.00	(98.00)	10.06	+206
+ 2.00	(97.00)	9.84	+184
+ 1.00	(96.00)	9.62	+162
+ 0	(95.00)	9.39	+139
− 1.00	(94.00)	9.17	+117
− 2.00	(93.00)	8.95	+95
− 3.00	(92.00)	8.72	+72
− 4.00	(91.00)	8.49	+49
− 5.00	(90.00)	8.26	+26

Adjustment Swap Using Interest Rate Swaps: Zero Coupon Swapped to Full Fixed Coupon

An investor is shown an attractive zero coupon 5-year note but wants a shorter duration and cash flow. A dealer's asset swap desk says that it will receive the zero flows and pay a full current coupon. This swap is summarized on the top of page 440.

The economics are based on the swap dealer's reinvestment assumptions. In this example, the investor pays the swap dealer 36.00% on an assumed $5 million investment. Using an 8.80% reinvestment rate (the Treasury rate plus the swap spread), the swap dealer will pay the investor on an amortizing basis every 6 months for 5 years. The investor would annually receive 9.05% (4.527% x 2). The cash flows would look as shown in Exhibit 22.

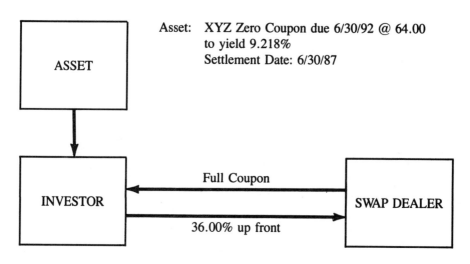

Asset: XYZ Zero Coupon due 6/30/92 @ 64.00
to yield 9.218%
Settlement Date: 6/30/87

$T_5 = 8.00\%$

EXHIBIT 22
CASH FLOWS ON FULL FIXED COUPON FROM INVESTOR'S PERSPECTIVE

Reinvestment Rate: 8.80%
Number of Payments: 10

6/30/87	−36.00%
12/31/87	+4.527%
6/30/88	+4.527%
•	•
•	•
•	•
12/31/91	+4.527%
6/30/92	+4.527%

IRR on Synthetic Asset: 9.05%

Double Swap Using Interest Rate Swaps

FASB 87 requires the assets and liabilities of pension funds to be marked to market annually. Most pension funds have assets with durations that are shorter than their liabilities. With the annual mark-to-market provision, the earnings volatility of the corporate parent could increase. Given this situation, a portfolio manager might want to extend asset duration in order to minimize the volatility of plan expense. Suppose a dealer recommends a number of alternatives. One of these, shown below, involves the double swap that an asset swap desk can create and execute.

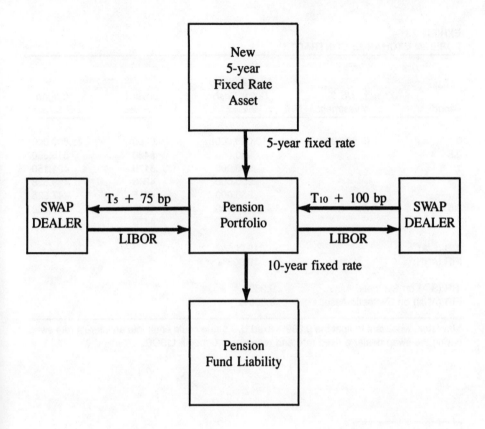

In the first 5 years, the pension fund will pay a fixed amount to the swap dealer of T_5 + 75 basis points and receive 3/6-month LIBOR. In the second 5 years, the pension fund will be left with a 5-year swap in which it will receive fixed at T_{10} + 100 basis points and pay 3/6-month LIBOR. The benefit will come from having a longer duration and from picking up 25 basis points on the swap curve plus picking up on a positively sloped Treasury curve.

Fully Hedged Fixed Using Currency Forwards

An investor purchases NZ$10 million of XYZ Corp. 19% U.S. domestic New Zealand dollar notes due 6/15/90 at par on 6/15/87. The investor purchases NZ$ in the spot foreign exchange market in order to purchase these securities and simultaneously contracts to sell the NZ$ coupon payments and principal repayment of the

EXHIBIT 23
FOREIGN EXCHANGE CONTRACTS

Period	US $ Investment	New Zealand Dollar Cash Flows	Forward FX Rates	Hedged US $ Asset
0	(5,800,000)	(10,000,000)	.5800	(5,800,000)
0.5		950,000	.5430	515,850
1		950,000	.5170	491,150
1.5		950,000	.4943	469,538
2		950,000	.4715	447,925
2.5		950,000	.4593	436,288
3		10,950,000	.4470	4,894,650
IRR (S/A)		19.000%		
IRR (ANN)		19.903%		
IRR (S/A) on Synthetic Asset:		9.289%*		
IRR (ANN) on Synthetic Asset:		9.505%		

* Investors who want to float the 9.289% fixed U.S.$ rate could enter into an interest rate swap, paying the swap dealer a fixed rate and receiving 3/6-month LIBOR.

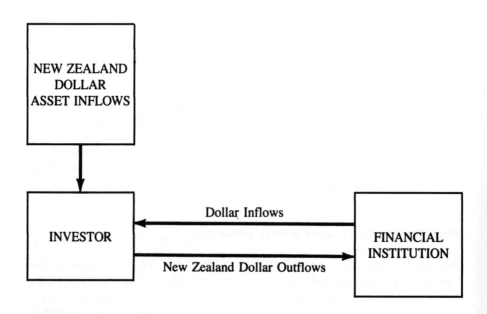

notes in the forward foreign exchange market for dollars to yield 9.289% semi-annually (Treasuries plus 100 basis points).[5] This transaction is summarized below and in Exhibit 23.

Fully Hedged Fixed Using Currency Swaps

As noted in the previous sections, an investor can convert a fixed rate NZ$10 million XYZ Corp. 19% U.S. domestic New Zealand dollar notes due 6/15/90 at par on 6/15/87 to U.S.$ LIBOR. An investor can also swap this issue from U.S.$ LIBOR to U.S.$ fixed, as shown in Exhibit 24.

---

[5]All future New Zealand dollar asset flows are sold at different exchange rates reflecting New Zealand dollar/U.S. dollar interest rate differentials.

EXHIBIT 24

(A) CURRENCY SWAP

Period	US $ Investment	New Zealand Dollar Cash Flows	Investor Pays New Zealand Dollars	Investor Receives U.S. Dollar LIBOR	Investor Net U.S. $ Cash Flows
0	(5,800,000)	(10,000,000)			(5,800,000)
0.5		950,000	950,000	LIBOR + 15	LIBOR + 15
1		950,000	950,000	LIBOR + 15	LIBOR + 15
1.5		950,000	950,000	LIBOR + 15	LIBOR + 15
2		950,000	950,000	LIBOR + 15	LIBOR + 15
2.5		950,000	950,000	LIBOR + 15	LIBOR + 15
3		10,950,000	10,950,000	LIBOR + 15	5,800,000

IRR (S/A) 9.762%
IRR (ANN) 10.000%

IRR on Synthetic Asset: LIBOR + 15 bp

(B) INTEREST RATE SWAP

Period	Investor Pays U.S. $ LIBOR	Investor Receives Fixed U.S. $	Investor Net U.S. $ Cash Flow
0			(5,800,000)
0.5	(LIBOR + 15)	269,410	269,410
1	(LIBOR + 15)	269,410	269,410
1.5	(LIBOR + 15)	269,410	269,410
2	(LIBOR + 15)	269,410	269,410
2.5	(LIBOR + 15)	269,410	269,410
3	(LIBOR + 15)	269,410	6,069,410

IRR (S/A) on Synthetic Asset: 9.290%
IRR (ANN) on Synthetic Asset: 9.506%

Chapter 21

Capping the Interest Rate Risk in Insurance Products

DAVID F. BABBEL, PH.D.
VICE PRESIDENT
GOLDMAN, SACHS & CO.
AND
ASSOCIATE PROFESSOR
WHARTON SCHOOL
UNIVERSITY OF PENNSYLVANIA

PETER BOUYOUCOS
ASSOCIATE
GOLDMAN, SACHS & CO.

ROBERT STRICKER
VICE PRESIDENT
GOLDMAN, SACHS & CO.

KEEPING RISK UNDER A CAP

During the past several years, interest rate caps have been increasingly sought by insurers. An interest rate cap is an agreement that provides protection against rising rates by making a payment to the holder when rates exceed a specified level. In this

The authors are grateful for helpful comments from Fischer Black, Artur Walther, Robert Kopprasch, Tom Montag, Mark Godin, Ron Krieger, Irwin Vanderhoof, and Andrew McKee.

chapter, we consider cap valuation and how cap strategies apply to other insurance products, such as SPDAs (single premium deferred annuities), universal life, and single premium life.[1] All these products contain an investment element, and the insurer has written a put option allowing policyholders to cash out of their policies based on book value rather than market value. An expected future cost has been incurred once the option is written, regardless of whether the insurer charges for it or chooses to hedge the risk associated with it.

In addition to these options on the liability side of the balance sheet, insurers also write options on the asset side in the form of callable corporate bonds and mortgage securities. This combination of options typically places insurers in a short straddle position, as we described in a recent paper on asset/liability management.[2] Economically, they are worse off if rates move too far in either direction. Because these options are often written out-of-the-money, and because book value accounting tends to mask the underlying economics, insurers were comfortable with a short straddle in the past when markets were less volatile. However, as volatility has increased, as policyholders have become more sophisticated, and as competition has become keener, insurers more than ever before now need to consider hedging their economic surplus against sudden, dramatic shifts in interest rates. This is especially pertinent to insurers doing business in New York because, as a result of Regulation 126, insurers are required to demonstrate the adequacy of their reserves under different interest rate scenarios.

The dramatic growth in recent years of interest rate sensitive products makes it especially important for insurers to adopt an effective asset/liability management strategy. To offer competitive yields, the insurer typically feels a need to extend out along the yield curve. The policyholder is generally given the option, however, to cash out early at predetermined surrender values. While early cashouts are not expected to be a problem for moderate increases in interest rates, a sudden spike in interest rates, especially in conjunction with an inverted yield curve, could create a serious surplus strain from these products.

A simulation of results for a typical SPDA product serves to illustrate the impact of interest rate volatility. Exhibit 1 shows accumulated surplus over 5, 10, 15, and 20 years, based on 40 random interest rate scenarios,[3] and also using the 7 scenarios

---

[1] In an earlier paper on caps for insurers, we described how interest rate caps could be used to hedge the lapse and policy loan risk on whole life policies. See David F. Babbel, "Capping the Risks of Life Insurance Policy Loans and Lapses," *Insurance Perspectives,* November 1986, Goldman, Sachs & Co.

[2] David F. Babbel, and Robert Stricker, "Asset/Liability Management for Insurers," *Insurance Perspectives,* May 1987, Goldman, Sachs & Co.

[3] The 40 random scenarios were generated by a two-factor equilibrium model of the term structure of interest rates originally proposed by Michael Brennan and Eduardo Schwartz in "A Continuous Approach to the Pricing of Bonds," *Journal of Banking and Finance,* 1979, pp. 133-155. They are considered more consistent with economic principles than the rather arbitrary New York Seven Scenarios. However, a more precise simulation would include several thousands of scenarios. The scenarios and SPDA analyses were provided by Tillinghast, and are used with its kind permission. Goldman Sachs performed the cap analysis using identical scenarios.

EXHIBIT 1
COMPARISON OF ACCUMULATED SPDA SURPLUS AND CAP PAYOFF

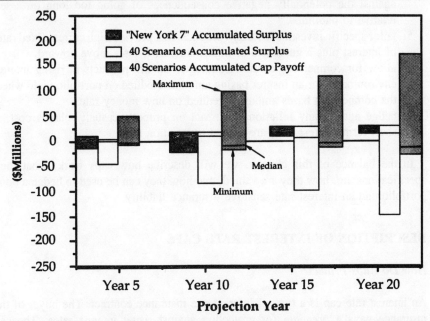

suggested by New York Regulation 126 for comparison. While the upside is comparable using both sets of assumptions, the 40-scenario simulation clearly illustrates the downside risk that stems from granting options in a volatile interest rate environment. Important to note is the ability of caps to hedge this downside risk. The cap payoff can be managed so as to offset the negative surplus impact of high interest rate scenarios.

As Exhibit 1 indicates, interest rate caps appear to offer one solution to help hedge products with policyholder options against a large increase in interest rates. Consequently, we anticipate that purchases of these instruments by insurers will increase.

Among the many potential applications of interest rate caps, insurers can use them to:

1. hedge against book value cashouts and adverse selection on interest rate sensitive products because of rising interest rates.
2. hedge against the risk of rising policy loan usage on traditional, fixed-loan-rate whole life policies.
3. offset a portion of the "negative convexity" risk of certain assets, such as high coupon collateral P.O.'s (principal only strips), that may suffer from a slowdown in prepayments when rates are high.

4. protect a portfolio against an upward shift in interest rates, while allowing it to capture the upside of long bond returns if interest rates decline—i.e., protect against the potentially negative consequences of going too long on assets relative to liabilities.

5. tailor specific investment-related products that provide high current fixed rates of interest plus a guarantee of higher interest if rates move upward.

6. allow for competitive crediting strategies on life products in rising interest environments for an insurer basing amounts credited on portfolio yield where the competition bases amounts credited on new money rates.

7. hedge against any inflationary impact on property-casualty claims cost, if short-term interest rates are related to inflation rates.

In the balance of this chapter, we will describe how caps work; what their specifications are, how they are valued, and how they can be used to hedge a bond portfolio and an interest rate sensitive insurance liability.

DESCRIPTION OF INTEREST RATE CAPS

How Do Caps Protect?

An interest rate cap is a type of interest rate insurance contract. The buyer of the insurance pays a *premium* for protection against rising interest rates. The cap provides this protection in two different ways.

First, the buyer of an interest rate cap will receive payments from the seller, to the extent that the underlying interest rate index rises above a prespecified trigger level. The difference between this trigger level and the initial market level of rates can be thought of as the *deductible*. The greater the difference, the larger the deductible. This implies less protection and hence lower cost. For example, if interest rates are currently 8% and a 10% cap is purchased, rates would need to rise 2 percentage points before any payments would be received from the cap. If a 12% cap were purchased, rates would have to increase by 4 percentage points before any payments were received. Naturally, the 10% cap costs more than the 12% cap because the buyer is receiving more protection. As with any insurance contract, the tradeoff between premium, amount of protection, and deductible is a function of your risk profile. The more risk averse you are, the greater the protection that you should purchase, and the lower the deductible should be.

Payment protection is available with a specified frequency, such as quarterly, that corresponds to the buyer's particular liabilities. Cap payments, for example, can be used to credit higher dividends to policyholders when rates rise, thereby making existing policies more attractive and reducing lapses and withdrawals.

The second form of protection—market value protection—arises from the fact that caps are marketable instruments. An interest rate cap will increase in value with the level of interest rates. This is particularly useful in situations where liabilities can be "put" back to the insurer in high interest rate environments. The gain from the sale of the cap can offset a portion of the loss on currently held assets, which may need to be liquidated to fund the unplanned payout on the liability. The gain will also help reduce the need to use new cash flows to retire old liabilities.

Both of these features, payment protection and market value protection, are very important to life insurance companies.

Cap Contract Specifications

Interest rate caps, like other over-the-counter instruments, can be custom-tailored to the particular needs of different buyers. By combining the various specifications, you can design virtually any level and pattern of protection (see Exhibit 2). The attributes you may specify include:

Underlying Index Underlying indexes may include LIBOR, commercial paper, U.S. Treasury bills, and the prime rate. LIBOR and commercial paper caps are the most prevalent. The index will typically have a term of 1, 3, or 6 months.

Frequency of Reset of Index The frequency of reset and the term of the index need not be identical, although generally they are. For instance, you could create a cap for a liability that floats off 3-month LIBOR and is repriced monthly. The determination of cap payments is made only on the actual reset dates. Reset periods range from daily to annually. When the reset dates are more frequent than the payment dates, the payment will be calculated based on the average of the underlying index on the reset dates.

Timing of Cap Payment Cap payments are typically made in arrears. For example, a standard 3-month LIBOR cap would have resets beginning on the effective date and ending 3 months prior to the maturity date. Payments on the cap would occur on each succeeding reset date (i.e., starting 3 months after the effective date and ending on the maturity date).

EXHIBIT 2
INTEREST RATE CAP CONTRACTS: SUMMARY OF FEATURES

1. Contract Type	Over-the-Counter
2. Underlying Index	LIBOR, CP, T-Bills, Prime (1-, 3-, 6-Month Rates)
3. Index Reset	Daily to Annually Over Term
4. Term of Contract	3 Months to 12 Years
5. Strike Level	Desired Index Level
6. Payment—Upfront	% of Notional Amount
—Amortized	Level Payment Over Entire Term

Term of Cap Agreement Interest rate caps typically have terms from 3 months to 12 years. The choice of term for the cap is based on the term of the underlying asset or liability being hedged, on the relative price of caps for various terms, and on the desired level of sensitivity to interest rates. Caps with longer terms will cost more and have greater dollar sensitivity to changes in interest rates than caps with shorter terms, all else being equal.

Strike Level The strike (trigger) level is the level of the underlying index above which the buyer receives payments. This will typically be a constant level for the life of the cap agreement, although this is not necessary. The higher the strike level, the higher the deductible. Since a higher strike level means the buyer must shoulder more of the risk of rising rates, this also implies a lower premium.

Notional Amount This is the underlying amount of principal on which cap payments are based. To fully cap the interest payments on a floating rate liability, the buyer would purchase caps with a notional amount equal to the total liability principal. Alternatively, the buyer may want to provide partial market value protection, assuming that only a portion of the liability will need to be repurchased when interest rates rise. (This is often the situation when offsetting a put option that has been granted to policy holders.) In this case, the notional amount (as well as other features, such as the strike level or time to expiration) may vary over time. This may be constructed as a single cap, or more likely, as a series of individual caps layered on top of one another.

Method of Payment The buyer will typically pay the seller an up-front sum equal to a percentage of the notional amount. For example, if the underlying amount is $100 million and the associated premium is 2.5%, the buyer will pay the seller $2.5 million.

Alternatively, the payment may be amortized over the term of the cap agreement. This method of payment exposes the writer to credit risk and is reflected in the price. If the contract is sold before expiration, the original buyer will need to reimburse the original seller for the present value of remaining payments.

Credit Risk Since interest rate caps are over-the-counter agreements, the buyer must be careful to assess default risk in choosing an appropriate counterparty. Counterparties spanning a range of creditworthiness are usually available.

Cap Payoff Characteristics

If, on the reset dates, the level of the underlying index is above the strike level of the cap, the seller must make a payment to the buyer. The payment will be calculated using the following formula:

$$\left(\begin{matrix} \text{Index} \\ \text{Level} \end{matrix} - \begin{matrix} \text{Strike} \\ \text{Level} \end{matrix} \right) \times \left(\begin{matrix} \text{Actual Days} \\ \text{in Period} \end{matrix} \Big/ 360 \right) \times \left(\begin{matrix} \text{Notional} \\ \text{Amount} \end{matrix} \right)$$

Thus, if 3-month LIBOR is at 11% on the reset date, the strike level is 10%, the number of days in the reset period is 91, and the notional amount is $100 million, the seller would pay the buyer

$$(11\% - 10\%) \times (91/360) \times (\$100,000,000) = \$252,778.$$

If 3-month LIBOR is at 10% or below on the reset date, no payment is due.

Exhibit 3 shows average monthly levels for 3-month LIBOR from January 1978 through December 1987. The two horizontal lines represent 8% and 10% strike levels for hypothetical 10-year caps purchased in January 1978. Exhibit 4 shows the actual payouts for $100 million notional amount of such caps. As you can see, substantial payouts at the assumed cap levels would have occurred during 1979-1982. Although the 8% cap pays out more frequently and in greater amounts than the 10% cap (as would be expected), the 8% cap's up-front premium would have been larger because of the lower deductible.

CONSIDERATIONS IN VALUING CAPS

An Interest Rate Cap as a Strip of Caps

How do the various contract specifications affect the value of interest rate caps? One way to think about this is to regard a cap of a certain term, e.g., 5 years, as a series of 1-period caps. We depict this in Exhibit 5. A 5-year cap on an index that resets semi-annually can be valued as nine separate caps, each covering different periods in the future. (Remember that there is no cap on the first period, since the interest rate is known when the cap is bought.) Because each potential cap payment occurs at different times, each with its own forward rate, a cap derives its value across the yield curve. This implies that the level and shape of the yield curve will be important determinants of cap values.

A second important point from Exhibit 5 is that the value of a cap should decline as it approaches maturity (assuming no changes in interest rates and volatility). Not only does the time value of each cap decline but, over time, there are fewer and fewer 1-period caps remaining. This also means that, all else equal, longer term caps are worth more than shorter term caps.

Impact of Expected Short Rate Volatility

Exhibit 6 portrays theoretical prices for caps of various terms and interest rate volatilities. Each line represents prices for various terms at each level of volatility.

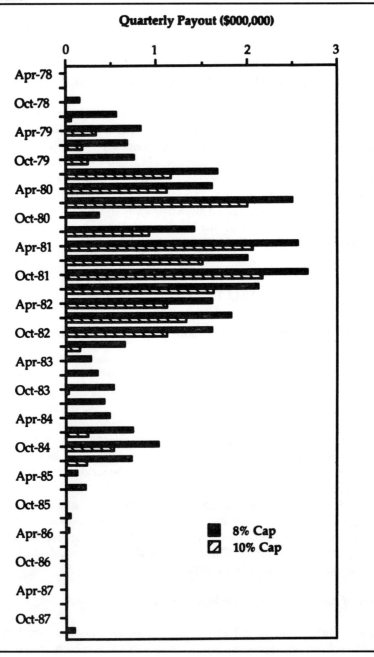

Quarterly Payout ($000,000)

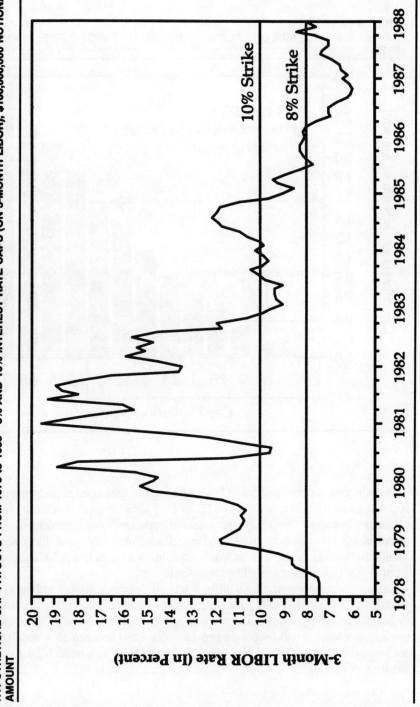

EXHIBIT 4
HYPOTHETICAL CAP PAYOUTS FROM 1978 to 1988—8% AND 10% INTEREST RATE CAPS (ON 3-MONTH LIBOR), $100,000,000 NOTIONAL AMOUNT

EXHIBIT 5
CAP VALUE EQUALS SUM OF 1 PERIOD CAPS—8% FLAT SPOT CURVE; 10% STRIKE LEVEL

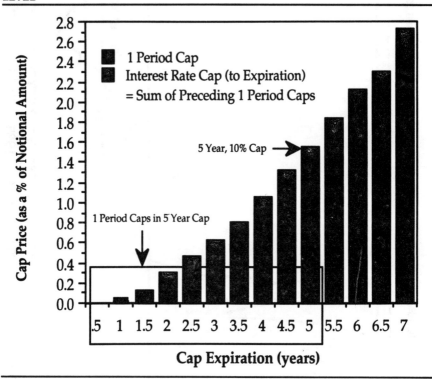

This main conclusions are that: (1) all else equal, greater expected volatility is correlated with higher cap values; and (2) as a cap ages, changes in volatility (as well as changes in interest rates) may have a greater impact on value than aging alone. For example, a 5-year cap currently valued at .8% assuming 16% volatility (point A in Exhibit 6) should theoretically be worth .65% in six months (point B), but could be worth 1.0% (point C) if volatility increases to 20%.

Exhibit 7 shows historical volatility levels. It depicts a 40-day rolling average volatility of 3-month LIBOR. Although a graph of implied volatilities (i.e., implied in actual market prices) would be more appropriate in assessing historical cap pricing, this chart is still useful. In general, volatilities between 15% and 30% are not unusual for 3-month LIBOR, (although short periods with much higher volatilities have occurred).

EXHIBIT 6
PRICE VERSUS EXPIRATION-VOLATILITY—8% FLAT SPOT CURVE; 10% STRIKE LEVEL

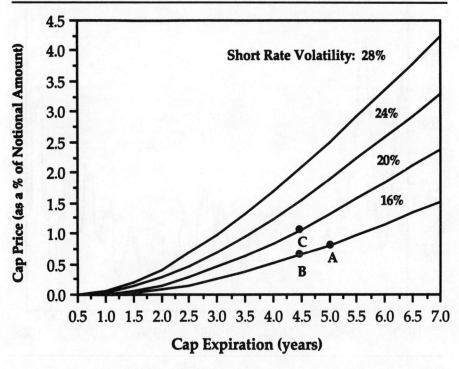

Impact of the Yield Curve

The general level of interest rates and the shape of the yield curve are important determinants of the value of caps. The unlimited number of combinations makes the precise impact quite difficult to summarize. However, if we focus on an "at-the-money" cap, an increase in the general level of interest rates should increase the value of the cap. The cap, in a sense, becomes more "in-the-money." The effect is directionally the same as lowering the strike level.

Steepening of the yield curve, while holding short-term rates at current levels for this same "at-the-money" cap, should also increase its value, all else equal. This is because a steeper yield curve contains higher implied forward short rates. The effect is to increase the degree to which future 1-period caps are near to or in the money.

EXHIBIT 7
HISTORY OF 3-MONTH LIBOR VOLATILITY—40-DAY ROLLING AVERAGE

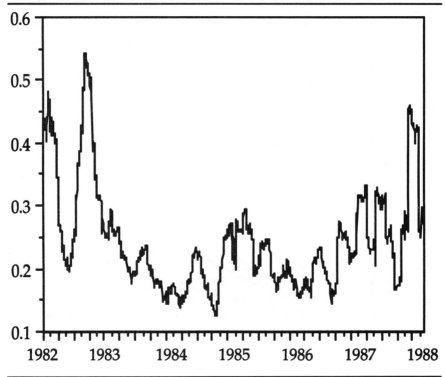

Relationship to Interest Rate Swaps and Floors

Interest rate swaps are arrangements whereby parties "swap" interest payments. There is no exchange of principal. The most common type of swap is one in which the two parties exchange fixed for floating payments. For example, if the rate to swap 5-year fixed for 3-month LIBOR is 10%, the fixed payer will make fixed payments equal to 10% annually and receive 3-month LIBOR. (This is considered a "fair swap" if the 10% fixed rate, over 5 years, corresponds to a combination of forward 3-month LIBOR rates implied in the swap yield curve over the same period.)

Interest rate floors are like caps, in that they are also interest rate insurance contracts. Unlike caps, however, floors provide protection against falling interest rates. Hence, a floor on 3-month LIBOR with a 10% strike level entitles the owner to payments from the seller if 3-month LIBOR falls below 10% on reset dates. Such payments would be based on the notional amount and the difference between 3-month LIBOR and the 10% strike level.

You can create an interest rate floor by entering into a swap (pay floating, receive fixed) and purchasing a cap. The swap will entitle the floating payer to receive 10% fixed payments in exchange for floating 3-month LIBOR. The cap will make payments to the holder whenever 3-month LIBOR is above 10%. Combining the two positions, for rates above 10%, the net payout is always zero because the cap payment received plus the fixed receipt will exactly equal the floating payment due of 3-month LIBOR. For rates below 10%, the cap does not make payments and the net cash received equals the difference between the 10% fixed rate received and the floating index paid. This payout pattern, across all levels of interest rates, is the same as that of an interest rate floor.

The general relationships[4] between swaps, caps and floors are:

Cap = Floor + Swap (Receive Floating, Pay Fixed)

Floor = Cap + Swap (Pay Floating, Receive Fixed)

Thus, floors can either be purchased outright or created synthetically with a swap and a cap. Another implication is that the valuation of caps and floors is related to interest rate swap market levels.

Price Sensitivity of Caps

Interest rate caps are highy convex instruments with very large negative durations that are rapidly changing.[5] Because caps increase in value with interest rates in increasing amounts, this negative duration and positive convexity serve to cushion the decline in value as rates fall, and to accelerate the increase in value as rates rise. This behavior is shown in Exhibits 8 and 9. These charts depict, for flat yield curves, the theoretical pricing of caps of different terms and strike levels. (Because the value of a cap also depends on a complex combination of volatility levels and the shape of the yield curve over the entire term, these simplified "price/yield" graphs can be misleading.)

Exhibit 8 shows the impact of term on price sensitivity. It shows caps of 3, 5, and 7 years with 10% strike levels across interest rates. Exhibit 8a shows cap prices as a function of interest rates for various maturities, while Exhibit 8b shows changes in cap prices for 100 basis point moves in interest rates. We can discern some general relationships. First, for all levels of interest rates, longer caps are worth more than those with shorter terms, all else equal. Second, for all caps, the actual price change accelerates as interest rates rise (although the curve straightens out beyond the strike level) and decelerates as rates fall. This effect is more pronounced the longer the term of the cap.

---

[4] These relationships hold most precisely for like term and strike levels and a flat yield curve.

[5] For a discussion of duration and convexity, see Frank J. Fabozzi, *Fixed Income Mathematics* (Chicago, IL: Probus Publishing, 1988), Chapters 10 and 11.

EXHIBIT 8a
PRICE SENSITIVITY BY TERM OF CAP—PRICE VERSUS INTEREST RATES

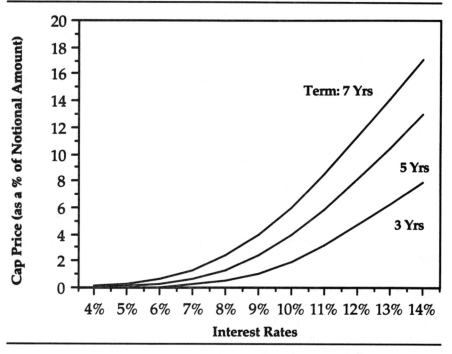

Exhibit 9 isolates the impact of strike level on price sensitivity. It shows 8%, 10%, and 12% strike levels for 5-year caps across interest rates. In general, the lower the strike level, the greater the price and its change across interest rates. In addition, as rates rise and the caps become more in-the-money, the change in price becomes close to linear.

These exhibits, although simplified by yield curve shape and volatility assumptions, are useful for understanding the price behavior of different caps. In particular, an asset/liability manager may determine that he will require about $10 million to offset a capital loss if rates rise to 11%. Based on his assumptions about price sensitivity, he determines the amounts of 8%, 10%, 12%, and layered combinations of 5-year caps that are necessary to reach the target. This is shown in Exhibit 10. If the hedge were initiated with interest rates at 8%, the cost of the hedge would vary inversely with the strike level. This makes sense, because the cap with a low strike level is more "in-the-money" and the probability of cap payouts is greater than for higher strike levels.

Another interesting point in this analysis is that for interest rate levels above 11%, the 12% caps become more valuable than the other hedge alternatives. This greater

EXHIBIT 8b
PRICE CHANGE VERSUS INTEREST RATE CHANGE

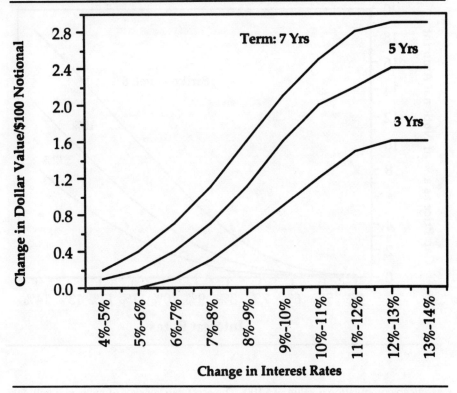

convexity of the 12% caps, compared with that of the 8% and 10% caps, is due to the greater amount of 12% caps needed for the hedge, as a result of their lower dollar sensitivity.

Finally, the sophisticated asset/liability manager understands that the hedge will under- or over-perform to the extent that the shape of the yield curve or the volatility changes during his hedging horizon. Thus, a cap position needs to be managed, just as an immunized bond portfolio needs to be managed over time because of duration drift.

ADDING CAPS TO A BOND PORTFOLIO

Interest rate caps can have an impact on both the cash flow and market value of a portfolio over time. Exhibit 11a shows market values, over a range of interest rates, of an asset (7-year noncallable 9% bond) and of a combination of the bond with a 7-year, 10% strike level, interest rate cap. At 9%, the bond has a value of $100 and the

EXHIBIT 9a
PRICE SENSITIVITY BY STRIKE LEVEL—PRICE VERSUS INTEREST RATES

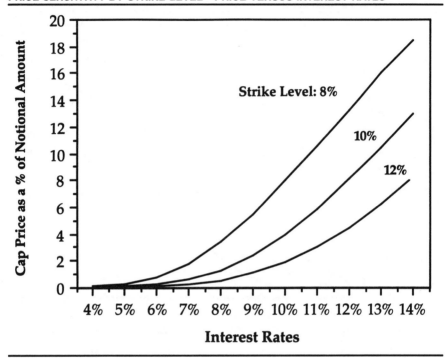

asset/cap combination a value of $100. The asset/cap consists of approximately $96 principal of the bond and $4 market value of the cap.

As rates fall below 9%, the 7-year bond steadily increases in value. The asset/cap also gains, although its value remains below that of the bond. This is because the cap value declines as rates fall, and the portfolio looks more and more like the bond with $96 principal. This "economic cost" is the upside potential foregone in exchange for protection against rising interest rates.

As rates rise, the chart becomes more interesting. Because the cap performs well in a rising rate environment, the asset/cap portfolio outperforms the bond.[6] Because the asset/cap portfolio is shorter in duration and more convex than the bond, it performs much better when rates rise.

In Exhibit 11b, we revisit the situation 4 years into its life. The asset is now a 3-year bond and the cap has 3 years remaining to expiration. Compared with the initial

---

[6]An interest rate range of 4% to 14% is consistent with a much higher level of volatility. Were the cap purchased in a 9% interest rate environment and at a volatility of 20%, and were interest rates suddenly to move plus or minus 500 basis points, the asset/cap combination would be worth considerably more than is indicated in Exhibit 11a.

EXHIBIT 9b
PRICE CHANGE VERSUS INTEREST RATE CHANGE

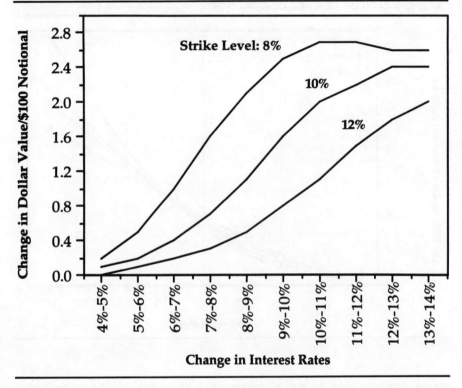

situation, the price/yield curves for the bond and asset/cap portfolios are much flatter.

Compared with Exhibit 11a, the asset/cap portfolio appears to perform below the bond for a much wider range of interest rates. This, of course, ignores any payments that may already have been received from the cap, and assumes no change in expected short rate volatility, general yield levels, or shape of the yield curve. To the extent these elements increase the value of the cap, the comparison would look much more favorable.

EXAMPLE: INTEREST-SENSITIVE LIFE INSURANCE

To illustrate the operational features of a cap hedge, we have selected an application geared toward single premium whole life insurance. The techniques discussed, however, can be modified and applied to other interest-sensitive and traditional life products to protect against surrenders from rising interest rates. We want to emphasize that hedging an interest rate sensitive life insurance product is not an exact

EXHIBIT 10
ALTERNATE WAYS TO HEDGE EXPECTED MARKET RISK AT 11%—8% CAPS, 10% CAPS, 12% CAPS OR LAYERED COMBINATION

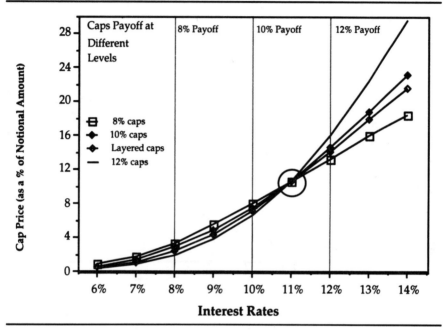

science. Not only must the option characteristics of the liabilities be approximated based on limited data, but the estimates of future cap payoffs are also subject to variation because underlying assumptions about volatility and shape of the yield curve change.

Consider a mutual insurer with a closed book of single premium whole life business. Such an insurer may have a clientele that consists of a time-varying portion of policyholders who are sensitive (in differing degrees) to interest rate spreads on competing products, and another portion who are, for practical purposes, insensitive to interest spreads. When interest rates spike, some among the interest rate sensitive portion of policyholders are likely to surrender their policies at the available cash-out value and redeploy elsewhere the funds obtained. This action could potentially produce a drain on surplus if assets are liquidated at a capital loss to accommodate the cash demands of surrendering policyholders.

To avoid this potential surplus drain, the insurer can do one of two things. First, it can base amounts credited to policyholders (in the form of dividends and increments to cash values) on new money rates (instead of portfolio yield) to minimize surrenders during periods of rising rates. But this has unfortunate consequences. To keep a segment of policyholders from lapsing, the insurer must provide higher credited

EXHIBIT 11a
7-YEAR CAP HEDGE—IMPACT ON PORTFOLIO OVER TIME (MARKET VALUE AT T(0)—
OVER CHANGING RATES)

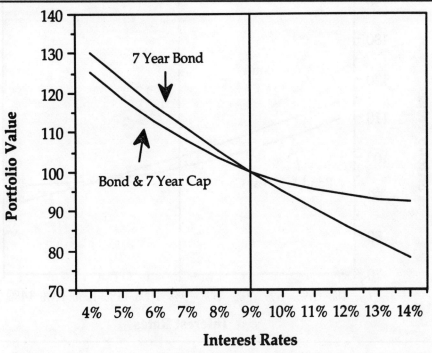

earnings to everybody when market yields rise, not just to the group that is prone to lapse. Moreover, unless the insurer has invested very short term, with the historically lower yields that such a strategy entails, it may be subjected to a large divergence between the new money rate and portfolio yield, i.e., the portfolio yield may be less than the new money rate on which dividends are based. This can have adverse economic consequences for the insurer. But if it does forgo the higher yields from investing long term, its policies may be unattractive during periods of steady or declining rates.

A second approach the insurer can take is to provide for sudden lapses when rates spike by having investments that provide capital gains when cash is needed most. One instrument available for accomplishing this objective is an interest rate cap. The key insight to keep in mind when using caps in such an application is that when a lapse occurs, a liability goes off the books. Thus, a group of assets can also be liquidated. Unlike the policy loan hedge, described elsewhere,[7] where periodic cap

---

[7]Babbel, "Capping the Risks of Life Insurance Policy Loans and Lapses."

EXHIBIT 11b
MARKET VALUE AFTER 4 YEARS—OVER CHANGING RATES

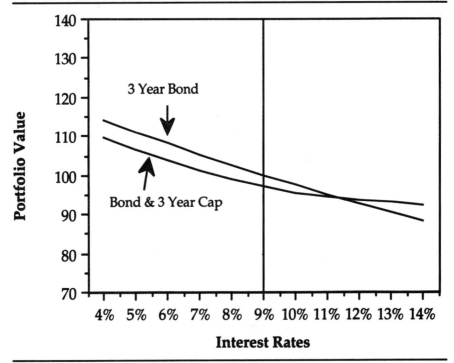

payments were relied on to offset entirely the lost interest on reserves placed in policy loans, a hedge against surrenders involves the liquidation of caps at their market value when cash demands require it. The caps are no longer required to hedge against surrenders, as a policyholder can surrender only once. In setting up an appropriate cap strategy, several steps may be followed. There are obviously varying degrees of fineness in the construction of an offsetting cap hedge, but the steps listed below are fundamental to any hedge strategy.

1. Set up a time profile of policy reserves on existing business, assuming normal surrenders and mortality. A hypothetical time profile of the total amount of policy reserves outstanding appears in Exhibit 12. Such a profile can be generated by company actuaries.

2. Estimate the amounts of reserves over time that would be subject to abnormal lapse experience resulting from interest sensitivity—"hot money." This is usually done by estimating the percentages of reserves likely to be subject to abnormally high lapses over time because of spikes in interest rates, and multiplying these percentages by the amounts of policy reserves scheduled to be outstanding at each point in time. The resulting products form a time profile of "hot money" that will be

EXHIBIT 12
INTEREST SPREAD SENSITIVITY MONEY PROFILE

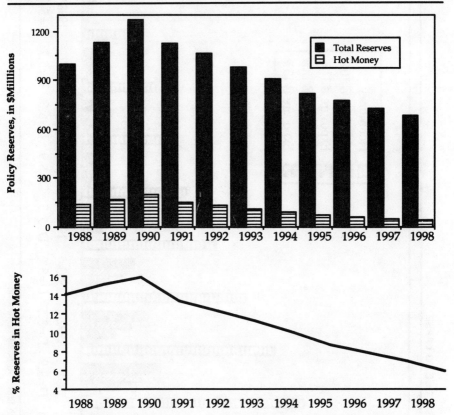

on the books *in the absence* of an interest rate spike. Once spreads between yields implied by dividends/cash value increments and those available elsewhere become of sufficient magnitude, policyholders representing the "hot money" will begin to surrender their policies until ultimately only the lethargic portion remains. Exhibit 12 also portrays an example of a schedule of potential hot money.

3. Determine the potential surplus drain associated with interest rate spikes of varying levels. There are several ways of going about this step. A first, broad brush approach is to compute the duration of assets supporting current and scheduled reserves at each point in time, and then to multiply the duration numbers by interest rate spreads that could give rise to excess surrenders. These products would then be multiplied by the amounts of hot money from the schedule of Step 2 to give the total potential surplus drain at each point in time. Exhibit 13 provides an example, which shows loss exposure beyond that which would be incurred from the first 100 basis

EXHIBIT 13
DURATION-IMPLIED EXPOSURE TO CAPITAL LOSS* DUE TO LAPSE

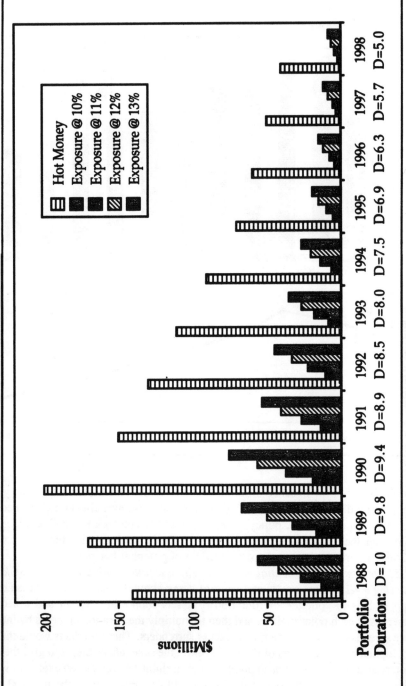

Legend:
- Hot Money
- Exposure @ 10%
- Exposure @ 11%
- Exposure @ 12%
- Exposure @ 13%

$Millions

Portfolio	1988	1989	1990	1991	1992	1993	1994	1995	1996	1997	1998
Duration:	D=10	D=9.8	D=9.4	D=8.9	D=8.5	D=8.0	D=7.5	D=6.9	D=6.3	D=5.7	D=5.0

*Assumes insurer absorbs capital loss associated with first 100 basis points move.

point rise in interest rates. (We assume the insurer is willing to absorb losses associated with a 100 basis point upward move.)

The broad brush approach is likely to exaggerate the levels of potential surplus drain, as it ignores the convexity of assets.

A more refined approach is to compute the actual implied (as distinguished from duration-implied) capital losses on the portion of the asset portfolio that would need to be liquidated in the event of sudden cash demands from surrendering policy-holders. These calculations would be made for various interest levels at various future times, and would take into account the evolution of portfolio value over time as assets came closer to maturity, and would incorporate reinvestment assumptions. In the stylized example that follows, we took the more refined approach.

4. Construct a payoff matrix of caps having maturities that span the period over which protection is desired. This step involves use of a cap pricing model, as the payoffs associated with a cap portfolio at any point in time include liquidation value as well as periodic payments. The payoff matrix would include the theoretical market values of caps at different interest rate levels, having varying remaining maturities and differing trigger levels. It would focus on how these values change under rising interest rates, and may include some periodic payment amounts as well. Exhibits 8 and 9 provide the type of information from which such a cap payoff matrix can be derived. Obviously, a good cap pricing model is required if the payoff matrix is to be viable. It is useful to include a few caps with trigger levels far out of the money, along with caps having triggers near those that engender surrenders, in order to hedge for any nonlinearities in the demand for cash.

5. Select that cap combination which provides for payoff amounts from Step 4 consistent with potential surplus drain from Step 3. There are several techniques that can be used to accomplish this step, ranging from careful eyeballing and experimentation to sophisticated dynamic programming. To determine the cap strategy illustrated in Exhibit 14, we used an approach in-between these two extremes in complexity, based on a simple spreadsheet backwards solution procedure. The procedure starts with buying sufficient caps to protect against abnormal surrenders during the final (10th year) period of the horizon.[8] These 10-year caps will be more than adequate to hedge the potential hot money existing in year 9, so some 9-year caps are sold until the net amount of remaining protection available in the 9th year is at the level desired. The portfolio manager then looks at how much net protection is already on the books for the 8th year from the purchase of 10-year caps and sale of 9-year caps, and either buys or sells 8-year caps based on the difference between desired and already existing cap protection. He follows this approach until reaching the current date.

---

[8] If the 10-year caps are bought with a trigger rate 100 basis points above the current rate, a notional amount of principal close to the product of the projected duration and the potential hot money would be sought. In the example, portfolio duration in the 10th year is projected to be 5.0 years, and potential hot money is $40 million; thus, a notional principal near $200 million would be sought for 10-year caps. If the caps are bought with triggers further out of the money, a higher notional principal would be needed.

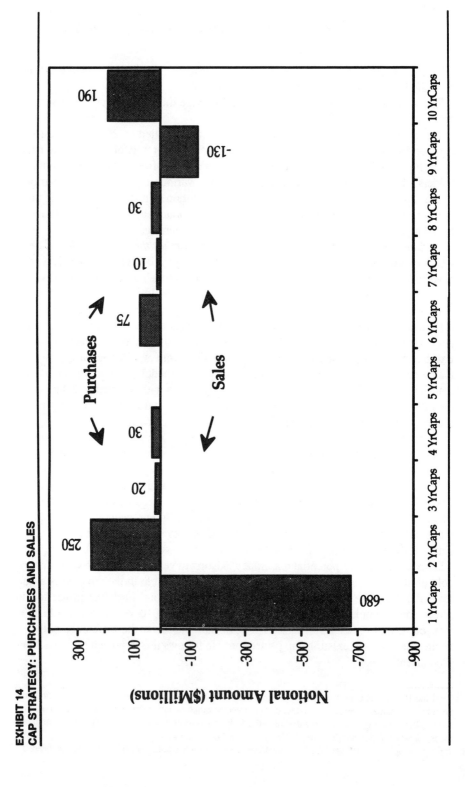

EXHIBIT 14
CAP STRATEGY: PURCHASES AND SALES

The illustration involves buying and selling caps of maturities ranging from 1 to 10 years, all at trigger levels of 9%. We refer to this strategy as a "full hedge" because our strategy utilizes the full range of cap maturities available and, apart from the first 100 basis point rise in interest rates, it aims at minimal surplus exposure. Exhibits 15a-d show how well this "full hedge" strategy offsets the potential surplus drain associated with expected policy surrenders resulting from future interest rate increases. Exhibit 15a illustrates a 200 basis point increase; Exhibit 15b, a 300 basis point increase; Exhibit 15c, a 400 basis point increase, and Exhibit 15d, a 500 basis point increase. The "full hedge" cap portfolio hedges well against surrenders, regardless of whether they occur sooner or later, and regardless of whether they occur at interest spreads of 200 basis points to 500 basis points, or beyond. If only a portion of the hot money leaves the company at a certain spread, only a pro-rata share of the cap portfolio is sold off to cover that portion, and the remainder is kept to cover subsequent lapses. The total estimated net cost of the illustrated cap strategy, assuming that the insurer is willing to absorb capital losses associated with the first 100 basis points rise in interest rates, is under $4.5 million for this hypothetical example. Viewing the upfront cap payment as a cost, however, is ignoring the expected return on that investment.[9] It is more proper to view the payment as an investment with a positive expected return and a payoff that behaves in a manner which offsets potential losses on other assets.

The amount of protection for any one year from the full hedge approach (as shown in Exhibits 15a-d) does not always exactly match the surplus exposure at every level of interest rates. More precision is available than that associated with the illustrated cap strategy by substituting some 9% caps with caps further out of the money. However, in practice, it is more likely that a portfolio manager will require less precision, which results in a simpler program with fewer caps. Furthermore, many insurers may be reluctant to sell off caps in those years where they have excess protection. At any point in time certain maturity and trigger level ranges of caps are more highly traded than others; for example, 2-, 3-, 5-, and 7-year caps that are 2% or 3% out of the money. To construct a simpler hedge using these more liquid caps, we used a backwards solution approach based on trial and error using a Lotus spreadsheet to calculate net exposure for each year for various combinations of caps. One such simplified hedge involves purchasing 10-year 9% caps with a notional amount of $110 million, 7-year 12% caps with a notional amount of $70 million, and 5-year 12% caps having a notional amount of about $500 million. While this simplified approach would not provide as uniform a pattern of protection as the full hedge strategy, it would still provide a very good hedge, does not require selling caps, would allow the insurer to operate in the more liquid segments of the market, and would have a cost somewhat lower than the full strategy (approximately $500,000 less in this particular case). As shown in Exhibits 15a-d, the "simple

---

[9]In the SPDA example of Exhibit 1, although the median return on the caps under the 40 random scenarios was negative, the expected return (average) was greater than zero. That is because of the asymmetric nature of returns on caps, which offer a large upside and limited downside potential.

EXHIBIT 15a
EXPOSURE AT 10% INTEREST RATES

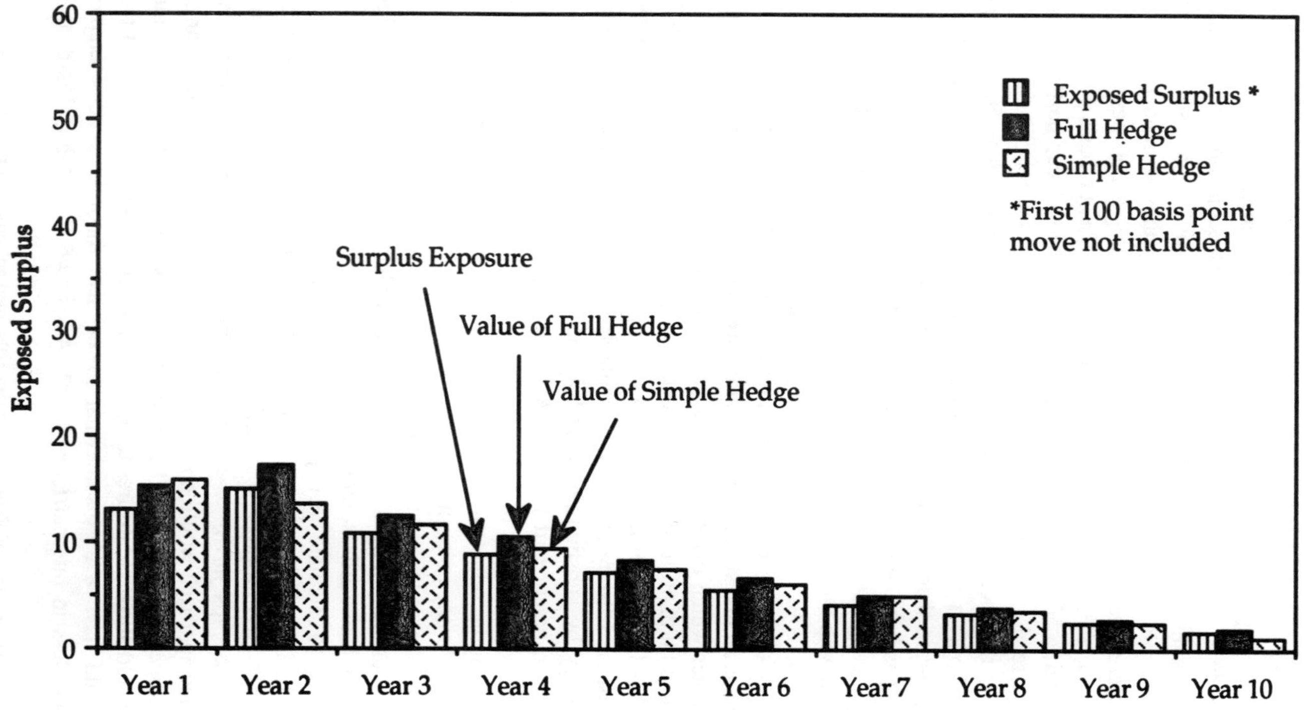

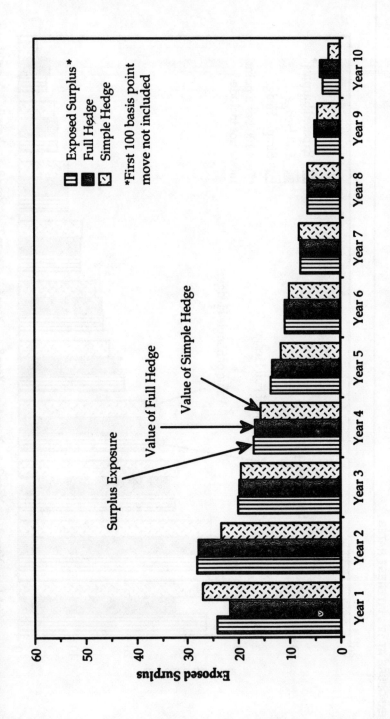

EXHIBIT 15c
EXPOSURE AT 12% INTEREST RATES

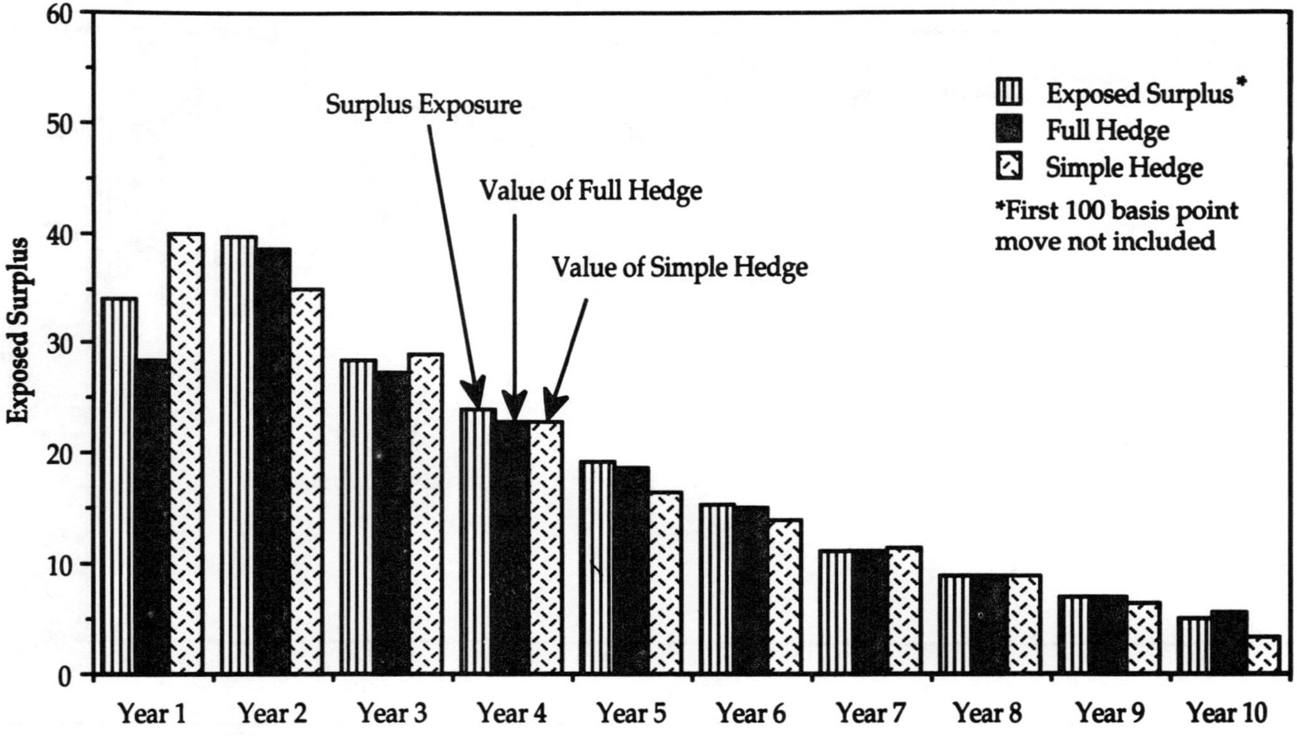

EXHIBIT 15d
EXPOSURE AT 13% INTEREST RATES

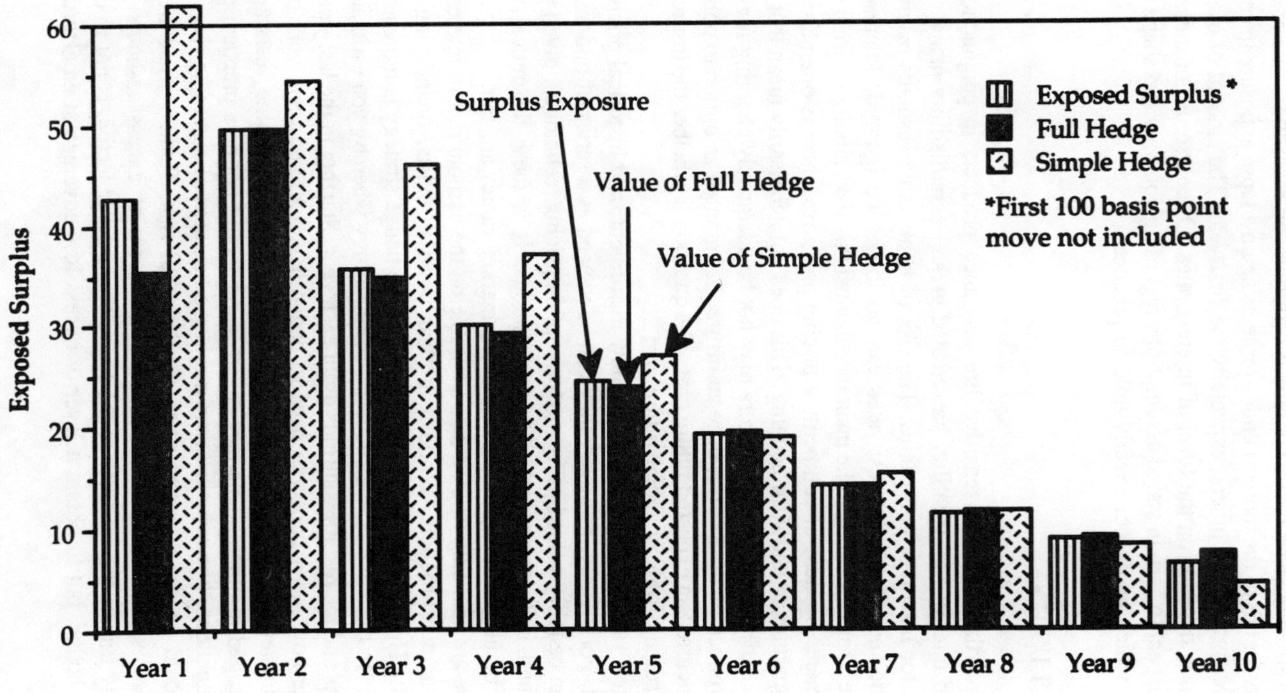

Exposed Surplus
60
50
40
30
20
10
0
Year 1
Year 2
Year 3
Year 4
Year 5
Year 6
Year 7
Year 8
Year 9
Year 10
Surplus Exposure
Value of Full Hedge
Value of Simple Hedge
Exposed Surplus *
Full Hedge
Simple Hedge
*First 100 basis point move not included

hedge" strategy (which utilizes only 3 different cap maturities, two of which have triggers far out of the money) under-protects against lapse exposure in certain years, and over-protects in others, especially the first year. The amount of over-or under-protection depends on the level of interest rates. Of course, all of these are shown with respect to certain stated assumptions regarding volatility and shape of the yield curve, which might not exactly hold in practice.

CONCLUSION

The growth of interest-sensitive life insurance products in conjunction with increased interest rate volatility has created greater asset/liability management challenges for insurance companies. The risk of book value cashouts resulting from a dramatic increase in interest rates can no longer be ignored. Interest rate caps provide a form of catastrophe insurance against this risk, albeit requiring an up-front investment. Because of competitive pricing pressures, there is often little room left in the margins to allow for hedging. This does not necessarily mean that the hedges are too expensive. Rather, insurers may not be adequately charging for this risk in their products. Nonetheless, once an insurer has granted an option to policyholders, it has incurred an expected future cost. The question is whether the insurer wishes to hedge some of this potential future cost.

Interest rate caps are a relatively new instrument, and historical pricing data are limited. Fortunately, however, they can be viewed as a series of options. As such, they can be fairly valued using modern option pricing techniques, given yield curve shape and interest rate volatility assumptions. It is these theoretical values that should be used to judge whether current market values are fair.

There are also only limited data available on the cashout risk of interest-sensitive life insurance products. While it is clear this risk exists, quantifying it is more difficult. Therefore, developing an appropriate hedge strategy is more an art than a science. In this chapter, we suggest a methodology whereby you estimate potential cashouts and the resulting surplus drain each year. Starting in the last year, you then estimate how many caps you need to hedge that risk, and then work backwards. Unfortunately, you will typically end up under-hedged in some years and perhaps over-hedged in others. This lack of precision should not be a practical problem in most situations, however. Insurers are in the business of accepting risk, and therefore would generally not want to eliminate all risk. Rather, what they want to eliminate is the risk of catastrophe, in the form of excess cashouts that could seriously impair the viability of the firm. Thus, the objective is not to construct a perfect hedge, but to obtain a layer of excess loss coverage at an affordable cost.

PART VII

International

Chapter 22

Structuring and Managing an International Bond Portfolio

ANDREW GORDON
VICE PRESIDENT
THE FIRST BOSTON CORPORATION

The desire for diversification and the potential for superior returns have encouraged increased U.S. investor involvement in the foreign bond markets. This represents the beginning of a trend. Nondollar bonds now comprise more than half of the global bond market, making it increasingly important for U.S. investors to consider the foreign currency sector (Exhibit 1). The increased sophistication, liquidity, and accessibility of foreign bond markets in recent years have made foreign bonds a viable investment for a large segment of U.S. investors.

Diverse investor groups comprise the U.S. institutional participation in the foreign bond markets. The proliferation of global bond funds and unit trusts reflects the increased retail investor demand for international bonds. Public and private pension funds have diversified into nondollar investments, while total return money managers have sought enhanced performance. High yield buyers also have been attracted to several sectors. Many investors are likely to explore portfolio diversification using foreign bonds in future years.

EXHIBIT 1
SIZE OF THE WORLD GOVERNMENT BOND MARKET

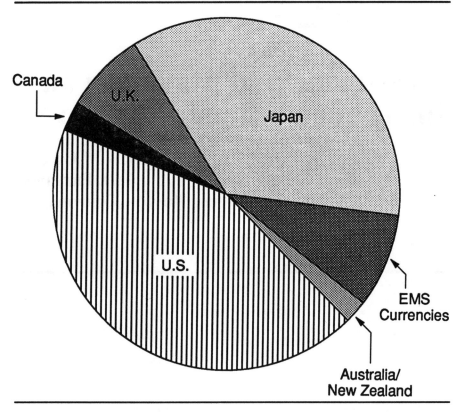

REASONS FOR NONDOLLAR INVESTMENTS

Total Return Potential

Nondollar bonds can outperform U.S. bonds in a variety of scenarios. During periods of U.S. dollar weakness, foreign currency appreciation boosts the total return of nondollar bonds. During periods of exchange market stability, investors should focus on the potential for superior local currency returns. This can arise from either higher coupon income or declining interest rates relative to the U.S. market. During periods of U.S. dollar strength, investors should take positions in attractive foreign bond markets in conjunction with currency hedges.

Diversification

International bonds provide portfolio diversification benefits as the major markets are not perfectly correlated. Exhibit 2 shows the correlation of monthly U.S. dollar

EXHIBIT 2
CORRELATION OF MONTHLY LOCAL CURRENCY RETURNS OF 10-YEAR BONDS
JANUARY 1978 to AUGUST 1988*

	U.S.	Japan	Germany	Canada	U.K.	Australia
U.S.	1	.31	.29	.73	.34	.10
Japan		1	.59	.36	.44	.22
Germany			1	.36	.50	.26
Canada				1	.46	.19
U.K.					1	.21
Australia						1

*A coefficient of 1 indicates a perfect positive linear relationship between the variables, while a coefficient of zero indicates no correlation.

total returns of 10-year government bonds for the January 1978 to August 1988 period. U.S. Treasuries had a correlation of .31 with Japanese bonds and .73 with Canadian securities. These statistical results reflect historical relationships and may be different in the future as the global markets become more integrated. Moreover, the correlation over the anticipated investment holding period may differ substantially from the long-term relationship.

There are also intuitive reasons to expect diversification benefits from foreign bonds. The year 1987 provides an excellent example, a period when all of the foreign bond markets dramatically outperformed U.S. Treasuries both in local currency and U.S. dollar terms. During the second quarter of 1987 the dollar's weakness heightened fears of inflation and monetary policy tightening in the U.S. and led interest rates to rise. Meanwhile, the major foreign bond markets rallied sharply amid speculation of monetary policy easing to preclude further dollar weakness.

TOTAL RETURN ANALYSIS

Calculating Total Return

The U.S. dollar total return from foreign currency bonds reflects the local currency return and the foreign exchange performance. Local currency return stems from the bond's coupon income and price appreciation or depreciation. Exhibit 3 shows that a local currency return of 5% and foreign currency gain of 10% leads to U.S. dollar total return of 15.5%. The cross product term reflects the exchange rate gain on the local currency return.

Historical Returns

Exhibit 4 shows recent local currency and U.S. dollar total returns from nondollar bonds. All of the foreign bond markets dramatically outperformed U.S. Treasuries

EXHIBIT 3
CALCULATING TOTAL RETURN

Example: Total Return from 10-year German
Bond, 6% coupon, 3-month Holding Period

Initial Price:	DM100.0	Initial Exchange Rate:	DM1.837/$
Ending Price:	DM103.5	Ending Exchange Rate:	DM1.670/$

	$		DM
Initial Cash Flow:	$54.437 ────────▶ DM1.837/$ ──────▶		DM100.00
			│
			▼
Ending Cash Flow:	$62.874 ◀──────── DM1.670/$ ◀────────		DM105.00*
Percent Return:	15.50%		5.00%

Total Return   = TR   = .1550
Local Currency Return = LC   = .0500
Exchange Rate Change = ER   = .1000

$$TR = LC + ER + (LC \times ER)$$

$$.1550 = .0500 + .1000 + (.0500 \times .1000)$$

---

*Reflects the assumed price appreciation and the accrued interest.

during 1987. Ten-year U.S. Treasuries provided a negative return, while positive local currency performance and the dollar's decline to historic lows boosted the returns on foreign bonds. During 1988, the dollar's appreciation caused the major nondollar markets to sharply underperform U.S. Treasuries. Meanwhile, the high yielding Canadian and Australian sectors continued to post excellent performance.

GENERAL GUIDELINES FOR PORTFOLIO MANAGEMENT

Setting Objectives

One management style approaches nondollar bonds as a core sector of a global portfolio. Managers whose objective is diversification or who are specifically allocated "international money" by plan sponsors should follow this approach. The manager must decide which markets to invest in and establish the duration and currency composition of the portfolio. Some managers advocate structuring a portfolio similar to a benchmark index to reflect market capitalizations and avoid market

EXHIBIT 4
LOCAL CURRENCY AND U.S. DOLLAR TOTAL RETURNS

Issue	1988			1987		
	Local Currency Return	Exchange Rate Change	Dollar Return	Local Currency Return	Exchange Rate Change	Dollar Return
United States	7.39%	—	7.39%	−2.25%	—	−2.25%
Germany	5.89	−11.20%	− 5.97	2.55	22.59%	−25.71
Japan	4.89	−3.08	1.66	10.72	30.73	44.71
United Kingdom	6.97	−4.08	2.61	15.63	27.25	47.14
Canada	9.71	9.15	19.75	1.78	6.31	8.20
Australia	13.26	18.12	33.78	17.18	8.72	27.40

Issue	1986			1985		
	Local Currency Return	Exchange Rate Change	Dollar Return	Local Currency Return	Exchange Rate Change	Dollar Return
United States	19.99%	—	19.99%	26.05%	—	26.05%
Germany	7.67	27.10%	36.85	10.28	28.81%	42.05
Japan	12.73	26.62	42.73	9.85	25.59	37.96
U.K.	12.41	2.57	15.29	13.53	24.68	41.55
Canada	12.58	1.20	13.94	21.31	−5.55	14.58
Australia	22.12	−2.40	19.19	6.05	−17.43	−12.43

timing decisions. However, global indexation strategies currently are not fequently used. More likely, managers underweight or overweight sectors based upon their market outlook. Global managers should be evaluated relative to a global or nondollar performance index.

Many U.S. investors involved in foreign bonds do not consider themselves to be global managers. These investors are motivated by the potential for superior total returns and pursue selective foreign bond strategies based upon a market outlook. The allocation to foreign bonds changes over time and can range from no exposure to a significant percentage of the portfolio. These investors should be judged against a traditional U.S. dollar index rather than a global index. The test of performance should be whether the foreign bond investment outperforms alternative U.S. dollar investments.

Developing an Outlook

Determining the portfolio composition lends itself to a top-down approach of portfolio management. The investor must develop both a currency and bond market

EXHIBIT 5
DEVELOPING AN OUTLOOK

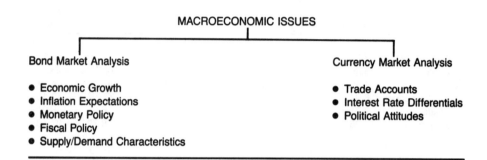

MACROECONOMIC ISSUES

Bond Market Analysis

- Economic Growth
- Inflation Expectations
- Monetary Policy
- Fiscal Policy
- Supply/Demand Characteristics

Currency Market Analysis

- Trade Accounts
- Interest Rate Differentials
- Political Attitudes

outlook based upon an analysis of broad macroeconomic issues and the economic conditions within each country. Basics include inflation and growth expectations, the stance of monetary and fiscal policy, and current account developments (see Exhibit 5). The particular area of focus may be different in each market and generally changes over time. Managers also should assess the technical position of the bond market and general market sentiment.

Formulating an investment outlook and understanding the idiosyncracies of each foreign market requires a significant effort at the beginning. However, investors can develop a market familiarity by monitoring yield changes and major developments daily. This information is accessible through electronic services and international newspapers, as well as global market makers. Moreover, investors will become increasingly familiar with subjects such as the stance of German monetary policy or the attitudes of Japanese investors as these factors continue to have an impact on the U.S. market.

INVESTMENT STRATEGIES

There are three basic investment strategies in the nondollar market. An outright bond investment provides nondollar bond market and foreign exchange market exposure. Bond investments in conjunction with a currency hedge in the short-dated forward market provides nondollar bond market exposure and limited currency exposure. Finally, fully hedged nondollar bonds periodically provide attractive yield pick-ups over comparable U.S. instruments. Exhibit 6 defines the risks and reward of these three strategies.

Widespread expectations for U.S. dollar depreciation following the September 1985 G-5 Plaza Accord encouraged outright bond investments in the nondollar

EXHIBIT 6
INVESTMENT STRATEGIES

Strategy	Mechanics	Exposure	Objective
Outright Bond Investment	Buy a nondollar bond and the foreign exchange to pay for it.	Nondollar bond and foreign exchange markets	Higher yield or Superior price performance or Currency appreciation
Bond Investment with Currency Hedge (Forward Hedged)	Buy a nondollar bond and the foreign exchange to pay for it. Simultaneously, sell the foreign currency in the short-dated forward exchange market. The short fx position hedges the long currency position stemming from the underlying bond investment.	Nondollar bond market	Higher yield or Superior price performance
Fully Hedged (Asset Swap)	Buy a nondollar bond and the foreign exchange to pay for it. Hedge all of the nondollar cash flows using currency swaps or a series of forward exchange rates. This creates a synthetic fixed or floating rate U.S. dollar instrument.	U.S. bond market	Yield pick-up over comparable U.S. investment

sectors by U.S. investors. However, the dollar's appreciation during 1988 and early 1989 has contributed to the popularity of forward hedged transactions. Recent studies suggest that hedged portfolios maintain their diversification benefits and have substantially lower variation of returns than unhedged portfolios.

When bond market exposure without currency exposure is desired, investors should match their long nondollar bond position with a short currency position in the foreign exchange market. The short position is established by selling the currency in the forward foreign exchange market. Exhibit 7 shows that currency depreciation would lead to an exchange rate loss on the long bond position and a gain on the short currency position. Alternatively, currency appreciation would lead to an exchange rate gain on the long position and a loss on the short position. Exposure in the nondollar bond market is maintained in each case.

EXHIBIT 7
THE HEDGING MATRIX

	Long Bond Market Position	Short Forward Currency Position
Currency Appreciation	Currency Gain	Currency Loss
Currency Depreciation	Currency Loss	Currency Gain

MARKET DIFFERENTIATION

Investors must differentiate among the markets in determining the portfolio composition. Within Europe, Dutch and French securities provide an alternative to German bonds, while U.K. gilts represent another option. The Japanese bond market is the world's second largest, and has several unique features. Many investors view the Canadian sector as a high yielding alternative to the U.S. market, given the high correlation of these sectors and the relatively stable C$/US$ relationship. Finally, the Australian and New Zealand sectors have an important and unique role in global portfolios.

Europe

European bond market and currency exposure generally represents an important component of global portfolios. The German government bond market is the largest in Continental Europe with DM175 billion of bonds outstanding. German bonds provide exposure to a traditionally hard currency, low inflation country. Over the last few years, expectations for currency appreciation and interest rate declines stemming from Germany's low inflation and large current account surpluses spurred foreign inflows.

Bonds denominated in other European Monetary System (EMS) currencies should be viewed as alternatives to DM bonds. EMS members include Germany, France, Belgium, Italy, Denmark, and the Netherlands. Unless there are formal realignments, the member currencies of the EMS are pegged to each other within specified bands (Exhibit 8). These currencies all provide similar foreign exchange exposure to U.S. investors during periods of EMS stability. Thus, it is often advantageous for investors to exploit the yield advantage of the traditionally weaker EMS currencies. Looking forward, the convergence of economic policies and conditions within Europe should lead to fewer and less dramatic realignments.

EXHIBIT 8
EXCHANGE RATES AGAINST THE DM

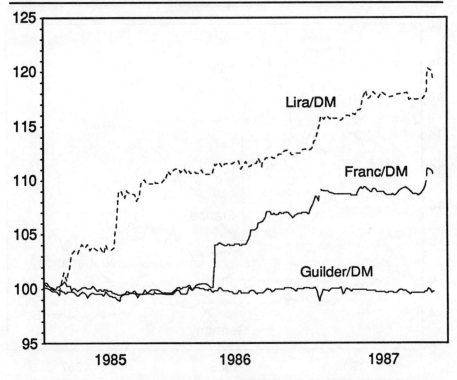

Dutch guilder and French franc bonds represent the most viable alternatives. Dutch guilder bonds generally provide yield advantages over German securities, especially in the short end of the yield curve (Exhibit 9). Moreover, the guilder-DM crossrate is historically stable, reflecting an implicit objective of Dutch monetary policy. In France, liberalizations to establish a system of primary dealers, standardize government bond issues, and develop the futures markets have improved the liquidity and sophistication of the market. The spread differential between French and German bonds reflects inflation differentials, perceived polititcal and currency risks, and other market factors.

U.K. government bonds (Gilt-Edged Stocks or Gilts) represent another important sector. "Big Bang" in October 1986 replaced an antiquated system of single capacity jobbers and brokers with a system of U.S. style primary dealers. This served to dramatically improve the liquidity and efficiency of the market. Sterling is not part of the EMS stabilization mechanism. However, the DM/£ crossrate is an important policy guide to the U.K. authorities, and investors should view sterling assets as an alternative to the EMS markets.

EXHIBIT 9
3-MONTH EUROCURRENCY RATES

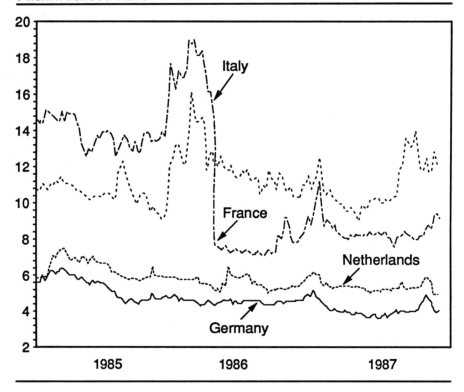

Japan

Investments in the Japanese sector provide exposure to a country that has had relatively low inflation and large external surpluses during the 1980s. The Japanese bond market is the world's second largest, with its strong growth reflecting larger Japanese budget deficits over the last decade. Market liberalizations, such as the development of the Euroyen sector and a liquid futures market also have led to advances in this sector. The Japanese market has several unique features. For example, a benchmark bond receives 75-95% of all trading volume, with large intraday moves on this bond routine. In addition, investor flows and the speculative nature of this sector often can exaggerate market moves. For example, a marked preference of Japanese investors to limit their U.S. dollar investments helped to push Japanese bond yields to historic lows during April 1987, which was followed by a severe market sell-off later in the year (Exhibit 10).

EXHIBIT 10
10-YEAR GOJ BOND YIELD

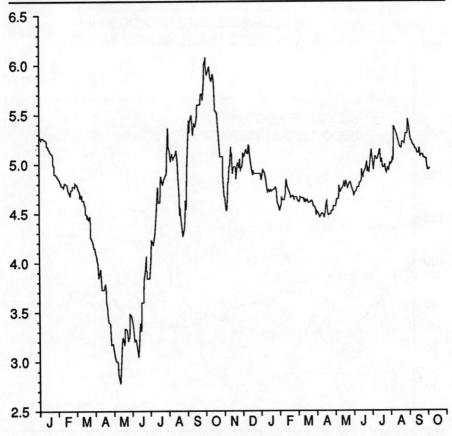

Canada

The correlation between the U.S. and Canadian sectors is relatively high. As a result, the Canadian market generally tracks the U.S. fixed income market in the absence of major local developments. Moreover, the C$/US$ relationship is historically relatively stable (Exhibit 11). While the Canadian sector provides minimal diversification benefits versus U.S. dollar investments, it does offer incremental yield opportunities. Canadian bonds also can outperform when the spread to U.S. Treasuries narrows. This occurred during 1987 when foreign inflows to Canada increased and the fundamental outlook improved. Short-term securities become particularly attractive when their yield advantage to U.S. Treasuries becomes sufficiently wide to underpin the C$ in the foreign exchange market.

488

EXHIBIT 11
C$ EXCHANGE RATE RELATIONSHIP

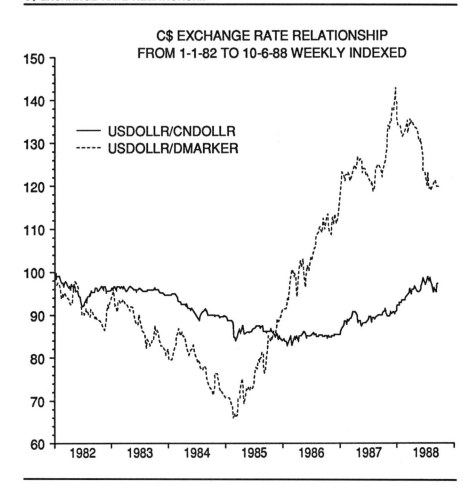

C$ EXCHANGE RATE RELATIONSHIP
FROM 1-1-82 TO 10-6-88 WEEKLY INDEXED

USDOLLR/CNDOLLR
USDOLLR/DMARKER

Australia and New Zealand

Although the Down Under sectors are relatively small in a global context, they receive disproportionate attention from international investors. Certainly, the high yields in these sectors help to capture investors' focus. More fundamentally, investors have responded to the implementation of pragmatic fiscal and monetary policies and economic reforms designed to address structural economic problems and large external deficits. These countries offer unique diversification given their role as commodity exporters. Rising commodity prices and global inflation fears helped both sectors during 1987.

RELATIVE VALUE ANALYSIS

Relative value analysis within each foreign market concludes the investment process. This entails selecting the desired maturity along the yield curve, the sector of the market, and the particular security. Given the recent dramatic movements in currency and interest rates, relative value analysis has not been emphasized by many managers. However, the pursuit of incremental total return within markets will become increasingly important as currency relationships become more stable. Moreover, index managers will need to emphasize relative value considerations given the overall portfolio duration and composition constraints.

Maturity Selection

Maturity selection obviously reflects the market outlook and objectives of the portfolio manager. The added twist in global management is to assess relative yield curve shapes. For example, the Canadian yield curve has been flatter than the U.S. yield curve over the recent period, making the yield advantage of Canadian securities wider at the short end. Short- to intermediate-term maturities therefore provided superior relative value. Short maturity U.K. securities have offered excellent relative value for investors desiring European currency exposure and a defensive bond market posture. The U.K. yield curve has been flat or inverted compared to the steep German yield curve, while the DM-£ crossrate has remained relatively stable. Finally, the inverted yield curve in New Zealand led yield conscious investors to favor the shorter maturities.

Sector Selection

Government bonds and foreign currency Yankee or Eurobond issues represent the most common investment alternatives. Many investors generally concentrate their activity in government bonds, which are considered the most liquid and the highest credit quality. Exhibit 12 depicts the alternative investments to government bonds within each nondollar market. These alternatives provide yield advantages and the potential for incremental total return from changing spread relationships. Moreover, Eurobonds and Yankee bonds are exempt from the withholding taxes applied on Japanese, Australian, New Zealand and other domestic securities. While U.S. investors can credit foreign withholding taxes against U.S. taxes (subject to constraints on foreign source income and other considerations), many investors nonetheless prefer the tax-free sectors.

EXHIBIT 12
ALTERNATIVES TO GOVERNMENT BONDS

	Domestic Alternatives	Foreign Currency[1] Yankee Bonds	Eurobonds
Japan	Samurai[2]	Isolated Issues	Active Market
Germany	Bundesbahn[3] Bundespost Pfandbriefe	None	Active Market
U.K.	Bulldogs[4]	None	Active Market
France	Provincials	None	Isolated Issues
Canada	Provincials	Isolated Issues	Increasingly Active Market
Australia	Semi-Governments Corporates	Active Market	Increasingly Active Market
New Zealand	N.A.	Active Market	Isolated Issues

[1]Issued in the U.S. capital market, SEC registered, and exempt from withholding taxes.
[2]Yen denominated bonds issued in Japan by non-Japanese issuers.
[3]Bundesbahn are bonds issued by the Federal Railway;
  Bundespost are issued by the Federal Post Office;
  Pfandbriefe are issued by private or public mortgage banks and collateralized by mortgages.
[4]Sterling denominated bonds issued in the U.K. by non-U.K. issuers.

For example, Australian Semi-Government securities often represent an attractive alternative to Commonwealth Bonds. Semi-Government Authorities are statutory authorities formed under an act of State or Federal parliament, and all Semi borrowings carry explicit guarantees of their respective governments. Top-tier issuers include New South Wales Treasury, Telecom, and Victoria Finance. Semis generally provide attractive yield pick-ups to Commonwealth issues (Exhibit 13). Moreover, Semis can outperform if the yield spread narrows as happened during the summer of 1987 when investor demand increased and the supply of Semi-Government issuance declined.

German bank mortgage bonds represent an alternative to Bundesrepublik issues. Phandbriefe bonds are issued by private and public mortgage banks and are collateralized by commercial mortgages. Importantly, the bank sector remains dominated by domestic investors, while the Bunds sector is heavily dependent on foreign participants. The Bank sector can outperform when anticipated DM weakness encourages foreign liquidations of German bonds. This factor has recently resulted in a substantial narrowing of the spread between these sectors (Exhibit 14).

EXHIBIT 13
COMMONWEALTH AND SEMI YIELD CURVES

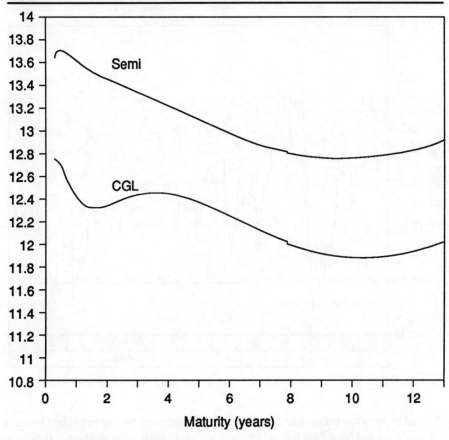

Security Selection

Actual security selection involves special considerations in some foreign markets. In Japan, for example, a benchmark bond generally receives 75-95% of all trading volume. The benchmark must have a large outstanding volume, an original maturity of 10-years, and a coupon close to current market rates. The benchmark bond displays the most volatility. Exhibit 15 shows that the spread between the benchmark and surrounding issues widened to 90 basis points during the Spring 1987 rally then contracted to 25 basis points during the summer setback. Investors bullish on the yen market should own the benchmark bond, while investors more neutral on the market

EXHIBIT 14
PHANDBRIEFE VS. BUNDS

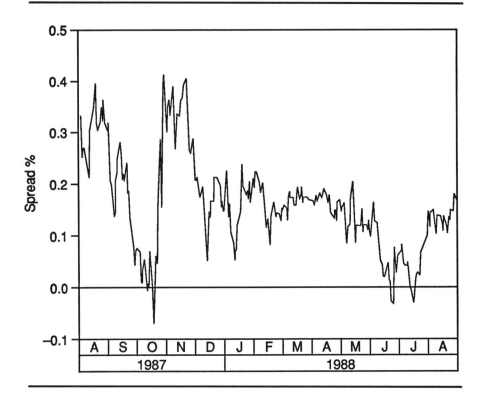

should concentrate on surrounding issues. A less dramatic benchmark effect prevails in Australia and New Zealand, while the situation in most other markets is similar to the on-the-run versus off-the-run characteristics of the U.S. Treasury market.

As another example, the U.K. market has several quirks related to security selection. The practice of the Bank of England to fund throughout the yield curve and to routinely re-open existing issues leads to numerous liquid on-the-run issues. Moreover, a U.S. investor should choose a "Section 99" bond which facilitates the process of gaining exemption from withholding tax. Finally, since there is no capital gains tax on gilts, U.K. residents prefer low coupon bonds. This generally makes discounts expensive relative to high coupon bonds in the gilt sector.

EXHIBIT 15
JAPANESE BENCHMARK VERSUS SIDE ISSUE YIELD SPREAD

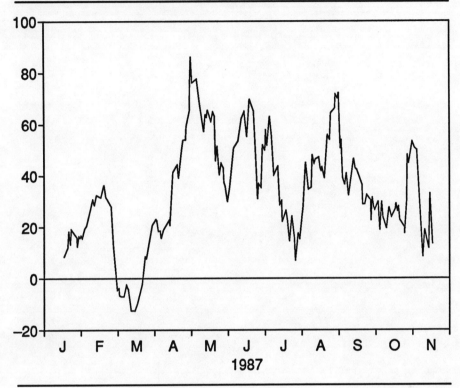

Chapter 23

Measuring the Yield of Currency Hedged Foreign Bonds: New Tools for International Fixed Income Investors

LEE R. THOMAS, III, PH.D.
INVESTCORP

Comparing foreign and domestic bond yields is fundamental to managing internationally diversified bond portfolios. In assessing relative values, international investors typically regard bond yields as the best single measure of a market's cheapness or richness. Yield comparisons are particularly important to investors engaging in a strategy now commonly referred to as "international arbitrage": buying a bond

Lee R. Thomas, III, was an Executive Director in the Financial Strategies Group at Goldman, Sachs & Co., London, when this chapter was written. The author would like to express his thanks to Tom Macirowski and Andrew Hudis, who provided many useful comments on this chapter; and to Edwin Robertson, who worked up the examples with his usual skill and expertise. He is also grateful to Ron Krieger for his tireless efforts in reviewing the structure and content of innumerable versions of this chapter, and to Diana Rich for her strong, professional editorial support.

denominated in one currency and simultaneously selling an otherwise similar bond denominated in another currency.[1]

Most sophisticated investors understand that when you execute international bond switches, you should do them on a currency hedged basis.[2] Unfortunately, however, you cannot apply conventional yield measures to currency hedged foreign bonds. This presents a problem: How do you compare bond yields internationally in a common, currency-neutral way?

To solve this problem, we recommend that investors and arbitragers alike use an alternative measure of a foreign bond's yield, one that we call "currency hedged yield," or simply "hedged yield." In this chapter and the one to follow, we will explain how this concept works and how it can help you to spot and exploit opportunities in the international bond markets.

INTERNATIONAL "ARBITRAGE"

We traditionally think of arbitrage, in the classical sense, as the simultaneous purchase and sale of identical or equivalent securities to exploit price discrepancies in different markets. Needless to say, such risk-free arbitrage opportunities have always been rare. Advances in communications technology have made them even rarer.

The "Arbitrage" Spectrum

In recent years, usage of the term arbitrage has broadened to include the simultaneous purchase and sale of *similar* securities in different markets. What investors now commonly refer to as "arbitrage" actually encompasses a spectrum of trades ranging from classical (or risk-free) arbitrage, in which the securities bought and sold are identical, to near outright speculation, in which the securities exchanged share only a few characteristics. The more alike the securities are in an arbitrage trade, the less risky the trade is likely to be.[3]

In the international bond markets, fully hedged swaps represent classical arbitrage trades; they carry no interest rate or exchange rate risks. To execute a fully hedged trade, an investor buys a debt security denominated in currency "X," converts each

---

[1] This trade is sometimes called an international "switch" or an international "swap." We will use these terms interchangeably.

[2] In particular, you would not ordinarily use a bond switch to change the currency composition of your portfolio. Instead, you can use forward foreign exchange contracts if your exchange rate views change. Use bond switches when you anticipate a change in relative interest rates or wish to exploit attractive yield opportunities.

[3] Specifically, the more highly correlated the returns to the securities, the lower the volatility that will result from taking a position that is long one security and short the other.

of its cash flows into currency "Y" using forward foreign exchange contracts or swaps, and then sells a portfolio of currency "Y" denominated bonds that has identical cash flows. The securities bought and sold promise the same payments; they are essentially identical instruments. As a consequence, if you execute the trades properly, the only risks on fully covered swaps are credit risk—the possibility that a bond issuer or the counterparty to the forward exchange contracts will default—and liquidity risk.

Unhedged international bond swaps represent the other end of the spectrum, where "arbitrage" is almost indistinguishable from outright speculation. You might enter into one of these trades when bond yields in one country appear to be "unreasonable" compared with bond yields in another country. Say, for example, that long-term government bond yields in country "X" are normally 250 basis points (bp) higher than those in country "Y." If the current differential is 400 bp, you, as a bond arbitrager or a fixed income portfolio manager, may consider positioning in anticipation that the spread will narrow. You do this by buying the "cheap" bonds and selling the "rich" ones. Since the bonds bought and sold are issued by different borrowers and are denominated in different currencies, these trades carry not only credit and liquidity risk, but also interest rate and exchange rate risk. The latter two hazards—interest rate risk and exchange rate risk—are usually substantial.

Evaluating Opportunities and Limiting Risk

One of the problems in identifying international bond arbitrage opportunities is that a simple comparison of yields on bonds in different countries may be misleading. Often the bonds differ in so many important ways that making a meaningful appraisal is almost impossible.

If the bonds were denomianted in the same currency, the task of comparing them would be much easier. You could then evaluate the arbitrage opportunity independently of your exchange rate views. The basic arbitrage position—long one bond and short the other—would not carry exchange rate risk.

We cannot literally redenominate one bond in the currency of another. But we can achieve a similar effect by combining the bond with forward foreign exchange contracts, using a rolling hedge design.[4] Currency hedging helps to make the bonds more comparable, and the resulting position generally is much less risky.

When bond positions are motivated by a view on relative interest rate movements, we recommend currency hedging to neutralize the foreign exchange rate risks on these trades. Currency hedging eliminates an element of risk from the trade, and it

---

[4]In Lee R. Thomas, III, *Managing Currency Risks in International Bond Portfolios*, Goldman Sachs December 1987, I show how to change the effective currency denomination of a bond by using rolling forward foreign exchange contracts. This strategy, in contrast to a fully hedged design, leaves the bond exposed to interest rate risk in its original currency.

simplifies the evaluation of arbitrage opportunities—once you have the right tool for comparing yields.

A word of warning is in order, however: Even when you currency hedge to eliminate your foreign exchange rate exposure, you should not underestimate the risks that may be associated with such arbitrage trades. For example, Exhibit 1, which shows the correlations between currency hedged foreign bond returns and the returns on U.S. Treasuries, illustrates how weak the linkages are between U.S. and foreign interest rates. While all of these correlations are, in statistical terms, significantly greater than zero, they are still small. This means that interest rate changes in the United States are not closely related to interest rate changes in other countries.[5] As a result, even when you do currency hedge to eliminate *exchange rate* risk, the *interest rate* risks on most U.S./foreign bond swaps are substantial.[6]

EXHIBIT 1
CORRELATIONS BETWEEN U.S. TREASURY AND FOREIGN BOND RETURNS*

	Japan	Germany	U.K.	France	Canada
U.S.	.32	.53	.35	.45	.83

*Based on monthly data (1983-87) for returns on currency hedged 10-year bonds.

TOWARD EASIER TRADING DECISIONS

Currency hedging a foreign bond by combining it with a forward foreign exchange contract is the recommended and relatively common practice in international bond switches and arbitrage trades. But unfortunately, you cannot apply conventional yield measures to the resulting bond-forward package. Hedged yield—the new measure of yield we develop in this paper—does allow us to compare domestic bonds with foreign bonds that we have currency hedged with rolling forward exchange contracts. In fact, we can use hedged yield to compare any pair of bonds denomianted in different currencies—hedged either back into your local currency or into any other common currency of your choice. This makes hedged yield a valuable

---

[5]Currency hedged international bond switches will be closest to classical arbitrage when the correlations between the hedged bond returns of the two countries involved are high and stable. Some of the most attractive candidates and their estimated return correlations are: Germany and the Netherlands: 0.74; Germany and France: 0.59; and the Netherlands and France: 0.63.

[6]In fact, the interest rate risks on international arbitrage trades involving U.S. Treasuries are generally only slightly less than the interest rate risks you assume with an outright long bond position. So "arbitrage" is a somewhat curious term for this kind of trade. You can mitigate these risks, however, by immunizing each leg of the trade against changes in the level of interest rates in that country. We describe the basic techniques for establishing an immunized, currency hedged position in the next chapter.

tool for international portfolio managers and for more aggressive arbitragers. As you will see, hedged yield is a straightforward notion and is relatively easy to calculate.

A Simple Example

To explain how the concept of hedged yield can simplify international bond investment decision, we will use the example of a basic cross-country exchange—10-year German Government bonds (Bundesanleihens, or "Bunds") for 10-year U.S. Treasuries. In mid-June, 1988, 10-year U.S. Treasury bonds were priced to yield 8.90%, while the yield on 10-year Bunds was 6.43%. (To foster comparability, we express both as annually compounded yields.)

Both of these bonds are govenment obligations, and the bonds' yields are substantially different. Is this therefore an attractive switch opportunity for a dollar-based investor? Before attempting an answer, let's first look at Exhibit 2, which lists the major risks associated with substituting one bond for another on an unhedged basis.

EXHIBIT 2
A 10-YEAR U.S. TREASURY VERSUS A 10-YEAR BUND

Characteristic	U.S. Treasury	Bund
Credit Risk	Negligible	Negligible
Interest Rate Risk	Exposed to increases in U.S. interest rates	Exposed to increases in German interest rates
Currency Risk	Denominated in U.S. dollars: No exchange rate risk	Denominated in German marks: Exposed to a depreciation of the mark

As you can see, U.S. Treasuries and Bunds differ in two major ways: interest rate risk and currency exposure. Hence a position established by buying one bond and shorting the other—or selling it out of your current portfolio—will carry *both* interest rate and exchange rate risk. The *unhedged* Treasury/Bund switch is thus risky and difficult to evaluate. Does the U.S. Treasury yield premium of 2.47% just compensate, overcompensate, or undercompensate for the exchange rate and interest rate risks you would bear by buying a U.S. Treasury and selling a Bund?

A Common Currency Denomination

We could better assess this potential bond trade if we could change the characteristics of one (or both) of the bonds to make them easier to compare. For example, we could effectively redenominate one or the other of the issues so that both carried the same currency exposure. Then the arbitrage position—long one bond, short the other—

would at least be free of exchange rate risk.[7] And as the overall risk of the arbitrage trade declines, the position will become closer in spirit to classical arbitrage and less like outright speculation. It will also become clearer whether the U.S./German yield differential represents a true opportunity—that is, whether interest rates in the two countries are truly out of line.

To compare the issues more readily we must synthetically change the effective denomination of one of the bonds: Either change the U.S. Treasury bond to German marks, or change the Bund to U.S. dollars. The outcomes are equivalent, so we can choose either approach. Here we will take the second; we will eliminate the Bund's exposure to changes in the dollar/mark exchange rate by combining it with forward foreign exchange contracts. We call the resulting composite security a "synthetic U.S. Treasury bond," a "currency hedged Bund," or simply a "hedged Bund." Exhibit 3 compares the risk characteristics of the two bonds.

EXHIBIT 3
A 10-YEAR U.S. TREASURY VERSUS A CURRENCY HEDGED 10-YEAR BUND

Characteristic	U.S. Treasury	Bund
Credit Risk	Negligible	Negligible
Interest Rate Risk	Exposed to increases in U.S. interest rates	Exposed to increases in German interest rates
Currency Risk	Denominated in U.S. dollars: No exchange rate risk	Effectively denominated in U.S. dollars: Negligible exchange rate risk

Both bonds represent sovereign credit risks, although the hedged Bund also carries some credit risk on its associated forward exchange contract. From a U.S. dollar investor's perspective, neither the U.S. Treasury nor the hedged Bund carries significant exchange rate risk.[8] As a result, the arbitrage trade—long one bond, short the other—is also essentially free of exchange rate risk, and an international asset manager who substitutes a synthetic Treasury for a U.S. Treasury (or vice versa) does not change his portfolio's exchange rate risk. The only important difference between these investments is their interest rate exposures. The U.S. Treasury is exposed to changes in long-term U.S. interest rates, while the hedged

---

[7]If you are a portfolio manager, you will execute the trade by buying one bond and selling the other out of your portfolio. You may think of this as adding the arbitrage position—long one bond, short the other—to your existing portfolio.

[8]If you hedge using conventional forward exchange contracts, the position retains some residual exchange rate risk. This is because you cannot predict how much the market price of the Bund will appreciate or depreciate in advance. Thus, you cannot design a perfect currency hedge. In practice, the resulting risk is small.

Bund is exposed to changes in German interest rates. Consequently, the arbitrage trade we would execute if the hedged Bund/U.S. Treasury yield difference became "unreasonable" would leave us exposed to changes in relative interest rates. This is exactly what we might want if we thought German interest rates were "too high" or "too low" compared with U.S. bond yields.

But to determine whether this kind of trade makes sense, we must be able to compare the yield on the U.S. Treasury with the yield on the hedged Bund. We call the difference between the hedged Bund's yield and the yield on the U.S. Treasury the "hedged yield spread," or simply the "hedged spread." To calculate it we must have some way of computing the yield on a hedged Bund—in essence, the yield on a portfolio consisting of a Bund and a forward foreign exchange contract.

MEASURES OF YIELD

We've already pointed out that conventional yield measures are not applicable to a hedged foreign bond. But whatever we substitute must still be *parallel* to the conventional measures of yield on a domestic issue if we are to make a valid comparison of the bonds in our prospective switch. In this section, we introduce two measures of hedged yield—one analogous to what we call the "yield to horizon" of a domestic bond, the other comparable to yield to maturity. Which one you use will depend on the circumstances underlying the contemplated trade—in particular, on the assumptions you are willing to make regarding what will happen to the relevant yield curves while you own the bonds.

We will first review the domestic bond measures of yield to maturity and yield to horizon. We will next relate each tool to its corresponding measure of hedged yield. Then, after explaining how to calcualte these new measures, we will go back and apply them to our Bund/U.S. Treasury example.

Yield to Maturity

Yield to maturity, the most commonly used measure of a bond's yield, is usually defined as the discount rate that makes the present value of a bond's promised cash flows equal to the bond's price. All other things being equal, investors prefer high yield to low because they believe that the higher the bond's yield to maturity, the higher the bond's probable return, even if they don't hold the issue until it matures.

It's important to note, however, that a bond's yield to maturity is guaranteed to equal its rate of return only under special circumstances, for example: (1) if you hold the bond to maturity, and (2) if you can reinvest the bond's coupons, as they are received, at a rate equal to the yield to maturity. Most bondholders do not routinely hold their bonds to maturity. Furthermore, even for those who do, the prospective return earned by holding a bond to maturity is usually extremely sensitive to the assumed coupon reinvestment rate.

The trades we are contemplating certainly do not involve holding bonds to maturity. Ordinarily, the holding period for an arbitrager will be weeks or months, not years. The investment horizons of international portfolio managers are likely to be a little longer, but few hold bonds to term. What, then, does yield to maturity tell an investor who does *not* intend to hold a bond to maturity? In particular, what is the relationship between a bond's yield to maturity and its total rate of return if the holding period is relatively short?

Yield to maturity can *still* equal the rate of return to a bond held over a short period, but again, only under very special circumstances: if the yield to maturity when the bond is eventually sold equals the yield to maturity when the bond was bought. That is, in an upward-sloping yield curve environment, the yield curve must rise by just enough to keep the yield to maturity of the bond constant as it ages and rolls down the curve.

For example, imagine that you buy a 10-year U.S. Treasury security on June 15, when it is priced to yield 8.90%. On July 15, you sell it. (Assume for simplicity that no coupons are paid during the intervening month.) If on the date of the sale the bond is still priced to yield 8.90% to maturity, then your annualized return on the completed transaction will be 8.90% (ignoring transaction costs). If on July 15 the bond is less than 8.90%, then your return will be less than 8.90%. If it is priced to yield less than 8.90%, your total return will be greater. If the original yield curve at the time of purchase on June 15 was upward sloping, then interest rates must shift upward to keep this bond's yield at 8.90% as it ages.

Yield to Horizon

What if, on the other hand, the yield does not change as the bond ages? What if, instead, the yield curve remains the same, and the yield changes as the bond rolls up or down the curve? Then, another yield measure, sometimes called the bond's "rolling yield," will be more useful than yield to maturity in assessing the bond's relative attractiveness. Since computing a bond's rolling yield requires using horizon analysis, we will call this yield measure the bond's "yield to horizon," or simply its "horizon yield."

Let's list the steps you would follow to compute a bond's yield to horizon:

1. First, you must select an appropriate investment horizon. The investment horizon represents a convenient hypothetical holding period for the bond.
2. Next, you assume that the yield curve will not shift or change shape over the period you hold the bond.
3. Finally, based on these assumptions, you compute the (annualized) rate of return to holding the bond from the present to the specified investment horizon.[9] This rate of return is the bond's yield to the horizon you selected in step 1.

---

[9]The rate of return takes into account all coupons, accrued interest, and capital gains or losses. The prospective capital gain or loss depends on the bond's price change as it ages and rolls up or down the (stationary) yield curve.

Remember, a bond's yield to horizon represents its prospective rate of return (including interest and capital gains) over a prespecified holding period only if the yield curve does not shift or change its shape.[10]

In practice, to compute a yield to horizon you must add accrued or realized coupon income (and reinvestment income, if a coupon is paid during the holding period) to the capital gain that will result as the bond rolls down the yield curve. In the event that the yield curve is inverted, the bond rolls up the curve and you must subtract the bond's prospective depreciation. Basically, yield to horizon equals a bond's yield to maturity plus a term that captures the effects of this capital gain or loss. Ordinarily, for long maturity bonds evaluated over short holding periods—the case in which we are primarily interested—the second term will be small. In this event, a bond's yield to horizon may not be very different from its yield to maturity.

In our example—the 10-year U.S. Treasury we are comparing with the 10-year Bund—the yield to maturity is 8.90%, while the one-month horizon yield is approximately 8.02%. Evaluated at a three-month holding period, this Treasury's horizon yield is approximately 7.80%. These horizon yields are based on the yield curve of June 15, 1988, which we show in Exhibit 4. Although the U.S. curve is *generally*

EXHIBIT 4
U.S. TREASURY YIELD CURVE, JUNE 15, 1988

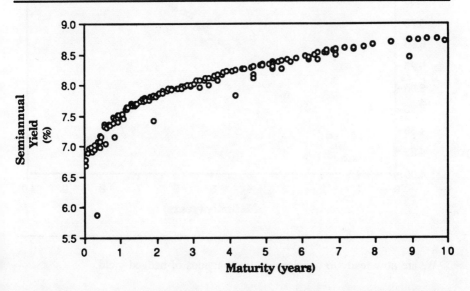

---

[10]Obviously, horizon yield does not tell us everything we need to know to evaluate a bond, or to compare two bonds. We ordinarily also want to know the prospective rate of return to a bond if the yield curve *does* shift or change shape in particular ways. We can generalize the concept of horizon yield (and the related horizon yield curve) to reflect these calculations, but this is not the place to describe how.

upward sloping, the yields to one-month and three-month horizons in this case are less than this bond's yield to maturity. This is because the U.S. yield curve is downward sloping for bonds in the 9¾- to 10-year maturity range.[11] As the 10-year Treasury ages, we expect its yield to rise by 1 bp at one month, or by 4 bp at three months, assuming no change in the U.S. interest rate environment.

For the Bunds, the yield curve is upward sloping in the 9¾- to 10-year region (see Exhibit 5). Under these circumstances, we would expect the Bund yield to fall as the bond aged. Accordingly, its mark-measured yield to a one-month horizon (6.56%) or a three-month horizon (6.97%) exceed its yield to maturity (6.43)%.

EXHIBIT 5
GERMAN GOVERNMENT BOND YIELD CURVE, JUNE 15, 1988

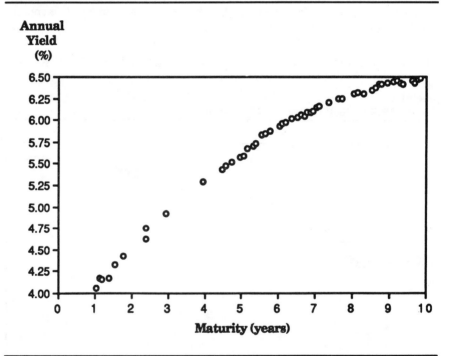

We are now ready to develop our two versions of hedged yield.

---

[11]In this case, we have used a simple visual approximation of the slope in this range. Ordinarily, you would employ a more sophisticated approach, via such methods as (1) running a simple regression equation or (2) decomposing the bonds into their underlying cash flows, estimating the zero coupon yield curve, and estimating—from the fitted curve—the prospective change in yield as the bond ages.

Hedged Horizon Yield

Like a domestic bond's yield to horizon, our first method of calculating the hedged yield on a foreign bond is based on horizon analysis.[12] This version represents the annualized return to a currency hedged foreign bond investment over a prespecified holding period, assuming that the relevant foreign yield curve does not shift or change its shape while you hold the position.[13] Notice that the interest rate assumption we use to compute hedged horizon yield—that the foreign yield curve does not shift or change shape—is identical to the assumption we make for a domestic bond when we compute its horizon yield. This makes it straight-forward to compare a domestic bond's horizon yield with a foreign bond's hedged horizon yield.

To see how hedged horizon yield works, refer back to the previous example. There we noted that on June 15 our 10-year Bund is priced to yield 6.43%; its yield evaluated at a one-month holding period, measured in German marks, is 6.56%. Suppose that you buy the Bund on that date, hold it for a month, and then sell it. Also imagine that the German yield curve does not shift or change shape during the intervening month. What will be your return?

For the German investor measuring the rate of return in marks, the answer is simple—6.56%. This is merely the horizon yield, applied to a 10-year Bund with a one-month investment horizon. But if you are a U.S. investor measuring the return in U.S. dollars, you must also consider what will happen to the mark/dollar exchange rate during the month. The dollar investor's return will equal 6.56% only if the exchange rate remains unchanged during the month.

What if you hedge your bond's currency exposure by selling marks one month forward for U.S. dollars when you buy the Bund? Then the trade bears no exchange rate risk, so you can ignore the appreciation or depreciation of the mark/dollar exchange rate. This, however, does not mean that you can ignore exchange rate considerations completely when computing the return to the position. Rather, since marks sell at a premium for one-month delivery, hedging by selling marks forward *increases* your dollar-measured return.

Say that on June 15, the one-month mark annualized forward premium is 3.77%. By hedging, you earn this certain return in addition to the Bund's mark-measured rate of return of 6.56% (if German interest rates do not change). Assuming that you hedge both the bond's future market value[14] and the prospective coupons or accrued interest, you can calculate the total return on the hedged Bund position as:

---

[12]This is perhaps the most obvious yield measure to use for a hedged foreign bond, since the forward contract used to strip away the bond's exchange rate risk defines a natural investment horizon. (Recall that the first step in calculating horizon yield is to select an investment horizon.)

[13]Remember that "currency hedged" here refers to bonds combined with a rolling hedge, rather than a cash-flow-by-cash-flow, fully hedged bond position. The differences between these hedge designs are detailed in *Managing Currency Risks in International Bond Portfolios*.

[14]Consistent with our assumptions, the future market value is taken to be the current market value, adjusted for its prospective capital gain or loss as it rolls up or down the stationary yield curve.

$$(1 + 0.0656)(1 + 0.0377) - 1 = 0.1058 = 10.58\%.$$

This is the Bund's hedged yield at a one-month horizon.

In short: *A foreign bond's hedged horizon yield shows the annualized return that you will earn over a prespecified holding period by buying a foreign bond, selling foreign currency forward (for domestic currency) for delivery at the end of the holding period, and then selling the bond at period end—if the foreign yield curve does not change.*

To calculate a foreign bond's hedged horizon yield, you need to know the foreign bond's horizon yield (measured in its local currency) and the appropriate forward exchange discount or premium. The formula is simply:

$$\left(\begin{array}{c} \text{Foreign Bond's} \\ 1 + \text{Horizon Yield} \end{array} \right) \times \left(\begin{array}{c} \text{Foreign Currency} \\ 1 + \text{Forward Premium} \\ \text{or Discount} \end{array} \right) - 1.$$

Another warning: Like a domestic bond's horizon yield, a foreign bond's hedged horizon yield is only a benchmark. In this case it is based on the critical assumption that the relevant foreign yield curve does not shift or change shape while you hold the bond. In fact, as we will see below, if we make a contrary assumption—for example, if we assume the yield curve will shift by just enough to keep the bond's yield to maturity constant—then hedged yield will come out to a different value.

Hedged Yield to Maturity

If you are willing to change the assumptions underlying your calculations—that is, if you are willing to assume that the foreign bond's *yield to maturity* will not change over your holding period, rather than that the foreign yield curve will not change—then you can compute hedged yield much more easily. While this new assumption may at first appear heroic, recall that when you use yield to maturity as a measure of a domestic bond's prospective return over a short holding period, you are implicitly making an analogous assumption about domestic interest rates. That is, you assume that the yield curve will shift by just enough to leave the bond's yield to maturity unchanged as it ages.[15]

Hedged yield to maturity is easy to compute. Recall the formula (above) for our first version of hedged yield—hedged horizon yield. In the same way, we can

---

[15]If you are using yield to maturity to measure return to a domestic bond held to term, your most important assumption is that coupons can be reinvested at a rate equal to the original yield. For hedged yield ot maturity to measure the return to a foreign bond held to term, you must make the same assumption plus one more: You must also assume that the forward exchange discount or premium does not change. (Ordinarily we would not use hedged yield to maturity to measure the return to a bond held to term, since it is designed to compare prospective returns over shorter holding periods.)

compute hedged yield to maturity, which assumes that the yield to maturity of the foreign bond does not change while you hold it:

$$\left(\begin{array}{c} \text{Foreign Bond's} \\ 1 + \text{Yield to Maturity} \end{array}\right) \times \left(\begin{array}{c} \text{Foreign Currency} \\ 1 + \text{Forward Premium} \\ \text{or Discount} \end{array}\right) - 1.$$

This second version of hedged yield will ordinarily be easier to calculate because you will normally *know* the foreign bond's yield to maturity, but you will have to *compute* its yield to a horizon. Hedged yield to horizon, on the other hand, is often more useful, since it can be used to directly calculate the carry on an international bond switch.[16]

One point to keep in mind: If you intend to compare bond yields in different countries, make sure that the yields to maturity you use are expressed on a comparable basis. For example, German bond yields are ordinarily quoted on an annual, rather than a semiannual, basis.

A Simple Approximation of Hedged Yield

We have already noted that one of the attractions of hedged yield is its ease of computation, particularly if you use the version based on yield to maturity rather than horizon yield. We can make it even easier, however. While we have defined both versions of hedged yield to be the *product* of (one plus) a foreign bond's yield and (one plus) the appropriate forward discount or premium (minus one), a foreign bond's hedged yield is also *approximately* equal to the *sum* of its yield and the appropriate forward premium or discount. This is because as long as the yield and the forward premium are small, you can get a good estimate by merely adding yield and the forward premium rather than using the multiplicative formula. Essentially, you are neglecting only the foreign premium or discount applied to the interest income on the bond, which is generally a small share of your total return.

Putting It All Together

Let's now apply the principles we've discussed to our Bund/U.S. Treasury example to determine whether this prospective trade makes sense.

First, we will compare horizon yields over the three months from June 15. Recall that the three-month horizon yield of our U.S. Treasury bond is 7.80%. For the Bund, measured in marks, the three-month horizon yield is 6.97%. The annualized forward premium you earn by selling German marks forward for three months is 3.78%. So the hedged horizon yield for the Bund is:

$$(1.0697)(1.0378) - 1 = 0.1101 = 11.01\%.$$

---

[16]See the next chapter.

In this instance, computing hedged yield has shown us that it is the Bund—not the U.S. Treasury—that is offering the higher yield, once we express the returns in a common currency. Recall that when we simply compared nominal yields, the U.S. Treasury seemed more attractive. In fact, at a three-month investment horizon, the Bund enjoys a significant hedged yield advantage—321 bp. Of course, the Bund's higher yield may reflect only a higher likelihood that German interest rates will rise. Remember, these calculations assumed that the yield curves in the United States and Germany would not change over the three-month investment horizon. If rates do change, then the total returns to these bonds will not equal 7.80% and 11.01%. Particularly, if rates rise in either country, the holder of the corresponding bond will earn a lower return than we have calculated. So even though the Bund has a higher hedged yield than a U.S. Treasury bond at three months, this is no guarantee that it will produce a higher total return after the fact.

However, comparing hedged yield with horizon yield shows us that if interest rates in both countries in fact do not change, then the investor who holds a currency hedged Bund will do significantly better than one who chooses a U.S. Treasury. So if on June 15 you bought U.S. Treasuries instead of currency hedged Bunds, you must have been expecting German interest rates to rise relative to U.S. rates.[17]

We can also compare the yield to maturity of the U.S. Treasury bond with the analogous hedged yield to maturity of the Bund. The yield to maturity of the U.S. Treasury is 8.90%. Measured in marks, the yield to maturity of the Bund is 6.43%. So, the *hedged* yield to maturity of the Bund is:

$$(1.0643)(1.0378) - 1 = 0.1045 = 10.45\%.$$

When we computed yield to horizon, we concluded that if interest rates do not shift, the hedged Bund will significantly outperform the U.S. Treasury bond. Comparing yields to maturity shows us that even if interest rates in both countries do shift by just enough to keep the yields to 10-year Treasuries and Bunds unchanged, the hedged Bund will still significantly outperform an investment in the U.S. alternative. In this case, the Bund's yield advantage is:

$$10.45\% - 8.90\% = 155 \text{ bp}$$

Once again we must emphasize that the hedged yield advantages offered by Bunds at a three-month horizon do not guarantee that they will outperform U.S. Treasuries on a total return basis. If yields rise sharply in Germany or fall sharply in the United

---

[17] The differences may also reflect a risk premium if the Bund is riskier than the U.S. Treasury bond. The riskiness of each bond depends on some easily measured variables, such as duration and the volatility of interest rates in the underlying currency, as well as on some not so easily measured variables, such as the correlation with the world wealth portfolio or consumption streams.

States, the hedged Bund investor could do significantly worse. But these calculations do show that, over our three-month investment horizon, hedged Bund investments would outperform similar maturity U.S. Treasuries *unless* interest rate changes in the two countries provided capital gains or losses to offset the hedged Bund's yield advantage.

In all, these results imply that international investors must have been betting that German rates would rise or that U.S. rates would fall during June 15-September 15. If you had held a different opinion, you could have expressed your view by buying Bunds, hedging their currency risk, and selling (or shorting) U.S. Treasury bonds.

SUMMING UP

International bond switches and "arbitrage" trades are usually motivated by a comparison of bond yields in two countries. Portfolio managers and arbitragers often hedge the exchange rate risks in these trades. Unfortunately, conventional yield measures do not apply to currency hedged foreign bonds.

What's needed are measures of yield that *can* be computed for currency-hedged foreign bonds. The measures must be comparable to conventional domestic yield measures. Hedged yield fits the bill.

We have developed two methods of calculating hedged yield. One is analogous to a domestic bond's yield to horizon. Like yield to horizon, it assumes that when you sell the bond, the foreign yield curve will look exactly as it did when you bought the bond. This measure takes into account your bond's roll down (or up) the yield curve as it ages. Hedged horizon yield seems most consistent with the idea that yield serves as a proxy for a bond's total prospective return over a predetermined holding period. In this case, the holding period corresponds to the hedge horizon.

The second measure of hedged yield is analogous to yield to maturity. It assumes that the yield to maturity on the foreign bond does not change while you hold it, so that the bond's yield also equals the return you earn by holding it. This version of hedged yield has two attractions: It is comparable to a domestic bond's yield to maturity, which is more commonly quoted than horizon yield; and in practice, it will usually be easier to compute.

Having explained what hedged yield is and how you can calculate it, we should also warn you of its limitations: Specifically, hedged yield cannot be applied as a mechanical formula for earning profits in the international bond markets. Hedged yield is a tool that can sharpen your market judgment; it is not a substitute for judgment. Hedged spreads highlight the yield opportunities offered by bonds in different countries. But it is still your responsibility to decide if international yield differences, hedged or unhedged, are reasonable in light of fundamental economic prospects and relative risks in different countries.

APPENDIX
HISTORICAL INTERNATIONAL BOND YIELD RELATIONSHIPS

To help you evaluate opportunities in the international bond markets, we illustrate here a bit of the historical evolution of hedged and unhedged spreads. We compare U.S. Treasuries with similar maturity (10-year) bonds issued by the governments of Germany, Japan, France, Great Britain, and Canada. Our data are representative of the five-year period spanning 1983-87. In each of these exhibits, we have used yield to maturity, rather than horizon yield, and we have computed hedged yields using the "shortcut" formula in the chapter. That is: A foreign bond's hedged yield is *approximately* equal to the *sum* of its yield to maturity and the appropriate forward premium or discount. We have estimated the relevant forward foreign exchange premium or discount using one-month Euro-deposit interest rates.

U.S. Treasuries versus German Bundesanleihen

Yields on U.S. Treasuries over the five-year period shown in Exhibit 6 consistently averaged between one and four percentage points higher than those on comparable Bunds. As a result, the unhedged spreads were predominantly negative. However, when we hedged U.S. and German bonds into a common currency, the average yield differential shrank considerably. Hedged, the yield difference between Bunds and Treasuries oscillated around a small positive value (0.38%).[18]

EXHIBIT 6
BUND LESS U.S. TREASURY YIELD—10-YEAR BONDS HEDGED AT 1 MONTH

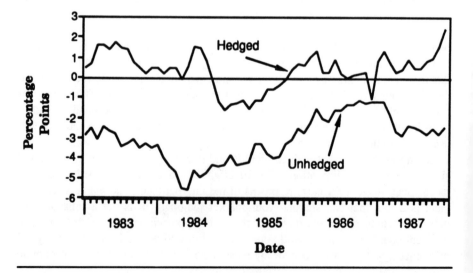

---

[18]The difference, though small, is statistically significant.

Let's delve a little more deeply into what this comparison between hedged and unhedged yields is telling us. The fact that currency hedging eliminated most of the yield differential suggests that, over this time period, most of the yield premium paid by U.S. bond issuers, compared with German bond issuers, stemmed from investors' preferences for holding marks rather than U.S. dollars. Unhedged, German bond yields appeared to be lower than those in the United States. Eliminating the currency factor, however, we see that investors—on average—demanded a slightly *higher* yield to hold German mark issues rather than U.S. dollar issues.

Why was this? One possible explanation is that investors expected German interest rates to rise faster than U.S. interest rates. On average, this would hand Bund investors an offsetting capital loss, so that expected *total returns* to hedged Bunds and to U.S. Treasuries could have been the same, even if *yields* more often favored Bunds.

This explanation, however, does not seem consistent with economic conditions during most of the period. For example, international investors had little reason to expect the inflation rate in Germany to rise faster than inflation in the United States. Moreover, a chronic government budget deficit was much more of a problem in the United States than in Germany. All in all, if investors expected German rates to rise by more than U.S. rates, they were wrong. Notice that the actual yield differential ended the period just about where it began—between two-and-a-half and three percentage points.

Another possible explanation for the disparity between bond yields in the United States and Germany is that the slightly higher covered yields on Bunds represented a risk premium. For example, investors may have preferred to hold U.S. Treasuries rather than hedged Bunds because they believed hedged Bund returns would be less volatile. But although assessing risk can be tricky, a simple, conventional risk measure—the standard deviation of monthly returns—strongly favored Bunds, not U.S. Treasuries. Over this period, the annualized standard deviation of returns to U.S. Treasuries was 9.66%, compared with 5.39% for currency hedged Bunds. So market risk is also not a persuasive explanation for higher hedged German yields.

We are forced into a third explanation: Hedged Bunds offered dollar investors higher risk-adjusted expected returns—on average—than did U.S. Treasuries. This implies that international capital markets are not perfectly integrated.[19] In other words, hedged Bunds offered a yield advantage because not enough dollar investors considered them to be alternatives to U.S. Treasuries. If that explanation is correct, the average hedged yield advantage we observed for Bunds over 1983-87 represented an opportunity that dollar investors failed to exploit.

U.S. Treasuries versus JGBs

Exhibit 7 shows unhedged and hedged Japanese government bond yield spreads. In one important way it is like—in another, quite unlike—the Bund exhibit. Notice

---

[19]Alternatively, Bunds may carry other risks that justify an expected return premium: liquidity or political risks, for example.

EXHIBIT 7
JGB LESS U.S. TREASURY YIELD—10-YEAR BONDS HEDGED AT 1 MONTH

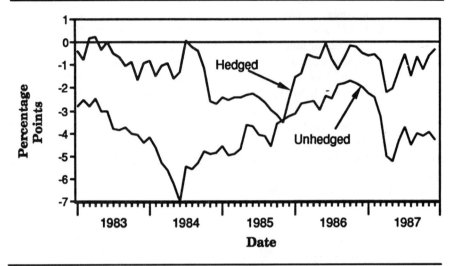

that, like Bund yield spreads, hedged JGB spreads were always closer to zero than were unhedged JGB spreads. This suggests that a currency effect partially explains the higher nominal yields on U.S. Treasuries: Investors preferred to hold yen rather than U.S. dollars. But currency preferences do not tell the whole story. Even after we hedged JGBs and U.S. Treasuries into a common currency (dollars), JGB yields were usually one to two percentage points lower than U.S. Treasury yields.

Japanese yields fell, but only slightly, relative to U.S. yields over 1983-87. Thus, the most likely explanation for the U.S. Treasury/hedged JGB yield differential is probably the same as in the case of Bunds: imperfect international integration of capital markets. The Japanese, high savers that they are, seem to have driven bond yields in Japan well below those in the United States, and by even more than the prospective appreciation of the yen justified.

If we expect this pattern to persist, it represents an opportunity for U.S. borrowers. The suggested strategy is to issue long-term liabilities in yen, to tap savings-rich Japanese investors, and then to hedge the effective currency exposure of those liabilities back into U.S. dollars using rolling short-dated forward foreign exchange contracts. Borrowers who employed this strategy over 1983-87 would have consistently saved roughly one-half to two percentage points in bond yields.[20]

---

[20]This *seems* to require the ability to issue in the Japanese market; some U.S. issuers may not have the name recognition there to do so. But, in fact, you need not issue in Japan at all. You could, for example, issue in U.S. dollars, swap the loan into fixed rate yen, and then hedge the resulting currency exposure with rolling forwards.

U.S. Treasuries versus French OATs

Exhibit 8 compares the yields on French government bonds (OATs) and U.S. Treasuries, hedged and unhedged. Unhedged, French yields were generally higher than U.S. yields. But currency hedging eliminated this difference. In fact, from 1983 through 1986, hedged French yields were usually less than U.S. yields. This indicates a simple explanation for most of the yield premium associated with French issues: the effects of the different currencies in which the bonds were denominated.

One feature of Exhibit 8 bears further explanation: the three sharp inverted spikes in early 1983, in 1984, and in early 1986. These represent periods of European Monetary System instability, when French short-term interest rates rose sharply. During these periods the cost of hedging by selling French francs forward rose sharply, because speculators selling francs in anticipation of a realignment of the French franc/German mark exchange rate had driven forward French franc values down dramatically. As a result, hedged OAT yields fell sharply.

U.S. Treasuries versus British Gilts

Until late 1984, both hedged and unhedged gilt and U.S. Treasury yields were relatively close—at least compared with subsequent levels (see Exhibit 9). Hedged gilt yields then fell sharply to about 500 bp less than U.S. rates in early 1985. They have slowly drifted back together again. At the same time, unhedged gilt yields were generally greater than U.S. yields, rising to a peak spread of about 400 bp in late

EXHIBIT 8
OATs LESS U.S. TREASURY YIELD—10-YEAR BONDS HEDGED AT 1 MONTH

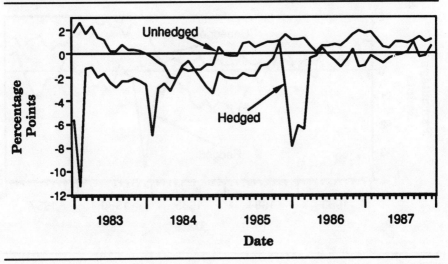

EXHIBIT 9
GILT LESS U.S. TREASURY YIELD—10-YEAR BONDS HEDGED AT 1 MONTH

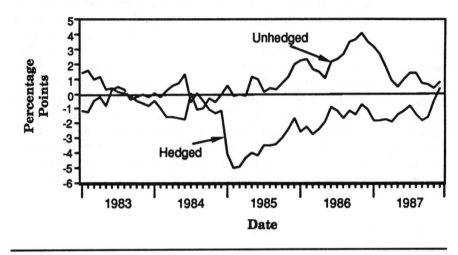

EXHIBIT 10
CANADIAN LESS U.S. TREASURY YIELD—10-YEAR BONDS HEDGED AT 1 MONTH

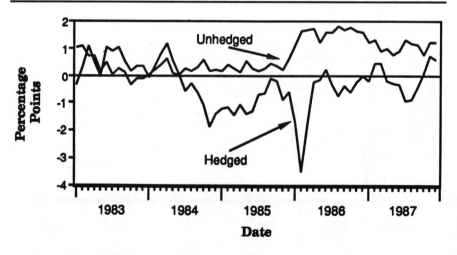

1986. The nominal differentials narrowed in early 1987. More recently, hedged and unhedged yields on 10-year gilts have been within 100 bp of 10-year U.S. Treasury yields.

U.S. Treasuries versus Canadian Treasury Bonds

Exhibit 10 compares Canadian and U.S. Treasury yields. Since Canadian financial markets are closely integrated with those in the United States, it is not surprising that both hedged and unhedged yields generally stayed within 200 bp of each other. The major difference since 1984: Unhedged Canadian yields have exceeded those of comparable U.S. issues. Hedged Canadian yields, in contrast, were less than U.S. yields from late 1984 through early 1986, and have been about the same as U.S. yields since then. Thus, we can safely attribute the recent yield premium commanded by Canadian bonds relative to U.S. bonds to currency differences.

Chapter 24

Tactical Trading Opportunities Using Currency Hedged Foreign Bonds

LEE R. THOMAS, III, PH.D.
INVESTCORP

EDWIN ROBERTSON
ANALYST
FINANCIAL STRATEGIES GROUP
GOLDMAN, SACHS & CO.

In the previous chapter, two new tools for making currency-neutral yield comparisons in international bond trades were introduced: hedged horizon yield and hedged yield to maturity. In that chapter, we explained how to calculate both of these hedged yields and discussed how each relates to conventional yield measures. In this chapter we will explain how to *use* hedged yields, both to identify tactical switch[1] opportunities in the international bond markets and to design hedged bond trades.

Lee R. Thomas, III, was an Executive Director in the Financial Strategies Group at Goldman, Sachs & Co., London, when this chapter was written. The authors would like to express their thanks to Andrew Hudis for his many useful comments on this chapter.

[1]We use the terms "switch" and "swap" interchangeably throughout this chapter to describe the strategy now commonly referred to as international "arbitrage." Unlike the classical usage of the term *arbitrage*, which refers to a riskless trade, this strategy consists of buying a bond denominated in one currency and simultaneously selling an otherwise similar bond denominated in another currency. For a more complete discussion of the spectrum of "arbitrage" trades, see the previous chapter.

To review, *hedged horizon yield* is comparable to the horizon yield (sometimes called rolling yield) on a domestic issue. It shows the return earned over a given investment horizon by holding a foreign bond hedged with a forward foreign exchange contract, assuming the foreign yield curve does not shift or change its shape while you hold the bond. *Hedged yield to maturity* is the currency hedged counterpart of a domestic bond's yield to maturity. It also shows the return to a currency hedged foreign bond over a specified horizon, but assumes that the foreign yield curve shifts by just enough to hold yield to maturity constant as the bond ages. Which measure you choose depends on the circumstances underlying the prospective trade and on your assumptions regarding future changes in the relevant yield curves.

In the discussion that follows, we will describe two kinds of trades and explain the circumstances under which each is appropriate.

A SIMPLE CURRENCY HEDGED BOND SWITCH

The first trade we examine relies on hedged horizon yield, specifically on the spread between a foreign bond's hedged horizon yield and the horizon yield on a comparable domestic bond. We call this the *hedged horizon yield spread*.[2] We recommend that international fixed income portfolio managers and arbitragers routinely monitor hedged yield spreads for anomalies that cannot be explained by underlying economic fundamentals, just as they regularly follow unhedged international spreads.

As you will see, the hedged horizon spread equals the carry of the simplest international hedged bond arbitrage position—a currency hedged bond swap. Carry is the profit or loss that accrues to a position solely as a result of the passage of time, rather than as a consequence of changes in market conditions; it is one important element to consider when evaluating a bond switch. However, a word of warning is in order here: favorable carry should not be the only consideration in your decision to enter into a particular trade; you must also consider the likelihood that interest rates will move against you.

Below, we describe the mechanics of a simple currency hedged bond switch. The resulting position is appropriate whenever the hedged horizon spread becomes wide and you expect the spread to remain wide for some time. In this case, the trade is used to earn favorable carry. This simple arbitrage trade is also appropriate if: (1) the hedged horizon spread is, in your opinion, unreasonable—because it is either abnormally wide or abnormally narrow—*and* (2) you expect the hedged horizon spread to change to a more reasonable value in the near future, *and* (3) you expect this change to result from changes in bond yields rather than forward foreign exchange rates. In

---

[2]In the previous chapter, we show how to compute the foreign bond's horizon yield and the domestic bond's horizon yield. Strictly speaking, neither of the bonds need to be a domestic issue. But it is convenient, and makes the exposition clearer, to refer to the bonds as the "domestic" and "foreign" issues.

this case, you expect to earn a return from capital gains on the underlying bonds, in addition to the carry.

A simple currency hedged bond switch involves virtually no exchange rate risk. Rather, its major risk is interest rate risk, since the position exposes you to relative changes in bond prices in two countries.

Spotting Opportunities

You can use hedged horizon yield to identify opportunities for a simple hedged switch. The conditions in the German Bund and U.S. Treasury bond markets in January 1988 provide an excellent example. On January 22, the three-month yield on a representative 10-year Bund (the 6⅜% of August 20, 1997) was 6.39%; hedged into U.S. dollars, the horizon yield was 10.38%. This compares with a three-month horizon yield of 8.43% on the 8⅞% U.S. Treasury of November 15, 1997. Both of these yields are based on a prospective three-month holding period beginning on January 22. These calculations imply that if the yield curves in the United States and Germany do not change from their January 22 positions, our currency hedged German Bund held over a three-month period will outperform its U.S. counterpart by the difference in yields, or by about 195 basis points (annualized).

Notice that our analysis assumes that we currency hedge the Bund. Thus, the difference in the bonds' yields cannot be explained by exchange rate risk; it can be attributed only to interest rate risk. In other words, this yield spread would be justified only if German interest rates were likely to rise by more than U.S. rates over the three-month period commencing January 22.[3] If German rates were to rise, the resulting capital loss on the Bund could offset its yield advantage.

Exhibits 1 and 2 illustrate the U.S. Treasury and German Bund yield curves on January 22. Using the data from those figures, we calculate a hedged horizon spread of 195 basis points. Exhibit 3 shows the history of the hedged Bund/U.S. Treasury horizon yield spread up to January 22. As you can see, the spread on that date was unusually wide. The width of this spread—and the rarity of a difference this great— would prompt you to examine this as a possible trading opportunity. If, after evaluating market conditions, you concluded that German rates were *not* likely to rise by more than U.S. rates—or at least not by enough to account for this large yield differential—your logical trade would be to buy the currency hedged Bund and sell the U.S. Treasury bond. The annualized carry on the trade would equal the hedged Bund's yield less the U.S. Treasury yield: 195 basis points—that is, the hedged spread on the trade.

Notice that in this case the favorable carry results from selling the relatively *high*

---

[3]There is one other way that the hedged yield spread could make sense: if German bonds carried a risk premium, so that their equilibrium expected return exceeded that of U.S. Treasury bonds. The risk premium could arise, for example, if there were liquidity differences between the Bund and U.S. Treasuries, or if there were political, tax, or regularly risks associated with the German issue.

EXHIBIT 1
U.S. TREASURY BOND YIELD CURVE, JANUARY 22, 1988

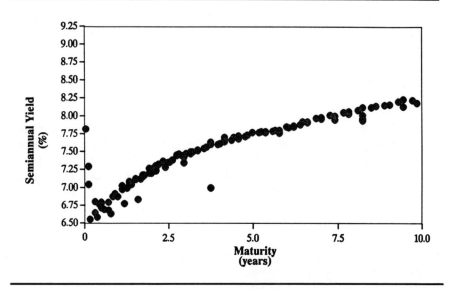

EXHIBIT 2
GERMAN GOVERNMENT BOND YIELD CURVE, JANUARY 22, 1988

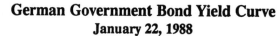

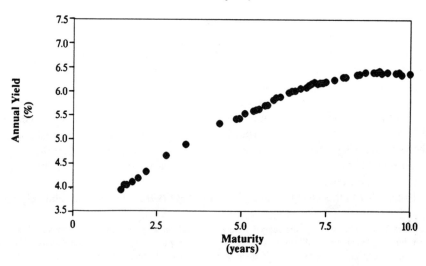

yielding bond—the Treasury yielding 8.43%—and buying the *lower* yielding one, the Bund yielding 6.39%. What seems to be a paradox is explained by the substantial premium on the forward sale of marks; this premium pushes the hedged yield on the Bund up to 10.38%.

Executing the Trade

Here is how you would administer the switch in practice. First, sell a U.S. Treasury bond from your inventory to raise the cash you will need to finance the trade. (If you do not own a portfolio of U.S. Treasury bonds, you can short a U.S. Treasury.) Next, buy the 6⅜% Bund of August 20, 1997. The price is DM 99.88; you acquire the German marks you need on the spot foreign exchange market. When you buy the marks spot, you simultaneously sell marks for three-month forward delivery. This substantially eliminates the exchange rate risk on the position and at the same time increases the Bund's dollar yield by approximately 374 basis points.

Exhibit 4 outlines the overall position based on $1 million of U.S. Treasury bonds sold.[4] To compute the number of marks to sell forward, you must project the Bund's value in three months. If the yield curve in Germany has not shifted or changed shape, the Bund will be worth DM 1.70 million. (This figure represents price plus accrued interest in three months.) If you sell this amount of marks forward for U.S. dollars, you eliminate most of your mark currency exposure. The resulting position will bear *some* exchange rate risk, but only on the difference between DM 1.70 million and the sum of the actual ending value of the Bund plus accrued interest.[5] In other words, you are currency exposed only on your foreign bond trade's profit or loss, not on the principal value of the bond.

Three months from January 22, your forward exchange contract expires. At that time you can sell the Bund, deliver the marks you receive to satisfy your maturing forward exchange contract, and repurchase your U.S. Treasury bond. Alternatively, if the hedged Bund/U.S. Treasury spread remains favorable, you can extend the position by "rolling" your forward contract forward. To do so, you buy marks spot

---

[4]As shown, the position involves buying and selling equal dollar amounts of the Bund and the U.S. Treasury. The resulting position is not symmetric, in the sense that a given change in U.S. rates has different profit implications from the same change in German rates. If you want the position to be symmetric, so that a 1 bp change in German bond yields has the same effect as a 1 bp change in U.S. yields, then you must consider the durations (interest rate sensitivities) of the two legs of the trade. The duration of the Bund is 7.22 years; with the hedge taken into account, the duration becomes 6.97 years. The duration of the 8⅞% U.S. Treasury of November 15, 1997 is 6.68 years; including the dollar cash flows from the forward contract, the duration is 6.43 years. So for each dollar invested in the hedged Bund, we should short $1.09 worth (6.97/6.43) of U.S. Treasuries.

[5]If you wished, you could secure an exact hedge by using a QUANTOS (quantity adjusting) forward foreign exchange contract. In this case you would sell forward the future value of the Bund, whatever it turns out to be. The resulting position would be completely free of exchange rate risk. For more information about these flexible forward exchange contracts, see *Quantity Adjusting Options and Forwards—QUANTOS*, published by J. Aron & Company, a member of the Goldman Sachs Group, 1986.

EXHIBIT 3
CURRENCY HEDGED SPREAD (10-YEAR BUND LESS U.S. TREASURY)

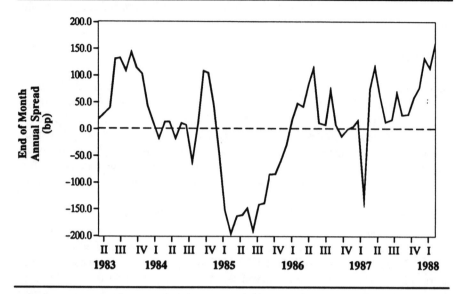

EXHIBIT 4
A SIMPLE HEDGED BUND/U.S. TREASURY ARBITRAGE ON JANUARY 22, 1988

Trade	Amount	Par Amount	Current Price
Sell 8⅞% U.S. Treasury of 11/15/97	$1.00 million	0.959	102.571
Buy 6% Bund of 8/20/97	DM 1.6755 million	1.631	99.881
Sell DM forward 3 months for U.S. dollars	DM 1.702 million		1.6602

(to deliver into your maturing forward contact) and sell marks forward. If the yield curves in the United States and Germany have not changed in three months, we can compute the profit on the position as in Exhibit 5.

Interest Rate Sensitivity

As we indicated earlier, the primary risk on the trade is that German interest rates could rise relative to U.S. interest rates while the position is in place. In fact, the

EXHIBIT 5
CALCULATION OF PROFIT WITH NO CHANGE IN GERMAN OR U.S. YIELD CURVES
(THOUSANDS)

U.S. Treasury		
Beginning value		$1,000.00
Capital gain		−0.89
Accrued interest		21.27
Ending value		1,020.38
Profit		−20.38
Bund		
Beginning value	DM 1,675.50	$1,000.00
Forward premium		9.22
Capital gain	DM 0.13	0.08
Accrued interest	DM 26.00	15.66
Ending value	DM 1,701.63	1,024.95
Profit on Bund	DM 26.13	24.95
Net profit:		**$4.58**

profitability of the position is highly sensitive to changes in relative yields. Suppose, for example, that German yields rise by 10 basis points and U.S. yields fall by 10 basis points, so that the yield spread narrows by 20 basis points. Then the capital loss on the bonds wipes out the favorable carry and results in a net loss on the trade, as Exhibit 6 shows.

Let's summarize the hedged Bund/U.S. Treasury switch opportunity. The current hedged yield differential is 195 basis points; this represents the carry on the switch. That is, if neither the German nor the U.S. yield curves change, then the position will produce profit at an annual rate of 1.95%. As Exhibit 5 shows, this translates into an ending profit of about $4,580 per $1 million of U.S. Treasuries sold. *But* if long-term German interest rates rise relative to U.S. interest rates during the holding period, then the profit will be rapidly eroded. For example, as we show in Exhibit 6, if German yields rise by 10 basis points and U.S. rates fall by 10 basis points, the trade loses $8,200. On the other hand, if German bond yields fall relative to U.S. bond yields, you can add a capital gain to your yield pickup.

Exhibit 7 shows the profitability of the trade at other ending spreads. We have calculated profits based on an ending exchange rate of DM 1.6602/$, equal to the January 22 forward rate. In addition, we show the profit or loss using other ending exchange rate assumptions, so you can see just how innocuous foreign currency risk is in such a trade.

Exhibit 7 emphasizes just how sensitive this switch position is to changes in U.S. or German bond yields. Clearly, interest rate changes in the bonds will quickly erode—or even eliminate—the trade's favorable carry. We reiterate the warning we made in the previous chapter: *hedged yield spreads do not offer a mechanical trading rule for earning profits in the international bond markets*. Rather, if you are

EXHIBIT 6
CALCULATION OF PROFIT WITH +10 bp SHIFT IN GERMAN YIELDS AND −10 bp SHIFT IN U.S. YIELDS (THOUSANDS)

Treasury	Beginning Value	$1,000.00
	Capital Gain	5.17
(in US$)	Accrued Interest	21.27
	Ending Value	1,026.44
	Profit on UST	−26.44
Bund	Beginning Value	DM 1,675.50
	Capital Gain	−11.02
(in DM)	Hedged Portion	0.13
	Unhedged Portion	−11.15
	Accrued Interest	26.00
	Ending Value	1,690.48
	Profit on Bund	14.98
Bund	Beginning Value	$1,000.00
	Forward Premium	9.22
(in US$)	Capital Gain	−6.63
	Hedged Portion	0.08
	Unhedged Portion	−6.71
	Accrued Interest	15.66
	Ending Value	1,018.24
	Profit on Bund	18.24
Net Profit:		**−$8.20**

considering these bond trades, you must do so in light of your interest rate expectations. In this case, if you believe that German bond yields are likely to fall or remain the same in relation to U.S. Treasury yields, then the trade will probably be attractive. On the other hand, if you think German rates are likely to rise relative to U.S. rates, you will want to carefully weigh the favorable carry against the prospect of a capital loss on the position.

AN IMMUNIZED, CURRENCY HEDGED BOND ARBITRAGE

The previous section showed how you can use hedged yield to evaluate a simple international bond switch. Ordinarily, this trade will not be attractive *unless* you believe that relative bond yields will move to your advantage—or will at least remain about where they are—since the favorable carry will quickly disappear if bond prices move adversely. In short, the simple hedged international bond swap exposes the portfolio manager or arbitrager to substantial interest rate risk. Consequently, even when the hedged yield spread is unusually wide, you may consider the trade to be prohibitively risky. You may instead prefer a trade motivated by the attractive hedged spread but one that you can also *immunize* against changes in the levels of foreign and domestic interest rates.

EXHIBIT 7
PROFITABILITY OF THE SIMPLE RISK ARBITRAGE (THOUSANDS OF DOLLARS)

Ending Spot Exchange Rate (DM/$)	Ending U.S. Treasury/Bund Yield Spread								
	−150	−100	−50	−20	0	+20	+50	+100	+150
1.56	−94.24	−61.35	−28.41	−8.63	4.58	17.79	37.64	70.80	104.07
1.61	−92.62	−60.26	−27.86	−8.41	4.58	17.57	37.08	69.66	102.35
1.66	−91.10	−59.23	−27.34	−8.20	4.58	17.36	36.55	68.59	100.72
1.71	−89.67	−58.27	−26.86	−8.00	4.58	17.16	36.05	67.58	99.19
1.76	−88.32	−57.36	−26.40	−7.82	4.58	16.97	35.58	66.63	97.75

There is another reason to consider an immunized trade. The simple hedged bond swap, described in the previous section, is not designed to generate a profit if the hedged yield spread narrows.[6] In fact, if the hedged spread collapses, you may well lose money on the trade. What can you do if the hedged yield spread is unreasonable, in your estimation, and you expect it to change soon? Suppose you want to profit *directly* if it does. The answer: you use the interest-rate immunized, currency hedged trade we will now describe.

In this particular case, the immunized hedged swap is designed to produce a profit directly if the hedged Bund/U.S. Treasury spread narrows.[7] Like the position described in the previous section, it is almost without exchange rate risk. But unlike the previous trade, it does not expose you to changes in relative interest rate levels.[8]

To examine the attractiveness of this position, we will use the second of the two tools described in the previous chapter: *hedged yield to maturity*.[9] Recall that this measure of the hedged yield of a currency hedged foreign bond is analogous to a domestic bond's yield to maturity. The hedged spread in this case is the difference between the domestic bond's yield to maturity and the foreign bond's hedged yield to maturity.

Dissecting the Hedged Spread

Before considering the design of this position, let's first take a closer look at the hedged spread itself, in particular at what causes it to change. This will help us determine what kind of arbitrage position to design to exploit a given set of currency hedged international bond yield disparities.

In the previous chapter, we presented a simple formula for approximating a foreign bond's hedged yield to maturity: take the bond's yield to maturity and add to it the appropriate forward foreign exchange premium or discount you receive or pay when you currency hedge. The spread between the hedged foreign bond and a U.S. Treasury bond then becomes (approximately) the foreign bond's yield to maturity plus the forward foreign currency exchange rate premium (or discount), less the U.S. Treasury yield to maturity. In brief:

$$\text{Hedged Spread} = \text{Foreign Bond Yield} + \text{Forward Exchange Premium} \qquad (1)$$
$$- \text{Treasury Yield.}$$

---

[6]The reason: the hedged yield spread depends on both the short-term U.S./German interest rate spread and the spread on German and U.S. bond prices. Your profit on the simple trade, however, depends on what happens only to bond prices, not to short-term interest rates.

[7]Obviously, we can construct a corresponding position if we expect the spread to widen.

[8]However, as we shall see, the trade described in this section is sensitive to changes in the *slopes* of the relevant yield curves. In fact, it is designed to be.

[9]The chief advantage of hedged yield to maturity is that it is usually easier to compute than hedged horizon yield, since it is based on the foreign bond's yield to maturity, which ordinarily will be widely quoted.

We also know that in accordance with covered interest rate parity—a fundamental international arbitrage relationship—the forward exchange premium rate is approximately equal to the difference between the one-month Eurodollar deposit rate and the one-month deposit rate on the relevant foreign currency. That is:

$$\text{Forward Exchange Premium} = \text{Eurodollar Rate} \qquad (2)$$
$$- \text{Relevant Eurodeposit Rate}$$

Putting relationships (1) and (2) together, we can express the hedged foreign bond/ U.S. Treasury spread entirely in terms of observable interest rates: the spread equals the difference between the yield on the foreign bond and the one-month foreign currency deposit rate, minus the difference between the yield on the U.S. Treasury and the one month Eurodollar deposit rate. More succinctly:

$$\text{Hedged Spread} = (\text{Foreign Bond Yield} - \text{Relevant Eurodeposit Rate}) \qquad (3)$$
$$- (\text{Treasury Yield} - \text{Eurodollar Rate}).$$

Equation (3) says, in effect, that the hedged foreign bond/U.S. Treasury spread is approximately equal to the slope of the foreign yield curve less the slope of the U.S. yield curve. In this particular case, we evaluate the slope from three months to 10 years.[10]

Positioning for Yield Curve Changes

In our example, the hedged Bund/U.S. Treasury spread is unusually wide because the German yield curve is unusually steep relative to the U.S. yield curve. Our task is to position ourselves to profit if the hedged Bund/U.S. Treasury spread narrows. According to equation (3), to do so we must design a trade that profits if the slope of the German yield curve flattens or the slope of the U.S. yield curve steepens. If we had access to bond and Eurodeposit futures contracts in both currencies, this would be easy. Germany's limited futures markets[11] make the design of such a position somewhat complex in the case of our Bund/U.S. Treasury example. So before we tackle that particular trade, we will first look at a simpler case.

Using the Futures Markets

Imagine that you expect a yield curve to flatten either at home or abroad. That is, after evaluating the economic fundamentals in a particular debt market, you believe

---

[10] The yield curves in question are unconventional, since they mix government bond and Eurodeposit interest rates.

[11] A futures contract on Bunds was scheduled to begin trading on September 29, 1988, on the London International Financial Futures Exchange. See James Andrew Hudis, Lee Thomas, III, and Karsten Schiebler, *Futures on German Government Bonds: An Introduction*, Goldman, Sachs & Co., September 1988.

that long-term interest rates will fall relative to short-term rates. One way to position yourself for the coming change would be to buy bond futures and sell Eurodeposit futures contracts.[12] Normally, if you had no view on the overall level of rates, you would choose to sell just enough Eurodeposit futures to duration-match your long bond futures position. That way, your position would be immunized against changes in the *level* of interest rates; your profit would then depend only on changes in the *slope* of the yield curve.

Similarly, if you wanted to bet that a yield curve was going to steepen, you would sell bond futures and buy Eurodeposit futures contracts. Again, you would ordinarily want to duration-match the long and short legs of the trade.

Putting it all together, if you expected the yield curve in one country to steepen relative to the yield curve in another country, you would execute both of these trades simultaneously. In one market you would buy bond futures and sell Eurodeposit (or bill) futures; in the second market, you would sell bond futures and buy Eurodeposit (or bill) futures.

Let's take a specific example. Imagine that you expected the French yield curve to flatten *relative to* the U.S. yield curve. Using equation (3), we can see that this is equivalent to expecting that the hedged yield spread between French Treasury bonds (OATs) and U.S. Treasuries will narrow. The easiest way to position yourself in such an instance would be to (1) buy a French bond futures contract and sell French bill contracts on the Paris futures exchange (MATIF);[13] and (2) simultaneously sell U.S. Treasury bond contracts while buying Eurodollar contracts in the U.S. futures markets.[14] To be duration matched on the U.S. side of the trade, you would want to buy about 3.2 bill contracts for each bond contract you sold. You would duration match the French leg of the trade by selling about 2.5 bill contracts per bond contract.

Using the Cash Markets

In our German Bund/U.S. Treasury example, you would not be able to execute the necessary trades in the futures markets because the German bond and Euromark futures contracts you would need do not exist.[15] You can, however, construct an

---

[12]Yet another way would be to use a specialized interest rate swap, in which you receive fixed and pay fixed less a constant spread. In fact, you can establish the immunized currency hedged bond position we derive in this section by executing a pair of these floating-off-of-government interest rate swaps, one in each currency. ·

[13]We use French bill contracts because futures contracts on Euro-French franc deposits are unavailable. Of course this means the trade does not conform exactly to equation (3). Rather, it has some TED spread basis risk.

[14]You might select the number of U.S. Treasury bond contracts to sell per French bond contract bought by comparing the durations of the cheapest-to-deliver U.S. and French bonds.

[15]These contracts did not exist in January, 1988, but they do now. As new contracts are developed it will become more practical to execute these curves in the futures markets.

equivalent position in the cash bond markets and the forward foreign exchange market. We will now show you how.

Defining Objectives and Setting Constraints: As it turns out, positioning for a prospective change in the hedged spread requires a rather complex set of trades. It may be helpful for us to first enumerate all the goals we have in mind in designing the position:

- We want the position to be symmetric, with a 1 basis point change in the slope of the German yield curve being equivalent (in profitability) to a 1 basis point change in the slope of the U.S. yield curve. Why? The hedged Bund/U.S. Treasury spread could narrow as a consequence of either a change in the German yield curve, a change in the U.S. yield curve, or both. And since we don't want to predict the source of the spread change, we must design a position that profits equally, regardless of the reason.
- Because we don't want to predict whether the general level of German interest rates will change, we must design a position that is immunized against a parallel shift in the German yield curve. To achieve this objective, we must match the durations of the position's long and short *mark* cash flows.
- Similarly, if we do not want to predict whether the general level of U.S. interest rates will change, we must design a position that is immunized against a parallel shift in the U.S. yield curve. This requires matching the durations of the position's long and short *dollar* cash flows.
- Since we are not predicting the direction of future changes in the mark/dollar exchange rate, we must design a position that is currency hedged. To accomplish this objective, we must see to it that the present values of the position's mark cash inflows and outflows sum to zero.

Sometimes, of course, you will have definite views on how interest rates or exchange rates will change. You can act on these views by relaxing one or more of the above conditions. The pure version of the trade, however, will meet all four objectives. Thus, as we said before, it is uncommonly complicated to design.

Designing the Position: The first step in formulating the position is to choose an investment horizon. We will design a position with an anticipated holding period of six months, bearing in mind that, if necessary, you can liquidate the position early or "roll" it forward.

In six months we wish to own the Bund. At that time we want the Bund effectively to be financed with a three-month Euromark deposit. We also want to be short the U.S. Treasury, with the funds invested in a three-month Eurodollar deposit. We want to contract *at today's prices* to take delivery of this position in six months, anticipating that by then the value of the position will have risen as the hedged spread narrowed.

The position is essentially two bond transactions: a currency hedge to eliminate exchange rate risk and forward-forward Eurodeposit trades that immunize the bonds' interest rate risks. One way to establish the forward-forward legs of the position is to contract to deposit U.S. dollars for three months starting in six months, and to contract to borrow marks for three months starting in six months. Alternatively— and, for most transactors, more easily—we can synthetically accomplish the borrowing and lending transactions by executing a forward foreign exchange swap. To execute a forward swap, we will buy marks for delivery (against dollars) in six months and sell marks for delivery (against dollars) in nine months. When six months have passed, this forward swap will have evolved into a three-month outright forward position. That is, in six months the swap will have become a synthetic three-month Eurodollar deposit combined with a synthetic three-month Euromark loan.

Exhibit 8 shows the details of the trades. Sometimes it will be necessary to add Eurodollar futures to these kinds of arbitrage positions to completely immunize your portfolio against U.S. dollar interest rate risk. However, in this particular case, the required Eurodollar futures position was small enough to neglect.

EXHIBIT 8
THE CURRENCY HEDGED BUND/TREASURY TRADE

Trade	Amount	Current Price
Sell 8⅞ of 11/15/97 UST	$1.00 million	102.57
Buy 6% of 8/20/97 Bund	DM 1.55 million	99.88
Sell DM forward 4 months	DM 44.63 million	1.6560
Buy DM forward 1 month	DM 42.70 million	1.6700

Net cash flow: $112,000

Calculating Profit Potential

How much can this arbitrage position make or lose? To illustrate how to compute the profit on the trade, we will assume that six months from setting up the trade, the three-month forward mark premium and the yields on the Bund and U.S. Treasury all remain unchanged from their current values. This simplifies the calculations, which we illustrate in Exhibit 9.

EXHIBIT 9
UNCHANGED COVERED SPREAD (THOUSANDS)

Ending value of Bund	$933.06
Ending value of Treasury	−1,000.79
$ takeout	75.27
Profit on currency swap	−20.02
Total profit	−$19.48

(Based on ending spot rate of 1.67 DM/$) on 1/1/88)

You can see that if nothing changes, the position will have lost $19,480. That is, this arbitrage position has negative carry. For it to earn a profit, the slopes of the U.S. or the German yield curve must change. Specifically, the hedged Bund/U.S. Treasury yield spread must narrow. But what are the prospects for this? The spread has exceeded 150 basis points on six occasions from 1983 to 1987. On three of these occasions it collapsed to zero (or below) within one month. On the other occasions, it took three, four, and six months to reach zero.

How would this trade do in a "best case" scenario? That is, how much would the position earn if the spread shrank to zero within six months?

For purposes of illustration, let's suppose that the Bund yield, 6.385% on January 22, falls to 5.985%, while the U.S. Treasury yield rises from 8.66% to 9.06%. At the same time, assume that the annualized three-month forward exchange premium, 3.74% on January 22, falls to 3.07% on July 22. Then the hedged spread will be zero.

Under these circumstances, the profit on the position can be computed as in Exhibit 10. The gross profit of $72,900 ignores transaction costs of approximately $12,000. When we factor in these costs, the net return falls to $60,900.

EXHIBIT 10
COVERED SPREAD NARROWS TO ZERO (THOUSANDS)

Ending value of Bund	$958.65
Ending value of Treasury	−983.78
$ takeout	75.27
Profit on currency swap	22.76
Total profit	$72.90

(Based on ending spot rate of 1.67 DM/$)

Exhibit 11 shows the profit or loss, including estimated transaction costs of $12,000, at other ending values of the hedged spread. To illustrate how insensitive the position is to currency changes, we also indicate the profit or loss at various ending mark/dollar exchange rates.

SUMMING UP: WHY USE HEDGED YIELD?

This chapter and the previous one have introduced two measures of yield that apply to foreign bonds currency hedged with forward foreign exchange contracts.

We suggested in the previous chapter that most international bond switches should be executed on a currency hedged basis, since currency hedging reduces the risk of this kind of trade.[16] Unfortunately, conventional yield measures do not apply to

---

[16]We argued that if you are considering a bond switch solely because of currency considerations, it is better to take an explicit currency position using forwards, futures, or Eurodeposits. Bond switches should be motivated by your views on prospective interest rate changes, not by exchange rate forecasts.

EXHIBIT 11
PROFIT OR LOSS (THOUSANDS OF DOLLARS)

Ending Spot Exchange Rate (DM/$)	Ending Covered Spread								
	306	266	226	186	146	106	66	26	−14
1.57	−166.26	−139.96	−113.63	−87.28	−60.91	−34.51	−8.08	18.38	44.87
1.62	−163.04	−137.35	−111.65	−95.92	−60.17	−34.39	−8.59	17.23	43.09
1.67	−160.01	−134.90	−109.78	−84.64	−59.48	34.29	−9.08	16.15	41.41
1.72	−157.15	−132.60	−108.02	−83.43	−58.82	−34.19	−9.54	15.13	39.83
1.77	−154.46	−130.42	−106.36	−82.29	−58.20	34.10	−9.97	14.17	38.34

foreign bonds hedged with rolling forward foreign exchange contracts. This makes it impossible to use these conventional measures to meaningfully compare the yield on a domestic bond with the yield on a currency hedged foreign bond. We introduced new yield measures specifically designed to apply to currency hedged foreign bonds.

In this chapter we demonstrated the practical application of these measures in identifying international bond switch opportunities and in designing hedged bond trades. We focused on two kinds of trading opportunities that might be identified by monitoring international hedged yield differences. We showed that hedged horizon yield spreads represent the carry on the first kind of trade, a simple hedged bond swap. This trade is most appropriate when you think that nominal yield differences are not likely to change much, and you want to earn the favorable carry that exists whenever the hedged horizon yield spread is large. Alternatively, the trade will also work if you expect the nominal bond yield spread to move in your favor, providing a capital gain to augment your carry profits.

You can also design trades that profit directly if hedged yield spreads change. In countries with well developed futures markets, the appropriate trade consists of establishing a long bond/short Eurodeposit position in one market and a short bond/long Eurodeposit position in the other. Although it involves a more complicated trade, you can carry out a comparable switch in the cash markets. In this instance, the appropriate arbitrage position is (1) a long position in one bond and a short position in the other, plus (2) a currency hedge for this bond position implemented using a forward foreign exchange contract, plus (3) a forward foreign exchange swap. We illustrated the techniques used to design these arbitrage positions, as well as the potential profits from these arbitrage trades, using the German and U.S. interest and exchange rates prevailing in January 1988.

We introduced the concept of hedged yield spread as an indicator of relative value—but one intended to augment, rather than to replace, such traditional indicators of relative value as the nominal (unhedged) yield spread. The unhedged spread tells you when international yield differences are out of line with their historical values. The hedged yield spread helps to tell you *why* they are out of line.

An unusually wide international yield spread can be attributed to conditions in the foreign exchange market or the bond market. Observing the unhedged spread alone does not tell you which.

The hedged spread, however, factors out the effects of currency differences between domestic and foreign bonds, so you can effectively eliminate exchange market considerations from your comparison of international yields. Anomalies in *hedged* international spreads can be attributed only to bond market conditions. This helps to isolate the trading opportunities—that is, unwarranted international yield differences arising from debt market anomalies, rather than from economic fundamentals.

Of course, what constitutes an unwarranted international yield difference remains a matter of opinion, even after we have factored exchange rates out of the analysis. What seems reasonable to one portfolio manager may seem unreasonable to another, even though they are evaluating the same economic fundamentals. That's why markets exist.

It is up to the individual portfolio manager to decide, on a case-by-case basis, if bond market fundamentals justify a particular hedged yield spread. If they do, even an historically wide spread does not signal a trading opportunity.

In short, we do *not* offer hedged spreads as the basis of a simple trading rule: buy whenever the level is low, sell whenever it is high. We have no faith in mechanical rules such as these. Rather, we have presented hedged spread analysis as one more tool you can use to sharpen your market judgment.

Chapter 25

The Role of Currency-Hedged Bonds in International Fixed-Income Diversification

VILAS GADKARI, Ph.D.
DIRECTOR–RESEARCH
SALOMON BROTHERS INC

SALVADOR DEMAFELIZ
RESEARCH ANALYST*
SALOMON BROTHERS INC

International investments offer participants the opportunity to diversify risk across several bond and currency markets. In recent years, increased currency market volatility has heightened the risk factor associated with foreign investments and, therefore, has somewhat reduced their appeal as diversification tools for lowering overall portfolio risk. Currency-hedged foreign investments, however, may

*Currently with the Australia New Zealand Bank.

The authors wish to thank Jeffrey Hanna and Nicholas Sargen for their insights and suggestions and Grace Burgess for her preparation of this manuscript.

allow investors to capture the diversification benefits of foreign bonds without incurring their currency risk.

Several hedging alternatives—such as forward exchange contracts and currency options or swaps—are available to investors. For bond investments, the currency exposure could be fully hedged with currency swaps or a series of forward exchange contracts covering each of the coupon payments as well as the principal repayment. Currency risk could also be hedged by using rolling shorter-dated forward or options contracts. The rolling hedges, however, cannot cover unexpected changes in the bond prices over the life of the hedging instrument and, therefore, are not perfect hedges.

In this chapter, we focus on only one of the hedging tools—rolling short-term forward exchange contracts. We analyze investments in the Japanese, West German, British, and Canadian Government bond markets. These four major nondollar markets account for 75% of the non-U.S. world bond markets, and they offer reasonable liquidity. A simulation of total returns for a U.S. dollar-based investor on hedged and unhedged market-weighted baskets of nondollar bonds over the December 1977 to March 1987 period produced the following key results:

- U.S. dollar total returns on the hedged basket of nondollar bonds were about the same as those on the unhedged basket, and total returns on both of these nondollar baskets were higher than those on U.S. Treasuries. *The volatility of those returns, however, was sharply lower for hedged bonds—about half that of U.S. Treasuries and only a third as much as most of the nondollar markets unhedged.* (Volatility is measured here as the standard deviation of monthly returns.)
- Correlations of returns on hedged nondollar bonds with U.S. Treasuries were generally higher than those of unhedged nondollar bonds and Treasuries but were not dramatically different from them. *This suggests that the hedged bonds preserve most of the diversification benefits of foreign bond investments. This is particularly important for dollar-based portfolio managers who do not wish to take currency risk because hedged bonds, as synthetic dollar instruments, offer much lower correlations than do such other alternatives as the corporate, mortgage or Eurodollar bonds.* Furthermore, the inclusion of the hedged basket in international fixed-income portfolios would have contributed significantly to reducing the overall risk of such portfolios.
- Rolling short-term forward exchange contracts was an effective currency hedge and, for the most part, removed the currency exposure. Therefore, *currency-hedged bonds should be viewed as synthetic dollar instruments. In light of the diversification benefits provided by currency-hedged nondollar bonds, investors who do not wish to take currency risk should include them as a new asset class in their portfolios.*
- From December 1977 to March 1987, the hedged bonds offered one of the most attractive risk/return payoffs among a broad spectrum of asset classes, includ-

EXHIBIT 1
HISTORICAL RISK/RETURN RELATIONSHIP: U.S. DOLLAR TOTAL RETURNS PER UNIT OF RISK (ANNUALIZED STANDARD DEVIATION OF MONTHLY RETURNS, DEC 77-MAR 87)

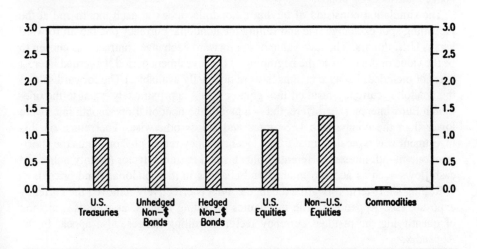

ing dollar and nondollar bonds, U.S. and non-U.S. equities, and commodities (see Exhibit 1). Returns per unit of risk—that is, U.S. dollar total return divided by volatility—were almost twice as high for hedged bonds than for most other asset classes.

The focus of traditional asset allocation models has been on the risk/return trade-off. Estimates of risk and return characteristics over the investment horizon are inputs to these models. Historical data on market risk seem to provide more information about future risk parameters than do data on total returns. Therefore, investors have typically used historical volatility and correlation data with their own expectations of future returns as inputs for asset allocation models. For the same reason, in this chapter, we focus more on the contribution of hedged bonds in reducing portfolio risk, and we analyze it in light of the historical data available through the Salomon Brothers World Bond Indexes.

HISTORICAL SIMULATION OF TOTAL RETURNS ON HEDGED NONDOLLAR BONDS

Using the monthly performance data from the Salomon Brothers World Bond Indexes, along with one-month forward exchange rates for the four major nondollar currencies, we simulated the performance of hedged nondollar bonds beginning in December 1977. Hedged bond indexes were created in the Japanese, West German, British, and Canadian bond markets, along with market-weighted baskets for unhedged and hedged bonds.

The simulation consisted of buying a nondollar index at each month-end at the prevailing spot exchange rate and selling the nondollar currency one month forward versus U.S. dollars. The face value of the forward exchange contract was chosen to be the value of the index at the beginning of the investment period. (Accrued interest was not included, because estimates were not easily available.) The forward sale of the nondollar currency resulted in a gain or a loss approximately equal to the one-month Euro-interest rate differential—a gain if the nondollar one-month rates were lower than the comparable U.S. rates and a loss otherwise. The return on this investment was typically equal to the local currency return plus or minus the short-term one-month interest differential plus a small currency factor (mainly unhedged cash flows such as accrued interest and changes in the nondollar bond prices).

Rolling short-term forward exchange contracts effectively removed the currency exposure (see Appendix). The mechanics of rolling hedges, as well as a method of quantifying the residual currency factor of rolling hedges, also appear in the Appendix.

COMPARISON OF TOTAL RETURNS

Over the December 1977 to March 1987 period, the hedged basket outperformed Treasuries by a wide margin—13.8% versus 10.7%, as measured by the annualized total returns in U.S. dollar terms. It also outdistanced the unhedged basket, but by a smaller margin—13.8% versus 13.5% (see Exhibit 2).

The hedged basket outperformed the unhedged basket in five of the nine years, and outperformed Treasuries in six of the nine years (see Exhibits 3 and 4). The unhedged basket turned in a stellar performance of about 110% for the past two years, as the U.S. dollar plummeted close to recent historical lows against some of the major nondollar currencies. The hedged basket, on the other hand, generated a steady performance with much lower volatility.

Hedged investments in lower-yielding currencies such as the Deutschemark and Japanese yen significantly outperformed hedged assets from such higher-yielding currencies as sterling and the Canadian dollar. It is interesting that the local currency returns in these lower-yielding currencies were among the lowest. However, the incremental return from the forward sale of these currencies added a large enough chunk to the hedged returns to make them one of the best performers in U.S. dollar terms.

The top performer for the period was the unhedged Japanese index, but the next four positions were captured by the four hedged indexes (see Exhibit 4).

EXHIBIT 2
GOVERNMENT BOND MARKET PERFORMANCE INDEXES OF U.S. TREASURIES AND THE HEDGED AND UNHEDGED MARKET-WEIGHTED BASKETS OF NONDOLLAR BONDS IN U.S. DOLLAR TERMS (BONDS WITH REMAINING MATURITIES OF AT LEAST FIVE YEARS; DEC 77-MAR 87)

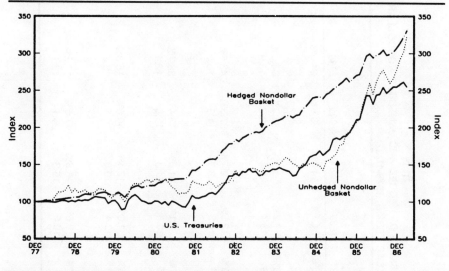

EXHIBIT 3
GOVERNMENT BOND MARKET PERFORMANCE INDEXES OF U.S. TREASURIES AND HEDGED NONDOLLAR MARKETS IN U.S. DOLLAR TERMS (BONDS WITH REMAINING MATURITIES OF AT LEAST FIVE YEARS; DEC 77-MAR 87)

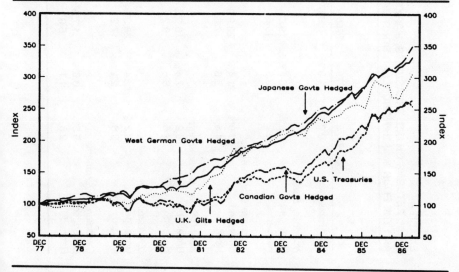

EXHIBIT 4

TOTAL RETURNS ON U.S. TREASURIES, MARKET-WEIGHTED BASKETS OF HEDGED AND UNHEDGED NONDOLLAR GOVERNMENT BONDS, AND THE FOUR MAJOR NONDOLLAR BOND MARKETS (U.S. DOLLAR TERMS; 1978-1Q87)

	1978	1979	1980	1981	1982	1983	1984	1985	1986	IQ 1987	Annual Rate of Return, Dec 77-Mar 87
U.S. Treasuries	0.0%	1.9%	-0.8%	3.9%	31.3%	4.1%	14.3%	28.5%	21.0%	0.1%	10.7%
Nondollar Basket											
Unhedged	17.0%	-6.5%	19.0%	-4.0%	13.9%	7.2%	-1.5%	37.9%	34.3%	14.9%	13.5%
Hedged	6.2	3.9	10.6	16.6	29.3	13.4	15.4	12.2	13.9	7.5	13.8
Japanese Governments											
Unhedged	31.9%	-21.4%	22.9%	5.5%	3.3%	12.5%	2.7%	37.3%	43.6%	16.1%	15.1%
Hedged	14.5	3.6	7.6	25.9	17.7	14.2	16.5	11.3	16.0	7.6	14.5
West German Governments											
Unhedged	16.2%	7.4%	-10.6%	-8.4%	14.1%	-8.1%	-1.0%	43.4%	38.7%	10.3%	9.6%
Hedged	7.5	8.6	9.2	12.5	27.5	10.6	21.3	15.8	12.4	4.2	13.9
U.K. Gilts											
Unhedged	3.2%	12.4%	28.9%	-19.0%	26.5%	1.0%	-13.1%	40.6%	15.3%	20.0%	11.0%
Hedged	-3.8	2.1	17.2	6.6	51.0	13.4	10.8	9.5	9.2	9.9	12.9
Canadian Governments											
Unhedged	-5.5%	-0.6%	1.7%	-2.4%	35.7%	9.6%	-8.8%	17.5%	17.2%	10.1%	9.4%
Hedged	2.8	-1.1	5.0	-4.5	40.1	10.6	15.3	24.1	13.1	3.8	11.1

VOLATILITY OF TOTAL RETURNS IN U.S. DOLLAR TERMS

Risk characteristics of an asset class can be analyzed by taking into account the volatility of returns on that asset and the correlation of those returns with other asset classes in a portfolio. In this section, we focus on the volatility aspects of currency-hedged nondollar bond investments.

- The volatility of the U.S. Treasury market, the widely accepted benchmark, was about 11% over the past 9¼ years. The U.K. gilt and the Canadian Government markets exhibited similar levels of volatility in local currency terms. *The West German and Japanese Government bond markets, on the other hand, were only about half as volatile as U.S. Treasuries in local currency terms (see Exhibit 5).*

EXHIBIT 5
ANNUALIZED VOLATILITY OF TOTAL RETURNS (JAN 78-MAR 87)

	Local Currency	U.S. Dollar Terms Hedged	U.S. Dollar Terms Unhedged
U.S. Treasuries	11.3%	—	—
Japanese Governments	5.2	5.3%	15.9%
West German Governments	5.5	5.5	16.2
U.K. Governments	10.8	10.7	18.5
Canadian Governments	11.4	11.4	13.8
Market-Weighted Basket	5.6	5.6	13.5

- An unhedged investment in a nondollar market is exposed to both currency and foreign bond market volatility. The currency volatility tends to dominate the volatility of U.S. dollar returns. In the case of West German and Japanese bond investments, it increased the volatility of U.S. dollar returns to about 16% from 5½% in local currency terms. For U.K. gilts, the volatility increased to 18½% from about 11%, and for the Canadian Government market, it rose to 13¾% from about 11½%. *Currency hedged nondollar bond investments, however, provided a way of capturing local currency interest rate exposure without incurring currency exposure, as volatility of U.S. dollar returns on hedged bonds was virtually identical to the volatility of local currency returns.*

CURRENCY-HEDGED NONDOLLAR BONDS IN AN ASSET ALLOCATION FRAMEWORK

In an asset allocation context, the inclusion of currency-hedged bonds would not only have enhanced the returns of an international fixed-income portfolio, but more importantly, it would also have improved its risk characteristics by introducing assets with lower volatilities and correlations. This has implications for single and multicurrency portfolio managers.

- *There is a highly compelling argument for including currency-hedged bonds in U.S. dollar-based portfolios when the investors do not wish to incur currency risk. As synthetic dollar assets, hedged bonds would provide a way to diversify interest rate risk across major world economies without incurring currency risk.* The correlations of Treasuries with hedged bonds—about 0.4-0.5 for Japanese, West German and British Governments—were much lower than with other dollar assets, such as U.S. corporates, mortgages or Eurodollar bonds; these tend to be around 0.9.
- *Hedged bonds are also attractive for multicurrency bond portfolio managers. The correlations of hedged bonds to Treasuries were higher than those of unhedged bonds by about 0.10-0.15 for the West German and Japanese markets and by about 0.05 for the Canadian market, while the two correlations were about the same for U.K. gilts (see Exhibit 6).* This suggests that removing the currency factor did not significantly reduce the diversification advantages. In the case of the gilt market, where the currency influence on the bond market is more pronounced, the diversification benefit remained unchanged.
- Using historical returns, we generated an illustration of the risk/return relationships between U.S. dollar cash (represented by the Salomon Brothers U.S. dollar Euro-Deposit Index), U.S. Treasuries, and the hedged and unhedged nondollar baskets (see Exhibits 7 and 8). In Exhibit 8, the curved line joining U.S. Treasuries and the unhedged nondollar basket indicates that, initially, increasing the weight of nondollar bonds would have improved both risk and return characteristics of a Treasury bond portfolio. Consider point A, which represents a portfolio with 60% Treasuries and 40% *unhedged* basket. From December 1977 to March 1987, U.S. dollar total returns on this portfolio would have been 12.0%, with a volatility of 10.3%. Compared with a portfolio comprising only of U.S. Treasuries, this portfolio would have provided better returns with lower volatility.

    Point B represents a portfolio of 60% Treasuries and 40% *hedged* basket. This portfolio would also have returned 12.0%, but with a volatility of 8.2%— almost 20% lower than portfolio A. The estimated reduction in portfolio risk with the addition of a new asset class or an increase in the weight of an asset

EXHIBIT 6
CORRELATIONS OF TOTAL RETURNS ON U.S. TREASURIES WITH U.S. DOLLAR RETURNS ON HEDGED AND UNHEDGED NONDOLLAR GOVERNMENT BONDS

	Japan	West Germany	U.K.	Canada	Market-Weighted Basket
Unhedged	0.31	0.37	0.38	0.73	0.45
Hedged	0.42	0.53	0.38	0.78	0.59

class is important to portfolio managers. The curved line in Exhibit 8 suggests that such risk reduction may not be linear. For example, in the case of a portfolio containing the unhedged basket and Treasuries, the portfolio volatility initially decreased as the weight of the unhedged basket increased to about 40%; after that, the volatility began to increase.

EXHIBIT 7
TOTAL RETURNS AND VOLATILITY IN U.S. DOLLARS AND LOCAL CURRENCY TERMS ON THE GOVERNMENT BOND MARKET PERFORMANCE INDEXES (MONTHLY DATA, JAN 78-MAR 87)

| | Local Currency | | U.S. Dollar Terms | | | |
| | | | Unhedged | | Rolling Hedge | |
	Returns	Volatility	Returns	Volatility	Returns	Volatility
U.S. Treasuries	10.7%	11.3%	—	—	—	—
Japanese Governments	9.1	5.2	15.1%	15.9%	14.5%	5.3%
West German Governments	7.8	5.5	9.6	16.2	13.9	5.5
·U.K. Governments	13.1	10.8	11.0	18.5	12.9	10.7
Canadian Governments	11.5	11.4	9.4	13.8	11.1	11.4
Market-Weighted Basket	10.3	5.6	13.5	13.5	13.8	5.6

EXHIBIT 8
HISTORICAL RISK/RETURN PROFILES FOR U.S. CASH, U.S. TREASURIES AND THE MARKET-WEIGHTED BASKETS OF HEDGED AND UNHEDGED NONDOLLAR BONDS

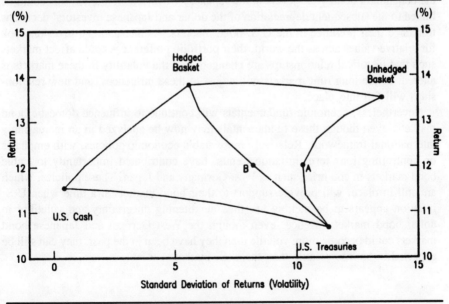

- The historical relationships shown in Exhibit 8 illustrate some points that may be specific to the time period we used. For example, U.S. cash had a higher return at a lower volatility than U.S. Treasuries, a relationship that does not hold over longer periods of time. Similarly, the hedged basket had a significantly higher return at a lower volatility than U.S. Treasuries. Even though the lower volatility may be justifiable given the presence of some of the more stable nondollar bond markets, it is not clear that the U.S. dollar total return on hedged nondollar bonds should necessarily be higher than Treasuries over long periods.

LOOKING AHEAD

What can be said about future risk/return relationships in international fixed-income markets?

The current environment of liberalization in international financial markets has altered the marketplace to some extent. Many domestic markets are experiencing an onslaught of international investors. The recent influence of Japanese investors in the U.S. Treasury market has been well documented, but there are similar instances found in other markets, as well: In the West German Government market, for example, foreign investors bought two thirds of last year's issuance. Following the Baker-Miyazawa agreement of October 1986, there were much larger fluctuations in the benchmark bond yield levels in the Japanese Government market; this could be linked to the subsequent depreciation of the dollar and Japanese investors' decisions to reduce their presence in the U.S. bond markets. As international investors look for relative values across the world, their portfolio preferences could affect markets such that historical relationships are changed, and the volatility in these markets is altered. In the long run, markets will adjust to these influences, and new relationships will fall into place.

Nevertheless, economic fundamentals will continue to influence domestic bond markets, even though these fundamentals may now be analyzed in an increasingly international framework. Relatively more stable economic policies, with emphasis on controlling long-term inflation trends, have contributed importantly to stable bond markets in countries such as West Germany and Japan. These policies, which are still in place, will provide support to their bond markets at a time when U.S. inflation appears to be picking up, thus heightening uncertainty and volatility in dollar bond markets. Hence, even though the West German and Japanese bond markets could become more volatile than they have been in the past, they can still be expected to be less volatile than the U.S. market.

APPENDIX

Effectiveness of Rolling Short-Term Forward Exchange Contracts as Currency Hedges

The rolling short-term forward exchange contracts that were used as currency hedges were not perfect hedges, since the nondollar bond price changes were left unhedged. However, we attempted to estimate the effectiveness of rolling hedges in two different ways, and concluded that they offer efficient means of hedging currency exposure.

First, we compared the volatilities of the U.S. dollar returns on hedged nondollar investments with the volatilities of those nondollar investments in their local currency terms—that is, without the currency hedge. If the two volatilities are very close, the currency hedge is effective. *The volatilities of the U.S. dollar returns on hedged nondollar investments were virtually identical to the volatilities of those investments in their local currencies, clearly indicating that the rolling short-term hedges were effective currency exposure management tools.* For example, the volatility of the West German Government bond index, in Deutschemark terms, was 5.5% over the past 9¼ years; this matched the volatility of U.S. dollar returns on the hedged index of West German Government bonds. (This was shown in Exhibit 5.)

Second, we measured the effect of over- or underhedging as a result of bond price changes by separating the residual currency factor from a U.S. dollar total return calculation and analyzing it independently. The U.S. dollar total return can be divided into three parts:

U.S.Dollar Total Return	=	Dollar Return for Static Market Conditions	+	Bond Price Return in Local Currency	+	Residual Currency Factor

The derivation of this formula is shown later in this appendix, which illustrates that *the "residual currency factor" that results from over- or underhedging as bond prices fluctuate is limited only to changes in nondollar bond prices multiplied by changes in currency values.* Thus, if the bond and currency prices both move by, say, 5% each, the currency risk is only 0.25%—small compared with the risk that an investor accepts with a bond investment. For example, a ten-year bond with 6% coupon would need a change in yields of only three to four basis points for the price to move by 0.25%. The results of a simulation of currency-hedged three-month rolling investments in ten-year West German Government bonds are shown in Exhibit A1. It depicts high, low and average quarterly fluctuations in the bond and currency values, again illustrating that the currency factor is small compared with the market risk that an investor accepts in ten-year bond investments.

EXHIBIT A1
SUMMARY STATISTICS FOR THE HISTORICAL SIMULATION OF CURRENCY-HEDGED QUARTERLY INVESTMENTS IN TEN-YEAR WEST GERMAN GOVERNMENT BONDS (TOTAL RETURNS IN U.S. DOLLAR TERMS, 4Q 77-1Q 87)

	High	Low	Mean Absolute Change
Change in Bond Price	11.88%	-11.80%	3.28%
Change in Exchange Rate	13.15	-22.22	5.44
Currency Factor	1.35	-0.30	0.21

If the July 16 price of the bond moves up or down from the DM101.875 purchase price, the hedged quarterly return will be higher or lower than the 2.20% shown in the example. If the Deutschemark value of the bond is greater (or less) than the Deutschemark amount hedged, the difference is the amount underhedged (or overhedged). The amount under- or overhedged is the investor's currency exposure to the spot rate at the end of the period.

The investor could decide to hedge an amount different from the price plus accrued interest that was hedged in the example. He could do one of the following: (1) choose to hedge the foreign currency purchase amount only, excluding the accrued interest earned for the hedging period; (2) take a view on the bond market and hedge based on the expected bond price at the end of the hedging period; or (3) put on a partial hedge, covering only some fraction of the foreign currency value of his bond position.

In our example, the forward currency exchange rate was at a premium to the spot rate, and the investor was able to lock in a foreign currency gain. However, forward exchange rates for some currencies may be at a discount to the spot rate, and the hedge transaction will have a "cost" in terms of a foreign currency loss. Currencies with Euro-interest rates lower (or higher) than the Eurodollar interest rate will sell at a forward premium (or discount). The forward premium/discount in annualized percentage terms is represented by the difference between the two Euro-interest rates.

The annualized return under static conditions, also known as yield to horizon, will approximately be the sum of the foreign bond yield and the short-term Euro-interest rate differential. Yield curves for the U.S. and West Germany and the three-month Eurodeposit rates for the U.S. dollar and Deutschemark are shown in Exhibit A2. Based on the Euro-rate differential of 3.00% and the West German bond yield of 5.74%, the yield to horizon for this example will be about 8.74%. Compared with the U.S. Treasury yield of 8.07%, the West German bond hedged into U.S. dollars provides a net yield pickup of about 67 basis points.

Mechanics of Rolling Hedges—An Example

Hedging Horizon: Three Months

Settlement Date: April 16, 1987

Bond: 6% of 3/20/97
West German Government
(Annual Coupon)

Bond Price: 101.875 (5.745% Yield
to Maturity, Annual Basis)
Plus 26 Days Accrued Interest
= Full Price of 102.308

DM/US$ Exchange Rates
- Spot: 1.8185
- Three-Month Forward: 1.8055
(to sell DM vs. US$)

Transaction Procedure
- Purchase DM1,000,000 Nominal of Bond @ Full Price
102.308 = DM1,023,080
- Purchase DM1,023,080 Spot @ 1.8185 DM/US$ for Settlement
April 16, 1987 = US$562,595
- Sell DM1,038,083 (Price Plus Accrued Interest After Three Months) @
1.8055 DM/US$ for Settlement July 16, 1987 = US$574,956

Bond Price (July 16, 1987): 101.875 (No Change)

Spot DM/US$ Exchange Rate (July 16, 1987): 1.8185 (No Change)

U.S. Dollar Return for Static Market
Conditions Over Investment Period: 2.20%

EXHIBIT A2
YIELD CURVES: U.S. AND WEST GERMAN GOVERNMENT BONDS
WITH THREE-MONTH EURO-INTEREST RATES

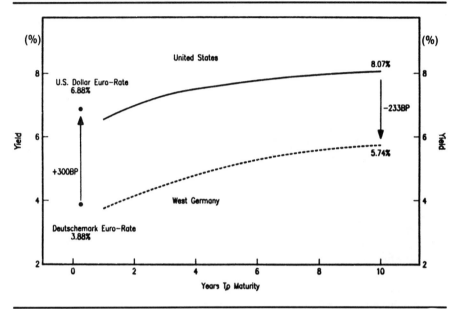

Forward currency sales for terms other than three months could also be used; one-, two-, six-, and 13-month hedges would be common, for example.

The bond position would not have to be liquidated in order to settle the forward currency contract at the end of the hedging period. It is possible to "roll" a forward exchange transaction at the maturity date of the forward currency contract by selling forward the maturing foreign currency amount for an additional three months.[1] In this "roll" transaction, the investor would give/receive a "difference check" for the dollar amount of the realized gain or loss on the forward currency contract.[2]

Quantifying the Currency Factor in the Rolling Hedge

$$\text{US\$ Return for Period (in \%)} = \left[\frac{\text{US\$ Final Proceeds}}{\text{US\$ Initial Investment}} - 1\right] \times 100$$

---

[1] Alternatively, the investor could increase the foreign currency amount hedged to reflect an additional amount of accrued interest, and as discussed previously, the foreign currency could be rolled forward for a term other than three months.

[2] This "gain" or "loss" would be calculated as the difference between US\$574,956 (the maturing dollar amount) and the value of DM1,038,083 (the amount hedged) at the spot DM/US\$ exchange rate at the maturity of the forward exchange contract.

US$ Final   = The US$ Amount of Nondollar Bond Price + Accrued
Proceeds   Interest Valued at Initial Forward Rate

+ The US$ Amount of Change in Nondollar Price Valued at Spot
Rate at End of the Investment Period (US$ Value of Amount
Under/Overhedged)

This can be represented as follows.[3]

US$ Final Proceeds $= (P_S + AI)E_F + \Delta P (E_S + \Delta E)$

where:
P_S = Purchase Price
AI = Accrued Interest Earned During Investment Period
E_S = Spot Rate (US$/Foreign Currency)
E_F = Forward Rate (US$/Foreign Currency)
ΔE = Change in Spot Rate by End of Investment
        Period (US$/Foreign Currency)
ΔP = Change in Bond Price by End of Investment Period

US $ Initial Investment = US$ Amount of Purchase Price of
                           Nondollar Bond Valued at Initial Spot Rate

This can be represented as:
U.S. Initial Investment $= P_S \times E_S$

US$ Return (in %) can be rewritten as:

$$= \left[\left[\frac{(P_s + AI)E_F + \Delta P (E_s + \Delta E)}{(P_s \times E_s)} \right] - 1 \right] \times 100$$

$$= \left[\frac{(P_s + AI)E_F}{P_s \times E_s} + \frac{\Delta P (E_s + \Delta E)}{P_s \times E_s} - 1 \right] \times 100$$

$$= \left[\frac{(P_s + AI)E_F}{P_s \times E_s} - 1 \right] \times 100 + \left[+ \frac{\Delta P (E_s + \Delta E)}{P_s \times E_s} \right] \times 100$$

$$\left[\left(\frac{P_s + AI}{P_s} \right) \left(\frac{E_F}{E_s} \right) - 1 \right] \times 100 + \left[\frac{\Delta P}{P_s} \right] \times 100 + \left[\left(\frac{\Delta P}{P_s} \right) \left(\frac{\Delta E}{E_s} \right) \right] \times 100$$

---

[3]For simplicity, we have assumed that initial accrued interest is zero.

The total US$ return for the period can be viewed as:

Dollar Return for Static Market Conditions	+	Bond Price Return in Local Currency	+	Residual Currency Factor

Therefore, the currency factor is the product of the change in the bond price divided by the purchase price and the change in the exchange rate divided by the initial spot rate. This product is expressed in percentage terms.

For the first quarter of 1987, for example, the changes in the ten-year West German Government bond and the Deutschemark-U.S. dollar exchange rate were as follows:

$$\text{Change in Bond Price} \quad = \quad 2.68\%$$
$$\text{Change in Spot Rate} \quad = \quad 6.54\%$$

Therefore, the currency factor was:
$$(0.0268)\,(0.0654) \quad \times \quad 100\%$$
$$= \quad 0.1753\%$$

PART VIII

Mutual Fund and GIC
Portfolio Management

Chapter 26

Mutual Funds and the Mortgage Market: The Impact of New SEC Rules Governing Performance Advertising on Mutual Fund Investment Strategies

SCOTT M. PINKUS
VICE PRESIDENT AND DIRECTOR
FIXED INCOME RESEARCH
GOLDMAN, SACHS & CO.

In 1988, the Securities and Exchange Commission (SEC) adopted new rules governing the advertising of performance measures by non-money market mutual funds.[1] These rules define, for the first time, a standardized formula for the calculation of the yield measure that mutual funds may use in advertisements. The SEC will also

The author would like to thank Hae Jin Baek, Lynn Bartholomew, Lorraine Justiniano, and Maria Pandolfo for their tremendous assistance on this chapter.

[1] These rules also pertain to insurance company separate accounts offering variable annuity contracts.

require that any yield quotation be accompanied by the fund's average annual total return for the most recent 1-year, 5-year, and 10-year periods. The rules became effective on May 1, 1988.

While at the time of this writing the full implications of the new SEC rules are not yet known, this chapter will review what we believe to be the most significant aspects of the new rules as they relate to a mutual fund's mortgage portfolio and the mortgage market in general. In addition, we will explore various restructuring strategies which might prove advantageous to the funds and the possible impact of any such strategies on relative values within the mortgage securities market.

SUMMARY OF NEW SEC RULES

Objective

The new rules adopted by the SEC were developed to "prevent misleading performance claims by funds and permit investors to make more meaningful comparisons among fund performance claims in advertisements."[2] The lack of standardized performance measures to date made it virtually impossible for investors to evaluate different funds on a consistent basis. The SEC has attempted to address this problem by requiring that the yield advertised by funds be computed on the basis of a standardized formula and that it be presented only in conjunction with historical total returns.

The Yield Calculation

Many, if not most, mutual funds currently advertise yields which reflect coupon income but do not consider the amortization of any premiums or discounts. This measure is usually referred to as the "current yield."[3] In addition, since there were previously no rules defining what could or could not be included in the advertised yield, many funds also consider such things as option premiums and short-term capital gains as income in their yield calculations. Although these other sources of income can still be included in any distributions to shareholders, they can no longer be counted toward income in the advertised yield.

The new rules require that, for non-installment debt (i.e., Treasury notes and bonds, but *not* mortgages), mutual funds recognize the amortization of any discount or premium in their yield calculation. Furthermore, the amortization of any discounts or premiums on these securities must be calculated on the basis of their *current market values* rather than historical or book costs. This results in a yield

---

[2]Securities and Exchange Commission, Release Number 33-6753, February 2, 1988, p.6.

[3]Current yield $= \dfrac{\text{Coupon}}{\text{Price}}$

figure which (excluding the impact of expenses) is approximately equal to the yield-to-maturity[4] on these instruments.[5]

For mortgage securities and other installment debt (e.g., asset-backed securities), the required yield calculations are somewhat different. The differences generally result from the fact that the effective maturity and principal paydown schedule of these instruments are not known with certainty, making it difficult to amortize any discount or premium in accordance with uniform accounting principles.

The formula for computing a yield on a mortgage-backed security is based on the net investment income earned over the most recent 30-day or 1-month period. Net investment income consists of the coupon income earned over the month adjusted for any gains or losses resulting from principal paydowns that occurred over the month, less expenses. Gains or losses from principal paydowns are determined on the basis of the *book cost* of each security and not the current market price. The resulting net investment income for the month can then be divided by the market value of a security and annualized (assuming semiannual compounding) to approximate the yield of an individual security.[6] The yield formula for mortgages (before expenses) is as follows:

$$\text{Mutual Fund Yield} = \left[\left(\frac{\frac{\text{Coupon}}{1200} + \left(\frac{\text{Principal}}{\text{Paydown}} \times \frac{(100 - \text{Book Cost})}{100} \right)}{\text{Market Value}} + 1 \right)^6 - 1 \right] \times 200$$

The SEC rules also state that a mutual fund may, at its option, amortize any discount or premium on the remaining balance of a mortgage security, after the receipt of a paydown. They do not, however, specify how this should be done or what assumptions could or should be made regarding future prepayments. Amortizing any discount or premium on the *remaining* balance of a mortgage security would

---

[4]On a callable corporate bond, yield-to-call should be used if the security is likely to be called.

[5]It is interesting to note that the required mutual fund yield calculation overstates the actual yield-to-maturity (YTM) of Treasury and corporate bonds by anywhere from 7 to 16 basis points. This is because the bond equivalent YTM on these instruments is used to accrue interest on a monthly basis, and the result is then converted back to a bond equivalent yield. Below is the formula that is used to compute the mutual fund yield on a Treasury or corporate bond.

$$\text{Mutual Fund Yield} = \left[\left(\frac{\frac{\text{YTM}}{1200} + \left(\frac{\text{Market}}{\text{Value}} \right)}{\text{Market Value}} + 1 \right)^6 - 1 \right] \times 200$$

If the yield-to-maturity on the bond is 8%, the mutual fund yield will be 8.13%.

[6]While we are attempting to show the impact of the new rules on the yield of an individual security, a mutual fund would actually report a single yield which reflects the net investment income of each security in their portfolio.

generally have only a small impact on the yield, once the gain or loss on the actual monthly paydown is taken into account.[7]

Exhibit 1 compares the current yield to the new mutual fund yield for selected GNMA securities. The book price is assumed to equal the market price for these issues on March 10, 1988, and the prepayment assumption used in the computation of the mutual fund yield is based on our 1-year forecast for each security on that date.[8]

The new mutual fund yield is slightly *higher* than the current yield for all GNMAs trading below par. For GNMAs assumed to be on the books at a premium, the mutual fund yield is significantly *lower* than the current yield. In both cases, the difference

EXHIBIT 1
THE MUTUAL FUND YIELD MEASURE

GNMA Coupon	Rem Term	Price * (3/10/88)	Projected 1-Year Avg CPR	Current Yield	Mutual Fund Yield	Difference (basis points)
7.5	353	88-22	2.1	8.61	9.00	39
8.0	353	91-12	2.3	8.92	9.22	30
8.5	352	94-04	2.6	9.20	9.42	22
9.0	350	96-30	3.3	9.47	9.60	13
9.5	350	99-20	3.8	9.73	9.74	2
10.0	350	102-16	4.5	9.96	9.83	−13
10.5	345	105-02	7.6	10.20	9.78	−42
11.0	330	107-04	15.0	10.49	9.34	−115
11.5	305	108-08	21.1	10.86	8.95	−191
12.0	316	109-08	25.9	11.24	8.59	−265
12.5	303	110-06	28.5	11.62	8.38	−323
13.0	301	111-06	30.0	11.98	8.25	−373

*Assumed to be both book cost and market price.

---

[7]For instance, consider the following example:
GNMA 12% coupon, 316-month remaining term, price of 109-08, assumed to prepay at a 25.9% CPR.
Current Yield = 11.24%
Mutual Fund Yield = 8.59%
Cash Flow Yield-to-Maturity = 8.40%
(assuming complete amortization of premium over the life of the security)
The difference between the current yield and the mutual fund yield, which recognizes gains or losses in a given month, is 284 basis points. Fully amortizing the entire premium over the life of the security would only reduce the mutual fund yield by an additional 19 basis points.

[8]Rather than show what the actual mutual fund yields would have been in March based on February prepayments, we want to focus on what the implications may be for advertised yields in future months. To do this, we have chosen to use our 1-year average prepayment forecast in the mutual fund yield calculation.

between these two yield measures reflects the gain or loss resulting from principal paydowns assumed to occur over the next month. Current yields increase along with the coupon, since this calculation ignores the unfavorable impact of paydowns on high coupon, premium securities. The new mutual fund yields, on the other hand, are highest for the current coupon and slight premium issues (i.e., the GNMA 9.5% through 10.5% coupons).

Total Return Disclosure

The SEC also requires that, beginning May 1, 1988, any performance data (including yield) advertised by a mutual fund be accompanied by a series of uniformly calculated historical returns. The funds are required to disclose their average total rates of return over the most recent 1-year, 5-year, and 10-year periods. The returns are rolling averages which must be updated at the end of each calendar quarter. They must reflect any changes in the value of a shareholder's account over the particular time period, including the impact of any sales loads (front-end or back-end) or advisory fees. In addition, the required total return data must be given equal or greater prominence than any other performance data presented in an advertisement.

The total return disclosure requirement is clearly an attempt to alert investors to the fact that the yield advertised by a non-money market mutual fund is not a measure of the total return one can expect to earn, as is generally the case with a money market fund. Implicitly, the SEC is also encouraging the investing public to recognize that yield is not the only number that should be considered when evaluating and comparing the performance of various funds.

Limitations on Advertising of Distribution Rates

The last key element of the new SEC rules that will be addressed in this chapter concerns the advertisement of distribution rates. The distribution rate reflects the actual distributions made to shareholders, which can include capital items such as option premiums and short-term capital gains. In the past, the yield advertised by many funds was, in fact, their distribution rate. Under the new rules, mutual funds are prohibited from using the distribution rate in advertisements. They are, however, permitted to include it in their prospectuses and sales literature as long as it is accompanied by proper disclosure and is presented in conjunction with the standard yield and total return information.

FACTORS INFLUENCING THE NEW YIELD MEASURE

In general, the new mutual fund yield is a far more realistic measure of economic value than most of the yield measures currently used in the industry, such as the current yield or the distribution rate. In the case of callable securities or any security with an embedded option, though, any yield measure in the spirit of a yield-to-maturity is inherently less meaningful. For mortgage securities, the use of book costs for computing gains or losses on paydowns and the method of accounting for paydowns each month further clouds the resulting yield.

The Impact of Book Cost

In the yield formula for mortgages, gains or losses on principal paydowns in a given month are computed on the basis of the historical or book cost of each security. Exhibit 2 illustrates the impact of book cost on the mutual fund yield of a GNMA 8% and a GNMA 12%. The book costs were chosen to roughly reflect the price range over which these two issues would most likely have been purchased by mutual funds.

Because of the relatively low prepayment rate assumed for the GNMA 8s, a 12 point variation in its book cost (88 to 100) results in its mutual fund yield varying by only about 42 basis points. For the GNMA 12s, on the other hand, a 12 point variation in its book cost (98 to 110) results in a 345 basis point change in their yield. Book costs have a dramatic impact on the calculated yield when prepayments and, more generally, principal paydowns are assumed to occur at a rapid pace. Regardless of the price at which a security is currently trading, the higher its book cost, the lower its mutual fund yield. When book cost is below par, any paydowns result in a

EXHIBIT 2
IMPACT OF BOOK COST ON YIELD

GNMA 8%		GNMA 12%	
Book Cost	Mutual Fund Yield	Book Cost	Mutual Fund Yield
88	9.34	98	11.82
90	9.27	100	11.24
91-12	9.22	102	10.66
92	9.20	104	10.09
94	9.13	106	9.52
96	9.06	108	8.94
98	8.99	109-08	8.59
100	8.92	110	8.37

Assumptions:

- 353-month remaining term
- Market price = 91-12
- Prepays at 2.3% CPR
  (1-year average forecast)

Assumptions:

- 316-month remaining term
- Market price = 109-08
- Prepays at 25.9% CPR
  (1-year average forecast)

gain and, therefore, an addition to income. Conversely, when book cost is above par, any paydowns result in a loss and reduce income.

Prepayment Variability

For a mortgage security purchased at any price other than par, the actual principal paydown that occurs in a given month will have a significant impact on a mutual fund's yield for that month. Although scheduled amortization of principal is included in the paydown, prepayments typically make up a much greater portion of actual paydowns each month. It is important to note that, for the purpose of the yield calculation, it is not the expected prepayment rate in the future that matters, but rather the actual prepayments (paydowns) that occur each month.

Exhibit 3 illustrates the impact of prepayments on the mutual fund yield of the same two GNMAs examined above. For the GNMA 8s, the actual prepayment rate for the month is assumed to fall between 0% and 10% CPR. Assuming both the book cost and market price of the security are 91 12/32nds, the yield ranges from a low of 8.99% (at 0% CPR) to a high of 10.02% (at 10% CPR).

Once again, the yield of the GNMA 12 is much more sensitive to the particular assumption chosen. Its book cost and market price are both assumed to be 109 8/32nds. However, prepayments on this security are assumed to vary between 10% and 40%, reflecting both the higher level of prepayments that would be expected and the greater variability of prepayments that would typically be experienced by such a high coupon mortgage security. At a 25% CPR, its yield is 8.69%, although it ranges from a high of 10.27% (at 10% CPR) to a low of 6.80% (at 40% CPR).

EXHIBIT 3
IMPACT OF PREPAYMENTS ON YIELD

GNMA 8%		GNMA 12%	
Assumed CPR	*Mutual Fund Yield*	*Assumed CPR*	*Mutual Fund Yield*
0	8.99	10	10.27
1	9.09	15	9.77
2	9.19	20	9.24
4	9.39	25	8.69
6	9.60	30	8.10
8	9.81	35	7.47
10	10.02	40	6.80

Assumptions:

- 353-month remaining term
- Book and market price = 91-12

Assumptions:

- 316-month remaining term
- Book and market price = 109-08

While the rapid prepayments on the GNMA 12s have a substantial negative impact on its yield, the *variability* of monthly prepayments may, in fact, pose the more serious problem. Even if interest rates remain relatively stable, seasonal factors alone would cause prepayments on GNMA 12s to vary considerably over the course of the year. Furthermore, given the extreme variability in prepayments among different pools of the same type and coupon, mutual funds must either own a large enough position in a given coupon to diversify away any pool-specific prepayment risk, or be subject to even greater prepayment and, therefore, yield variability.[9] To demonstrate this point, Exhibit 4 shows the monthly prepayment rates for all GNMA 12s over the last 12 months, as well as those of two specific 12% pools. As the exhibit illustrates, monthly prepayments across all 12% pools varied from 15.2% to 48.1% over the last year, while for the individual pools shown prepayments varied over an even greater range.

IMPLICATIONS OF THE NEW SEC RULES

Total Return Orientation

By requiring that historical total returns be prominently displayed in any advertisements, prospectuses, or sales literature, the new rules will inevitably cause funds to

EXHIBIT 4
HISTORICAL PREPAYMENT VARIABILITY (CPRs)

Month	All GNMA 12% Pools	Pool 104751 (GNMA 12%)	Pool 67591 (GNMA 12%)
Mar 1988	16.6	0.0	0.7
Feb 1988	15.2	9.0	0.7
Jan 1988	18.3	19.9	0.5
Dec 1987	16.1	8.1	0.5
Nov 1987	19.9	20.0	62.1
Oct 1987	23.3	0.0	24.9
Sep 1987	24.9	8.0	60.6
Aug 1987	30.8	33.9	0.4
Jul 1987	37.2	56.6	48.2
Jun 1987	40.7	54.8	51.4
May 1987	48.1	41.6	36.0
Apr 1987	46.8	30.8	30.6
3-month average	16.7	10.0	0.6
6-month average	18.3	9.9	19.2
12-month average	29.2	26.2	30.7

[9]Owning a $1 million piece of a $200 million pool could offer the same degree of diversification as owning 200 $1 million pools.

focus more on these figures. While the overwhelming majority of bond funds claim as their primary objective the maximization of current income, most also profess to having total return maximization as their second objective. Total return may simply become a more significant second objective.

A greater emphasis on total return will lead funds to become more concerned with the fundamental economic values of securities and relatively less concerned purely with their impact on accounting income and yield. As a result, funds will be more likely to consider swaps and other trading strategies which may enhance their total returns. In addition, they should become more sensitive to the durations of their portfolios, as that will have a significant, if not dominant, impact on their total return performance as interest rates vary. This change in emphasis should have a positive impact on the mortgage market, in that liquidity may be marginally improved and securities may trade more in accordance with their fundamental values.

Coupon Preference

Yield advertising has always been important to bond funds. This was particularly true prior to 1987 when the funds were experiencing their most rapid growth in assets. Although yield advertising is somewhat less significant in the current environment, it is still an important marketing tool for many funds.

For the purpose of mutual fund advertising, the yields associated with most fixed income securities will be significantly different under the new SEC rules than they were under the yield calculations most commonly used in the industry. Most significant, perhaps, is the impact of the new yield calculations on the relative attractiveness of high coupon securities. Under the old "current yield" calculation, high coupon securities appear to offer unusually attractive yields, since the amortization of their (often substantial) premiums is ignored. For Treasury and corporate bonds, though, the new rules require that premiums (and discounts) be fully amortized into income using a yield-to-maturity calculation. The end result is that the yields on high coupon Treasuries and corporates will no longer look outstanding relative to lower coupons, but rather will be comparable to the yields on otherwise-similar lower coupon issues. Mutual funds may continue to prefer high coupon issues in these sectors, however, since they offer roughly the same yields as lower coupon issues, while the higher coupon would permit the funds to pay out more in distributions, if they so chose.

Coupon preferences in the mortgage market, on the other hand, may change substantially. As was shown in Exhibit 1, the high coupon GNMAs had much higher yields than the lower coupons when they were computed on the basis of the "current yield" formula. When the new formula was used, though, high coupon yields were significantly below those of the current and slight premium coupons. The yield of the GNMA 12, for instance, went from 128 basis points higher than the yield on the GNMA 10 (under the "current yield" formula) to 124 basis points lower (under the new formula). In addition to the relatively lower yields associated with high coupon mortgage securities, their monthly prepayment and yield variability may pose a serious problem for mutual funds holding sizeable positions in these issues. Everything else being equal, funds will have less of an incentive to own high coupon mortgages. How much less, though, depends partially on other factors.

As was discussed previously, the historical or book cost of a mortgage security will have a large impact on the new mutual fund yield. The higher the book cost associated with a particular security position, the lower the mutual fund yield. Whether or not a high coupon mortgage security that is already held in portfolio will continue to appear attractive on the basis of its yield depends largely on its book price. High coupons purchased at relatively low premiums will continue to offer attractive yields and, as a result, are unlikely to be sold by mutual funds. Referring back to the examples used in Exhibit 1 and 2, GNMA 12s at the market price shown do not offer a particularly attractive mutual fund yield. At a book price of 104, however, they would offer a significantly higher yield than any other GNMA coupon.

Another important consideration for mutual funds is their distribution rate. Even if a high coupon mortgage security does not offer the highest yield in its sector, it may still be attractive to a mutual fund since its entire coupon can be distributed.[10] Each individual fund will have to evaluate the tradeoff between the yield they can advertise and their desired distribution rate. Somewhat reducing the importance of the distribution rate, though, is the fact that it can no longer be advertised and that, even when it can be quoted, it must be presented along with the standardized yield and historical total returns.

Capital gains or losses resulting from any portfolio restructuring will generally also impact a fund's distribution rate. This consideration will influence how bond funds react to the new SEC rules and, in particular, the probability that they will significantly reduce their exposure to high coupon mortgage securities. Of course, this only affects securities already in portfolio. Since new purchase decisions are free from this constraint, it is likely that the average coupon purchased will gradually shift toward the current and slight premium coupons.

Prepayment-Motivated Trading Strategies

The sensitivity of the mutual fund yield measure to the actual prepayments that occur in any given month suggests certain strategies that mutual funds may want to consider. Seasonal swapping would be one such strategy. To take advantage of the fact that prepayments typically speed up during the summer months and slow down during the winter months, mutual funds should consider selling premiums (and/or purchasing discounts) in the spring and repurchasing (selling) them in the late fall.

---

[10]The new SEC rules do not address the manner in which funds determine their distributions. While the gain or loss associated with a principal paydown may be reflected in distributable income, many (if not most) funds do not treat this as an adjustment to income.

While it is naive to think that the market as a whole does not recognize this effect and adjust prices accordingly (such that there is no real economic benefit to this trade), the yield benefit to a fund could be substantial. Referring back to Exhibit 3, if, everything else being equal, GNMA 12s are expected to prepay at 15% CPR during the winter months and at 35% CPR during the summer months, the mutual fund yield of that security would fluctuate between 9.77% (during the winter) and 7.47% (during the summer). It is possible that the yield benefits associated with this strategy may be so significant for mutual funds that they could, conceivably, cause the relative values of high and low coupon mortgage securities to fluctuate on a seasonal basis. The result would be that premiums may tend to be relatively cheap in the summer and rich in the winter, while discounts may tend to be rich in the summer and cheap in the winter.

Another strategy involves taking advantage of the sensitivity of prepayments to the age of a security. Prepayments on all but the highest coupon mortgage securities are highly sensitive to the age of the underlying mortgages (i.e., their degree of seasoning). Newly-originated loans tend to prepay at a significantly slower rate than more seasoned loans. To the extent that funds can purchase premium securities that are backed by relatively young mortgages, their yield will benefit.

For example, consider the case of the GNMA 11, issued in 1987, shown in Exhibit 5. Given that it is backed by relatively new mortgages (assumed to be about 7 months old), its prepayments are expected to be relatively low initially and

EXHIBIT 5
THE IMPACT OF SEASONING ON YIELD

GNMA 11%
(Price = 107-04)

Month	Rem Term	Assumed CPR*	Mutual Fund Yield	Month	Rem Term	Assumed CPR*	Mutual Fund Yield
Apr 1988	353	3.5	10.22	Apr 1989	341	9.5	9.77
May 1988	352	4.0	10.18	May 1989	340	10.0	9.73
Jun 1988	351	4.5	10.14	Jun 1989	339	10.5	9.69
Jul 1988	350	5.0	10.11	Jul 1989	338	11.0	9.65
Aug 1988	349	5.5	10.07	Aug 1989	337	11.5	9.62
Sep 1988	348	6.0	10.03	Sep 1989	336	12.0	9.58
Oct 1988	347	6.5	10.00	Oct 1989	335	12.5	9.54
Nov 1988	346	7.0	9.96	Nov 1989	334	13.0	9.50
Dec 1988	345	7.5	9.92	Dec 1989	333	13.5	9.46
Jan 1989	344	8.0	9.88	Jan 1990	332	14.0	9.42
Feb 1989	343	8.5	9.85	Feb 1990	331	14.5	9.38
Mar 1989	342	9.0	9.81	Mar 1990	330	15.0	9.34

*Based on 250% PSA.

increase gradually over the next 2 to 3 years. The figure shows what the mutual fund yield would be on the security each month, if it actually prepaid at the varying monthly rates (CPRs) implied by a 250% PSA assumption.[11] The yield on the security would start at 10.22% in April 1988 and gradually decline each month until it reached a low of 9.34% in March 1990. To the extent that the market does not differentiate the prices of moderately high coupon mortgage securities according to their degree of seasoning, mutual funds may have an opportunity to increase their advertised yields by selectively purchasing newly-originated issues.

New Product Focus

The fact that the SEC rules do not require the amortization of premiums (or discounts) on installment debt may present mutual funds with some unusual opportunities. From a yield perspective, the ideal security for a mutual fund is one that has a high coupon, is not subject to monthly prepayments (or significant scheduled principal prepayments), and can be treated as installment debt. Such instruments as receivable-backed securities, project loans (with lock-outs or significant prepayment penalties), and conceivably even PAC tranches of other longer tranches of CMOs (depending on a particular fund's accounting treatment) may come very close to fitting the bill.[12] Mutual funds should explore these and other less traditional products, as they could prove to be valuable additions to their portfolios.

PORTFOLIO RESTRUCTURING: AN EXAMPLE

This section will review a hypothetical restructuring of a "typical" mutual fund mortgage portfolio. We will start with a mortgage portfolio which is somewhat representative of those held by government/agency-oriented bond funds. The portfolio consists of a wide variety of positions across the GNMA, FNMA and FHLMC 30-year sectors. The range of book costs associated with the positions reflect purchases that were assumed to have been made at varying times over the last 2 years. After examining what the impact of the new SEC rules would be on the advertised yield of the portfolio, we will explore how the portfolio could be restructured given the objectives and constaints of the (hypothetical) fund. The analysis is intended to provide an example of the types of strategies that mutual funds may be considering over the near term.[13]

---

[11]For an explanation of the PSA Standard Prepayment Model, see Scott M. Pinkus, Susan Mara Hunter, and Richard Roll, "An Introduction to the Mortgage Market and Mortgage Analysis," in Frank J. Fabozzi and T. Dessa Garlicki-Fabozzi (eds), *Advances in Bond Analysis and Portfolio Strategies* (Chicago, IL; Probus Publishing, 1987).

[12]There are significant differences across funds as to what securities they are permitted to own and, for many of them, how they are treated for accounting purposes.

[13]Because of the complexity of this analysis, a complete discussion of the methodology as well as all of the assumptions used is beyond the scope of this chapter.

Evaluating the Original Portfolio

The original portfolio that will be examined is shown in Exhibits 6a and 6b. Exhibit 6a details the actual holdings of the fund, as well as the book cost and market price (as of 3/10/88) of each position. In addition, the static cash flow yield-to-maturity, the current yield, and the new mutual fund yield are shown for each individual bond and for the entire portfolio.[14] In some instances the book cost of a particular position is higher than its market price, as is the case with the GNMA 9% and FHLMC PC (PC GUAR) 8% positions, while in other instances the book cost is below the market price, as in the GNMA 11% and FHLMC 11.5% positions.

The book price of each security has a significant impact on the relationship between its mutual fund yield and its static cash flow yield and current yield. In most cases, when the book price is greater than the market price, the mutual fund yield is lower than the static cash flow yield, and vice versa. Relative to the current yield, the mutual fund yield is always higher when the book price is less than par, and always lower when the book price is at a premium. For the entire portfolio, the current yield is 10.05%, while the mutual fund yield is only 9.23%. This reflects the fact that the average book cost of the portfolio is above par. The advertised yield of our hypothetical fund would, therefore, decline by 82 basis points after the new SEC rules become effective.

EXHIBIT 6a
ORIGINAL PORTFOLIO: YIELD ANALYSIS

Security Type	Coupon	Rem Term	Par Value	Book Price	Market Price 3/10/88	Proj 1-YR CPR	Static CF Yield	Current Yield (At Mkt)	Mutual Fund Yield
GNMA SF	7.50	353	55,000	92-07	88-22	2.1	9.37	8.61	8.88
GNMA SF	8.00	353	60,000	94-08	91-13	2.3	9.48	8.93	9.13
GNMA SF	9.00	350	70,000	102-13	96-30	3.3	9.64	9.47	9.36
GNMA SF	9.50	350	70,000	97-10	99-20	3.8	9.69	9.73	9.85
GNMA SF	10.00	350	25,000	102-16	102-16	4.5	9.66	9.96	9.83
GNMA SF	10.50	345	12,000	106-00	105-02	7.6	9.55	10.20	9.70
GNMA SF	11.00	330	35,000	102-00	107-04	15.0	9.21	10.49	10.17
GNMA SF	11.50	305	60,000	108-00	108-08	21.1	8.80	10.86	9.01
GNMA SF	12.00	316	55,000	108-24	109-08	25.9	8.44	11.24	8.73
GNMA SF	12.50	303	64,000	109-24	110-06	28.5	8.23	11.62	8.52
GNMA SF	13.00	301	11,000	110-14	111-06	30.0	8.09	11.98	8.50
FNMA	8.00	348	35,000	97-24	92-13	4.5	9.44	8.82	8.95
FNMA	8.50	345	25,000	100-06	95-01	5.7	9.50	9.11	9.10
FNMA	10.50	310	3,000	105-13	104-04	17.9	9.26	10.30	9.22
FNMA	11.50	279	4,000	106-20	106-14	30.4	8.48	11.05	9.06
PC GUAR	8.00	348	48,000	97-16	92-03	4.5	9.40	8.85	9.00
PC GUAR	9.50	350	20,000	101-02	99-12	5.9	9.58	9.75	9.68
PC GUAR	11.00	298	14,000	104-28	105-10	24.4	8.76	10.68	9.31
PC GUAR	11.50	276	25,000	102-02	106-04	30.4	8.40	11.08	10.34
PORTFOLIO 1			**691,000**				**9.31**	**10.05**	**9.23**

[14]The static cash flow yield is based on our long-term prepayment forecast for each security on the pricing date, while the mutual fund yield is based on our 1-year average forecast.

EXHIBIT 6b

ORIGINAL PORTFOLIO: PERFORMANCE CHARACTERISTICS

Security Type	Coupon	Rem Term	Price (Mar) 3/10/88	Par Value (000)	Mkt Value (000)	Port %	Mutual Fund Yield	Static CF Yield	Static Sprd	Opt Adj Spd	Opt Cost	Dur	Scenario Return Profile -200	-100	0	100	200	Exp Ret
GNMA SF	7.50	353	88-22	55,000	48,778	7.0	8.88	9.37	85	60	35	6.23	20.59	15.03	9.38	5.83	-1.45	9.06
GNMA SF	8.00	353	91-12	60,000	54,826	7.9	9.12	9.48	96	56	41	6.00	19.92	14.86	9.45	4.09	-1.06	9.11
GNMA SF	9.00	350	96-30	70,000	67,856	9.8	9.36	9.64	115	54	69	5.36	17.84	14.11	9.68	4.74	-0.11	9.11
GNMA SF	9.50	350	99-20	70,000	69,738	10.1	9.85	9.69	123	53	71	4.97	16.62	13.61	9.60	5.09	0.45	9.06
GNMA SF	10.00	350	102-16	25,000	25,625	3.7	9.83	9.66	124	38	57	4.52	15.23	12.90	9.54	5.45	1.06	8.93
GNMA SF	10.50	345	105-02	12,000	12,608	1.8	9.70	9.55	122	21	101	3.87	13.46	11.88	9.40	5.96	1.96	8.73
GNMA SF	11.00	330	107-04	35,000	37,494	5.4	10.17	9.21	104	2	103	3.04	11.72	10.53	9.04	6.47	3.08	8.38
GNMA SF	11.50	305	108-08	60,000	64,950	9.4	9.01	8.80	84	7	77	2.60	11.07	9.96	8.61	6.77	3.96	8.17
GNMA SF	12.00	316	109-08	55,000	60,088	8.7	8.73	8.44	60	10	60	2.38	10.77	9.61	8.26	6.76	4.45	8.00
GNMA SF	12.50	303	110-06	64,000	70,520	10.2	8.52	8.22	46	14	32	2.24	10.59	9.31	8.05	6.72	4.98	7.88
GNMA SF	13.00	301	111-08	11,000	12,231	1.8	8.50	8.09	36	14	22	2.16	10.48	9.20	7.93	6.63	5.17	7.80
FNMA	8.00	348	92-12	35,000	32,331	4.7	8.96	9.44	100	62	38	5.47	18.27	14.10	9.38	4.52	-0.25	8.99
FNMA	8.50	346	94-01	25,000	23,758	3.4	9.10	9.50	107	58	48	6.17	17.21	13.72	9.47	4.90	0.50	9.01
FNMA	10.50	310	104-04	3,000	3,124	0.5	9.22	9.36	119	21	98	2.95	11.39	10.48	9.06	6.57	3.36	8.43
FNMA	11.50	279	106-14	4,000	4,268	0.6	9.06	8.48	76	19	57	3.11	10.03	9.18	8.27	7.02	4.96	7.98
PC GUAR	8.00	348	92-03	43,000	44,205	6.4	9.00	9.40	96	58	38	5.52	18.35	14.14	9.37	4.46	-0.36	8.97
PC GUAR	9.50	350	99-12	20,000	19,875	2.9	9.68	9.68	124	51	74	4.53	16.19	12.86	9.49	5.47	1.17	8.91
PC GUAR	11.00	298	105-10	14,000	14,744	2.1	9.31	8.76	88	7	81	2.46	10.47	9.61	8.60	6.83	4.16	8.11
PC GUAR	11.50	276	106-04	25,000	26,531	3.8	10.34	8.40	69	13	65	2.18	10.06	9.18	8.24	6.96	4.85	7.94
PORTFOLIO 1				691,000	693,537	100.0	9.23	9.51	92	38	57	4.13	14.91	12.17	9.02	6.66	1.79	8.62

Exhibit 6b analyzes the performance characteristics of each of the securities in the portfolio as well as of the portfolio as a whole. The static spread, option-adjusted spread, and option cost of each security is shown along with a measure of price sensitivity, the option-adjusted duration. All of these measures are generated using our simulation model. In addition to these summary measures of performance, a scenario return profile is shown for each security and for the portfolio. The returns are generated over a 1-year holding period for each of the interest rate scenarios shown, assuming cash flows are reinvested in short-term instruments and that the securities are repriced at the end of the holding period at their option-adjusted spread. Also shown is an expected return, which is a probability-weighted average of the individual scenario returns.[15]

The portfolio has a duration of 4.1 years and consists of coupons ranging from 7.5% to 13% across the GNMA, FNMA, and FHLMC 30-year sectors. Many of the positions look attractive based on their wide option-adjusted spreads and high expected returns relative to other comparable duration issues. Other positions, though, do not appear to offer attractive relative values when compared to alternative investments. Beyond the pure economics, however, the relatively low book costs associated with some of the high coupon positions may make them an important component of the portfolio, given the positive impact they have on the mutual fund yield.

Restructuring the Portfolio

The most difficult part of any portfolio restructuring analysis is determining the appropriate objectives and constraints. The goal of the analysis is to find the optimal portfolio, that is, the one which satisfies all of the constraints and maximizes the defined objective. For the purpose of this analysis, the objective will be to restructure the portfolio in such a way as to provide the highest expected return that could be generated, while satisfying certain other requirements. The other requirements, however, are particularly onerous. The new restructured portfolio must have a mutual fund yield which is 50 basis points higher than that of the original portfolio (9.23 + 0.50 = 9.73). This constraint is, in fact, so severe that it almost overrides the primary objective (i.e., maximizing expected return). Any new portfolio must first satisfy the yield constraint before the "best" one (from an expected return perspective) is chosen. The other critical constraint concerns the duration of the new portfolio. We have (arbitrarily) decided that the new portfolio must have the same duration as the original portfolio (4.1 years).

The universe of securities that we will examine for possible inclusion in the portfolio consists of the most liquid generic GNMA, FNMA and FHLMC securities. Among the 30-year securities, we include the coupons between 7.5% and 13%,

---

[15]For a definition of terms and a list of all of the assumptions used in the simulation analysis, see *Mortgage Market Comment*, Goldman, Sachs & Co., Mortgage Securities Research, March 11, 1988.

while in the 15-year area we will focus on the coupons between 7.5% and 10%. So that the portfolio is not too heavily weighted toward one security or a few positions, we will impose an additional constraint that limits any new security position (over and above current holdings) to no more than 10% of the entire portfolio. In addition, total holdings in the 15-year area are limited to 15% of the portfolio.

Given the objectives and constraints discussed above, the optimal restructured portfolio was selected and is shown in Exhibits 7a and 7b. The top portion of each of the exhibits (i.e., the 6 securities shown above the double line) shows what would remain of the original positions held in portfolio. The bottom portion shows the new purchases that would be made. The book costs associated with what remains of the original positions are in most cases different from the market prices shown. The book prices of the newly purchased positions, on the other hand, are by definition equal to current market prices.

The restructuring analysis indicates that about one-quarter of the original portfolio should continue to be held, while the remaining 75% should be sold, with the proceeds used to purchase other securities which better meet the objectives and constraints. To forster an intuitive understanding of how the new portfolio was created, we will compare the two portfolios and highlight the steps involved in restructuring the original portfolio.

The first step in the restructuring would be to sell all of the discount positions held in the original portfolio, that is, those with coupons of 9% and below. While these securities generally appear to offer reasonable value, their mutual fund yields (even at current market prices) are relatively low comapred to the required yield of 9.73% for the portfolio. Furthermore, the book costs of the original positions in these securities are all above current market prices, causing their mutual fund yields to be

EXHIBIT 7a
OPTIMAL PORTFOLIO: YIELD ANALYSIS

Security Type	Coupon	Rem Term	Par Value	Book Price	Market Price 3/10/88	Proj 1-YR CPR	Static CF Yield	Current Yield (At Mkt)	Mutual Fund Yield
GNMA SF	9.50	350	70,000	97-10	99-20	3.8	9.69	9.73	9.85
GNMA SF	10.00	350	25,000	102-16	102-16	4.5	9.66	9.96	9.83
GNMA SF	10.50	345	12,000	106-00	105-02	7.6	9.55	10.20	9.70
GNMA SF	11.00	330	35,000	102-00	107-04	15.0	9.21	10.49	10.17
PC GUAR	9.50	350	20,000	101-02	99-12	5.9	9.58	9.75	9.68
PC GUAR	11.50	276	1,091	102-02	106-04	30.4	8.40	11.08	10.34
GNMA SF	9.50	350	69,615	99-20	99-20	3.8	9.69	9.73	9.74
GNMA SF	10.00	350	67,662	102-16	102-16	4.5	9.66	9.96	9.83
GNMA SF	10.50	345	66,012	105-02	105-02	7.6	9.55	10.20	9.78
FNMA	9.00	350	4,931	97-10	97-10	5.0	9.58	9.43	9.59
FNMA	9.50	350	69,462	99-27	99-27	5.9	9.59	9.71	9.72
FNMA	10.50	310	2,006	104-04	104-04	17.9	9.26	10.30	9.47
PC GUAR	9.50	350	69,790	99-12	99-12	5.9	9.58	9.75	9.80
PC GUAR	10.50	300	66,827	103-25	103-25	17.9	9.21	10.33	9.57
PC 15YR	9.50	160	68,923	100-20	100-20	11.0	9.18	9.63	9.53
GNMES	9.50	165	34,461	100-20	100-20	9.0	9.19	9.63	9.55
PORTFOLIO 2			**682,780**				**9.53**	**9.90**	**9.73**

EXHIBIT 7b

OPTIMAL PORTFOLIO: PERFORMANCE CHARACTERISTICS

Security Type	Coupon	Rem Term	Price (Mar) 3/10/88	Par Value (000)	Mkt Value (000)	Port %	Mutual Fund Yield	Static CF Yield	Static Sprd	Opt Adj Spd	Opt Cost	Dur	Scenario Return Profile					Exp Ret
													-200	-100	0	100	200	
GNMA SF	9.50	360	99-20	70,000	69,730	10.1	9.86	9.69	123	53	71	4.97	16.62	13.61	9.60	5.09	0.45	9.06
GNMA SF	10.00	360	102-16	25,000	25,625	3.7	9.83	9.66	124	38	87	4.53	15.23	12.90	9.54	5.45	1.06	8.93
GNMA SF	10.50	345	105-03	12,000	12,608	1.8	9.70	9.65	122	21	101	3.87	13.46	11.85	9.40	5.95	1.96	8.72
GNMA SF	11.00	330	107-04	35,000	37,494	5.4	10.17	9.21	104	3	103	3.04	11.72	10.53	9.04	6.47	3.08	8.38
PC GUAR	9.50	360	99-12	20,000	19,875	2.9	9.63	9.53	124	51	74	4.52	16.19	12.85	9.49	5.47	1.17	8.91
PC GUAR	11.50	276	105-04	1,091	1,158	0.3	10.34	8.40	69	13	55	2.16	10.06	9.18	8.24	6.96	4.85	7.94
GNMA SF	9.50	360	99-20	69,615	69,354	10.0	9.74	9.69	123	53	71	4.97	16.62	13.61	9.60	5.09	0.45	9.06
GNMA SF	10.00	360	102-16	67,662	69,384	10.0	9.83	9.66	124	38	87	4.53	15.23	12.90	9.54	5.45	1.06	8.93
GNMA SF	10.50	345	105-03	66,012	69,384	10.0	9.78	9.65	122	21	101	3.97	13.46	11.85	9.40	5.95	1.96	8.72
FNMA	9.00	360	97-10	4,931	4,798	0.7	9.59	9.58	119	60	60	4.88	16.34	13.39	9.52	5.16	0.66	9.00
FNMA	9.50	360	99-27	69,462	69,353	10.0	9.73	9.59	125	51	75	4.46	16.06	12.77	9.48	5.61	1.25	8.90
FNMA	10.50	310	104-04	2,006	2,089	0.3	9.47	9.26	119	21	98	2.95	11.59	10.48	9.06	6.57	3.36	8.42
PC GUAR	9.50	360	99-12	69,700	69,354	10.0	9.80	9.58	124	51	74	4.52	16.19	12.85	9.49	5.47	1.17	8.91
PC GUAR	10.50	300	103-16	66,837	69,384	10.0	9.67	9.21	114	19	96	2.97	11.43	10.50	9.05	6.54	3.31	8.41
PC 15YR	9.50	180	100-20	64,923	69,354	10.0	9.53	9.18	113	60	52	3.23	12.40	11.21	9.21	6.52	3.49	8.71
GNOMES	9.50	165	100-20	34,461	34,676	5.0	9.55	9.19	112	60	53	3.36	12.71	11.37	9.25	6.44	3.29	8.74
PORTFOLIO 3				652,780	693,536	100.0	9.73	9.63	120	41	79	4.10	14.29	12.28	9.40	5.77	1.76	8.81

even less attractive than if they were purchased at market. Most of the very high coupon positions would also be sold, with two exceptions, which will be discussed shortly. The coupons 11% and above do not appear to offer high enough yields and/ or expected returns to make them desirable for the new portfolio.

Of the 25% of the original portfolio that would be retained after the restructuring, the holdings are predominately in the 9.5%, 10% and 10.5% coupon area. This should come as no surprise since these coupons were shown in Exhibit 1 to have the highest mutual fund yields (based on 3/10/88 prices). The book costs associated with these positions are, in general, fairly close to market prices. The 9.5% coupons and, to a lesser extent, the 10% securities also appear to offer reasonable value in terms of their option-adjusted spreads and expected returns relative to other comparable duration issues. In fact, not only are the original positions in these coupons maintained, but new purchases of these securities would be made for the optimal portfolio (in many cases reaching the 10% limit for a given security). Other purchases that would be made in the restructuring are also concentrated in the 9% through 10.5% coupons. In addition, 15-year securities in this coupon range appear very attractive, so much so that new purchases would be made up to the 15% limit.

The only high coupon positions that would continue to be held after the restructuring are the GNMA 11% and FHLMC 11.5% positions. The book costs associated with each of these positions are well below their market prices, causing them to have unusually attractive mutual fund yields. While no additional purchases are to be made in this coupon area (since the book price would equal the market price), the optimal portfolio contains the entire GNMA 11 position as well as a small portion of the FHLMC 11.5 position.

Finally, one other point of note involves the FNMA 10.5% position. While the entire original position would be sold, two-thirds of the balance would then be repurchased for the new portfolio. This results from the fact that the original position in this security has a book cost which is 1¼ points above the current market price. Given the book price of the original position, the security is not attractive, although at the lower market price its yield is higher and a small amount would be selected for the optimal portfolio. To establish a lower book price for this security, however, 30 days must pass between the time it is sold and the time it is repurchased, otherwise it is considered a *wash sale* and a new book price is *not* established. The wash sale rule, though, only applies to purchases of the exact same coupon in the same sector.

The Bottom Line

The new restructured portfolio is, by almost every measure, superior to the original portfolio. The mutual fund yield of the new portfolio is 50 basis points higher than that of the original portfolio. Furthermore, the expected return and the average option-adjusted spread of the new portfolio are both higher than on the original portfolio, by 19 and 6 basis points, respectively.

Comparing the scenario return profiles of the two portfolios also offers some interesting information. These results can be seen graphically in Exhibit 8. The new (optimal) portfolio offers a substantially higher return over a 1-year holding period than the original portfolio when interest rates are assumed to be unchanged or vary by as much as 100 basis points in either direction. When interest rates are assumed to rise by 200 basis points, the two portfolios offer equivalent returns. More significantly, when rates are assumed to fall by 200 basis points, the new portfolio underperforms the original portfolio by a substantial margin.

The scenario analysis vividly illustrates that the new portfolio has greater negative convexity associated with it than the original portfolio. The higher option cost of the new portfolio is another indication of this. While negative convexity is clearly an undesirable property, like anything, at a price it is worth bearing. The simulation model and the scenario return analysis, in fact, both attempt to evaluate the performance costs associated with negative convexity and determine the value of different securities net of these costs. The results of both of these analyses indicate that the new portfolio is fundamentally more valuable than the original portfolio. Whether or

EXHIBIT 8
SCENARIO RETURN PROFILE—ORIGINAL PORTFOLIO VS OPTIMAL PORTFOLIO

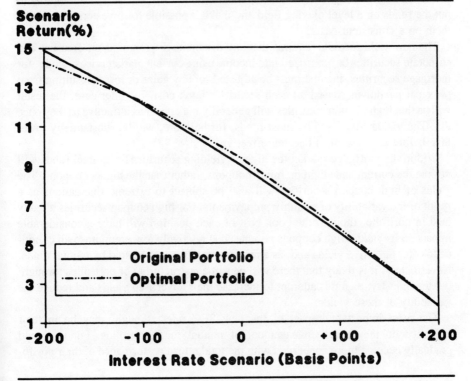

not this was the case, though, the new portfolio was structured as such largely to satisfy the requirement that it yield 50 basis points more than the original portfolio. If it also happens to be a more valuable portfolio, so much the better.

The hypothetical portfolio restructuring reviewed in this section was intended to familiarize non-mutual fund readers with the types of strategies that mutual funds will be considering over the next several months. For mutual fund readers, the section was designed to provide an example of how a fund can systematically consider and evaluate tradeoffs among its multiple objectives. As a result of the new SEC rules, mutual funds are more likely than ever to reevaluate their existing portfolios. The approach described in this section may provide a useful guide.

CONCLUSION

The new SEC rules governing performance advertising by mutual funds will undoubtly have a significant impact on the mutual fund industry and will likely have an impact on the mortgage market as well. By requiring that the yield advertised by mutual funds be computed on the basis of a standardized formula and that it be presented only in conjunction with historical total returns, the SEC is attempting to put the funds on a level playing field and make it possible for investors to evaluate them on a consistent basis.

The new yield formula requires that any discounts or premiums on Treasury and corporate securities be amortized into income using current market prices, while, for mortgage securities, income must be adjusted for any gains or losses resulting from principal paydowns, based on each security's book cost. In either case, the result will be that high coupon securities will generally not appear as attractive as they once did. The yields advertised by most funds, furthermore, will be substantially lower than before the new rules became effective.

Within the mortgage market the highest yielding securities for mutual funds will now be the current and slight premium coupons, rather than the higher coupons. The yields of high coupon securities will also be subject to extreme fluctuations as a result of the variability of monthly prepayments. For high coupon securities already held in portfolio, though, the book cost of each position will have a considerable impact on its yield. High coupons purchased at relatively low premiums will continue to offer attractive yields and, as a result, are unlikely to be sold by mutual funds. Nevertheless, it is likely that there will be some restructuring of portfolios throughout the industry, as funds attempt to increase their advertised yields and reduce the variability of these yields.

The most important impact of the new SEC rules, though, may be in their influence on the overall management of mutual fund portfolios. Funds should gradually become more concerned with the total return performance of their portfolios, rather than focusing only on their distribution rates or advertised yields. As a result, they will become more sensitive to and more actively manage the durations of their portfolios and, in addition, will be more apt to take advantage of attractive trading opportunities in the marketplace.

Chapter 27

GIC Portfolio Management

DAVID M. PERRY
PRESIDENT
CERTUS FINANCIAL CORPORATION

Guaranteed Investment Contracts (GICs) have their origin as far back as the mid-1950's when life insurance companies began offering Deposit Administration (DA) contracts. The DA products were inflexible and crude in structure but did provide retirement plan sponsors with guarantees of principal which were backed by the life insurance carrier's general assets. Life insurance companies adjusted yields credited to these contracts annually at their discretion. Expense charges associated with maintaining DAs were determined by the life insurer as well. The contracts had no maturity dates although they were capable of paying out benefits to individual participants who were retiring. Non-retirement benefit payouts provoked substantial early termination penalties.

In the 1960's, Immediate Participating Guarantee (IPG) products replaced the DA contracts. With IPGs, the North American life insurers moved to the forefront of the burgeoning pension investment business. IPGs were similar to DAs in that assets were backed by the life insurer's general account. They were different, however, in that credited yields tracked prevailing interest rates, and a minimum or floor rate was typically a contract feature. Contract expenses could be increased but were limited to stipulated maximum amounts. While IPGs contained no fixed termination date, individual participants could withdraw money for a number of purposes besides retirement without incurring any penalties.

In the 1970's, the GIC, a product which soon was to become a mainstay in employee benefit programs, was introduced. In the early part of the decade, several of the largest life insurers issued GICs primarily to sponsors of defined benefit pension plans. In their inaugural phase, GICs were attractive because of their ability to account for earnings on a "book" rather than "market" value basis. The principal and interest of GICs were backed by the general assets of the issuing life insurer. However, for the first time, insured investment products had stated maturity dates instead of being open-ended, perpetual agreements. Amounts needed for participant-directed withdrawals were made with few restrictions.

In the 1980's, with the advent of the 401(k) feature into defined contribution plans, the popularity of GICs exploded. Funds comprised primarily of GICs became the most favored investment option in 401(k) plans. Estimates on the total dollars invested into GICs within these programs ranged as high as $150 billion. By 1988, there were approximately 75 North American life insurance companies issuing some form of insured investment contract. In addition, a growing number of commercial banks and savings and loans began to offer products with comparable features. These contracts, known as BICs and SLICs, conceivably have the added protection of federal deposit insurance.

Because GICs are not considered securities, but are viewed as group annuity contracts, they remain exempt from SEC registration. This enables GICs to be priced at book value and this single characteristic explains why the product has achieved such phenomenal growth. Participants investing assets into GICs are assured that their balances will not be negatively affected by moving interest rates. In volatile economic times, the ability to know that principal will continue to earn interest at predictable rates of return is a very appealing feature. In addition, the fact that through 1988, there had never been a single default on a GIC, underscores the overall security of the life insurance industry.

GIC Funds, also known as Guaranteed Fixed-Income Funds, Guaranteed Asset Funds, Fixed-Rate Funds and Interest Guarantee Funds, are usually the most favored investment option in employee-directed benefit programs. They accept ongoing deposits and make ongoing disbursements. They provide plan participants with stable, secure, reasonably predictable rates of return.

However, pronounced differences exist in how plan sponsors manage GIC fund portfolios. Some sponsors conduct annual searches and commit a full year's worth of cash flow to one issuer on one date. Others hire consultants to assist in making more frequent purchase decisions, but still retain ultimate responsibility over contract selection. Still others engage registered investments advisors to manage GIC portfolios and purchase contracts throughout the year on a discretionary basis.

This chapter will not retrace the evolution of the GIC product into its present format. Rather, it will: 1) elicit the fundamental considerations affecting plan sponsors that have established GIC funds as one of the investment options in an employee-directed benefit program; 2) describe proven investment management strategies which more successful GIC fund managers utilize; and 3) illustrate several investment management techniques which enhance GIC fund performance.

MANAGEMENT CONSIDERATIONS

Whether a GIC portfolio is handled in-house or by an external GIC manager, the following are fundamental concerns that can affect performance:

Credit Quality. Clearly, the most important component of any GIC fund is its credit quality. The acronym GIC stands for *guaranteed* investment contract. The strength of the underlying assets which back this guarantee is the manager's principal concern. Moreover, managers should also explore to what extent, if any, federal or state regulatory entities would provide adjunct protection. Since there has never been a default by a GIC issuer, this consideration may sometimes be overlooked as unnecessary. This is a mistake, particularly in volatile economic and political times. Maintaining a portfolio of high credit quality should always be the manager's chief priority.

Diversification. Diversification may be approached from two perspectives: the overall diversification of the portfolio among different life insurers, and the diversification of the portfolio among different industries. The emergence of commercial banks and savings and loans as contract vendors now makes it possible to diversify GIC portfolios on an industry-wide basis as well. For the most part, however, contracts continue to be underwritten by North American life insurance companies. The diversification aspect of a GIC fund is also sometimes not considered by managers. Many GIC funds have invested 100% of their portfolio with one issuer — something which would never happen in a stock or bond fund. Diversification of the portfolio makes good sense.

Yield. GIC managers continually seek ways to increase their portfolios' yields. Sometimes, this is attempted within the context of established investment guidelines. Other managers accomplish this simply by selecting the highest yielding contracts available, irrespective of credit quality or diversification concerns. In either case, GIC returns are primarily a function of prevailing interest rates at the time of purchase commitments. Occasionally, managers enter into longer term commitments to capture what they perceive as especially attractive rates. Unless the manager is willing to accept responsibility for timing interest rates as a function of the portfolio's performance, this should be discouraged.

GIC yields are most often compared to U.S. Treasuries of comparable durations. Spreads between these two instruments have narrowed considerably in the past few years (see Exhibits 1A and 1B).

Duration. Durations of GIC portfolios also vary considerably from one fund to another. Some managers simply elect to purchase contracts of identical duration at the same time each year. Other managers establish an overall target duration objective, but select contracts of different durations by examining yield curves and yield spreads throughout the year. Most GIC funds have durations between two and five years. In the past, individual contracts of longer durations (as long as twelve years) were placed. This practice has become almost non-existent as managers look for their portfolios to turn over more frequently.

EXHIBIT 1A
3-YEAR GIC AVERAGE VERSUS TREASURIES

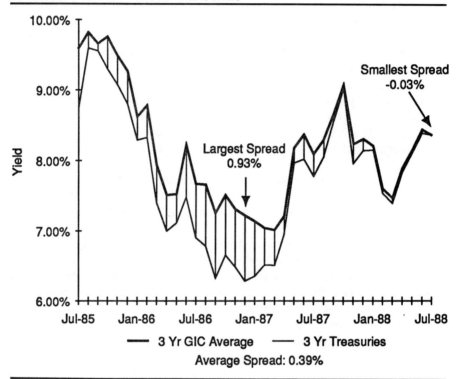

3 Yr GIC Average ——   —— 3 Yr Treasuries
Average Spread: 0.39%

Liquidity. The liquidity issue may be analyzed from two perspectives: the portfolio's liquidity needs for bona fide benefit disbursements for transfers, withdrawals, loans and retirement, and the need for some cash in case above-market opportunities occur or in anticipation of rising interest rates. Maintenance of cash equivalents within a portfolio would appear to lower the fund's rate of return. However, many managers have created ways of using cash to their advantage, either for benefit payouts or investment opportunities.

Communication to Participants. The manner in which a GIC Fund is communicated to participants can affect a manager's strategy. If a "class year" approach[1] is communicated, it severely limits the products and durations of products the manager can consider. This stems from the need to broadcast the fund's actual yield over a several year period of time. If a "blended"[2] approach is communicated, the need to

---

[1]Under this method, interest is allocated to individual "cells" each year. In most cases, this translates into one contract per year. Participants, therefore, all end up with their own individual GIC fund rate.

[2]Under this method, interest is blended among all products within the GIC fund on a pro rata basis. There is no limit to the number or type of products utilized within the fund. All participants are credited with the same interest rate.

EXHIBIT 1B
5-YEAR GIC AVERAGE VERSUS TREASURIES

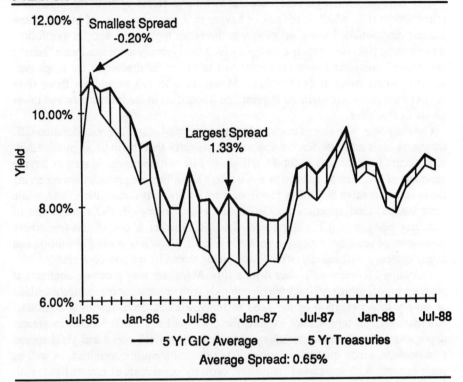

Source: Certus Financial Corporation

broadcast a minimum or guaranteed rate for some period of time can also affect a manager's options. Far more flexibility exists with the "blended" approach.

Product Variation. Assuming the "blended" method is used, the manager may select from a wide variety of contract types. These include the generically-named "window"[3] and "bullet"[4] contracts as well as floating-rate, enhanced liquidity, convertible, advance commitment and participating contracts. Product selection by the manager can influence the fund's performance in tangible ways, including yield, liquidity, maturity, duration and assignability. GIC product terms can be individually drafted to comply with the manager's specific guidelines and objectives.

Portfolio Structure/Cash Flow Analysis. Some managers structure a GIC fund's portfolio simply, so that contracts are purchased one year and all benefit disbursements are made on a LIFO basis. Other managers create and then maintain more complex portfolio structures, with layered liquidity tiers that are more closely tied to

[3]Typically, "window" contracts refer to contracts with deposit periods that can extend from one month to five years. Most common are contracts with six or twelve month "window" periods.

[4]Typically, "bullet" contracts refer to contracts with lump sum deposits.

the actual cash flow needs of the plan. The manager's assessment and corresponding reaction to the cash flow both into and out of a GIC fund can affect results.

Risk Analysis. Managers may address two basic forms of risk: the portfolio's reinvestment risk, which is the risk of having to invest large sums of money at low interest rates and/or having no money to invest at high rates; and the portfolio's underwriting risk, i.e., expense charges which are typically associated with "benefit responsive" contracts (contracts earmarked to make disbursements for employee-directed withdrawals at book value). Managers who fail to address these risks subject their funds to enormous interest rate fluctuation in the former case and lower yields in the latter.

Contract Size. The size of contracts being negotiated is another consideration GIC managers must address. Recent experience indicates that the most aggressive bidding occurs for contracts in the $1 million to $10 million range. Managers buying contracts of less than $1 million or more than $10 million are probably not receiving the most competitive bids. Very few issuers are consistently competitive. And, while most issuers' total appetites for GIC business has increased, the average size of contracts being issued has decreased. The GIC market is one of the few where economies of scale are capped at such a low level. Contracts in the $25 million and larger category will usually offer lower yields than $10 million contracts.

Execution Techniques/Product Availability. Managers may purchase contracts at predetermined, arbitrary times which coincide with investment committee meetings or simply in anticipation of the need to reinvest assets from maturing contracts. Alternatively, managers may explore the GIC market's inefficiencies in greater depth and make purchase decisions after evaluating yield curve and yield spread relationships, credit quality mispricings, pre-commitment opportunities, as well as other factors. With increasing frequency, capacity constraints of issuers limit product availability. Managers may position their funds to buy simply when it is convenient and hope sufficient competition exists for their business. They may also respond by positioning their funds to buy whenever they perceive it is advantageous to do so.

Coordination with Trustee and Employee Benefits Personnel. The manager must serve as a central administrative source for the fund, coordinating with bank trustees, plan recordkeepers and employee benefit personnel. In some plans, administrative and recordkeeping concerns are the main considerations in making contract selection decisions.

MANAGEMENT STRATEGIES

GIC managers respond to the issues above in a variety of ways. Many still employ reactive or passive strategies that are capable of producing satisfactory results. Several others have decided that more carefully conceived and well-researched strategies lead to superior performance. Described below are four simple and straightforward guidelines that managers of more successful GIC portfolios typically employ.

Establish Credit Quality and Diversification Guidelines

It would be inconceivable for a stock or bond manager to invest 100% of a portfolio's assets with any one entity. This is the case even considering the ability to trade stocks or bonds in an open market. Nevertheless, some GIC managers do not consider the pitfalls of investing all of their GIC portfolio's assets with a single issuer. In many cases, the size of a GIC fund eclipses the size of other funds by large margins. And yet, very often, the sponsor has not adopted any formal investment policy guidelines for the GIC portfolio.

Today, various rating agencies including Moody's, Standard & Poor's and Duff & Phelps have joined A.M. Best as arbiters of life insurers that issue GICs. Even though contradictory information has been published concerning the credit quality of many issuers, GIC managers must still make their own distinctions on this issue. Credit quality standards must be developed and followed. Diversification of a portfolio is not only prudent; it is essential in volatile economic times.

Purchase Contracts Throughout the Year

In turbulent interest rate environments such as these, selecting contracts only once or twice a year subjects GIC fund performance to a huge interest rate gamble. Historically, many plan sponsors have purchased new "window" contracts in the fall for the subsequent calendar year's cash flow. This combines the interest rate gamble with possible capacity constraints, which can limit product availability.

Obviously, the total size of a GIC fund and available cash for individual placements dictate to a great extent how often a plan sponsor can enter the market. There is no question that smaller investors are at a disadvantage and that purchasing GICs of smaller sizes is not advantageous. (For these investors, pooled funds of GICs[5] are an appropriate vehicle to consider. These can be managed as creatively and opportunistically as individually managed funds.)

The intent of most GIC funds is to earn higher yields when interest rates rise and lower yields when interest rates fall. This is not achieved as easily if contracts are secured only once or twice a year. Selection periods may or may not coincide with the best times to be in the market. In 1987, for example, if a manager purchased a GIC in mid-October before the stock market's crash, the year's highest nominal yield was probably achieved. Only 30 to 60 days later, a contract of identical duration would have earned anywhere from 100 to 200 basis points less.

---

[5]Pooled funds of GICs are a fairly recent innovation which are very similar to a mutual fund comprised of cash equivalents and insured investment contraacts. Offered by numerous bank trusts, they are especially popular for smaller plans. These funds are priced at "book" value.

The only way to offset the interest rate gamble and avoid selecting contracts when attractive products are scarce is to be in the market more frequently. By being in position to purchase GICs throughout the year, the manager can select contracts more opportunistically and limit large spikes up or down in a GIC portfolio. By being able to wait until the higher quality issuers offer the more attractive products, managers using this strategy can also improve a portfolio's overall credit quality.

Minimize Underwriting Risk Charges

In the past few years, GIC issuers have become far more sophisticated in their ability to underwrite investment contracts. This trend does produce more issuer caution and lower yields. However, in the long run, it is an advantage to plan sponsors because it reflects the issuers' continued ability to maintain profitability in the GIC product area.

In general, issuers measure underwriting risk in the following simplistic way: how much and over what period of time does the issuer expect to receive money; how much and over what period of time does the issuer expect to pay out money; and what level of confidence does the issuer have that these expectations are valid.

If an issuer were assured of receiving a lump sum contribution on one date and agreed to return 100% of the principal and interest on another date without any potential for early withdrawals, the underwriting risk would be virtually non-existent.

However, since most GICs placed into 401(k) plans are benefit-responsive, risk charges almost always are of some consequence. Transfers to other investment options, early retirement offers and loans are only a few examples of events which can trigger the need to invade a contract for benefit liquidity purposes. In addition, many plan sponsors continue to utilize window contracts which have variable deposits during periods of extended length. The risk charges for benefit-responsive, window contracts vary from one issuer to another. However, the unpredictable nature of cash flow into and/or out of a GIC can, in the worst scenario, discourage issuers from quoting at all. At best, rates will be reduced.

GIC managers seeking improved performance should make efforts to reduce or, if possible, negate entirely the underwriting risk charges which adversely impact GIC yields. By assuaging underwriters' concerns on cash flow instability, both into and out of contracts, managers secure higher yields for the portfolio. There are several ways to do this. The creation of liquidity tiers (explained later in the chapter) is one of the more effective methods.

Limit Reinvestment Risk

Another typical problem of GIC funds is the reinvestment risk that is caused by large, single date maturing pieces. New contracts that are selected should be structured so that maturities occur over a period of time, as opposed to on one day when it may subject the fund to undue reinvestment risk. Older, in-force contracts should be examined to determine whether revised payouts can be achieved without affecting the duration. Quite often, issuers are more than willing to do this, because it can improve their own investment portfolios.

Limiting a portfolio's reinvestment risk enables the GIC fund's yield to be more compatible with prevailing interest rates. A sound strategy is to have between 10%-30% of the total portfolio available for investment/reinvestment each year. Ideally, these would be fairly evenly distributed by quarter as well. If a manager positions the fund to buy contracts of comparable size through all interest rate cycles, chances of sharp increases or decreases in yield are very unlikely. Instead, the GIC fund will function comparably to a money market fund, only with higher rates.

MANAGEMENT TECHNIQUES

Retention of outside GIC managers is still a fairly recent phenomenon. For the most part, however, their implementation of management strategies has been more progressive and creative than that of their in-house counterparts. Four specific techniques which some outside managers utilize to improve fund performance are discussed below.

Creation of Liquidity Tiers

One of the strategies previously mentioned that GIC managers should pursue is to minimize underwriting risk charges. An ideal way to accomplish this is by creating a three-tiered liquidity structure for all fund disbursements.

Very simply, it works like this: The manager divides the fund's assets into three categories or tiers. The first tier is comprised essentially of cash equivalents. This tier is the first one accessed for employee-directed withdrawals. The second tier is comprised of a diversified pool of GICs. This tier is accessed on a pro rata basis after 100% of the first tier has been depleted. The third tier is comprised of non-benefit responsive GICs and "insulated"[6] GICs which are depleted only after the first two tiers are completely exhausted. The percentage size of each tier should be determined after the manager carefully analyzes the historical and projected cash flows into the GIC fund.

In practice, this system operates extremely well. The amount of money maintained in the first tier should be sufficient to cover all normal, expected disbursements. It should be an amount that is not too large, because in most interest rate environments, the overall yield of assets within this tier will be less than the rest of the portfolio. In a growing plan, the amount should be approximately 5% of the total

---

[6]"Insulated" GICs refer to a generic product which are benefit-responsive GICs after all contracts within the second tier are depleted. An increasing number of GIC vendors offer these products.

portfolio. In some funds, the first tier is limited to a specific dollar amount rather than to a percentage.

The GICs within the second tier would be the next ones accessed for benefit needs. These payouts would come on a pro rata basis from all contracts within this tier. In most cases, there will never be the need to go into this tier for any money, since adequate cash would be available from the first tier.

Finally, the third tier contracts would include non-benefit responsive GICs and "insulated" GICs that would be accessed once the first two tiers were fully depleted. The third tier would only be accessed as a result of a major plan restructuring or termination, both events which could provoke a market value adjustment anyway. In effect, creating these three liquidity tiers (see Exhibit 2) accomplishes the following:

1. Assuages underwriters' concerns since contracts will be disbursed only after the first tier has been depleted. This gives them assurances by either a percentage or dollar limit amount of what the fund's needs would be before money from their contracts are actually needed. This reduces risk charges.

EXHIBIT 2
LIQUIDITY TIER ILLUSTRATION (DESCRIPTION OF ASSETS)

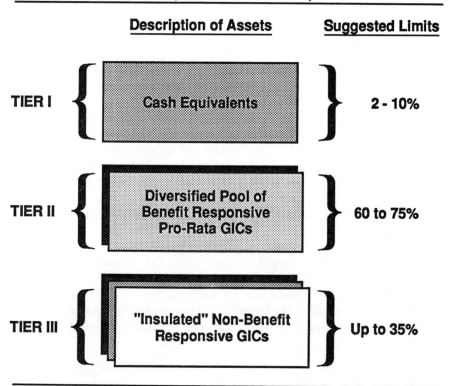

	Description of Assets	**Suggested Limits**
TIER I	Cash Equivalents	2 - 10%
TIER II	Diversified Pool of Benefit Responsive Pro-Rata GICs	60 to 75%
TIER III	"Insulated" Non-Benefit Responsive GICs	Up to 35%

2. Improves the portfolio's yield in two ways: by reducing the risk charges associated with contracts in the second tier, and by purchasing contracts which are either non-benefit responsive (no risk charges) or only benefit responsive after the first two tiers are exhausted. The small percentage of money typically maintained in the first tier is usually lower yielding. However, the yields of contracts within the second tier are higher than those when a first tier does not exist. The contracts in the third tier can be significantly higher. (See Exhibits 3A and 3B.) There is no indication that yields for second tier contracts are reduced by creating a third tier. The buffer maintained in the first tier is sufficient to make underwriters comfortable that assets from contracts within the second tier are unlikely to be withdrawn.

EXHIBIT 3A
TIER II VERSUS TIER III RATES

Issuer	Tier II Yield	Tier III Yield	Rate Differential
A	8.46%	8.51%	.05
B	8.29%	8.48%	.19
C	8.20%	8.35%	.15
D	8.49%	8.54%	.05
E	8.30%	8.57%	.27
Average	8.35%	8.49%	.14

Placement Date:	January 7, 1988	
Contract Amount:	$5 Million	
Duration:	3.82 Years	

EXHIBIT 3B
TIER II VERSUS TIER III RATES

Issuer	Tier II Yield	Tier III Yield	Rate Differential
A	8.20%	8.50%	.30
B	8.48%	8.55%	.07
C	8.15%	8.53%	.38
D	8.55%	8.30%	.20
E	8.40%	8.62%	.07
F	8.34%	8.64%	.30
Average	8.30%	8.52%	.22

Placement Date:	January 7,1988	
Contract Amount:	$3 Million	
Duration:	4.25 Years	

Source: Certus Financial Corporation

Utilization of Risk-Adjusted Premiums

One factor which GIC managers review in every GIC purchase consideration is the nominal yield which a contract offers. If every issuer were of equal credit quality, analyzing the nominal yields alone would be sufficient. It would make purchase decisions relatively easy. In the GIC marketplace, however, this is most definitely not the case. Methodologies and rankings differ widely among rating agencies. As a result, inconclusive credit evaluations emerge. (See Exhibit 4.)

A sensible management technique is to compare the nominal yields of issuers and then adjust these relative to the credit quality of the issuer. This approach requires the manager to establish a credit ranking for each issuer competing for business. The manager can then purchase contracts on a more preferential basis from the more creditworthy issuers. It also enables the manager to expect a higher return when moving down on the credit quality scale.

Clearly, the most difficult aspect of utilizing "risk-adjusted" premiums is in the establishment of proper credit rankings. One approach which can be utilized is to place issuers into four quartiles of credit risk. The higher-ranked issuers from a solvency perspective are in the first quartile, the next highest in the second, etc. The manager can then suggest guidelines which incorporate risk-adjusted premiums into the quoted nominal yields. The adjustments utilized in this approach can vary depending upon individual portfolio guidelines and maturities being reviewed.

When risk-adjusted premiums are used, two immediate consequences result. First, issuers know where they stand. A second-quartile issuer knows what it needs to outperform a first-quartile issuer in order to win a piece of business. Second, managers who select contracts from lower-quartile issuers can be assured of premiums in the form of higher yields. Managers can incorporate maximum durations by quartile into this approach, as well, to limit the time exposure to the less creditworthy issuers. For example, fourth quartile issuers would not be able to quote on contracts with durations of five years or longer in the hypothetical example listed in this chapter. (See Exhibit 5.)

EXHIBIT 5
HYPOTHETICAL SUGGESTED RISK-ADJUSTED RANGE PREMIUM

Quartile	No Adjustment	Not Acceptable	Not Acceptable
1	No Adjustment	No Adjustment	No Adjustment
2	5 BP Decrease	10 BP Decrease	15 BP Decrease
3	10 BP Decrease	15 BP Decrease	Not Acceptable
4	15 BP Decrease	Not Acceptable	Not Acceptable

EXHIBIT 4
SAMPLES OF RATING AGENCY DISCREPANCIES

Insurer	A.M. Best	Duff & Phelps (CPA)*	Moody's (CPA)*	S&P (CPA)*
Highest Rating	A+	13	Aaa	AAA
Equitable Life Assurance of the U.S.	A+	4	Aa3	Not Rated
Executive Life Insurance of CA	A+	9	A3	AAA
Home Life Insurance Co.	A+	Not Rated	Aa3	Not Rated
Lincoln National Pension Insurance Co.	A	Not Rated	Not Rated	AAA
Penn Mutual Life Insurance Co.	A+	Not Rated	A2	Not Rated
Peoples Security Life Insurance Co.	A+	2	Aa3	AAA
Provident National Assurance Co.	A	3	Aa1	AA+
Sun Life Insurance Co. of America	A+	Not Rated	A3	A+

*CPA - Claims Paying Ability

EXHIBIT 6
PRE-COMMITMENT OPPORTUNITIES

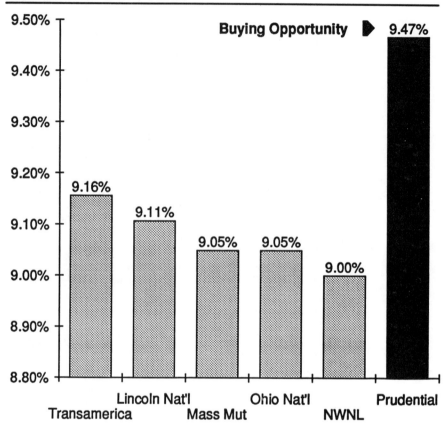

Highest Quotes on $5 Million, 6 Year Simple Interest Bullet Contracts on June 28, 1988, Versus Actual Pre-Commitment Rate for Funds Available October 31, 1988 and January 2, 1988.

Exploit Pre-Commitment Opportunities

In light of the increased demand for GICs, many issuers have expanded their appetite for GIC business. Nevertheless, capacity constraints are quite common, particularly in the fall when much of the traditional "window" business takes place. One technique which is particularly effective in avoiding capacity limitations and taking advantage of above-market opportunities is committing to purchase decisions weeks or even months prior to the time when money will actually be deposited.

This technique requires the manager to notify potential issuers in advance of portfolio requirements. The underwriters and investment personnel at life insurance companies are quite willing and, in some cases, even eager to secure GIC assets well in advance of actual deposit dates. This technique not only provides the issuers with the manager's anticipated GIC activity, it enables the issuers to bid aggressively for certain accounts of stature at times when they might otherwise be uncompetitive. (See Exhibit 6.)

Renegotiate Large, Lump Sum Maturities

In the previous section, we suggested that limiting a portfolio's reinvestment risk enables a GIC fund's yield to be more in synch with prevailing interest rate levels. One technique which can be effective in limiting the reinvestment risk is renegotiating the payout of a large, lump sum maturity.

Issuers are quite often inclined to do this to improve their own investment portfolio and typically will offer the manager a contract with a comparable overall duration without any sacrifice in yield. Occasionally, it is even possible to renegotiate preferred rates when the renegotiation includes a commitment of new cash flow. (See Exhibits 7A and 7B.)

SUMMARY

The concept of GIC portfolio management has gained a great deal of acceptance in recent years. Buyers of these products have come a long way from the one-sided, open-ended agreements of DA contracts and IPGs. GIC market specialists have emerged and have had a profound effect on the distribution system of the product. Even so, at this writing, a large majority of plan sponsors continue to manage their GIC funds in the same primitive ways as they did many years ago.

One of the more unique aspects of GIC portfolio management is the lack of any accepted barometer or index to measure performance. This does, indeed, make it difficult to ascertain how any GIC portfolio is truly faring. In the absence of such an index, many GIC managers erroneously believe that their funds are doing extremely well or, conversely, extremely poorly. In truth, it is very hard to assess a fund's performance without at the very least establishing investment guidelines.

In the near future, it is likely that it will continue to be difficult to measure GIC fund performance in a uniform way. Understanding the considerations, strategies and techniques of GIC portfolio management, however, is a valuable first step. It enables the manager to at least recognize and respond to the fundamentals of GIC portfolio management. It can also help plan sponsors decide whether their in-house capabilities are sufficient to optimize their GIC fund performance or whether outside market specialists are better suited to manage the portfolio.

EXHIBIT 7A
REINVESTMENT RISK BEFORE RENEGOTIATION

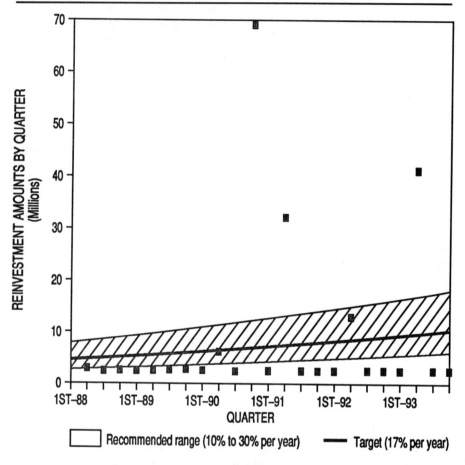

Actual $100 Million Portfolio. Data Points Represent Scheduled Payouts.

Clearly, as the GIC marketplace continues to evolve, numerous other consider-ations, strategies and techniques will surface. GIC managers, both those who are hired as outside market specialists and those who manage their institution's plans internally, need to keep apprised of charges which affect GIC performance. Only by doing so can they be confident that their portfolios are being managed competently and professionally.

EXHIBIT 7B
REINVESTMENT RISK AFTER RENEGOTIATION

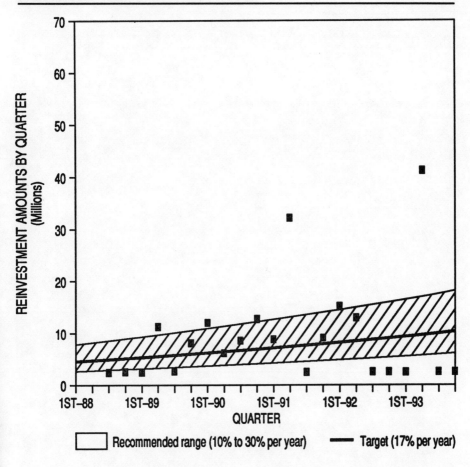

Same Portfolio After Renegotiation of Existing Contracts. Similar Portfolio Duration was Maintained.

The art of GIC portfolio management is still in its infancy. The explosive growth of GIC funds seems destined to continue. Proper management of these funds requires plan sponsors to approach GICs in the same way as other asset classes—developing and implementing sound investment strategies.

PART IX

Normal Portfolios

Chapter 28

Fixed Income Normal Portfolios and Their Application to Fund Management

EDGAR A. ROBIE, JR.
MANAGING DIRECTOR
WESTERN ASSET MANAGEMENT COMPANY

PETER C. LAMBERT
DODGE & COX

With the increased volatility of the bond markets and the plethora of management styles, plan sponsors who have a portion of their assets invested in the fixed income markets have found themselves carefully scrutinizing both the manager's investment process and his performance. Such evaluation usually takes the form of total return measurement and its comparison to market indices or other portfolios from the manager's "peer group." Total return measurement tells a sponsor little about a manager's investment process and its contribution to the total return. Moreover, this focus on short-term total return leads to a situation in which manager performance is measured against a bogey that is inappropriate for the task. The result is not only that performance is incorrectly evaluated but the original rationale for including fixed income investments in the fund is forgotten. What is needed is a benchmark that accurately reflects the objectives of a manager's portfolio and its contribution to the total fund.

The purpose of this chapter is to propose the use of normal portfolios as a practical tool for the objectification and quantification of a fixed income manager's investment process and to demonstrate the applicability of its use in fund management. The identification of a manager's normal portfolio provides a basis for evaluating portfolio performance with respect to its stated objectives.

Until quite recently, the use of the normal portfolio concept has been confined to equity managers and fund sponsors. The notion of specifically identifying the goals of fixed income portfolio management and relating the portfolio's short-term performance to its long-term goals was suggested by Leibowitz in an article which establishes the usefulness of "baseline" or normal portfolios.[1]

In that same article it was suggested that the investment process may be characterized by four major steps.[2] The process could also be illustrated as shown in Exhibit 1.

The first step involves the plan sponsor's allocation of funds to broad asset classes (e.g., fixed income). The second step involves the selection of managers according to their investment processes identified by their long-run exposure to specific market characteristics. The third step is the manager's active management process in which portfolio holdings are adjusted vis-a-vis their long-run exposure in response to current market conditions. The fourth step reviews and evaluates the contribution of the strategic decisions to the manager's stated objectives in order to ensure that the

EXHIBIT 1
OVERVIEW OF THE INVESTMENT MANAGEMENT PROCESS

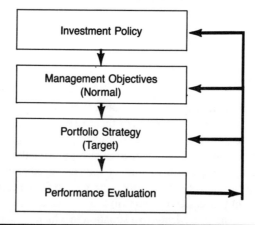

---

[1]Martin L. Leibowitz, "Goal Oriented Bond Portfolio Management," *Journal of Portfolio Management*, Summer 1979, pp. 13-18.

[2]*Ibid.*

portfolio performance and associated risk are in line with the sponsor's original expectations.

THE EVOLUTION OF THE NORMAL PORTFOLIO

The construction of the normal portfolio includes the definition and quantification of both the passive and active components of the manager's investment process. It begins with the identification of the broad universe of investable fixed income securities and, proceeding through several stages, establishes the average exposures to specific market characteristics (e.g., duration, sector, coupon and quality) over a long-run investment horizon. Because it is often difficult for managers to articulate their investment process and identify these average, long-run characteristics, it may be useful to consider the investment process in three stages. These stages correspond to portfolios whose attributes can be defined with increasing specificity and reflect the strategic decision-making process inherent in active management. These three stages may be defined as follows:

1. *Definition of the benchmark portfolio.* This is the appropriate universe of investable fixed income securities from which the manager selects securities for inclusion in his portfolios. For practical application it is usually sufficient to use one (or a combination) of the several publicly available bond indices (e.g. The Salomon Brothers Broad Investment-Grade Bond Index, the Shearson/Lehman Composite Index or the Merrill Lynch High Yield Index). Plan sponsors have traditionally used these "portfolios" as benchmarks for evaluating managers' total rate-of-return performance.
2. *Identification of the manager's normal portfolio.* This portfolio represents the set of "passive" or "neutral" investment positions which best depicts the manager's long-run strategy and average exposures to market characteristics. Through its exposure to market characteristics such as duration, sector, coupon and quality, the normal portfolio serves as the best predictor of the expected risk and return of the manager's portfolios. The normal portfolio captures the essence of a manager's long-run investment style and so serves as a point of reference for evaluating the success of his active investment decisions.
3. *Identification of the target portfolio.* The target portfolio is an objective depiction of the manager's investment strategy at a given point-in-time. The target portfolio's deviations from the normal portfolio represent the manager's responses to current market conditions. The target portfolio is the manager's optimal portfolio at a given point-in-time based upon his expectations and constrained by his overall investment policy or style.

These three stages of portfolio construction mirror the underlying investment process and provide a framework for use in constructing the normal portfolio.

CONSTRUCTION OF THE NORMAL PORTFOLIO

The construction of a manager's normal portfolio is no simple task. It requires the manager to identify his long-run objectives and to distinguish between the passive and active components of his investment style. The first step is to characterize the manager's investment philosophy from which his investment process or "style" is derived. Such a characterization might include the following statements of objectives:

1. As a broad-scale or "core" fixed income manager, the fixed income component of an investment fund is a "stabilizing force" which should be relatively free from the volatility and economic risks associated with the equity components of the fund. To this end, the investment philosophy calls for holdings in most of the major sectors of the fixed income markets but excludes lower quality securities. Emphasis should be on those sectors which consistently offer opportunities to capture excess returns by exploiting inefficiencies.
2. The fixed income component of a client's fund should be a provider of stable cash flow that may be depended upon under virtually any economic condition. Consequently, investment concentration is in those securities which provide stable total returns irrespective of the current interest rate environment.
3. Recognizing the impossibility of consistently predicting the movement of interest rates, the investment strategy limits unnecessary exposure to interest rate risk. Hence, our portfolios will, on average, maintain a duration equal to that of the benchmark portfolio; at no time will a portfolio's duration deviate from the duration of the benchmark portfolio by more than 20%.

Using such general objectives as guidelines, the next step is to specifically identify the manager's exposure to sectors of the fixed income market. A manager's sector exposures may be thought of as his "preferred habitat" for making active investment decisions. A further requirement of the normal portfolio definition is that its holdings reflect the average holdings in a manager's portfolios over a relatively long period of time.

The following is an example of how a manager's investment exposure to the broad market sectors may be characterized. Note that sector weightings are specified with respect to the benchmark portfolio and that the stated rationale for each sector exposure supports this manager's overall investment policy and objectives.

Normal Portfolio Characteristics

A. *Governments and agencies* (Underweighting: 25%; SBBI[3] = 57%): A deliberate under-allocation is made to governments and agencies in the normal portfolio as

---

[3]Salomon Brothers Broad Investment-Grade Bond Index.

they traditionally do not provide the yields available from other sectors. However, due to the liquidity of this sector, they provide a convenient means of effecting changes in portfolio duration. They also provide additional diversification to the portfolio and mitigate a portion of the credit risk assumed in other market sectors.

B. *Corporates* (Overweighting: 30%; SBBI = 22%): A substantial emphasis on corporates in the normal portfolio is due to the attractive opportunities provided by inefficiencies which exist within this sector (i.e., credit perception, structural qualities and technical factors) as well as the generous yield-to-maturity characteristics of the sector.

C. *Mortgage pass-throughs* (Overweighting: 40%; SBBI = 21%): A high concentration is allocated to mortgage pass-throughs in the normal portfolio due to both the securities' cash-flow characteristics which provide generous yields compared to other broad market sectors and the numerous inefficiencies created by the continual introduction of new types of mortgage securities.

D. *Cash equivalents* (Strategic Allocation: 5%; SBBI = 0%): While cash equivalents constitute a small fraction of the normal portfolio, as a sector it provides funds for investment opportunities and added flexibility in making the duration decision.

E. *Duration* (Equal to benchmark; may vary ±20%): The duration of the normal portfolio is equal to the benchmark (SBBI) portfolio. In times in which no strong convictions can be made about the direction of interest rates, a neutral position (normal portfolio duration = benchmark portfolio duration) represents the point at which economic and volatility risk equal that of the market.

The normal portfolio characteristics stated above provide an example of how any fixed income manager may go about constructing his own normal portfolio. Depending upon a particular manager's investment objectives and strategies, more specific characterizations may be required. Some managers may maintain explicit concentrations in some subsector of the broad sectors mentioned. For instance, a manager's exposure to corporate bonds may be primarily concentrated in the utility sector; the manager's normal portfolio should reflect this fact. Similarly, a manager who desires a high-level of call protection may exclude high-coupon bonds priced at a premium to par.

A note of caution is appropriate here; when constructing a normal portfolio to be compared with one of the existing benchmark indices, it is crucial that all characteristics be specified according to the same methods of calculation. For instance, when determining the duration of the mortgage pass-through component, one's prepayment assumptions must match those used in the calculation of the benchmark portfolio's durations.

FUNCTIONS OF THE NORMAL PORTFOLIO

The use of normal portfolios by fixed income investment managers provides a tremendous amount of information about the investment process that has previously been extremely difficult for the fund sponsor to define. We highlight three ways that the normal portfolio can contribute to the dialogue between the fund sponsor and his managers:

The normal portfolio:

1. Provides a mutual vantage point from which the success of a manager's active investment decisions can be evaluated with respect to the stated objectives of the fund.
2. Serves as the appropriate benchmark against which a manager's actual returns should be compared.
3. Provides an analytic description of a manager's investment process which a sponsor may employ to assess the appropriateness of a particular manager's style to his fund's overall investment objectives.

EVALUATION OF ACTIVE MANAGEMENT

Given the normal portfolio depicts a manager's long-term "neutral" or "passive" investment strategy, departures from the normal portfolio represent his strategic (active) investment decisions. Such departures are made in response to changes in current market conditions with the expectation of capturing excess returns or of protecting the value of the portfolio in adverse market conditions. The increasing tendency to focus on short-term total returns may cause managers to accept greater risks in pursuit of short-term returns than is appropriate in view of the fund's overall investment objectives. The use of a normal portfolio allows a manager's active investment strategies to be evaluated in terms of their contribution to the fund's overall risk and return profile.

The sum effect of a manager's active strategies on the portfolio's composition is embodied in the target portfolio discussed above. This portfolio may be illustrated by a matrix showing the percentage of the portfolio that is invested in each sector and the distribution of the durations of each of the sector holdings as in Exhibit 2.

The target portfolio serves as the model around which a manager's fully discretionary portfolios are constructed and maintained. As market conditions change, the composition of the target portfolio will adjust to take advantage of those changes.

Technological developments have resulted in quantitative tools that allow for the decomposition of a fixed income portfolio's return into its several sources.[4] Similar capabilities have been available for use in equity portfolios since the early 1970s.[5]

---

[4]Gifford H. Fong, Charles Pearson, and Oldrich Vasicek, "Bond Performance: Analyzing Sources of Return," *Journal of Portfolio Management,* Spring 1983, pp. 46-50.

[5]Eugene F. Fama, "Components of Investment Performance," *Journal of Finance,* June 1972, pp. 551-67.

EXHIBIT 2
PORTFOLIO CHARACTERISTICS MATRIX—JANUARY 1986

Sector	Benchmark	Normal	Duration Distribution					Target	Average Duration
			0-1	1-3	3-5	5-7	7+		
Governments & Agencies	60	25		10	5	30	10	15	
Mortgage Instruments	20	40				25	5	40	
Corporates	20	30						30	
Cash & Cash Equivalents	0	5	15					15	
Target Portfolio			15	10	5	55	15	100	5.1 Yrs.
Normal Portfolio			10	20	20	30	20	100	4.6 Yrs.
Benchmark Portfolio			1	33	32	12	22	100	4.6 Yrs.

Percent of Portfolio

One such "return attribution" system provides a method for attributing returns to the "external" interest rate environment and to the components of the active management process; maturity/duration management, sector/quality management and individual security selection. Performing a return attribution analysis on both the normal and the target portfolios allows one to determine the marginal value added by deviations from the normal portfolio. To the extent that such deviations add to the portfolio's risk exposure, the contribution of the added risk to portfolio returns can be assessed. Using the normal portfolio as a guide allows the portfolio manager to focus more clearly on his day-to-day activities on the fund sponsor's behalf.

THE NORMAL PORTFOLIO AS THE MANAGER'S APPROPRIATE BOGEY

While choosing the correct benchmark index is an important first step towards meaningful performance evaluation, the normal portfolio improves upon indices in that it is a customized benchmark for a particular manager. If we accept the normal portfolio as representative of the passive component of a manager's strategy that could be adopted as is, and view the active management decisions as deviations from his "normal" strategy, then the normal portfolio is the correct benchmark against which a manager's performance should be measured. To the extent that the returns on a manager's target or actual portfolios exceed those earned by his normal portfolio, then his active management strategies may be considered successful. However, if a manager's returns are less than those of his normal portfolio, he would have been better-off investing in a portfolio designed to replicate the characteristics of the normal portfolio.

We have tracked the normal portfolio described above for the six year period beginning January 1, 1980 and ending December 31, 1985. The returns on this normal portfolio were compared to the benchmark portfolio, in this case the Salomon Brothers Broad Investment-Grade Bond Index, and to a composite portfolio of 10 fully discretionary portfolios which serves as a proxy for the target portfolio. Over this period, the normal portfolio returned 49 basis points above the benchmark index on an annualized basis; the proxy target portfolio returned another 127 basis points more than the normal portfolio on the same annualized basis. While the total rate-of-return volatility of the normal portfolio was slightly higher than that of the benchmark index (13.29% vs. 12.18% in annual standard deviation), the volatility of the target portfolio was less than that of both the normal and benchmark portfolios (11.59%). These results are summarized in Exhibits 3a and 3b along with the comparable statistics for the four broad sectors.

In this example, the active strategies followed by the managers, as exemplified by the proxy target portfolio, have decidedly been successful. Not only has total rate-of-return volatility been reduced (in accordance with the manager's stated objectives presented in Exhibit 3), but returns have been significantly enhanced.

EXHIBIT 3a
RISK/RETURN ANALYSIS—JANUARY 1, 1980–DECEMBER 21, 1985

Sector/Portfolio	Annual Geometric Mean Return	Annual Standard Deviation
Treasury/Agency*	13.75	9.94
Corporates*	14.20	15.03
Mortgage Pass-throughs*	15.04	15.89
3-Month T-Bill	10.31	1.17
SBBI*	13.99	12.18
Normal Portfolio	14.48	13.29
Target Portfolio	15.75	11.59

*Source: Salomon Brothers Inc

EXHIBIT 3b
RISK/RETURN ANALYSIS—JANUARY 1, 1980–DECEMBER 31, 1985

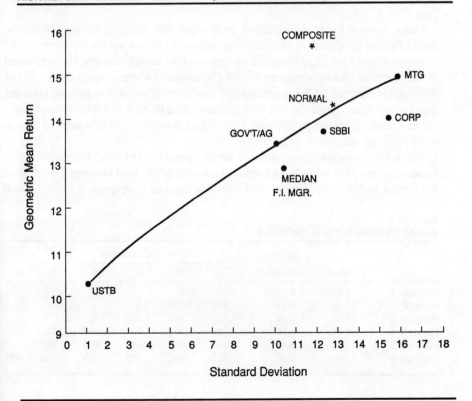

USING THE NORMAL PORTFOLIO TO SELECT MANAGERS

As fund sponsors increase the number of managers in a multiple-manager environment, the aggregate holdings of the fund's active managers tend to resemble the market portfolio of investable assets. While this provides the fund with the benefits of maximum risk diversification, it mitigates the original intention of hiring "specialty" managers. In short, as the fund assumes the risk profile of the market, it will assume the market's return profile.

The normal portfolio describes the manager's average or "normal" exposure to market characteristics. As such, it is the best prediction of the expected risk and return of a manager's portfolio. To the extent that a plan sponsor attempts to select the "optimal" mix of managers for a multiple-manager fund, the normal portfolio is the best available input to such a process. Sponsors can use managers' normal portfolios to select the allocations to various managers that will provide the fund with the desired diversification benefits while maintaining a greater than market exposure to certain characteristics (e.g., high-yield securities or discount securities). A combination of qualitative judgement and quantitative techniques may be used to select that mix of managers which best fits the overall goals and objectives of the fund.

Using mean-variance optimization techniques, the sponsor can determine the most efficient allocation to his active managers. Exhibit 4 shows the normal risk/return profiles of six fixed income managers and the correlation among them based on five years of quarterly returns. In order to ensure that some minimum number of managers is selected by the optimizer, the maximum allocation to any one manager may be constrained by an appropriate percentage. Exhibit 5 and 6 have constrained the maximum allocation to 25% and 33%, which provides for a minimum of four or three different managers, respectively.

These exhibits show how managers are eliminated as the allocation constraint is increased from 25% to 33%. In Exhibit 5 a manager can hold no more than 25% of the corpus and in Exhibit 6 no more than one third of the corpus. As the risk and

EXHIBIT 4
MANAGER RISK/RETURN PROFILES

	Return	Standard Deviation	Correlation					
			(1)	(2)	(3)	(4)	(5)	(6)
Manager 1	18.92%	5.05%	1.000					
Manager 2	14.49	4.39	.766	1.000				
Manager 3	15.06	5.28	.750	.965	1.000			
Manager 4	17.11	6.50	.748	.945	.920	1.000		
Manager 5	14.81	5.46	.706	.926	.935	.954	1.000	
Manager 6	15.92	5.22	.785	.966	.975	.949	.942	1.000

EXHIBIT 5
OPTIMIZATION RESULTS AND EFFICIENT FRONTIER (25% ALLOCATION CONSTRAINT)

					Allocations					
	Min. Risk	(2)	(3)	(4)	(5)	(6)	(7)	(8)	(9)	Max. Return
Manager 1	25.0	25.0	25.0	25.0	25.0	25.0	25.0	25.0	25.0	25.0
Manager 2	25.0	25.0	25.0	25.0	25.0	25.0	25.0	25.0	15.1	0.0
Manager 3	17.2	22.0	21.2	16.9	13.4	8.7	4.0	0.0	9.9	25.0
Manager 4	0.0	0.0	3.8	8.1	11.6	16.3	21.0	25.0	25.0	25.0
Manager 5	12.4	3.0	0.0	0.0	0.0	0.0	0.0	0.0	0.0	0.0
Manager 6	20.4	25.0	25.0	25.0	25.0	25.0	25.0	25.0	25.0	25.0
Expected Return	16.0	16.1	16.2	16.3	16.3	16.4	16.5	16.6	16.7	16.8
Std. Deviation	4.7	4.7	4.8	4.8	4.9	4.9	5.0	5.0	5.1	5.2

EXHIBIT 6
OPTIMIZATION RESULTS AND EFFICIENT FRONTIER (33% ALLOCATION CONSTRAINT)

					Allocations					
	Min. Risk	(2)	(3)	(4)	(5)	(6)	(7)	(8)	(9)	Max. Return
Manager 1	33.0	33.0	33.0	33.0	33.0	33.0	33.0	33.0	33.0	33.0
Manager 2	33.0	33.0	33.0	30.2	25.1	19.7	15.6	11.0	5.8	0.0
Manager 3	16.0	8.5	0.3	0.0	0.0	0.0	0.0	0.0	0.0	0.0
Manager 4	0.0	0.0	0.0	3.8	8.9	14.3	18.4	23.0	28.2	33.3
Manager 5	13.4	10.4	0.7	0.0	0.0	0.0	0.0	0.0	0.0	0.0
Manager 6	4.6	15.1	33.0	33.0	33.0	33.0	33.0	33.0	33.0	33.3
Expected Return	16.2	16.2	16.4	16.5	16.7	16.8	16.9	17.0	17.2	17.3
Std. Deviation	4.6	4.6	4.6	4.7	4.8	4.9	5.0	5.1	5.2	5.3

expected return increase, the weaker performing managers are eliminated. This analysis suggests that greater returns can be achieved (50 basis points) for about the same level of risk with fewer as opposed to a greater number of managers. The reduction in managers is further enhanced by lower fees and transaction costs. The sponsor may choose which efficient mix of managers is right for his fund.

The point of this example is to show how the information provided by managers' normal portfolios can be used with quantitative techniques to select the optimal mix of managers. The allocation of funds to each manager should, in the aggregate, provide the risk and return characteristics desired for the fixed income component of the fund.

SUMMARY

Normal portfolios can be extremely useful to both the plan sponsor and the manager. Advantages of using this approach include defining the investment process of the manager and eliminating fuzzy generalities, providing a mutual vantage point for interpreting the *actual* returns and increasing the level of discussion between the sponsor and the manager. The normal portfolio is an objective point of reference which ensures continuity of understanding over any investment horizon between the sponsor and his managers.

Index

Toyota economic model
of inventory